LEGAL RESEARCH, ANALYSIS, AND WRITING

D1299369

SECOND EDITION

LEGAL RESEARCH, ANALYSIS, AND WRITING

An Integrated Approach

Joanne Banker Hames

Yvonne Ekern

Pearson
Prentice Hall
Legal Series

PEARSON

Prentice
Hall

Upper Saddle River, New Jersey 07458

Library of Congress Cataloging-in-Publication Data

Hames, Joanne Banker.
    Legal research, analysis, and writing : an integrated approach / Joanne Banker Hames,
Yvonne Ekern.— 2nd ed.
        p. cm.
    Includes index.
    ISBN 0–13–118888–7
    1. Legal research—United States. 2. Legal composition. 3. Legal assistants—United
States—Handbooks, manuals, etc. I. Ekern, Yvonne. II. Title.
    KF240.H36 2006
    340'.072'073—dc22

                                                        2005005490

Director of Production and Manufacturing: Bruce Johnson
Senior Acquisitions Editor: Gary Bauer
Editorial Assistant: Jacqueline Knapke
Consulting Editors: Athena Group, Inc.
Senior Marketing Manager: Leigh Ann Sims
Managing Editor—Production: Mary Carnis
Manufacturing Buyer: Ilene Sanford
Production Liaison: Denise Brown
Production Editor: Melissa Westley/Carlisle Publishers Services
Composition: Carlisle Communications, Ltd.
Senior Design Coordinator: Christopher Weigand
Cover Design: Kevin Kall
Cover Printer: Phoenix Color
Printer/Binder: Banta-Harrisonburg

The information provided in this text is not intended as legal advice for specific situations, but is meant solely for educational and informational purposes. Readers should retain and seek the advice of their own legal counsel in handling specific legal matters.

Copyright © 2006, 2000 by Pearson Education, Upper Saddle River, New Jersey 07458. Pearson Prentice Hall. All rights reserved. Printed in the United States of America. This publication is protected by Copyright and permission should be obtained from the publisher prior to any prohibited reproduction, storage in a retrieval system, or transmission in any form or by any means, electronic, mechanical, photocopying, recording, or likewise. For information regarding permission(s), write to: Rights and Permissions Department.

Pearson Prentice Hall™ is a trademark of Pearson Education, Inc.
Pearson® is a registered trademark of Pearson plc
Prentice Hall® is a registered trademark of Pearson Education, Inc.

Pearson Education Ltd.
Pearson Education Singapore Pte. Ltd.
Pearson Education Canada, Ltd.
Pearson Education—Japan

Pearson Education Australia Pty. Limited
Pearson Education North Asia Ltd.
Pearson Educación de Mexico, S. A. de C.V.
Pearson Education Malaysia Pte. Ltd.
Pearson Education, Upper Saddle River, New Jersey

10 9 8 7 6 5 4 3 2
ISBN 0-13-118888-7

BRIEF CONTENTS

PEARSON LEGAL SERIES

Pearson Legal Series provides paralegal/legal studies students and educators with the publishing industry's finest content and best service. We offer an extensive selection of products for over 70 titles and we continue to grow with more new titles each year. We also provide:

- online resources for instructors and students
- state-specific materials
- custom publishing options from Pearson Custom Publishing group

To locate your local Pearson Prentice Hall representative, visit www.prenhall.com

To view Pearson Legal Series titles and to discover a wide array of resources for both instructors and students, please visit our website at:

www.prenhall.com/legal_studies

Pearson
Prentice Hall
Legal Series

CONTENTS

CHAPTER 3
THE STARTING POINT: ANALYZING FACTS AND
IDENTIFYING LEGAL ISSUES   33

Chapter 4
FINDING AND ANALYZING CASE LAW   55

Chapter 5
HOW TO BRIEF A CASE   95

CHAPTER 6

CONSTITUTIONS, STATUTES, AND
ADMINISTRATIVE REGULATIONS   113

CHAPTER 7

STATUTORY AND CONSTITUTIONAL ANALYSIS   **151**

CHAPTER 8

SECONDARY SOURCES   **182**

CHAPTER 9
DIGESTS AND MISCELLANEOUS RESEARCH TOOLS   221

CHAPTER 10
VALIDATING YOUR RESEARCH: USING *SHEPARD'S* AND OTHER CITATORS   252

CHAPTER 11
COMPUTER ASSISTED LEGAL RESEARCH (CALR)   278

CHAPTER 12
HOW TO CREATE RESEARCH STRATEGIES   296

CHAPTER 13
BASIC LEGAL WRITING TOOLS   339

CHAPTER 14
LEGAL WRITING: WRITING TO INFORM   349

CHAPTER 15

WRITING TO THE COURT   380

PREFACE

GOALS

Beginning legal researchers generally ask three questions:

- How do I find the law?
- How do I know that I found the right law?
- What do I do with the law now that I've found it?

Experienced legal researchers know that successful research requires the ability to answer each of these questions.

They also know that researching the law requires more than knowledge of law books. It requires the ability to analyze factual and legal disputes; the ability to understand the written law, whether found in cases or statutory materials; the ability to apply the law to the factual disputes; and the ability to communicate one's findings. Our purpose in writing this book is to give students the basic knowledge and tools they need in order to research and analyze a problem and to communicate the results of that research and analysis to the appropriate person. This text, therefore, integrates three areas: legal research, legal analysis, and legal writing.

Our experience in teaching legal research classes in both law school and paralegal programs confirms that all programs cover the same topics and assign similar projects. A review of the model curriculum for legal research and writing recommended by the American Association for Paralegal Association further illustrates the similarity. However, even within law schools or paralegal programs the way in which legal research and writing is taught often differs. Some programs teach separate courses in legal research, legal writing, and legal analysis. Some programs recommend research before writing, while others require writing courses before research. We believe that these differences stem from the fact that in practice the process of legal research, analysis, and writing is an integrated one. This text reflects that practice. However, this text is appropriate for a variety of instructional approaches to legal research, analysis, and writing and realizing that there are legitimate reasons for different organizations we offer suggestions for using the text with different approaches to teaching the subject.

ORGANIZATION OF *LEGAL RESEARCH, ANALYSIS AND WRITING: AN INTEGRATED APPROACH*

- Chapters 1 and 2 present an introduction to legal research and writing as well as an overview of the legal system, with an emphasis on the way that laws originate. The distinction between federal and state laws is explained. This material provides even beginning students with the basic information and concepts needed to successfully undertake legal research.
- Chapter 3 introduces students to the beginning steps of legal research—analyzing the facts and issues to be researched.
- Chapters 4 through 7 explore the primary sources of law, cases, statutes, and constitutions. These chapters explain the publication and organization of these materials as well as how the laws should be read and analyzed. Case briefing, statutory analysis, and the IRAC method of analysis are covered.
- Chapters 8 and 9 explore numerous secondary sources.
- Chapter 10 explains *Shepard's* and other citators.
- Chapter 11 introduces the students to Computer Assisted Legal Research, although the use of the Internet as a research tool is included in all chapters.
- Chapter 12 reviews the numerous research materials covered in prior chapters and presents ways to create successful research strategies using these materials.
- Chapters 13 through 15 cover the different types of legal writing (memorandum of law, memorandum of points and authorities, trial briefs and appellate briefs.) These chapters also review the basic analysis methods (e.g., IRAC) introduced in earlier chapters and show how these methods are incorporated into more formal legal writing.

For courses covering only legal writing the following chapters are appropriate:

- Chapters 1, 2 and 3   Introductory Material (These chapters may be quickly reviewed depending on the students' educational background)
- Chapter 5   How to Brief a Case
- Chapter 7   Statutory and Constitutional Analysis
- Chapters 13   Basic Legal Writing Tools
- Chapter 14   Legal Writing: Writing to Inform
- Chapter 15   Writing to the Court

For courses covering only legal research the following chapters are appropriate:

- Chapters 1, 2 and 3   Introductory Material (These chapters may be quickly reviewed depending on the students' educational background)
- Chapter 4   Finding and Analyzing Case Law
- Chapter 6   Constitutions, Statutes, and Administrative Regulations
- Chapter 8   Secondary Sources
- Chapter 9   Digests and Miscellaneous Research Tools
- Chapter 10   Validating Your Research: Using *Shepard's* and Other Citators
- Chapter 11   Computer Assisted Legal Research (CALR)
- Chapter 12   How to Create Research Strategies

THE SECOND EDITION OF *LEGAL RESEARCH, ANALYSIS, AND WRITING*

When we first wrote *Legal Research, Analysis, and Writing,* we were convinced that students needed a text that integrated research, analysis, and writing skills. We remain convinced of that, and, therefore, our basic approach to the subject matter did not change. However, legal research materials and the methods of doing legal research have changed considerably over the past few years. The availability of legal resources through the Internet has tremendous influence on the way research is conducted. No longer are researchers confined to a law library. The widespread use of all forms of computer assisted legal research requires that legal researchers develop new skills. However, the law has not abandoned the written word and, as any experienced researcher knows, books are often preferred. The new skills that researchers must develop, therefore, cannot supplant traditional research skills, but must complement them. Chapter 11, Computer Assisted Legal Research, was substantially revised to reflect current trends in legal research. Most chapters were revised in less substantial ways for the same reason.

In the second edition we added several features to help students develop basic research, writing, and analysis skills. Recognizing that students are often frustrated and overwhelmed by the complexities of legal citation, we added a feature in each chapter called Citation Matters, introducing the student to one facet of legal citation. This allows students to gradually develop important citation skills. We also now include a statement of Chapter Objectives in each chapter so that students are better able to focus on the reading material. In order to provide students with more opportunities for legal analysis and writing, several shorter hypothetical research problems were added to the appendix material.

PRACTICAL APPROACH

Regardless of which instructional approach is followed, this text assists the instructor in presenting material in a practical and relevant way.

Each chapter opens with an **Interoffice Memorandum** that contains a hypothetical factual situation to be researched and analyzed by a fictional research associate. The memorandum approach helps to introduce the topic of the chapter and to engage the student's imagination. Furthermore, because learning to do legal research requires hands-on experience, at the end of each chapter three additional features appear. **Research Assignments and Activities** contains research, analysis, and writing problems that students must often use a law library to complete. **Can You Figure It Out?** makes use of the numerous sample law book pages found in the chapters. In this section, students are asked practical research questions that can be answered by referring to the appropriate sample page in the text. Students can begin a practical approach to learning legal research even before entering the law library.

The **Case Project** allows students and instructors to select one hypothetical case (many of which are found in Appendix A) and to perform some research, analysis, or writing project in each chapter. In this way, students see how the material covered in the different chapters is integrated.

FEATURES

A variety of features helps students and instructors.

- **Legal vocabulary** is identified in boldface type. The key terms are defined in the margins of the text where the terms appear. A comprehensive **glossary** is also included.

- **Chapter Objectives** are listed at the beginning of each chapter, helping students recognize the main points of the chapter.

- **Citation Matters,** a feature that appears in each chapter, is a brief overview of major citation rules affecting legal writing.

- As previously stated, an **Interoffice Memorandum** opens the text of each chapter. This memorandum serves as an introduction to the subject matter, encouraging the student to think about the subject matter in a practical setting.

- A **Technology Corner** appears in each chapter. This feature exposes the student to the ways in which technology relates to the subject matter of the chapter and provides a list of useful Internet sites, allowing the student to actually utilize technology skills.

- **Research checklists** are found in several chapters, providing a quick, easy-to-read summary of the material found in the text.

- **Sample pages** from an assortment of law books are included in the research chapters. Practical exercises at the end of the chapter, found in the section **Can You Figure It Out?**, give students the opportunity to practice research skills *before* going to the library.

- Examples of actual **research memoranda** appear in appropriate chapters.

- A **Chapter Summary** is included in every chapter; it provides a short overview of the major concepts covered in the chapter.

- Basic **Questions for Review** follow the chapter summary. These questions are designed to focus the student in on the most important concepts presented in the chapter.

- **Research Assignments and Activities** are included at the end of each chapter. This feature includes library research problems, analysis exercises, and writing assignments.

- Most chapters include a feature we call **A Point to Remember.** This practical information is fashioned to help students focus on the skills and concepts that will help them in doing legal research, writing, and analysis.

- **Appendix A** includes several research problems that can be used as a basis for assignments for all chapters, giving students the opportunity to see the entire research process as it relates to one factual problem. Other appendixes include a **short citation guide,** a **research strategies outline,** a **memorandum of points and authorities,** and an **appellate brief.**

- An **Instructor's Manual** is available, including answers to library research projects, answers to questions found in the feature Can You Figure It Out?, a test bank, transparency masters, and additional research problems.

- Icons in the table of contents and on the individual chapter outlines identify the chapter as primarily a research chapter (a book icon), a writing and analysis chapter (a pen icon), or a chapter emphasizing computer assisted legal research.

ACKNOWLEDGMENTS

Special thanks are extended to several individuals whose assistance and encouragement were invaluable: to Dean Gerald Uelman, who graciously shared with us his considerable research experiences, insight, and documents; to Delene Waltrip, senior paralegal with the Santa Clara Country District Attorney's Office; Kenneth Rosenblatt, Deputy District Attorney and author of *High-Technology Crime;* and Mark Hames, Deputy District Attorney, who also shared with us the fruits of their legal research and writing. Finally we thank our husbands, Bill Ekern and Mark Hames. Each has contributed special talents and expertise to improving this text and each continues to be a source of encouragement and support.

Special thanks to the reviewers of this text: Lora Clark, Pitt Community College, Winterville NC; Robert Loomis, Spokane Community College, Spokane WA.

ABOUT THE AUTHORS

Yvonne Ekern is a full-time member of the Legal Analysis, Research, and Writing faculty at Santa Clara University's School of Law. For seven years she was the chairperson of the West Valley College Paralegal Program (ABA approved). Prior to attending law school, she taught high school English and math in California and Missouri. She graduated from the University of Idaho School of Law in 1985. While working in criminal and family law offices, she taught part-time in several Silicon Valley paralegal programs. Among the classes she has taught are Legal Research and Writing, Advanced Legal Research and Writing, Advanced Legal Research and Writing Using LEXIS, and Legal Analysis. She has over twenty years teaching experience. She is a principal and co-founder of Continuing Education for the Legal Assistant, a company dedicated to providing quality educational opportunities for working legal assistants. She is also the principal of Simply Legal, a consulting firm providing services to law offices and medical-legal offices. In recent years, she has been a guest speaker at AAfPE conferences, chaired the AAfPE committee that developed the model curriculum for legal research, and was a member of the committee that developed the model curriculum for Introduction to Law. She is the co-author of the texts *Introduction to Law,* and *Constitutional Law: Principles and Practice.*

Joanne Banker Hames is an attorney and paralegal educator who has been actively involved in paralegal education since 1977. She is an instructor in and the former coordinator for the ABA-approved paralegal program at DeAnza Community College in Cupertino, California. She earned her J. D. degree from Santa Clara University Law School and has been an active member of the California Bar since 1972. As an attorney, she has been involved in research and writing for legal memoranda and appellate briefs. Among the classes she has taught are Legal Research and Writing, Advanced Legal Research and Writing, and Advanced Legal Research Using LEXIS. She is the co-author of *Civil Litigation, Introduction to Law,* and *Constitutional Law: Principles and Practice.*

INTRODUCTION TO LEGAL RESEARCH, WRITING, AND ANALYSIS

CHAPTER OUTLINE

CHAPTER OBJECTIVES

When you complete this chapter you should be able to

- Discuss the role of a research associate.
- Explain the difference between a primary and a secondary source of law.
- List the types of materials often found in law libraries.
- List the common features of law books.

CITATION MATTERS

WHY LEGAL CITATION MATTERS

The term *citation* refers to special information provided by the author of a document. A legal citation shows the reader the origin of the cited authority. Everyone is familiar with the use of quotations. When you use a quote you must indicate the origin of the quote. Generally, the citation to the original material follows the quoted language. The same is true in legal writing, only we take it a bit further. Most legal writing is designed to inform or convince. The best way to do that is to show the reader where the ideas originated, whether or not a quote is used.

In legal research, for example, we may search for a case addressing the "issue" (the legal problem) raised in a client's case. If there is a "case" (a legal decision written by a judge) that deals with similar factual issues and that case reaches a result that would be advantageous for the client, then the researcher may want to "cite to" that case as *precedent*. Our legal system is based on the concept of precedent. This means that when we search for answers to legal questions, we look back to see how courts have dealt with the same or similar problems in the past. Previous cases carry what we call a "weight of authority"—something that personal opinion does not carry. A court is not interested in personal opinions. It is interested in the legal authority that supports the opinion.

Case law provides good examples of citation use in legal writing. Sometimes it seems as though every sentence has a citation following it. That can make reading legal material tedious and slow. But because legal citations alert the reader to the origin of the material, they are a critical element of legal writing. In your legal writing, you should strive to cite carefully and completely. Appendix B provides a basic overview of citation. Read it carefully and begin to learn the basic rules of legal citation. Review the use of legal citations below:

> The United States Constitution guarantees the right to trial by jury in order to prevent oppression by the government. U.S. CONST. amend.VI and XIV; *Duncan v. State of La.*, 391 U.S. 145, 194 (1968).

This sentence is a statement of law, not an opinion: "The United States Constitution guarantees the right to trial by jury in order to prevent oppression by the government." The writer shows his audience that the guarantee of a jury trial is found in the United States Constitution under Amendments Six and Fourteen. This same statement is further supported by the citation to a United States Supreme Court case. Notice that the two citations are separated by a semicolon and followed by a period. The second sentence is called a *citation sentence*.

The *name* of the case is *Duncan v. State of La.* The name of a case is italicized or underlined, never both.

This case is found in the United States Reports. *U.S.* is the proper abbreviation for the *Official reporter* of United States Supreme Court case law.

This case is located in *volume* 391, and the *first page* of the case is 145. The writer also provided a "pinpoint cite" for the page in the case where the Court addresses the right to trial by jury. The pinpoint cite is to page 194.

The *year of the decision* is 1968. Notice that the year is placed at the end of the citation, and it must be placed in parentheses.

The citation manual used in the preparation of this text is THE BLUEBOOK: A UNIFORM SYSTEM OF CITATION (Columbia Law Review Ass'n et al. eds., 18th ed. 2000).

INTEROFFICE MEMORANDUM

TO: Research Associate

FROM: Supervising Attorney

RE: Research Assignment

Attached is a Memo of P. & A.s in support of a motion for summary judgment recently filed by the other side in the Rambeaux civil matter. We need to file our own memo and declarations as soon as possible. Please read all the cases and statutes cited in the document. Shepardize everything to make sure it is good law. Do this online to make sure it's current. Then brief each of the cited cases. Be sure to clearly state the holding and rationale of the cases. Pay close attention to the *Catlette* case found at 132 F.2d 902. I think the memo misinterprets and misapplies the court's ruling in the case. When you finish reviewing the opposing memo, please find law that supports our side of the case. Discuss your findings in an interoffice memorandum. You should be able to do most of this work in our office law library and by accessing either LEXIS or Westlaw. However, the opposing memo cites some rarely used secondary sources. You may have to go to the county law library to check these out.

1-1 INTRODUCTION

Interoffice memoranda like the one at the beginning of this chapter are common in law offices. Lawyers and their assistants, usually paralegals and law clerks, are constantly required to find and analyze the law and to communicate their findings in some legal document. Undoubtedly, one of the most important skills for anyone working in the law is the ability to perform legal research.

Even though legal research is a task usually associated with lawyers and their staff, many other professions find that the ability to do some legal research is a useful tool. Police officers, for example, must often refer to code sections and case law in their jobs. Individuals in the business or corporate world also find that they need to answer legal questions. Questions of contract law and environmental regulations arise constantly in this setting.

Although this textbook is intended primarily for students pursuing a career in the legal environment, it provides a basic framework for legal research that any student should be able to follow. The subject matter of each chapter is introduced in an "Interoffice Memorandum" based on a hypothetical factual scenario. As you go through the text you will learn where and how laws are published, how to analyze

a factual situation and apply the relevant legal principles, and how to communicate your findings to clients, other attorneys, and the court. At the end of each chapter are several practical research or writing exercises. Some of these can be completed with material that is in the text. Others require that you visit a law library. In addition, Appendix A contains several hypothetical situations that form the basis of some of the research and writing exercises.

1-2 LEGAL RESEARCH AND LAW PRACTICE

Although legal professionals and paraprofessionals spend considerable time studying the law before working in the field, they do not know the answer to every legal question. Even the most experienced lawyers must research the law. Laws change constantly. Legislatures routinely enact, amend, or repeal statutes. Courts decide new cases every day. Even constitutions are amended. When lawyers make legal arguments in court or give legal advice to clients, they must be certain about the current state of the law. Because laws are not the same throughout the various states, lawyers must be certain about the law in their jurisdiction. The process of finding the law is known as *legal research.*

When lawyers or their assistants perform legal research, it is usually in relation to a specific case that the law firm is handling. Legal professionals rarely research the law out of academic curiosity. Furthermore, when legal research is performed for a client, the researcher's job does not stop when he or she finds the appropriate law. The law must then be analyzed in relation to the facts of the particular case and the results of the research and analysis explained, usually in written form, to the appropriate person. This may be a client, another attorney, or a judge.

As you read the chapters in this text, therefore, you will see how legal research, analysis, and writing occur in connection with several hypothetical cases, including the Rambeaux case discussed in this chapter. Read Case 1 in Appendix A and familiarize yourself with all the facts of this case. This case involves allegations of use of excessive force by a police officer, Randy Rambeaux.

Randy Rambeaux hired a law firm to represent him because of legal problems he could not handle. Rambeaux's attorneys must research several different areas of law in order to give proper advice. There are questions of **criminal law,** questions of **civil law,** and questions of **administrative procedures.** Along with finding the law, Rambeaux's legal representatives must analyze the law and the facts of their particular case to determine their applicability. Eventually, the law firm will be required to convey its findings and opinions in writing, either to its client, to opposing counsel, or to the court. The entire process of finding the appropriate law, applying it to a particular factual dispute, and then conveying the results in writing is referred to as *legal research, legal analysis, and legal writing.*

criminal law. The area of law dealing with prosecution and defense of crimes.

civil law. The area of law dealing with private disputes between parties.

administrative procedures. Procedures used by agencies and boards.

BOX 1-1

THE LEGAL RESEARCH PROCESS

√ Identify factual question to research.

√ Find law that applies to factual question.

√ Analyze law in relationship to factual question.

√ Communicate findings.

1-3 THE ROLE OF THE RESEARCH ASSOCIATE

Unless you are an attorney, you are not allowed to give legal advice to clients. Therefore, if you are a paralegal or law clerk, any legal research you perform should be under the general supervision of an attorney. Before any client is advised of the findings of your legal research, an attorney should review it.

Many attorneys have very definite opinions about non-lawyers, especially paralegals, performing legal research. Some, in fact, are strongly opposed, believing that only law school graduates have the capacity to do research adequately. Others rely heavily on paralegals and law clerks. If you do legal research for an attorney, realize that he or she always expects accuracy and thoroughness. The attorney often relies on your research when advising clients or when arguing matters in court.

Even if your job responsibilities do not include working as a research associate for an attorney, if you work in a law office in any capacity, you will undoubtedly find yourself doing legal research for your own benefit. Legal research, analysis, and writing skills contribute greatly to your success in a law office.

⇨ **A Point to Remember**   A paralegal or a law clerk cannot give legal advice. To do so is the unauthorized practice of law and is unethical, not to mention illegal. Paralegals or clerks who do legal research should report their findings to their supervising attorney. All legal advice to a client must come from the attorney.

1-4 LEGAL PUBLICATIONS

Law is found in the same types of materials as any other information, i.e., books, periodicals such as magazines or newspapers, and electronic media. Published law is called either a **primary source** of law or a **secondary source** of law. The former is a work that contains the law itself, such as publications of constitutions, cases, statutes, and administrative regulations. Publications of cases are called **case reporters.** Publications of statutes are sometimes called **code books.** Secondary sources of law are publications that explain or discuss the law, for example legal encyclopedias and journals. Often secondary sources are helpful in finding and understanding the primary law. The goal of legal research is always to find a primary source of law controlling your factual situation.

Until recently, the term *law publication* referred to books or magazines. Today, a broader definition is necessary. Primary and secondary sources of law are found not only in books, but also in electric form. **CD-ROM libraries** containing both primary and secondary sources are common. Furthermore, legal researchers can read primary and secondary sources of the law through online services such as **LEXIS, Westlaw,** and the Internet.

primary source.   A work that contains the law itself.

secondary source.   A tool used to help understand the law; one such tool is a legal encyclopedia that explains the law.

case reporters.   Books that contain case decisions from the courts.

code books.   Books that contain codes or statutes.

CD-ROM libraries.   Legal materials, either primary or secondary sources, stored on CD-ROM.

LEXIS.   A computer-assisted legal research service.

Westlaw.   A computer-assisted legal research service.

1-5 THE LAW LIBRARY

Types of Libraries

One of the prerequisites to doing legal research is familiarity with the **law library,** which is one dedicated to legal resource material. If you work in a law firm, you will probably find that the firm maintains its own library. Law libraries maintained by law firms may contain either small collections of basic law books or extensive collections of legal research material. Some firms even employ law librarians to maintain their libraries.

law library.   A library that is dedicated to legal resource material.

⇨ **A Point to Remember**   You should make every effort to become familiar with your firm's law library as soon as possible. Knowing what resources are immediately available can save you time and worry.

If you need a more comprehensive legal library, you may be able to use a county law library or that of a nearby law school. These libraries probably contain more material than you will ever need, most likely material not only related to the law of your state and the laws of the United States, but also information concerning the laws of other states and of foreign nations. County law libraries are often open to the public. Law school libraries, on the other hand, may only be available to you if your law firm has a special arrangement with the school.

In addition to the traditional law library, today's researcher has access to material through the computer online sources LEXIS and Westlaw, which are large databases of legal materials. In a sense, they are large virtual law libraries where researchers can find legal material from the convenience of their own desk at almost any time of the day or night. All that is needed is a computer, Internet connection, and a subscription to the service. Unlike the traditional library, LEXIS and Westlaw charge fees for use of their resources.

Law libraries contain legal material as their primary content. However, many general libraries also contain legal collections. Even your local library may have copies of your state codes, federal codes, or case law. Many university or college libraries, as well as the Internet, contain a wide array of legal materials.

BOX 1-2

LEGAL RESOURCES ON THE INTERNET

The following Web sites contain extensive primary and secondary sources of the law.

http://www.loc.gov/law/public/law.html	The Law Library of Congress
www.findlaw.com	FindLaw
www.lexisone.com	lexisONE

---

table of contents. An outline of the material covered in the book or document.

index. A list of words and phrases that reflect the topics covered in the book.

table of cases. A common feature of legal publications containing the names of all cases cited in the book or document.

table of statutes. A common feature of legal publications containing a list of all statutes or codes that are referenced in the book.

table of abbreviations. A common feature of legal publications containing an explanation of all abbreviations found in the book.

Types of Materials Found in Law Libraries

When you visit a law library, you find books and periodicals such as legal journals, magazines, and newspapers. See Figure 1-1 for a list of the specific types of books found in most law libraries.

In many law libraries, you find electronically stored information. Today legal materials are found not only in print, but also on disk and CD-ROM, and many law libraries make these available to researchers.

Learning to do legal research requires a great deal of time and effort. However, law books and periodicals are often similar to non-legal materials. Most law books (except for case reporters) have an extensive **table of contents** and **index.** The table of contents, like that of any book, is an outline of the material covered in the book. The index is a list of words and phrases that reflect the topics covered. Using both enables you to find any particular topic in the book. When using legal periodicals, you can locate specific topics in indexes that resemble the *Reader's Guide to Periodical Literature* that you probably used when writing research papers in high school and college.

Many law books contain various tables, either in the front or the back, such as a **table of cases,** a **table of statutes,** and a **table of abbreviations.** These generally include references cited within the book.

Case Reporters	Large sets of books containing written case decisions or opinions from state and federal courts
Code Books	Sets of books containing either federal or state statutory law organized in a topical order; also may contain copies of the federal or state constitution
Encyclopedias	Multivolume sets of books that explain the law; they are organized alphabetically by topic; some explain American law in general, others are limited to explanations of laws in a single state
Digests	Multivolume sets of books that act as a detailed topical index to case reporters; are organized topically and contain short summaries of cases
Looseleaf Service	A type of legal work, usually concerning a single legal topic (such as family law), where the written material is kept in a pull-apart binder. The material is continually updated. When laws are changed the publisher sends replacement pages to the subscribers of the service. Pages with the old law are removed and replaced with new pages that reflect the changes in the law.
Treatises	Usually single books published on one legal subject
Form Books	Books containing forms that lawyers use to prepare legal documents; sometimes referred to as *practice books*
Legal Periodicals	Magazines, journals, and newspapers related to the practice of law; included are law reviews, and journals published regularly by law schools

FIGURE 1-1 Types of Legal Materials

One aspect of law books is fairly unique, however: they must be current. Because the law is constantly changing, law books must reflect those changes. Many law books are therefore supplemented regularly by **pocket part** supplements that contain recent changes in the law and slip into an opening on the inside of the back binding.

pocket part. A removable supplement; includes all changes or additions to the material contained in the hardbound volume.

➡ **A Point to Remember** When using any law book, always check the back to see if there is a pocket part supplement. If so, be sure to read any section addressing your topic.

BOX 1-3

COMMON FEATURES OF LAW BOOKS

Most law publications contain:
- √ directions about how to use the book or set
- √ explanation of abbreviations used in the book
- √ table of contents
- √ index
- √ table of cases
- √ table of statutes
- √ pocket part supplements

1-6 THE LANGUAGE OF THE LAW

You have probably heard the expression, "He talks just like a lawyer." Unfortunately, this is usually not a compliment. Instead, it reflects the fact that lawyers and other legal professionals often use unique jargon and terminology understood only by other legal professionals. When you work with an attorney as a paralegal or a law clerk, especially if you are doing legal research, you become familiar with some special terms and phrases. For example, in the interoffice memorandum at the beginning of this chapter, the supervising attorney used many terms common to legal professionals engaged in legal research. The research associate to whom the memo was addressed would be lost if he or she did not understand the terms *Memo of P. and A.s, brief, holding, rationale,* and *Shepardizing.* The research associate would also be unable to function without understanding the meaning of the citation "132 F.2d 902."

As you go through the chapters in this text, you will become familiar with the terminology used by legal researchers. You will learn what a *memorandum of points and authorities* is, and will probably even write one yourself. You will learn how to brief cases and identify a *holding and rationale.* You will learn all about *Shepardizing.*

Although you will become familiar with the terms used by legal researchers, the language of the law may still present problems for you. When doing legal research, you are usually reading cases, statutes, or other legal source material written by lawyers (or judges) for other lawyers. For example, consider the following passage from a case in which the author (a judge) is discussing whether a homeowner has discriminated against a family renting the home by putting a limit on the number of people who could live in the home.

The government argues that the Pfaffs' numerical occupancy restriction has a disparate impact on families with children which is prima facie discriminatory, and that the Pfaffs have failed to rebut this prima facie case.... To establish a prima facie case of disparate impact under the FHA, 'a plaintiff must show at least that the defendant's actions had a discriminatory effect.' *Pfaff v. Dept. of Housing and Urban Development,* 88 F.3d 739, 745 (1996).

Many terms used in the law are not common to everyday language. Some legal concepts or ideas are expressed by using the Latin terminology. Many words that you *think* you know have special meanings when used in a legal context. It is essential, therefore, to have and use a **legal dictionary,** which is one that defines and explains legal terms. Another tool is a **legal thesaurus,** which provides synonyms for legal terms. This is particularly helpful when you use an index. Common legal terms used in case law are found in Table 1-1. Look over this list and see how many you understand.

In addition to understanding the unique vocabulary of the law, a legal researcher also must be familiar with special abbreviations, known as **legal citations,** used to describe resource material.

legal dictionary. A dictionary defining and explaining legal terms.

legal thesaurus. A book providing synonyms for legal words.

legal citations. Special abbreviations used to describe resource material.

Citing the Law

If you have ever written a term paper and used footnotes or a bibliography, you know that there are standard abbreviations for research sources such as books, magazines, and encyclopedias. The same is true for legal resource materials. An abbreviated or shorthand way of referring to a particular legal source is called a *legal citation.* The leading authority for legal citation form is *A Uniform System of Citation,* published by

TABLE 1-1　Legal Terminology

Affirm	Precedent
Appeal	Real party in interest
Appellant	Remand
Appellee	Respondent
Civil	Reverse
Criminal	*Stare decisis*
Defendant	Writ of certiorari
Motion for summary judgment	Writ of habeas corpus
Plaintiff	Writ of mandate

the Harvard Law Review Association and commonly referred to as *The Bluebook* or the *Harvard Bluebook*. This book provides citation format and accepted abbreviations for almost all legal materials, both federal and state. While it is the most commonly used authority for citations, it is not the only one. The *ALWD Citation Manual,* created by the Association of Legal Writing Directors, is another popular citation guide. Your state may publish its own style manual. In addition, you must know local court rules. Many may have rules dictating which style manual should be followed in documents filed with those courts.

TECHNOLOGY CORNER

Many of us use the Internet every day. The Internet provides a great deal of information. Some of this information is useful and accurate. We must remember that the Internet provides a huge self-publishing environment. Anyone can create and maintain his or her own Web page. Be careful to evaluate the source of the information you locate.

Using the Internet and performing legal research on the Internet are not the same activity. Legal research on the Internet is still evolving. Some of the information is accurate and *current*. Some of the information is either inaccurate or out-of-date. Always check to see who publishes the information you want to use and when it was last updated.

Consider beginning an Internet notebook. Keep track of the sites you find most useful and user friendly. Create a simple template and fill it in each time you wish to add a new site to your notebook. Your template might include the following information:

Site Visit Summary

Address (URL):

Name of Site:

Description of the information available:

List of best links to other sites (if available):

It is impossible to provide a complete and accurate list of great legal research sites. However, this text suggests certain Web sites and provides tips to help you navigate the Internet successfully.

The following law school Web sites may prove useful during your studies. Law schools are often tremendous sources of accurate information.

www.law.cornell.edu

www.law.indiana.edu

www.washburnlaw.edu

Always remember: Sites on the Internet come and go and their quality may vary greatly over a two-year period.

CHAPTER SUMMARY

Legal research usually involves finding the law that applies to a specific factual question. Because lawyers must know the current law in their jurisdiction, even the most experienced legal practitioners do research before advising a client or arguing a matter before a court. Paralegals and law clerks often do legal research; indeed many non-legal professionals find this competency to be an important tool.

The total process of legal research involves identifying the factual issue, finding the law, applying the law to the factual situation, and communicating these findings. While paralegals and law clerks often perform the research, they should do so under the supervision of a lawyer. Accuracy and thoroughness are essential. Paralegals and other non-attorneys must be careful not to give legal advice to a client because to do so constitutes the unauthorized practice of law and is unethical and illegal.

Legal publications include primary and secondary sources of the law. A primary source includes the law itself (constitutions, cases, statutes, and administrative regulations). Secondary sources, such as legal encyclopedias and journals, help explain and find the primary source of law. Legal publications are found in printed as well as in electronic format.

Legal research is usually conducted in law libraries found in most law offices. Counties and law schools also maintain large law libraries. Materials there resemble materials found in any library. Law books contain many of the same features found in reference books, such as a table of contents and an index. In addition, many law books contain tables of cases, tables of statutes, and tables of abbreviations used in the book. Some books also include pocket part supplements that keep the work up-to-date.

Legal research requires a familiarity with legal terminology and with the way that law is cited. A law dictionary is essential for any new researcher.

TERMS TO REMEMBER

criminal law	law library
civil law	table of contents
administrative procedures	index
primary source	table of cases
secondary source	table of statutes
case reporters	table of abbreviations
code books	pocket part

CD-ROM libraries   legal dictionary
LEXIS   legal thesaurus
Westlaw   legal citations

QUESTIONS FOR REVIEW

1. Explain the process of legal research, analysis, and writing.
2. Discuss the various sources of U.S. law.
3. What is the difference between a primary source of law and a secondary source?
4. What types of legal materials are found in law libraries?
5. Describe some of the common features of legal publications.

CAN YOU FIGURE IT OUT?

Refer to Figure 1-1, Types of Legal Materials. The Interoffice Memorandum at the beginning of this chapter refers to the *Catlette* case found at 132 F.2d 902. In what type of legal material would you expect to find this authority?

RESEARCH ASSIGNMENTS AND ACTIVITIES

1. Using a legal dictionary, define the terms in Table 1-1.
2. Using a legal thesaurus, find different words for each of the terms in Table 1-1.
3. Visit the law library that you will use to do your legal research assignments. Locate the following legal sources:

   The United States Codes

   A case reporter containing decisions from the United States Supreme Court

   Your state code

   Case reporters containing case law from your state.

   Review the list of common features of law books found in Box 1-3 earlier in the chapter. Which of these features is found in each of the above-listed legal sources?
4. Review the Web sites listed in Box 1-2. List the primary sources of law found on each of the sites.

CASE PROJECT

Select one hypothetical case from those found in Appendix A. You will be asked to work on this hypothetical case throughout this text. Read the facts carefully and make a list of all legal terms found in the factual scenario. Which of these terms appear in Table 1-1? Define all legal terms found in the factual situation.

BEFORE YOU BEGIN

CHAPTER OUTLINE

CHAPTER OBJECTIVES

When you complete this chapter you should be able to

- List the sources of U.S. law.
- Explain the relationship between state and federal law.
- Explain the appeal process.
- Describe the relationship between the sources of law.
- Compare and contrast the West Topic and Key Number System with the Lawyers Cooperative Total Client-Service Library.
- Explain the concept of *stare decisis*
- Explain the difference between mandatory and persuasive authority.

CITATION MATTERS

UNITED STATES SUPREME COURT CASE LAW

THE BLUEBOOK — RULE 8

Capitalize "Court" when referring to the United States Supreme Court.

> The Court stated that all immigrants are entitled to due process. (referring to the United States Supreme Court)

THE BLUEBOOK — RULE 10

United States Supreme Court Case Law Citation Analyzed

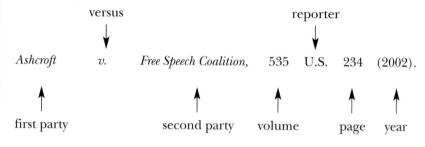

This is a *citation sentence* and a period is placed at the end.

THE BLUEBOOK - TABLE 1 (T.1)

Cite to the *U.S. Reports* unless the official citation is not yet assigned. This is often the situation with very new cases. When there is no U.S. citation, cite to the *Supreme Court Reporter* (S. Ct.), *Lawyer's Edition* (L. Ed., L. Ed. 2d), or *United States Law Week* (U.S.L.W.), in that order of preference.

The *U.S. Reports* is the official reporter of United States Supreme Court case law. It is "official" because it is published by the federal government. The *Supreme Court Reporter, Lawyer's Edition,* and *United States Law Week* are all unofficial reporters of United States Supreme Court case law. That simply means these collections of U.S. Supreme Court case law are not published by the federal government. The *case law decisions* in these sets are identical. The differences are found in the editorial enhancements. Chapter 4 explains some of the features found in the unofficial publications. Take a trip to your local law library. Locate the following volumes.

> 491 U.S. 397
> 109 S. Ct. 2533
> 105 L. Ed. 2d 342

Open all of them to the first page of the *Texas v. Johnson* case. Remember, the first number is the volume number, the second number is the first page of the case. Notice that the prefatory material varies from one publication to the next. You may use any of these volumes during your research.

However, you must cite to the official publication (the U.S.). Notice that the unofficial publications indicate the page breaks for the *U.S. Reports*. That means it is not necessary to actually read the official publication because you can easily cite to it from the unofficial publications.

Look at Figure 4-4 on page 66. Notice that in the first column the word *prohibited* is broken with what looks like an upside down T. It is breaking the word *prohibited*, and there is a number following *ited*. This shows that page 398, in the official reporter (U.S.), begins with "ited on the basis that . . . ."

Look at Figure 4-5 on page 70. Notice that the first column opens with "[491 US 399]." This publication lets the reader know that the material following the bracketed citation is the beginning of page 399 in the official reporter. Remember, this is done so that the researcher may use the unofficial publications and still cite to the official publication.

A researcher may quote from material *in* the opinion. A researcher should never quote from anything added by a publisher. That material (the editorial enhancements) is there to help, but it is not part of the decision, so it cannot be cited.

OTHER FEDERAL REPORTERS

The *Federal Reporter* publishes the United States Court of Appeals cases for the Federal Circuits. This is an example of a *Federal Reporter* citation:

Free Speech Coalition v. Reno, 220 F.3d 1113 (9th Cir. 200).

There is no space between the *F.* and *3d*.

The *Federal Supplement* publishes the United States trial court cases for the Federal Districts. This is an example of a *Federal Supplement* citation:

EEOC v. Rotary Corp., 297 F. Supp. 2d 643 (N.D.N.Y. 2003).

There is a space between *F.* and *Supp.*

Other reporters of federal case law are listed in Table 1 (T.1) of THE BLUEBOOK.

INTEROFFICE MEMORANDUM

TO: Research Associate

FROM: Supervising Attorney

RE: Research Assignment—*Rambeaux* Case

I am afraid that our local prosecutor is about to go to the grand jury and ask for a criminal indictment against our client, Rambeaux. Please research the law and let me know what possible criminal charges our county prosecutor can bring against Rambeaux.

2-1 INTRODUCTION

Visiting a law library and beginning legal research on any project can be an intimidating experience. Before you start any research, you should have a general understanding of some basic legal concepts, particularly of the organization of the U.S. legal system and the various sources of law. Because case law is an important source of law, you should also understand how case law develops and how it applies. Finally, before you begin to research you should know about the features developed by two legal publishers, West Group and Lawyers Cooperative Publishing. Although you will undoubtedly study these matters in detail in other classes, this chapter provides you with a brief review of these concepts and explains how they affect your legal research.

2-2 LAW AND U.S. GOVERNMENT

In the previous chapter, you were introduced to the way legal materials are published. A key feature of legal publications is that separate publications often exist for federal law and for that of each individual state. While some secondary sources attempt to discuss all laws, many legal publications (especially primary sources of law) contain law related only to a specific jurisdiction, that is, only federal law, or only the law of one state. When you begin your research you can save time, and be more accurate, if you focus on publications that contain the proper law. For example, suppose you were asked to research the following question: "If Mary divorces John, and they are both California residents, is she entitled to one-half of his pension?" Because the question clearly indicates that the parties are California residents, the state law of California controls, and you must begin your research in books that contain California state law. This is a question related to family law (sometimes called *domestic relations*) and is controlled by state law rather than federal law. Every time you have a research question, you must make this type of determination, according to your knowledge of the organization and operation of the American legal system.

In the United States, government operates under a principle called **federalism,** which means that two separate governments, federal and state, regulate citizens. Each government is responsible for making its own laws. When researching an issue, you are therefore faced with different sets of laws for each state and for the federal government. A general understanding of the types of laws that are likely to be found in the collection of federal laws versus the types of laws that are likely to be found in the collection of state laws will help you with your research.

federalism. A system of government in which the people are regulated by both federal and state governments.

Federal Laws

The power of the federal government to regulate or make laws is not unlimited. It has only that power given to it in the United States Constitution, which grants it the **express powers** to regulate such matters as the coining of money, the post office, and the military. (See Table 2-1 for a more complete list.) Along with express powers, the federal government is also given the power to make all laws that are necessary and proper for carrying into execution any of the stated powers. These are known as **implied powers.**

express powers. Powers given to the federal government that are expressly stated in the Constitution.

implied powers. Powers to make all laws that are necessary and proper for carrying into execution any of the stated or express powers of the government.

TABLE 2-1   Article 1 Section 8 of the United States Constitution

Powers Granted to U.S. Congress

1. Collect taxes; pay debts; provide for common defense and welfare of U.S.
2. Borrow money
3. Regulate commerce with foreign nations and between states
4. Establish rules for naturalization and bankruptcy
5. Coin and regulate money
6. Punish counterfeiting
7. Establish post offices
8. Establish copyright and patents
9. Establish inferior courts
10. Define and punish piracies and felonies on the high seas
11. Declare war
12. Raise and support armies
13. Maintain a navy
14. Regulate land and naval forces
15. Call forth a militia
16. Organize, arm, and train a militia
17. Govern the area to become seat of federal government
18. To make all laws necessary to carry out foregoing powers

State Laws

States have very broad powers to make laws that control within the state boundaries. Some of the more common areas regulated by state laws include family law, contractual relationships, tort liability, real estate transactions, and corporate law.

Relationship Between State and Federal Law

In some cases your research may show that both state and federal laws apply. Unfortunately, sometimes these laws are different. Where a conflict exists, federal law controls. This is because of the "Supremacy Clause" of the Constitution (Article VI): "This Constitution, and the Laws of the United States which shall be made in Pursuance thereof . . . shall be the supreme Law of the Land; and the Judges in every State shall be bound thereby, any Thing in the Constitution or Laws of any State to the Contrary notwithstanding." When a state passes a law that conflicts with the Constitution, the United States Supreme Court has the power to declare that state law unconstitutional and unenforceable.

However, not all differences between state and federal laws mean that there is a conflict. This is clearly seen in the area of "search and seizure." The U.S. Supreme Court has decided many cases dealing with the legality of various types of searches. If the Supreme Court has held that certain police conduct violates the Constitution, then no state can allow that conduct to occur. However, states do have the right to prevent police searches that have been approved by the U.S. Supreme Court. This is because states are allowed to grant residents more rights than those found in the Bill of Rights. You must understand federal law to determine if a conflict exists with state law.

Following is a U.S. Supreme Court case, *Ohio v. Robinette*, which illustrates how different state and federal laws can apply to the same case. The case involved a traffic

stop and subsequent search made by a state police officer. During the search, the officer found contraband and the driver was charged with possession of drugs under Ohio statutory law. The case was tried in state court. However, a procedural issue arose in the case concerning the legality of the search. Read the opinion of the Court written by Justice Rehnquist along with the concurring opinion of Justice Ginsburg. Then answer the questions for analysis following the case.

CASE 2-1

Ohio v. Robinette
519 U.S. 33 (1996)
OPINION: CHIEF JUSTICE REHNQUIST delivered the opinion of the Court.

We are here presented with the question whether the Fourth Amendment requires that a lawfully seized defendant must be advised that he is "free to go" before his consent to search will be recognized as voluntary. We hold that it does not.

This case arose on a stretch of Interstate 70 north of Dayton, Ohio, where the posted speed limit was 45 miles per hour because of construction. Respondent Robert D. Robinette was clocked at 69 miles per hour as he drove his car along this stretch of road, and was stopped by Deputy Roger Newsome of the Montgomery County Sheriff's office. Newsome asked for and was handed Robinette's driver's license, and he ran a computer check which indicated that Robinette had no previous violations. Newsome then asked Robinette to step out of his car, turned on his mounted video camera, issued a verbal warning to Robinette, and returned his license.

At this point, Newsome asked, "One question before you get gone: Are you carrying any illegal contraband in your car? Any weapon of any kind, drugs, anything like that?" App. To Brief for Respondent 2 [internal quotation marks omitted]. Robinette answered "no" to these questions, after which Deputy Newsome asked if he could search the car. Robinette consented. In the car, Deputy Newsome discovered a small amount of marijuana and, in a film container, a pill which was later determined to be methylenedioxymethamphetamine (MDMA). Robinette was then arrested and charged with knowing possession of a controlled substance, MDMA, in violation of Ohio Rev. Code Ann. § 2925.11(A) (1993).

Before trial, Robinette unsuccessfully sought to suppress this evidence. He then pleaded "no contest," and was found guilty. On appeal, the Ohio court of appeals reversed, ruling that the search resulted from an unlawful detention. The Supreme Court of Ohio, by a divided vote, affirmed. 73 Ohio St. 3d 65, 653 N.E.2d 695 (1995). In its opinion, that court established a bright-line prerequisite for consensual interrogation under these circumstances:

"The right, guaranteed by the federal and Ohio Constitutions, to be secure in one's person and property requires that citizens stopped for traffic offenses be clearly informed by the detaining officer when they are free to go after a valid detention, before an officer attempts to engage in a consensual interrogation. Any attempt at consensual interrogation must be preceded by the phrase 'At this time you legally are free to go' or by words of similar import." *Id.*, at 650–651, 653 N.E. 2d at 696.

We granted certiorari, 516 U.S. _____ (1996), to review this *per se* rule, and we now reverse.

We must first consider whether we have jurisdiction to review the Ohio Supreme Court's decision. Respondent contends that we lack such jurisdiction because the Ohio decision rested upon the Ohio Constitution, in addition to the Federal Constitution. Under *Michigan v. Long,* 463 U.S. 1032 (1983), when "a state court decision fairly appears to rest primarily on federal law, or to be interwoven with the federal law, and when the adequacy and independence of any possible state law

ground is not clear from the face of the opinion, we will accept as the most reasonable explanation that the state court decided the case the way it did because it believed that federal law required it to do so." *Id.,* at 1040–1041. Although the opinion below mentions Article I, Section 14 of the Ohio Constitution in passing (a section which reads identically to the Fourth Amendment), the opinion clearly relies on federal law nevertheless. Indeed, the only cases it discusses or even cites are federal cases, except for one state case which itself applies the federal constitution.

Our jurisdiction is not defeated by the fact that these citations appear in the body of the opinion, while, under Ohio law, "the Supreme Court speaks as a court only through the syllabi of its cases." *See Ohio v. Gallagher,* 425 U.S. 257, 259 (1976). When the syllabus, as here, speaks only in general terms of "the federal and Ohio Constitutions," it is permissible for us to turn to the body of the opinion to discern the grounds for decision. *Zacchini v. Scripps-Howard Broadcasting Co.,* 433 U.S. 562, 566 (1977).

Respondent Robinette also contends that we may not reach the question presented in the petition because the Supreme Court of Ohio also held, as set out in the syllabus (1): "When the motivation behind a police officer's continued detention of a person stopped for a traffic violation is not related to the purpose of the original, constitutional stop, and when that continued detention is not based on articulable facts giving rise to a suspicion of some separate illegal activity justifying an extension of the detention, the continued detention constitutes an illegal seizure," 73 Ohio St. 3d at 650, 653 N.E.2d at 696.

In reliance on this ground, the Supreme Court of Ohio held that when Newsome returned to Robinette's car and asked him to get out of the car, after he had determined in his own mind not to give Robinette a ticket, the detention then became unlawful.

Respondent failed to make any such argument in his brief in opposition to certiorari. *See* this Court's Rule 15.2. We believe the issue as to the continuing legality of the detention is a "predicate to an intelligent resolution" of the question presented, and therefore "fairly included therein." This Court's rule 14.1 (a); *Vance v. Terrazas,* 444 U.S. 252, 258–259, n. 5 (1960). The parties

have briefed this issue, and we proceed to decide it.

We think that under our recent decision in *Whren v. United States,* 517 U.S. _____ (1996) (decided after the Supreme Court of Ohio decided the present case), the subjective intentions of the officer did not make the continued detention of respondent illegal under the Fourth Amendment. As we made clear in *Whren,* " 'the fact that [an] officer does not have the state of mind which is hypothecated by the reasons which provide the legal justification for the officer's action does not invalidate the action taken as long as the circumstances, viewed objectively, justify that action' . . . Subjective intentions play no role in ordinary, probable-cause Fourth Amendment analysis." *Id.,* at _____ (slip op. at 6–7) (quoting *Scott v. United States,* 436 U.S. 128, 138 (1978)). And there is no question that, in light of the admitted probable cause to stop Robinette for speeding, Deputy Newsome was objectively justified in asking Robinette to get out of the car, subjective thoughts notwithstanding. *See Pennsylvania v. Mimms,* 434 U.S. 106, 111, n. 6 (1977) ("We hold . . . that once a motor vehicle has been lawfully detained for traffic violation, the police officers may order the driver to get out of the vehicle without violating the Fourth Amendment's proscription of unreasonable searches and seizures.")

We now turn to the merits of the question presented. We have long held that the "touchstone of the Fourth Amendment is reasonableness." *Florida v. Jimeno,* 500 U.S. 248, 250 (1991). Reasonableness, in turn is measured in objective terms by examining the totality of the circumstances.

In applying this test we have consistently eschewed bright-line rules, instead emphasizing the fact-specific nature of the reasonableness inquiry. Thus, in *Florida v. Royer,* 460 U.S. 491 (1983), we expressly disavowed any "litmus-paper test" or single "sentence or . . . paragraph . . . rule," in recognition of the "endless variations in the facts and circumstances" implicating the Fourth Amendment. *Id.,* at 506. Then in *Michigan v. Chesternut,* 486 U.S. 567 (1988), when both parties urged "bright-line rules applicable to all investigatory pursuits," we rejected both proposed rules as contrary to our "traditional contextual approach." *Id.,* at 572–573. And again, in *Florida v. Bostick,* 501 U.S. 429 (1991), when the Florida

Supreme Court adopted a per se rule that questioning abroad a bus always constitutes a seizure, we reversed, reiterating that the proper inquiry necessitates a consideration of "all the circumstances surrounding the encounter." *Id.*, at 439.

We have previously rejected a per se rule very similar to that adopted by the Supreme Court of Ohio in determining the validity of a consent to search. In *Schneckloth v. Bustamonte*, 412 U.S. 218 (1973), it was argued that such a consent could not be valid unless the defendant knew that he had a right to refuse the request. We rejected this argument: "While knowledge of the right to refuse consent is one factor to be taken into account, the government need not establish such knowledge as the *sine qua non* of an effective consent." *Id.*, at 227. And just as it "would be thoroughly impractical to impose on the normal consent search the detailed requirements of an effective warning," *Id.*, at 231, so too would it be unrealistic to require police officers to always inform detainees that they are free to go before a consent to search may be deemed voluntary.

The Fourth Amendment test for a valid consent to a search is that the consent be voluntary, and "voluntariness is a question of fact to be determined from all the circumstances," *Id.*, at 248–249. The Supreme Court of Ohio having held otherwise, its judgment is reversed, and the case is remanded for further proceedings not inconsistent with this opinion.

It is so ordered.

CONCUR: JUSTICE GINSBURG, concurring in the judgment.

Robert Robinette's traffic stop for a speeding violation on an interstate highway in Ohio served as a prelude to a search of his automobile for illegal drugs. Robinette's experience was not uncommon in Ohio. As the Ohio Supreme Court related, the sheriff's deputy who detained Robinette for speeding and then asked Robinette for permission to search his vehicle "was on drug interdiction patrol at the time." 73 Ohio St. 3d 650, 651, 653 N.E. 2d 695, 696 (1995). The deputy testified in Robinette's case that he routinely requested permission to search automobiles he stopped for traffic violations. *Ibid.* According to the deputy's testimony in another prosecution, he requested consent to search in 786 traffic stops in 1992, the year of Robinette's arrest. *State v. Retherford*,

93 Ohio App. 3d 586, 594, n. 3, 639 N.E. 2d 498, 503 n. 3, *dism'd*, 69 Ohio St. 3d 1488, 635 N.E. 2d 43 (1994).

From their unique vantage point, Ohio's courts observed that traffic stops in the State were regularly giving way to contraband searches, characterized as consensual, even when officers had no reason to suspect illegal activity. One Ohio appellate court noted: "Hundreds, and perhaps thousands of Ohio citizens are being routinely delayed in their travels and asked to relinquish to uniformed police officers their right to privacy in their automobiles and luggage, sometimes for no better reason than to provide an officer the opportunity to "practice" his drug interdiction technique." 932 Ohio App. 3d at 594, 639 N.E. 2d, at 503 (footnote omitted).

Against this background, the Ohio Supreme Court determined, and announced in Robinette's case, that the federal and state constitutional rights of Ohio citizens to be secure in their persons and property called for the protection of a clear-cut instruction to the State's police officers: An officer wishing to engage in consensual interrogation of a motorist at the conclusion of a traffic stop must first tell the motorist that he or she is free to go. The Ohio Supreme Court described the need for its first—tell-then-ask rule this way:

"The transition between detention and a consensual exchange can be so seamless that the untrained eye may not notice that it has occurred . . . .

"Most people believe that they are validly in a police officer's custody as long as the officer continues to interrogate them. The police officer retains the upper hand and the accouterments of authority. That the officer lacks legal license to continue to detain them is unknown to most citizens, and a reasonable person would not feel free to walk away as the officer continues to address him.

"While the legality of consensual encounters between police and citizens should be preserved, we do not believe that this legality should be used by police officers to turn a routine traffic stop into a fishing expedition for unrelated criminal activity. The Fourth Amendment to the federal Constitution and Section 14, Article I of the Ohio Constitution exist to protect citizens against such an unreasonable interference with their liberty." 73 Ohio St. 3d at 654–655, 653 N.E. 2d at 698–699.

Today's opinion reversing the decision of the Ohio Supreme Court does not pass judgment on the wisdom of the first-tell-then-ask rule. This Court's opinion simply clarifies that the Ohio Supreme Court's instruction to police officers in Ohio is not, under this Court's controlling jurisprudent the command of the Federal Constitution. *See ante*, at 5–6. The Ohio Supreme Court invoked both the Federal Constitution and the Ohio Constitution without clearly indicating whether state law, standing alone, independently justified the court's rule. The ambiguity in the Ohio Supreme Court's decision renders this Court's exercise of jurisdiction proper under *Michigan v. Long*, 463 U.S. 1032, 1040–1042 (1983), and this Court's decision on the merits is consistent with the Court's "totality of the circumstances" Fourth Amendment precents, *see ante*, at 5. I therefore concur in the Court's judgment.

I write separately, however, because it seems to me improbable that the Ohio Supreme Court understood its first-tell-then-ask rule to be the Federal Constitution's mandate for the Nation as a whole. "[A] State is free as a matter of its own law to impose greater restrictions on police activity than those this Court holds to be necessary upon federal constitutional standards." *Oregon v. Haas*, 420 U.S. 714, 719. But ordinarily, when a state high court grounds a rule of criminal procedure in the Federal Constitution, the court thereby signals its view that the Nation's Constitution would require the rule in all 50 States. Given this Court's decisions in consent-to-search cases such as *Schneckloth v. Bustamonte*, 412 U.S. 218 (1973), and *Florida v. Bostick*, 501 U.S. 429 (1991), however, I suspect that the Ohio Supreme Court may not have homed in on the implication ordinarily to be drawn from a state court's reliance on the Federal constitution. In other words, I question whether the Ohio court thought of the strict rule it announced as a rule for the governance of police conduct not only in Miami County, Ohio, but also in Miami, Florida.

The first-tell-then-ask rule seems to be a prophylactic measure not so much extracted from the text of any constitutional provision as crafted by the Ohio Supreme Court to reduce the number of violations of textually guaranteed rights. In *Miranda v. Arizona*, 384 U.S. 436 (1966), this Court announced a similarly motivated rule as a minimal national requirement without

suggesting that the text of the Federal Constitution required the precise measures the Court's opinion set forth. *See id.*, at 467 ("The *Miranda* exclusionary rule . . . sweeps more broadly than the Fifth Amendment itself".) Although all parts of the United States fall within this Court's domain, the Ohio Supreme Court is not similarly situated. That court can declare prophylactic rules governing the conduct of officials in Ohio, but it cannot command the police forces of sister States. The very ease with which the Court today disposes of the federal leg of the Ohio Supreme Court's decision strengthens my impression that the Ohio Supreme Court saw its rule as a measure made for Ohio, designed to reinforce in that State the right of the people to be secure against unreasonable searches and seizures.

The Ohio Supreme Court's syllabus and opinion, however, were ambiguous. Under *Long*, the existence of ambiguity regarding the federal- or state-law basis of a state court decision will trigger this Court's jurisdiction. *Long* governs even when, all things considered, the more plausible reading of the state court's decision may be that the state court did not regard the Federal Constitution alone as a sufficient basis for its ruling. Compare *Arizona v. Evens*, 514 U.S. _____ (1995) (slip op., at 4–7), with *id.*, at _____ (slip op., at 10–11) (GINSBURG, J., dissenting).

It is incumbent on a state court, therefore, when it determines that its State's laws call for protection more complete than the Federal constitution demands, to be clear about its ultimate reliance on state law. Similarly, a state court announcing a new legal rule arguably derived from both federal and state law can definitively render state law an adequate and independent ground for its decision by a simple declaration to that effect. A recent Montana Supreme Court opinion on the scope of an individual's privilege against self-incrimination includes such a declaration:

"While we have devoted considerable time to a lengthy discussion of the application of the Fifth Amendment to the United States constitution, it is to be noted that this holding is also based separately and independently on [the defendant's] right to remain silent pursuant to Article II, Section 25 of the Montana Constitution." *State v. Fuller*, _____ Mont. _____ 915 P.2d 809, 816, *cert. denied*, 519 U.S. _____ (1996).

An explanation of this order meets the Court's instruction in *Long* that "if the state court decision indicates clearly and expressly that it is alternatively based on bona fide separate, adequate, and independent grounds, [this Court] will not undertake to review the decision." *Long*, 463 U.S. at 1041.

On remand, the Ohio Supreme Court may choose to clarify that its instructions to law-enforcement officers in Ohio find adequate and independent support in state law, and that in issuing these instructions, the court endeavored to state dispositively only the law applicable in Ohio. *See Evans*, 514 U.S. at _____ (slip op., at 8–12) (GINSBURG, J., dissenting). To avoid misunderstanding, the Ohio Supreme Court must itself speak with the clarity it sought to require of its State's police officers. The efficacy of its endeavor to safeguard the liberties of Ohioans without disarming the State's police can then be tested in the precise way Our Federalism was designed to work. *See e.g., Kaye, State Courts at the Dawn of a New Century: Common Law Courts Reading Statutes and Constitutions*, 70 N.Y.U.L. Rev. 1, 11–18 (1995); Linda, *First Things First: Rediscovering the States' Bills of Rights*, 9 U. Ballet. L. Rev. 379, 392–396 (1980).

Questions for Analysis

1. Did federal drug laws apply to this case? Why or why not?

2. What law is the Court interpreting in this case?

3. This case was remanded to the Ohio Supreme Court. Must the Supreme Court of Ohio find the search illegal? Explain.

4. On remand, suppose the Ohio Supreme Court decides that the Ohio state constitution requires a tell rule. If you were researching a similar case in Ohio in the future, would you rely on the U.S. Supreme Court case of *Ohio v. Robinette?* Explain.

5. Is there a conflict between the state and federal search and seizure laws in this case?

6. If you were researching a similar search and seizure issue in your state, would you rely on the case of *Ohio v. Robinette* if (a) the issue revolved around your state's constitution or if (b) the issue revolved around the meaning of the U.S. Constitution?

Cases you research are normally controlled either by federal law or state law because federal laws usually govern areas different from those governed by state laws. In part, this is because the United States Constitution limits the types of matters that can be controlled by the federal government. However, there are times when one case may involve questions of both federal and state law. For example, recall the Rodney King incident that occurred a number of years ago. In that case, the police officers were originally tried in state court for violating state laws relating to assault and battery and use of excessive force by police officers. After a jury found the officers not guilty in a state court proceeding, they were then charged in federal court for violating federal law (violating King's civil rights). There are also times when state courts are required to use federal law and when federal courts are required to use state laws. Consider the following situations.

(1) Jackson is arrested for possession of narcotics. The drugs were found after Jackson was stopped for speeding. The officer states that as he was writing a ticket for Jackson, the officer noted the smell of marijuana, ordered the driver out of the car, searched the vehicle, and found the drugs. Jackson is charged with possession of marijuana, a state crime. The case is filed in state court. If Jackson's attorney claims that the search was unconstitutional, the state court must look at federal law regarding the legality of the search, because this involves a constitutional right.

(2) Adams, a resident of Texas, is involved in an automobile accident with Brown, a resident of California. The accident is Adams' fault and Brown is

injured. The accident occurred in California. Normally lawsuits arising out of automobile accidents are filed in state court and are governed by that state's law regarding negligence. However, in this case, Brown could file a lawsuit to recover his damages in federal court because the federal courts have jurisdiction when the lawsuit is between citizens of different states and the plaintiff is claiming more than $75,000 in damages. This is known as *diversity of citizenship.* However, although the case will be tried in a federal court, the state substantive law applies.

Before you begin any research, determine if you are researching state law (and if so, which state), federal law, or both. You must research the law of the jurisdiction that controls the situation. Laws from other jurisdictions do not control. Sometimes, the determination of which law applies to a situation is itself a major issue in the case, requiring extensive research!

⇨ **A Point to Remember**   Where conflicts exist between federal and state laws, the federal law controls. However, not all differences result in a conflict. Do not *assume* that federal law always controls.

BOX 2-1

RESEARCH CHECKLIST: BEFORE YOU BEGIN

√ Review the factual situation.

√ Determine if the factual situation is controlled by federal law, by state law, or by both.

√ Use research materials that contain the proper law.

2-3 SOURCES OF U.S. LAW

Whether you are researching state law or federal law, you find some basic similarities because in both systems the laws come from the same types of sources. All governments, state and federal, have constitutions that are published in numerous sources. Other laws generally come from our legislatures, courts, and administrative agencies. Both the federal and state legislatures enact statutory laws. As a researcher, you most often use code books of the appropriate jurisdiction to find these laws. Federal courts and state courts are responsible for case law found in case reporters. Administrative agencies exist on both federal and state levels from which we derive administrative rules or regulations. U.S. law is thus found in four sources: constitutions, statutes, administrative rules or regulations, and case law decisions. Separate sources exist for the federal government and for each of the states.

Constitutional Law

The federal government and all states have constitutions, documents whose primary purpose is to establish the government and define its functions and obligations in relation to the people. The U.S. Constitution establishes and defines the role of the

federal government and its relation to the people of the United States. The U.S. Constitution applies only to the federal government, unless expressly made applicable to individual states. Each state constitution establishes and defines the role of state government and its relationship to citizens of that state. The various constitutions are published in numerous ways, often with the statutory law for the jurisdiction. In other words, the U.S. Consitution can be found with the U.S. Codes and state constitutions are usually found with the state codes.

Statutory Law

Statutory law results from legislative action. The federal and state legislatures enact laws that are then sent to the chief executive (the President or governor) for approval. After they are signed (or a veto properly overridden) the laws are organized and published in codes. The code for the United States is known as the *United States Code.* Legislatures also empower the courts to enact rules, known as *rules of court,* which govern practice in the courts. In addition, local governing bodies (cities and counties) enact laws, often known as *local ordinances* or *municipal codes.*

Administrative Regulations

In order for government to perform all of its tasks, it has become necessary for legislatures to create various agencies to handle specific jobs. For example, Congress created the Securities Exchange Commission (S.E.C.) to handle corporate stock transactions. In addition to creating these agencies, legislatures give these agencies or boards the right to make regulations that are necessary to function; these are known as *administrative regulations.* Administrative agencies exist in the federal government as well as in each state.

Case Law

U.S. law is based primarily on the English **common law,** a system in which laws developed through the courts and through case decisions. The common law was based on the concept of **precedent** or *stare decisis.* It was *not* based on a set of written laws or rules enacted by the government. Until a factual dispute arose and was resolved in the courts, there was no rule or law that controlled. When parties had a legal problem, their dispute was presented to a judge who decided the case. The decision then became precedent. Then, if the same type of factual dispute was presented to a court in the future, the judge followed the decision of the first case. Precedent is also referred to as *stare decisis.*

> **common law.** Body of law developed through the courts.
>
> **precedent.** The example set by the decision of an earlier court for similar cases or similar legal questions which arise in later cases.
>
> *stare decisis.* "It stands decided"; another term for precedent.

In the U.S. legal system, case law does not result every time any court decides a case. It results from decisions made by various *appellate* courts, including the Supreme Court. Because it comes from the courts, you should review the basic organization of the court system. In the federal system, there are three levels of courts: district courts, appellate courts, and the Supreme Court.

United States district courts are **trial courts.** This is where federal cases originate. The factual dispute is resolved at a trial. If the case is appealed, it proceeds to the United States circuit court of appeals where a three-judge panel reviews the proceedings of the trial court to determine if any serious legal errors occurred. If one of the parties is still not satisfied with the result, that party can request a hearing in the Supreme Court, usually by filing a document called a **petition for writ of certiorari.** In most cases, the Supreme Court has the option to hear or not to hear the case.

> **trial courts.** This is where cases originate and where the factual dispute is resolved at a trial.
>
> **petition for writ of certiorari.** A request for a hearing in the Supreme Court.

```
+------------------------------------------------------------+
|                                                            |
|                    SUPREME COURT                           |
|                                                            |
|             (written opinions are case law)                |
|                          ↓                                 |
|           INTERMEDIATE APPELLATE COURTS                    |
|                                                            |
|   (written opinions are case law if published and if final)|
|                          ↓                                 |
|                     TRIAL COURTS                           |
|                                                            |
|            (written opinions are not case law)             |
|                                                            |
+------------------------------------------------------------+
```

FIGURE 2-1   Courts and Case Law

Most states pattern their court systems after the federal system, although some states only have one level of appellate courts. See Figure 2-1.

Case law originates with a controversy or dispute between two or more parties. The parties bring that controversy before a court asking for resolution. A trial court resolves that dispute, but the resolution will not result in case law. That will happen only if the case is appealed. If a dissatisfied party does **appeal,** the decision of the appellate court may become case law, but not if a higher court agrees to hear a further appeal. Also, in some jurisdictions, not all final appellate court decisions become case law; they become case law only if the court orders that they be published. Unpublished appellate court decisions are not case law and cannot be cited as precedent. Decisions of the United States Supreme Court, as well as those from the highest state courts, always result in case law.

appeal.   Review of a lower court decision.

▷ **A Point to Remember**   Case law comes from appellate decisions, that is, decisions from courts of appeals or Supreme Courts. It does not come from trial court decisions.

Case law is discussed in detail in Chapter 4.

```
+------------------------------------------------------------+
|                                                            |
|  BOX 2-2                                                   |
|                      SOURCES OF LAW                        |
|                                                            |
|       Federal Law                                          |
|            U.S. Constitution                               |
|            United States Codes                             |
|            Federal Administrative Regulations              |
|            Federal Cases                                   |
|       State Law                                            |
|            State Cases                                     |
|            State Constitution                              |
|            State Codes                                     |
|            State Administrative Regulations                |
|                                                            |
+------------------------------------------------------------+
```

2-4 THE APPEAL PROCESS

Because all case law comes from appellate courts, before reading case law you should be familiar with the appeal process; see Figure 2-2. An appeal results when one party to an action is dissatisfied with the result and asks a higher court to review the trial. In general, in a civil case either party has the right to appeal. In a criminal trial, however, only the defendant has the right to appeal because of the **double jeopardy** clause of the Constitution. An appeal usually takes place only after a final judgment in the trial court. That is, parties are not generally allowed to appeal before the case is over. This is to avoid multiple appeals from the same case and to avoid useless appeals.

Parties cannot appeal just because they are not satisfied with the result of the trial court. Appeals must be based on a claim of **legal error** that was so substantial it led to a miscarriage of justice. Such claims are reviewed in two ways. First the appellate court usually receives both a **clerk's transcript** and **reporter transcript** of the trial court proceedings. The appellate court can read for itself what happened. Second, the parties in the case file **appellate briefs** with the court citing and discussing the primary legal authorities that support their position. Attorneys may also be allowed to argue their positions orally before the court.

After reviewing these authorities, and sometimes researching its own authorities, the court renders its decision. The appellate court can **affirm** the

double jeopardy. Clause in the U.S. Constitution that generally prevents the government from trying a person more than once for the same offense.

legal error. Application of law to a case in a mistaken way.

clerk's transcript. A record containing copies of documents filed in connection with a court proceeding prepared by a court clerk.

reporter's transcript. A verbatim record of the oral proceedings in court prepared by the court reporter.

appellate brief. Written document containing factual and legal contentions prepared by attorneys dealing with an appeal in a case.

affirm. To uphold: in connection with an appeal to uphold the lower court's decision.

Factual dispute is resolved at trial court ↓	No case law results
Losing party files appeal in intermediate appellate court (exception: prosecutor in criminal case cannot appeal guilty verdict) ↓	
Appellate court reviews case and renders a written opinion ↓	Opinion becomes case law if published and if there is no further appeal
Losing party can seek further review in highest court (often by filing petition for writ of certiorari) ↓	
High court has discretion to grant or deny review ↓	
If high court grants a hearing, it reviews actions in lower courts and renders a written opinion ↓	Opinion becomes case law if final
If case contains a constitutional issue, losing party can request hearing in U.S. Supreme Court ↓	
If Court grants a hearing, it reviews state court actions and renders a written opinion	Opinion becomes case law

FIGURE 2-2
Appellate Process — State Action

reverse. To change.
remand. To send back.

decision, **reverse** the decision, or reverse and **remand** the decision. When the court affirms the decision, it lets the lower court decision stand. When it reverses the case, it overturns or changes the lower court decision. When it reverses and remands the case, it overturns the lower court decision, but sends it back to the trial court for a retrial. In any case, the appellate court always renders a written decision in which it explains its reasons. It discusses the claims made by each of the parties and also reviews and analyzes the various primary legal authorities cited by the parties. The parties are often referred to as the **appellant,** the one who appealed, and the **appellee,** the other party.

appellant. One who appeals.
appellee. Party in an appeal who did not file the appeal.

In the federal legal system and in many states, a supreme court also exists. This court plays a role in the appellate process. If a party is still not satisfied after a hearing in the appellate court, parties can petition the highest court in their legal system for a hearing. If a case was originally tried in the state courts, the parties can petition for a hearing in the U.S. Supreme Court if a federal issue is involved. Such a request is called a *petition for a writ of certiorari.* Before requesting a hearing in the highest court, a party can request a rehearing in the appellate court, but rehearings are rarely granted.

Writs of Mandate

Even though parties are not allowed to appeal until the case is final, special procedures allow parties to ask the appellate court to intervene while the case is still pending in the trial court. The most common of these is known as a petition for a **writ of mandate.** When you read a court of appeals decision in this type of case, it reads the same as a decision in a true appeal. One major difference, however, concerns the name or title of the case. The party requesting the petition is called a **petitioner.** Because a petition for writ of mandate asks the appellate court to order the lower court to do something or to refrain from doing something, the trial court becomes the **respondent.** The other party at the trial level is called the **real party in interest,** although this name is not included in the title of the case.

writ of mandate. Order from higher court to lower court to take some action.

petitioner. The person who files a petition with the court.

respondent. The party who answers the petitioner's petition.

real party in interest. A party who has a true interest in the action.

Consider the following situation. Green sues ABC Corp. for trade secret infringement in a state superior court. At trial, ABC Corp. makes a discovery motion that is denied by the trial court. ABC Corp. believes the trial court has erred and that, if the motion is not granted, it will be irreparably harmed at trial. ABC Corp. therefore files a petition for writ of mandate in the appellate court. If the court grants the writ and renders a decision, the case name will be *ABC Corp. v. Superior Court.* The court will call Green the real party in interest, although Green's name does not appear in the title to the case. When reading a decision in this type of case, always be careful to identify the parties and the role each played at the trial court level.

Writs of Habeas Corpus

writ of habeas corpus. An order directing the release of one who is in custody.

In criminal cases, you sometimes read appellate court decisions that stem from a **writ of habeas corpus** rather than an appeal. A petition for a writ of habeas corpus is a request that the court order the release of one who is imprisoned or otherwise confined.

Legal Error

The basis for any appeal is a legal error. This means that at the trial court, the law was not followed. Often this stems from the trial judge's ruling regarding the admissibility of evidence, or from the instructions given to the jury by the judge at the end of the trial. Legal errors can also stem from the court's ruling on various

motions that attorneys make in the case. One motion that often results in an appeal is a **motion for summary judgment,** which is a request that the trial court decide the case without a **trial.** The basis for the motion is that there are no triable issues of fact. When you read case law, always be sure that you understand the nature of the proceedings in the trial court. If the appellate court describes unfamiliar procedures be sure to use a dictionary or other resource.

motion. A request for an order from the court.

motion for summary judgment. A request that the trial court decide the case without a trial.

trial. A court proceeding before a judge or a jury where each side presents evidence of the facts that form the basis for the lawsuit or the defense to the lawsuit.

2-5 *STARE DECISIS*

Case law is based on the concept of *stare decisis,* which means "it stands decided." Case law is also known as *precedent.* This concept, which is the basis of English Common Law, means that once a court has decided a particular factual dispute, other courts should follow the same ruling when presented with the same facts. It is meant to give stability and uniformity to the legal system. Case law in the United States follows this idea, with some qualifications.

- First, *stare decisis* applies only to published case decisions that come from appellate or supreme courts. Decisions from trial courts, even if they are published, do not create case law that other courts must follow.

- Second, as a general rule, *stare decisis* applies only to cases within the same jurisdiction. For example, if the California Supreme Court decides a case, that decision is not binding, or *stare decisis,* in the other 49 states. Of course, if, in deciding a case, the United States Supreme Court interprets a federal law or the United States Constitution, that interpretation is binding in all states.

- Third, *stare decisis* requires that courts follow case decisions of *higher* courts. For example, if a court of appeals decides a particular dispute, all of the trial courts within that jurisdiction must follow the decision. Other appellate courts in that jurisdiction do not have to follow the decision.

Mandatory Authority and Persuasive Authority

When a case is truly *stare decisis,* lower courts in the same jurisdiction must follow the decision. The case is **mandatory authority,** sometimes called **binding authority.** However, this does not mean that a court cannot consider published cases from other courts. In fact, many courts consider non-binding case law when deciding an issue. Non-binding case law is sometimes called **persuasive authority.**

mandatory authority. Case law that must be followed by a court.

binding authority. Another term for *mandatory authority.*

persuasive authority. Non-binding case law that nevertheless is considered by a court.

2-6 RELATIONSHIP BETWEEN SOURCES OF LAW

When you research an issue, you often find yourself referring to more than one of the primary sources of law. This is because there is often a connection between the various sources. The supreme law of this land is the U.S. Constitution. Thus, whenever the U.S. Congress or a state legislature enacts statutory law, that statutory law cannot conflict with the Constitution. U.S. courts (and ultimately the U.S. Supreme Court) usually determine if a statute conflicts with the Constitution because the courts have the power to interpret both the Constitution and statutory law. If your question is answered in a statute, you must always determine how the courts have interpreted that statute to see if it is valid, and if so, what it means.

2-7 TOPIC AND KEY NUMBER SYSTEM AND TOTAL CLIENT-SERVICE LIBRARY

To help the legal researcher, two publishers, West Group and Lawyers Cooperative Publishing Company, developed systems to integrate and coordinate material found in different books on the same subject. West took the body of U.S. law found in cases and categorized it into numerous legal topics and subtopics. To each category, West assigned a number preceded by a symbol resembling a key. This system is primarily useful for finding case law and is discussed further in Chapter 4. Lawyers Cooperative Publishing, on the other hand, annotated its resource material with references to other sources. It refers to this integrated system as the Total Client-Service Library. See Figures 2-3 and 2-4 for examples.

Recently, West Group was acquired by the large publishing house, International Thomson Publishing Company, which already owned Lawyers Cooperative Publishing Company. However, both the topic and key number system and the total client library service remain.

ANNOTATION
WHEN DOES POLICE OFFICER'S USE OF FORCE
DURING ARREST BECOME SO EXCESSIVE AS TO
CONSTITUTE VIOLATION OF CONSTITUTIONAL
RIGHTS, IMPOSING LIABILITY UNDER FEDERAL
CIVIL RIGHTS ACT OF 1871 (42 USCS § 1983)

by

Richard P. Shafer, J. D.

REFERENCES give you citations to other legal authorities that deal with the same subject.

TOTAL CLIENT-SERVICE LIBRARY® REFERENCES

5 Am Jur 2d, Arrest §§ 80-85, 114; 6 Am Jur 2d, Assault and Battery §§ 125, 148; 15 Am Jur 2d, Civil Rights §§ 11-21, 263-287; 40 Am Jur 2d, Homicide §§ 134-137

Annotations: See the related matters listed in the annotation, infrm.

6 Federal Procedure L Ed, Civil Rights §§ 11:146-11:187

5 Federal Procedural Forms L Ed, Civil Rights §§ 10.41, 42, 47, 48, 50

5 Am Jur Pl & Pr Forms (Rev), Civil Rights, Form 2.4 (Supp); 22 Am Jur Pl & Pr Forms (Rev), Sheriffs, Police, and Constables, Forms 135-137

9 Am Jur Proof of Facts 2nd 363, Police Officer's Use of Excessive Force in Making Arrest

15 Am Jur Trials 555, Police Misconduct Litigation—Plaintiff's Remedies

42 USCS § 1983

US L Ed Digest, Civil Rights § 12.5

L Ed Index to Annos, Arrest; Assault and Battery; Civil Rights; Police

ALR Quick Index, Arrest; Assault and Battery; Discrimination; Force and Violence; Police

Federal Quick Index, Arrest; Assault and Battery; Civil Rights; Force or Violence; Police

Consult POCKET PART in the volume for later cases

204

FIGURE 2-3 The Total Client-Service Library

Reprinted with permission of Thomson/West

14. Process ⬿— 171

One can no more seek compensatory damages for outstanding criminal conviction in action for abuse of process than in one for malicious prosecution.

15. Civil Rights ⬿— 131

To recover damages for allegedly unconstitutional conviction or imprisonment, or for other harm caused by actions whose unlawfulness would render conviction or sentence invalid, § 1983 plaintiff must prove that conviction or sentence has been reversed on direct appeal, expunged by executive order, declared invalid by state tribunal authorized to make such determination, or called into quesiton by federal court's issuance of writ of habeas corpus. 42 U.S.C.A. § 1983; 28 U.S.C.A. §2264.

16. Civil Rights ⬿— 134

Claim for damages for allegedly unconditional conviction or imprisonment, or for other harm caused by actions whose unlawfulness would render conviction or sentence invalid, that has not been reversed on direct appeal, expunged by executive order, declared invalid by state tribunal authorized to make such determination, or called into question by federal court's issuance of writ of habeas corpus, is not cognizable under § 1983. 42 U.S.C.A. § 1983; 28 U.S.C.A. § 2264.

17. Civil Rights ⬿— 134

When state prisoner seeks damages in § 1983 suit, district court must consider whether judgment in favor of prisoner would necessarily imply invalidity of his conviction or sentence; if it would, complaint must be dismissed unless prisoner can demonstrate that conviction or sentence has already been invalidated. 42 U.S.C.A. § 1983.

18. Civil Rights ⬿— 134

If district court determines that § 1983 plaintiff's action even if successful, will not demonstrate invalidity of any outstanding criminal judgment against plaintiff, action should be allowed to proceed, in absence of some other bar to suit. 42 U.S.C.A. § 1983.

19. Civil Rights ⬿— 132.1

Suit for damages attributable to allegedly unreasonable search may lie even if challenged search produced evidence that was introduced in state criminal trial resulting in § 1983 plaintiff's still outstanding conviction, as under doctrines like independent source, inevitable discovery, and harmless error, § 1983 action, even if successful, would not necessarily imply that plaintiff's conviction was unlawful, 42 U.S.C.A. § 1983; U.S.C.A. Const.Amend. 4.

20. Civil Rights ⬿— 132.1

To recover compensatory damages based on allegedly unreasonable search, § 1983 plaintiff must prove not only that search was unlawful, but that it caused him actual, compensable injury, which does not encompass injury of being convicted and imprisoned (until his conviction has been overturned). 42 U.S.C.A. § 1983.

21. Federal Courts ⬿— 48

If state criminal defendant brings federal civil rights lawsuit during pendency of his criminal trial, appeal, or state habeas action, abstention may be appropriate response to parallel state court proceeding. 42 U.S.C.A. § 1983.

22. Courts ⬿— 97(1)

State courts are bound to apply federal rules in determining preclusive effect of federal court decisions on issues of federal law.

23. Judgment ⬿— 631

Federal rules on subject of issue and claim preclusion, unlike those relating to exhaustion of state remedies are almost entirely judge-made, and in developing them courts can and should be guided by federal policies reflected in congressional enactments.

24. Judgment ⬿— 828.21(1)

Court-made issue and claim preclusion rules may, as judicial application of categorical mandate of § 1983 may not, take account of policy embodied in federal habeas corpus statute's exhaustion requirement, that state courts be given first opportunity to review.

Reprinted with permission of Thomson/West

West organized the law into numerous topics and sub-topics. It assigned names to each topic, for example, "Civil Rights" or "Federal Courts" or "Judgment." Sub-topics are organized by number. Because each number is preceded by a "key" symbol, the number is referred to as a key number. The page to the left is a copy of headnotes to a case reported in a West reporter. Researchers can use the topics and key numbers to find other cases on the same topic and sub-topic.

FIGURE 2-4   Key Number System

TECHNOLOGY CORNER

When using the Internet, capitalization counts. Occasionally, you will encounter the message "URL not found." This may occur because you have capitalized a character or a word. Pay close attention to upper and lower case letters. As a reminder, many Web servers use the Unix operating system. When using Unix, case is important. Once you have located

the site, bookmark it, if it is useful. Then you will not need to type in the URL the next time you visit the site.

Locate the following Web sites and add them to your Internet Notebook if they appear to be generally useful

www.usdoj.gov (U.S. Department of Justice home page—links to Attorney General's Office and the Justice Department resources)

www.whitehouse.gov (Home page and welcome to the White House in Washington, D.C.)

CHAPTER SUMMARY

Before you begin any legal research you must understand the United States legal system. This system is founded on the principle of federalism, which means that two separate governments, federal and state, regulate citizens. The laws of each government are usually found in separate publications. When you research a factual issue it is generally controlled by either federal or state law, although at times both may apply. Determining which law applies to a factual question is one of the first decisions a researcher must make.

All laws, whether state or federal, are found in constitutions, statutes or codes, cases, and administrative regulations. Case law stems from the English Common Law, a system where laws developed through the courts and through case decisions. The common law was based on the concept of precedent or *stare decisis,* which means that once a court decided a factual dispute, the same factual dispute in the future had to be decided in the same way. In the United States today, case law results from final decisions from the appellate and supreme courts in the federal and state systems as long as those decisions are published. Case law is usually the result of an appeal. Appeals are filed by a dissatisfied party when the case is finished in the trial court.

Asking a court to review an order of the trial court before the case is over can be done by filing a petition for writ of mandate in the appellate court. Review by the appellate court in such a case is discretionary. Appellate courts can also review cases when parties in a criminal case file a petition for writ of habeas corpus.

Case law is binding, or mandatory authority, when it is applied to the same factual dispute within the jurisdiction in which the case law was decided. Cases with similar, but not exact facts, or cases from other jurisdictions are persuasive authority.

Researching a factual issue often requires you to consult several, if not all, of the primary sources of laws. In order to facilitate the research process, two publishers developed their own systems: the Topic and Key Number system, and the Total Client-Service Library.

TERMS TO REMEMBER

federalism	precedent
express powers	*stare decisis*
implied powers	trial courts
common law	petition for writ of certiorari

appeal	writ of mandate
double jeopardy	petitioner
legal error	respondent
clerk's transcript	real party in interest
reporter's transcript	writ of habeas corpus
appellate brief	motion
affirm	motion for summary judgment
reverse	trial
remand	mandatory authority
appellant	binding authority
appellee	persuasive authority

QUESTIONS FOR REVIEW

1. Explain the concept of federalism and how it affects legal research.
2. Describe situations where both state and federal law apply to the same situation.
3. How does the Supremacy Clause of the U.S. Constitution affect legal research?
4. What are the sources of primary law in the United States?
5. Explain the English Common Law.
6. How is case law in the United States today similar to the English Common Law? How is it different?
7. Describe the appeal process.
8. What is a petition for a writ of mandate?
9. What is the difference between mandatory authority and persuasive authority?
10. Describe the West Topic and Key Number System and the Total Client-Service Library of Lawyers Cooperative Publishing.

CAN YOU FIGURE IT OUT?

1. Review Figure 2-2, Appellate Process — State Action. Using this as a guide, trace the appellate process of *Ohio v. Robinette* reprinted in this chapter. Be specific as to courts and parties.
2. Refer to Figure 2-3. The symbol § appears frequently. What does this stand for?
3. Refer to Figure 2-3. What is the topic of the article found in 15 *Am. Jur. Trials* 555?
4. Refer to Figure 2-4. What is the rule of law found in the West topic "courts" and key number 97(1)?

RESEARCH ASSIGNMENTS AND ACTIVITIES

1. Review the Interoffice Memorandum at the beginning of this chapter. Would you begin your research in federal law or state law? Explain your reasoning.

2. Consider the following questions and state whether you would begin your research in state or federal sources.

   a. Can a client who filed bankruptcy five years ago file for bankruptcy again?

   b. If a person took $10,000 from an employer without permission, but paid it back when discovered, could that person be charged with any crime?

   c. What are the elements of the crime of counterfeiting?

   d. Mary's boss told her that if she did not have sex with him, she would not get a raise. What are Mary's options?

   e. Terry is a word processor and developed carpal tunnel syndrome. Terry's doctor says it is a result of Terry's job. What rights does Terry have?

3. Review the following Internet site: www.supremecourtus.gov. Find and summarize information about Supreme Court opinions.

4. Write a summary of both the Rehnquist majority opinion and the Ginsburg concurring opinion of the *Robinette* case found in this chapter.

CASE PROJECT

Review the hypothetical case you selected in Chapter 1. Is the case likely to be controlled by state law or federal law? Write a short memo stating your reasons.

THE STARTING POINT:
Analyzing Facts and Identifying Legal Issues

CHAPTER OUTLINE

CHAPTER OBJECTIVES

When you complete this chapter you should be able to

- State and describe the three basic factual categories.
- Explain how to compare case law facts with a client's factual situation.
- Describe how to identify legal issues in a client's factual situation.
- Describe how to identify legal issues in a reported case law decision.
- Provide examples of good issue statements.

CITATION MATTERS

LEGAL DICTIONARIES

THE BLUEBOOK — RULE 15.8

A legal dictionary requires a special citation form.
BLACK'S LAW DICTIONARY 657 (7th ed. 1999).
BALLENTINE'S LAW DICTIONARY 243 (3d ed. 1969).

Dictionary Citation Analyzed

title	page	edition and year

BLACK'S LAW DICTIONARY   657   (7th ed. 1999).

The *title* of the dictionary is placed first. Notice the use of large and small capital letters.

The *page* from where the material was borrowed comes next. Notice there is no comma used here.

The *edition* is placed in parentheses at the end of the citation sentence. There is a space between the *3d* and the *ed.* There is also a space before the year.

A good legal dictionary is an essential research tool. All students of law need one. If you use a definition from the dictionary, you need to place a citation behind the definition.

Researchers also need a good legal thesaurus. These tools are often used together. If you look up your term in both resources, you are much more likely to understand it. Law libraries make legal dictionaries and legal thesauri available. These are resources you need to acquire for your personal use.

INTEROFFICE MEMORANDUM

TO: Research Associate

FROM: Supervising Attorney

RE: Sanchez Research Assignment

Ms. Grace Sanchez, a new client, states the following. Ms. Sanchez was recently dismissed from her position as Day Manager of Helman's, a large local department store. Ms. Sanchez is sixty-four years old. She was with the company for over thirty years. She began her career at Helman's as a clerk in the jewelry department. Ms. Sanchez believes Helman's dismissed her because she is approaching retirement age and they do not want to pay her a pension. I am not current on this area of the law. You need to research employment discrimination. Begin the research in a secondary source such as a legal encyclopedia. After you locate case law on this topic compare the cases with the facts and issues of Ms. Sanchez's situation.

3-1 INTRODUCTION

As described in the previous chapters, the legal research process consists of finding law, analyzing the law and the facts of your case, and communicating the results of your research and analysis to interested parties. The research process usually begins with obtaining and understanding the facts involved in your client's case and with identifying the legal question or issues in that case. This chapter discusses the importance of the facts and legal issues to the research process and provides some methods of analyzing the facts and identifying the issues.

At the beginning of the research process, a clear understanding of the facts involved in a client's situation is essential. No legal research is productive until the researcher acquires a good picture of the client's facts. A good client interview produces a factually rich picture of the events and people involved in the client's situation. Before any legal research begins, all *relevant* facts must be acquired and placed into perspective. Students who are new to the law may be tempted to begin research projects prior to establishing a clear picture of the events involved in the case. This is a time-consuming error. Until the facts are well established, it is impossible to research the law. Contrary to what one might initially think, the facts determine the area of law to be researched. Facts are found in many places: client interviews, witness interviews, relevant documentation, and depositions. A thorough understanding of the facts enables the researcher to focus on those most significant, thereby leading the researcher to pinpoint the area of law to be reviewed.

3-2 KNOW AND ANALYZE THE FACTS

Your office accepted a new client. The attorney who accepted the Sanchez case and conducted the initial interview with the client sends you the memo found at the beginning of this chapter and asks you to conduct some initial research. This is usually performed as a direct result of a set of facts: the facts come first, then the law is applied to those facts. The researcher should categorize or analyze the known facts.

Obviously, some are more important than others. Your research assists you in determining which ones are *most* relevant. There are three basic fact categories:

- Relevant facts
- Explanatory facts
- Legally unimportant facts

Once you gather all of the known facts, the next step is to place them into one of these categories. However, determining relevant facts requires that the researcher have at least a general understanding of the legal principles governing the case. You cannot determine what facts are legally important if you are totally unfamiliar with the law. For example, if you know nothing about employment law, you would not know whether the client's thirty-year tenure with the company is legally relevant. You might not even know if her actual age (sixty-four) is relevant. If you are unfamiliar with the area of law, you must perform some general legal research first. Become familiar with the basic legal principles and then analyze your client's facts. As your research continues, you might also have to reevaluate how to categorize the facts.

Relevant Facts: Relevant facts are absolutely essential; they cannot be ignored. They are legally and factually important. There may be several ways to identify them in a factual situation: (1) remove the fact and ask yourself if it *significantly* changes the situation; (2) change the fact and ask yourself if it *significantly* changes the situation. If either alters the fact situation, it is probably a relevant fact.

Explanatory Facts: Explanatory facts clarify the relevant facts. They enable us to get the entire picture of the events by supplementing and explaining the relevant facts. They often provide color or depth of understanding to the situation.

Legally Unimportant Facts: Legally unimportant facts should be put aside during legal research. They play no real role in the legal situation. There are several ways to identify them: (1) remove the fact and ask yourself if it significantly changes the situation; (2) change the fact and ask yourself if it significantly changes the situation. If the answer to either question is "no, it does not alter the fact situation," the fact is probably legally unimportant.

3-3 HOW TO SORT THE FACTS OF A CLIENT'S CASE

Categorizing your client's facts helps you focus your research. Remember from the previous chapter, when you research you look for primary law (case law, statutory law, and constitutional law.) Because of the rule of *stare decisis*, relevant case law includes cases where the courts have decided the same or similar factual questions. Relevant statutory law includes laws or rules that can be applied to your factual situation. In any event, the relevant facts in your client's case must be identified.

The ultimate sorting of the facts is best left to those trained in the law. Clients are often ill equipped to categorize facts. What is important to a client may be legally irrelevant. However, always let the client tell the entire story. Do not encourage a client to edit the facts. Sometimes facts that appear unimportant initially take on special significance as the litigation or the case moves forward.

⇨ **A Point to Remember**   The relevant and explanatory facts are the focal points for the researcher. The key here is to recognize and put aside the legally unimportant facts. Sorting the facts enables you to zoom in on the relevant facts and highlight missing facts.

3-4 HOW TO COMPARE CASE LAW FACTS WITH YOUR CLIENT'S FACTS

If your research is focused on case law, you must compare your client's factual situation with those found in published cases. Before determining that specific cases apply to your client's situation, you must determine that the nature of the dispute or the issue is similar. The researcher looks for factually and legally similar cases to compare to the client's case. Identifying issues is discussed later in this chapter.

A process of comparison of relevant facts is a good starting place in the legal analysis process. Factual comparison usually takes place after the researcher clarifies the client facts and locates case law that may be applicable to the client's legal situation. The effective legal researcher works to locate **case law** that is as factually similar to the client facts as possible. Because our legal system is based on **precedent,** the sorting and comparison of facts are essential **legal analysis** skills.

case law.   A collection of reported cases.
precedent.   The example set by the decision of an earlier court for similar cases or similar legal questions that arise in later cases.
legal analysis.   The process of comparing and contrasting facts and legal issues.

SORTING THE FACTS

Consider the following factual situation.

Rimma is traveling at 40 miles per hour on a city street when Emerson, moving at 65 miles per hour, runs into the back of Rimma's vehicle. Emerson's vehicle is a new black Jeep Cherokee. Rimma was driving a four-year-old green Volvo. Emerson did not notice that traffic was slowing and that Rimma's brake lights were on. Emerson was talking on a cellular phone and was in a hurry to get to his office. He was returning from an appointment with his physician. Emerson took a strong sedative about 30 minutes prior to the accident. He has been under a great deal of stress recently. Rimma's car is badly damaged and she is injured. As a result of the accident Rimma could not get to her job that evening, due to lack of transportation. Rimma is a twenty-two-year-old exotic dancer. She had a contract for a special engagement that evening that would have paid her $1,000.00. Emerson is an automobile salesperson. Your office represents Rimma in an action against Emerson.

It is not always clear in which category a particular fact belongs. What is most important is that you begin to sort them. You are not discarding them, only sorting them. As research continues, the researcher may move the facts from one category to another.

Sort the facts above into the three categories.

Relevant Facts

1. Emerson was driving under the influence of a narcotic.
2. Emerson was exceeding safe driving speed under the conditions.
3. Emerson's vehicle struck Rimma's vehicle.
4. Rimma's vehicle was damaged as a result of Emerson's actions.
5. Rimma lost wages as a result of Emerson's actions.

Explanatory Facts

1. Emerson was hurrying while returning to his office.
2. Emerson was talking on his cellular phone.
3. Emerson was returning from a visit to his physician.

4. Emerson was traveling at 65 mph while Rimma slowed to 40 mph.

5. Emerson did not notice that traffic was slowing down and did not see Rimma's brake lights.

Legally Unimportant Facts

1. Rimma is an exotic dancer.

2. Emerson is a car salesperson.

3. Rimma's car is a green Volvo.

4. Emerson's car is a new black Jeep Cherokee.

The fact category for any given fact may change if the fact pattern is altered. For example: Does the fact pattern change if Emerson's car was malfunctioning and the accelerator was stuck? Does the fact pattern change if Rimma is traveling 40 miles per hour in a 65 mile per hour zone and she is legally intoxicated? Obviously, the answer to both questions is "of course that changes the situation." You can see that changes in the facts may change the overall factual analysis of the case.

Factual comparison may at first seem confusing and somewhat arbitrary. However, once you establish a process, the confusion dissolves. When you compare the client's facts with those of a reported case look for the following:

- Factual similarities
- Factual unknowns
- Factual differences

	Client's Case	*Published Case*
Factual Similarities		
Factual Unknowns		
Factual Differences		

This chart enables you to easily compare and contrast the facts of your client's case with those of a reported case. A good number of similarities of relevant facts indicates that the case *may* apply in your client's situation. Conversely, a good number of differences in the relevant facts indicates that the case *may not* apply. When there are significant gaps or unknown facts, the reported case probably does not apply to your client's case. As a legal researcher, you are looking for cases that are factually and legally very similar to the one you are researching.

➪ **Exercise**   Reread the Interoffice Memorandum located at the beginning of the chapter. Imagine that you locate the *Cancellier* case that follows. Use the process set forth previously for sorting and comparing facts of the Sanchez case with *Cancellier.*

CASE 3-1

Cancellier v. Federated Department Stores
672 F.2d 1312 (9th Cir. 1981)

PRIOR HISTORY:
Appeal from the United States District Court for the Northern District of California.

OPINION:
The plaintiffs below and appellants here, Philip D. Cancellier, John W. Costello, and Zelma Smith Ritter, are former employees of I. Magnin, the defendant below and cross-appellant here. They won a jury verdict in the district court totaling $1.9 million, plus court-awarded attorneys' fees of $400,000, on their claims under the Age Discrimination in Employment Act (ADEA), 29 U.S.C. §§ 621-634 (1976 & Supp. II 1978) and pendent state claims. They appeal denial of their motions for reinstatement and for an injunction against I. Magnin. I. Magnin cross-appeals the judgment primarily on grounds of improper ADEA instructions, use of a general verdict, and an erroneous award of compensatory and punitive damages for breach of the implied covenant. We affirm.

FACTS
Plaintiffs-appellants are former executives of I. Magnin. Cancellier was vice president for stores and operations. Costello was divisional merchandise manager for accessories. Ritter was a buyer of sportswear. In early 1978 they were terminated after having been employed at I. Magnin for twenty-five, seventeen, and eighteen years, respectively. In July 1979 they brought this action in the United States District Court for the Northern District of California alleging that their terminations violated the ADEA. They sought back pay, liquidated damages, reinstatement to their former positions, and an injunction against further age discrimination at I. Magnin. Appellants also raised claims under California law for breach of employment contract and breach of the implied covenant of good faith and fair dealing. Costello sought additional relief claiming fraud in connection with a promise of future employment at I. Magnin.

After a six-week trial the jury returned general verdicts in favor of Cancellier in the amount of $800,000, Costello in the amount of $600,000, and Ritter in the amount of $500,000. The jury also returned verdicts in favor of I. Magnin on Costello's fraud claims. Both sides appeal. For convenience, I. Magnin's cross-appeal is discussed first.

II.

I. MAGNIN'S CROSS-APPEAL

A. ADEA   "Determining   Factor" Standard
The ADEA makes it unlawful for an employer to discharge any individual because of such individual's age. 29 U.S.C. § 623(a) (1976). In *Kelly v. American Standard, Inc.,* 640 F.2d 974, 984-85 (9th Cir. 1981), this court set out the requirements for a proper jury instruction on age discrimination. We adopted the "determining factor" test established in *Laugesen v. Anaconda,* 510 F.2d 307, 317 (6th Cir. 1975), and restated as a "but for" test in *Loeb v. Textron,* 600 F.2d 1003, 1019 (1st Cir. 1979). We rejected the argument that plaintiff must prove age was the sole factor in his discharge, and upheld a jury instruction stating that plaintiff has the burden of proving that one of the reasons he was terminated was because of his age, and that he should prevail if this factor "made a difference" in determining whether the plaintiff was retained or discharged.

The essence of a proper jury instruction under *Kelly* is that it requires the jury to focus on the marginal effect of the age factor. Age need not be the sole factor in a discharge or other discriminatory practice. Conversely, it is not enough that age discrimination be present or even that it figure in the decision to fire; age must "make a difference" between termination and retention of the employee in the sense that, but for the presence of age discrimination, the employee would not have been discharged.

Here the district judge instructed the jury that "age must be a determining factor in an employer's personnel policies or practices before violation of the Act occurs." The district judge completely failed to give any guidance as to the meaning of "determining factor" in lawsuits under the ADEA, or to refer to the *Laugesen* and *Loeb* test we adopted in *Kelly v. American Standard, Inc.* This was error. The words "determining factor" are not self-explanatory. In general, fair application of the Act requires the trial judge to formulate precisely what employer conduct the ADEA redresses and what employer conduct it leaves undisturbed. Because the attribute with which the statute is concerned comes to each of us in time, it will inevitably be present in a multitude of employee discharges. It will be a factor in many and a determining factor in some. It is only this last group that can obtain relief under the ADEA, even though, in the broad sense, it aims to benefit the entire aged employment force.

However, a careful reading of the transcript and record convinces us that in this case the instruction does not require reversal. Giving it was harmless error. There is little or no indication in the proceedings that the outcome would have changed if the *Kelly* jury instruction had been given. This case was not decided by a hairsbreadth. There was ample evidence that consideration of age "made a difference" in the termination of Cancellier, Costello, and Ritter. Moreover, it was conceded at oral argument that the challenged instruction was fashioned by the judge from language submitted by I. Magnin. While we are extremely reluctant to affirm verdicts based on jury instructions different from those approved in *Kelly* or their equivalent, we find that on the facts of this case refusing a new trial is consistent with substantial justice. Fed.R.Civ.P. 61; *Ginsburg v. Ginsburg*, 276 F.2d 94, 96 n.2 (9th Cir. 1960); 7 J. Moore & J. Lucas, Moore's Federal Practice P 61.11 & n.1a (2d ed. 1979). The instruction approved in *Kelly* adequately protects against mistaken inferences either that age must be the sole factor in the discharge, or that age may be less than a "but for" cause of the discharge. It is strongly preferred. Here, however, we find the error harmless.

B. Use of General Verdict

I. Magnin contends that the district court committed reversible error by using simple general verdict forms without requiring special interrogatories or any breakdown of the verdict by source of damages. Thus, I. Magnin contends, the possibility of punitive damages not recoverable under the ADEA in this lawsuit or of duplicative damages in the pendent state claims requires a new trial.

Submission of special interrogatories is a matter committed to the discretion of the district judge. Fed.R.Civ.P. 49(b); *Monsma v. Central Mutual Insurance Co.*, 392 F.2d 49 (9th Cir. 1968); 5A J. Moore & J. Lucas, Moore's Federal Practice P 49.04 & n.3 (2d ed. 1981). A jury generally is not required to itemize the components that enter into an award of damages. *Neal v. Saga Shipping Co.*, 407 F.2d 481, 489 (5th Cir.), *cert. denied*, 395 U.S. 986, 89 S. Ct. 2143, 23 L. Ed. 2d 775 (1969), cited in *Frito-Lay, Inc. v. Local 137, International Brotherhood of Teamsters*, 623 F.2d 1354, 1365 (9th Cir. 1980), *cert. denied*, 449 U.S. 1013, 101 S. Ct. 571, 66 L. Ed. 2d 472 (1981), and *cert. denied*, 449 U.S. 1112, 101 S. Ct. 922, 66 L. Ed. 2d 841 (1981) (district court sitting as trier of fact not required to itemize damage award).

When state claims for breach of the implied covenant of good faith and fair dealing are joined to claims of age discrimination under the ADEA, however, review of jury verdicts presents special difficulty to appellate courts. A general verdict may conceal punitive damages which may not be allowed under the ADEA. If the state claims are flawed, the entire verdict may have to be reversed. For these reasons, a separate verdict for each claim and a separate verdict on punitive damages is strongly preferred.

Nevertheless, failure to submit special interrogatories was not an abuse of discretion. The amounts awarded here are consistent with a reasonable award on the ADEA and pendent state claims. We find no reversible error. I. Magnin's claim that it is impossible to tell which plaintiffs prevailed on which of their claims is unpersuasive. The court submitted general verdict forms in favor of the defendant on each claim. The jury returned general verdict forms in favor of I. Magnin on Costello's fraud claim and Costello's negligent misrepresentation claim; clearly, all other claims were resolved in favor of the plaintiffs. The verdict is clear

THE STARTING POINT: ANALYZING FACTS AND IDENTIFYING LEGAL ISSUES

as to which plaintiffs prevailed on which claims.

C. Tort Damages for Breach of the Implied Covenant

Breach of the Implied Covenant

I. Magnin contends that a claim for breach of the implied covenant under the circumstances here is contrary to California law. The contention is without merit.

California law recognizes an implied covenant of good faith and fair dealing in certain contracts that neither party will do anything to deprive the other of the benefit of the contract. *See, e.g., Gruenberg v. Aetna Insurance Co.,* 9 Cal.3d 566, 578, 108 Cal.Rptr. 480, 510 P.2d 1032 (1973) (*en banc*); *Comunale v. Traders & General Insurance Co.,* 50 Cal.2d 654, 658, 328 P.2d 198 (1958). California courts have recently applied the duty created by the implied covenant to the situation where the employee alleges no more than long service and the existence of personnel policies or oral representations showing an implied promise by the employer not to act arbitrarily in dealing with its employees. Such claims sound in both contract and tort and may give rise to emotional distress damages and punitive damages. *Pugh v. See's Candies, Inc.,* 116 Cal.App.3d 311, 171 Cal.Rptr. 917 (1981); *Cleary v. American Air Lines,* 111 Cal.App.3d 443, 168 Cal.Rptr. 722 (1980) (alternative holding). *See Tameny v. Atlantic Richfield Co.,* 27 Cal.3d 167, 179 n.12, 164 Cal.Rptr. 839, 610 P.2d 1330 (1980) (dicta). Cf. Note, Defining Public Policy Torts in At-Will Dismissals, 34 Stan.L.Rev. 153 (1981) (arguing against application of implied covenant to employment context).

Preemption

The ADEA does not preempt the award of tort damages on pendent state claims. *Kelly v. American Standard, Inc.,* 640 F.2d 974, 983 (9th Cir. 1981) (upholding emotional distress damages under state age discrimination statute). The award of tort damages on state claims here did not duplicate ADEA relief. Plaintiffs' ADEA claims were based on age discrimination in firing. Plaintiffs' contract and covenant claims were based on I. Magnin's obligation not to deal arbitrarily or unfairly in terminating plaintiff's employment, an obligation created by I. Magnin's personnel policies and the fact of long service by the employee. Punitive and emotional distress damages for this violation, unavailable under the ADEA, do not duplicate the ADEA award for back pay, lost benefits, and liquidated damages. While the wisdom of allowing open-ended state claims for breach of the implied covenant to coexist with ADEA claims whose financial redress Congress has carefully limited to specific damage elements, *see* 29 U.S.C. § 626(b) (1976); *Kelly v. American Standard, Inc.,* 640 F.2d at 983, is arguable, it is for Congress, not us, to decide whether state common law remedies trench too closely on the federal scheme. Pendent jurisdication, of course, is a doctrine of discretion. We recognize that in appropriate circumstances dismissal of the state claims without prejudice is proper. *United Mineworkers v. Gibbs,* 383 U.S. 715, 726-27, 86 S. Ct. 1130, 1139, 16 L. Ed. 2d 218 (1966). Such circumstances may exist, for example, where the trial judge finds that the state issues predominate in terms of the comprehensiveness of the remedy sought, or that there is a sufficient likelihood of jury confusion in treating divergent legal theories of relief to justify separating state and federal claims. *Id.*

Punitive Damages

A jury may award punitive damages if it finds by a preponderance of the evidence that defendant was guilty of malice, oppression, or fraud. Cal.Civ.Code § 3294 (West 1981); *Egan v. Mutual of Omaha Insurance Co.,* 24 Cal.3d 809, 819, 169 Cal.Rptr. 691, 620 P.2d 141 (1979). It is a question for the jury whether defendant's conduct was fraudulent, malicious, or oppressive. *Id.* at 821, 169 Cal.Rptr. 691, 620 P.2d 141. The evidence before the jury adequately supported a finding against I. Magnin on the issue of punitive damages.

D. Other Alleged Errors

I. Magnin's additional claims of error are without merit. A thorough review of the record below establishes that the trial was fairly and properly conducted.

III.

APPEAL OF CANCELLIER, COSTELLO, AND RITTER

A. Reinstatement and Injunction

The ADEA provides that "in any action brought to enforce (the Act) the

court shall have jurisdiction to grant such legal or equitable relief as may be appropriate . . . including without limitation judgments compelling employment, reinstatement or promotion. . . ." 29 U.S.C. § 626(b) (1976). Reinstatement is not a mandatory remedy; it lies within the discretion of the trial court after careful consideration of the particular facts of the case. *Combes v. Griffin Television, Inc.,* 421 F. Supp. 841, 846 (W.D.Okl.1976). Ordinarily a verdict for plaintiff on the age discrimination claim is res judicata on plaintiff's equitable reinstatement claim. *Cleverly v. Western Electric Co.,* 450 F. Supp. 507, 511 (W.D.Mo.1978), aff'd, 594 F.2d 638 (8th Cir. 1979). However, courts have refused to grant reinstatement where the employer continued a reduction in force for permissible business reasons, *id.,* or where discord and antagonism between the parties made it preferable to fashion relief from other available remedies, *Combes v. Griffin Television, Inc., supra,* at 846-47.

Damages in lieu of reinstatement may be awarded in addition to liquidated damages. However, the value of reinstatement is often speculative. Thus, availability of a substantial liquidated damages award may be a proper consideration in denying additional damages in lieu of reinstatement. *Loeb v. Textron, Inc.,* 600 F.2d 1003, 1021-23 (1st Cir. 1979).

The trial judge in this case denied reinstatement because he found evidence of acrimony in the record and because he was "fully satisfied that (the verdict) has made the plaintiffs whole." Clerk's Record 124. The court noted the testimony of an I. Magnin officer who referred to plaintiff Ritter as a "cancer." I. Magnin's numerous attacks during the trial on plaintiffs' abilities support the trial judge's conclusion that plaintiffs and I. Magnin could no longer "co-exist in a business relationship that would be productive to the consumer, community or to the business itself." Clerk's Record 125. By virtue of his position in conducting the trial, the judge was peculiarly well-situated to observe the demeanor of plaintiffs and defendants in making this determination. Moreover, in view of the substantial verdict the judge did not abuse his discretion in finding that it had made the plaintiffs whole.

Like the reinstatement remedy, injunctive relief is available under the ADEA when appropriate. The trial judge found that the $2.3 million judgment against I. Magnin, including attorneys' fees, was sufficient to discourage I. Magnin from practicing age discrimination in the future. This finding was not an abuse of discretion.

B. Attorneys' Fees on Appeal

A grant of fees on appeal is within the discretion of the appellate court. *Kelly v. American Standard, Inc.,* 640 F.2d 974, 986 (9th Cir. 1981). Although plaintiffs did not prevail on their reinstatement and injunction claims, an award of fees on appeal in some amount is appropriate to reflect successful defense of the verdict below. *See id.; Cleverly v. Western Electric Co.,* 594 F.2d 638, 642 (8th Cir. 1979) (fees awarded to plaintiff denied reinstatement). We remand to the district court for a determination of the proper amount.

IV.

CONCLUSION

While the instructions approved in *Kelly v. American Standard, Inc., supra,* and separate verdict forms for each claim, as well as a separate verdict form for punitive damages, are preferred, the trial judge did not commit reversible error in instructing the jury on "determining factor" under the ADEA, in using a general verdict, or in allowing tort damages on pendent state claims. Nor was denial of plaintiffs' motions for reinstatement and for injunctive relief against continuing age discrimination at I. Magnin an abuse of discretion. Plaintiffs are entitled to reasonable attorneys' fees in light of the outcome on appeal. The judgment of the district court is affirmed.

AFFIRMED.

Take a moment here to create a chart similar to the one found in section 3-4 earlier in the chapter. Fill in the chart using the *Cancellier* case.

3-5 LEGAL ISSUES

Once the client's factual situation is clear, it is time to consider what the issues may be. Ask yourself the following question as you begin each legal research assignment: Do I understand the client's problems? If the answer is yes, you are ready to attempt to identify the issues or problems presented by the client's facts. If you are unclear on the legal issues, ask your supervisor for guidance.

Legal issues are specific questions raised by the facts. Think of it this way: An incident occurs, and now you need to give the factual situation a legal label. Properly identifying these "legal labels" helps you locate relevant law. After careful review of a fact pattern, the legal researcher must begin to identify the area of law involved. Once this is known (for example, contract law, tort law, or family law) identification of the issues must occur. Review the factual situation in the case of *Rimma v. Emerson* described earlier in this chapter. This case involves the general area of tort law. The issue is therefore related to tort law. In very general terms, a question raised by these facts is "Did Emerson commit a tort?" This question or issue is much too broad and will not help you in your research. It must be more specifically identified and stated. A more specific area of law involved here is negligence, a part of tort law. However, asking "Was Emerson negligent?" is also too broad. The issue must be more specifically stated in relationship to the facts of the case. A better way to state the issue might be "Was Emerson negligent when he drove his car on a city street at 65 miles per hour while he was under the influence of drugs, and rear-ended a vehicle driven by Rimma, damaging the car and injuring Rimma?" This is a more complete issue statement. To simply ask "Was Emerson negligent?" is not enough; the facts are missing.

Another way to think of issues is that they are the questions the parties to a lawsuit bring to the court for resolution. The court resolves the legal issues. Sometimes issues are also called **questions presented**—meaning the questions presented to the court for resolution.

questions presented. A statement of the legal issue presented to the court for resolution.

3-6 HOW TO IDENTIFY THE LEGAL ISSUES

Issues in Your Client's Case

If **pleadings** have been filed in a case, go to the pleadings and read about the causes of action involved to help establish the issues. Issues are found in **causes of action** or **affirmative defenses** in pleadings. For example, if you read the complaint filed by Rimma against Emerson you would probably find a cause of action labeled "negligence." When you read this cause of action you see that Rimma claims (1) that Emerson was driving his car on a public road, (2) that he drove negligently in that he was under the influence of drugs and was not paying attention to traffic, (3) that he rear-ended the vehicle driven by Rimma, and (4) that he caused damage to the car and injury to Rimma. In this type of civil lawsuit, one of the questions the court is asked to decide is whether Emerson was negligent, if Rimma's claims are true. Let's look again at this issue statement: "Was Emerson negligent when he drove his car on a city street at 65 miles per hour while he was under the influence of drugs, and rear-ended a vehicle driven by Rimma, damaging the car and injuring Rimma?" Note how the claims or allegations in a cause of action relate to the way a proper issue statement is phrased. Of course, not all legal issues relate to the existence of a cause of action. Sometimes procedural

pleadings. The formal written allegations filed with the court by both sides to a lawsuit; claims and defenses are clearly set out so that both parties are placed on notice of the position of the opposing party.

causes of action. The basis upon which a lawsuit may be brought to the court.

affirmative defenses. Defenses raised by the defendant in the answer; reasons why the plaintiff should not recover even if all of the allegations of the complaint are true.

problems or questions of the admissibility of evidence may also be a legal issue in a case. If you are in doubt about the specific legal issue you are asked to research, always ask your supervisor for initial guidance. As with your analysis of relevant facts, your specific legal questions may change as you do more research and find out more about the law.

Issues in a Reported Case

judicial history. The legal (courtroom) history of a case.

Once you identify the issues in your client's case, you must look for case law dealing with the same issue and similar fact pattern. In reported cases, the court explains the legal issues. Usually, the issues are stated after the court has explained the factual background of the case and the **judicial history** of the case. The court in some instances actually states "The first issue is" or "The question before this court involves." This is the clearest indication of the issue. Many cases involve more than one issue. The court usually indicates when it is moving from one issue to the next. The *Lopez* case that follows provides a typical example of the way in which a court introduces issues.

➯ **A Point to Remember**   Case law is often written to instruct the legal community. It is written not so much for the parties involved in the litigation as for those who will read it in search of case law relevant to their client's situation. The parties to the litigation are primarily concerned with the outcome of the case. The legal researcher is concerned with the legal reasoning or legal analysis provided by the court.

3-7 HOW ISSUE STATEMENTS ARE WRITTEN

An issue statement sets forth the legal question *and* it provides the reader with the most significant facts. The issue is often stated as a question. Remember, it is the question presented to the court for resolution.

For example: John is the second baseman of the Hidden Valley Ranger softball team. He is its best hitter. After striking out, he carelessly tosses the wooden bat sixteen feet behind him, hitting and injuring Rachael, a ten-year-old spectator. The Rangers lost the final game of the season due to John's striking out.

elements. The components of a cause of action or of a statute.

Your initial research tells you that a cause of action for negligence has four **elements:** (1) a duty on the part of the defendant to act in a safe manner; (2) breach of the duty to behave in a safe manner; (3) causation (of the injury or damage); and (4) damage to the plaintiff. On a very basic level, the question in the fact pattern above is this: "Was John negligent?" However, this question does not provide the reader with enough information. A better, more specific issue statement is this: "Was John negligent when he carelessly tossed a wooden baseball bat into the crowd injuring a spectator standing sixteen feet away?" This question or issue statement provides the reader with a clear picture of what happened. By placing the most relevant facts into the issue, the reader may easily look at the four elements of negligence and decide whether or not the plaintiff makes a

***prima facie* case.** On first view or on its face; for example, the plaintiff presented a strong *prima facie* case for establishing the negligence of the defendant.

prima facie case for negligence.

Read the *Lopez* case, looking for facts and issues.

CASE 3-2

United States v. Lopez
514 U.S. 549 (1995)

SYLLABUS:

After respondent, then a 12th-grade student, carried a concealed handgun into his high school, he was charged with violating the Gun-Free School Zones Act of 1990, which forbids "any individual knowingly to possess a firearm at a place that [he] knows . . . is a school zone," 18 U.S.C. § 922(q)(1)(A). The District Court denied his motion to dismiss the indictment, concluding that Section 922(q) is a constitutional exercise of Congress' power to regulate activities in and affecting commerce. In reversing, the Court of Appeals held that, in light of what it characterized as insufficient congressional findings and legislative history, § 922(q) is invalid as beyond Congress' power under the Commerce Clause.

Held:

The Act exceeds Congress' Commerce Clause authority. First, although this Court has upheld a wide variety of congressional Acts regulating intrastate economic activity that substantially affected interstate commerce, the possession of a gun in a local school zone is in no sense an economic activity that might, through repetition elsewhere, have such a substantial effect on interstate commerce. Section 922(q) is a criminal statute that by its terms has nothing to do with "commerce" or any sort of economic enterprise, however broadly those terms are defined. Nor is it an essential part of a larger regulation of economic activity, in which the regulatory scheme could be undercut unless the intrastate activity were regulated. It cannot, therefore, be sustained under the Court's cases upholding regulations of activities that arise out of or are connected with a commercial transaction, which viewed in the aggregate, substantially affects interstate commerce. Second, § 922(q) contains no jurisdictional element which would ensure, through case-by-case inquiry, that the firearms possession in question has the requisite nexus with interstate commerce. Respondent was a local student at a local school; there is no indication that he had

recently moved in interstate commerce, and there is no requirement that his possession of the firearm have any concrete tie to interstate commerce. To uphold the Government's contention that Section 922(q) is justified because firearms possession in a local school zone does indeed substantially affect interstate commerce would require this Court to pile inference upon inference in a manner that would bid fair to convert congressional Commerce Clause authority to a general police power of the sort held only by the States.

OPINION: CHIEF JUSTICE REHNQUIST delivered the opinion of the Court.

In the Gun-Free School Zones Act of 1990, Congress made it a federal offense "for any individual knowingly to possess a firearm at a place that the individual knows, or has reasonable cause to believe, is a school zone." 18 U.S.C. § 922 (q)(1)(A) (1988, Supp. V). The Act neither regulates a commercial activity nor contains a requirement that the possession be connected in any way to interstate commerce. We hold that the Act exceeds the authority of Congress "to regulate Commerce . . . among the several States. . . ." U.S. Const., Art. I, § 8, cl. 3.

On March 10, 1992, respondent, who was then a 12th-grade student, arrived at Edison High School in San Antonio, Texas, carrying a concealed .38 caliber handgun and five bullets. Acting upon an anonymous tip, school authorities confronted respondent, who admitted that he was carrying the weapon. He was arrested and charged under Texas law with firearm possession on school premises. *See* Tex. Penal Code Ann. § 46.03(a)(1) (Supp. 1994). The next day, the state charges were dismissed after federal agents charged respondent by complaint with violating the Gun-Free School Zones Act of 1990. 18 U.S.C. § 922(q)(1)(A) (1988, Supp. V).

A federal grand jury indicted respondent on one count of knowing possession of a firearm at a school zone, in violation of

§ 922(q). Respondent moved to dismiss his federal indictment on the ground that § 922(q) "is unconstitutional as it is beyond the power of Congress to legislate control over our public schools." The District Court denied the motion, concluding that § 922(q) "is a constitutional exercise of Congress' well-defined power to regulate activities in and affecting commerce, and the 'business' of elementary, middle and high schools . . . affects interstate commerce." App. to Pet. for Cert. 55a. Respondent waived his right to a jury trial. The District Court conducted a bench trial, found him guilty of violating Section 922(q), and sentenced him to six months' imprisonment and two years' supervised release.

On appeal, respondent challenged his conviction based on his claim that Section 922(q) exceeded Congress' power to legislate under the Commerce Clause. The Court of Appeals for the Fifth Circuit agreed and reversed respondent's conviction. It held that, in light of what it characterized as insufficient congressional findings and legislative history, "section 922(q), in the full reach of its terms, is invalid as beyond the power of Congress under the Commerce Clause." 2 F.3d 1342, 1367–1368 (1993). Because of the importance of the issue, we granted *certiorari*, 511 U.S. _____ (1994), and we now affirm.

We start with first principles. The Constitution creates a Federal Government of enumerated powers. *See* U.S. Const., Art. I, § 8. As James Madison wrote, "the powers delegated by the proposed Constitution to the federal government are few and defined. Those which are to remain in the State governments are numerous and indefinite." The Federalist No. 45, pp. 292–293 (C. Rossiter ed. 1961). This constitutionally mandated division of authority "was adopted by the Framers to ensure protection of our fundamental liberties." *Gregory v. Ashcroft*, 501 U.S. 452, 458 (1991) (internal quotation marks omitted). "Just as the separation and independence of the coordinate branches of the Federal Government serves to prevent the accumulation of excessive power in any one branch, a healthy balance of power between the States and the Federal Government will reduce the risk of tyranny and abuse from either front." *Ibid.*

The Constitution delegates to Congress the power "to regulate Commerce with foreign Nations, and among the several States, and with the Indian Tribes." U.S. Const., Art. I, § 8, cl. 3. The Court, through Chief Justice Marshall, first defined the nature of Congress' commerce power in *Gibbons v. Ogden*, 22 U.S. 1, 9 Wheat. 1, 189-190, 6 L. Ed. 23 (1824):

"Commerce, undoubtedly, is traffic, but it is something more: it is intercourse. It describes the commercial intercourse between nations, and parts of nations, in all its branches, and is regulated by prescribing rules for carrying on that intercourse."

The commerce power "is the power to regulate; that is, to prescribe the rule by which commerce is to be governed. This power, like all others vested in Congress, is complete in itself, may be exercised to its utmost extent, and acknowledges no limitations, other than are prescribed in the constitution." *Id.*, at 196. The *Gibbons* Court, however, acknowledged that limitations on the commerce power are inherent in the very language of the Commerce Clause.

"It is not intended to say that these words comprehend that commerce, which is completely internal, which is carried on between man and man in a State, or between different parts of the same State, and which does not extend to or affect other States. Such a power would be inconvenient, and is certainly unnecessary.

"Comprehensive as the word 'among' is, it may very properly be restricted to that commerce which concerns more States than one. . . . The enumeration presupposes something not enumerated; and that something, if we regard the language or the subject of the sentence, must be the exclusively internal commerce of a State." *Id.*, at 194-195.

For nearly a century thereafter, the Court's Commerce Clause decisions dealt but rarely with the extent of Congress' power, and almost entirely with the Commerce Clause as a limit on state legislation that discriminated against interstate commerce. *See, e.g., Veazie v. Moor,* 55 U.S. 568, 14 HOW 568, 573-575, 14 L. Ed. 545 (1853) (upholding a state-created steamboat monopoly because it involved regulation of wholly internal commerce); *Kidd v. Pearson,* 128 U.S. 1, 17, 20-22 (1888) (upholding a state prohibition on the manufacture of intoxicating liquor because the commerce power "does not comprehend the purely domestic commerce of a State

which is carried on between man and man within a State or between different parts of the same State"); *see also* L. Tribe, American Constitutional Law 306 (2d ed. 1988). Under this line of precedent, the Court held that certain categories of activity such as "production," "manufacturing," and "mining" were within the province of state governments, and thus were beyond the power of Congress under the Commerce Clause. *See Wickard v. Filburn,* 317 U.S. 111, 121 (1942) (describing development of Commerce Clause jurisprudence).

In 1887, Congress enacted the Interstate Commerce Act, 24 Stat. 379, and in 1890, Congress enacted the Sherman Antitrust Act, 26 Stat. 209, as amended, 15 U.S.C. § 1 *et seq.* These laws ushered in a new era of federal regulation under the commerce power. When cases involving these laws first reached this Court, we imported from our negative Commerce Clause cases the approach that Congress could not regulate activities such as "production," "manufacturing," and "mining." *See, e.g., United States v. E. C. Knight Co.,* 156 U.S. 1, 12 (1895) ("Commerce succeeds to manufacture, and is not part of it"); *Carter v. Carter Coal Co.,* 298 U.S. 238, 304 (1936) ("Mining brings the subject matter of commerce into existence. Commerce disposes of it"). Simultaneously, however, the Court held that, where the interstate and intrastate aspects of commerce were so mingled together that full regulation of interstate commerce required incidental regulation of intrastate commerce, the Commerce Clause authorized such regulation. *See, e.g., Houston, E. & W.T.R. Co. v. United States,* 234 U.S. 342 (1914) (*Shreveport Rate Cases*).

In A. L. A. *Schechter Poultry Corp. v. United States,* 295 U.S. 495, 550 (1935), the Court struck down regulations that fixed the hours and wages of individuals employed by an intrastate business because the activity being regulated related to interstate commerce only indirectly. In doing so, the Court characterized the distinction between direct and indirect effects of intrastate transactions upon interstate commerce as "a fundamental one, essential to the maintenance of our constitutional system." *Id.,* at 548. Activities that affected interstate commerce directly were within Congress' power; activities that affected interstate commerce indirectly were beyond Congress' reach. *Id.,* at 546. The justification for this formal

distinction was rooted in the fear that otherwise "there would be virtually no limit to the federal power and for all practical purposes we should have a completely centralized government." *Id.,* at 548.

Two years later, in the watershed case of *NLRB v. Jones & Laughlin Steel Corp.,* 301 U.S. 1 (1937), the Court upheld the National Labor Relations Act against a Commerce Clause challenge, and in the process, departed from the distinction between "direct" and "indirect" effects on interstate commerce. *Id.,* at 36-38 ("The question [of the scope of Congress' power] is necessarily one of degree"). The Court held that intrastate activities that "have such a close and substantial relation to interstate commerce that their control is essential or appropriate to protect that commerce from burdens and obstructions" are within Congress' power to regulate. *Id.,* at 37.

In *United States v. Darby,* 312 U.S. 100 (1941), the Court upheld the Fair Labor Standards Act, stating:

"The power of Congress over interstate commerce is not confined to the regulation of commerce among the states. It extends to those activities intrastate which so affect interstate commerce or the exercise of the power of Congress over it as to make regulation of them appropriate means to the attainment of a legitimate end, the exercise of the granted power of Congress to regulate interstate commerce." *Id.,* at 118.

See also United States v. Wrightwood Dairy Co., 315 U.S. 110 (1942) (the commerce power "extends to those intrastate activities which in a substantial way interfere with or obstruct the exercise of the granted power").

In *Wickard v. Filburn,* the Court upheld the application of amendments to the Agricultural Adjustment Act of 1938 to the production and consumption of home-grown wheat. 317 U.S., at 128-129. The *Wickard* Court explicitly rejected earlier distinctions between direct and indirect effects on interstate commerce, stating:

"Even if appellee's activity be local and though it may not be regarded as commerce, it may still, whatever its nature, be reached by Congress if it exerts a substantial economic effect on interstate commerce, and this irrespective of whether such effect is what might at some earlier time have been defined as 'direct' or 'indirect.'" *Id.,* at 125.

The *Wickard* Court emphasized that although Filburn's own contribution to the demand for wheat may have been trivial by itself, that was not "enough to remove him from the scope of federal regulation where, as here, his contribution, taken together with that of many others similarly situated, is far from trivial." *Id.,* at 127-128.

Jones & Laughlin Steel, Darby, and *Wickard* ushered in an era of Commerce Clause jurisprudence that greatly expanded the previously defined authority of Congress under that Clause. In part, this was a recognition of the great changes that had occurred in the way business was carried on in this country. Enterprises that had once been local or at most regional in nature had become national in scope. But the doctrinal change also reflected a view that earlier Commerce Clause cases artificially had constrained the authority of Congress to regulate interstate commerce.

But even these modern-era precedents which have expanded congressional power under the Commerce Clause confirm that this power is subject to outer limits.

In *Jones & Laughlin Steel,* the Court warned that the scope of the interstate commerce power "must be considered in the light of our dual system of government and may not be extended so as to embrace effects upon interstate commerce so indirect and remote that to embrace them, in view of our complex society, would effectually obliterate the distinction between what is national and what is local and create a completely centralized government." 301 U.S., at 37; *see also Darby, supra,* at 119-120 (Congress may regulate intrastate activity that has a "substantial effect" on interstate commerce); *Wickard, supra,* at 125 (Congress may regulate activity that "exerts a substantial economic effect on interstate commerce"). Since that time, the Court has heeded that warning and undertaken to decide whether a rational basis existed for concluding that a regulated activity sufficiently affected interstate commerce. *See e.g., Hodel v. Virginia Surface Mining & Reclamation Assn., Inc.,* 452 U.S. 264, 276-280 (1981); *Perez v. United States,* 402 U.S. 146, 155-156 (1971); *Katzenbach v. McClung,* 379 U.S. 294 (1964); *Heart of Atlanta Motel, Inc. v. United States,* 379 U.S. 241, 252-253 (1964).

Similarly, in *Maryland v. Wirtz,* 392 U.S. 183 (1968), the Court reaffirmed that "the power to regulate commerce, though broad indeed, has limits" that "the Court has ample power" to enforce. *Id.,* at 196, overruled on other grounds, *National League of Cities v. Usery,* 426 U.S. 833 (1976), overruled by *Garcia v. San Antonio Metropolitan Transit Authority,* 469 U.S. 528 (1985). In response to the dissent's warnings that the Court was powerless to enforce the limitations on Congress' commerce powers because "all activities affecting commerce, even in the minutest degree, [*Wickard*], may be regulated and controlled by Congress," 392 U.S., at 204 (Douglas, J., dissenting), the *Wirtz* Court replied that the dissent had misread precedent as "neither here nor in *Wickard* has the Court declared that Congress may use a relatively trivial impact on commerce as an excuse for broad general regulation of state or private activities," *id.,* at 197, n. 27. Rather, "the Court has said only that where a general regulatory statute bears a substantial relation to commerce, the de minimis character of individual instances arising under that statute is of no consequence." *Ibid.*

Consistent with this structure, we have identified three broad categories of activity that Congress may regulate under its commerce power. *Perez v. United States, supra,* at 150; *see also Hodel v. Virginia Surface Mining & Reclamation Assn., supra,* at 276-277. First, Congress may regulate the use of the channels of interstate commerce. *See, e.g., Darby,* 312 U.S., at 114; *Heart of Atlanta Motel, supra,* at 256 ("'The authority of Congress to keep the channels of interstate commerce free from immoral and injurious uses has been frequently sustained, and is no longer open to question.'" (*quoting Caminetti v. United States,* 242 U.S. 470, 491 (1917)). Second, Congress is empowered to regulate and protect the instrumentalities of interstate commerce, or persons or things in interstate commerce, even though the threat may come only from intrastate activities. *See, e.g., Shreveport Rate Cases,* 234 U.S. 342 (1914); *Southern R. Co. v. United States,* 222 U.S. 20 (upholding amendments to Safety Appliance Act as applied to vehicles used in intrastate commerce); *Perez, supra,* at 150 ("For example, the destruction of an aircraft (18 U.S.C. § 32), or . . . thefts from interstate shipments (18 U.S.C. Section 659)"). Finally, Congress' commerce authority includes the power to regulate those activities having a substantial relation to interstate commerce, *Jones & Laughlin*

Steel, 301 U.S., at 37, i.e., those activities that substantially affect interstate commerce. *Wirtz, supra,* at 196, n. 27.

Within this final category, admittedly, our case law has not been clear whether an activity must "affect" or "substantially affect" interstate commerce in order to be within Congress' power to regulate it under the Commerce Clause. *Compare Preseault v. ICC,* 494 U.S. 1, 17 (1990), with *Wirtz, supra,* at 196, (the Court has never declared that "Congress may use a relatively trivial impact on commerce as an excuse for broad general regulation of state or private activities.") We conclude, consistent with the great weight of our case law, that the proper test requires an analysis of whether the regulated activity "substantially affects" interstate commerce.

We now turn to consider the power of Congress, in the light of this framework, to enact § 922 (q). The first two categories of authority may be quickly disposed of: § 922(q) is not a regulation of the use of the channels of interstate commerce, nor is it an attempt to prohibit the interstate transportation of a commodity through the channels of commerce; nor can § 922(q) be justified as a regulation by which Congress has sought to protect an instrumentality of interstate commerce or a thing in interstate commerce. Thus, if Section 922(q) is to be sustained, it must be under the third category as a regulation of an activity that substantially affects interstate commerce.

First, we have upheld a wide variety of congressional Acts regulating intrastate economic activity where we have concluded that the activity substantially affected interstate commerce. Examples include the regulation of intrastate coal mining; *Hodel, supra,* intrastate extortionate credit transactions, *Perez, supra,* restaurants utilizing substantial interstate supplies, *McClung, supra,* inns and hotels catering to interstate guests, *Heart of Atlanta Motel, supra,* and production and consumption of home-grown wheat, *Wickard v. Filburn,* 317 U.S. 111 (1942). These examples are by no means exhaustive, but the pattern is clear. Where economic activity substantially affects interstate commerce, legislation regulating that activity will be sustained.

Even *Wickard,* which is perhaps the most far reaching example of Commerce Clause authority over intrastate activity, involved economic activity in a way that the possession of a gun in a school zone does not. Roscoe Filburn operated a small farm in Ohio, on which, in the year involved, he raised 23 acres of wheat. It was his practice to sow winter wheat in the fall, and after harvesting it in July to sell a portion of the crop, to feed part of it to poultry and livestock on the farm, to use some in making flour for home consumption, and to keep the remainder for seeding future crops. The Secretary of Agriculture assessed a penalty against him under the Agricultural Adjustment Act of 1938 because he harvested about 12 acres more wheat than his allotment under the Act permitted. The Act was designed to regulate the volume of wheat moving in interstate and foreign commerce in order to avoid surpluses and shortages, and concomitant fluctuation in wheat prices, which ahd previously obtained. The Court said, in an opinion sustaining the application of the Act to Filburn's activity:

"One of the primary purposes of the Act in question was to increase the market price of wheat and to that end to limit the volume thereof that could affect the market. It can hardly be denied that a factor of such volume and variability as home-consumed wheat would have a substantial influence on price and market conditions. This may arise because being in marketable condition such wheat overhangs the market and, if induced by rising prices, tends to flow into the market and check price increases. But if we assume that it is never marketed, it supplies a need of the man who grew it which would otherwise be reflected by purchases in the open market. Home-grown wheat in this sense competes with wheat in commerce." 317 U.S., at 128.

Section 922(q) is a criminal statute that by its terms has nothing to do with "commerce" or any sort of economic enterprise, however broadly one might define those terms. Section 922(q) is not an essential part of a larger regulation of economic activity, in which the regulatory scheme could be undercut unless the intrastate activity were regulated. It cannot, therefore, be sustained under our cases upholding regulations of activities that arise out of or are connected with a commercial transaction, which viewed in the aggregate, substantially affects interstate commerce.

Second, § 922(q) contains no jurisdictional element which would ensure,

through case-by-case inquiry, that the firearm possession in question affects interstate commerce. For example, in *United States v. Bass*, 404 U.S. 336 (1971), the Court interpreted former 18 U.S.C. § 1202(a), which made it a crime for a felon to "receive, possess, or transport in commerce or affecting commerce . . . any firearm." 404 U.S., at 337. The Court interpreted the possession component of § 1202(a) to require an additional nexus to interstate commerce both because the statute was ambiguous and because "unless Congress conveys its purpose clearly, it will not be deemed to have significantly changed the federal-state balance." *Id.,* at 349. The *Bass* Court set aside the conviction because although the Government had demonstrated that Bass had possessed a firearm, it had failed "to show the requisite nexus with interstate commerce." *Id.,* at 347. The Court thus interpreted the statute to reserve the constitutional question whether Congress could regulate, without more, the "mere possession" of firearms. *See id.,* at 339; *see also United States v. Five Gambling Devices,* 346 U.S. 441, 448 (1953) (plurality opinion) ("The principle is old and deeply imbedded in our jurisprudence that this Court will construe a statute in a manner that requires decision of serious constitutional questions only if the statutory language leaves no reasonable alternative"). Unlike the statute in *Bass,* § 922(q) has no express jurisdictional element which might limit its reach to a discrete set of firearm possessions that additionally have an explicit connection with or effect on interstate commerce.

Although as part of our independent evaluation of constitutionality under the Commerce Clause we of course consider legislative findings, and indeed even congressional committee findings, regarding effect on interstate commerce, *see, e.g., Preseault v. ICC,* 494 U.S. 1, 17 (1990), the Government concedes that "neither the statute nor its legislative history contains express congressional findings regarding the effects upon interstate commerce of gun possession in a school zone." Brief for United States 5-6. We agree with the Government that Congress normally is not required to make formal findings as to the substantial burdens that an activity has on interstate commerce. *See McClung,* 379 U.S., at 304; *see also Perez,* 402 U.S., at 156 ("Congress need [not] make particularized

findings in order to legislate"). But to the extent that congressional findings would enable us to evaluate the legislative judgment that the activity in question substantially affected interstate commerce, even though no such substantial effect was visible to the naked eye, they are lacking here.

The Government argues that Congress has accumulated institutional expertise regarding the regulation of firearms through previous enactments. *Cf. Fullilove v. Klutznick,* 448 U.S. 448, 503 (1980) (Powell, J., concurring). We agree, however, with the Fifth Circuit that importation of previous findings to justify § 922(q) is especially inappropriate here because the "prior federal enactments or Congressional findings [do not] speak to the subject matter of section 922(q) or its relationship to interstate commerce. Indeed, § 922(q) plows thoroughly new ground and represents a sharp break with the long-standing pattern of federal firearms legislation." 2 F.3d at 1366.

The Government's essential contention, in fact, is that we may determine here that § 922(q) is valid because possession of a firearm in a local school zone does indeed substantially affect interstate commerce. Brief for United States 17. The Government argues that possession of a firearm in a school zone may result in violent crime and that violent crime can be expected to affect the functioning of the national economy in two ways. First, the costs of violent crime are substantial, and, through the mechanism of insurance, those costs are spread throughout the population. *See United States v. Evans,* 928 F.2d 858, 862 (CA9 1991). Second, violent crime reduces the willingness of individuals to travel to areas within the country that are perceived to be unsafe. *Cf. Heart of Atlanta Motel,* 379 U.S., at 253. The Government also argues that the presence of guns in schools poses a substantial threat to the educational process by threatening the learning environment. A handicapped educational process, in turn, will result in a less productive citizenry. That, in turn, would have an adverse effect on the Nation's economic well-being. As a result, the Government argues that Congress could rationally have concluded that § 922(q) substantially affects interstate commerce.

We pause to consider the implications of the Government's arguments. The Government admits, under its "costs of crime" reasoning, that Congress could

regulate not only all violent crime, but all activities that might lead to violent crime, regardless of how tenuously they relate to interstate commerce. *See* Tr. of Oral Arg. 8-9. Similarly, under the Government's "national productivity" reasoning, Congress could regulate any activity that it found was related to the economic productivity of individual citizens: family law (including marriage, divorce, and child custody), for example. Under the theories that the Government presents in support of § 922(q), it is difficult to perceive any limitation on federal power, even in areas such as criminal law enforcement or education where States historically have been sovereign. Thus, if we were to accept the Government's arguments, we are hard-pressed to posit any activity by an individual that Congress is without power to regulate.

Although JUSTICE BREYER argues that acceptance of the Government's rationales would not authorize a general federal police power, he is unable to identify any activity that the States may regulate but Congress may not. JUSTICE BREYER posits that there might be some limitations on Congress' commerce power such as family law or certain aspects of education. These suggested limitations, when viewed in light of the dissent's expansive analysis, are devoid of substance.

JUSTICE BREYER focuses, for the most part, on the threat that firearm possession in and near schools poses to the educational process and the potential economic consequences flowing from that threat. Specifically, the dissent reasons that (1) gun-related violence is a serious problem; (2) that problem, in turn, has an adverse effect on classroom learning; and (3) that adverse effect on classroom learning, in turn, represents a substantial threat to trade and commerce. This analysis would be equally applicable, if not more so, to subjects such as family law and direct regulation of education.

For instance, if Congress can, pursuant to its Commerce Clause power, regulate activities that adversely affect the learning environment, then, *a fortiori,* it also can regulate the educational process directly. Congress could determine that a school's curriculum has a "significant" effect on the extent of classroom learning. As a result, Congress could mandate a federal curriculum for local elementary and secondary schools because what is taught in local schools has a significant "effect on classroom learning," and that, in turn, has a substantial effect on interstate commerce.

JUSTICE BREYER rejects our reading of precedent and argues that "Congress . . . could rationally conclude that schools fall on the commercial side of the line." Again, JUSTICE BREYER's rationale lacks any real limits because, depending on the level of generality, any activity can be looked upon as commercial. Under the dissent's rationale, Congress could just as easily look at child rearing as "falling on the commercial side of the line" because it provides a "valuable service—namely, to equip [children] with the skills they need to survive in life and, more specifically, in the workplace." *Ibid.* We do not doubt that Congress has authority under the Commerce Clause to regulate numerous commercial activities that substantially affect interstate commerce and also affect the educational process. That authority, though broad, does not include the authority to regulate each and every aspect of local schools.

Admittedly, a determination whether an intrastate activity is commercial or noncommercial may in some cases result in legal uncertainty. But, so long as Congress' authority is limited to those powers enumerated in the Constitution, and so long as those enumerated powers are interpreted as having judicially enforceable outer limits, congressional legislation under the Commerce Clause always will engender "legal uncertainty." As Chief Justice Marshall stated in *McCulloch v. Maryland,* 17 U.S. 316, 4 Wheat. 316, 4 L. Ed. 579 (1819):

"The [federal] government is acknowledged by all to be one of enumerated powers. The principle, that it can exercise only the powers granted to it . . . is now universally admitted. But the question respecting the extent of the powers actually granted, is perpetually arising, and will probably continue to arise, as long as our system shall exist." *Id.,* at 405.

See also Gibbons v. Ogden, 9 Wheat., at 195 ("The enumeration presupposes something not enumerated"). The Constitution mandates this uncertainty by withholding from Congress a plenary police power that would authorize enactment of every type of legislation. *See* U.S. Const., Art. I, § 8. Congress has operated within this framework of legal uncertainty ever since this

Court determined that it was the judiciary's duty "to say what the law is." *Marbury v. Madison,* 5 U.S. 137, 1 Cranch. 137, 177 (Marshall, C. J.). Any possible benefit from eliminating this "legal uncertainty" would be at the expense of the Constitution's system of enumerated powers.

In *Jones & Laughlin Steel,* 301 U.S., at 37, we held that the question of congressional power under the Commerce Clause "is necessarily one of degree." To the same effect is the concurring opinion of Justice Cardozo in *Schechter Poultry:*

"There is a view of causation that would obliterate the distinction of what is national and what is local in the activities of commerce. Motion at the outer rim is communicated perceptibly, though minutely, to recording instruments at the center. A society such as ours 'is an elastic medium which transmits all tremors throughout its territory; the only question is of their size.'" 295 U.S., at 554 (*quoting United States v. A.L.A. Schechter Poultry Corp.,* 76 F.2d 617, 624 (CA2 1935) (L. Hand, J., concurring)).

These are not precise formulations, and in the nature of things they cannot be. But we think they point the way to a correct decision of this case. The possession of a gun in a local school zone is in no sense an economic activity that might, through repetition elsewhere, substantially affect any sort of interstate commerce. Respondent was a local student at a local school; there is no indication that he had recently moved in interstate commerce, and there is no requirement that his possession of the firearm have any concrete tie to interstate commerce.

To uphold the Government's contentions here, we would have to pile inference upon inference in a manner that would bid fair to convert congressional authority under the Commerce Clause to a general police power of the sort retained by the States. Admittedly, some of our prior cases have taken long steps down that road, giving great deference to congressional action. The broad language in these opinions has suggested the possibility of additional expansion, but we decline here to proceed any further. To do so would require us to conclude that the Constitution's enumeration of powers does not presuppose something not enumerated, *cf. Gibbons v. Ogden, supra,* at 195, and that there never will be a distinction between what is truly national and what is truly local, *cf. Jones & Laughlin Steel, supra,* at 30. This we are unwilling to do.

For the foregoing reasons the judgment of the Court of Appeals is affirmed.

TECHNOLOGY CORNER

At times we need information but we are not sure about how to locate it. A library provides several options: the computerized filings of the library collection, the card catalog, and the librarian. The Internet also provides choices. Sometimes you want to perform a search but are not sure which sites contain good information.

The following list represents some of the major search engines used for legal research. These search engines search many Web sites at one time and then provide you with a great many options. Caution: Practice writing your searches. A poorly written search results in a great deal of unwanted information. A search with carefully chosen terms produces finely focused information. Practice with creating searches is essential. Many search engines and the Web sites provide help with how to use their site. Always check this information: you may be amazed at what is new since the last time you used the resource.

Some of the major search engines follow.

Yahoo:	www.yahoo.com
AltaVista	www.altavista.com
Lycos:	www.lycos.com
Excite:	www.excite.com
FindLaw:	www.findlaw.com
LawCrawler:	www.lawcrawler.com
HotBot:	www.hotbot.com
WebCrawler:	www.webcrawler.com

Be sure to add these to your Internet Notebook.

CHAPTER SUMMARY

The identification of relevant facts is an essential step in both reading the law and researching the law. Understanding the facts is the first step toward analysis of the legal problem. Until the facts are known and understood, no research should begin. Facts may be categorized as relevant, explanatory, or legally unimportant. Once this categorization takes place, you are ready to determine the legal issues. Factual analysis arises in two frameworks. First, one must analyze the client's facts. The second involves categorizing the facts in a reported case. When you compare your client's facts with the facts in a reported case, look for similarities, unknowns (gaps), and differences. The legal issues are stated as questions. A good issue statement contains a legal question surrounded by the relevant facts.

TERMS TO REMEMBER

case law	causes of action
precedent	affirmative defenses
legal analysis	judicial history
questions presented	elements
pleadings	*prima facie* case

QUESTIONS FOR REVIEW

1. Why is the client's factual situation important?
2. State and describe the three basic fact categories.
3. Explain the process for factual comparison.
4. What is a legal issue?
5. How do you identify the issues in a case in which pleadings have been filed?
6. How do you identify the issues in a case in which no pleadings have been filed?
7. How do you identify the issues in a reported case?
8. What does a good issue statement contain?

CAN YOU FIGURE IT OUT?

1. Using the *United States v. Lopez* case (located in this chapter), can you find the name of Title 18 of the United States Code § 922?
2. In the *Cancellier* case, I. Magnin files a "cross-appeal." What is a cross-appeal?

RESEARCH ASSIGNMENTS AND ACTIVITIES

1. Create a chart of relevant, explanatory, and legally unimportant facts for the *United States v. Lopez* case.
2. Create a chart of the relevant, explanatory, and legally unimportant facts for the Sanchez fact pattern as presented in the Interoffice Memorandum at the beginning of this chapter.
3. What is the legal issue in the Sanchez case?
4. What was the legal issue in the *Cancellier* case?

CASE PROJECT

Review the hypothetical case you selected in Chapter 1. Try to identify the relevant facts, explanatory facts, and legally unimportant facts. Also, try to identify the legal issues. Remember that this may change after you have researched the case.

FINDING AND ANALYZING CASE LAW

CHAPTER OUTLINE

CHAPTER OBJECTIVES

When you complete this chapter you should be able to

- List where case law may be located.
- Explain the purpose of case law.
- Explain the elements of a case law citation.
- List the print publications containing U.S. Supreme Court case law.
- Explain the differences between the official publication of U.S. Supreme Court case law and the unofficial publications of the same material.
- List other federal reporters.
- Explain the purpose of a regional reporter.
- List and define the components of a case.
- Compare and contrast the facts of a reported case with a client's factual situation.

CITATION MATTERS

STATE CASE LAW

THE BLUEBOOK — RULE 10

THE BLUEBOOK - Table 1 (T.1)

State case law is cited in the same basic format that the U.S. Supreme Court cases are cited. In many instances, state case law is published in two or three reporters. Some states publish their own case law reporters; those are the official reporters. Unofficial reporters also publish these cases. For example, in California the state authorizes one publication of all California Supreme Court and Appellate Court cases. All California cases are also published in the *California Reporter* (unofficial). In addition, the California Supreme Court cases are included in the *Pacific Reporter,* the regional reporter for California (this is also an unofficial reporter). Be sure to check Table 1 to review the publications and proper abbreviations for the state case law you need to cite.

INTEROFFICE MEMORANDUM

TO: Research Associate

FROM: Supervising Attorney

RE: Research Assignment

The office needs to begin case law research in the *Rambeaux* case. Look for California and United States Supreme Court case law to support our client's position. Review the file before you begin. Please check with me if you need clarification. [Reread the Interoffice Memorandum and Figure 1-1 in Chapter 1.] Create a list of the cases you locate, include a brief summary of each case on your list.

4-1 OVERVIEW OF CASE LAW AND THE CONCEPT OF *STARE DECISIS*

Case law is **primary authority.** Cases are written by judges. Once a case is presented to the court and the legal and factual issues are resolved, the judge writes a **decision,** which is sometimes called an **opinion.** This written decision is case law. At the state and federal level decisions are reported for many appellate and all supreme court cases. At the federal level even some of the trial court cases are reported. Once you become familiar with case citations you will know the level of the court deciding the case with just a glance at the reporter abbreviation in the case citation.

Our legal system is, in part, based on the concept of **precedent** or *stare decisis.* The court looks to what other courts in the same jurisdiction have done with the same or similar legal and factual issues.

4-2 WHERE TO FIND CASE LAW

Cases are published by several publishers and may be located in a number of resources. Each state publishes, or arranges to have published, its appellate and supreme court cases. States such as New York, Texas, Florida, New Jersey, Washington, California, and many others publish their opinions in what are known as official publications of their case law. Other states, such as North Dakota, have arranged with the West Group to publish their case law in the appropriate **regional reporters.** A concise guide to the appropriate resources is found in the ***Uniform System of Citation*** (*THE BLUEBOOK*). In addition to the traditional paper publications, most state case law is available on various CD-ROM products and through the online legal databases of **LEXIS** and **Westlaw.** Increasing collections of state and federal case law are found at various sites on the Internet.

Case Law Reporters

Case law reporters are books filled with decisions. They exist for most states; in addition, there are large sets of books known as *regional reporters* that publish selected case law from a geographical region of the United States. Those are discussed in Section 4-6.

---

primary authority. The resources that provide the actual law; laws are found in constitutions, statutes, case law, and some administrative materials.

decision. The formal written resolution of a case; it explains the legal and factual issues, the resolution of the case, and the law used by the court in reaching its resolution.

opinion. A decision is sometimes referred to as an opinion.

precedent. The example set by the decision of an earlier court for similar cases or similar legal questions that arise in later cases.

stare decisis. "It stands decided"; another term for precedent.

regional reporters. A set of published volumes of cases by courts in specific regions of the United States; for example, the *Pacific Reporter* or the *North Eastern Reporter.*

Uniform System of Citation. A reference manual; it contains the rules for proper citation format; often called *THE BLUEBOOK.*

LEXIS. A computer-assisted legal research service.

Westlaw. A computer-assisted legal research service.

Case law reporters. Sets of published volumes of cases decided by various courts.

LEXIS and Westlaw

LEXIS and Westlaw are huge online legal databases. Use of these services is through contract with the publishers. Both services should be used only by persons trained to search in large legal databases. Case law is only one of the many resources they provide.

CD-ROM Products

Several publishers now offer case law on CD-ROM. These products often combine the ease of using books with the speed of using an online database.

Internet

There are Internet sites for case law retrieval. Many of these are provided in the Technology Corners. Because the Internet is growing and changing at a rapid rate, it is difficult to offer a reliable list of research sites. Some law schools continue to maintain consistently reliable Web sites. Try the following Internet site for U.S. Supreme Court case law: http://www.law.cornell.edu/.

4-3 WHAT IS A CASE?

A case is a decision, sometimes called an *opinion,* written by a judge (the court). Judges write opinions designed to inform and instruct those who read the decisions. The parties to most litigation are interested in the outcome of the case. But they may not be interested in the court's legal reasoning, although, on appeal that may be important.

In the course of legal research, we read case law to attempt to understand the factual and legal issues and a court's resolution of those issues. Judges rely on previous decisions, the Constitution, statutory law, and administrative regulations in rendering decisions and writing opinions. Judges are acutely aware that legal researchers read reported case law looking for opinions that may apply to their client's situation. That is why judges are so careful to provide detailed facts and lengthy analysis of the factual and legal issues. It is not enough for a court to state, "Plaintiff, you win; defendant, you lose."

The importance of case law is apparent when we recall that the U.S. legal system relies on precedent. The court must look to past decisions to aid it in making current decisions. Therefore, researchers must do the same to locate case law similar to the factual and legal situation being researched.

When you read a case decision, keep in mind that the decision usually comes from a panel of judges. At the appellate level, three justices hear and decide a case; at the Supreme Court level, nine justices hear and decide a case. In many instances, the decision of the court is not unanimous. One or more justices may disagree entirely with the decision. In such a case, that justice may write a dissenting opinion in which the justice explains his or her position. Sometimes one or more justices may agree with the ultimate result of the case but not with the reasoning of the majority. That justice may write a concurring opinion, an opinion in which the justice explains his or her reasoning. Although concurring and dissenting opinions are published with the majority opinion, they do not result in "case law." Case law is found only in the majority opinion.

4-4 CASE CITATIONS

The name of the case is either italicized or underlined and placed at the beginning of any case law citation, which is arranged in the following format. The volume number is first, the abbreviation for the name of the reporter is next, and the page on which the case begins follows the reporter abbreviation. The year of the decision will be placed either at the very end of the citation or in some instances just after the name of the case (see Figure 4-1).

Marvin v. Marvin (1976) 18 Cal. 3d 660, 557 P. 2d.106, 134 Cal. Rptr. 815

or

Marvin v. Marvin, 18 Cal. 3d 660, 557 P. 2d.106, 134 Cal. Rptr. 815 (1976)

FIGURE 4-1

The year is always placed in parentheses. The *Uniform System of Citation (THE BLUEBOOK)* provides a comprehensive guide to proper citation format. Check your state citation rules for the proper placement of the year. Appendix B provides a Basic Citation Reference Guide.

⇨ **A Point to Remember**   When looking in a case reporter, check the very top of the first full page of the case for the proper case citation. This will be the proper abbreviation of the case name. See Figure 4-2. *Illinois v. Gates,* 462 U.S. 213 (1983) is the accepted citation for this case. Usually it is shorter than the full names of all of the parties. Compare the full names of the parties in the *Texas v. Johnson* case with the short version at the top of the page (Figures 4-3 through 4-5).

Sometimes, a case is reported in several publications. It is the same case, just different publishers. The **official citation** is always listed first; this is followed by the parallel (and unofficial) citations. For example: the *United States Reports,* abbreviated as U.S., is the official reporter of all U.S. Supreme Court case law. There are, however, other publishers of all U.S. Supreme Court case law. This is discussed in Section 4-5.

⇨ **A Point to Remember**   Sometimes in **secondary sources** the citations are incomplete. For example, the year may be omitted or the reporter abbreviation may differ from that suggested in the *Uniform System of Citation* or your state **style manual**. Once the case is retrieved, you are able to complete and, if necessary, correct the citation.

official citation. This is the citation to the official publication of case law for a particular jurisdiction (this is usually a government publication); the official citation includes the name of the case, volume number in which the case is located, the first page of the case, and the year of the decision.

secondary sources. Tools used to understand the law; one such tool is a legal encyclopedia, which explains the law.

style manual. A manual illustrating the proper citation format for a particular state.

4-5 FEDERAL CASE LAW

Cases decided by federal courts are published in various federal case law reporters. For example, U.S. Supreme Court cases are available in written format from several publishers.

United States Supreme Court Case Law

This is a Supreme Court case citation with **parallel citations:**

Meritor Sav. Bank, FSB v. Vinson, 477 U.S. 57, 106 S.Ct. 2399, 91 L.Ed.2d 49 (1986)

parallel citations. Many case citations include references to unofficial publications as well as the official citation. These additional references are parallel citations; simply stated—you may find the exact case in more than one publication.

③ **This is the proper short form of the case name.**

③
→ ILLINOIS *v.* GATES

①
213 ← **This is the page number of the first page of the case.**

①

Syllabus ② ←

②
This is a summary of the case; is *not* part of the Court's opinion.

ILLINOIS *v.* GATES ET UX.

CERTIORARI TO THE SUPREME COURT OF ILLINOIS

No. 81–430.   Argued October 13, 1982—Reargued March 1, 1983—
Decided June 8, 1983

On May 3, 1978, the Police Department of Bloomingdale, Ill., received an anonymous letter which included statements that respondents, husband and wife, were engaged in selling drugs; that the wife would drive their car to Florida on May 3 to be loaded with drugs, and the husband would fly down in a few days to drive the car back; that the car's trunk would be loaded with drugs; and that respondents presently had over $100,000 worth of drugs in their basement.   Acting on the tip, a police officer determined respondents' address and learned that the husband made a reservation on a May 5 flight to Florida.   Arrangements for surveillance of the flight were made with an agent of the Drug Enforcement Administration (DEA), and the surveillance disclosed that the husband took the flight, stayed overnight in a motel room registered in the wife's name, and left the following morning with a woman in a car bearing an Illinois license plate issued to the husband, heading north on an interstate highway used by travelers to the Bloomingdale area.   A search warrant for respondents' residence and automobile was then obtained from an Illinois state-court judge, based on the Bloomingdale police officer's affidavit setting forth the foregoing facts and a copy of the anonymous letter. When respondents arrived at their home, the police were waiting and discovered marihuana and other contraband in respondents' car trunk and home.   Prior to respondents' trial on charges of violating state drug laws, the trial court ordered suppression of all the items seized, and the Illinois Appellate Court affirmed.   The Illinois Supreme Court also affirmed, holding that the letter and affidavit were inadequate to sustain a determination of probable cause for issuance of the search warrant under *Aguilar* v. *Texas,* 378 U. S. 108, and *Spinelli* v. *United States,* 393 U. S. 410, since they failed to satisfy the "two-pronged test" of (1) revealing the informant's "basis of knowledge" and (2) providing sufficient facts to establish either the informant's "veracity" or the "reliability" of the informant's report.

⑤   ⑤
Notice that the factual story is followed by the judicial (procedural) history.

④ **This is still part of the syllabus.**

→ ④ *Held:*

1. The question—which this Court requested the parties to address—whether the rule requiring the exclusion at a criminal trial of evidence obtained in violation of the Fourth Amendment should be modified so as, for example, not to require exclusion of evidence obtained in the reason-

FIGURE 4-2 Sample Published Case

214   OCTOBER TERM, 1982   ①

Syllabus   462 U. S.

able belief that the search and seizure at issue was consistent with the Fourth Amendment will not be decided in this case, since it was not presented to or decided by the Illinois courts. Although prior decisions interpreting the "not pressed or passed on below" rule have not involved a State's failure to raise a defense to a federal right or remedy asserted below, the purposes underlying the rule are, for the most part, as applicable in such a case as in one where a party fails to assert a federal right. The fact that the Illinois courts affirmatively applied the federal exclusionary rule does not affect the application of the "not pressed or passed on below" rule. Nor does the State's repeated opposition to respondents' substantive Fourth Amendment claims suffice to have raised the separate question whether the exclusionary rule should be modified. The extent of the continued vitality of the rule is an issue of unusual significance, and adhering scrupulously to the customary limitations on this Court's discretion promotes respect for its adjudicatory process and the stability of its decisions, and lessens the threat of untoward practical ramifications not foreseen at the time of decision. Pp. 217–224. ②

2. The rigid "two-pronged test" under *Aguilar* and *Spinelli* for determining whether an informant's tip establishes probable cause for issuance of a warrant is abandoned, and the "totality of the circumstances" approach that traditionally has informed probable-cause determinations is substituted in its place. The elements under the "two-pronged test" concerning the informant's "veracity," "reliability," and "basis of knowledge" should be understood simply as closely intertwined issues that may usefully illuminate the common-sense, practical question whether there is "probable cause" to believe that contraband or evidence is located in a particular place. The task of the issuing magistrate is simply to make a practical, common-sense decision whether, given all the circumstances set forth in the affidavit before him, there is a fair probability that contraband or evidence of a crime will be found in a particular place. And the duty of a reviewing court is simply to ensure that the magistrate had a substantial basis for concluding that probable cause existed. This flexible, easily applied standard will better achieve the accommodation of public and private interests that the Fourth Amendment requires than does the approach that has developed from *Aguilar* and *Spinelli*. Pp. 230–241.

3. The judge issuing the warrant had a substantial basis for concluding that probable cause to search respondents' home and car existed. Under the "totality of the circumstances" analysis, corroboration of details of an informant's tip by independent police work is of significant value. Cf. *Draper* v. *United States*, 358 U. S. 307. Here, even standing alone, the facts obtained through the independent investigation of the Bloomingdale police officer and the DEA at least suggested that

FIGURE 4-2   (continued)

① ← **This is the volume number of the *United States Reports*.**

② ← **Pages 217–224 of this case present the material covered in the first section of the Syllabus.**

United States Reports

United States Reports.
Official publication of all
United States Supreme
Court case law; published
by the federal government.

This is the official publication of all U.S. Supreme Court case law. It is published by the federal government. The proper citation format for the **United States Reports** is U.S. Figure 4-3 is the first page of the *Texas v. Johnson* case as it appears in the *United States Reports*.

Supreme Court Reporter

unofficial publication.
Material not published by a
government entity or a government designee.
editorial enhancements.
Helpful information
included in many unoffi-
cial publications; the
enhancements assist the
researcher to understand
the material. Most official
publications have little or
no editorial enhancements.
digest topics. Topics included in an index (digest)
to reported case law,
arranged by subject.
key numbers. A research
aid unique to the West
Group materials; these
numbers allow a researcher
to quickly access specific
material in a digest.
Supreme Court Reporter.
Printed by West Group, this
is an unofficial publication
of all United States
Supreme Court case law.
Lawyers' Edition. LEXIS
Law Publishing publishes
this unofficial (nongovern-
ment) printing of all U.S.
Supreme Court case law.

This is an **unofficial publication** of all Supreme Court case law. It is published by West Group. The cases are identical to those published in the *United States Reports*. The only differences are in the format in which the cases are published and the **editorial enhancements.** The primary editorial enhancement worth noting in all West case reporter publications is the inclusion of **digest topics** and **key numbers.** Digests are discussed in Chapter 9. These tools enable the researcher to quickly and easily expand the research. The West publications are linked together through the use of the digest topics and the key numbers. The proper citation format for the **Supreme Court Reporter** is S. Ct. Notice the different format of the *Supreme Court Reporter* publication of *Texas v. Johnson* (Figure 4-4) starting in the second column on page 66.

Lawyers' Edition

This is also an unofficial publication of all Supreme Court cases published by LEXIS Law Publishing. It was previously published by Lawyers' Cooperative Publishing. The case law is identical to that in the *United States Reports* and the *Supreme Court Reporter*. Again, the differences involve format and editorial comments. The proper citation format for the **Lawyers' Edition** is L. Ed. Always be sure to include the edition of the report for example, 91 L.Ed.2d 49. Compare the *Lawyers' Edition* publication of *Texas v. Johnson* with the other versions. It is the same case; the differences lie in publication format and editorial enhancements. Over time, you will develop a preference for one publication over the other two. See Figure 4-5.

These are the three most common printed sources in which a researcher may locate all United States Supreme Court case law. The text of the opinion, what the justices wrote, is identical in each source. The differences are the editorial enhancements and the speed of publication. The official reporter, the *United States Reports,* is published later than all other reporters.

Other Federal Reporters

Federal Reporter. The set
containing all of the federal appellate decisions.
Federal Supplement. The
set containing the cases
argued and determined in
the United States District
Courts, the United States
Court of International
Trade, and the rulings
of the Judicial Panel on
Multidistrict Litigation.

There are several reporters publishing federal case law. Most important to the beginning legal researcher are the **Federal Reporter** and the **Federal Supplement.** The *Federal Reporter* publishes the United States Circuit Court of Appeals opinions. The *Federal Supplement* includes cases from the U.S. District Courts and some special courts.

Federal Reporter West's *Federal Reporter* is a set of federal appellate decisions. Because it is published by West Group, it uses the Key Number Digest System. There is also a specific digest for federal decisions. You will learn more about the Key Number Digest System and digests in general in Chapter 9. Figure 4-6 is a sample cover page from the *Federal Reporter*.

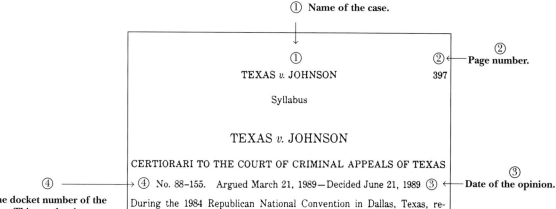

① Name of the case.

①
TEXAS *v.* JOHNSON   ②   ← **Page number.**
397

Syllabus

TEXAS *v.* JOHNSON

CERTIORARI TO THE COURT OF CRIMINAL APPEALS OF TEXAS

④ → ④ No. 88-155. Argued March 21, 1989—Decided June 21, 1989 ③ ← **Date of the opinion.**

The docket number of the case. This number is assigned by the Court.

During the 1984 Republican National Convention in Dallas, Texas, respondent Johnson participated in a political demonstration to protest the policies of the Reagan administration and some Dallas-based corporations. After a march through the city streets, Johnson burned an American flag while protesters chanted. No one was physically injured or threatened with injury, although several witnesses were seriously offended by the flag burning. Johnson was convicted of desecration of a venerated object in violation of a Texas statute, and a State Court of Appeals affirmed. However, the Texas Court of Criminal Appeals reversed, holding that the State, consistent with the First Amendment, could not punish Johnson for burning the flag in these circumstances. The court first found that Johnson's burning of the flag was expressive conduct protected by the First Amendment. The court concluded that the State could not criminally sanction flag desecration in order to preserve the flag as a symbol of national unity. It also held that the statute did not meet the State's goal of preventing breaches of the peace, since it was not drawn narrowly enough to encompass only those flag burnings that would likely result in a serious disturbance, and since the flag burning in this case did not threaten such a reaction. Further, it stressed that another Texas statute prohibited breaches of the peace and could be used to prevent disturbances without punishing this flag desecration.

Held: Johnson's conviction for flag desecration is inconsistent with the First Amendment. Pp. 402–420.

(a) Under the circumstances, Johnson's burning of the flag constituted expressive conduct, permitting him to invoke the First Amendment. The State conceded that the conduct was expressive. Occurring as it did at the end of a demonstration coinciding with the Republican National Convention, the expressive, overtly political nature of the conduct was both intentional and overwhelmingly apparent. Pp. 402–406.

(b) Texas has not asserted an interest in support of Johnson's conviction that is unrelated to the suppression of expression and would therefore permit application of the test set forth in *United States* v. *O'Brien,* 391 U. S. 367, whereby an important governmental interest in regulating nonspeech can justify incidental limitations on First Amendment freedoms when speech and nonspeech elements are combined in the same course of conduct. An interest in preventing breaches of the peace is not implicated on this record. Expression may not be prohib-

FIGURE 4-3 *Texas v. Johnson, from U.S. Reports*

Page Number.

①
398

OCTOBER TERM, 1988

② ②

Volume number and reporter. (*United States Reports*)

Syllabus   491 U. S.

ited on the basis that an audience that takes serious offense to the expression may disturb the peace, since the government cannot assume that every expression of a provocative idea will incite a riot but must look to the actual circumstances surrounding the expression. Johnson's expression of dissatisfaction with the Federal Government's policies also does not fall within the class of "fighting words" likely to be seen as a direct personal insult or an invitation to exchange fisticuffs. This Court's holding does not forbid a State to prevent "imminent lawless action" and, in fact, Texas has a law specifically prohibiting breaches of the peace. Texas' interest in preserving the flag as a symbol of nationhood and national unity is related to expression in this case and, thus, falls outside the *O'Brien* test. Pp. 406–410.

(c) The latter interest does not justify Johnson's conviction. The restriction on Johnson's political expression is content based, since the Texas statute is not aimed at protecting the physical integrity of the flag in all circumstances, but is designed to protect it from intentional and knowing abuse that causes serious offense to others. It is therefore subject to "the most exacting scrutiny." *Boos* v. *Barry*, 485 U. S. 312. The government may not prohibit the verbal or nonverbal expression of an idea merely because society finds the idea offensive or disagreeable, even where our flag is involved. Nor may a State foster its own view of the flag by prohibiting expressive conduct relating to it, since the government may not permit designated symbols to be used to communicate a limited set of messages. Moreover, this Court will not create an exception to these principles protected by the First Amendment for the American flag alone. Pp. 410–422.

③
End of Syllabus. →

755 S. W. 2d 92, affirmed. ③

④

List of justices participating in the opinion.

BRENNAN, J., delivered the opinion of the Court, in which MARSHALL, ④
BLACKMUN, SCALIA, and KENNEDY, JJ., joined. KENNEDY, J., filed a concurring opinion, *post*, p. 420. REHNQUIST, C. J., filed a dissenting opinion, in which WHITE and O'CONNOR, JJ., joined, *post*, p. 421. STEVENS, J., filed a dissenting opinion, *post*, p. 436.

Kathi Alyce Drew argued the cause for petitioner. With her on the briefs were *John Vance* and *Dolena T. Westergard*. ⑤

⑤

Lawyers.

William M. Kunstler argued the cause for respondent. With him on the brief was *David D. Cole*.*

⑥ *Briefs of *amici curiae* urging reversal were filed for the Legal Affairs Council by *Wyatt B. Durrette, Jr.*, and *Bradley B. Cavedo;* and for the Washington Legal Foundation by *Daniel J. Popeo* and *Paul D. Kamenar.*

⑥

Footnote.

Briefs of *amici curiae* urging affirmance were filed for the American Civil Liberties Union et al. by *Peter Linzer, James C. Harrington*, and

FIGURE 4-3
(continued)

TEXAS *v.* JOHNSON 399

① → ① Page number.

397 Opinion of the Court

② JUSTICE BRENNAN delivered the opinion of the Court.

② → The opinion begins here. All material before this is prefatory and *not* written by one of the justices.

After publicly burning an American flag as a means of political protest, Gregory Lee Johnson was convicted of desecrating a flag in violation of Texas law. This case presents the question whether his conviction is consistent with the First Amendment. We hold that it is not.

I ③ ← ③ Always pay attention to how the Court organizes the opinion.

While the Republican National Convention was taking place in Dallas in 1984, respondent Johnson participated in a political demonstration dubbed the "Republican War Chest Tour." As explained in literature distributed by the demonstrators and in speeches made by them, the purpose of this event was to protest the policies of the Reagan administration and of certain Dallas-based corporations. The demonstrators marched through the Dallas streets, chanting political slogans and stopping at several corporate locations to stage "die-ins" intended to dramatize the consequences of nuclear war. On several occasions they spray-painted the walls of buildings and overturned potted plants, but Johnson himself took no part in such activities. He did, however, accept an American flag handed to him by a fellow protestor who had taken it from a flagpole outside one of the targeted buildings.

The demonstration ended in front of Dallas City Hall, where Johnson unfurled the American flag, doused it with kerosene, and set it on fire. While the flag burned, the protestors chanted: "America, the red, white, and blue, we spit on you." After the demonstrators dispersed, a witness to the flag burning collected the flag's remains and buried them in his backyard. No one was physically injured or threatened with injury, though several witnesses testified that they had been seriously offended by the flag burning.

Steven R. Shapiro; for the Christic Institute et al. by *James C. Goodale;* and for Jasper Johns et al. by *Robert G. Sugarman* and *Gloria C. Phares.*

FIGURE 4-3
(continued)

① This is the official citation for this case.

491 U.S. 397

TEXAS v. JOHNSON ④

③ **Cite as 109 S.Ct. 2533 (1989)**

2533

② Page number in the *Supreme Court Reporter.*

④ Case name.

trial court originally sentenced the defendant only to the term of imprisonment. When the court realized its mistake five hours later, it recalled the defendant for resentencing and imposed the $100 fine as well. We held that the resentencing did not violate the defendant's rights under the Double Jeopardy Clause. There, as in *DiFrancesco*, the defendant could not argue that his *legitimate* expectation of finality in the original sentence had been violated, because he was charged with knowledge that the court lacked statutory authority to impose the subminimum sentence in the first instance. See 330 U.S., at 166, 167, 67 S.Ct., at 648, 649. See also *United States v. Arrellano–Rios*, 799 F.2d 520, 524 (CA9 1986) (stating that defendant can have no legitimate expectation of finality in an illegal sentence); *United States v. Edmondson*, 792 F.2d 1492, 1496, n. 4 (CA9 1986) (same).

Applying *DiFrancesco* and *Bozza* here, it seems to me respondent must prevail. There is no doubt that the court had *authority* to impose the 15–year sentence, and respondent therefore had a legitimate expectation of its finality. There are only two grounds on which that could possibly be contested: (1) that the court had authority to impose a 15–year sentence, but not *both* a 15–year sentence and life, or (2) that his legitimate expectation was not necessarily 15 years, but rather *either* 15 years (on the one sentence) *or* life (on the other sentence). But at least where, as here, the one sentence has been fully served, these alternative approaches to defining his legitimate expectation are ruled out by *Bradley*. There also it could have been said that the court had no authority to impose both the $500 fine and the six months' imprisonment; and there also it could have been said that the defendant's legitimate expectation was not necessarily a $500 fine, but either a $500 fine or six months' imprisonment. But we in effect rejected those approaches, holding that once the fine had been paid a subsequent proceeding could

* I agree with the Court, *ante*, at 2527, n. 3, that the Court of Appeals erred in saying that the

not replace₃₉₆ it with the alternative penalty. There is simply no basis for departing from that holding here.

The Double Jeopardy Clause is and has always been, not a provision designed to assure reason and justice in the particular case, but the embodiment of technical, prophylactic rules that require the Government to turn square corners. Whenever it is applied to release a criminal deserving of punishment it frustrates justice in the particular case, but for the greater purpose of assuring repose in the totality of criminal prosecutions and sentences. There are many ways in which these technical rules might be designed. We chose one approach in *Bradley* —undoubtedly not the only possible approach, but also not one that can be said to be clearly wrong. (The fact that it produces a "windfall" separates it not at all from other applications of the double jeopardy guarantee.) With technical rules, above all others, it is imperative that we adhere strictly to what we have stated the rules to be. A technical rule with equitable exceptions is no rule at all. Three strikes is out. The State broke the rules here, and must abide by the result.

For these reasons, I believe the Court of Appeals was correct to set aside respondent's life sentence. I would therefore affirm the judgment of the Court of Appeals, and respectfully dissent from the Court's disposition of this case.*

⑤

⑤ In the West reporters, a key symbol is used to mark the end of one case and the beginning of the next case.

O-W·E·S·T KEY NUMBER SYSTEM ⑤

⑦

491 U.S. 397, 105 L.Ed.2d 342

⌐₃₉₇**TEXAS, Petitioner**

v.

Gregory Lee JOHNSON.

No. 88–155.

Argued March 21, 1989.

Decided June 21, 1989.

⑦ References to the *Lawyers' Edition* citation for this case, an unofficial reporter citation.

⑥

Defendant was convicted in the County Criminal Court No. 8, Dallas County, John

State could not resentence or retry respondent for a non-jeopardy-barred lesser included of-

FIGURE 4-4
Texas v. Johnson, from *Supreme Court Reporter*

⑥ The beginning of the West editor's summary, an editorial enhancement.

① Reference to the volume and name of the reporter.

2534 ① **109 SUPREME COURT REPORTER** 491 U.S. 397

C. Hendrik, J., of desecration of venerated object, and he appealed. The Dallas Court of Appeals, Fifth Supreme Judicial District, 706 S.W.2d 120, Vance, J., affirmed, and defendant petitioned for discretionary review. The Texas Court of Criminal Appeals, 755 S.W.2d 92, Campbell, J., reversed and remanded, and certiorari was granted. The Supreme Court, Justice Brennan, held that: (1) defendant's act of burning American flag during protest rally was expressive conduct within protection of First Amendment, and (2) State could not justify prosecution of defendant based on interest in preventing breaches of peace or to preserve flag as symbol of nationhood and national unity.

② Affirmed.

Justice Kennedy concurred and filed an opinion.

Chief Justice Rehnquist dissented and filed an opinion in which Justice White and Justice O'Connor joined.

Justice Stevens dissented and filed an opinion.

③

1. Constitutional Law ⬅90(1), 274.1(1)

Conduct may be sufficiently imbued with elements of communication to fall within scope of First and Fourteenth Amendments. U.S.C.A. Const.Amends. 1, 14.

2. Constitutional Law ⬅90.1(1)

In deciding whether particular conduct possesses sufficient communicative elements to bring First Amendment into play, it is necessary to determine whether there was an intent to convey a particularized message and whether likelihood was great that message would be understood by those who viewed it. U.S.C.A. Const. Amend. 1.

fense, see *Morris v. Mathews*, 475 U.S. 237, 106 S.Ct. 1032, 89 L.Ed.2d 187 (1986). Since it is undisputed, however, that the State has made

3. Constitutional Law ⬅90.1(1)

Any action taken with respect to American flag is not automatically expressive; rather, in characterizing such action for First Amendment purposes, Supreme Court considers context in which conduct occurred. U.S.C.A. Const.Amend. 1.

4. Constitutional Law ⬅90.1(2)

In prosecution for desecration of venerated object, defendant's burning of American flag as part of political demonstration that coincided with convening of political party and renomination of incumbent for President was expressive conduct subject to First Amendment protection. U.S.C.A. Const.Amend. 1; V.T.C.A., Penal Code § 42.09(a)(3).

5. Constitutional Law ⬅90(3)

Government generally has freer hand in restricting expressive conduct than it has in restricting written or spoken word, but it may not proscribe particular conduct because it has expressive elements; law directed at communicative nature of conduct must, like law directed at speech itself, be justified by substantial showing of need that First Amendment requires. U.S.C.A. Const.Amend. 1.

6. Constitutional Law ⬅90(1)

Principal function of free speech under our system of government is to invite dispute; it may indeed best serve its high purpose when it induces condition of unrest, creates dissatisfaction with conditions as they are, or even stirs people to anger. U.S.C.A. Const.Amend. 1.

7. Constitutional Law ⬅90.1(2)
United States ⬅5½

State's interest in preventing breaches of peace did not justify defendant's conviction for violation of Texas flag desecration

no attempt to do that, that portion of the Court of Appeals' opinion was the purest dictum, and no basis for reversal of its judgment.

FIGURE 4-4 (continued)

① Reference to the volume and name of the reporter.

② End of editor's summary.

③ This is a West digest topic and corresponding key numbers. These are editorial enhancements. These digest topics and key numbers are called *headnotes*.

statute when he burned American flag as part of protest; no actual breach of peace occurred at time of flag burning or in response to flag burning, and mere potential for breach of peace could not serve to justify prosecution. U.S.C.A. Const. Amend. 1; V.T.C.A., Penal Code § 42.-09(a)(3).

8. Constitutional Law ☜90.1(2)

In prosecution for violation of Texas flag desecration statute based on defendant's burning of American flag during protest rally, state's asserted interest in preserving special symbolic character of American flag would be subject to the most exacting scrutiny since defendant's political expression was restricted by prosecution because of content and message he conveyed. U.S.C.A. Const.Amend. 1; V.T.C.A., Penal Code, § 42.09(a)(3).

9. Constitutional Law ☜90(1)

If there is a bedrock principle underlying the First Amendment, it is that government may not prohibit expression of an idea simply because society finds idea itself offensive or disagreeable. U.S.C.A. Const. Amend. 1.

10. Constitutional Law ☜90.1(2)

State of Texas could not justify criminal prosecution under flag desecration statute of defendant who burned American flag at protest rally based on interest in preserving flag as symbol of nationhood and national unity. U.S.C.A. Const.Amend. 1; V.T.C.A., Penal Code § 42.09(a)(3).

①

The Syllabus, provided, by the *United States Reports*, follows the headnotes.

① ⟶ ①

Syllabus *

During the 1984 Republican National Convention in Dallas, Texas, respondent Johnson participated in a political demonstration to protest the policies of the Reagan administration and some Dallas-based

* The syllabus constitutes no part of the opinion of the Court but has been prepared by the Reporter of Decisions for the convenience of the

corporations. After a march through the city streets, Johnson burned an American flag while protesters chanted. No one was physically injured or threatened with injury, although several witnesses were seriously offended by the flag burning. Johnson was convicted of desecration of a venerated object in violation of a Texas statute, and a State Court of Appeals affirmed. However, the Texas Court of Criminal Appeals reversed, holding that the State, consistent with the First Amendment, could not punish Johnson for burning the flag in these circumstances. The court first found that Johnson's burning of the flag was expressive conduct protected by the First Amendment. The court concluded that the State could not criminally sanction flag desecration in order to preserve the flag as a symbol of national unity. It also held that the statute did not meet the State's goal of preventing breaches of the peace, since it was not drawn narrowly enough to encompass only those flag burnings that would likely result in a serious disturbance, and since the flag burning in this case did not threaten such a reaction. Further, it stressed that another Texas statute prohibited breaches of the peace and could be used to prevent disturbances without punishing this flag desecration.

Held: Johnson's conviction for flag desecration is inconsistent with the First Amendment. Pp. 2538–2548.

(a) Under the circumstances, Johnson's burning of the flag constituted expressive conduct, permitting him to invoke the First Amendment. The State conceded that the conduct was expressive. Occurring as it did at the end of a demonstration coinciding with the Republican National Convention, the expressive, overtly political nature of the conduct was both intentional and overwhelmingly apparent. Pp. 2538–2540.

reader. See *United States v. Detroit Lumber Co.,* 200 U.S. 321, 337, 26 S.Ct. 282, 287, 50 L.Ed. 499.

FIGURE 4-4
(continued)

2536   **109 SUPREME COURT REPORTER**   491 U.S. 397

(b) Texas has not asserted an interest in support of Johnson's conviction that is unrelated to the suppression of expression and would therefore permit application of the test set forth in *United States v. O'Brien*, 391 U.S. 367, 88 S.Ct. 1673, 20 L.Ed.2d 672, whereby an important governmental interest in regulating nonspeech can justify incidental limitations on First Amendment freedoms when speech and nonspeech elements are combined in the same course of conduct. An interest in preventing breaches of the peace is not implicated on this record. Expression may not be prohibited₃₉₈ on the basis that an audience that takes serious offense to the expression may disturb the peace, since the government cannot assume that every expression of a provocative idea will incite a riot but must look to the actual circumstances surrounding the expression. Johnson's expression of dissatisfaction with the Federal Government's policies also does not fall within the class of "fighting words" likely to be seen as a direct personal insult or an invitation to exchange fisticuffs. This Court's holding does not forbid a State to prevent "imminent lawless action" and, in fact, Texas has a law specifically prohibiting breaches of the peace. Texas' interest in preserving the flag as a symbol of nationhood and national unity is related to expression in this case and, thus, falls outside the *O'Brien* test. Pp. 2540–2542.

(c) The latter interest does not justify Johnson's conviction. The restriction on Johnson's political expression is content based, since the Texas statute is not aimed at protecting the physical integrity of the flag in all circumstances, but is designed to protect it from intentional and knowing abuse that causes serious offense to others. It is therefore subject to "the most exacting scrutiny." *Boos v. Barry*, 485 U.S. 312, 108 S.Ct. 1157, 99 L.Ed.2d 333. The government may not prohibit the verbal or nonverbal expression of an idea merely because society finds the idea offensive or disagreeable, even where our flag is

involved. Nor may a State foster its own view of the flag by prohibiting expressive conduct relating to it, since the government may not permit designated symbols to be used to communicate a limited set of messages. Moreover, this Court will not create an exception to these principles protected by the First Amendment for the American flag alone. Pp. 2542–2548.

755 S.W.2d 92, (Tex.Cr.App.1988), affirmed.

BRENNAN, J., delivered the opinion of the Court, in which MARSHALL, BLACKMUN, SCALIA, and KENNEDY, JJ., joined. KENNEDY, J., filed a concurring opinion, *post*, p. 2548. REHNQUIST, C.J., filed a dissenting opinion, in which WHITE and O'CONNOR, JJ., joined, *post*, p. 2549. STEVENS, J., filed a dissenting opinion, *post*, p. 2556.

———————

Kathi Alyce Drew, Dallas, Tex., for petitioner.

William M. Kunstler, New York City, for respondent.

⊥₃₉₉Justice BRENNAN delivered the opinion of the Court.

After publicly burning an American flag as a means of political protest, Gregory Lee Johnson was convicted of desecrating a flag in violation of Texas law. This case presents the question whether his conviction is consistent with the First Amendment. We hold that it is not.

I

While the Republican National Convention was taking place in Dallas in 1984, respondent Johnson participated in a political demonstration dubbed the "Republican War Chest Tour." As explained in literature distributed by the demonstrators and

Reprinted with permission of Thomson/West

Annotations (margin):

① Page 398, in the *United States Reports* begins here: "ited."

② ⊥ 399 indicates where page 399 in the *United States Reports* begins (official reporter).

③ The Court's opinion begins here.

FIGURE 4-4
(continued)

① The volume
and reporter.
(*Lawyers'
Edition 2d.*)

U.S. SUPREME COURT REPORTS   105 L Ed 2d ← ①

[491 US 397]
TEXAS, Petitioner

② Full name/
designation of
parties. Look at
the top of the
next page for the
proper short
name of the
case. Always cite
the case using
the short name.

② ───────────→ ②   v

GREGORY LEE JOHNSON

491 US 397, 105 L Ed 2d 342, 109 S Ct 2533

[No. 88-155]

Argued March 21, 1989. Decided June 21, 1989.

Decision: Conviction of protester for burning American flag as part of
political demonstration held to violate Federal Constitution's First
Amendment.
③

③ Summary
of the case,
written by an
editor.

SUMMARY ←──────────────────────── ③

While the 1984 Republican National Convention was taking place in
Dallas, Texas, a group of people staged a political demonstration in Dallas
to protest the policies of the President of the United States, who was being
nominated by the Convention for re-election, and of certain Dallas-based
corporations. During the course of that demonstration, one of the protesters
(1) accepted an American flag handed to him by a fellow protester, who had
taken the flag from a pole outside one of the targeted buildings, (2) doused
the flag with kerosene, and (3) set the flag on fire. While the flag burned, the
protesters chanted, "America, the red, white, and blue, we spit on you." The
protester who allegedly had burned the flag was subsequently prosecuted in
a Texas trial court for that act and was convicted of violating a state statute
which (1) prohibited the desecration of, among other things, a state or
national flag, and (2) defined desecration as the physical mistreatment of
such objects in a way which the actor knows will seriously offend one or
more persons likely to observe or discover the act. Several witnesses testified
that they had been seriously offended by the flag burning. The defendant
protester appealed his conviction on the ground, among others, that the
application of the state statute violated his right to freedom of speech under
the Federal Constitution's First Amendment. In affirming the conviction,
the Court of Appeals for the Fifth District of Texas at Dallas ruled that the
defendant protester's flag burning constituted symbolic speech requiring
First Amendment scrutiny, but concluded that the desecration statute
nevertheless could be upheld as a legitimate and constitutional means of (1)

④ References to
supplemental
material
available at
the end of
this volume.

④

SUBJECT OF ANNOTATION

Beginning on page 809, infra

Supreme Court's views as to constitutionality of laws prohibiting, or of criminal convictions for, desecration, defiance, disre-
spect, or misuse of American flag

④

⑤ ───→ ⑤ Briefs of Counsel, p 807, infra.

⑤ The briefs filed
with the Court
are available to
the researcher in
this publication.

342

FIGURE 4-5   *Texas v. Johnson,* from *Lawyers' Edition*

①
TEXAS v JOHNSON
② (1989) 491 US 397, 105 L Ed 2d 342, 109 S Ct 2533 ← ─────── ②

protecting the public peace, because acts of flag desecration are, of themselves, so inherently inflammatory that the state may act to prevent breaches of the peace, and (2) realizing the state's legitimate and substantial interest in protecting the flag as a symbol of national unity (706 SW2d 120). The Court of Criminal Appeals of Texas, however, held that the desecration statute as applied violated the defendant protester's First Amendment rights, because the statute (1) was too broad for First Amendment purposes as it related to breaches of the peace, and (2) was not adequately supported by the state's purported interest in preserving a symbol of unity; therefore, the court reversed the decisions below and remanded the case to the trial court with instructions to dismiss the information (755 SW2d 92).

On certiorari, the United States Supreme Court affirmed. In an opinion by BRENNAN, J., joined by MARSHALL, BLACKMUN, SCALIA, and KENNEDY, JJ., it was held that the conviction of the defendant protester was inconsistent with the First Amendment under the particular circumstances presented, because (1) the protester's conduct was sufficiently imbued with elements of communication to implicate the First Amendment, given that this flag burning was the culmination of a political demonstration and that the state conceded that the protester's conduct was expressive; (2) the state's interest in preventing breaches of the peace was not implicated on the record in this case, since (a) no disturbance of the peace actually occurred or threatened to occur because of the flag burning, (b) it cannot be presumed that an audience which takes serious offense at a particular expression is necessarily likely to disturb the peace, and (c) the flag burning does not fall within the small class of "fighting words" that are likely to provoke the average person to retaliation and thereby cause a breach of the peace; and (3) the state's asserted interest in preserving the flag as a symbol of nationhood and national unity does not justify the conviction, since (a) the attempted restriction on expression is content-based, and thus subject to the most exacting scrutiny, given that the flag-desecration statute is aimed not at protecting the physical integrity of the flag in all circumstances, but only against impairments that would cause serious offense to others, and is aimed at protecting onlookers from being offended by the ideas expressed by the prohibited activity, and (b) although the state has a legitimate interest in encouraging proper treatment of the flag, it may not foster its own view of the flag by prohibiting expressive conduct relating to it and by criminally punishing a person for burning the flag as a means of political protest.

KENNEDY, J., concurred, expressing the view that the First Amendment compels the result reached in this case, regardless of how distasteful that result may be to the Justices who announce it, because the defendant protester's acts were speech in both the technical and the fundamental meaning of the Federal Constitution.

REHNQUIST, Ch. J., joined by WHITE and O'CONNOR, JJ., dissented, expressing the view that (1) the Texas statute is not invalid under the First Amendment as applied in this case, because (a) the American flag has come to be the visible symbol embodying our nation and is not simply another

343 ←

FIGURE 4-5
(continued)

U.S. SUPREME COURT REPORTS   105 L Ed 2d

idea or point of view competing for recognition in the marketplace of ideas, and (b) the public burning of the American flag in this case was no essential part of any exposition of ideas and had a tendency to incite a breach of the peace, for flag burning is the equivalent of an inarticulate grunt or roar that is most likely to be indulged in not to express any particular idea, but to antagonize others, and the statute thus deprived the defendant protester of only one rather inarticulate symbolic form of protest—a form of protest that was profoundly offensive to many—and left him with a full panoply of other symbols and every conceivable form of verbal expression to express his deep disapproval of national policy; and (2) the statute is not unconstitutionally vague or overbroad.

STEVENS, J., dissented, expressing the view that (1) sanctioning the desecration of the flag will tarnish its value as a national symbol, a tarnish which is not justified by the trivial burden on free expression that is occasioned by requiring that alternative modes of expression be employed; (2) the flag-desecration statute does not prescribe orthodox views or compel any conduct or expression of respect for any idea or symbol; and (3) the defendant protester in this case was prosecuted not for his criticism of government policies, but for the method he chose to express those views, and a prohibition against that method is supported by a legitimate interest in preserving the quality of an important national asset.

FIGURE 4-5
(continued)

TEXAS v JOHNSON

(1989) 491 US 397, 105 L Ed 2d 342, 109 S Ct 2533

HEADNOTES

Classified to U.S. Supreme Court Digest, Lawyers' Edition

Constitutional Law §§ 934, 935, 960; Evidence § 419 — free speech — flag burning — provoking public disturbance — presumption

1a-1i. The conviction of a protester for burning an American flag, in violation of a state statute which prohibits the desecration of the flag and which defines desecration as physical mistreatment which the actor knows will seriously offend one or more persons likely to observe or discover the action, is inconsistent with the free speech guarantee of the Federal Constitution's First Amendment under the particular circumstances presented, where (1) the protester's conduct is sufficiently imbued with elements of communication to implicate the First Amendment, given that this flag burning was the culmination of a political demonstration protesting the policies of a President of the United States who was then being nominated for re-election in the city where the demonstration occurred, and the policies of various corporations based in

---

TOTAL CLIENT-SERVICE LIBRARY® REFERENCES

12 Am Jur 2d, Breach of Peace and Disorderly Conduct § 8; 16A Am Jur 2d, Constitutional Law §§ 507-511, 513, 514, 516; 35 Am Jur 2d, Flag §§ 3-5

USCS, Constitution, Amendment 1

US L Ed Digest, Constitutional Law §§ 934, 935, 960

Index to Annotations, Breach of Peace and Disorderly Conduct; Fighting Words; Flags; Freedom of Speech and Press

Auto-Cite®: Cases and annotations referred to herein can be further researched through the Auto-Cite® computer-assisted research service. Use Auto-Cite to check citations for form, parallel references, prior and later history, and annotation references.

ANNOTATION REFERENCES

Supreme Court's view as to the protection or lack of protection, under the Federal Constitution, of the utterance of "fighting words." 39 L Ed 2d 925.

The Supreme Court and the right of free speech and press. 93 L Ed 1151, 2 L Ed 2d 1706, 11 L Ed 2d 1116, 16 L Ed 2d 1053, 21 L Ed 2d 976.

What constitutes violation of flag desecration statutes. 41 ALR3d 502.

345

FIGURE 4-5
(continued)

U.S. SUPREME COURT REPORTS   105 L Ed 2d

that city, and given that the state conceded that the protester's conduct was expressive; (2) the interest in preventing breaches of the peace, asserted by the state as justifying the individual's conviction, is not implicated on the record in this case, because (a) no disturbance of the peace actually occurred or threatened to occur because of the flag burning, (b) the only evidence as to onlookers' reactions was the testimony of several persons who were seriously offended by the flag burning, (c) it cannot be presumed that an audience which takes serious offense at a particular expression is necessarily likely to disturb the peace, and (d) the flag burning does not fall within the small class of "fighting words" that are likely to provoke the average person to retaliation and thereby cause a breach of the peace; and (3) the state's asserted interest in preserving the flag as a symbol of nationhood and national unity does not justify the protester's conviction, since (a) the attempted restriction on expression is content-based, and thus subject to the most exacting scrutiny, given that the flag-desecration statute is aimed not at protecting the physical integrity of the flag in all circumstances, but only against impairments that would cause serious offense to others, and is aimed at protecting onlookers from being offended by the ideas expressed by the prohibited activity, and (b) although the state has a legitimate interest in encouraging proper treatment of the flag, it may not foster its own view of the flag by prohibiting expressive conduct relating to it and by criminally punishing a person for burning the flag as a means of political protest. (Rehnquist, Ch. J., and White, O'Connor, and Stevens, JJ., dissented from this holding.)

[See annotation p 809, infra]

Appeal § 1600; Constitutional Law § 960; Trial § 288 — free speech — flag burning — related speech — instruction on aiding and abetting — reversible error

2a, 2b. Although the jury, in the state court prosecution of a protester for burning the American flag—in violation of a state statute which makes it a crime to desecrate the flag, but does not on its face permit conviction for remarks critical of the flag or its referents—was instructed in accordance with the state's law of parties that a person is criminally responsible for an act committed by another if he or she solicits, encourages, directs, aids, or attempts to aid the other person to commit the offense with the intent of promoting or assisting the commission of the offense, this instruction could not have led the jury, in violation of the individual's rights under the Federal Constitution's First Amendment, to convict the protester solely for his words in leading chants denouncing the flag while it burned, where (1) this instruction was offered by the prosecution, because the individual's defense was that he was not the person who had burned the flag in question, (2) the instruction does not permit a conviction merely for the pejorative nature of the individual's words, and (3) the words themselves —"America, the red, white, and blue, we spit on you"—do not encourage the burning of the flag as the instruction seems to require; given the additional fact that the bulk of the prosecutor's argument, which mentioned that the individual had led this chant, was premised on the individual's culpability as a sole actor, it is too unlikely that the jury

346

FIGURE 4-5
(continued)

TEXAS v JOHNSON
(1989) 491 US 397, 105 L Ed 2d 342, 109 S Ct 2533

convicted the individual on the basis of this alternative theory for the conviction to be reversed on this ground.

Appeal § 732 — United States Supreme Court — review of state court decision — validity of state statute

3a, 3b. Although an individual who has been convicted in a state court of desecrating the American flag by burning it raises a claim that the state statute under which he was convicted violates on its face the free speech provisions of the Federal Constitution's First Amendment, the United States Supreme Court, in reviewing the individual's conviction on certiorari, will address only the alternative claim that the statute violates the First Amendment as applied to political expression like that engaged in by the individual—who allegedly burned the flag, to the accompaniment of the chant "America, the red, white, and blue, we spit on you," in the course of a demonstration protesting the policies of the incumbent President of the United States, who was then being nominated for a second term in the city where the demonstration was held, and of various corporations based in that city—because (1) although one violates the statute, according to its terms, only if one knows that one's physical mistreatment of the flag will seriously offend one or more persons likely to observe or discover this action, this does not necessarily mean that the statute applies only to expressive conduct protected by the First Amendment; (2) the prosecution of a person who had not engaged in expressive conduct would pose a different case; and (3) the case can be disposed of on narrower grounds.

Constitutional Law § 934 — free speech — regulation of expressive conduct

4. Under the Federal Constitution's First Amendment, the government generally has a freer hand in restricting expressive conduct than it has in restricting the written or spoken word, but it may not proscribe particular conduct because that conduct has expressive elements; a law directed at the communicative nature of conduct must, like a law directed at speech itself, be justified by the substantial showing of need that the First Amendment requires; in short, it is not simply the verbal or nonverbal nature of the expression, but the governmental interest at stake, that helps to determine whether a restriction on that expression is valid.

Appeal § 1662 — effect of decision on other grounds

5a, 5b. The United States Supreme Court—in reviewing on certiorari the state court criminal conviction of an individual who is charged with desecrating an American flag by burning it and who claims that his act was expressive conduct protected by the Federal Constitution's First Amendment—need not consider the individual's argument that the state's interest in preventing breaches of the peace, asserted as justifying the conviction, is related to the suppression of free expression in that the violent reaction to flag burnings feared by the state would be the result of the message conveyed by them, where the Supreme Court finds that this interest is not implicated on the particular facts of the case.

Constitutional Law § 934 — free speech — prosecution for expressive conduct

6. Under the Federal Constitu-

347

FIGURE 4-5
(continued)

U.S. SUPREME COURT REPORTS 105 L Ed 2d

tion's First Amendment, where a court is confronted with a case of prosecution for the expression of an idea through activity, the court must examine with particular care the interests advanced to support the prosecution.

Constitutional Law §§ 935, 960 — free speech — flag burning — audience reaction

7a, 7b. For purposes of the free speech clause of the Federal Constitution's First Amendment, there is no distinction of constitutional significance between (1) a state flag-desecration statute which is violated only when one physically mistreats the American flag in a way that he or she "knows" will offend others—so that a conviction for flag burning under that statute purportedly does not depend on onlookers' actual reactions, but on the actor's intent—and (2) a statute which depends on actual audience reaction.
[See annotation p 809, infra]

Constitutional Law § 935 — free speech — offensiveness

8. Under the Federal Constitu-

tion's First Amendment, the government may not prohibit the expression of an idea simply because society finds the idea itself offensive or disagreeable.

Constitutional Law §§ 925, 961 — freedom of speech and religion

9. Under the Federal Constitution, no official, high or petty, can prescribe what shall be orthodox in politics, nationalism, religion, or other matters of opinion or force citizens to confess by word or act their faith therein.

Constitutional Law § 934 — free speech — regulation — mode of expression

10. The rule, under the Federal Constitution's First Amendment, that the government may not prohibit expression simply because it disagrees with its message, is not dependent on the particular mode in which one chooses to express an idea.

SYLLABUS BY REPORTER OF DECISIONS

During the 1984 Republican National Convention, respondent Johnson participated in a political demonstration to protest the policies of the Reagan administration and some Dallas-based corporations. After a march through the city streets, Johnson burned an American flag while protesters chanted. No one was physically injured or threatened with injury, although several witnesses were seriously offended by the flag burning. Johnson was convicted of desecration of a venerated object in violation of a Texas statute, and a state court of appeals affirmed. However, the Texas Court of Criminal Appeals reversed, holding that the

State, consistent with the First Amendment, could not punish Johnson for burning the flag in these circumstances. The court first found that Johnson's burning of the flag was expressive conduct protected by the First Amendment. The court concluded that the State could not criminally sanction flag desecration in order to preserve the flag as a symbol of national unity. It also held that the statute did not meet the State's goal of preventing breaches of the peace, since it was not drawn narrowly enough to encompass only those flag burnings that would likely result in a serious disturbance, and since the flag burning in this case

FIGURE 4-5
(continued)

TEXAS v JOHNSON
(1989) 491 US 397, 105 L Ed 2d 342, 109 S Ct 2533

did not threaten such a reaction. Further, it stressed that another Texas statute prohibited breaches of the peace and could be used to prevent disturbances without punishing this flag desecration.

Held: Johnson's conviction for flag desecration is inconsistent with the First Amendment.

(a) Under the circumstances, Johnson's burning of the flag constituted expressive conduct, permitting him to invoke the First Amendment. The State conceded that the conduct was expressive. Occurring as it did at the end of a demonstration coinciding with the Republican National Convention, the expressive, overtly political nature of the conduct was both intentional and overwhelmingly apparent.

(b) Texas has not asserted an interest in support of Johnson's conviction that is unrelated to the suppression of expression and would therefore permit application of the test set forth in United States v O'Brien, 391 US 367, 20 L Ed 2d 672, 88 S Ct 1673, whereby an important governmental interest in regulating nonspeech can justify incidental limitations on First Amendment freedoms when speech and nonspeech elements are combined in the same course of conduct. An interest in preventing breaches of the peace is not implicated on this record. Expression may not be prohibited on the basis that an audience that takes serious offense to the expression may disturb the peace, since the Government cannot assume that every expression of a provocative idea will incite a riot but must look to the actual circumstances surrounding the expression. Johnson's expression of dissatisfaction with the Federal Government's policies also does not fall within the class of "fighting

words" likely to be seen as a direct personal insult or an invitation to exchange fisticuffs. This Court's holding does not forbid a State to prevent "imminent lawless action" and, in fact, Texas has a law specifically prohibiting breaches of the peace. Texas' interest in preserving the flag as a symbol of nationhood and national unity is related to expression in this case and, thus, falls outside the O'Brien test.

(c) The latter interest does not justify Johnson's conviction. The restriction on Johnson's political expression is content based, since the Texas statute is not aimed at protecting the physical integrity of the flag in all circumstances, but is designed to protect it from intentional and knowing abuse that causes serious offense to others. It is therefore subject to "the most exacting scrutiny." Boos v Barry, 485 US 312, 99 L Ed 2d 333, 108 S Ct 1157. The Government may not prohibit the verbal or nonverbal expression of an idea merely because society finds the idea offensive or disagreeable, even where our flag is involved. Nor may a State foster its own view of the flag by prohibiting expressive conduct relating to it, since the Government may not permit designated symbols to be used to communicate a limited set of messages. Moreover, this Court will not create an exception to these principles protected by the First Amendment for the American flag alone.

755 SW2d 92, affirmed.

Brennan, J., delivered the opinion of the Court, in which Marshall, Blackmun, Scalia, and Kennedy, JJ., joined. Kennedy, J., filed a concurring opinion. Rehnquist, C.J., filed a dissenting opinion, in which White and O'Connor, JJ., joined. Stevens, J., filed a dissenting opinion.

349

FIGURE 4-5
(continued)

U.S. SUPREME COURT REPORTS   105 L Ed 2d

APPEARANCES OF COUNSEL

Kathi Alyce Drew argued the cause for petitioner.
William M. Kunstler argued the cause for respondent.
Briefs of Counsel, p 807, infra.

OPINION OF THE COURT

[491 US 399]

① The Court's opinion begins here.

① Justice **Brennan** delivered the opinion of the Court.

[1a] After publicly burning an American flag as a means of political protest, Gregory Lee Johnson was convicted of desecrating a flag in violation of Texas law. This case presents the question whether his conviction is consistent with the First Amendment. We hold that it is not.

I

While the Republican National Convention was taking place in Dallas in 1984, respondent Johnson participated in a political demonstration dubbed the "Republican War Chest Tour." As explained in literature distributed by the demonstrators and in speeches made by them, the purpose of this event was to protest the policies of the Reagan administration and of certain Dallas-based corporations. The demonstrators marched through the Dallas streets, chanting political slogans and stopping at several corporate locations to stage "die-ins" intended to dramatize the consequences of nuclear war. On several occasions they spray-painted the walls of buildings and overturned potted plants, but Johnson himself took no part in

such activities. He did, however, accept an American flag handed to him by a fellow protestor who had taken it from a flag pole outside one of the targeted buildings.

The demonstration ended in front of Dallas City Hall, where Johnson unfurled the American flag, doused it with kerosene, and set it on fire. While the flag burned, the protestors chanted, "America, the red, white, and blue, we spit on you." After the demonstrators dispersed, a witness to the flag burning collected the flag's remains and buried them in his backyard. No one was physically injured or threatened with injury, though several witnesses testified that they had been seriously offended by the flag burning.

[491 US 400] ②

② Page 400 in the *United States Reports* begins here.

Of the approximately 100 demonstrators, Johnson alone was charged with a crime. The only criminal offense with which he was charged was the desecration of a venerated object in violation of Tex Penal Code Ann § 42.09(a)(3) (1989).[1] After a trial, he was convicted, sentenced to one year in prison, and fined $2,000. The Court of Appeals for the Fifth District of Texas at Dallas affirmed Johnson's conviction, 706 SW2d 120③ (1986), but the Texas Court of Criminal Appeals reversed, 755 SW2d 92

③ Courts do not always follow THE BLUEBOOK citation format.

---

1. Tex Penal Code Ann § 42.09 (1989) provides in full:

"§ 42.09. Desecration of Venerated Object

"(a) A person commits an offense if he intentionally or knowingly desecrates:

"(1) a public monument;

"(2) a place of worship or burial; or

"(3) a state or national flag.

"(b) For purposes of this section, 'desecrate' means deface, damage, or otherwise physically mistreat in a way that the actor knows will seriously offend one or more persons likely to observe or discover his action.

"(c) An offense under this section is a Class A misdemeanor."

350

FIGURE 4-5
(continued)

Reprinted from *United States Supreme Court Reports, Lawyers' Edition 2d.* Copyright 1993 Matthew Bender & Company, Inc., a member of the LexisNexis Group. All Rights Reserved. Reprinted with permission.

West's
FEDERAL REPORTER

Third Series
A Unit of the National Reporter System

Volume 311 F.3d

Cases Argued and Determined
in the

UNITED STATES COURTS OF APPEALS

Mat # 40121287

FIGURE 4-6   Cover
Page, *Federal Reporter*

Reprinted with permission of Thomson/West

Federal Rules Decisions.
The set containing federal opinions, decisions, and rulings involving the Federal Rules of Civil Procedure and the Federal Rules of Criminal Procedure.

Federal Rules Decisions   West's ***Federal Rules Decisions*** collects federal opinions, decisions, and rulings involving the Federal Rules of Civil Procedure and the Federal Rules of Criminal Procedure. Figure 4-7 is a sample cover page from *Federal Rules Decisions.*

Federal Supplement   The *Federal Supplement* reports the cases argued and determined in the U.S. District Courts (trial courts), the United States Court of International Trade, and the rulings of the Judicial Panel on Multidistrict Litigation. This is a very large set, also published by West Group. Decisions from the *Federal Supplement* are digested in the *Federal Digest.* Figure 4-8 is a cover page from the *Federal Supplement.*

Specialized Reporters

specialized reporters.
Collections of cases grouped by specific topics rather than by level of court or jurisdiction.

West also publishes numerous **specialized reporters.** For example, the *Military Justice Reporter* provides opinions of the United States Courts of Appeals for the Armed Forces and selected opinions of the Courts of Criminal Appeals. Figure 4-9 is a cover page from this reporter. The *Bankruptcy Reporter* includes bankruptcy cases decided in the United States Bankruptcy Courts, the United States Bankruptcy Appellate Panels, the United States District Courts, the United States Courts of Appeals, and the Supreme Court of the United States. Figure 4-10 is a sample cover page from this reporter.

LEXIS and Westlaw

All U.S. Supreme Court case law may be found in either LEXIS or Westlaw. These large legal databases make retrieval of case law fast and extremely simple. The researcher may locate a case by its name, its citation, or its facts and legal issues. Computer Assisted Legal Research is addressed in Chapter 11.

Internet   U.S. Supreme Court case law is readily available on the Internet. New sites appear rapidly; look for changes and additions to the sites you already frequent. Cornell Law School's Legal Information Institute offers U.S. Supreme Court decisions on the day the decision is handed down. You may visit this site at http://www.law.cornell.edu. Another good site is http://www.findlaw.com.

4-6 STATE CASE LAW

State court cases are published in state and regional reporters. For example, in California, state cases are printed in the official reporters, *California Reports* (California Supreme Court case law) or *California Appellate Reports,* and in the unofficial reporter, *California Reporter.* In addition, selected cases are found in the regional reporter, the *Pacific Reporter,* which includes cases from a number of western states, including California. Therefore, in California, all cases are found in at least two reporters, and some are found in a third.

Regional Reporters

There are seven regional reporters, each of which covers the case law of a specific region of the United States. For example, the following states are included in the Pacific Region:

PACIFIC REGION
Alaska, Arizona, California, Colorado, Hawaii, Idaho, Kansas, Montana, Nevada, New Mexico, Oklahoma, Oregon, Utah, and Washington.

West's
FEDERAL RULES
DECISIONS

A Unit of the National Reporter System

Volume 210

*Opinions, Decisions and Rulings
involving the*

**FEDERAL RULES OF CIVIL PROCEDURE
AND
FEDERAL RULES OF CRIMINAL PROCEDURE**

Mat # 40119221

Reprinted with permission of Thomson/West

FIGURE 4-7
Cover Page, *Federal
Rules Decisions*

West's
FEDERAL
SUPPLEMENT

Second Series
A Unit of the National Reporter System

Volume 228 F.Supp.2d

Cases Argued and Determined
in the

UNITED STATES DISTRICT COURTS

UNITED STATES COURT OF
INTERNATIONAL TRADE

and Rulings of the

JUDICIAL PANEL ON MULTIDISTRICT
LITIGATION

FIGURE 4-8 Cover
Page, *Federal Supplement*

Mat # 40121564

Reprinted with permission of Thomson/West

West's

MILITARY JUSTICE

REPORTER

A Unit of the National Reporter System

Volume 56

OPINIONS OF THE UNITED STATES COURT

OF APPEALS FOR THE ARMED FORCES

AND

SELECTED OPINIONS OF THE COURTS OF

CRIMINAL APPEALS

Mat # 18217538

Reprinted with permission of Thomson/West

FIGURE 4-9   Cover Page, *Military Justice Reporter*

West's
BANKRUPTCY REPORTER

A Unit of the National Reporter System

Volume 285

Covering

285 West's Bankruptcy Reporter
123 S.Ct. 477–583
309 F.3d 1 to 311 F.3d 424

———————

Bankruptcy Cases Decided in the

UNITED STATES BANKRUPTCY COURTS
UNITED STATES BANKRUPTCY APPELLATE PANELS
UNITED STATES DISTRICT COURTS
UNITED STATES COURTS OF APPEALS
SUPREME COURT OF THE UNITED STATES

THOMSON
———————✳———————™
WEST

Mat # 40119654

FIGURE 4-10   *Cover Page, Bankruptcy Reporter*

Reprinted with permission of Thomson/West

Official Reporters

Some states, such as Montana, do not have a state **official reporter.** For such states, *all* cases are reported in the appropriate regional reporter. These states contract with West to print all of their cases. In this way, the state avoids the expense and delay of a government publication. Other states print their own official reports. In these instances, West publishes only the state Supreme Court cases in the regional reporter. Figures 4-11 and 4-12 show sample cover pages from two of the regional reporters.

official reporters. Sets of case law published by the government or the designee of the government.

Unofficial Reporters

Unofficial reporters are collections of printed decisions, usually from a specific state, that are not government publications and are not authorized by the government. The publisher cannot change the text of the decision, but it adds useful information, which often includes a short summary of the facts of the case, the legal issue, and the outcome. In addition, **headnotes** are added to assist the researcher to find additional case law on a given topic. For these reasons, researchers often find these unofficial reporters extremely helpful.

unofficial reporters. Collections of printed decisions that are not government publications.

headnote. Editorial enhancement added to the front material of a case; useful summary of most of the legal topics addressed in the case.

▷ **A Point to Remember**　At first, the concept of headnotes may be confusing. However, as your research skills improve and the importance of a digest becomes clear, you will find headnotes to be an important research aid. Always read them and the summary provided by the editors; this information is designed to help you understand the case you are about to read. The information is there to provide focus. However, you may not quote from the editorial material. All quotes must originate within the actual opinion of the court.

Remember, wherever you locate the case, no matter who published it, the actual language in the decision is *identical* in every source. Go back and look at the *Texas v. Johnson* case. Once the opinion begins, the language is identical.

Other Sources

State case law is also available on LEXIS and Westlaw. Some may be found on the Internet. Many states publish their case law on CD-ROM disks.

▷ **A Point to Remember**　When performing legal research, one must be conscious of the jurisdiction in which the cause of action (the client's legal problem) arose. In general, if your client lives in Florida and the cause of action arose in Florida, your research takes place in the Florida codes, cases, and practice guides. Similarly, if the cause of action involves a federal issue, all research is performed in the federal research sources.

4-7 HOW TO READ A CASE

Most cases are compiled in a similar format; this format becomes familiar as one reads more. Knowing what to expect and looking for the basic components of a case helps you to read a case once rather than over and over in a seemingly vain attempt to master the court's reasoning.

West's
PACIFIC REPORTER

Third Series
A Unit of the National Reporter System

Volume 57 P.3d

Cases Argued and Determined
in the Courts of

ALASKA	**MONTANA**
ARIZONA	**NEVADA**
CALIFORNIA	**NEW MEXICO**
COLORADO	**OKLAHOMA**
HAWAI'I	**OREGON**
IDAHO	**UTAH**
KANSAS	**WASHINGTON**

WYOMING

THOMSON
WEST

Mat # 40122566

FIGURE 4-11 Cover
Page, *Pacific Reporter*

Reprinted with permission of Thomson/West

West's
SOUTH EASTERN
REPORTER

Second Series
A Unit of the National Reporter System

Volume 571 S.E.2d

Cases Argued and Determined
in the Courts of

GEORGIA   **SOUTH CAROLINA**
NORTH CAROLINA   **VIRGINIA**
WEST VIRGINIA

Mat # 40037910

Reprinted with permission of Thomson/West

FIGURE 4-12 Cover Page, *South Eastern Reporter*

Components of a Case

Initially, some students find case law difficult to read and understand. Each case must be approached with a plan. Case law contains each of the following components.

Facts   The key facts, provided by the court, are essential to the researcher. In legal research, you read case law to locate those cases that are similar, factually and legally, to your client's case. Without the facts, no effective comparisons may take place. Many judges provide the reader with the facts at the very beginning of the case.

Judicial History   The judicial history explains the prior proceedings—what happened in the lower court(s). This component is usually included early in the case.

Issues   Issues are the legal questions before the reviewing court.

Rules   Rules are the primary law relied upon by the court in the analysis or reasoning component of the case.

Analysis   The analysis or reasoning component of most cases will be the longest section. It usually follows the facts, judicial history, and a basic statement of the issues. This component contains a discussion of the facts, issues, and appropriate rules or laws relied upon by the court.

Conclusion   The conclusion—the holding of the court—is the legal outcome of the case.

Many students of the law learn to read cases looking for issues, rules, analysis, and a conclusion. Known as the *IRAC method,* it prepares the researcher to effectively summarize or "brief" the case. Add the relevant facts and the basic judicial history and you have a complete summary.

Each paragraph of a case includes one or more of these six components: (1) judicial history, (2) facts, (3) issues, (4) rules, (5) analysis, and (6) conclusion. As you read, identify the components of every paragraph. This allows you to focus and sort out the case while you read, rather than going back and rereading. Some of the paragraphs contain more than one element; for example, paragraphs of analysis almost always contain rules/law and possibly some relevant facts.

⇨ **A Point to Remember**   It is not possible, nor is it prudent, to give only one label to each paragraph of a decision. But remember: Each paragraph must contain at least one of the six components listed above. Do not become frustrated if you find four elements in one paragraph. Rather, congratulate yourself on careful analysis.

The first two pages of *United States v. Virginia* follows. Use margin notes to identify the components of the case.

CASE 4-1

United States v. Virginia
518 U.S. 515 (1996)

OPINION: JUSTICE GINSBURG delivered the opinion of the Court.

Virginia's public institutions of higher learning include an incomparable military college, Virginia Military Institute (VMI). The United States maintains that the Constitution's equal protection guarantee precludes Virginia from reserving exclusively to men the unique educational opportunities VMI affords. We agree.

I

Founded in 1839, VMI is today the sole single-sex school among Virginia's 15 public institutions of higher learning. VMI's distinctive mission is to produce "citizen-soldiers," men prepared for leadership in civilian life and in military service. VMI pursues this mission through pervasive training of a kind not available anywhere else in Virginia. Assigning prime place to character development, VMI uses an "adversative method" modeled on English public schools and once characteristic of military instruction. VMI constantly endeavors to instill physical and mental discipline in its cadets and impart to them a strong moral code. The school's graduates leave VMI with heightened comprehension of their capacity to deal with duress and stress, and a large sense of accomplishment for completing the hazardous course.

VMI has notably succeeded in its mission to produce leaders; among its alumni are military generals, Members of Congress, and business executives. The school's alumni overwhelmingly perceive that their VMI training helped them to realize their personal goals. VMI's endowment reflects the loyalty of its graduates; VMI has the largest per-student endowment of all public undergraduate institutions in the Nation.

Neither the goal of producing citizen-soldiers nor VMI's implementing methodology is inherently unsuitable to women. And the school's impressive record in producing leaders has made admission desirable to some women. Nevertheless, Virginia has elected to preserve exclusively for men the advantages and opportunities a VMI education affords.

II

A

From its establishment in 1839 as one of the Nation's first state military colleges, *see* 1839 Va. Acts, ch. 20, VMI has remained financially supported by Virginia and "subject to the control of the [Virginia] General Assembly," Va. Code Ann. § 23–92 (1993). First southern college to teach engineering and industrial chemistry, *see* H. Wise, Drawing Out the Man: The VMI Story 13 (1978) (The VMI Story), VMI once provided teachers for the State's schools, *see* 1842 Va. Acts, ch. 24, § 2 (requiring every cadet to teach in one of the Commonwealth's schools for a 2-year period). Civil War strife threatened the school's vitality, but a resourceful superintendent regained legislative support by highlighting "VMI's great potential [,] through its technical know-how," to advance Virginia's postwar recovery. The VMI Story 47.

VMI today enrolls about 1,300 men as cadets. Its academic offerings in the liberal arts, sciences, and engineering are also available at other public colleges and universities in Virginia. But VMI's mission is special. It is the mission of the school "'to produce educated and honorable men, prepared for the varied work of civil life, imbued with love of learning, confident in the functions and attitudes of leadership, possessing a high sense of public service, advocates of the American democracy and free enterprise system, and ready as citizen-soldiers to defend their country in time of national peril.'" 766 F. Supp. 1407, 1425 (WD Va. 1991) (*quoting* Mission Study Committee of the VMI Board of Visitors, Report, May 16, 1986).

In contrast to the federal service academies, institutions maintained "to prepare cadets for career service in the armed forces," VMI's program "is directed

at preparation for both military and civilian life"; "only about 15% of VMI cadets enter career military service." 766 F. Supp. at 1432.

VMI produces its "citizen-soldiers" through "an adversative, or doubting, model of education" which features "physical rigor, mental stress, absolute equality of treatment, absence of privacy, minute regulation of behavior, and indoctrination in desirable values." *Id.,* at 1421. As one Commandant of Cadets described it, the adversative method "dissects the young student," and makes him aware of his "limits and capabilities," so that he knows "how far he can go with his anger, . . . how much he can take under stress, . . . exactly what he can do when he is physically exhausted." *Id.,* at 1421-1422 (*quoting* Col. N. Bissell).

VMI cadets live in spartan barracks where surveillance is constant and privacy nonexistent; they wear uniforms, eat together in the mess hall, and regularly participate in drills. *Id.,* at 1424, 1432. Entering students are incessantly exposed to the rat line, "an extreme form of the adversative model," comparable in intensity to Marine Corps boot camp. *Id.,* at 1422. Tormenting and punishing, the rat line bonds new cadets to their fellow sufferers and, when they have completed the 7-month experience, to their former tormentors. *Id.*

The appeals court greeted with skepticism Virginia's assertion that it offers single-sex education at VMI as a facet of the State's overarching and undisputed policy to advance "autonomy and diversity." The court underscored Virginia's nondiscrimination commitment: "'It is extremely important that [colleges and universities] deal with faculty, staff, and students without regard to sex, race, or ethnic origin.'" *Id.,* at 899 (*quoting* 1990 Report of the Virginia Commission on the University of the 21st Century). "That statement," the Court of Appeals said, "is the only explicit one that we have found in the record in which the Commonwealth has expressed itself with respect to gender distinctions." *Ibid.* Furthermore, the appeals court observed, in urging "diversity" to justify an all-male VMI, the State had supplied "no explanation for the movement away from [single-sex education] in Virginia by public colleges and universities." *Ibid.* In short, the court concluded, "[a] policy of diversity which aims to provide an array of educational opportunities, including single-gender institutions, must do more than favor one gender." *Ibid.*

The parties agreed that "some women can meet the physical standards now imposed on men," *Id.,* at 896, and the court was satisfied that "neither the goal of producing citizen soldiers nor VMI's implementing methodology is inherently unsuitable to women," *Id.,* at 899. The Court of Appeals, however, accepted the District Court's finding that "at least these three aspects of VMI's program—physical training, the absence of privacy, and the adversative approach—would be materially affected by coeducation." *Id.,* at 896-897. Remanding the case, the appeals court assigned to Virginia, in the first instance, responsibility for selecting a remedial course. The court suggested these options for the State: Admit women to VMI; establish parallel institutions or programs; or abandon state support, leaving VMI free to pursue its policies as a private institution. *Id.,* at 900. In May 1993, this Court denied certiorari. *See* 508 U.S. 946.

⇨ **A Point to Remember**   While you are learning to read case law effectively, make a copy of the case and note in the margins which components are in each paragraph. This will help you to remain focused while you read.

Official and Unofficial Publications

When citing to case law, always cite to the official citation first; the parallel/unofficial citation follows the official. In most citation formats the year follows the last parallel citation.

⇨ **A Point to Remember** Sometimes the unofficial publishers go to press so quickly that they publish cases the Court has decided to **de-publish** in whole or in part. When a case has been de-published, it cannot be used as case precedent. Always check to make sure that the case has an official citation. One good method to ensure that you do not miss a de-published case is to carefully Shepardize all cases you research. Shepardizing will be presented in detail in Chapter 10.

de-publish. In rare instances, a court will decide a case, write and release a decision, *but before it is published in the official reporter,* the court decides not to publish some or all of the case decision. A de-published case cannot be used as precedent.

4-8 HOW TO USE CASE LAW

Compare and Contrast the Facts of a Reported Case with Your Client's Facts

The doctrine of precedent mandates that when you use case law you must show factual similarities between your client's situation and the case law found in your research.

First

Compare the facts of the cases you locate in your research with those of your client's situation. If both sets are similar, or easily analogous, the case *may* be considered precedent.

Second

Contrast the facts of the cases you research with those of your client's situation. Significant factual differences probably mean that the case should *not* be used in an attempt to support your client's position.

After comparison of the facts, compare the legal issues. Ask yourself: Are my client's problems the same as, or similar to, the problems in the case I located? If the answer is yes, the case *may* be considered precedent.

Consider the following fact pattern:

A public high school in your city decided to become an all-female campus. The school proposes to focus on the education of young women with an emphasis on female leadership roles in American society. The school notified all parents of existing students of this plan. Over 80% of the parents, including those of male students, support the proposed plan. The school has already set in motion plans to transfer all male students beginning next semester. Neighboring schools are in vigorous support of the plan. Any female students not wishing to attend the all-female school may transfer at any time. The school officials report donations of $75,000 have already been received, with further substantial donations expected. The superintendent of the school district has come to your office, just to make sure this is "all legal." Compare this fact pattern with *United States v. Virginia*. What advice, based on *United States v. Virginia,* will your office most likely give the school district?

⇨ **A Point to Remember** In legal research, never lose sight of the fact that you are researching on behalf of a client. The more you understand about the client's factual situation, the better you are able to focus the research. Take a second look at the fact statement from the *BMW v. Gore* case in Chapter 3. Notice the factual details.

TECHNOLOGY CORNER

The major law schools often provide access to some case law. Try these sites:

www.law.cornell.edu

www.law.indiana.edu

www.washburnlaw.edu

This is only a starting place. Explore as your time permits.

You will find court opinions on the following sites:

www.findlaw.com/casecode/supreme.html (great resource for U.S. Supreme Court case law)

www.findlaw.com/casecode/courts/index.html (federal circuit court opinions)

www.statelocalgov.net/index.cfm (directory to state court case law)

www.fedworld.gov/supcourt/index.htm (older U.S. Supreme Court case law)

www.usscplus.com (Database of U.S. Supreme Court case law)

Note: Each Circuit also has its own site. These sites are usually maintained by a law school in the Circuit.

Searching for case law on the Internet is most likely to be successful if you are looking for U.S. Supreme Court cases, very recent cases, or cases of high interest. The very best sources of online accurate case law are LEXIS and Westlaw. However, these are not free resources. You may visit their Web sites to read about their services and try some of their resources. There are other pay-per-view providers of case law. You see most of them advertised in legal newspapers, bar journals, and legal periodicals.

www.lexis.com

www.westlaw.com

CHAPTER SUMMARY

Case law is primary authority. Cases are presented to the court. Once the legal and factual issues are resolved by the court, the judge writes a decision, often called an *opinion*. The concept of *stare decisis,* or precedent, requires that courts look to what other courts in the same jurisdiction have done with the same or similar legal and factual issues.

Case law is published in large sets of books often referred to as *reporters*. Most states publish their own case law. In addition to the government publications (official reporter), several independent publishers (unofficial reporters) quickly add editorial enhancements and publish well ahead of the government publications. Case law is also easily located on LEXIS, Westlaw, and the Internet.

Learning to cite the law properly is essential. Review of a style manual or the *Uniform System of Citation* is required of anyone citing to legal references. Many citations contain official and unofficial references. All citations must include the short

name of the case followed by the volume, the abbreviation for the reporter, the number of the first page of the case, and the year of the decision.

All U.S. Supreme Court cases are published in three separate publications. The official reporter is the *United States Reports* (U.S.). The two unofficial reporters are the *Supreme Court Reporter* (S. Ct.) and the *Lawyers' Edition* (L. Ed.). Other federal case law is found in the *Federal Reporter, Federal Rules Decisions, Federal Supplement* and various specialized reporters. The Internet is also a good resource for some case law.

State case law is usually published by the state government; this is the official reporter. There is also a regional reporter system, which breaks up the United States into geographic regions.

As you read a case, always focus on the six components of a decision: (1) facts, (2) judicial history, (3) issues, (4) rules, (5) analysis, and (6) conclusion. In your research, remain focused on the doctrine of precedent. When you use or cite case law you must show factual similarities between your client's situation and the case law found in your research.

TERMS TO REMEMBER

primary authority	unofficial publication
decision	editorial enhancements
opinion	digest topics
precedent	key numbers
stare decisis	*Supreme Court Reporter*
regional reporters	*Lawyers' Edition*
Uniform System of Citation	*Federal Reporter*
LEXIS	*Federal Supplement*
Westlaw	*Federal Rules Decisions*
case law reporters	specialized reporters
official citation	official reporters
secondary sources	unofficial reporters
style manual	headnote
parallel citations	de-publish
United States Reports	

QUESTIONS FOR REVIEW

1. Discuss the importance of precedent or *stare decisis*.
2. What is a case law reporter?
3. Explain what is meant by "official citation."
4. Discuss the differences between the three publishers of United States Supreme Court case law.
5. What is a parallel citation?
6. Why will a researcher choose to read an unofficial reporter?
7. List, with brief explanations, the various publications of federal case law.
8. What is a regional reporter?
9. List, with brief explanations, the six components of a case.
10. Why is factual analysis so important?

CAN YOU FIGURE IT OUT?

1. Which regional reporter reports Virginia state case law (Figure 4-12)?
2. What cases are reported in the *Military Justice Reporter* (Figure 4-9)?
3. Which reporter listed in the *Marvin v. Marvin* case citation is the official cite (Figure 4-1)?
4. State four highly relevant facts from the *United States v. Virginia* case.
5. State the factual similarities between the fact pattern in Section 4-8 and the *United States v. Virginia* case.

RESEARCH ASSIGNMENTS AND ACTIVITIES

1. Locate the following U.S. Supreme Court cases. For each case, write the name of the case (the short form of the name), the official citation, and the year. Use the *Uniform System of Citation* format:

   Gideon v. Wainwright, 372 U.S. 335 (1963).

   Cases to be located:

   491 U.S. 274

   387 U.S. 1

   367 U.S. 568

   384 U.S. 436

   471 U.S. 1

2. Locate and read *United States v. Virginia,* 518 U.S. 515, 116 S.Ct. 2264, 135 L.Ed.2d, 735 (1996). Summarize the case using the components set forth in Section 4-7 of this chapter.

3. Locate the following cases: *U.S. v. Dean,* 722 F.2d 92 (1983) and *Gray v. Spellman,* 925 F.2d 90 (1991). Read and summarize each case using the components in Section 4-7.

4. Compare the facts of the Rambeaux case with the facts of each case you summarized.

⇨ **A Point to Remember** When you receive instructions, be sure to complete each part of the assignment. For example, in Research Assignments 3 and 4 above you are asked to complete more than one task. In fact, you are asked to do several separate tasks: (1) read case number 1; (2) read case number 2; (3) summarize case number 1; (4) summarize case number 2; (5) compare the facts of the Rambeaux case with the facts of case number 1; (6) compare the facts of the Rambeaux case with the facts of case number 2.

Your completed written project should clearly set out the two summaries and the two factual comparisons. Avoid making your reader guess. Use simple titles or headings. Make your written work very easy to follow.

CASE PROJECT

Review the hypothetical case you selected in Chapter 1. List the numerous case reporters that contain mandatory authority for the situation.

HOW TO BRIEF A CASE

CHAPTER OBJECTIVES

When you complete this chapter you should be able to

- Explain the purpose of a case brief.
- List the components of a case brief.
- Describe the components of a case brief.
- Explain how to systematically approach a daunting project.

CITATION MATTERS

QUOTATIONS

THE BLUEBOOK — RULE 5

Quotations are an important part of legal writing. When you quote, you *must* alert the reader that you are using quoted language. This means, in most instances, you need quotation marks. A citation must follow a quote. This citation lets the reader know where the borrowed material originated.

Quotations of fifty words or more are *blocked* and no quotation marks are used. A blocked quote is single spaced and slightly indented on the left and right margins. The citation that follows a blocked quote is placed on the line below the last line of the blocked quote and it is drawn all the way over to the left margin. Good examples are included under *THE BLUEBOOK* Rule 5.

Example of a blocked quote:

> The *Ferber* case upheld a prohibition on the distribution and sale of child pornography, as well as its production, because these acts were "intrinsically related" to the sexual abuse of children in two ways. *New York v. Ferber*, 458 U.S. 747, 759 (1982). First, as a permanent record of a child's abuse, the continued circulation itself would harm the child who had participated. *See id.* Second, because the traffic in child pornography was an economic motive for its production, the State had an interest in closing the distribution network. *Id.* at 760.

Quotes of forty-nine words or fewer should be placed in quotation marks, but not set off from the remainder of the text. Place periods and commas inside the quotation marks. Other punctuation is placed inside the quotation marks *only* if it is part of the quoted excerpt.

INTEROFFICE MEMORANDUM

TO:　　　Research Associate

FROM:　　Supervising Attorney

RE:　　　Read and Brief *Richards v. Wisconsin*

Please read *Richards v. Wisconsin* (copy attached) and brief it for me. This is a somewhat recent U.S. Supreme Court decision; I have not had time to get to this and we need to be familiar with the legal reasoning in this case. For now, just read and summarize the case. Later we will compare and contrast the *Richards* case with our client's facts in the Nguyen situation.

5-1 PURPOSE OF A CASE BRIEF

Simply stated, a **case brief** is a short summary of a **reported case.** It may serve several purposes. Students of the law write case briefs to summarize the cases they read for class in an effort to keep track of the large number of cases they are required to read and analyze. During legal research, case briefs serve to help the researcher keep track of the cases read and analyzed, and may serve as the foundation for legal arguments in **trial briefs** or other documents filed with the court. An attorney may hear about a case and ask a legal assistant to read and brief or summarize the case. The overall purpose is to concisely summarize the components of a case.

You will recall from Chapter 4 that case law is written by judges to inform and educate the legal community. If we focus on the purpose of case law, it is easier to understand the purpose of a case brief. A well-written case brief simplifies and condenses the reported case. Most case law is written in a specific format using certain components. Once you realize that all cases contain the same or very similar components, the mystery of reading cases begins to fade.

case brief. A short summary of a reported case.

reported case. A published judicial decision.

trial brief. A document submitted to the court; the trial brief contains a statement of facts, the issues and the party's legal argument.

5-2 THE COMPONENTS OF A CASE BRIEF

A judge, writing to inform the legal community, has certain goals in every reported case. It is important that the reader of any case understand the following.

Who are the parties?

What happened in the lower court(s)—if the case is an appeal?

What happened to bring these parties into court in the first place?

What is the legal question before *this* court?

What rules (primary law) did the court rely on in reaching its decision?

How did the court analyze the facts in light of the legal question and the rules?

How did the court resolve the dispute?

These questions lay the foundation for the components of a case brief.

▷ **A Point to Remember**   Whenever possible, make a copy of the case you plan to brief. Note in the margins, for each paragraph, which component (or components) of the brief is included in that paragraph. This technique helps you focus as you read and provides organization as you begin writing the brief.

These components may be divided into the following elements: name and citation of the case, judicial history, facts, issue(s), rule(s), analysis or reasoning, and conclusion or holding.

Name and Citation of the Case

The name of the case, the citation, and the year are essential. Always provide the name and full citation of the case at the beginning of the case brief.

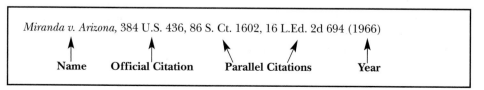

When you cite a U.S. Supreme Court case, you need only give the official citation. However, in a case brief you should include the full citation, including parallel citations.

Judicial History

The judicial history explains how the case traveled through the courts. The reader of the brief needs to know who sued whom and why. Let the reader know what happened in each of the courts.

Facts

Include only the facts that are relevant to the court's reasoning and decision. Tell a story about what happened to bring these parties before the court. If possible, tell a story about people. Leave the legal terminology *out* of this section.

Issue(s)

The issue is the question presented to the court for resolution. It should be one sentence long and is best written as a question. Most of the cases you read will have judicial history. This means that lower courts have already adjudicated these issues. The case you are briefing is probably an appeal of what the lower court decided. Many times the issue is stated in the format of "Did the lower court err when it held . . . ?" This issue asks: "Did the last court to hear this case make one or more mistakes in its resolution of the legal issues?"

Rule(s)

primary sources. The resources that provide the actual law; laws are found in constitutions, statutes, case law, and some administrative materials.

The rules section is usually a listing of the laws the court relied on in the analysis or reasoning. This might include statutes, case law, articles or amendments from the Constitution, or other **primary sources** of the law. This section does not include every source discussed by the court, just the relevant primary sources. Each constitutional reference, statute, or case, should include a very brief statement including the title of the constitutional reference, the topic of the statute, and the relevance of the case law cited.

Analysis or Reasoning

This will be the lengthiest and also the most important section of most case briefs. The analysis *incorporates* much of the information from the facts, issues, and rules into a focused discussion. If you are asked to read and brief a case for someone else, that person has not read the case. The reader must understand why the court resolved the issues as it did. This section never includes the writer's personal analysis or opinions. Think of the analysis as a summary of how the court analyzed the facts and issues. Notice the laws used or discussed by the court. All of this provides the court's **rationale** or reasoning supporting its ultimate holding or conclusion.

rationale. The reasoning or explanation for the court's ultimate resolution of the case.

Conclusion or Holding

holding. The legal principle to be taken from the court's decision.

The conclusion or **holding** is the court's answer to the issue or question presented. Each issue has a conclusion. It is easiest to list each issue with its answer. Keep this section short and to the point. This is not a discussion section.

⇨ **A Point to Remember**   A case brief does not include the writer's personal opinion. The brief is a summary of (1) what the court said, and (2) the action of the court. There is no room for the pronoun "I" in a good case brief. Pay close attention to the facts stressed by the court. Notice when one or more facts are discussed at length or in more than one context. This is a clue for the reader that the court views these facts as relevant; they are essential to an overall understanding of the case.

Apply the notes-in-the-margin technique from Chapter 4 with the *Gideon v. Wainwright* case. As you read the case locate the following:

The name and the citation of the case: Name of litigants and correct legal citation for this reported case.

The judicial history: What happened in the lower court(s)?

The facts: What happened to bring the parties before the court?

The issues: What is the legal question before *this* court?

The rules: What rules (primary law) did the court rely on in reaching its decision?

The analysis: How did the court analyze the facts in light of the legal question and the rules?

The conclusion: How did the court resolve the dispute?

CASE 5-1

Gideon v. Wainwright
372 U.S. 335 (1963)

SYLLABUS:

Charged in a Florida State Court with a non-capital felony, petitioner appeared without funds and without counsel and asked the Court to appoint counsel for him; but this was denied on the ground that the state law permitted appointment of counsel for indigent defendants in capital cases only. Petitioner conducted his own defense about as well as could be expected of a layman; but he was convicted and sentenced to imprisonment. Subsequently, he applied to the State Supreme Court for a writ of *habeas corpus*, on the ground that his conviction violated his rights under the Federal Constitution. The State Supreme Court denied all relief.

Held:

The right of an indigent defendant in a criminal trial to have the assistance of counsel is a fundamental right essential to a fair trial, and petitioner's trial and conviction without the assistance of counsel violated the Fourteenth Amendment. *Betts v. Brady,* 316 U.S. 455.

OPINION: MR. JUSTICE BLACK delivered the opinion of the Court.

Petitioner was charged in a Florida state court with having broken and entered a poolroom with intent to commit a misdemeanor. This offense is a felony under Florida law. Appearing in court without funds and without a lawyer, petitioner asked the court to appoint counsel for him, whereupon the following colloquy took place:

"The COURT: Mr. Gideon, I am sorry, but I cannot appoint Counsel to represent you in this case. Under the laws of the State of Florida, the only time the Court can appoint Counsel to represent a Defendant is when that person is charged with a capital offense. I am sorry, but I will have to deny your request to appoint Counsel to defend you in this case.

"The DEFENDANT: The United States Supreme Court says I am entitled to be represented by Counsel."

Put to trial before a jury, Gideon conducted his defense about as well as could be expected from a layman. He made an opening statement to the jury, cross-examined

the State's witnesses, presented witnesses in his own defense, declined to testify himself, and made a short argument "emphasizing his innocence to the charge contained in the Information filed in this case." The jury returned a verdict of guilty, and petitioner was sentenced to serve five years in the state prison. Later, petitioner filed in the Florida Supreme Court this *habeas corpus* petition attacking his conviction and sentence on the ground that the trial court's refusal to appoint counsel for him denied him rights "guaranteed by the Constitution and the Bill of Rights by the United States Government." Treating the petition for *habeas corpus* as properly before it, the State Supreme Court, "upon consideration thereof" but without an opinion, denied all relief. Since 1942, when *Betts v. Brady,* 316 U.S. 455, was decided by a divided Court, the problem of a defendant's federal constitutional right to counsel in a state court has been a continuing source of controversy and litigation in both state and federal courts. To give this problem another review here, we granted *certiorari.* 370 U.S. 908. Since Gideon was proceeding *in forma pauperis,* we appointed counsel to represent him and requested both sides to discuss in their briefs and oral arguments the following: "Should this Court's holding in *Betts v. Brady,* 316 U.S. 455, be reconsidered?"

I.

The facts upon which Betts claimed that he had been unconstitutionally denied the right to have counsel appointed to assist him are strikingly like the facts upon which Gideon here bases his federal constitutional claim. Betts was indicted for robbery in a Maryland state court. On arraignment, he told the trial judge of his lack of funds to hire a lawyer and asked the court to appoint one for him. Betts was advised that it was not the practice in that country to appoint counsel for indigent defendants except in murder and rape cases. He then pleaded not guilty, had witnesses summoned, cross-examined the State's witnesses, examined his own, and chose not to testify himself. He was found guilty by the judge, sitting without a jury, and sentenced to eight years in prison. Like Gideon, Betts sought release by *habeas corpus,* alleging that he had been denied the right to assistance of counsel in violation of the Fourteenth Amendment. Betts was denied any relief, and on review

this Court affirmed. It was held that a refusal to appoint counsel for an indigent defendant charged with a felony did not necessarily violate the Due Process Clause of the Fourteenth Amendment, which for reasons given the Court deemed to be the only applicable federal constitutional provision. The Court said:

"Asserted denial [of due process] is to be tested by an appraisal of the totality of facts in a given case. That which may, in one setting, constitute a denial of fundamental fairness, shocking to the universal sense of justice, may, in other circumstances, and in the light of other considerations, fall short of such denial." 316 U.S., at 462.

Treating due process as "a concept less rigid and more fluid than those envisaged in other specific and particular provisions of the Bill of Rights," the Court held that refusal to appoint counsel under the particular facts and circumstances in the Betts case was not so "offensive to the common and fundamental ideas of fairness" as to amount to a denial of due process. Since the facts and circumstances of the two cases are so nearly indistinguishable, we think the *Betts v. Brady* holding if left standing would require us to reject Gideon's claim that the Constitution guarantees him the assistance of counsel. Upon full reconsideration we conclude that *Betts v. Brady* should be overruled.

II.

The Sixth Amendment provides, "In all criminal prosecutions, the accused shall enjoy the right . . . to have the Assistance of Counsel for his defense." We have construed this to mean that in federal courts counsel must be provided for defendants unable to employ counsel unless the right is competently and intelligently waived. Betts argued that this right is extended to indigent defendants in state courts by the Fourteenth Amendment. In response the Court stated that, while the Sixth Amendment laid down "no rule for the conduct of the States, the question recurs whether the constraint laid by the Amendment upon the national courts expresses a rule so fundamental and essential to a fair trial, and so, to due process of law, that it is made obligatory upon the States by the Fourteenth Amendment." 316 U.S., at 465. In order to decide whether the Sixth Amendment's guarantee of counsel is of this fundamental

nature, the Court in *Betts* set out and considered "relevant data on the subject . . . afforded by constitutional and statutory provisions subsisting in the colonies and the States prior to the inclusion of the Bill of Rights in the national Constitution, and in the constitutional, legislative, and judicial history of the States to the present date." 316 U.S., at 465. On the basis of this historical data the Court concluded that "appointment of counsel is not a fundamental right, essential to a fair trial." 316 U.S., at 471. It was for this reason the *Betts* Court refused to accept the contention that the Sixth Amendment's guarantee of counsel for indigent federal defendants was extended to or, in the words of that Court, "made obligatory upon the States by the Fourteenth Amendment." Plainly, had the Court concluded that appointment of counsel for an indigent criminal defendant was "a fundamental right, essential to a fair trial," it would have held that the Fourteenth Amendment requires appointment of counsel in a state court, just as the Sixth Amendment requires in a federal court.

　　We think the Court in *Betts* had ample precedent for acknowledging that those guarantees of the Bill of Rights which are fundamental safeguards of liberty immune from federal abridgment are equally protected against state invasion by the Due Process Clause of the Fourteenth Amendment. This same principle was recognized, explained, and applied in *Powell v. Alabama,* 287 U.S. 45 (1932), a case upholding the right of counsel, where the Court held that despite sweeping language to the contrary in *Hurtado v. California,* 110 U.S. 516 (1884), the Fourteenth Amendment "embraced" those " [lsquo]fundamental principles of liberty and justice which lie at the base of all our civil and political institutions," even though they had been "specifically dealt with in another part of the federal Constitution." 287 U.S., at 67. In many cases other than *Powell* and *Betts,* this Court has looked to the fundamental nature of original Bill of Rights guarantees to decide whether the Fourteenth Amendment makes them obligatory on the States. Explicitly recognized to be of this "fundamental nature" and therefore made immune from state invasion by the Fourteenth, or some part of it, are the First Amendment's freedoms of speech, press, religion, assembly, association, and petition for redress of grievances. For the same reason, though not always in precisely the same terminology, the Court has made obligatory on the States the Fifth Amendment's command that private property shall not be taken for public use without just compensation, the Fourth Amendment's prohibition of unreasonable searches and seizures, and the Eighth's ban on cruel and unusual punishment. On the other hand, this Court in *Palko v. Connecticut,* 302 U.S. 319 (1937), refused to hold that the Fourteenth Amendment made the double jeopardy provision of the Fifth Amendment obligatory on the States. In so refusing, however, the Court, speaking through Mr. Justice Cardozo, was careful to emphasize that "immunities that are valid as against the federal government by force of the specific pledges of particular amendments have been found to be implicit in the concept of ordered liberty, and thus, through the Fourteenth Amendment, become valid as against the states" and that guarantees "in their origin . . . effective against the federal government alone" had by prior cases "been taken over from the earlier articles of the federal bill of rights and brought within the Fourteenth Amendment by a process of absorption." 302 U.S., at 324–325, 326.

　　We accept *Betts v. Brady's* assumption, based as it was on our prior cases, that a provision of the Bill of Rights which is "fundamental and essential to a fair trial" is made obligatory upon the States by the Fourteenth Amendment. We think the Court in *Betts* was wrong, however, in concluding that the Sixth Amendment's guarantee of counsel is not one of these fundamental rights. Ten years before *Betts v. Brady,* this Court, after full consideration of all the historical data examined in *Betts,* had unequivocally declared that "the right to the aid of counsel is of this fundamental character." *Powell v. Alabama,* 287 U.S. 45, 68 (1932). While the Court at the close of its *Powell* opinion did by its language, as this Court frequently does, limit its holding to the particular facts and circumstances of that case, its conclusions about the fundamental nature of the right to counsel are unmistakable. Several years later, in 1936, the Court reemphasized what it had said about the fundamental nature of the right to counsel in this language:

"We concluded that certain fundamental rights, safeguarded by the first eight amendments against federal action, were also safeguarded against state action by the due process of law clause of the Fourteenth Amendment, and among them the fundamental right of the accused to the aid of counsel in a criminal prosecution." 297 U.S. 233, 243–244 (1936).

And again in 1938 this Court said:

"[The assistance of counsel] is one of the safeguards of the Sixth Amendment deemed necessary to insure fundamental human rights of life and liberty. . . . The Sixth Amendment stands as a constant admonition that if the constitutional safeguards it provides be lost, justice will not 'still be done.'" *Johnson v. Zerbst*, 304 U.S. 458, 462 (1938). To the same effect, *see Avery v. Alabama*, 308 U.S. 444 (1940), and *Smith v. O'Grady*, 312 U.S. 329 (1941).

In light of these and many other prior decisions of this Court, it is not surprising that the *Betts* Court, when faced with the contention that "one charged with crime, who is unable to obtain counsel, must be furnished counsel by the State," conceded that "expressions in the opinions of this court lend color to the argument. . . . " 316 U.S., at 462–463. The fact is that in deciding as it did—that "appointment of counsel is not a fundamental right, essential to a fair trial"—the Court in *Betts v. Brady* made an abrupt break with its own well-considered precedents. In returning to these old precedents, sounder we believe than the new, we but restore constitutional principles established to achieve a fair system of justice. Not only these precedents but also reason and reflection require us to recognize that in our adversary system of criminal justice, any person haled into court, who is too poor to hire a lawyer, cannot be assured a fair trial unless counsel is provided for him. This seems to us to be an obvious truth. Governments, both state and federal, quite properly spend vast sums of money to establish machinery to try defendants accused of crime. Lawyers to prosecute are everywhere deemed essential to protect the public's interest in an orderly society. Similarly, there are few defendants charged with crime, few indeed, who fail to hire the best lawyers they can get to prepare and present their defenses. That government hires lawyers to prosecute and defendants who have the money hire lawyers to defend are the strongest indications of the widespread belief that lawyers in criminal courts are necessities, not luxuries. The right of one charged with crime to counsel may not be deemed fundamental and essential to fair trials in some countries, but it is in ours. From the very beginning, our state and national consititutions and laws have laid great emphasis on procedural and substantive safeguards designed to assure fair trials before impartial tribunals in which every defendant stands equal before the law. This noble ideal cannot be realized if the poor man charged with crime has to face his accusers without a lawyer to assist him. A defendant's need for a lawyer is nowhere better stated than in the moving words of Mr. Justice Sutherland in *Powell v. Alabama:*

"The right to be heard would be, in many cases, of little avail if it did not comprehend the right to be heard by counsel. Even the intelligent and educated layman has small and sometimes no skill in the science of law. If charged with crime, he is incapable, generally, of determining for himself whether the indictment is good or bad. He is unfamiliar with the rules of evidence. Left without the aid of counsel he may be put on trial without a proper charge, and convicted upon incompetent evidence, or evidence irrelevant to the issue or otherwise inadmissible. He lacks both the skill and knowledge adequately to prepare his defense, even though he have a perfect one. He requires the guiding hand of counsel at every step in the proceedings against him. Without it, though he be not guilty, he faces the danger of conviction because he does not know how to establish his innocence." 287 U.S., at 68–69.

The Court in *Betts v. Brady* departed from the sound wisdom upon which the Court's holding in *Powell v. Alabama* rested. Florida, supported by two other States, has asked that *Betts v. Brady* be left intact. Twenty-two States, as friends of the Court, argue that Betts was "an anachronism when handed down" and that it should now be overruled. We agree.

The judgment is reversed and the cause is remanded to the Supreme Court of Florida for further action not inconsistent with this opinion.

Reversed.

5-3 HOW TO WRITE A CASE BRIEF

Each of the components should be set forth as separate sections of the case brief. Paragraphs explaining the component follow each section heading. The analysis, or reasoning, section combines or synthesizes much of what is included in the facts, issues, and rules sections. As a writer, you may detect that there is a certain degree of redundancy.

A brief or summary of the *Gideon* case might look like this:

Gideon v. Wainwright, 372 U.S. 335 (1963)

Judicial History

The trial court denied Gideon's request for appointment of defense counsel. As a result of this denial, he conducted his own defense. The jury found him guilty. The Florida State Supreme Court denied Gideon's request for relief.

Facts

Gideon was charged with breaking and entering a poolroom.

Issues

1. Did Gideon's trial and conviction violate his rights under the Fourteenth Amendment?

2. Should *Betts v. Brady* be overruled? (This issue was raised by the Court. Both parties were asked to argue this issue.)

Rules

Fourteenth Amendment: due process clause

Sixth Amendment: "In all criminal prosecutions, the accused shall enjoy the right . . . to have the Assistance of Counsel for his defense."

Betts v. Brady, 316 U.S. 455 (1942): "appointment of counsel is not a fundamental right, essential to a fair trial. . . . " (*Betts* is reconsidered by the Court in *Gideon* and overruled.)

Powell v. Alabama 287 U.S. 45 (1932): the right to counsel is fundamental and essential to a fair trial. (Followed in *Gideon.*)

Analysis

The facts of the *Gideon* case are very similar to the facts of the *Betts v. Brady* case. The *Betts* case held that "a refusal to appoint counsel for an indigent defendant charged with a felony did not necessarily violate the due process clause of the Fourteenth Amendment." The Court overruled *Betts v. Brady.* Relying on the Sixth Amendment, the Court found that "counsel must be provided for defendants unable to employ counsel unless the right is competently and intelligently waived." The fundamental safeguards of liberty are protected by the due process clause of the Fourteenth Amendment. The Sixth Amendment guarantee of counsel is one of these fundamental safeguards. The Court cites the sound wisdom upon which the *Powell v. Alabama* case was decided. In *Powell,* the Court explained that a criminal defendant needs the "guiding hand of counsel at every step in the proceedings against him."

Conclusion

The judgment of the Florida State Supreme Court was reversed. The cause was remanded to the Florida courts for "further action not inconsistent with this opinion." *Betts v. Brady* was overruled.

This is only one approach to briefing the *Gideon* case. While no two people will write exactly the same brief, and the actual format for the brief may differ, the information contained generally falls into the categories set forth in this sample brief. The following case brief contains the same basic information, but it is arranged differently.

Gideon v. Wainwright, 372 U.S. 335 (1963)

Facts

Gideon was charged with breaking and entering a poolroom. The trial court denied Gideon's request for defense counsel. As a result of this denial he conducted his own defense. The jury found him guilty. The Florida State Supreme Court denied Gideon's request for relief.

Issues

(1) Did Gideon's trial and conviction violate his rights under the Fourteenth Amendment?

(2) Should *Betts v. Brady* be overruled? (This issue was raised by the Court. Both parties were asked to argue this issue.)

Holding

The judgment of the Florida State Supreme Court was reversed. The cause was remanded to the Florida courts for "further action not inconsistent with this opinion." *Betts v. Brady* was overruled.

Rationale

The facts of the *Gideon* case are very similar to the facts of the *Betts v. Brady*, 316 U.S. 455 (1942) case. The *Betts* case held that "a refusal to appoint counsel for an indigent defendant charged with a felony did not necessarily violate the due process clause of the Fourteenth Amendment." The Court overruled *Betts v. Brady*. Relying on the Sixth Amendment, the Court found that "counsel must be provided for defendants unable to employ counsel unless the right is competently and intelligently waived." The fundamental safeguards of liberty are protected by the due process clause of the Fourteenth Amendment. The Sixth Amendment guarantee of counsel is one of these fundamental safeguards. The Court cites the sound wisdom upon which the *Powell v. Alabama*, 287 U.S. 45 (1932) case was decided. In *Powell*, the Court explained that a criminal defendant needs the "guiding hand of counsel at every step in the proceedings against him."

➪ **A Point to Remember**   Some cases include concurring opinions and dissenting opinions. You need to include a section explaining the concurrence or dissent only if there is something of importance that your reader needs to know. Read *Richards v. Wisconsin*. Take notes on the judicial history, facts, issues, rules, analysis, and conclusion/holding.

CASE 5-1

Richards v. Wisconsin
520 U.S. 385 (1997)

STEVENS, J., delivered the opinion for a unanimous Court.

In *Wilson v. Arkansas*, 514 U.S. 927, 131 L. Ed. 2d 976, 115 S. Ct. 1914 (1995), we

held that the Fourth Amendment incorporates the common law requirement that police officers entering a dwelling must knock on the door and announce their identity and purpose before attempting forcible entry. At the same time, we recognized that the "flexible requirement of reasonableness should not be read to mandate a rigid rule of announcement that ignores countervailing law enforcement interests," *id.*, at 934, and left "to the lower courts the task of determining the circumstances under which an unannounced entry is reasonable under the Fourth Amendment." *Id.*, 936.

In this case, the Wisconsin Supreme Court concluded that police officers are never required to knock and announce their presence when executing a search warrant in a felony drug investigation. In so doing, it reaffirmed a pre-*Wilson* holding and concluded that *Wilson* did not preclude this *per se* rule. We disagree with the court's conclusion that the Fourth Amendment permits a blanket exception to the knock-and-announce requirement for this entire category of criminal activity. But because the evidence presented to support the officers' actions in this case establishes that the decision not to knock and announce was a reasonable one under the circumstances, we affirm the judgment of the Wisconsin court.

I

On December 31, 1991, police officers in Madison, Wisconsin obtained a warrant to search Steiney Richards' hotel room for drugs and related paraphernalia. The search warrant was the culmination of an investigation that had uncovered substantial evidence that Richards was one of several individuals dealing drugs out of hotel rooms in Madison. The police requested a warrant that would have given advance authorization for a "no-knock" entry into the hotel room, but the magistrate explicitly deleted those portions of the warrant.

The officers arrived at the hotel room at 3:40 a.m. Officer Pharo, dressed as a maintenance man, led the team. With him were several plainclothes officers and at least one man in uniform. Officer Pharo knocked on Richards' door and, responding to the query from inside the room, stated that he was a maintenance man. With the chain still on the door, Richards cracked it open. Although there is some dispute as

to what occurred next, Richards acknowledges that when he opened the door he saw the man in uniform standing behind Officer Pharo. He quickly slammed the door closed and, after waiting two or three seconds, the officers began kicking and ramming the door to gain entry to the locked room. At trial, the officers testified that they identified themselves as police while they were kicking the door in. When they finally did break into the room, the officers caught Richards trying to escape through the window. They also found cash and cocaine hidden in plastic bags above the bathroom ceiling tiles.

Richards sought to have the evidence from his hotel room suppressed on the ground that the officers had failed to knock and announce their presence prior to forcing entry into the room. The trial court denied the motion, concluding that the officers could gather from Richards' strange behavior when they first sought entry that he knew they were police officers and that he might try to destroy evidence or to escape. *Id.*, at 54. The judge emphasized that the easily disposable nature of the drugs the police were searching for further justified their decision to identify themselves as they crossed the threshold instead of announcing their presence before seeking entry. *Id.*, at 55. Richards appealed the decision to the Wisconsin Supreme Court and that court affirmed. 201 Wis. 2d 845, 549 N.W.2d 218 (1996).

The Wisconsin Supreme Court did not delve into the events underlying Richards' arrest in any detail, but accepted the following facts: "On December 31, 1991, police executed a search warrant for the motel room of the defendant seeking evidence of the felonious crime of Possession with Intent to Deliver a Controlled Substance in violation of Wis. Stat. Section 161.41 (lm) (1991–92). They did not knock and announce prior to their entry. Drugs were seized." *Id.*, at 849, 549 N.W.2d at 220.

Assuming these facts, the court proceeded to consider whether our decision in *Wilson* required the court to abandon its decision in *State v. Stevens*, 181 Wis. 2d 410, 511 N.W.2d 591 (1994), *cert. denied*, 515 U.S. 1102 (1995), which held that "when the police have a search warrant, supported by probable cause, to search a residence for evidence of delivery of drugs or evidence of possession with intent to deliver drugs, they

necessarily have reasonable cause to believe exigent circumstances exist" to justify a no-knock entry. 201 Wis. 2d at 852, 549 N.W.2d at 221. The court concluded that nothing in *Wilson's* acknowledgment that the knock-and-announce rule was an element of the Fourth Amendment "reasonableness" requirement would prohibit application of a per se exception to that rule in a category of cases. 201 Wis. 2d at 854–855, 549 N.W.2d at 220. In reaching this conclusion, the Wisconsin court found it reasonable—after considering criminal conduct surveys, newspaper articles, and other judicial opinions—to assume that all felony drug crimes will involve "an extremely high risk of serious if not deadly injury to the police as well as the potential for the disposal of drugs by the occupants prior to entry by the police." *Id.*, at 847–848, 549 N.W.2d at 219. Notwithstanding its acknowledgment that in "some cases, police officers will undoubtedly decide that their safety, the safety of others, and the effective execution of the warrant dictate that they knock and announce," *Id.*, at 863, 549 N.W.2d at 225, the court concluded that exigent circumstances justifying a no-knock entry are always present in felony drug cases. Further, the court reasoned that the violation of privacy that occurs when officers who have a search warrant forcibly enter a residence without first announcing their presence is minimal, given that the residents would ultimately be without authority to refuse the police entry. The principal intrusion on individual privacy interests in such a situation, the court concluded, comes from the issuance of the search warrant, not the manner in which it is executed. *Id.*, at 864–865, 549 N.W.2d at 226. Accordingly, the court determined that police in Wisconsin do not need specific information about dangerousness, or the possible destruction of drugs in a particular case, in order to dispense with the knock-and-announce requirement in felony drug cases.

Justice Abrahamson concurred in the judgment because, in her view, the facts found by the trial judge justified a no-knock entry. *Id.*, at 866–868, 549 N.W.2d at 227. Specifically, she noted that Richards' actions in slamming the door when he saw the uniformed man standing behind Officer Pharo indicated that he already knew that the people knocking on his door were police officers. Under these circumstances,

any further announcement of their presence would have been a useless gesture. *Id.*, at 868–869, n. 3, 549 N.W.2d at 228. While agreeing with the outcome, Justice Abrahamson took issue with her colleagues' affirmation of the blanket exception to the knock-and-announce requirement in drug felony cases. She observed that the constitutional reasonableness of a search has generally been a matter left to the court, rather than to the officers who conducted the search, and she objected to the creation of a blanket rule that insulated searches in a particular category of crime from the neutral oversight of a reviewing judge. *Id.*, at 868–875, 549 N.W.2d at 228–230.

II

We recognized in *Wilson* that the knock-and-announce requirement could give way "under circumstances presenting a threat of physical violence," or "where police officers have reason to believe that evidence would likely be destroyed if advance notice were given." 514 U.S. at 936. It is indisputable that felony drug investigations may frequently involve both of these circumstances. The question we must resolve is whether this fact justifies dispensing with case-by-case evaluation of the manner in which a search was executed.

The Wisconsin court explained its blanket exception as necessitated by the special circumstances of today's drug culture, 201 Wis. 2d at 863–866, 549 N.W.2d at 226–227, and the State asserted at oral argument that the blanket exception was reasonable in "felony drug cases because of the convergence in a violent and dangerous form of commerce of weapons and the destruction of drugs." Tr. of Oral Arg. 26. But creating exceptions to the knock-and-announce rule based on the "culture" surrounding a general category of criminal behavior presents at least two serious concerns.

First, the exception contains considerable over-generalization. For example, while drug investigation frequently does pose special risks to officer safety and the preservation of evidence, not every drug investigation will pose these risks to a substantial degree. For example, a search could be conducted at a time when the only individuals present in a residence have no connection with the drug activity and thus will be

unlikely to threaten officers or destroy evidence. Or the police could know that the drugs being searched for were of a type or in a location that made them impossible to destroy quickly. In those situations, the asserted governmental interests in preserving evidence and maintaining safety may not outweigh the individual privacy interests intruded upon by a no-knock entry. Wisconsin's blanket rule impermissibly insulates these cases from judicial review.

A second difficulty with permitting a criminal-category exception to the knock-and-announce requirement is that the reasons for creating an exception in one category can, relatively easily, be applied to others. Armed bank robbers, for example, are, by definition, likely to have weapons, and the fruits of their crime may be destroyed without too much difficulty. If a per se exception were allowed for each category of criminal investigation that included a considerable—albeit hypothetical—risk of danger to officers or destruction of evidence, the knock-and-announce element of the Fourth Amendment's reasonableness requirement would be meaningless.

Thus, the fact that felony drug investigations may frequently present circumstances warranting a no-knock entry cannot remove from the neutral scrutiny of a reviewing court the reasonableness of the police decision not to knock and announce in a particular case. Instead, in each case, it is the duty of a court confronted with the question to determine whether the facts and circumstances of the particular entry justified dispensing with the knock-and-announce requirement.

In order to justify a "no-knock" entry, the police must have a reasonable suspicion that knocking and announcing their presence, under the particular circumstances, would be dangerous or futile, or that it would inhibit the effective investigation of the crime by, for example, allowing the destruction of evidence. This standard—as opposed to a probable cause requirement—strikes the appropriate balance between the legitimate law enforcement concerns at issue in the execution of search warrants and the individual privacy interests affected by no-knock entries. *Cf. Maryland v. Buie*, 494 U.S. 325, 337, 108 L. Ed. 2d 276, 110 S. Ct. 1093 (1990) (allowing a protective sweep of a house during an arrest where the officers have "a reasonable

belief based on specific and articulable facts that the area to be swept harbors an individual posing a danger to those on the arrest scene"); *Terry v. Ohio*, 392 U.S. 1, 30, 20 L. Ed. 2d 889, 88 S. Ct. 1868 (1968) (requiring a reasonable and articulable suspicion of danger to justify a pat-down search). This showing is not high, but the police should be required to make it whenever the reasonableless of a no-knock entry is challenged.

III

Although we reject the Wisconsin court's blanket exception to the knock-and-announce requirement, we conclude that the officers' no-knock entry into Richards' hotel room did not violate the Fourth Amendment. We agree with the trial court, and with Justice Abrahamson, that the circumstances in this case show that the officers had a reasonable suspicion that Richards might destroy evidence if given further opportunity to do so. The judge who heard testimony at Richards' suppression hearing concluded that it was reasonable for the officers executing the warrant to believe that Richards knew, after opening the door to his hotel room the first time, that the men seeking entry to his room were the police. Once the officers reasonably believed that Richards knew who they were, the court concluded, it was reasonable for them to force entry immediately given the disposable nature of the drugs. *Id.*, at 55.

In arguing that the officers' entry was unreasonable, Richards places great emphasis on the fact that the magistrate who signed the search warrant for his hotel room deleted the portions of the proposed warrant that would have given the officers permission to execute a no-knock entry. But this fact does not alter the reasonableless of the officers' decision, which must be evaluated as of the time they entered the hotel room. At the time the officers obtained the warrant, they did not have evidence sufficient, in the judgment of the magistrate, to justify a no-knock warrant. Of course, the magistrate could not have anticipated in every particular the circumstances that would confront the officers when they arrived at Richards' hotel room. These actual circumstances— petitioner's apparent recognition of the officers combined with the easily

disposable nature of the drugs—justified the officers' ultimate decision to enter without first announcing their presence and authority.

Accordingly, although we reject the blanket exception to the knock-and-announce requirement for felony drug investigations, the judgment of the Wisconsin Supreme Court is affirmed.

It is so ordered.

Case Questions

1. Summarize the facts in the *Richards* case.
2. What are the legal issues?
3. Which rules/law did the Court rely upon most?

5-4 ANALYSIS AND THE CASE BRIEF

The brief or summary of a reported case is only the starting point. The legal researcher reads law looking for primary law that is applicable to a client's situation. When you begin serious research, you are armed with the facts of your client's case. These facts provide the initial foundation for your research and your research plan or strategy. The facts help the researcher identify and articulate the legal issues involved in the client's case. Always attempt to identify the most relevant facts involved in your client's situation.

When researching, you are searching for primary law that is very similar to the facts of your client's case. In Chapter 3 you learned to separate facts into the following categories:

Relevant

Explanatory

Legally unimportant

Once the facts of a case you have researched are categorized, you are ready to compare and contrast the facts of the reported decision with those of your client's situation. This process of comparing the facts of a client's case with those of a reported case is an essential analytical skill. As you begin the comparison process, be sure to look for the following:

Similarities

Unknowns (gaps)

Differences

5-5 AN APPROACH TO A DAUNTING PROJECT

Briefing cases is often part of a larger research project. Sometimes this larger project seems to be daunting. If so, try the following approach.

1. Re-read the *directions.* Ask yourself:

Do I fully understand what I have been asked to do?
If not, get clarification.

Do I have a mental picture of the document I must create?

If not, get an example.

Do I have a deadline?

Do I have special instructions?

2. Begin the project *only* after framing clear answers to the preceding questions.

3. Begin the project in a ***logical fashion.***

   Create an outline of the material to be covered. Leave plenty of space between the sections. Do this on the word processor. In this way, the project has officially begun.

   Fill in the outline with key words and phrases.

   Make a separate list of problem areas.

   Identify the easy parts of the project.
      Consider doing these portions first.

   Identify the difficult part of the project.
      Create a special approach for this part of the project.

4. Choose one section of the project and begin writing. Do not worry about spelling, grammar, consistency, or anything else at this point. Just get your ideas on paper. There will be plenty of time to edit your work. Remember, your word processor will probably do much of this simple editing for you!

5. Complete one section before you move on to another section of the project. Try to accomplish closure of small portions of the project. This will serve you well in the workplace. Because it is easy to show your supervisor small portions of a project, the supervisor has the opportunity to see that you are organized and proceeding in a logical fashion.

6. Consider this: Will placing material into a chronology help you? Will the chronology help the reader? If it helps you, do it in an effort to get your ideas on paper. If a chronology will not be particularly helpful to the reader, do not use it in the final copy.

   A chronology may help the writer sort out a large number of facts or events. Creation of a "list" is often helpful. This list probably does not belong in the final written product, but it is a good outlining tool during the drafting stage.

   As you look at a long, often very detailed list, you may begin to see where you may combine facts or events. Or you may begin to see a pattern emerge.

   For example: If you have a series of judicial events, think about lumping them into a time frame, **or** addressing the happenings at each court level, **or** saying "Petitioner's various motions to re-open the case were repeatedly denied" **or** "Defendant's motions were heard favorably in the appellate court, but the State Supreme Court was not so lenient. . . . "

   Remember, not all judicial events are equal in importance; even the number of hearings or trials may not be significant. In a summary, the writer cannot possibly cover everything in the original document and therefore must make choices based on knowledge and analytical skill. Such choices are learned through practice.

7. If you are summarizing a document, is there a specific format or order in which it is written?

   If there is a specific format or order, adopt it if at all possible.

Until you fully understand the document, you will not be able to create an effective summary.

Ask yourself the following questions:

On what does the author of the document focus?

On what does the author spend the most time?

What seems most critical to the author of the document?

(*not* what do *you* think is most important?)

Follow the lead of the original document.

8. Remember, a summary should *reflect* the original. Think about this. A summary synthesizes or condenses the original document.

9. Avoid creating confusion. We are often our own worst enemies.

10. Go back to the directions. Are you still focused?

Have you done what you were asked to do?

Is your document clear and concise?

Is it in the appropriate format?

When is the deadline?

11. At this point, put your draft away for 24 to 48 hours. Just let it sit; avoid even thinking about it.

Then: (a) Get out a bright color pen (felt pens are hard to miss).

(b) Re-read the directions (yes, again).

(c) Start reading at the beginning, marking as you go.

Look for errors (spelling, grammar, etc.).

Look for passive voice (use active voice, if possible).

Look for long sentences (count the words!).

Look for topic sentences (make sure you have them).

Look for format consistency.

Look for internal consistency.

Look for vagueness.

Look for redundancy.

12. At this point, you should have marked all sorts of things. Make the necessary corrections and put the document aside. You are done. Going over and over a document is not realistic. Of course, we all strive for some degree of perfection, but the sheer reality of the working world often precludes perfection in all aspects of every project. Remember: Sometimes our changes are just changes, not improvements. You can over-think and over-edit your work.

13. Closure is a good thing!

 # **T**ECHNOLOGY CORNER

There are a growing number of large, inclusive showcases on the Web. These mega search engines search groups of other search engines. The following sites represent only two of the more successful mega search engines.

www.hg.org

www.dogpile.com

A caution: Searching a large group of search engines is a great idea and often works reasonably well. But remember, the form in which you write a search for one site or search engine may vary from others. This variation could cause you to miss otherwise available information. Sometimes valuable information may not be retrieved because not all of the search engines used by these inclusive showcases are able to understand or properly assimilate the search request. Just because you do not retrieve data does not mean you should not search again. You may change your search terms and you may target certain search engines.

CHAPTER SUMMARY

A case brief is a summary of a reported case. Briefs serve many purposes: Some are written as a reminder for the writer; others for someone who did not read the case. A good case brief simplifies and condenses the reported case. It must be broken down into components that enable the reader to follow the information easily. The most common components of a case brief are (1) name of the case, (2) judicial history, (3) facts, (4) issues, (5) rules, (6) analysis or reasoning, and (7) conclusion or holding. Making notes in the margin while reading the case is an effective method of initial summarization.

Analysis of your client's situation involves placing facts into categories. Facts should be categorized as (1) relevant, (2) explanatory, and (3) legally unimportant. Then you can compare and contrast them.

A daunting project requires advance planning. A logical approach to the project saves time and helps the writer create the structure of the document early in the drafting process. Editing your own work is a skill you should work on with every document you produce.

TERMS TO REMEMBER

case brief	primary sources
reported case	rationale
trial brief	holding

QUESTIONS FOR REVIEW

1. Discuss the various uses of case law briefs.
2. What is the purpose of a case brief?
3. What questions lay the foundation for the components of a case brief?
4. List and explain the components of a case brief.
5. What clues might a court provide as to which facts are most important?
6. When comparing facts, what categories help in the compare and contrast process?

CAN YOU FIGURE IT OUT?

1. Use your citation manual to define the following.

   Cf.

   Id., at 847

   Cert. Denied

2. What is the first page of the *Miranda v. Arizona* case in the official reporter? (See Section 5-2.)

3. What is the first page of the *Miranda v. Arizona* case in the *Supreme Court Reporter?*

RESEARCH ASSIGNMENTS AND ACTIVITIES

1. Write a brief of the *Richards v. Wisconsin* case. Use the six components of a case brief.

2. Re-read the Interoffice Memorandum at the beginning of this chapter. Our client, Mr. Nguyen, was arrested three weeks ago under the following circumstances: Mr. Nguyen rents one-half of a duplex on North 15th Street. Apparently, Mr. Nguyen's residence was under surveillance for several days prior to the arrest that took place three weeks ago. The police received a tip that large numbers of automatic weapons were being sold out of Mr. Nguyen's residence. The officers believe that the sale and purchase of the weapons is gang-related. A search warrant was obtained for the residence several hours prior to the arrest. Two uniformed officers, armed with a properly executed search warrant, approached the residence while other officers positioned themselves around the duplex. As the officers stepped onto the porch, Mr. Nguyen's brother opened the front door; upon seeing the officers he began to yell over his shoulder and retreated into the home. Without announcing their intent or purpose, five officers rushed the doors of the duplex at that time. The front and back doors were broken down and the officers entered the duplex. Many weapons were seized and our client was arrested. Apply the *Richards* decision to Mr. Nguyen's situation.

CONSTITUTIONS, STATUTES, AND ADMINISTRATIVE REGULATIONS

CHAPTER OUTLINE

CHAPTER OBJECTIVES

When you complete this chapter you should be able to

- Explain how federal statutory law is enacted.
- Discuss the differences between public laws and private laws.
- Compare and contrast the United States Codes publications.
- Explain the use of pocket part supplements.
- Explain the purpose of the *Statutes at Large.*
- Discuss the differences between the *Code of Federal Regulations* and the *United States Code.*
- Explain how to find administrative regulations and rules of court.

CITATION MATTERS

UNITED STATES CONSTITUTION AND UNITED STATES CODE

THE BLUEBOOK — RULE 11

This is the correct format for a citation to the Fourteenth Amendment to the United States Constitution:

U.S. CONST. amend. XIV.

United States Constitution Citation Analyzed

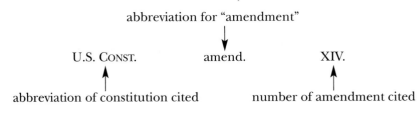

Other examples:

U.S. CONST. amend. XIV, § 2.
U.S. CONST. art. I, § 9, cl. 2.

When you refer to one of the constitutional amendments, it is best to use the number spelled out. The number and the term *amendment* are capitalized; for example: Fourteenth Amendment.

THE UNITED STATES CODE

THE BLUEBOOK — **RULE 12**

18 U.S.C. § 242 (2000)
Occupational Safety and Health Act (OSHA) of 1970, 29 U.S.C. § 651 (1988 & Supp. V 1993)

The *United States Code* (U.S.C.) is the official federal code. There are two popular unofficial federal codes. They are the *United States Code Service* (U.S.C.S) and the *United States Code Annotated (U.S.C.A.).* You should cite to the official code when possible.

United States Code Citation Analyzed

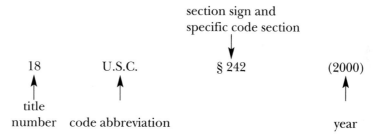

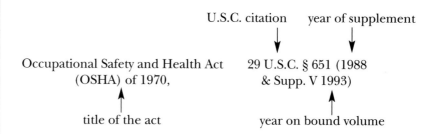

THE BLUEBOOK rules for citing the United States Code are detailed and complex. However, between Rule 12 and Table 1 (T.1), most situations are addressed.

STATE CODES

THE BLUEBOOK — **RULE 12**

THE BLUEBOOK — **TABLE 1 (T.1)**

State codes are cited in much the same way the federal codes are cited. Each state has its own code. Each state has a specific format and special abbreviations. Look up the state in Table 1; examples are provided.

COURT RULES

THE BLUEBOOK — RULE 12.8.3

This is the correct format for a citation to Rule 26 of the Federal Rules of Civil Procedure:

FED. R. CIV. P. 26

This is the correct format for a citation to Rule 6 of the Federal Rules of Criminal Procedure:

FED. R. CRIM. P. 6

This is the correct format for a citation to Rule 301 of the Federal Rules of Evidence:

FED. R. EVID. 301

INTEROFFICE MEMORANDUM

TO: Research Associate

FROM: Supervising Attorney

RE: Our Client, Randy Rambeaux

We finally received a copy of the criminal complaint against Rambeaux. The complaint alleges that Rambeaux violated 18 U.S.C. § 242. Please find that code section and make a copy for me. We do not have the U.S. Codes in our office library so you may have to go to the county law library to find the section. You may also be able to find this on the Internet. Try that before making a trip to the library.

6-1 INTRODUCTION

Although the legal system in the United States relies heavily on common law principles, case law is not the only source of law in this country. Constitutions, statutes, and administrative regulations are other sources as well. The U.S. legal system relies on these various rules and regulations. Unlike case law, these rules are not created after disputes arise. They are in place and provide guidelines to parties *before* a dispute arises. Furthermore, when disputes do arise between parties, courts look to constitutional provisions, statutory law, or administrative regulations in deciding how to resolve the dispute. If appropriate law exists, the court must apply it to the factual dispute.

6-2 CONSTITUTIONS

The United States Constitution, the supreme law of the land, provides the framework for the establishment of the federal government. It describes what powers the government has and places limits on that power. The United States Constitution also sets out rights that people have in relationship to the federal government. This part of the Constitution is referred to as the **Bill of Rights.**

The Constitution has three main parts: the preamble, the body, and the amendments. The body of the Constitution is divided into articles that are further subdivided into clauses and sections. The amendments are changes to the original Constitution. See Figure 6-1 for examples of the various parts of the Constitution.

The United States Constitution is published in numerous sources. It is published as a single pamphlet and in connection with other works. The Constitution is located in several sources on the Internet. It is also published in the various editions of the United States Codes. For legal researchers, the *United States Code Annotated* and *United States Code Service* publications are important for two reasons. First, the Constitution is **indexed** with the code. This enables researchers to locate appropriate provisions of the Constitution when researching a specific topic. Second, it is published in an **annotated** format, with the annotated codes discussed below. In an annotated format, the publisher provides not only the exact text of the Constitution but also references to cases that have interpreted the Constitution. See Figure 6-2 for an example of an annotated Constitutional provision. An annotated U.S. Constitution can also be found on the Internet at http://www.gpoaccess.gov/constitution/index.html. This document was prepared under the direction of the Library of Congress. A copy is also found on www.findlaw.com.

Each state has a constitution. Like the U.S. Constitution, state constitutions are published either on their own or with the state codes. They may also be found on the Internet.

> **A Point to Remember** State constitutions should always be reviewed when researching a constitutional question. In Chapter 2 you read about the relationship between the state and federal constitutions. Remember that when you are researching an issue controlled by the Bill of Rights, your state constitution may give an individual more rights than he or she may have under the U.S. Constitution. If this is the case, your research must focus on your state constitution and on cases that interpret your state constitution.

6-3 FEDERAL STATUTORY LAW

Enactment of Statutory Law

In the U.S. system of government, legislative bodies have the power to make laws. These laws are described as **statutory law.** Unlike case law, statutory law is not enacted to resolve a specific factual dispute. Instead, legislative bodies make rules or laws they believe are needed by society in general. These laws establish many of our rights and obligations in our dealings with one another and with society. Statutory law describes requirements for areas such as crimes, contracts, and corporations.

Bill of Rights. First ten amendments to United States Constitution.

index. A list of words and phrases that reflect the topics covered in the book.

annotated. A brief summary of a statute or a case.

statutory law. Law enacted through the legislative process.

① **Preamble**

② **Articles**

FIGURE 6-1

U.S. Constitution

CONSTITUTION OF THE UNITED STATES OF AMERICA—1787[1]

①

WE THE PEOPLE of the United States, in Order to form a more perfect Union, establish Justice, insure domestic Tranquility, provide for the common defence, promote the general Welfare, and secure the Blessings of Liberty to ourselves and our Posterity, do ordain and establish this Constitution for the United States of America.

②ARTICLE. I.

SECTION 1. All legislative Powers herein granted shall be vested in a Congress of the United States, which shall consist of a Senate and House of Representatives.

SECTION. 2. [1]The House of Representatives shall be composed of Members chosen every second Year by the People of the several States, and the Elector in each State shall have the Qualifications requisite for Electors of the most numerous Branch of the State Legislature.

[2]No Person shall be a Representative who shall not have attained to the Age of twenty five Years, and been seven Years a Citizen of the United States, and who shall not, when elected, be an Inhabitant of that State in which he shall be chosen.

[3]Representatives and direct Taxes shall be apportioned among the several States which may be included within this Union, according to their respective Numbers, which shall be determined by adding to the whole Number of free Persons, including those bound to Service for a Term of Years, and excluding Indians not taxed, three fifths of all other Persons.[2] The actual Enumeration shall be made within three Years after the first Meeting of the Congress of the United States, and within every subsequent Term of ten Years, in such Manner as they shall by Law direct. The Number of Representatives shall not exceed one for every thirty Thousand, but each State shall have at Least one Representative; and until such enumeration shall be made, the State of New Hampshire shall be entitled to chuse three, Massachusetts eight, Rhode-Island and Providence Plantations one, Connecticut five, New-York six, New Jersey four, Pennsylvania eight, Delaware one, Maryland six, Virginia ten, North Carolina five, South Carolina five, and Georgia three.

[4]When vacancies happen in the Representation from any State, the Executive Authority thereof shall issue Writs of Election to fill such Vacancies.

SECTION 4. The President, Vice President and all civil Officers of the United States, shall be removed from Office on Impeachment for, and Conviction of, Treason, Bribery, or other high Crimes and Misdemeanors.

ARTICLE. II.

SECTION. 1.

CLAUSE 1: The executive Power shall be vested in a President of the United States of America. He shall hold his Office during the Term of four Years, and, together with the Vice President, chosen for the same Term, be elected, as follows

CLAUSE 2: Each State shall appoint, in such Manner as the Legislature thereof may direct a Number of Electors, equal to the whole Number of Senators and representatives to which the State may be entitled in the Congress: but no Senator or Representative, or Person holding an Office of Trust or Profit under the United States, shall be appointed an Elector.

CLAUSE 3: The Electors shall meet in their respective States, and vote by Ballot for two Persons, of whom one at least shall not be an Inhabitant of the same State with themselves. And they shall make a List of all the Persons voted for, and of the Number of Votes for each; which List they shall sign and certify, and transmit sealed to the Seat of the Government of the United States, directed to the President of the Senate. The President of the Senate shall, in the Presence of the Senate and House of Representatives, open all the Certificates, and the Votes shall then be counted. The Person having the greatest Number of Votes shall be the President, if such Number be a Majority of the whole Number of Electors appointed; and if there be more than one who have such Majority, and have an equal Number of Votes, then the House of Representatives shall immediately chuse by Ballot one of them for President; and if no Person have a Majority, then from the five highest on the List the said House shall in like Manner chuse the President. But in chusing the President, the Votes shall be taken by States, the Representation from each State having one Vote: A quorum for this Purpose shall consist of a Member or Members from two thirds of the States, and a Majority of all the States shall be necessary to a Choice. In every Case, after the Choice of the President, the Person having the greatest Number of Votes of the Electors shall be the Vice President. But if there should remain two or more who have equal Votes, the Senate shall chuse from them by Ballot the Vice President.

CLAUSE 4: The Congress may determine the Time of chusing the Electors, and the Day on which they shall give their Votes; which Day shall be the same throughout the United States.

CLAUSE 5: No Person except a natural born Citizen, or a Citizen of the United States, at the time of the Adoption of this Constitution, shall be eligible to the Office of the President; neither shall any Person be eligible to that Office who shall not have attained to the Age of thirty five Years, and been fourteen Years a Resident within the United States.

CLAUSE 6: In Case of the Removal of the President from Office, or of his Death, Resignation, or Inability to discharge the Powers and Duties of the said Office (*See Note 9*) the Same shall devolve on the Vice President, and the Congress may by Law provide for the Case of Removal, Death, Resignation or Inability, both of the President and Vice President,

declaring what Officer shall then act as President, and such Officer shall act accordingly, until the Disability be removed, or a President shall be elected.

CLAUSE 7: The President shall, at stated Times, receive for his Services, a Compensation, which shall neither be encreased nor diminished during the Period for which he shall have been elected, and he shall not receive within that Period any other Emolument from the United States, or any of them.

CLAUSE 8: Before he enter on the Execution of his Office, he shall take the following Oath or affirmation:—"I do solemnly swear (or affirm) that I will faithfully execute the Office of President of the United States, and will to the best of my Ability, preserve, protect and defend the Constitution of the United States."

SECTION. 2.

CLAUSE 1: The President shall be Commander in Chief of the Army and Navy of the United States, of the Militia of the several States, when called into the actual Service of the United States; he may require the Opinion, in writing, of the principal Officer in each of the executive Departments, upon any Subject relating to the Duties of their respective Offices, and he shall have Power to grant Reprieves and Pardons for Offences against the United States, except in Cases of Impeachment.

CLAUSE 2: He shall have Power, by and with the Advice and Consent of the Senate, to make Treaties, provided two thirds of the Senators present concur; and he shall nominate and by and with the Advice and Consent of the Senate, shall appoint Ambassadors, other public Ministers and Consuls, Judges of the supreme Court, and all other Officers of the United States, whose Appointments are not herein otherwise provided for, and which shall be established by Law: but the Congress may by Law vest the Appointment of such inferior Officers, as they think proper, in the President alone, in the Courts of Law, or in the Heads of Departments.

CLAUSE 3: The President shall have Power to fill up all Vacancies that may happen during the Recess of the Senate, by granting Commissions which shall expire at the End of their next Session.

SECTION. 3.

He shall from time to time give to the Congress Information of the State of the Union, and recommend to their Consideration such Measures as he shall judge necessary and expedient; he may, on extraordinary Occasions, convene both Houses, or either of them, and in Case of Disagreement between them, with Respect to the Time of Adjournment, he may adjourn them to such Time as he shall think proper; he shall receive Ambassadors and other public Ministers; he shall take Care that the Laws be faithfully executed, and shall Commission all the Officers of the United States.

SECTION. 4.

The President, Vice President and all civil Officers of the United States, shall be removed from Office on Impeachment for, and Conviction of, Treason, Bribery, or other high Crimes and Misdemeanors.

ARTICLE. III.

SECTION. 1. The judicial Power of the United States, shall be vested in one supreme Court, and in such inferior Courts as the Congress may from time to time ordain and establish. The Judges, both of the supreme and inferior Courts, shall hold their Offices during good Behaviour, and shall, at stated Times, receive for their Services, a Compensation, which shall not be diminished during their Continuance in Office.

SECTION. 2. [1]The judicial Power shall extend to all Cases, in Law and Equity, arising under this Constitution, the Laws of the United States, and Treaties made, or which shall be made, under their Authority;—to all Cases affecting Ambassadors, other public Ministers and Consuls;—to all Cases of admiralty and maritime Jurisdiction;—to Controversies to which the United States shall be a Party;—to Controversies between two or more States;—between a State and Citizens of another State; [10]—between Citizens of different States,—between Citizens of the same State claiming Lands under Grants of different States, and between a State, or the Citizens thereof, and foreign States, Citizens or Subjects.

[2]In all Cases affecting Ambassadors, other public Ministers and Consuls, and those in which a State shall be Party, the supreme Court shall have original Jurisdiction. In all the other Cases before mentioned, the supreme Court shall have appellate Jurisdiction, both as to Law and Fact, with such Exceptions, and under such Regulations as the Congress shall make.

[3]The Trial of all Crimes, except in Cases of Impeachment, shall be by Jury; and such Trial shall be held in the State where the said Crimes shall have been committed; but when not committed within any State, the Trial shall be at such Place or Places as the Congress may by Law have directed.

SECTION. 3. [1]Treason against the United States, shall consist only in levying War against them, or in adhering to their Enemies, giving them Aid and Comfort. No Person shall be convicted of Treason unless on the Testimony of two Witnesses to the same overt Act, or on Confession in open Court.

[2]The Congress shall have Power to declare the Punishment of Treason, but no Attainder of Treason shall work Corruption of Blood, or Forfeiture except during the Life of the Person attainted.

ARTICLE. IV.

SECTION. 1. Full Faith and Credit shall be given in each State to the public Acts, Records, and judicial Proceedings of every other State. And the Congress may by general Laws prescribe the Manner in which such Acts, Records and Proceedings shall be proved, and the Effect thereof.

SECTION. 2. [1]The Citizens of each State shall be entitled to all Privileges and Immunities of Citizens in the several States.

[2]A Person charged in any State with Treason, Felony, or other Crime, who shall flee from Justice,

FIGURE 6-1
(continued)

and be found in another State, shall on Demand of the executive Authority of the State from which he fled, be delivered up, to be removed to the State having Jurisdiction of the Crime.

³No Person held to Service or Labour in one State, under the Laws thereof, escaping into another, shall, in Consequence of any Law or Regulation therein, be discharged from such Service or Labour, but shall be delivered up on Claim of the Party to whom such Service or Labour may be due.[11]

SECTION. 3. ¹New States may be admitted by the Congress into this Union; but no new State shall be formed or erected within the Jurisdiction of any other State; nor any State be formed by the Junction of two or more States, or Parts of States, without the Consent of the Legislatures of the States concerned as well as of the Congress.

²The Congress shall have Power to dispose of and make all needful Rules and Regulations respecting the Territory or other Property belonging to the United States; and nothing in this Constitution shall be so construed as to Prejudice any Claims of the United States, or of any particular State.

SECTION. 4. The United States shall guarantee to every State in this Union a Republican Form of Government, and shall protect each of them against Invasion; and on Application of the Legislature, or of the Executive (when the Legislature cannot be convened) against domestic Violence.

ARTICLE. V.

The Congress, whenever two thirds of both Houses shall deem it necessary, shall propose Amendments to this Constitution, or, on the Application of the Legislatures of two thirds of the several States, shall call a Convention for proposing Amendments, which, in either Case, shall be valid to all Intents and Purposes, as Part of this Constitution, when ratified by the Legislatures of three fourths of the several States, or by Conventions in three fourths thereof, as the one or the other Mode of Ratification may be proposed by the Congress; Provided that no Amendment which may be made prior to the Year One thousand eight hundred and eight shall in any Manner affect the first and fourth Clauses in the Ninth Section of the first Article; and that no State, without its Consent, shall be deprived of its equal Suffrage in the Senate.

ARTICLE. VI.

¹All Debts contracted and Engagements entered into, before the Adoption of this Constitution, shall be as valid against the United States under this Constitution, as under the Confederation.

²This Constitution, and the Laws of the United States which shall be made in Pursuance thereof; and all Treaties made, or which shall be made, under the Authority of the United States, shall be the supreme Law of the Land; and the Judges in every State shall be bound thereby, any Thing in the Constitution or Laws of any State to the Contrary notwithstanding.

³The Senators and Representatives before mentioned, and the Members of the several State Legislatures, and all executive and judicial Officers, both of the United States and of the several States, shall be bound by Oath or Affirmation, to support this Constitution; but no religious Test shall ever be required as a Qualification to any Office or public Trust under the United States.

ARTICLE. VII.

The Ratification of the Conventions of nine States, shall be sufficient for the Establishment of this Constitution between the States so ratifying the Same.

DONE in Convention by the Unanimous Consent of the States present the Seventeenth Day of September in the Year of our Lord one thousand seven hundred and Eighty seven and of the Independence of the United States of America the Twelfth IN WITNESS whereof We have hereunto subscribed our Names,

G.º WASHINGTON—*Presid*ᵗ.
and deputy from Virgina

[Signed also by the deputies of twelve States.]

New Hampshire

JOHN LANGDON
NICHOLAS GILMAN

Massachusetts

NATHANIEL GORHAM
RUFUS KING

Connecticut

Wᴹ. SAMᴸ· JOHNSON
ROGER SHERMAN

New York

ALEXANDER HAMILTON

New Jersey

WIL: LIVINGSTON
DAVID BREARLEY.
Wᴹ. PATERSON.
JONA: DAYTON

Pennsylvania

B FRANKLIN
THOMAS MIFFLIN
ROBᵀ MORRIS
GEO. CLYMER
THOˢ. FITZSIMONS
JARED INGERSOLL
JAMES WILSON.
GOUV MORRIS

Delaware

GEO: READ
GUNNING BEDFORD jun
JOHN DICKINSON
RICHARD BASSETT
JACO: BROOM

FIGURE 6-1
(continued)

Maryland

JAMES M^C^HENRY

DAN OF S^T^ THO^S^. JENIFER

DAN^L^ CARROLL.

Virginia

JOHN BLAIR—

JAMES MADISON JR.

North Carolina

W^M^ BLOUNT

RICH^D^. DOBBS SPAIGHT.

HU WILLIAMSON

South Carolina

J. RUTLEDGE

CHARLES COTESWORTH PINCKNEY

CHARLES PINCKNEY

PIERCE BUTLER.

Georgia

WILLIAM FEW

ABR BALDWIN

Attest   WILLIAM JACKSON *Secretary*

ARTICLES IN ADDITION TO, AND AMEND-
MENT OF, THE CONSTITUTION OF THE
UNITED STATES OF AMERICA, PROPOSED
BY CONGRESS, AND RATIFIED BY THE
LEGISLATURES OF THE SEVERAL STATES,
PURSUANT TO THE FIFTH ARTICLE OF THE
ORIGINAL CONSTITUTION[12]

③ ARTICLE [I.][13]

Congress shall make no law respecting an establishment of religion, or prohibiting the free exercise thereof; or abridging the freedom of speech, or
of the press; or the right of the people peaceably to assemble, and to petition the Government for a redress
of grievances.

ARTICLE [II.]

A well regulated Militia, being necessary to the
security of a free State, the right of the people to keep
and bear Arms, shall not be infringed.

ARTICLE [III.]

No soldier shall, in time of peace be quartered in
any house, without the consent of the owner, nor in
time of war, but in a manner to be prescribed by law.

ARTICLE [IV.]

The right of the people to be secure in their persons, houses, papers, and effects, against unreasonable searches and seizures, shall not be violated, and
no Warrants shall issue, but upon probable cause,
supported by oath or affirmation, and particularly describing the place to be searched, and the persons or
things to be seized.

ARTICLE [V.]

No person shall be held to answer for a capital,
or otherwise infamous crime, unless on a presentment or indictment of a Grand Jury, except in cases
arising in the land or naval forces, or in the Militia,
when in actual service in time of War or public danger; nor shall any person be subject for the same offence to be twice put in jeopardy of life or limb; nor
shall be compelled in any criminal case to be a witness against himself, nor be deprived of life, liberty,
or property, without due process of law; nor shall private property be taken for public use, without just
compensation.

ARTICLE [VI.]

In all criminal prosecutions, the accused shall
enjoy the right to a speedy and public trial, by an impartial jury of the State and district wherein the crime
shall have been committed, which district shall have
been previously ascertained by law, and to be informed of the nature and cause of the accusation; to
be confronted with the witnesses against him; to have
compulsory process for obtaining witnesses in his
favor, and to have the Assistance of Counsel for his
defence.

ARTICLE [VII.]

In Suits as common law, where the value in controversy shall exceed twenty dollars, the right of trial
by jury shall be preserved, and no fact tried by a jury,
shall be otherwise re-examined in any Court of the
United States, than according to the rules of the common law.

ARTICLE [VIII.]

Excessive bail shall not be required, nor excessive fines imposed, nor cruel and unusual punishments inflicted.

ARTICLE [IX.]

The enumeration in the Constitution, of certain
rights, shall not be construed to deny or disparage
others retained by the people.

ARTICLE [X.]

The powers not delegated to the United States by
the Constitution, nor prohibited by it to the States, are
reserved to the States respectively, or to the people.

ARTICLE [XI.]

The Judicial power of the United States shall not
be construed to extend to any suit in law or equity,
commenced or prosecuted against one of the United
States by Citizens of another State, or by Citizens or
Subjects of any Foreign State.

PROPOSAL AND RATIFICATION

The eleventh amendment to the Constitution of
the United States was proposed to the legislatures of
the several States by the Third Congress, on the 4th
of March 1794; and was declared in a message from
the President to Congress, dated the 8th of January,
1798, to have been ratified by the legislatures of
three-fourths of the States. The dates of ratification

③ **Amendments**

FIGURE 6-1
(continued)

PREAMBLE

Preamble to → Constitution

WE THE PEOPLE of the United States, in Order to form a more perfect Union, establish Justice, insure domestic Tranquility, provide for the common defence, promote the general Welfare, and secure the Blessings of Liberty to ourselves and our Posterity, do ordain and establish this CONSTITUTION for the United States of America.

WESTLAW ELECTRONIC RESEARCH

Editorial → enhancement

WESTLAW supplements U.S.C.A. electronically and is useful for additional research. Enter a citation in INSTA–CITE for display of parallel citations and case history. Enter a constitution, statute or rule citation in a case law database for cases of interest.

Example query for INSTA–CITE: 790 F.2d 978

Example query for United States Constitution:

(first +6 amendment) + S religion

Example query for statute: "42 U.S.C.*" + 4 1983

Also, see the WESTLAW guide following the Explanation pages of this volume.

NOTES OF DECISIONS

Annotations →

Formation of more perfect Union   3
Nature and function of Preamble   1
Ordainment and establishment of Constitution   7
   Promotion of general welfare   5
   Provision for common defense   4
   Securing of liberty   6
   United States of America   8
   We the People   2

1. Nature and function of Preamble

The Preamble can never be resorted to, to enlarge the powers confided to the general government and can never be the legitimate source of any implied power, when otherwise drawn from the Constitution; its true office is to expound the nature, extent, and application of the powers actually conferred by the Constitution and not substantively to create them. U.S. v. Boyer, D.C.Mo. 1898, 85 F. 425.

2. We the People

In our system, while sovereign powers are delegated to the agencies of government, sovereignty itself remains with the people, by whom and for whom all government exists and acts. Yick Wo v. Hopkins, Cal.1886, 6 S.Ct. 1064, 118 U.S. 369, 30 L.Ed. 220.

The Constitution of the United States was made by, and for the protection of, the people of the United States. Leggue v. De Young, Tex.1850, 52 U.S. 203, 11 How. 203, 13 L.Ed. 657.

The Constitution was ordained and established by the people of the United States for themselves, for their own government and not for the government of the individual states; the people of the United States framed such a government for the United States as they supposed best adapted to their situation and best calculated to promote their interests. Barron v. Baltimore, Md.1833, 32 U.S. 247, 7 Pet. 247, 8. L.Ed. 672.

The Constitution emanated from the people, and was not the act of sovereign and independent states. M'Culloch v. Maryland, Md.1819, 17 U.S. 403, 4 Wheat. 403, 4 L.Ed. 579.

FIGURE 6-2
Annotated
Constitution

Reprinted with permission of Thomson/West

It also regulates such areas as marriage and divorce. Statutory law comes from federal, state, and local governing bodies.

Federal statutory law includes those laws enacted by the United States Congress. Congress meets for two-year terms, each separate term given a number. For example, the Congress that met for the years 1995–96 was referred to as the 104th Congress. Each year of Congress constitutes a separate session. One of the primary responsibilities of each Congress is the enactment of new legislation, which consists of the following steps.

Legislation Proposed   All federal laws begin with a proposal, known as a *bill.*

Bill Introduced   The bill is introduced into either the House of Representatives or the Senate and immediately assigned a number. This number is preceded by "H.R." if the bill is introduced into the House of Representatives, or "S" if the bill is introduced into the Senate. The bill retains this number throughout the legislative process. These numbers are important when researching the **legislative history** of any statute. Legislative histories are discussed later in this chapter.

legislative history. The proceedings that relate to a bill before it becomes law.

Bill Referred to Committee   After a bill is introduced, it is referred to the appropriate committee for consideration. Both the House and the Senate have a number of standing committees that concentrate on certain matters. Once the bill is referred, the proper committee reviews and discusses the proposal, sometimes holding public hearings on the bill. If a committee looks favorably on a bill, it prepares a committee report with its recommendations and analysis of the bill.

Vote by Legislators   If a report is issued, the whole house then considers the bill and votes on it. If it receives a majority vote of approval, it is passed and sent to the other house.

Action by Other House   When referred to the other house, the bill goes through much the same process again. If the bill is amended or changed, a joint conference from both houses may convene to work out differences. Both houses must approve the same bill before it can be submitted to the President. Once passed by both houses, the bill is sent to the President for approval.

Executive Action   The President has the power to approve or to veto the bill. If the President does nothing with the bill, it is deemed approved after ten days unless Congress should adjourn within that ten-day period. If this happens, the bill is considered vetoed (pocket veto). If the President vetoes a bill, it can still be enacted as law if a two-thirds majority of each house votes to override the veto.

Initial Publication of Statutes

Laws enacted by Congress are categorized as either public laws or private laws. **Public laws** are those that concern the general public. For example, read the code section referred to in the memorandum at the beginning of this chapter (see Figure 6-5). It is a public law because it regulates the general public. It is not limited to specific individuals or groups.

public laws. Laws enacted by Congress that affect the public in general.

   Private laws are those that concern single individuals or groups. Private laws usually deal with matters such as naturalization or settlement of a claim by the government. See Figure 6-3 for an example of a private law. This law affects only the person named in the law.

private laws. Laws enacted by Congress that affect only selected individuals.

   After a bill completes the legislative process and is signed by the President (or a veto properly overridden), the law is labeled as either a public law or a private law and assigned a number. The number includes the number of the Congress and the chronological number of the bill. Thus, the first public law enacted by the 104th Congress is identified as Public Law 104-1. Remember that, at this point, the legislation has two numerical references: the original number of the bill (i.e., H.R. 1234) and the public or private law number assigned after passage.

   As each law is passed, it is published by the government in pamphlet form, known as **slip law.** At the end of each session of Congress, all of these laws are published in a book referred to as the *Statutes at Large.* The *Statutes at Large* publishes laws in chronological order. They are not organized according to topic or subject

slip law. First publication of a law; usually in pamphlet form.

PRIVATE LAW 103-7—OCT. 22, 1994   108 STAT. 506

Private Law 103–6
103d Congress

An Act

FOR THE RELIEF OF ORLANDO WAYNE NARAYSINGH.   Oct. 22, 1994
                                                      [H.R. 2266]

Be it enacted by the Senate and House of Representatives of the United States of America in Congress assembled,

SECTION 1. IMMEDIATE RELATIVE STATUS FOR ORLANDO WAYNE NARAYSINGH.

① **Note that private law applies only to named individual.**

(a) IN GENERAL.—Orlando Wayne Naraysingh shall be classified as a child under section 101(b)(1)(E) of the Immigration and Nationality Act for purposes of approval of a relative visa petition filed under section 204 of such Act by his adoptive parent and the filing of an application for an immigrant visa or adjustment of status.

(b) ADJUSTMENT OF STATUS.—If Orlando Wayne Naraysingh enters the United States before the filing deadline specified in subsection (c), he shall be considered to have entered and remained lawfully and shall, if otherwise eligible, be eligible for adjustment of status under section 245 of the Immigration and Nationality Act as of the date of the enactment of this Act.

(c) DEADLINE FOR APPLICATION AND PAYMENT OF FEES.—Subsections (a) and (b) shall apply only if the petition and the application for issuance of an immigrant visa or the application for adjustment of status are filed with appropriate fees within 2 years after the date of the enactment of this Act.

(d) REDUCTION OF IMMIGRANT VISA NUMBER.—Upon the granting of an immigrant visa or permanent residence to Orlando Wayne Naraysingh, the Secretary of State shall instruct the proper officer to reduce by 1, for the current or next following fiscal year, the worldwide level of family-sponsored immigrants under section 201(c)(1)(A) of the Immigration and Nationality Act.

(e) DENIAL OF PREFERENTIAL IMMIGRATION TREATMENT FOR CERTAIN RELATIVES.—The natural parents, brothers, and sisters of Orlando Wayne Naraysingh shall not, by virtue of such relationship, be accorded any right, privilege, or status under the Immigration and Nationality Act.

Approved October 22, 1994.

Private Law 103–7
103d Congress

An Act

For the relief of Leteane Clement Monatei.   Oct. 22, 1994
                                                     [H.R. 2411]

Be it enacted by the Senate and House of Representatives of the United States of America in Congress assembled,

SECTION 1. IMMEDIATE RELATIVE STATUS FOR LETEANE CLEMENT MONATSI

(a) IN GENERAL.—Leteane Clement Monatsi shall be classified as a child under section 101(b)(1)(E) of the Immigration and Nationality Act for purposes of approval of a relative visa

FIGURE 6-3
Private Law

code. A topical organization of statutes.

matter. As a result, the *Statutes at Large* (and slip laws) is extremely difficult to research. In order to alleviate this problem, federal statutes are codified (put into codes). A **code** is an organization by subject matter of all of the public laws found in statutes. Because of the way Congress works, it is not uncommon for one statute to contain many different kinds of laws that end up in different code sections. In recent years, when *Statutes at Large* is published it contains margin references to the codes in which the

PUBLIC LAW 103-322—SEPT. 13, 1994 ①   ① 108 STAT. 1970

"(1) for murder, by death or life imprisonment, or a fine of not more than $250,000, or both; and for kidnapping, by imprisonment for any term of years or for life, or a fine of not more than $250,000, or both;".

(13) GENOCIDE.—Section 1091(b)(1) of title 18, United States Code, is amended by striking " a fine of not more than $1,000,000 or imprisonment for life," and inserting ", where death results, by death or imprisonment for life and a fine of not more than $1,000,000, or both;".

(14) CARJACKING.—Section 2119(3) of title 18, United States Code, is amended by striking the period after "both" and inserting ", or sentenced to death."; and by striking ", possessing a firearm as defined in section 921 of this title, and inserting ", with the intent to cause death or serious bodily harm". (b) CONFORMING AMENDMENT TO FEDERAL AVIATION ACT OF 1954.—Chapter 465 of title 49, United States Code, is amended—

(1) in the chapter analysis by striking "Death penalty sentencing procedure for aircraft piracy" and inserting "Repealed"; and

(2) by striking section 46503.

SEC. 60004. APPLICABILITY TO UNIFORM CODE OF MILITARY JUSTICE.   18 USC 3591
                                                       note

Chapter 228 of title 18, United States Code, as added by this title, shall not apply to prosecutions under the Uniform Code of Military Justice (10 U.S.C. 801).

SEC. 60005. DEATH PENALTY FOR MURDER BY A FEDERAL PRISONER.

(a) IN GENERAL.—Chapter 51 of title 18, United States Code, is amended by adding at the end the following new section:

"§ 1118. Murder by a Federal prisoner

"(a) OFFENSE.—A person who, while confined in a Federal correctional institution under a sentence for a term of life imprisonment, commits the murder of another shall be punished by death or by life imprisonment.

"(b) DEFINITIONS.—In this section—

"'Federal correctional institution' means any Federal prison, Federal correctional facility, Federal community program center, or Federal halfway house.

"'murder' means a first degree or second degree murder (as defined in section 1111).

"'term of life imprisonment' means a sentence for the term of natural life, a sentence commuted to natural life, an indeterminate term of a minimum of at least fifteen years and a maximum of life, or an unexecuted sentence of death.".

(b) TECHNICAL AMENDMENT.—The chapter analysis for chapter 51 of title 18, United States Code, is amended by adding at the end the following new item:

"1118. Murder by a Federal prisoner.".

SEC. 60006. DEATH PENALTY FOR CIVIL RIGHTS MURDERS.

(a) CONSPIRACY AGAINST RIGHTS.—Section 241 of title 18, United States Code, is amended by striking the period at the end of the last sentence and inserting ", or may be sentenced to death.".

②(b) DEPRIVATION OF RIGHTS UNDER COLOR OF LAW.—Section 242 of title 18, United States Code, is amended by striking the period at the end of the last sentence and inserting ", or may be sentenced to death.".

① **Note two references to same law.**

② **This section amends 18 USC §242.**

FIGURE 6-4   Pages from *Statutes at Large,* Volume 108, pages 1970 and 1971

section of the statute will be included. See Figure 6-4 for a sample of a law found in the *Statutes at Large.* Note the different code sections affected by the one statute.

6-4 UNITED STATES CODES

The United States Codes contain a consolidation of the general and permanent laws of the United States arranged topically. (Private laws are not included in the code.) The laws are organized according to subject matter in fifty separate title headings.

108 STAT. 1970   PUBLIC LAW 103-322—SEPT. 13, 1994

(c) Federally Protected Activities.— Section 245(b) of title 18, United States Code, is amended in the matter following paragraph (5) by inserting ", or may be sentenced to death" after "or for life".

(d) Damage to Religious Property; Obstruction of the Free Exercise of Religious Rights.—Section 247(c)(1) of title 18, United States Code, is amended by inserting ", or may be sentenced to death" after "or both".

SEC. 60007. death penalty for the murder of federal law enforcement officials.

Section 1114 of title 18, United States Code, is amended by striking "punished as provided under sections 1111 and 1112 of this title," and inserting "punished, in the case of murder, as provided under section 1111, or, in the case of manslaughter, as provided under section 1112.".

Drive-By Shooting Prevention Act of 1994. 18 USC 36 note.

SEC. 60008. new offense for the indiscriminate use of weapons to further drug conspiracies.

(a) Short Title.—This section may be cited as the "Drive-By Shooting Prevention Act of 1994".

(b) In General.—Chapter 2 of title 18, United States Code, is amended by adding at the end the following new section:

"§ 36. Drive-by-shooting

"(a) Definition.—In this section, 'major drug offense' means—

"(1) a continuing criminal enterprise punishable under section 403(c) of the Controlled Substances Act (21 U.S.C. 848(c));

"(2) a conspiracy to distribute controlled substances punishable under section 406 of the Controlled Substances Act (21 U.S.C. 846) section 1013 of the Controlled Substances Import and Export Control Act (21 U.S.C. 963); or

"(3) an offense involving major quantities of drugs and punishable under section 401(b)(1)(A) of the Controlled Substances Act (21 U.S.C. 841(b)(1)(A)) or section 1010(b)(1) of the Controlled Substances Import and Export Act (21 U.S.C. 960(b)(1)).

"(b) Offense and Penalties.—(1) A person who, in furtherance or to escape detection of a major drug offense and with the intent to intimidate, harass, injure, or maim, fires a weapon into a group of two or more persons and who, in the course of such conduct, causes grave risk to any human life shall be punished by a term of no more than 25 years, by fine under this title, or both.

"(2) A person who, in furtherance or to escape detection of a major drug offense and with the intent to intimidate, harass, injure, or maim, fires a weapon into a group of 2 or more persons and who, in the course of such conduct, kills any person shall, if the killing—

"(A) is a first degree murder (as defined in section 1111(a)), be punished by death or imprisonment for any term of years or for life, fined under this title, or both; or

"(B) is a murder other than a first degree murder (as defined in section 1111(a)), be fined under this title, imprisoned for any term of years or for life, or both."

FIGURE 6-4
(continued)

For example, all laws regarding bankruptcy are arranged under the general topical heading of bankruptcy or Title 11 (see Table 6-1 for list of subject matter headings). The general topics are arranged alphabetically. However, the titles are officially referred to numerically rather than by the topical name. Titles are further divided into sections. Each section is a separate law. Laws are referred to and cited by title and section.

For example, if you refer to the code section at the beginning of the chapter, you say, "Title 18, section 242 of the *United States Code*." Of course, in speaking, lawyers often refer to the various codes by their more popular names, such as the Bankruptcy Code. The code books contain popular name indexes so that researchers can find code sections by their common or popular name.

TABLE 6-1　Title Headings for U.S. Code and Administrative Regulations

U.S. Code	Administrative Regulations
Topic Heading	Topic Heading
1. General Provisions	1. General Provisions
2. The Congress	2. The Congress (reserved)
3. The President	3. The President
4. Flag and Seal, Seat of Government, and the States	4. Accounts
5. Government Organization and Employees	5. Administrative Personnel
6. Surety Bonds (repealed by the enactment of Title 31)	6. Economic Stabilization
7. Agriculture	7. Agriculture
8. Aliens and Nationality	8. Aliens and Nationality
9. Arbitration	9. Animals and Animal Products
10. Armed Forces	10. Energy
11. Bankruptcy	11. Federal Elections
12. Banks and Banking	12. Banks and Banking
13. Census	13. Business Credit and Assistance
14. Coast Guard	14. Aeronautics and Space
15. Commerce and Trade	15. Commerce and Foreign Trade
16. Conservation	16. Commercial Practices
17. Copyrights	17. Commodity and Securities Exchange
18. Crimes and Criminal Procedure	18. Conservation of Power and Water Resources
19. Customs Duties	19. Customs Duties
20. Education	20. Employees' Benefits
21. Food and Drugs	21. Food and Drugs
22. Foreign Relations and Intercourse	22. Foreign Relations
23. Highways	23. Highways
24. Hospitals and Asylums	24. Housing and Urban Development
25. Indians	25. Indians
26. Internal Revenue Code	26. Internal Revenue
27. Intoxicating Liquors	27. Alcohol, Tobacco Products and Firearms
28. Judiciary and Judicial procedure	28. Judicial Administration
29. Labor	29. Labor
30. Mineral Lands and Mining	30. Mineral Resources
31. Money and Finance	31. Money and Finance: Treasury
32. National Guard	32. National Defense
33. Navigation and Navigable Waters	33. Navigation and Navigable Waters
34. Navy (eliminated by the enactment of Title 10)	34. Education
35. Patents	35. Panama Canal (reserved)

(continued)

TABLE 6-1   (continued)

U.S. Code	Administrative Regulations
Topic Heading	Topic Heading
36. Patriotic Societies and Observations	36. Parks, Forests, and Public Property
37. Pay and Allowances of the Uniformed Services	37. Patents, Trademarks and Copyrights
38. Veterans' Benefits	38. Pensions, Bonuses, and Veterans' Relief
39. Postal Service	39. Postal Service
40. Public Buildings, Property, and Works	40. Protection of the Environment
41. Public Contracts	41. Public Contracts and Property Management
42. The Public Health and Welfare	42. Public Health
43. Public Lands	43. Public Lands: Interior
44. Public Printing and Documents	44. Emergency Management and Assistance
45. Railroads	45. Public Welfare
46. Shipping	46. Shipping
47. Telegraphs, Telephones, and Radiotelegraphs	47. Telecommunications
48. Territories and Insular Possessions	48. Federal Acquisition Regulations System
49. Transportation	49. Transportation
50. War and National Defense	50. Wildlife and Fisheries

positive law.   Codes that have been enacted into law by Congress.

In researching statutory law, legal researchers generally search the codes rather than the *Statutes at Large.* This is because the index makes the codes much easier to use. When statutory law is organized and put into appropriate codes, differences between the language of the statute and the language of the code occasionally occur. The law is the language that was approved by Congress. To eliminate confusion, Congress began reenacting the various code titles so researchers could rely on the code rather than the difficult-to-use *Statutes at Large.* Once approved, the code becomes the law and is called **positive law.**

Congressional approval of the codes is a cumbersome process and is not yet complete. Some titles remain to be approved. Code titles that have not been reenacted are considered evidence of what the law is. That means that you can cite the code sections to a court. However, if someone shows that the statute at large is different, it controls.

Legislative Histories

legislative intent.   The purpose of the legislature in passing a law.

Once in a while, a legal dispute arises regarding the meaning of a particular code section. When this happens in connection with a factual dispute, the court is called upon to interpret the code section. The court gives great weight to the **legislative intent** behind the law. The legislative intent is what the legislature intended to accomplish by passing the law. While no one can absolutely prove what was in the minds of all the legislators when the law was enacted, various documents help the

court make this determination. The original language of the bill and changes made to that language often provide evidence of intent. Transcripts of committee hearings and transcripts of debates on the bill also help.

Rather than seeking the originals of these records, a researcher can use *United States Code and Congressional and Administrative News* (U.S.C.C.A.N.). This contains the legislative history of statutes, federal regulations, and court rules. It contains bills in their original format, changes, and committee hearings and discussions. Determining the meaning of any code section is more involved than simply looking at legislative intent. The following chapter discusses this in more detail.

United States Code Publications

There are three main publications of the Unites States Code: the *United States Code,* published by the Government Printing Office, the *United States Code Annotated,* published by West, and the *United States Code Service,* originally published by Lawyers Cooperative Publishing and now published by LEXIS Law Publishing. The *United States Code* (abbreviated U.S.C.) contains only the statutory language of the code. On the other hand, both *United States Code Annotated* (abbreviated U.S.C.A.) and the *United States Code Service* (abbreviated U.S.C.S.) are annotated editions of the code. An annotated version of a code contains references to cases that interpret the code section along with references to other legal sources that explain the code section. The annotations that are not part of the code are added by the publisher and are intended to assist the researcher. See Figure 6-5 for examples of a code section found in each of these three sources.

BOX 6-1

COMMON FEATURES OF AN ANNOTATED CODE

- History of law
- Cross reference to similar laws
- References to secondary authorities
- References to case decisions

There is, however, one difference between the *United States Code Annotated* and the *United States Code Service.* The U.S.C.A. uses the exact language found in the *United States Code.* The U.S.C.S. uses the exact language found in the *Statutes at Large.* In most cases, this presents no problem to the researcher who can usually use either source.

Pocket Part Supplements

Laws change every year and code publications must be kept up-to-date to reflect these changes. This is done by the use of **pocket part supplements,** which are replaced each year and contain all changes to the law. When a code is **repealed** or **amended,** that change is found in the pocket part supplement. In annotated codes, the pocket part supplement also contains the latest cases to interpret the statute. Thus, even if a code section has not been changed, it is important to check the pocket part supplement to see if any recent case decisions have affected the interpretation of the law. Occasionally, supplemental material becomes too voluminous for a pocket part supplement. When this happens, a separately

pocket part supplement. A removable supplement; includes all changes or additions to the material contained in the hardbound volume.
repeal. To undo; to declare a law no longer in effect.
amend. To change.

CHAPTER 13—CIVIL RIGHTS

Sec.
241. Conspiracy against rights.
242. Deprivation of rights under color of law.
243. Exclusion of jurors on account of race or color.
244. Discrimination against person wearing uniform of armed forces.
245. Federally protected activities.
246. Deprivation of relief benefits.
247. Damage to religious property; obstruction of persons in the free exercise of religious beliefs.
248. Freedom of access to clinic entrances.

AMENDMENTS

1994—Pub. L. 103–322, title XXXIII, § 330023(a)(1), Sept. 13, 1994, 108 Stat. 2150, substituted "Freedom of access to clinic entrances" for "Blocking access to reproductive health services" in item 248.

Pub. L. 103–259, § 4, May 26, 1994, 108 Stat. 697, added item 248.

1988—Pub. L. 100–690, title VII, § 7018(b)(2), Nov. 18, 1988, 102 Stat. 4396, struck out "of citizens" after "rights" in item 241.

Pub. L. 100–346, § 3, June 24, 1988, 102 Stat. 645, added item 247.

1976—Pub. L. 94–453, § 4(b), Oct. 2, 1976, 90 Stat. 1517, added item 246.

1968—Pub. L. 90–284, title I, § 102, Apr. 11, 1968, 82 Stat. 75, added item 245.

§ 241. Conspiracy against rights

If two or more persons conspire to injure, oppress, threaten, or intimidate any person in any State, Territory, or District in the free exercise or enjoyment of any right or privilege secured to him by the Constitution or laws of the United States, or because of his having so exercised the same; or

If two or more persons go in disguise on the highway, or on the premises of another, with intent to prevent or hinder his free exercise or enjoyment of any right or privilege so secured—

They shall be fined under this title or imprisoned not more than ten years, or both; and if death results from the acts committed in violation of this section or if such acts include kidnapping or an attempt to kidnap, aggravated sexual abuse or an attempt to commit aggravated sexual abuse, or an attempt to kill, they shall be fined under this title or imprisoned for any term of years or for life, or both, or <u>may be sentenced to death.</u>   ②

(June 25, 1948, ch. 645, 62 Stat. 696; Apr. 11, 1968, Pub. L. 90–284, title I, § 103(a), 82 Stat. 75; Nov. 18, 1988, Pub. L. 100–690, title VII, § 7018(a), (b)(1), 102 Stat. 4396; Sept. 13, 1994, <u>Pub. L. 103–322</u>, title ② VI, § 60006(a), title XXXII, §§ 320103(a), 320201(a), title XXXIII, § 330016(1)(L), 108 Stat. 1970, 2109, 2113, 2147.)

HISTORICAL AND REVISION NOTES

Based on title 18, U.S.C., 1940 ed., § 51 (Mar. 4, 1909, ch. 321, § 19, 35 Stat. 1092).

Clause making conspirator ineligible to hold office was omitted as incongruous because it attaches ineligibility to hold office to a person who may be a private citizen and who was convicted of conspiracy to violate a specific statute. There seems to be no reason for imposing such a penalty in the case of one individual crime, in view of the fact that other crimes do not carry such a severe consequence. The experience of the Department of Justice is that this unusual penalty has been an obstacle to successful prosecutions for violations of the act.

Mandatory punishment provision was rephrased in the alternative.

Minor changes in phraseology were made.

AMENDMENTS

1994—Pub. L. 103–322, § 320201(a), substituted "person in any State" for "inhabitant of any State" in first par.

Pub. L. 103–322, §§ 320103(a)(1), 330016(I)(L), amended section identically, substituting "They shall be fined under this title" for "They shall be fined not more than $10,000" in third par.

Pub. L. 103–322, § 320103(a)(2)–(4), in third par., substituted "results from the acts committed in violation of this section or if such acts include kidnapping or an attempt to kidnap, aggravated sexual abuse or an attempt to commit aggravated sexual abuse, or an attempt to kill, they shall be fined under this title or imprisoned for any term of years or for life, or both" for "results, they shall be subject to imprisonment for any term of years or for life".

Pub. L. 103–322, § 60006(a), substituted ", or may be sentenced to death." for period at end of third par.

1988—Pub. L. 100–690 struck out "of citizens" after "rights" in section catchline and substituted "inhabitant of any State, Territory, or District" for "citizen" in text.

1968—Pub. L. 90–284 increased limitation on fines from $5,000 to $10,000 and provided for imprisonment for any term of years or for life when death results.

CROSS REFERENCES ①

Action for neglect to prevent, see section 1986 of Title 42, The Public Health and Welfare.

Conspiracy to commit offense or to defraud United States, see section 371 of this title.

Conspiracy to interfere with civil rights, see section 1985 of Title 42, The Public Health and Welfare.

Proceedings in vindication of civil rights, see section 1988 of Title 42.

§ 242. Deprivation of rights under color of law ②

Whoever, under color of any law, statute, ordinance, regulation, or custom, willfully subjects any

---

① **U.S. Code provides amendments and cross annotations but no case decisions.**

② **Note amendment from Pub. L 103–322 (Figure 6-4).**

FIGURE 6-5A U.S.C. (United States Code)

person in any State, Territory, or District to the deprivation of any rights, privileges or immunities secured or protected by the Constitution or laws of the United States, or to different punishments, pains, or penalties, on account of such person being an alien, or by reason of his color, or race, than are prescribed for the punishment of citizens, shall be fined under this title or imprisoned not more than one year, or both; and if bodily injury results from the acts committed in violation of this section or if such acts include the use, attempted use, or threatened use of a dangerous weapon, explosives, or fire, shall be fined under this title or imprisoned not more than ten years, or both; and if death results from the acts committed in violation of this section or if such acts include kidnapping or an attempt to kidnap, aggravated sexual abuse, or an attempt to commit aggravated sexual abuse, or an attempt to kill, shall be fined under this title, or imprisoned for any term of years or for life, or both, or may be sentenced to death.

(June 25, 1948, ch. 645, 62 Stat. 696; Apr. 11, 1968, Pub. L. 90–284, title I, § 103(b), 82 Stat. 75; Nov. 18, 1988, Pub. L. 100–690, title VII, § 7019, 102 Stat. 4396; Sept. 13, 1994, Pub. L. 103–322, title VI, § 60006(b), title XXXII, §§ 320103(b), 320201(b), title XXXIII, § 330016(1)(H), 108 Stat. 1970, 2109, 2113, 2147.)

HISTORICAL AND REVISION NOTES

Based on title 18, U.S.C., 1940 ed., § 52 (Mar. 4, 1909, ch. 321, § 20, 35 Stat. 1092).

Reference to persons causing or procuring was omitted as unnecessary in view of definition of "principal" in section 2 of this title.

A minor change was made in phraseology.

AMENDMENTS

1994—Pub. L. 103–322, § 320201(b), substituted "any person in any State" for "any inhabitant of any State" and "on account of such person" for "on account of such inhabitant".

Pub. L. 103–322, §§ 320103(b)(1), 330016(1)(H), amended section identically, substituting "shall be fined under this title" for "shall be fined not more than $1,000" after "citizens,".

Pub. L. 103–322, § 320103(b)(2)–(5), substituted "bodily injury results from the acts committed in violation of this section or if such acts include the use, attempted use, or threatened use of a dangerous weapon, explosives, or fire, shall be fined under this title or imprisoned not more than ten years, or both; and if death results from the acts committed in violation of this section or if such acts include kidnapping or an attempt to kidnap, aggravated sexual abuse, or an attempt to commit aggravated sexual abuse, or an attempt to kill, shall be fined under this title, or imprisoned for any term of years or for life, or both" for "bodily injury results shall be fined under this title or imprisoned nor more than ten years, or both; and if

death results shall be subject to imprisonment for any term of years or for life".

Pub. L. 103–322, § 60006(b), inserted before period at end ", or may be sentenced to death".

1988—Pub. L. 100–690 inserted "and if bodily injury results shall be fined under this title or imprisoned not more than ten years, or both;" after "or both;".

1968—Pub. L. 90–284 provided for imprisonment for any term of years or for life when death results.

CROSS REFERENCES

Civil action for deprivation of rights, see section 1983 of Title 42, The Public Health and Welfare.

Equal rights under the law, see section 1981 of Title 42.

Minor offenses tried by United States magistrate judges as excluding offenses punishable under this section, see section 3401 of this title.

Proceedings in vindication of civil rights, see section 1988 of Title 42, The Public Health and Welfare.

§ 243. Exclusion of jurors on account of race or color

No citizen possessing all other qualifications which are or may be prescribed by law shall be disqualified for service as grand or petit juror in any court of the United States, or of any State on account of race, color, or previous condition of servitude; and whoever, being an officer or other person charged with any duty in the selection or summoning of jurors, excludes or fails to summon any citizen for such cause, shall be fined not more than $5,000.

(June 25, 1948, ch. 645, 62 Stat. 696.)

HISTORICAL AND REVISION NOTES

Based on section 44 of title 8, U.S.C., 1940 ed., Aliens and Nationality (Mar. 1, 1875, ch. 114, §4, 18 Stat 336).

Words "be deemed guilty of a misdemeanor, and" were deleted as unnecessary in view of definition of misdemeanor in section 1 of this title.

Words "on conviction thereof" were omitted as unnecessary, since punishment follows only after conviction.

Minimum punishment provisions were omitted. (See reviser's note under section 203 of this title.)

Minor changes in phraseology were made.

FEDERAL RULES OF CIVIL PROCEDURE

Jurors, see rule 47, Title 28, Appendix, Judiciary and Judicial Procedure.

FEDERAL RULES OF CRIMINAL PROCEDURE

Grand jury, see rule 6, Appendix to this title.
Trial jurors, see rule 24.

FIGURE 6-5A
(continued)

CROSS REFERENCES

Bribery of public officials and witnesses, see section 201 of this title.

Civil rights generally, see section 1981 et seq. of Title 42, The Public Health and Welfare.

Exclusion or excuse from jury service, see section 1863 of Title 28, Judiciary and Judicial Procedure.

Grand jurors, number of and summoning additional jurors, see section 3321 of this title.

Juries generally, see section 1861 et seq. of Title 28, Judiciary and Judicial Procedure.

Manner of drawing jurors, see section 1864 of Title 28.

Qualifications of jurors, see section 1861 of Title 28.

Summoning jurors, see section 1867 of Title 28.

§ 244. Discrimination against person wearing uniform of armed forces

Whoever, being a proprietor, manager, or employee of a theater or other public place of entertainment or amusement in the District of Columbia, or in any Territory, or Possession of the United States, causes any person wearing the uniform of any of the armed forces of the United States to be discriminated against because of that uniform, shall be fined under this title.

(June 25, 1948, ch. 645, 62 Stat. 697; May 24, 1949, ch. 139, § 5, 63 Stat. 90; Sept. 13, 1994, Pub. L. 103–322, title XXXIII, § 330016(1)(G), 108 Stat. 2147.)

HISTORICAL AND REVISION NOTES

1948 ACT

Based on title 18, U.S.C., 1940 ed., § 523 (Mar. 1, 1911, ch. 187, 36 Stat. 963; Aug. 24, 1912, ch. 387, § 1, 37 Stat. 512; Jan. 28, 1915, ch. 20, § 1, 38 Stat. 800).

Words "guilty of a misdemeanor", following "shall be", were omitted as unnecessary in view of definition of "misdemeanor" in section 1 of this title. (See revisioner's note under section 212 of this title.)

Changes were made in phraseology.

1949 ACT

This section [section 5] substitutes, in section 244 of title 18, U.S.C., "any of the armed forces of the United States" for the enumeration of specific branches and thereby includes the Air Force, formerly part of the Army. This clarification is necessary because of the establishment of the Air Force as a separate branch of the Armed Forces by the act of July 26, 1947.

AMENDMENTS

1994—Pub. L. 103–322 substituted "fined under this title" for "fined not more than $500".

1949—Act May 24, 1949, substituted "any of the armed forces of the United States" for enumeration of the specific branches.

CROSS REFERENCES

Uniforms, wearing without authority, see section 702 of this title.

FIGURE 6-5A
(continued)

---

said sections, Watson v. Devlin, D.C. Mich.1958, 107 F.Supp. 638.

This section and section 242 of this title, providing punishment by fine or imprisonment for persons conspiring to injure, oppress, threaten or intimidate any citizen in the free exercise and enjoyment of any right or privilege secured by the Constitution or federal laws, and like punishment of person who under color of law willfully subjects any citizen to the deprivation of such rights, privileges or immunities, or to different punishments on account of being an alien or by reason of color or race, have no application to the plaintiff's proposed civil action for damages. Mattheis v. Hoyt, D.C.Mich.1955, 136 F. Supp. 110.

This section has no application to a civil action for money damages for alleged violation of those

rights. Copley v. Sweet, D.C.Mich.1955, 133 F.Supp. 502, affirmed 234 F.2d 660, certiorari denied 77 S.Ct. 138, 352 U.S. 887, 1 L.Ed.2d 91.

Plaintiff in a civil conspiracy case has the burden of proving the existence of a conspiracy which it alleges exists. United Elec. Radio & Mach. Workers of America v. General Elec. Co., D.C.D.C:1954, 127 F.Supp. 934, affirmed in part, vacated in part on other grounds 231 F.2d 257, 97 U.S.App.D.C. 306, certiorari denied 77 S. Ct. 95, 352 U.S. 872, 1 L.Ed.2d 76.

Civil actions against superintendent and physician of State Farm for injuries sustained by inmate could not be based on former sections 51, 52 of this title [now this section and section 242 of this title] making it a crime for one person to deprive another of civil rights. Gordon v. Garrson, D.C.Ill.1948, 77 F.Supp. 477.

① **U.S.C.A. same code as U.S.C., but features are added.**

§242. Deprivation of rights under color of law ①

Whoever, under color of any law, statute, ordinance, regulation, or custom, willfully subjects any inhabitant of any State, Territory, or District to the deprivation of any rights, privileges, or immunities secured or protected by the Constitution or laws of the United States, or to different punishments, pains, or penalties, on account of such inhabitant being an alien, or by reason of his

FIGURE 6-5B
U.S.C.A. (United States Code Annotated)

color, or race, not more than $1,000 or imprisoned not more than one year, or both; and if death results shall be subject to imprisonment for any term of years or for life.

June 25, 1948, c. 645, 62 Stat. 696; Apr. 11, 1968, Pub.L.90–284, Title I, § 103(b), 82 Stat. 75.

HISTORICAL AND REVISION NOTES

Reviser's Note. Based on Title 18, U.S.C., 1940 ed., § 52 (Mar. 4, 1909, c. 321, § 20, 35 Stat. 1092 [Derived from R.S. § 5510]).

Reference to persons causing or procuring was omitted as unnecessary in view of definition of "principal" in section 2 of this title.

A minor change was made in phraseology. 80th Congress House Report No. 304.

1968 Amendment. Pub.L. 90–284 provided for imprisonment for any term of years or for life when death results.

Legislative History. For legislative history and purpose of Pub.L. 90–284, see 1968 U.S.Code Cong. and Adm.News, p. 1837.

CROSS REFERENCES

Civil action for deprivation of rights, see section 1983 of Title 42, The Public Health and Welfare.
Equal rights under the law, see section 1981 of Title 42.
Minor offenses tried by United States magistrates as excluding offenses punishable under this section, see section 3401 of this title.
Proceedings in vindication of civil rights, see section 1988 of Title 42, The Public Health and Welfare.

LIBRARY REFERENCES

Civil Rights ⚷— 2.   C.J.S. Civil Rights § 3.

NOTES OF DECISIONS ② ←

② **Case decisions are added. These case decisions interpret or refer to § 242.**

Generally **4**
Admissibility of evidence **27**
Amendment of indictment **19**
Arrest, deprivation of rights **10**
Assault and battery, deprivation of rights **11**
Bill of particulars **22**
Civil remedies **37**
Color of law **6**
Conspiracy **16**
Constitutionality **1**
Construction with other laws **2**
Defenses **24**
Deprivation of rights **9–15**
  Generally **9**
  Arrest **10**
  Assault and battery **11**
  Education **12**
  Elections **13**
  Homicide **14**
  Particular acts **15**
Education, deprivation of rights **12**
Elections, deprivation of rights **13**
Evidence
  Admissibility **27**
  Sufficiency **28**
Homicide, deprivation of rights **14**
Indictment **18–20**
  Generally **18**
  Amendment **19**
  Sufficiency **20**

Information **21**
Inhabitants **8**
Instructions **32**
Judicial notice **29**
Jurisdiction **17**
Jury trial **26**
Limitations **25**
Mistrial **33**
Motion to dismiss **23**
New trial **34**
Persons to institute prosecution **5**
Purpose **3**
Questions for jury **31**
Review **36**
Sufficiency of
  Evidence **28**
  Indictment **20**
Vacation of sentence **38**
Variance **30**
Verdict **35**
Wilfulness **7**

―――――――

1. Constitutionality

This section, as applied to sustain a conviction for obtaining a confession by use of force and violence by private detective acting under semblance of policeman's power, was not unconstitutional on theory that no specific standard of guilt was provided. Williams v. U. S., Fla. 1951, 71 S.Ct. 576, 341 U.S. 97, 95 L.Ed. 774.

FIGURE 6-5B
(continued)

The states, in adopting U.S.C.A.Const. Amend. 14, expressly delegated to Congress the power to provide for the enforcement of its provisions by appropriate legislation, and former section 52 of this title [now this section] was enacted in the exercise of such power.   Culp v. U.S., C.C.A.Ark.1942, 131 F.2d 93.

A right or immunity, whether created by federal constitution or only guaranteed thereby, even without any express delegation of power, may be protected by Congress.   Id.

2. Construction with other laws

This section, section 241 of this title, and sections 1981 and 1985 of Title 42, creating civil claims or imposing criminal penalties for deprivation of constitutional rights are not laws providing for equal rights nor do they confer "color of authority" for exercise of those rights within civil rights removal statute. People of State of N.Y. v. Galamison, C.A. N.Y.1965, 342 F.2d 255, 8 A.L.R.3d 263, certiorari denied 85 S.Ct. 1342, 380 U.S. 977, 14 L.Ed.2d 272.

3. Purpose

Purpose of this section calling for imposition of penalties for depriving anyone under color of law of rights protected by the constitution is to procure criminal remedies or imposition of penalties. Sinchak v. Parente, D.C.Pa.1966, 262 F.Supp. 79.

This section prohibiting anyone, under color of any law, from willfully depriving inhabitant of state of any right protected by Constitution or laws of United States was enacted to enforce U.S.C.A. Const. Amend. 14. U. S. v. Cooney, D.C. Colo. 1963, 217 F.Supp. 417.

4. Generally

Former section 52 of this title [now this section] authorized the punishment of two different offenses, one of which was willfully subjecting any inhabitant to the deprivation of rights secured by the constitution and laws and the other willfully subjecting any inhabitant to different punishments on account of his color or race than were prescribed for the punishment of citizens. U. S. v. Classic, La.1941, 61 S.Ct. 1031, 313 U.S. 299, 85 L.Ed. 1368, rehearing denied 62 S.Ct. 51, 314 U.S. 707, 86 L.Ed. 565. See, also, Culp v. U.S., C.C.A.Ark.1942, 131 F.2d 93.

Under former section 52 of this title [now this section] the qualification with respect to alienage, color, and race referred only to differences in punishment and not to deprivations of any rights or privileges secured by the constitution and laws. U.S. v. Classic, La.1941, 61 S.Ct. 1031, 313 U.S. 299, 85 L.Ed. 1368, rehearing denied 62 S.Ct. 51, 314 U.S. 707, 86 L.Ed. 565.

This section does not come into play merely because the federal law or the state law under which

the officer purports to act is violated, but it is applicable only when some one is deprived of a federal right by that action. U. S. v. Walker, D.C.Fla.1954, 121 F.Supp. 458. reversed on other grounds 216 F.2d 683, certiorari denied 75 S.Ct. 450, 348 U.S. 959, 99 L.Ed. 748.

Former section 52 of this title [now this section] did not create or add to rights of one citizen as against another, but was rather a guaranty against encroachment by the state and its authorized agents upon the rights of the citizen under the federal Constitution. U. S. v. Trierweiler, D.C.Ill.1943, 52 F.Supp. 4.

5. Persons to institute prosecution

Prisoner could not properly personally institute criminal proceeding against state and its officers for violation of his rights under color of law and any such complaint should have been sent to United States attorney. Dixon v. State of Md. by Carter, D.C.Md.1966, 261 F.Supp. 746.

6. Color of law

To act "under color" of law for purposes of this section prohibiting, under color of law, willfully subjecting any inhabitant of any state to deprivation of any rights, privileges or immunities secured or protected by Constitution or laws of United States does not require that accused be officer of state and it is enough that he is a willful participant in joint activity with state or its agents. U.S. v. Price, Miss.1966, 86 S.Ct. 1152, 383 U.S. 787, 16 L.Ed.2d 267.

Private persons, jointly engaged with state officials in prohibited action, are acting "under color of law" for purposes of this section prohibiting, under color of law, willfully subjecting any inhabitant of any state to deprivation of any rights, privileges or immunities secured or protected by Constitution or laws of United States. Id.

If release of three men from county jail, interception of them on highway and assault and murder of them was joint activity of state officers and nonofficial defendants, nonofficial defendants were acting, under color of law, in violation of this section providing punishment for whoever, under color of law, subjects any inhabitant of any state to deprivation of rights, privileges, or immunities secured or protected by Constitution or laws of United States. Id.

Where detective hired by lumber company to ascertain identity of thieves held special police officer's card issued by city, and took suspects to shack on company's premises and obtained confessions by forcing a suspect to look at bright light, by repeatedly hitting him with rubber hose and sash cord, by knocking another from chair and hitting him in the stomach, by beating, threatening and punishing suspects, and by flashing his badge and city policeman sent by his superior was present to lend authority to the proceedings, jury could properly find that detective was

FIGURE 6-5B
(continued)

acting under "color of law" within this section. Williams v. U. S., Fla.1951, 71 S.Ct. 576, 341 U.S. 97, 95 L.Ed. 774.

Under this section, "color of law" includes misuse of power possessed by virtue of state law and

made possible only because wrongdoer is clothed with authority of state law. Id.

Misuse of power, possessed by virtue of state law and made possible only because the wrongdoer is clothed with the

Reprinted with permission of Thomson/West

FIGURE 6-5B
(continued)

---

18 USCS § 241, n 71   CRIMES & CRIMINAL PROCEDURE

Evidence of victims' reactions to cross-burning, including photographs of security measures they took afterwards and son's testimony he began to sleep with baseball bat, was admissible, since it was probative of defendant's intent under 18 USCS §§ 241 and 844. United States v Magleby (2001, CA10 Utah) 241 F3d 1306.

73. —Sufficiency

Evidence that defendants resorted to acts which are not constitutionally protected, including bottle throwing, brandishing knives and verbally threatening, in order to prevent black persons from using public park was sufficient to prove violation of 18 USCS § 241. United States v McDermott (1994, CA8 Iowa) 29 F3d 404.

Evidence was sufficient to prove that defendant intended to threaten victims of cross burning with physical violence, where he made racial derogatory statements while constructing cross and testified at trial that his purpose was to scare victims so they would move out of town, in addition to which victim testified that she and her children felt physically threatened. United States v Pospisil (1999, CA8 Mo) 186 F3d 1023, reh en banc, den (1999, CA8) 1999 US App LEXIS 22128.

Evidence was sufficient to convict defendant of conspiring to violate 18 USCS § 241, despite fact that he did not directly participate in cross burning, where on afternoon of cross burning men waited to discuss defendant's altercation with victim until defendant arrived, defendant not only knew about, discussed, and encouraged action but initiated it, defendant was informed when mission was accomplished, and his credibility was suspect. United States v Whitney (2000, CA 10 Kan) 229 F3d 1296, 2000 Colo J C A R 5742.

Jury could infer that defendant intended to oppress, threaten, and intimidate victims in free exercise of their federal right to occupy property, where

he, understanding meaning of burning cross to general public, had placed one in their yard. United States v Magleby (2001, CA10 Utah) 241 F3d 1306.

Juvenile delinquents are guilty beyond reasonable doubt of violation of 18 USCS § 241, where they were all active members of skinhead group New Dawn Hammerskins, which desecrated several Jewish temples and vandalized car of Jewish teacher, because U.S. has proven that defendants had specific intent to interfere with federal right of Jewish inhabitants to hold and use property. United States v Three Juveniles (1995, DC Mass) 886 F Supp 934.

75. Instructions

In prosecution of police officers for alleged use of excessive force in making arrests, jury instructions did not constructively amend indictment, which could be read in due process terms, whereas instruction alleged Fourth Amendment violation, since proof was same and defendants' substantial rights were not affected; instructions adequately distinguished specific intent and violation of constitutional rights as elements of proof. United States v Reese (1993, CA9 Cal) 2 F3d 870, 93 CDOS 5642, 93 Daily Journal DAR 9617, petition for certiorari filed (Oct 28, 1993) and (among conflicting authorities noted in United States v Lilly (CA1) 1994 US App LEXIS 69).

District court did not err in instructing jury that, while victim's reaction to cross-burning was not conclusive evidence of defendant's intent in burning cross in yard of Afro-American, it could be considered as some evidence of it. United States v Hartbarger (1998, CA7 Ind) 148 F3d 777, 49 Fed Rules Evid Serv 783, reh en banc, den (1998, CA7 Ind) 1998 US App LEXIS 177724.

District court properly instructed jury that victims' reactions to cross-burning could be considered by trier of fact as relevant evidence of defendant's intent under 18 USCS § 241. United States v Magleby (2001, CA10 Utah) 241 F3d 1306.

§ 242. Deprivation of rights under color of law ①

Whoever, under color of any law, statute, ordinance, regulation, or custom, willfully subjects any person in any State, Territory, Commonwealth, Possession, or District to the deprivation of any rights, privileges, or immunities secured or protected by the Constitution or laws of the United States, or to different punishments, pains, or penalties, on account of such person being an alien, or by reason of his color, or race, than are prescribed for the punishment of citizens, shall be fined

① **Same code as U.S.C. but features are added**

FIGURE 6-5C
U.S.C.S. (United States Code Service)

under this title or imprisoned not more than one year, or both; and if bodily injury results from the acts committed in violation of this section or if such acts include the use, attempted use, or threatened use of a dangerous weapon, explosives, or fire, shall be fined under this title or imprisoned not more than ten years or both; and if death results from the acts committed in violation of this section or if such acts include kidnapping or an attempt to kidnap, aggravated sexual abuse, or an attempt to commit aggravated sexual abuse, or an attempt to kill, shall be fined under this title, or imprisoned for any term of years or for life, or both, or may be sentenced to death.

(As amended Sept. 13, 1994, P. L. 103-322, Title VI, § 60006(b), Title XXXII, Subtitle A, § 320103(b), Subtitle B, § 320201(b), Title XXXIII, § 330016(1)(H), 108 Stat. 1970, 2109, 2113, 2147; Oct. 11, 1996, P. L. 104-294, Title VI, §§ 604(b)(14)(B), 607(a), 110 Stat. 3507, 3511.)

CRIMES

HISTORY; ANCILLARY LAWS AND DIRECTIVES

Amendments:

1994. Act Sept. 13, 1994, substituted "person in" for "inhabitant of", substituted "such person" for "such inhabitant", and inserted ", or may be sentenced to death".

Section 320103(b), as amended by Act Oct. 11, 1996 (effective on 9/13/94, pursuant to § 604(d) of such Act, which appears as 18 USCS § 13 note), inserted "from the acts committed in violation of this section or if such acts include the use, attempted use, or threatened use of a dangerous weapon, explosives, or fire", inserted "from the acts committed in violation of this section or if such acts include kidnapping or an attempt to kidnap, aggravated sexual abuse, or an attempt to commit aggravated sexual abuse, or an attempt to kill, shall be fined under this title, or", substituted "imprisoned" for "shall be subject to imprisonment", and inserted ", or both".

Section 330016(1)(H) of such Act substituted "under this title" for "not more than $1,000". 1996, Act Oct 11, 1996 (effective on 9/13/94, pursuant to § 604(d) of such Act, which appears at 18 USCS § 13 note) (amended § 320103(b) of Act Sept. 13, 1994, which amended this section.

Such Act further substituted "any State, Territory, Commonwealth, Possession, or District" for "any State, Territory, or District".

CROSS REFERENCES

Sentencing Guidelines for the United States Courts, 18 USCS Appx §§ 2H1.1, 2H2.1.

RESEARCH GUIDE

Federal Procedure:

12 Fed Proc L Ed, Evidence § 33:209.

Am Jur:

15 Am Jur 2d, Civil Rights §§ 205–215.

29 Am Jur 2d, Evidence § 441.

Immigration:

1 Immigration Law and Procedure (Matthew Bender rev. ed.), Aliens' Rights, Privileges and Liabilities § 6.02.

6 Immigration Law and Procedure (Matthew Bender rev. ed.), Procedure in Deportation Cases § 72.03.

8 Immigration Law and Procedure (Matthew Bender rev. ed.), Judicial Review § 104.11.

Annotations:

Validity, construction, and application of 18 USCS §§ 241 and 242 (and similar predecessor provisions), providing criminal liability for conspiring to deprive, or depriving, person of civil rights—Supreme Court cases. 137 L Ed 2d 1091.

Law Review Articles:

To serve and protect: police civil liability. 41 Fed B News & June 1994.

Fink; Rohr. Scylla and Charybdis: charting a course for law enforcement officers caught between 42 U.S.C. § 1983 and 18 U.S.C. §§ 241 and 242. 41 Fed B News & J, June 1994.

INTERPRETIVE NOTES AND DECISIONS

I. IN GENERAL

1. Generally

There is no private right of action under either 18 USCS § 242 or 18 USCS § 1385. Robinson v Overseas Military Sales Corp. (1994, CA2, NY) 21 F3d 502, 64 BNA FEP Cas 638, 64 CCH EPD ¶ 42973.

6. Construction, generally

Criminal liability may be imposed under 18 USCS § 242 for deprivation of federal constitutional

FIGURE 6-5C
(continued)

right only if, in light of pre-existing law, unlawfulness under Constitution is apparent; where unlawfulness is apparent, constitutional requirement of fair warning of § 242 liability is satisfied; single standard for fair warning does not point a single level of specificity, for (1) in some circumstances, as when earlier case expressly leaves open whether general rule applies to conduct at issue, very high degree of prior factual particularity may be necessary, while (2) in other instances, general constitutional rule already identified in decisional law may apply with obvious clarity to conduct in question, even though conduct has not previously been held unlawful. United States v Lanier (1997, US) 137 L Ed 2d 432, S Ct 1219, 97 CDOS 2350, 97 Daily Journal DAR 4168, 10 FLW Fed S 388.

7. Relationship with other laws

General terms of 18 USCS § 242 incorporate constitutional law by reference, in lieu of describing specific conduct forbidden, and thus, neither statute nor good many of its constitutional references delineate range of forbidden conduct with particularity.

8. Civil liability

Former federal employee's 18 USCS §§ 242 and 371 claims against federal judges were dismissed because it was impermissible to bring private cause of action under those statutes. Rockefeller v United States Court of Appeals Office (2003, DC Dist Col) 248 F Supp 2d 17.

II. ELEMENTS OF CRIME

10. Deprivation of rights protected by Federal Constitution or laws

Test of whether officers violated arrestees' or detainees' Fourth Amendment rights by use of excessive force—as distinct from determination of specific intent—is objective one. United States v Reese (1993, CA9 Cal) 2 F3d 870, 93 CDOS 5642, 93 Daily Journal DAR 9617, petition for certiorari filed (Oct 28, 1993) and (among conflicting authorities noted in United States v Lilly (CA1) 1994 US App LEXIS 69). United States v Lanier (1997, US) 137 L Ed 2d 432, 117 S Ct 1219, 97 CDOS 2350, 97 Daily Journal DAR 4168, 10 FLW Fed S 388.

Because 18 USCS § 242 is merely criminal analog of 42 USCS § 1983, and because Congress intended both statutes to apply similarly in similar situations, civil precedents are equally persuasive in criminal context. United States v Mohr (2003, CA4 Md) 318 F3d 613.

Double jeopardy does not bar federal prosecution of former police officer for violation of 18 USCS § 242, where he allegedly used excessive force and assaulted person while attempting to arrest him, even though he was found guilty of criminally negligent homicide in state trial, because (1) § 242 and state crime require proof of different elements and (2) doctrine of dual sovereignty allows federal indictment charging conduct that was previously subject of state prosecution. United States v Livoti (1998, SD NY) 8 F Supp 2d 246.

FIGURE 6-5C
(continued)

Reprinted from *United States Code Service.* Copyright © 1995, Matthew Bender & Company, Inc., a member of the LexisNexis Group. All Rights Reserved. Reprinted with permission.

bound volume known as a *bound supplement,* is produced. Every six years, new editions of the code are published. See Figure 6-6 for an example of a pocket part supplement.

In addition to the publications of the United States Codes in book form, the codes are on Westlaw, LEXIS, and the Internet.

6-5 STATE STATUTORY LAW

Every state has statutory law enacted by the state legislature and then codified. Because state governments are largely patterned after the federal government, the legislative process is similar.

Publication of state laws is similar to that of federal law. In general, statutes are published first as slip laws. At the end of the state congressional session, all laws are published in chronological fashion in works similar to the *Statutes at Large.* Although differences exist from state to state in what these works are called, they are often referred to as **session laws.** Finally, state laws are organized and arranged topically in a code.

session laws. Laws from state legislatures, published in chronological order.

§ 242. Deprivation of rights under color of law

Whoever, under color of any law, statute, ordinance, regulation, or custom, willfully subjects any person in any State, Territory, or District to the deprivation of any rights, privileges, or immunities secured or protected by the Constitution or laws of the United States, or to different punishments, pains, or penalties, on account of such person being an alien, or by reason of his color, or race, than are prescribed for the punishment of citizens, shall be fined under this title or imprisoned not more than one year, or both; and if bodily injury results from the acts committed in violation of this section or if such acts include the use, attempted use, or threatened use of a dangerous weapon, explosives, or fire, shall be fined under this title or imprisoned not more than ten years, or both; and if death results from the acts committed in violation of this section or if such acts include kidnapping or an attempt to kidnap, aggravated sexual abuse, or an attempt to commit aggravated sexual abuse, or an attempt to kill, shall be fined under this title, or imprisoned for any term of years or for life, or both, or may be sentenced to death.

(As amended Nov. 18, 1988, Pub.L. 100–690, Title VII, § 7019, 102 Stat. 4396; Sept. 13, 1994, Pub.L. 103–322, Title VI, § 60006(b), Title XXXII, §§ 320103(b), 320201(b), Title XXXIII, § 330016(1)(H), 108 Stat. 1970, 2109, 2113, 2147.)

HISTORICAL AND STATUTORY NOTES

① Note reference to 1994 amendments.

1994 Amendments ①

Pub.L. 103–322, §§ 60006(b), 320103(b), 320201(b), amended section generally. Prior to amendment section read as follows: "Whoever, under color of any law, statute, ordinance regulations, or custom, willfully subjects any inhabitant of any State, Territory, or District to the deprivation of any rights, privileges, or immunities secured or protected by the Constitution or laws of the United States, or to different punishments, pains, or penalties, on account of such inhabitant being an alien, or by reason of his color, or race, than are prescribed for the punishment of citizens, shall be fined not more than $1,000 or imprisoned not more than one year, or both; and if bodily injury results shall be fined under this title or imprisoned not more than ten years, or both; and if death results, shall be subject to imprisonment for any term of years or for life."

Pub.L. 103–322, § 330016(1)(H), directed that, in text, the phrase "under this title" be substituted for the phrase "not more than $1,000" after "punishment of citizens, shall be fined". The amendment could not be executed due to the prior identical amendment by section 320103(b)(1) of Pub.L. 103–322.

1988 Amendment

Pub.L. 100–690 inserted "and if bodily injury results shall be fined under this title or imprisoned not more than ten years, or both;" after "or both;".

Legislative History

For legislative history and purpose of Pub.L. 100–690, see 1988 U.S. Code Cong. and Adm. News, p. 5937. See, also, Pub.L. 103–322, 1994 U.S. Code Cong. and Adm. News, p. 1801.

CROSS REFERENCES

Misdemeanors tried by United States magistrates as excluding offenses punishable under this section, see 18 USCA § 3401.

FEDERAL SENTENCING GUIDELINES

See §§ 2H1.4, 2H2.1.

FEDERAL PRACTICE AND PROCEDURE

Construction of under color of law by courts, see Wright, Miller & Cooper: Jurisdiction § 3573.

FEDERAL JURY PRACTICE AND INSTRUCTIONS

Civil rights—deprivation under color of state law, see Devitt and Blackmar § 27.01 et seq.

WEST'S FEDERAL PRACTICE MANUAL

Civil liability of local officials, see § 12124. Voting rights, see § 12281 et seq.

CRIMINAL PROCEDURE

Illegally seized evidence, exclusionary rule, see LaFave and Israel § 3.1.

FIGURE 6-6 Pocket Part Supplement to 18 U.S.C.A. § 242

CRIMINAL LAW DEFENSES

Mistake or ignorance of law as defense, see Robinson § 62.

LAW REVIEW COMMENTARIES

Balancing the Fourth Amendment scales: The bad-faith "exception" to exclusionary rule limitations. George C. Thomas III, and Barry S. Pollack, 45 Hastings L.J. 21 (1993).

Criminalization of employer fraud against alien employees? A national priority. Roshani M. Gunewardene, 25 New Eng.L.Rev. 795 (1991).

Decertification of police: An alternative to traditional remedies for police misconduct. Roger Goldman and Steven Puro, 15 Hast. Const.L.Q. 51 (1987).

NOTES OF DECISIONS ②

Bodily injury   45
Burden of proof   26a
Contraband   39
Cross-examination   29a
Deprivation of rights Arrest   10
Discipline of attorneys   40
Double jeopardy   24a
Elements of offense   6a
Evidentiary hearing   23a
Harmless or prejudicial error   44
Official witnesses   42
Pre-trial suspension   41
Res judicata   43
Selective prosecution   5a
State criminal laws   37a

1. Constitutionality

Amendments to criminal statutes prohibiting conspiracies to deprive another person of his civil rights and proscribing actual deprivation of civil rights of another person, to set punishment in instances in which "death results," did not have effect of creating new "death resulting" crimes having similar elements, but were intended to add "death resulting" as factor that would justify enhanced sentences; victim's death was not element of either offense, but simply aggravating circumstance, which gave district court authority to impose harsher punishment. Catala Fonfrias v. U.S., C.A.1 (Puerto Rico) 1991, 951 F.2d 423, certiorari denied 113 S.Ct. 105, 506 U.S. 834, 121 L.Ed.2d 64.

This section making it a crime to, under color of law, subject a person to the deprivation of any federal right, privilege or immunity on account of said person's color or race is not unconstitutionally vague in further providing "* * * if death results shall be subject to imprisonment for any term of years or for life," notwithstanding defendant's argument that the law does not provide any means to follow the causal connections between the death and the acts of violating civil rights. U. S. v. Hayes, C.A.5 (Tex.) 1979, 589 F.2d 811, rehearing denied 591 F.2d 1343, certiorari denied 100 S.Ct. 93, 444 U.S. 847, 62 L.Ed.2d 60.

This section prohibiting depriving persons of constitutional rights under color of law is not unconstitutionally vague. U. S. v. Shafer, D.C.Ohio 1974, 384 F.Supp. 483.

2. Construction with other laws

United States is no part of class for whose special benefit was enacted section 241 of this title providing penalty for conspiracy against rights of citizens or this section providing penalty for deprivation of rights under color of law, and neither this section nor section 241 of this title creates federal right in favor of government, nor is other statutory authority to be implied. U.S. v. City of Philadelphia, C.A.3 (Pa.) 1980, 644 F.2d 187.

This section and section 241 of this title proscribing conspiracy against rights of citizens and deprivation of rights under color of law provided no basis for civil suit under federal Civil Rights Act, section 1983 of Title 42. Aldabe v. Aldabe, C.A.9 (Cal.) 1980, 616 F.2d 1089.

Section 241 of this title proscribing conspiracies against the rights of citizens and this section proscribing deprivation of rights under color of law are concerned only with deprivations of rights guaranteed by federal law or the Constitution. U.S. v. O'Dell, C.A.6 (Tenn.) 1972, 462 F.2d 224.

This chapter providing for punishment by fine or imprisonment for deprivation of certain federal rights, privilege or immunities have no application to a civil suit under the Federal Civil Rights Act, section 1981 et seq. of Title 42. Shaffer v. Jennings, D.C.Pa.1970, 317 F.Supp. 446.

4. Generally

Section 241 of this title providing penalty for conspiracy against rights of citizens and this section providing penalties for deprivation of rights under color of law were designed to prevent violations of all rights under U.S.C.A. Const. Amend. 14, including both due process and equal protection. U.S. v. City of Philadelphia, C.A.3 (Pa.) 1980, 644 F.2d 187.

This section which imposes criminal sanctions on "whoever, under color of any law, statute, ordinance, regulation, or custom," deprives any "inhabitant" of his or her civil rights applies to action of

② **Note cases. All of these cases were decided after main volume was published.**

FIGURE 6-6
(continued)

FIGURE 6-6
(continued)

federal officer taken under color of federal law. U. S. v. Otherson, C.A.9 (Cal.) 1980, 637 F.2d 1276, certiorari denied 102 S.Ct. 149, 454 U.S. 840, 70 L.Ed.2d 123.

Once a due process right has been defined and made specific by court decisions, the right is encompassed by this section making it a crime to, under color of law, subject a person to the deprivation of any federal right, privilege or immunity on account of said person's color or race. U. S. v. Hayes, C.A.5 (Tex.) 1979, 589 F.2d 811, rehearing denied 591 F.2d

1343, certiorari denied 100 S.Ct. 93, 444 U.S. 847, 62 L.Ed.2d 60.

Proof that defendant actually knew that it was a constitutional right that he was violating or was conspiring against is not essential to conviction of violation of this section and section 241 of this title. U.S. v. O'Dell, C.A.6 (Tenn.) 1972, 462 F.2d 224.

This section relating to deprivation of rights under color of law does not create a private right of action, but rather is a criminal provision

Reprinted with permission of Thomson/West

Differences exist from state to state regarding the names of the codes. In some states individual codes are assigned separate names and are cited by those names; for example, California Penal Code §187. On the other hand, some states follow the federal pattern and refer to the codes only by the state name and section number. Citation manuals such as the *The Bluebook* explain how state codes are cited. Also, like the United States Codes, state codes are published in both annotated and unannotated form.

State codes are kept up-to-date by the use of pocket part supplements. In addition to publications that contain the entire state code, many publishers produce books containing selected titles from the total code, for example, the state's penal code. These are particularly useful to lawyers or paralegals who specialize in an area of law and want easy access to frequently needed codes. However, these are usually not annotated and not supplemented. Instead, each year a new volume is published and the old volume is discarded.

6-6 LOCAL ORDINANCES

The right to make laws belongs not only to federal and state governments but also to local governing bodies. These municipal or county ordinances, which may be organized into municipal or county codes, are not as widely published as state and federal codes. Generally, they can be located in the local county law library or they may be available in the local public libraries. Many local ordinances are now online.

6-7 ADMINISTRATIVE REGULATIONS

Much of the work of the federal government is done through the creation of boards or agencies, known as *administrative agencies*. These agencies are empowered by Congress to make rules or regulations to carry out their functions. As administrative rules and regulations are adopted, they are printed in the *Federal Register*. The *Federal Register* is a daily government publication (except for weekends and holidays) that keeps the public informed of actions taken by administrative agencies. Included in the publication are the following:

1. enacted or amended rules or regulations
2. proposed rules

3. notices of administrative hearings

4. Presidential proclamations

Like the *Statutes at Large,* the *Federal Register* is a chronological organization of rules and notices and therefore difficult to use. In order to allow easier access to administrative rules, like the statutes, the administrative rules or regulations are topically organized in the *Code of Federal Regulations* (abbreviated C.F.R.). This code is organized in a manner similar to the United States Codes. There are fifty titles, whose topics closely parallel the topics of the fifty titles of the United States Codes. See Table 6-1 for a comparison of the title topics.

A major difference between the *Code of Federal Regulations* and the *United States Code* is the way in which the laws are updated. The *United States Code* is updated with pocket part supplements. The *Code of Federal Regulations* is not. Checking the current state of administrative regulations is a cumbersome process. You must use a separate publication titled "LSA-List of CFR Sections Affected." This is a monthly update of federal regulations that tells you if any section of the *Code of Federal Regulations* has been changed. The LSA only tells you *if* the section has been changed. It refers you to the *Federal Register* where you can see *what* the change is.

Because states have administrative agencies, administrative rules and regulations are also found at the state level.

The *Federal Register,* the *Code of Federal Regulations,* and the "List of Sections Affected" can be accessed online through the Web site for the Government Printing Office:

Federal Register	http://www.gpoaccess.gov/fr/index.html
C.F.R.	http://www.gpoaccess.gov/cfr/index.html
LSA	http://www.gpoaccess.gov/lsa/index.html

6-8 COURT RULES

Congress gave the courts the right to make rules for practice within the courts. These are known as court rules or **rules of court.** The federal court adopted several rules for practice in the federal courts, including the following.

rules of court.
Procedural rules adopted by all courts regulating practice in the court.

Federal Rules of Civil Procedure

Federal Rules of Bankruptcy Practice

Federal Rules of Evidence

Federal Rules for Appellate Procedure

Federal Rules of Criminal Procedure

The rules of court are published with the codes. In addition to the rules of court that apply in all federal courts, each court is allowed to adopt its own **local rules of court.**

local rules of court.
Procedural rules adopted by an individual court for practice in that specific court.

State courts also have state rules of court as well as local rules of court for individual courts. You will probably find state rules of court with your state codes. A local law library should have copies of the local rules of court. These are often kept at the reference desk.

The Federal Rules can be accessed online through the Web site for the United States Courts at http://www.uscourts.gov/rules/newrules4.html.

6-9 UNIFORM LAWS AND MODEL CODES

Because each state makes its own laws, a number of differences exist in the law from state to state. In order to promote more uniformity among the states, representatives from the states have drafted proposed laws known as *uniform laws* and *model codes*. The most noted uniform law is the Uniform Commercial Code, a code that regulates contracts for the sale of goods. There are over 175 proposed uniform laws. A uniform law or model code, however, is *not* law in any state unless it has been enacted by the state's legislature. The **uniform laws** and **model codes** are published in an annotated form by West. These books closely resemble other code books. The case annotations to uniform laws come from all jurisdictions.

When researching statutory law, you must refer to your state's code and not the uniform law or model code. If your state has enacted a uniform law or model code, you can check the annotations in the uniform laws to find case law that controls your factual situation. Remember, however, if you find a case and it does not come from your state, it is only persuasive authority.

uniform laws. Similar laws that are enacted by the legislatures of different states (i.e., Uniform Commercial Code); intended to create uniformity in the law.

model codes. A collection of sample laws; created for the states to adopt in whole or in part; helps to create uniformity in law.

6-10 FINDING CONSTITUTIONAL PROVISIONS, STATUTORY LAW, ADMINISTRATIVE REGULATIONS, AND RULES OF COURT

Finding the Law

Locating a constitutional provision, code section, or rule of court when you have the citation is an easy task. (Refer to Citation Matters at the beginning of the chapter.) The outside binding of each volume of all of these published materials identifies the laws found within the volume.

The more difficult research problem is locating the *proper* law when you have a factual situation or problem and are looking for an answer to the problem. For example, consider the "Interoffice Memorandum" at the beginning of this chapter. Suppose you are asked to locate any code sections that might provide a basis for federal criminal charges against Rambeaux. In such a case, you must first identify the controlling law. A number of different methods can be used to do this. Probably the most common way is to use the index at the end of the code. The *United States Code*, the *United States Code Annotated*, and the *United States Code Service* all contain topical indexes that refer the reader to code sections that deal with the topic. The key here is to properly identify the topics and vocabulary used in the index. A legal dictionary and thesaurus can help. See Figure 6-7 for an example of an index. In this case, the topic "civil rights" was checked to locate statutes relating to the Rambeaux case.

⇨ **A Point to Remember**   Indexes are prepared by the publishers of the works and differ from edition to edition. If you are not successful in one index, check another.

In addition to topical indexes, the various editions of the code contain popular name tables. When laws are passed, many of them have popular names, such as "Civil Rights Act of 1968." By checking this name in the table of popular names, you learn the proper citation and are able to find the law. (See Figure 6-8.) In addition to indexes, statutory law is located using secondary sources. These are discussed in Chapters 8 and 9.

CIVIL RIGHTS—Continued

Contempt—Continued

Demand for jury trial, criminal contempt proceedings, 42 § 2000h

Double jeopardy, specific crimes and criminal contempt, 42 § 2000h–1

Exceptions, jury trial in criminal contempt proceedings, 42 § 2000h

Intent, criminal contempt, 42 § 2000h

Jury trial, 42 § 1995

Penalties, criminal contempt proceedings, 42 § 2000h

Refusal by officer of election to permit qualified persons to vote, 42 § 1971

Correctional facilities, State facilities, etc. Institutionalized persons, generally, post, this heading

Counselors. Attorneys and counselors, generally, ante, this heading

Court orders, obstruction, 18 § 1509

Court powers, without jury, in civil contempt proceedings unaffected, 42 § 2000h

Courts of Appeals, this index

Crimes and offenses,

    Conspiracy, 18 § 241; 42 § 1985

    Definitions, 18 § 248

    Deprivation of rights under color of law, 18 § 242

    Discrimination against person wearing uniform of Armed Forces, 18 § 244

    Exclusion of jurors on account of race or color, 18 § 243

    Federally protected activities, intimidation or interference with, 18 § 245

    Freedom of access to clinic entrances, reproductive health services, 18 § 248

        Congressional purpose, 18 § 248 note

    Precautionary measures, failure to take, 42 § 1986

    Severability, freedom of access to clinic entrances, reproductive health services, 18 § 248 note

    Speedy trial of offenders, 42 § 1992

Criminal contempt. Contempt, generally, ante, this heading

Criminal practice, conformity with, jury trial in criminal contempt proceedings, 42 § 2000h

Damages, compensatory and punitive, intentional employment discrimination, standard of proof, exclusions, limitations, etc., 42 § 1981a

Dangerous weapon,

    Deprivation of rights under color of law, penalties, 18 § 242

    Intimidation, interference with federally protected activities, penalties, 18 § 351

    Obstruction of free exercise of religious beliefs, penalties, 18 § 247

De jure or de facto segregation, federally assisted education programs, guidelines, 42 § 2000d–6

Defense housing or public works, acquisition of property for not to affect, 42 § 1547

Defense in contempt cases for violations, assignment of counsel, witnesses, etc., 42 § 1971

Definitions, 42 § 1971

Demand for jury trial, criminal contempt proceedings, 42 § 2000h

Deprivation,

    Civil action for, 42 § 1983

    <u>Color of law, under, 18 § 242</u>

Deputy Attorney General, certification, prosecution by U.S. of offenses concerning interference, etc., with federally protected activities, 18 § 245

Desegregation,

    Public education, post, this heading,

    Public facilities, post, this heading

Discrimination,

    Against language minorities, voting rights, 42 § 1973b

    On account of race, color, etc.,

    Highways, prohibition of discrimination on basis of sex in federally assisted programs, etc., 23 § 324

    Participation in federally protected activities, willful intimidation, etc., with, penalties, 18 § 245

Discriminatory practice, defined, intentional discrimination in employment, damages 42 § 1981a

District courts,

    Action concerning voting rights, 42 § 1971

    Appointment of voting referees, 42 § 1971

    Equal employment opportunity, post, this heading

    Institutionalized persons, civil action for equitable relief, 42 § 1997a

    Jurisdiction, 28 § 1343

    Twenty-sixth amendment, enforcement, 42 § 1973bb

Domestic Volunteer Services, nondiscrimination provisions, 42 § 5057

Double jeopardy, specific crimes and criminal contempts, 42 § 2000h–1

Education,

    Desegregation. Public education, generally, post, this heading

    General education provisions, programs, applicability of, 20 § 1221

    National policy with respect to equal educational opportunity, 20 § 1221–1

Elective franchise, jurisdiction of district court, 28 § 1343

Equal educational opportunities for students.

    Students, generally, this index

⟵ **18 U.S.C. § 242 contains the terms "under color of law" and "deprivation of civil rights."**

FIGURE 6-7   Index to Code

Civil Liberties Act Amendments of 1992

Pub. L. 102–371, Sept. 27, 1992, 106 Stat. 1167

Civil Obedience Act of 1968

Pub. L. 90–284, title X, Apr. 11, 1968, 82 Stat. 90 (Title 18, §§ 231–233)

Civil Relief Act (Soldiers and Sailors)

See Soldiers' and Sailors' Civil Relief Acts of 1918 and 1940

Civil Rights Acts

See Title 42, §§ 1971 et seq., 1981 et seq.

Apr. 9, 1866, ch. 31, 14 Stat. 27

May 31, 1870, ch. 114, 16 Stat. 140

Feb. 28, 1871, ch. 99, 16 Stat. 433

Apr. 20, 1871, ch. 22, 17 Stat. 13

Mar. 1, 1875, ch. 114, §§ 3–5, 18 Stat. 336, 337

Civil Rights Act of 1957

Pub. L. 85–315, Sept. 9, 1957, 71 Stat. 634 (Title 28, §§ 1343, 1861; Title 42, §§ 1971, 1971 note, 1975–1975e, 1995)

Pub. L. 86–383, title IV, § 401, Sept. 28, 1959, 73 Stat. 724

Pub. L. 86–449, May 6, 1960, titles IV, VI, 74 Stat. 89, 90

Pub. L. 87–264, title IV, Sept. 21, 1961, 75 Stat. 559

Pub. L. 88–152, § 2, Oct. 17, 1963, 77 Stat. 271

Pub. L. 88–352, title V, July 2, 1964, 78 Stat. 249

Pub. L. 90–198, § 1, Dec. 14, 1967, 81 Stat. 582

Pub. L. 91–521, Nov. 25, 1970, 84 Stat. 1356

Pub. L. 92–64, Aug. 4, 1971, 85 Stat. 166

Pub. L. 92–496, Oct. 14, 1972, 86 Stat. 913

Pub. L. 94–292, § 2, May 27, 1976, 90 Stat. 524

Pub. L. 95–132, § 2, Oct. 13, 1977, 91 Stat. 1157

Pub. L. 95–444, §§ 2–7, Oct. 10, 1978, 92 Stat. 1067, 1068

Pub. L. 96–81, §§ 2, 3, Oct. 6, 1979, 93 Stat. 642

Pub. L. 96–447, § 2, Oct. 13, 1980, 94 Stat. 1894

Civil Rights Act of 1960

Pub. L. 86–449, May 6, 1960, 74 Stat. 86 (Title 18, §§ 837, 1074, 1509; Title 20, §§ 241, 640; Title 42, §§ 1971, 1974–1974e, 1975d)

Civil Rights Act of 1964

Pub. L. 88–352, July 2, 1964, 78 Stat. 241 (Title 28, § 1447; Title 42, §§ 1971, 1975a–1975d, 2000a et seq.)

Pub. L. 92–261, §§ 2–8, 10, 11, 13, Mar. 24, 1972, 86 Stat. 103–113

Pub. L. 92–318, title IX, § 906(a), June 23, 1972, 86 Stat. 375

Pub. L. 93–608, § 3(1), Jan. 2, 1975, 88 Stat. 1972

Pub. L. 94–273, § 3(24), Apr. 21, 1976, 90 Stat. 377

Pub. L. 95–251, § 2(a)(11), Mar. 27, 1978, 92 Stat. 183

Pub. L. 95–555, § 1, Oct. 31, 1978, 92 Stat. 2076

Pub. L. 95–598, title III, § 330, Nov. 6, 1978, 92 Stat. 2679

Pub. L. 95–624, § 5, Nov. 9, 1978, 92 Stat. 3462

Pub. L. 96–191, § 8(g), Feb. 15, 1980, 94 Stat. 34

Pub. L. 100–259, § 6, Mar. 22, 1988, 102 Stat. 31

Pub. L. 102–166, title I, §§ 104, 105(a), 106–108, 109(a), (b)(1), 110(a), 111, 112, 113(b), 114, Nov. 21, 1991, 105 Stat. 1074–1079

Pub. L. 102–411, § 2, Oct. 14, 1992, 106 Stat. 2102

Pub. L. 103–382, title III, § 391(q), Oct. 20, 1994, 108 Stat. 4024

Civil Rights Act of 1968 ①

Pub. L. 90–284, Apr. 11, 1968, 82 Stat. 73–92 (Title 18, §§ 231–233, 241, 242, 245, 1153, 2101, 2102; Title 25, § 1301 et seq.; Title 28, § 1360 note; Title 42, §§ 1973j, 3533, 3535, 3601 et seq.)

Pub. L. 93–265, Apr. 12, 1974, 88 Stat. 84

Pub. L. 93–383, title VIII, § 808(b), Aug. 22, 1974, 88 Stat. 729

Pub. L. 100–430, §§ 4, 5, 6(a), (b)(1), (2), (c)–(e), 7–10, 15, Sept. 13, 1988, 102 Stat. 1619–1636

Pub. L. 101–511, title VIII, § 8077(b), (c), Nov. 5, 1990, 104 Stat. 1892

Civil Rights Act of 1991

Pub. L. 102–166, Nov. 21, 1991, 105 Stat. 1071

Pub. L. 102–392, title III, § 316, Oct. 6, 1992, 106 Stat. 1724

Pub. L. 103–50, § 1204(a), July 2, 1993, 107 Stat. 268

Pub. L. 103–283, title III, § 312(f)(1)–(3), July 22, 1994, 108 Stat. 1446

Civil Rights Attorney's Fees Awards Act of 1976

Pub. L. 94–559, Oct. 19, 1976, 90 Stat. 2641 (Title 42, §§ 1981 note, 1988)

Civil Rights Commission Act of 1978

Pub. L. 95–444, Oct. 10, 1978, 92 Stat. 1067 (Title 42, §§ 1975 note, 1975b–1975e)

Civil Rights Commission Act of 1983

Pub. L. 98–183, Nov. 30, 1983, 97 Stat. 1301 (title 42, § 1975 et seq.)

Pub. L. 101–180, § 2, Nov. 28, 1989, 103 Stat. 1325

Pub. L. 102–167, §§ 2–5, Nov. 26, 1991, 105 Stat. 1101

Pub. L. 102–400, § 2, Oct. 7, 1992, 106 Stat. 1955

Pub. L. 103–419, § 2, Oct. 25, 1994, 108 Stat. 4338

Civil Rights Commission Amendments Act of 1994

Pub. L. 103–419, Oct. 25, 1994, 108 Stat. 4338

① **18 U.S.C. § 242 is popularly called "Civil Rights Act of 1968." If you know that, you check the popular name and it refers you to 18 U.S.C. § 242.**

FIGURE 6-8
Popular Name Index

Civil Rights Commission Authorization Act of 1976	Civil Rights Commission Authorization Act of 1979
Pub. L. 94–292, May 27, 1976, 90 Stat. 524	Pub. L. 96–81, Oct. 6, 1979, 93 Stat. 642
Civil Rights Commission Authorization Act of 1977	
Pub. L. 95–132, Oct. 13, 1977, 91 Stat. 1157	

FIGURE 6-8
(continued)

After locating the code section in the main volume, remember to check any pocket part or bound supplement. This tells you if any changes in the law have occurred. It also gives you citations to new cases interpreting the statute.

 A Point to Remember   Before you start researching, try to determine if your factual situation is one that is governed by federal law or by state law. Federal and state laws are published separately.

Searching for code sections on the online services such as LEXIS and Westlaw or even the Internet requires different research techniques, especially if you do not have the exact citation. When you search these sources, the computer searches the codes for words or combinations of words that you specify. There are no indexes. You can generally search either the entire text of the code or the table of contents to the code for selected words or phrases. This is discussed in more detail in Chapter 11.

Finding Administrative Regulations and Rules of Court

Finding a particular topic in the *Code of Federal Regulations* is similar to finding a topic in the U.S. Codes. That is, topics are checked in an index that leads you to appropriate titles and sections. Verifying that the law is current, however, cannot be done as it is with the codes. Unfortunately, the *Code of Federal Regulations* is not regularly supplemented with pocket part supplements. Because the code publications are revised only every four years, some method of updating is essential. This can be done by referring to the "LSA: List of CFR Sections Affected," a monthly publication listing regulations that have changed and telling you where to find the change in the *Federal Register*.

Finding a constitutional provision, code section, administrative regulation, or court rule is only the beginning of your research. These laws must also be analyzed, interpreted, and applied to your factual situation before your research is complete. That process is discussed in the next chapter.

TECHNOLOGY CORNER

The following Internet Web sites may prove useful when working with constitutions, statutes, and administrative regulations.

U.S. Government Printing Office	www.gpoaccess.gov/index.html
Securities and Exchange Commission	www.sec.gov
Food and Drug Administration	www.fda.gov
U.S. Patent and Trademark Office	www.uspto.gov

U.S. Environmental Protection Agency   www.epa.gov

Federal Bureau of Investigation   www.fbi.gov

Note: The U.S. Constitution and the U.S. Codes are found on, or may be linked to, from most law school Web sites. All states now provide access to state codes from one of their government Web pages. Look for the state government page or the senate page for the state in which your research is performed.

This site offers the full U.S. Code, the U.S. Constitution, the Code of Federal Regulations, and the Federal Rules of Evidence:

www.law.cornell.edu

CHAPTER SUMMARY

In addition to case law, primary law is found in constitutions, statutes or codes, administrative regulations, and court rules. All of these sources exist on both the federal and state level. The United States Constitution, which is the supreme law of the land, can be located in numerous sources, including publications of the *United States Code.* In these sources the Constitution is indexed. The Constitution that is published with the annotated codes is also annotated, containing references to cases interpreting the various Constitutional provisions or amendments.

Laws enacted by legislative bodies are known as *statutory laws.* Federal statutory law results from action by the United States Congress. Congress enacts both public laws and private laws. Public laws affect the general population. Private laws affect only named individuals or groups. When federal statutory law is enacted, it is first published in pamphlet form and is known as *slip law.* At the end of each session of Congress, all of the public laws are published in chronological order in *Statutes at Large,* and then topically organized and published as a code known as the *United States Code.* The *United States Code* is also published in annotated form by two private publishers, West, which publishes the *United States Code Annotated,* and LEXIS Law Publishing, which now publishes the *United States Code Service.* In annotated format, the codes contain references to other legal resources, including cases that help with understanding the code. All codes are indexed and kept up-to-date by the use of pocket part supplements. All states have statutory law found in state codes. Many local governments enact statutory law often known as *municipal ordinances* or *codes.*

Federal administrative agencies, created by Congress, often enact rules or regulations to carry out their functions. They are authorized by Congress to make these rules. Administrative rules or regulations are first published in the *Federal Register,* a monthly publication of the U.S. Government. The regulations are topically organized and published in the *Code of Federal Regulations.* Courts are empowered by Congress to make rules for practice within the courts. These are known as *rules of court* and are published with the United States Codes. States also have administrative regulations and rules of court.

Finding sections of the Constitution, codes, administrative regulations, or court rules requires that you know the citation. The citation can be found by analyzing your factual situation and identifying topics and key words. Those terms are then checked in a general index, which gives you the citation you need to find the law.

BOX 6-2

RESEARCH CHECKLIST: FINDING THE CODES

√ Analyze factual situation and identify key words or terms.

√ Consider synonyms and/or related terms for key words.

√ Check index to code for words or terms.

√ If unsuccessful, check index to alternate publication of code.

√ Read code section.

√ Check pocket part or bound supplement.

BOX 6-3

FEDERAL STATUTORY RESEARCH MATERIAL

- SLIP LAWS: publication of single statute in pamphlet form
- STATUTES AT LARGE: cumulative chronological publication of laws enacted by Congress during a congressional session
- UNITED STATES CODE: topical organization of public statutory law
- UNITED STATES CODE ANNOTATED: topical organization of public statutory law with references to related legal materials
- UNITED STATES CODE SERVICE: topical organization of public statutory law with references to related legal materials

---

BOX 6-4

ADMINISTRATIVE REGULATIONS—RESEARCH MATERIAL

- CODE OF FEDERAL REGULATIONS: topical organization of federal administrative regulations
- FEDERAL REGISTER: monthly publication of all changes and proposed changes to administrative regulations
- LSA—LIST OF SECTIONS AFFECTED: monthly publication containing list of all administrative regulations that have changed

---

TERMS TO REMEMBER

Bill of Rights	legislative intent
index	pocket part supplement
annotated	repeal
statutory law	amend
legislative history	session laws
public laws	rules of court

private laws   local rules of court
slip law   uniform laws
code   model codes
positive law

QUESTIONS FOR REVIEW

1. What are the three parts of the U.S. Constitution?
2. Where will you find publications of the U.S. Constitution?
3. Describe the steps in the enactment of statutory law.
4. What do the following abbreviations mean?
   a. H.R. 346
   b. S. 123
   c. Public Law 104-398
5. What is a slip law?
6. What is contained in the *Statutes at Large?*
7. What are the similarities and differences among the *United States Code,* the *United States Code Annotated* and the *United States Code Service?*
8. Explain the concept of positive law.
9. What is the importance of a pocket part supplement?
10. Describe the *Federal Register,* the *Code of Federal Regulations,* and "LSA—List of Sections Affected."
11. What are court rules?
12. How do you find a code section if you do not have the citation?

CAN YOU FIGURE IT OUT?

1. Refer to Figure 6-2 (annotated Constitution). Does the preamble to the Constitution give powers to the federal government? Give the source of your answer.
2. Refer to Figure 6-3.
   a. What is the subject matter of Private Law 103–6?
   b. Was this act first introduced in the House of Representatives or the Senate? How do you know?
3. Refer to Figure 6-4.
   a. Give the *Statutes at Large* citation for Public Law 103-322.
   b. Give the citation for the code sections affected by Public Law 103-322.
4. Refer to Figure 6-5A.
   a. What is the number of the Public Law from the 103rd Congress that amended 18 U.S.C. §242?
   b. How did Public Law 103-322 §60006(b) amend this law?
   c. What is the year of this amendment?
   d. What is the code section for a civil lawsuit based on a deprivation of rights?
5. Refer to Figure 6-5B.
   a. Cite one case that explains the purpose of 18 U.S.C.A. § 242.
   b. Cite one case that explains the term "color of law."

6. Refer to Figure 6-5C. Give a citation to a 1998 case that discusses 18 U.S.C.S. § 242.

7. Refer to Figure 6-7.
   a. What is the main topic indexed in this figure?
   b. Look at the subtopic "Desegregation." Under this, it states, "Public education, post, this heading." What does this mean?
   c. Look under the subtopic "Counselors." Here it states, "Attorneys and counselors, generally, ante, this heading." What does this mean?
   d. Look at the subtopic "Courts of Appeals." Here it says, "this index." What does this mean?
   e. What code section deals with obstruction of court orders?

8. Refer to Figure 6-8. Give the Public Law number and *Statutes at Large* citation for the Civil Rights Attorneys Fee Awards Act of 1976.

RESEARCH ASSIGNMENTS AND ACTIVITIES

1. Find the following sections of the law. Summarize each in your own words.
   a. 18 U.S.C. § 6002
   b. 2 U.S.C. § 192
   c. 11 U.S.C. § 541
   d. 11 U.S.C. § 541 (a)(2)
   e. 11 U.S.C. § 541 (b)(3)

2. Using the U.S. Codes, answer the following questions and cite the source of your answer.
   a. Review the Rambeaux case. If the victims want to sue for civil damages in federal court, what code section provides authority?
   b. Can a court award costs and attorney fees to successful litigants in a copyright infringement case?
   c. Can one place an advertisement on the U.S. flag in Washington D.C.?
   d. Can a state impose income tax on retirement income of an individual not a resident or domicile of that state?
   e. Which governmental entity or entities have the right to regulate the importation of honeybees into the United States? Why is it regulated? What is the punishment for unlawful importation?
   f. When is failure to pay child support a federal crime?
   g. Using the Popular Name table, find the Home Health Care and Alzheimer Disease Amendment of 1990. Where is this found in the U.S. Code? Is this a public law or a private law? How do you know?

3. Using an annotated U.S. Code answer the following.
   a. What code section makes it a crime for anyone to desecrate the flag? How has the Supreme Court considered this statute? Give the name and citation of a Supreme Court case or cases.
   b. What is the punishment for counterfeiting? Review annotations in the U.S.C.S. and answer the following questions, providing full case citations using *THE BLUEBOOK*.
      1. Can states also have counterfeiting laws?
      2. Is it counterfeiting to insert a black and white photocopy of a $1 bill into a coin change machine?

4. Using the United States Constitution, answer the following questions.
   a. What does U.S. Const. art. IV, § 1 provide?
   b. What does U.S. Const. art. 1, § 2, cl.2 provide?
   c. What does U.S. Const. amend. XXV provide?
   d. How often must Congress assemble and when does the meeting begin? Give the authority for your answer.
   e. Who has the power of impeachment? Give the authority for your answer.
5. Use the Rules of Court and the *Code of Federal Regulations* to answer the following.
   a. Summarize the following.
      1. Fed. R. Civ. Proc. 56
      2. Fed. R Crim. Proc. 6
      3. 27 C.F.R. § 555.180
   b. Which federal rule sets out the requirement for the use of interrogatories in civil cases?
   c. Can a deposition be used in a criminal case in federal court? Cite your authority.

CASE PROJECT

Research federal and/or state codes for your Appendix A hypothetical case. List any relevant code sections and give a short summary of any code sections you find. List all terms that you checked in the index to the codes.

STATUTORY AND CONSTITUTIONAL ANALYSIS

CHAPTER OUTLINE

CHAPTER OBJECTIVES

When you complete this chapter you should be able to

- Explain why it is helpful to outline statutory language.
- Discuss why it is helpful to review case law that interprets code provisions.
- Explain the importance of legislative history.
- List the four steps used in the IRAC approach.
- Discuss how to determine whether the U.S. Constitution or a state constitution applies to a factual situation arising under state law.

CITATION MATTERS

CAPITALIZATION

THE BLUEBOOK — RULE 8

In titles and headings, capitalize the first word, the word following a colon, and all other words except articles, prepositions of four or fewer letters, and conjunctions of four or fewer letters. Capitalize nouns referring to groups or people only when they identify specific, groups, persons, government offices, or government bodies or groups:

the President
Congress
the Agency
the FBI

Capitalize *act* only when referring to a specific act:

Labor Management Relations Act
the Act

Capitalize *circuit* only when used with the circuit number:

the Ninth Circuit

Capitalize *code* only when referring to the *specific* code:

the 1956 and 1962 Codes

Capitalize *constitution* only when naming a constitution in full and when referring to the U.S. Constitution. Always capitalize components of the United States Constitution when using them in textual sentences:

Fourteenth Amendment
Supremacy Clause
Article I, Section 8, Clause 17 of the Constitution

However, this is the proper capitalization in a *citation:*

U.S. CONST. art I, & § 8, cl. 17

Capitalize *judge* only when using the name of a specific justice or judge, or when referring to a United States Supreme Court Justice:

Judge Murphy
Justice Marshall
the Justice (used as a reference to a United States Supreme Court Justice)

INTEROFFICE MEMORANDUM

TO: Research Associate

FROM: Supervising Attorney

RE: Rambeaux

Our client, Rambeaux, has asked us to explain his position regarding criminal and civil liability. The applicable code sections are 18 U.S.C. § 242 and 42 U.S.C. § 1983. Copies of those sections are attached to this memo. Review the facts in this case and write a brief memo explaining how these sections apply to Rambeaux.

---

18 U.S.C. § 242

Whoever, under color of any law, statute, ordinance, regulation, or custom, willfully subjects any person in any State, Territory, Commonwealth, Possession, or District to the deprivation of any rights, privileges, or immunities secured or protected by the Constitution or laws of the United States, or to different punishments, pains, or penalties, on account of such person being an alien, or by reason of his color, or race, than are prescribed for the punishment of citizens, shall be fined under this title or imprisoned not more than one year, or both; and if bodily injury results from the acts committed in violation of this section or if such acts include the use, attempted use, or threatened use of a dangerous weapon, explosives, or fire, shall be fined under this title or imprisoned not more than ten years, or both; and if death results from the acts committed in violation of this section or if such acts include kidnapping or an attempt to kidnap, aggravated sexual abuse, or an attempt to commit aggravated sexual abuse, or an attempt to kill, shall be fined under this title, or imprisoned for any term of years or for life, or both, or may be sentenced to death.

42 U.S.C. § 1983

Every person who, under color of any statute, ordinance, regulation, custom, or usage, of any State or Territory or the District of Columbia, subjects, or causes to be subjected, any citizen of the United States or other person within the jurisdiction thereof to the deprivation of any rights, privileges, or immunities secured by the Constitution and laws, shall be liable to the party injured in an action at law, suit in equity, or other proper proceeding for redress, except that in any action brought against a judicial officer for an act or omission taken in such officer's judicial capacity, injunctive relief shall not be granted unless a declaratory decree was violated or declaratory relief was unavailable. For the purposes of this section, any Act of Congress applicable exclusively to the District of Columbia shall be considered to be a statute of the District of Columbia.

7-1 INTRODUCTION

Researching statutes, constitutions, and administrative regulations requires more than merely locating code sections, constitutional provisions, or specific regulations, just as researching case law requires more than just finding a case. Researchers must be able to understand and explain how any law applies to a factual situation. This requires legal analysis. A substantial part of legal research and analysis is based on the concept of **stare decisis.** This involves finding case law that contains the same factual dispute as the one you are researching. Your analysis of the situation requires that you compare your factual situation with the facts of the cases you find. If your factual situation and

stare decisis. It stands decided; another term for *precedent.*

issue are the same as that in the cases, and the cases are controlling in your jurisdiction, then the holdings or rules of law found in the cases apply to your case. However, as you read in the previous chapter, not all U.S. law is found in cases. Laws are also found in constitutions, statutes, and administrative rules and regulations. Unlike case law, these sources of law contain general rules that are not stated in reference to a specific factual situation. Because you have no facts to compare, your analysis of these types of laws is somewhat different from situations where case law controls.

Whether you analyze constitutional provisions, statutes, or administrative regulations, the basic approach is similar. Start by analyzing the language of the law to determine its meaning. In determining the meaning of the law, the researcher often goes beyond the words contained in the law. Case law may play a role in interpretation and analysis. If a court has interpreted a law, that interpretation is binding if the case is **mandatory authority.** In some cases, interpreting statutory provisions or administrative regulations requires a determination of the legislative intent behind the enactment of the law. You do this by researching the legislative history of the law. In this chapter you will see how to analyze constitutional provisions, statutes, and administrative regulations.

mandatory authority.
Authority that a court must
follow.

7-2 STATUTORY ANALYSIS

Outline Statutory Language

A starting point in statutory analysis is to develop a clear understanding of what a particular code section means. This is not always easy. Unfortunately, statutory language is often cumbersome and confusing. To be understood, statutes must be carefully read and analyzed. Remember, they are laws that are often written to establish various rights, liabilities, and obligations. In order for that right or obligation to exist, the statute usually sets forth various requirements that must be met. For example, consider the statute set out at the beginning of this chapter. That statute creates criminal liability if certain requirements are met. These are sometimes called **statutory requirements.** In the Rambeaux case, the criminal statute (18 U.S.C. § 242) requires the following before any criminal responsibility exists:

statutory requirements.
Various requirements or
elements of a statute that
must be met before the
statute applies to a
situation.

1. Someone must act under color of law *and*
2. Act willfully *and*
3. Deprive another of rights granted under the Constitution *or* laws of U.S.
4. *Or* subject another to different punishments, pains or penalties, *and* do this because of race *or* color *or* because of being an alien.

This statutory analysis involves breaking a statute down into its elements. To analyze a statute, you must pay close attention to all "connectors" and "qualifiers" such as *shall, and, or, except, unless,* and *provided that.* These tell you if all or only some of the elements or requirements must be met before a statute applies to a set of facts.

Before listing the elements of a statute be sure to identify the issue or question you are researching. The above elements answer the question "When does basic criminal responsibility occur?" If your question is different (for example, "What is Rambeaux's potential punishment?"), your analysis is different. To answer this question you must include the punishment described in the statute.

Breaking down a statute like this does not always specifically answer the researcher's problem. Words or phrases in a statute are sometimes unclear or

ambiguous. Solving these ambiguities or uncertainties is the job of the researcher. This is done in different ways.

Review Case Law That Interprets Code Provisions

One of the most important ways to determine the proper interpretation of a code section is to see if the law, or any part of it, has been interpreted by the courts. If case law explains a statute and that case law is controlling law in the jurisdiction, the rule of *stare decisis* requires that the court's interpretation be followed. Reading the annotations following the statute helps you locate relevant cases. Consider again the Rambeaux case and the criminal liability statute. A number of questions arise depending on the facts of the case. For example, what does the phrase "under color of any law" mean? Does it include a police officer? What if Rambeaux is off duty at the time of the shooting? Is he still acting under color of law? Also, consider the clause "on account of such person being an alien, or by reason of his color, or race." Does this clause require a racial motivation if an action is based on a deprivation of constitutional rights, or does this clause relate only to a situation where an individual is subject to "different punishments, pains, or penalties"? To answer these questions, it is necessary to see how the courts have interpreted the statute. Look at Figure 7-1, a copy of some of the annotations following 18 U.S.C.S. § 242. Looking at the annotations in Figure 7-1 you see that case law provides interpretations. Of course, you cannot rely on reading only the annotation. You must read the entire case.

⇨ **A Point to Remember**   Always check the pocket part or bound supplement. Even if a code section has not been amended, new case decisions may add to the interpretation of the statute.

Even if you think that the words of a statute are clear and that your facts obviously fit the language of the statute, your research should include case law. If courts have applied a particular code section to a factual situation that parallels your factual dispute, this gives added support to your analysis. The rule of *stare decisis* prevents a court from adopting a different interpretation of the law, unless the court overrules its prior decisions.

Review Other Code Sections

Sometimes terms used in a code section are defined in another section of the same code. See the example found in Figure 7-2.

When these defined terms appear in later code sections, the researcher can refer back to earlier sections to determine their meanings.

In addition, many codes provide general rules to aid in the interpretation of the language of the code. For example, the following are two basic rules to help us understand the language of the statute.

1. Statutes are to be read as promoting the common law.
2. Particular or specific provisions control over general statements.

Later in this chapter is a recent United States Court case, *Robinson v. Shell Oil*, in which the Court interpreted the term *employee* in a statute. Read the case and see what rules the Court followed in making its interpretation.

(1984, ED Pa) 595 F Supp 178, aff'd without op (1985, CA3 Pa) 774 F2d 1150 and aff'd without op (1985, CA3 Pa) 774 F2d 1150 and aff'd without op (185, CA3 Pa) 774 F2d 1150.

18 USCS § 242 is penal statute and gives rise to no civil action for damages. Watson v Devlin (1958, DC Mich) 167 F Supp 638, aff'd (1959, CA6 Mich) 268 F2d 211.

Purpose of 18 USCS §§ 241 and 242 is to procure criminal remedies only; sections may not be used as bases for civil actions for damages. Sinchak v Parente (1966, WD Pa) 262 F Supp 79.

18 USCS § 242 does not create private right of action; it is criminal provision for deprivation of civil rights under color of law. Williams v Halperin (1973, SD NY) 360 F Supp 554.

Neither 18 USCS § 241 nor 242 create private rights of action for their violation. Moriani v Hunter (1978, SD NY) 462 F Supp 353.

Statutes providing criminal penalty for violation of constitutional rights do not provide for private right of action. Sauls v Bristol-Myers Co. (1978, SD NY) 462 F Supp 887, 18 BNA FEP Cas 1529, 18 CCH EPD ¶ 8824.

There is no civil cause of action for violation of 18 USCS §§ 241, 242, 371 or 1001. Fiorino v Turner (1979, DC Mass) 476 F Supp 962.

18 USCS §§ 241 and 242 neither authorize any civil suit nor create any civil liability; thus, United States Attorney General was not given implied authority by statutes to maintain law suit which sought to bring about fundamental change in administration of Philadelphia police force based on department's allegedly unconstitutional practices and policies. Untied States v Philadelphia (1979, ED Pa) 482 F Supp 1248, supp op (1979, ED Pa) 482 F Supp 1274, aff'd (1980, CA3 Pa) 644 F2d 187, later proceeding (1984, ED Pa) 595 F Supp 178, aff'd without op (1985, CA 3 Pa) 774 F2d 1150 and aff'd without op (1985, CA3 Pa) 774 F2d 1150 and aff'd without op (1985, CA 3 Pa) 774 F2d 1150.

No private right of action inheres in 18 USCS §§ 241, 242. Pawelek v Paramount Studios Corp. (1983, ND III) 571 F Supp 1082.

There is no private right of action under 18 USCS § 242. Fundiller v Cooper City (1984, SD Fla) 578 F Supp 303, revd on other grounds (1985), CA11 Fla) 777 F2d 1436.

18 USCS §§ 241, 242 do not create civil cause of action. Richcreek v Grecu (1985, SD Ind) 612 F Supp 111, 85-2 USTC ¶ 9520, 56 AFTR 2d 85-5732.

18 USCS §§ 241, 242, 245 relate to deprivation of civil rights, however there is no private right of action under any of these statutes. Dugan v Coughlin (1985, SD NY) 613 F Supp 849.

Neither 18 USCS §§ 241 nor 242 rise to civil action for damages or authorize individual to institute criminal proceedings. Lewis v Green (1986, DC Dist Col) 629 F Supp 546.

Federal fraud defendant has no valid damage claims under 18 USCS § 242 or USCS §§ 1983 and 1985, because (1) § 242 is criminal statute which provides no private cause of action, and (2) §§ 1983 and 1985 address only constitutional deprivations made under state law while alleged actions of Assistant United States Attorney and 2 private attorneys that represented defendant in Federal court matters could only have been taken under color of federal law. Lovelace v Whitney (1988, ND III) 684 F Supp 1438, aff'd without op (1989, CA7 III) 886 F2d 332.

II. ELEMENTS OF CRIME

9. GENERALLY

Provision in predecessor of 18 USCS § 212 that "whoever, under color of any law . . . wilfully subjects . . . any inhabitant of any state . . . to the deprivation of any rights . . . protected by the Constitution and laws of the United States, or to different punishments, pains, or penalties on account of such inhabitant being an alien, or by reason of his color, or race, than are prescribed for the punishment of citizens," applies to any deprivation of constitutional right, not merely to deprivations "on account of such inhabitant being an alien or by reason of his color, or race," latter qualification having reference only to words "different punishments, pains, or penalties," and not to clause "rights . . . protected by the Constitution and laws of the United States." United States v Classic (1941) 313 US 299, 85 L Ed 1368, 61 S Ct 1031, reh den (1941), 314 US 707, 96 L Ed 565, 62 S Ct 51 and (ovrld on other grounds by Monell v Department of Social Services (1978) 436 US 658, 56 L Ed 2d 611, 98 S Ct 2018, 17 BNA FEP Cas 873, 16 CCH EPD ¶ 8345) as stated in Scott v Rosenberg (1983, CA9 Cal) 702 F2d 1263, cert den (1984) 465 US 1078, 79 L Ed 2d 760, 104 S Ct 1439, later proceeding (1984, CA9 Cal) 739 F2d 1464, 39 FR Serv 2d 1295 and later proceeding (1984, CA9 Cal) 746 F2d 1377.

Physical abuse or violence is not necessary element of offense under 18 USCS § 242. United States v Ramey (1964, CA4 W Va) 336 F2d 512, cert den (1965) 379 US 972, 13 L Ed 2d 564, 65 S Ct 649.

Elements of offense described in 18 USCS § 242 are: defendant's acts must have deprived someone of right secured or protected by Constitution or laws of United States; defendant's illegal acts must have been committed under color of law; person deprived of his rights must have been inhabitant of state, territory, or district; and defendant must have acted wilfully. United States v Senak (1973, CA7 Ind) 477 F2d 304, cert den (1973) 414 US 856, 38 L Ed 2d 105, 94 S Ct 157 and appeal after remand (1975, CA7 Ind) 527 F2d 129m cert den (1976) 425 US 907, 47 L Ed 2d 758, 96 S Ct 1500.

In any prosecution under 18 USCS § 242, following elements must be established by government, namely: (1) that defendants' acts must have

FIGURE 7-1

18 U.S.C.S. § 242
Annotations from
Main Volume and 2004
Supplement

18 USCS § 242, n 9

deprived someone of right secured or protected by Constitution or laws of United States; (2) that defendants' illegal acts must have been committed under color of law; (3) that person deprived of his rights must have been inhabitant of state, territory, or district; and (4) that defendants must have acted willfully. United States v Shafer (1974, DC Ohio) 384 F Supp 496.

Elements of offense under 18 USCS § 242 are (1) that action was taken under color of state law, (2) wilfully to deprive rights protected by Constitution and laws of United States, (3) from inhabitant of any state of United States. United States v Fleming (1975, ED Mo) 399 F Supp 77, revd on other grounds (1975, CA8 Mo) 526 F2d 191, cert dismd (1976) 423 US 1082, 47 L Ed 2d 93, 96 S Ct 872.

10. Deprivation of rights protected by Federal Constitution or laws

Predecessor of 18 USCS § 242 making it federal offense wilfully to deprive any person under color of law of any rights, privileges, or immunities secured or protected by Constitution and laws of United States, does not come into play merely because law under which officer purports to act is violated, but is applicable only when some one is deprived of Federal right by such action. Screws v United States (1945) 325 US 91,89 L Ed 1495, 65 S Ct 1031, 162 ALR 1330.

Both 18 USCS § 241, which makes conspiracy to interfere with citizen's free exercise or enjoyment of any right or privilege secured to him by Constitution or laws of United States federal offense, and 18 USCS § 242, which makes it federal offense wilfully to deprive any person under color of law of same rights include, presumably, all of Constitution and laws of United States. United States v Price (1966) 383 US 787, 16 L Ed 2d 267, 86 S Ct 1152 (ovrld on other grounds by Adickesv S. H. Kress & Co. (1970) 398 US 144, 26 L Ed 2d, 142, 90 S Ct 1598) as stated in Gresham Park Community Organization v Howell (1981, CA5 Ga) 652 F2d 1227.

Federal court had jurisdiction where defendant was charged with depriving named person of rights and privileges under Constitution of United States, even though acts of defendants also violated laws of state. Williams v United States (1950, CA5 Fla) 179 F2d 656m aff'd (1951) 341 US 97, 95 Ed 774, 71 S Ct 576.

18 USCS § 242 is concerned only with deprivation of rights guaranteed by federal law or Constitution. United States v O'Dell (1972, CA6 Tenn) 462 F2d 224.

Once due process right has been defined and made specific by court decisions, right is encompassed by 18 USCS § 242. United States v Hayes (1979, CA5 Tex) 589 F2d 811, reh den (1979, CA5 Tex) 591 F2d 1343 and cert den (1979) 444 US 847, 62 L Ed 2d 60, 100 S Ct 93.

Acts done under color of state law do not violate federal law if only local rights are involved, since constitutional right must be violated before federal law is involved. Arkansas use of Temple v Central Surety & Ins. Corp. (1952, DC Ark) 102 F Supp 444.

11. Illegal act committed under color of law, generally

Predecessor to 18 USCS § 242 required actions under color of state law. United States v Powell (1909) 212 US 564, 53 L Ed 653, 29 S Ct 690.

It is immaterial, for purposes of predecessor to 18 USCS § 242, whether acts committed under color of state law are authorized by state law. Guinn v United States (1915) 238 US 347, 59 L Ed 1340, 35 S Ct 926.

Misuse of power, possessed by virtue of state law and made possible only because wrongdoer is clothed with authority of state law, is action taken "under color of" state law, within meaning of predecessor of 18 USCS § 242 making it offense to deprive inhabitant of state of his constitutional rights "under color or" any law. United States v Classic (1941) 313 US 299, 85 L Ed 1368, 61 S Ct 1031, reh den (1941) 314 US 707, 86 L Ed 565, 62 S Ct 51 and (ovrld on other grounds by Monell v Department of Social Services (1978) 436 US 658, 56 L Ed 2d 611, 98 S Ct 2018, 17 BNA FEP Cas 873, 16 CCH EPD ¶ 8345) as stated in Scott v Rosenberg (1983, CA9 Cal) 702 F2d 1263, cert den (1984) 465 US 1078, 79 L Ed 2d 760, 104 S Ct 1439, later proceeding (1984, CA9 Cal) 739 F2d 1464, 39 FR Serv 2d 1295 and later proceeding (1984, Ca9 Cal) 746 F2d 1377.

Question was not whether state law had been violated but whether inhabitant of state had been deprived of federal right by one who acted under color of any law. Screws v United States (1945) 325 US 91, 89 L Ed 1495, 65 S Ct 1031, 162 ALR 1330.

Phrase "under color of any statute, ordinance, regulation, or custom" should be accorded same construction in both 18 USC § 242, which provides for criminal punishment of, and Rev Stat § 1979 (42 USC § 1983), which gives right of action against, person who, "under color of" state law, subjects another to deprivation of any rights, privileges, or immunities secured by Federal Constitution. Monroe v Pape (1961) 365 US 167, 5 L Ed 2d 492, 81 S Ct 473 (ovrld on other grounds by Monell v Department of Social Services (1978) 436 US 658, 56 L Ed 2d 611, 98 S Ct 2018, 17 BNA FEP Cas 873, 16 CCH EPD ¶ 8345) and (ovrld on other grounds by Ingraham v Wright (1977) 430 US 651, 51 L Ed 2d 711, 97 S Ct 1401) as stated in Suess Builders Co v Beaverton (1982) 294 Or 254, 656 P2d 306, appeal after remand (1986) 77 Or App 440, 714 P2d 229, review den (1986) 300 Or 722, 717 P2d 630 and (ovrld on other grounds by Parratt v Taylor (1981) 451 US 527, 68 L Ed 2d 420, 101 S Ct 1908) as stated in Elliott v University of Tennessee (1985, CA6 Tenn) 766 F2d 982,

Note the number of cases that interpret the term *color of law.*

FIGURE 7-1
(continued)

CRIMES   **18 USCS § 242, n 12**

38 BNA FEP Cas 522, 37 CCH EPD¶ 35419, cert gr (1985) 474 US 1004, 88 L Ed 2d 455, 106 S Ct 522 an aff'd in part and revd on other grounds in part (1986) 478 US 788, 92 L Ed 2d 635, 106 S Ct 3220, 41 BNA FEP Cas 177, 40 CCH EPD ¶ 36205 and (ovrld on other grounds by air Assessment in real Estate Assoc. v McNary (1981) 454 US 100, 70 L Ed 2d 271, 102 S Ct 177) as stated in Winicki v Mallard (1986, CA11 Fla) 783 F2d 1567, cert den (1986) 479 US 815, 93 L Ed 2d 27, 107 S Ct 70.

Color of law, as used in 18 USCS § 242, means pretense of law; it may include, but does not necessarily mean, under authority of law. United States v Jones (1953, CA5 Fla) 207 F2d 785.

Under 18 USCS § 242, "color of law" includes misuse of power possessed by virtue of state law and made possible only because wrongdoer is clothed with authority of state law. United States v Ramsey (1964, CA4 W Va) 336 F2d 512, cert den (1965) 379 US 972, 13 L Ed 2d 564, 85 S Ct 649.

Tests for state action under 42 USCS § 1983 and 18 USCS § 242 are identical. Potenza v Schoessling (1976, CA7 Ill) 541 F2d 670, 93 BNA LRRM 2556, 81 CCH LC § 13126.

Requirement of "state action" is essential jurisdictional predicate in prosecution for violation of 18 USCS § 242; test for state action is same under 18 USCS § 242 and 42 USCS § 1983. Robinson v Bergstrom (1978, CA7 Ill) 579 F2d 401 (disapproved on other grounds Polk County v Dobson, 454 US 312, 70 L Ed 2d 509, 102 S Ct 445).

18 USCS § 242 applies to actions taken under color or both state and federal law. United States v Otherson (1980, CA9 Cal) 637 F2d 1276, cert den (1981) 445 US 840, 70 L Ed 2d 123, 102 S Ct 149.

Excessive force can be basis of conviction under 18 USCS § 242. United States v Dean (1983, CA5 La) 722 F2d 92.

Police officer was acting under color of law rather than as jealous husband when he attacked individual who had had affair with his wife, even through he never threatened arrest, where he claimed that he could kill individual because he was officer of law, and summoned another police officer, running him out of town in their squad car, since presence of police and air of official authority pervaded entire assault incident. United States v Tarpley (1991, CA5 Tex) 945 F2d 806, reh den (1991, CA5) 1991 US App LEXIS 27427 and cert den (1992, US) 118 L Ed 2d 562, 112 S Ct 1960.

Officer proceeds under color of state law if proceeding in official capacity, even though acts committed are not within his authority, or are in excess of his authority. Arkansas use of Temple v Central Surety & Ins. Corp. (1952, DC Ark) 102 F Supp 444.

Phase "color of state law," whether used in context of 42 USCS § 1983 or in context of its criminal counterpart, 18 USCS § 242, is synonymous with concept of "state action" under Fourteenth Amendment. Timson v Weiner (1975, SD Ohio) 395 F Supp 1344.

12. —Miscellaneous

Misuse of power, possessed by virtue of state law and made possible only because wrongdoer is clothed with authority of state law, is action taken "under color" of state law, within meaning of predecessor to 18 USCS § 242, making it offense to deprive inhabitant of state of his constitutional rights "under color of" any law. Williams v United States (1951) 341 US 97, 95 L Ed 774, 71 Ct 576.

Every beating by state officer, no matter how wilfully administered, was not deprivation of federal right; beating had to be administered under color of law and with purpose to deprive prisoner of constitutional right. Pullen v United States (1947, CA5 Tex) 164 F2d 756.

Failure of Florida state attorney to procure release of prisoner for whom trial judge had directed verdict of not guilty on charge of murder, following which prisoner had been detained until state could prepare information charging him as accessory after facts, did not subject him to prosecution under 18 USCS § 242, as no legal duty existed under Florida statutes, decisions of its courts, or principle of common law for prosecutor to make application to trial judge for release of prisoner. United States v Hunter (1954, CA5 Fla) 214 F2d 356, cert den (1954) 348 US 888, 99 Ed 698, 75 S Ct 208.

Evidence that defendant railroad police officers, who were charged with violations of 18 USCS § 242, assaulted vagrants found on railroad property while they were on duty and were armed with service revolvers while possessing, by virtue of state law, some powers as city police, was sufficient to support finding that they were acting under color of state law. United States v Hoffman (1974, CA7 Ill) 498 F2d 879.

Civil rights of civilian are violated where state undercover policemen, dressed in civilian clothes and driving unmarked car, kicks and hits civilian in attempt to try to effectuate arrest without first identifying themselves as police officers. United States v McQueeney (1982, CA1) 674 F2d 109.

Sheriff and deputy were guilty of depriving parties seized and beaten by "klansmen" of due process and equal protection under color of law where

11. Illegal act committed under color of law, generally

Government need not prove that police officers who allegedly used excessive force acted for ostensible government purpose rather than for personal reasons, since their acts were committed "under color of law." United States v Reese (1993, CA9 Cal) 2 F3d 870, 93 CDOS 5642, 93 Daily Journal DAR 9617, petition for certiorari filed (Oct 28, 1993) and (among conflicting authorities noted in United States v Lilly (CA1) 1994 US App LEXIS 69).

These annotations are in pocket-part supplement. Note the newer cases.

FIGURE 7-1
(continued)

18 USCS § 242, n 11   CRIMES & CRIMINAL PROCEDURE

12. –Miscellaneous

Off-duty police officer who admitted to beating prisoner in city jail, using his official authority to get prisoner out of jail cell in order to attack him, and threatening to arrest prisoner every time he saw him in future was guilty of violating 18 USCS § 242 under color of state law, even though he was off-duty at time had his motivation was personal. United States v Colbert (1999, CA8 Mo) 172 F3d 594.

Convictions of police officer, drug dealer, and his associate for conspiracy to violate 18 USCS § 241 and violation of 18 USCS §§ 242, 1512 regarding murder of individual who filed complaint against police officer were for conduct "under color of state law," where officer abused his official power to access police station, police car, and police radio to plan, execute, and cover up murder, and his codefenders jointly engaged with him in these prohibited actions. Untied States v Causey (1999, CA5 La) 185 F3d 407.

14. Willfulness; Intent

In determining whether police officers assigned to special drug task force had specific intent to use excessive force in arresting and detaining individuals, it was not necessary to prove that they knew their conduct was unlawful. United States v Reese (1993, CA9 Cal) 2 F3d 870, 93 CDOS 5642, 93 Daily Journal DAR 9617, petition for certiorari filed (Oct 28, 1993) and (among conflicting authorities noted in United States v Lilly (CA1) 1994 US App LEXIS 69).

In order to convict under 18 USCS § 242, government must show that defendant had particular purpose of violating protected right made definite by rule of law recklessly disregarded risk that he would violate such right; government does not need to show that defendant knowingly violated any right. United States v Johnstone (1997, CA3 NJ) 107 F3d 200.

"Willfulness" under USCS § 242 essentially requires that defendant intended to commit unconstitutional act without necessarily intending to do that act for specific purpose of depriving another of constitutional right; in other words, to act "willfully" in § 242 sense, defendant must intend to commit act that results in deprivation of established constitutional right as reasonable person would understand that right. United States v Bradley (1999, CA7 III) 196 F3d 762.

Evidence that defendant, police officer, released defendant's police dog on another suspect at later date was probative of willfulness by suggesting that, at least on one other occasion, defendant used dog in reckless disregard of another's right to be free from excessive force and was admissible under FRE 404(b), and was not unduly prejudicial under FRE 403 merely because it was pointed out that suspect was African-American; defendant's conviction under 18 USCS § 242 was affirmed. United States v Mohr (2003, CA4 Md) 318 F3d 613.

Actions of 400-pound correctional officer in stepping on prison inmate's penis on 3 separate occasions were subjectively wanton and malicious, violating inmate's Eighth Amendment rights and satisfying subjective element of conviction of criminal deprivation of rights under color of law pursuant to 18 USCS § 242, sine there was n need for application of force used, there was no threat reasonably perceived by officer given that inmate was in his cell, and officer made no effort to temper severity of his forceful response. United States v Walsh (1998, WD NY) 27 F Supp 2d 186.

III. RIGHTS AND PRIVILEGES SECURED OR PROTECTED

16. Freedom from unlawful arrest

Criminal liability may be imposed on commanding police officer who failed to prevent use of excessive force by officers under has command, since individuals have constitutional right to protect from assaults by police officers, as has been made clear in civil actions under 42 USCS § 1983, and it is right, not fact that criminal conviction may flow from its willful abrogation, that must be made clear. Untied States v Reese (1993, CA9 Cal) 2 F3d 870, 93 CDOS 5642, 93 Daily Journal DAR 9617, petition for certiorari filed (Oct 28, 1993) and (among conflicting authorities noted in United States v Lilly (CA1) 1994 US App Lexis 69).

17. Freedom from unlawful search and seizure

Police officer's act of shooting into vehicle of person who had run red light constituted "seizure" under Fourth Amendment in violation of 18 USCS § 242, where there was both show of authority and use of force which caused fleeing suspect to stop attempting to escape. United States v Bradley (1999, CA7 III) 196 F3d 762.

21. Miscellaneous

Proposal that Congress never intended 18 USCS § 242 to extend to "newly-created constitutional rights" is belied by fact that Congress has increased penalties for § 242's violation several times since Screws v United States (1945) 325 US 91, 89 Led 1495, 65 S Ct 1031—which originally set forth § 242 process as to whether rights have been made specific for fair-warning purposes—was decided, without contracting § 242's substantive scope. United States v Lanier (1997, US) 137 L Ed 2d 432, 117 S Ct 1219, 97 CDOS 2350, 97 Daily Journal DAR 4168, 10 FLW Fed S 388.

State court judge who sexually assaulted women deprived them of their constitutional right to bodily integrity under Fourteenth Amendment and right to personal security under Fourth Amendment for purposes of 18 USCS § 242. United States v Lanier (1994, CA6 Tenn) 33 F3d 639, 1994 FED App 305P.

FIGURE 7-1
(continued)

Sexual assault of state employees and litigants by state judge may not be prosecuted as violation of constitutional substantive due process right to bodily integrity under 18 USCS § 242, even if limited to acts which shock conscience, since that judicial standard cannot be made element of offense, where legislative history, case law, long established tradition of restraint in extension of criminal statues, and lack of notice to public all points against such expansive reading of ambiguous statute. United States v Lanier (1996, CA6 Tenn) 73 F3d 1380.

V. PERSONS COVERED

26. State or Federal officers

Even if there has never been 42 USCS § 1983 case accusing welfare officials of selling foster children

FIGURE 7-1 (continued)

Reprinted from *United States Code Service.* Copyright © 2005, Matthew Bender & Company, Inc., a member of the LexisNexis Group. All Rights Reserved. Reprinted with permission.

Signification of Certain Words

Words used in this code in the present tense include the future as well as the present; words used in the masculine gender include the feminine and neuter; the singular number includes the plural and the plural the singular; the word "person" includes a corporation as well as a natural person; the word "county" includes "city and county"; and the words "judicial district" include "city and county"; writing includes printing and typewriting; "oath" includes affirmation or declaration; and every mode of oral statement, under oath or affirmation, is embraced by the term "testify," and every written one in the term "depose"; signature or subscription includes mark, when the person cannot write, his or her name or her being written near it by a person who writes his or her own name as a witness; provided, that when a signature is by mark it must, in order that the same may be acknowledged or may serve as the signature to any sworn statement, be witnessed by two persons who must subscribe their own names as witness thereto.

The following words have in this code the signification attached to them in this section, unless otherwise apparent from the context:

1. The word "property" includes both real and personal property;

2. The words "real property" are coextensive with lands, tenements, and hereditaments;

3. The words "personal property" include money, goods, chattels, things in action, and evidences of debt;

4. The word "month" means a calendar month, unless otherwise expressed;

5. The word "will" includes codicil;

6. The word "writ" signifies an order or precept in writing, issued in the name of the people, or of a court or judicial officer; and the word "process" a writ or summons issued in the course of judicial proceedings;

7. The word "state," when applied to the different parts of the United States, includes the District of Columbia and the territories; and the words "United States" may include the district and territories;

8. The word "section" whenever hereinafter employed, refers to a section of this code, unless some other code or statute is expressly mentioned;

9. The word "affinity" when applied to the marriage relation, signifies the connection existing in consequence of marriage, between each of the married persons and the blood relatives of the other;

10. The word "sheriff" shall include "marshal."

Calif. Code Civ. Proc. § 17

FIGURE 7-2 Sample Codes Illustrating Rules for Statutory Interpretation

Construction of Statutes and Instruments; General Rule

In the construction of a statute or instrument, the office of the judge is simply to ascertain and declare what is in terms or in substance contained therein, not to insert what has been omitted, or to omit what has been inserted; and where there are several provisions or particulars, such a construction is, if possible, to be adopted as will give effect to all.

Calif. Code Civ. Proc. § 1858

The Intention of the Legislature or Parties

In the construction of a statute the intention of the Legislature, and in the construction of the instrument the intention of the parties, is to be pursued, if possible; and when a general and [a] particular provision are inconsistent, the latter is paramount to the former. So a particular intent will control a general one that is inconsistent with it.

Calif. Code Civ. Proc. § 1859

FIGURE 7-2
(continued)

CASE 7-1

Robinson v. Shell Oil Company
519 U.S. 337, 117 S. Ct. 843, 136 L. Ed. 2d 808 (1997)

OPINION: JUSTICE THOMAS delivered the opinion of the Court.

Section 704(a) of Title VII of the Civil Rights Act of 1964 makes it unlawful "for an employer to discriminate against any of his employees or applicants for employment" who have either availed themselves of Title VII's protections or assisted others in so doing. 78 Stat. 257, as amended, 42 U.S.C. § 2000e-3(a). We are asked to decide in this case whether the term "employees," as used in § 704(a), includes former employees, such that petitioner may bring suit against his former employer for postemployment actions allegedly taken in retaliation for petitioner's having filed a charge with the Equal Employment Opportunity Commission (EEOC). The United States Court of Appeals for the Fourth Circuit, sitting *en banc*, held that the term "employees" in § 704(a) referred only to current employees and therefore petitioner's claim was not cognizable under Title VII. We granted *certiorari*, 517 U.S. 1154 (1996), and now reverse.

I.
Respondent Shell Oil Co. fired petitioner Charles T. Robinson, Sr., in 1991. Shortly thereafter, petitioner filed a charge with the EEOC, alleging that respondent had discharged him because of his race. While that charge was pending, petitioner applied for a job with another company. That company contacted respondent, as petitioner's former employer, for an employment reference. Petitioner claims that respondent gave him a negative reference in retaliation for his having filed the EEOC charge.

Petitioner subsequently sued under § 704(a), alleging retaliatory discrimination. On respondent's motion, the District Court dismissed the action, adhering to previous Fourth Circuit precedent holding that § 704(a) does not apply to former employees. Petitioner appealed, and a divided panel of the Fourth Circuit reversed the District Court. The Fourth Circuit granted rehearing *en banc*, vacated the panel decision, and thereafter affirmed the District Court's determination that former employees may not bring suit under § 704(a) for retaliation occurring after termination of their employment. 70 F.3d 325 (1995) *(en banc)*.

We granted *certiorari* in order to resolve a conflict among the Circuits on this issue.[1]

II.

A

Our first step in interpreting a statute is to determine whether the language at issue has a plain and unambiguous meaning with regard to the particular dispute in the case. Our inquiry must cease if the statutory language is unambiguous and "the statutory scheme is coherent and consistent." *United States v. Ron Pair Enterprises, Inc.,* 489 U.S. 235, 240 (1989); *see also Connecticut Nat. Bank v. Germain,* 503 U.S. 249, 253–254 (1992).

The plainness or ambiguity of statutory language is determined by reference to the language itself, the specific context in which that language is used, and the broader context of the statute as a whole. *Estate of Cowart v. Nicklos Drilling* Co., 505 U.S. 469, 477 (1992); *McCarthy v. Bronson,* 500 U.S. 136, 139 (1991). In this case, consideration of those factors leads us to conclude that the term "employees," as used in § 704(a), is ambiguous as to whether it excludes former employees.

At first blush, the term "employees" in § 704(a) would seem to refer to those having an existing employment relationship with the employer in question. *Cf. Walters v. Metropolitan Ed. Enterprises, Inc.,* 519 U.S._____ (1997) (slip op., at 5) (interpreting the term "employees" in § 701 (b), 42 U.S.C. § 2000e(b)). This initial impression, however, does not withstand scrutiny in the context of § 704(a). First, there is no temporal qualifier in the statute such as would make plain that § 704(a) protects only persons still employed at the time of the retaliation. That the statute could have expressly included the phrase "former employees" does not aid our inquiry. Congress also could have used the phrase "current employees." But nowhere in Title VII is either phrase used—even where the specific context otherwise makes clear an intent to cover current or former employees.[2] Similarly, that other statues have been more specific in their coverage of "employees" and "former employees," *see, e.g.,* 2 U.S.C. § 1301(4) (1994 ed., Supp. I) (defining "employee" to include "former employee"); 5 U.S.C. § 1212(a)(1) (including "employees, former employees, and applicants for employment" in the operative provision), proves only that Congress can use the unqualified term "employees" to refer only to current employees, not that it did so in this particular statute.

Second, Title VII's definition of "employee" likewise lacks any temporal qualifier and is consistent with either current or past employment. Section 701(f) defines "employee" for purposes of Title VII as "an individual employed by an employer." 42 U.S.C. § 2000e(f). The argument that the term "employed," as used in § 701(f), is commonly used to mean "performing work under an employer-employee relationship," *Black's Law Dictionary* 525 (6th ed. 1990), begs the question by implicitly reading the word "employed" to mean "is employed." But the word "employed" is not so limited in its possible meanings, and could just as easily be read to mean "was employed."

---

[1] The other Courts of Appeals to have considered this issue have held that the term "employees" in § 704(a) does include former employees. *See Charlton v. Paramus Bd. of Educ.,* 25 F.3d 194, 198–200 (CA3 1994), *cert. denied,* 513 U.S. 1022 (1994); *Bailey v. USX Corp.,* 850 F.2d 1506, 1509 (CA11 1988); *O'Brien v. Sky Chefs, Inc.,* 670 F.2d 864, 869 (CA9 1982), overruled on other grounds by *Atonio v. Wards Cove Packing Co.,* 810 F.2d 1477, 1481–1482 (CA9 1987) (*en banc*); *Pantchenko v. C. B. Dolge Co.,* 581 F.2d 1052, 1055 (CA2 1978); *Rutherford v. American Bank of Commerce,* 565 F.2d 1162, 1165 (CA10 1977). The Fourth Circuit indicated that it joined the approach taken by the Seventh Circuit in *Reed v. Shepard,* 939 F.2d 484, 492–493 (CA7 1991). But the Seventh Circuit has since repudiated the Fourth Circuit's view of *Reed. See Veprinsky v. Fluor Daniel, Inc.,* 87 F.3d 881, 886 (CA7 1996).

[2] Our recent decision in *Walters v. Metropolitan Ed. Enterprises, Inc.,* 519 U.S. (1997), held that the term "employees" in §701(b), 42 U.S.C. §2000e(b), referred to those persons with whom an employer has an existing employment relationship. *See* 519 U.S. at (slip op., at 5). But § 701(b) has two significant temporal qualifiers. The provision, which delimits Title VII's coverage, states that the Act applies to any employer "who has fifteen or more employees for each working day in each of twenty or more calendar weeks in the current or preceding calendar year." 42 U.S.C. §2000e(b) [emphasis added]. The emphasized words specify the time frame in which the employment relationship must exist, and thus the specific context of that section did not present the particular ambiguity at issue in the present case.

STATUTORY AND CONSTITUTIONAL ANALYSIS

Third, a number of other provisions in Title VII use the term "employees" to mean something more inclusive or different than "current employees." For example, §§ 706(g)(1) and 717(b) both authorize affirmative remedial action (by a court or EEOC, respectively) "which may include . . . reinstatement or hiring of employees." 42 U.S.C. §§2000e-5(g)(1) and 2000e-16(b). As petitioner notes, because one does not "reinstate" current employees, that language necessarily refers to former employees. Likewise, one may hire individuals to be employees, but one does not typically hire persons who already are employees.

Section 717(b) requires federal departments and agencies to have equal employment opportunity policies and rules, "which shall include a provision that an employee or applicant for employment shall be notified of any final action taken on any complaint of discrimination filed by him thereunder." 42 U.S.C. § 2000e-16(b). If the complaint involves discriminatory discharge, as it often does, the "employee" who must be notified is necessarily a former employee. Similarly, § 717(c) provides that an "employee or applicant for employment, if aggrieved by the final disposition of his complain, . . . may file a civil action. . . . " 42 U.S.C. § 2000e-16(c). Again, given that discriminatory discharge is a forbidden "personnel action affecting employees," *see* § 717(a), 42 U.S.C. § 2000e-16(a), the term "employee" in § 717(c) necessarily includes a former employee. *See Loeffler v. Frank*, 486 U.S. 549 (1988) (involving a discriminatory discharge action successfully brought under § 717 by a former Postal Service employee).[3]

Of course, there are sections of Title VII where, in context, use of the term "employee" refers unambiguously to a current employee, for example those sections

addressing salary or promotions. *See* § 703(h), 42 U.S.C. § 2000e-2(h) (allowing different standards of compensation for "employees who work in different locations"); § 717(b), 42 U.S.C. § 2000e-16(b) (directing federal agencies to establish a plan "to provide a maximum opportunity for employees to advance so as to perform at their highest potential").

But those examples at most demonstrate that the term "employees" may have a plain meaning in the context of a particular section—not that the term has the same meaning in all other sections and in all other contexts. Once it is established that the term "employees" includes former employees in some sections, but not in others, the term standing alone is necessarily ambiguous and each section must be analyzed to determine whether the context gives the term a further meaning that would resolve the issue in dispute.[4]

Respondent argues that the addition of the word "his" before "employees" narrows the scope of the provision. Brief for Respondent 19. That argument is true, so far as it goes, but it does not resolve the question before us—namely, in what time frame must the employment relationship exist. The phrase "his employees" could include "his" former employees, but still exclude persons who have never worked for the particular employer being charged with retaliation.

Nor are we convinced by respondent's argument that Congress' inclusion in § 704(a) of "applicants for employment" as persons distinct from "employees," coupled with its failure to include "former employees," is evidence of congressional intent not to include former employees. The use of the term "applicants" in § 704(a) does not serve to confine, by negative inference, the temporal scope of the term "employees." Respondent's argument rests on the incorrect premise that the term

---

[3]Other sections also seem to use the term "employees" to mean something other than current employees. Section 701(c) defines "employment agency" as "any person regularly undertaking . . . to procure employees for an employer or to procure for employees opportunities to work for an employer . . ." 42 U.S.C. § 2000e(c). This language most naturally is read to mean "prospective employees." Section 701(e) uses identical language when providing that a labor organization affects commerce if it "operates a hiring hall or hiring office which procures employees for an employer. . . ." 42 U.S.C. § 2000e(e).

[4]Petitioner's examples of non-Title VII cases using the term "employee" to refer to a former employee are largely irrelevant, except to the extent they tend to rebut a claim that the term "employee" has some intrinsically plain meaning. *See, e.g., Richardson v. Belcher*, 404 U.S. 78, 81, 83 (1971) (unemployed disabled worker); *Nash v. Florida Industrial Comm'n*, 389 U.S. 235, 239, 19 L. Ed. 2d 438, 88 S. Ct. 362 (1967) (individual who had been fired); *Flemming v. Nestor*, 363 U.S. 603, 611 (1960) (retired worker).

"applicants" is equivalent to the phrase "future employees." But the term "applicants" would seem to cover many persons who will not become employees. Unsuccessful applicants or those who turn down a job offer, for example, would have been applicants, but not future employees. And the term fails to cover certain future employees who may be offered and will accept jobs without having to apply for those jobs. Because the term "applicants" in § 704(a) is not synonymous with the phrase "future employees," there is no basis for engaging in the further (and questionable) negative inference that inclusion of the term "applicants" demonstrates intentional exclusion of former employees.

Finally, the use of the term "individual" in § 704(a), as well as in § 703(a), 42 U.S.C. § 2000e-2(a), provides no meaningful assistance in resolving this case. To be sure, "individual" is a broader term than "employee" and would facially seem to cover a former employee. But it would also encompass a present employee as well as other persons who have never had an employment relationship with the employer at issue. The term "individual," therefore, does not seem designed to capture former employees, as distinct from current employees, and its use provides no insight into whether the term "employees" is limited only to current employees.

B

Finding that the term "employees" in § 704(a) is ambiguous, we are left to resolve that ambiguity. The broader context provided by other sections of the statute provides considerable assistance in this regard. As noted above, several sections of the statute plainly contemplate that former employees will make use of the remedial mechanisms of Title VII. *See supra,* at 4–5. Indeed, § 703(a) expressly includes discriminatory "discharge" as one of the unlawful employment practices against which Title VII is directed. 42 U.S.C. § 2000e-2(a). Insofar as § 704(a) expressly protects employees from retaliation for filing a "charge" under Title VII, and a charge under § 703(a) alleging unlawful discharge would necessarily be brought by a former employee, it is far more consistent to include former employees within the scope of "employees" protected by § 704(a).

In further support of this view, petitioner argues that the word "employees" includes former employees because to hold otherwise would effectively vitiate much of the protection afforded by § 704(a). *See* Brief for Petitioner 20–30. This is also the position taken by EEOC. *See* Brief for United States and EEOC as Amici Curiae 16–25; *see also* 2 EEOC Compliance Manual § 614.7(f). According to EEOC, exclusion of former employees from the protection of § 704(a) would undermine the effectiveness of Title VII by allowing the threat of post-employment retaliation to deter victims of discrimination from complaining to EEOC, and would provide a perverse incentive for employers to fire employees who might bring Title VII claims. Brief for United States and EEOC as Amici Curiae 18–21.

Those arguments carry persuasive force given their coherence and their consistency with a primary purpose of antiretaliation provisions: Maintaining unfettered access to statutory remedial mechanisms. *Cf. NLRB v. Scrivener,* 405 U.S. 117, 121–122 (1972) (National Labor Relations Act); *Mitchell v. Robert DeMario Jewelry, Inc.,* 361 U.S. 288, 292–293 (1960) (Fair Labor Standards Act). EEOC quite persuasively maintains that it would be destructive of this purpose of the antiretaliation provision for an employer to be able to retaliate with impunity against an entire class of acts under Title VII—for example, complaints regarding discriminatory termination. We agree with these contentions and find that they support the inclusive interpretation of "employees" in § 704(a) that is already suggested by the broader context of Title VII.

III.

We hold that the term "employees," as used in § 704(a) of Title VII, is ambiguous as to whether it includes former employees. It being more consistent with the broader context of Title VII and the primary purpose of § 704(a), we hold that former employees are included within § 704(a)'s coverage. Accordingly, the decision of the Fourth Circuit is reversed.

It is so ordered.

Watch Your Dates

When a factual dispute is controlled by both statutory law and case law, differences may exist between the two sources of law. When this happens, it is important to check the dates of the statute and the case. If a statute is passed after a case is decided, that statute probably controls over the case, unless the issue is Constitutional. If the issue is Constitutional, then the case probably controls, regardless of the dates, unless the Constitution has been amended. If there is a Constitutional amendment after a case decision, then the Constitutional amendment controls.

Read Box 7-1, which sets out the development of the law in California regarding the liability of bar owners and social hosts for furnishing too much alcohol to someone who injures another.

BOX 7-1

CHANGES IN THE LAW—STATUTES AND CASES

Reconciling Statutes and Case Law

Research Question: Is a person who furnishes alcohol to another liable to a third person who is injured by an intoxicated individual to whom alcohol was furnished?

Research Findings:

Prior to 1971, common law was followed. Common law provides that there is no liability on the part of the one who furnishes alcohol because that person is not the proximate cause of the injuries.

1971—State Supreme Court decides that the common law rule should not be followed as to commercial providers of alcohol (bars) and that they should be liable to third persons who are injured by one to whom alcohol was provided.

1978—State Supreme Court extends rule of liability to non-commercial providers of alcohol.

1978—State legislature amends statutes, expressly abrogates above holdings of State Supreme Court and provides that commercial and non-commercial providers of alcohol to intoxicated persons are not the proximate cause of injuries suffered by a third person injured by the intoxicated individual.

Analysis: Based on the above case and statute, how would you answer the research question?

Legislative History

Another source used to aid in statutory interpretation is the legislative history of the statute. The legislative history helps the researcher determine the intent of the legislature in passing the law. A bill goes through several stages before becoming law. At each step there are records of what happened. These records include copies of the bill with deletions, additions, and changes noted. They might include transcripts of hearings and discussions on the bill. Rather than seeking the originals of these records, you can use a source such as *United States Code and Congressional and Administrative News* (U.S.C.C.A.N.). This contains the legislative history of statutes, federal regulations, and court rules. It contains bills in their original format, changes, and committee hearings and discussions. See Figure 7-3 for an example of the contents of U.S.C.C.A.N.

OKLAHOMA CITY NATIONAL MEMORIAL ACT OF 1997

PUBLIC LAW 105–58, see page 111 Stat. 1261

DATES OF CONSIDERATION AND PASSAGE

Senate: July 31, 1997

House: September 23, 1997

Cong. Record Vol. 143 (1997)

Senate Report (Energy and Natural Resources Committee)
No. 105–71, July 30, 1997
[To accompany S. 871]

House Report (Resources Committee)
No. 105–316, October 8, 1997
[To accompany H.R. 1849]

The Senate Report is set out below.

SENATE REPORT NO. 105–71

[page 1]

The Committee on Energy and Natural Resources, to which was referred the bill (S. 871) to establish the Oklahoma City National Memorial as a unit of the National Park System; to designate the Oklahoma City Memorial Trust, and for other purposes, having considered the same, reports favorably thereon without amendment and recommends that the bill do pass.

PURPOSE OF THE MEASURE

The purpose of S. 871 is to establish the Oklahoma City National Memorial as a unit of the National Park System and to establish the Oklahoma City Memorial Trust and to manage the Memorial.

BACKGROUND AND NEED

One hundred and sixty-eight Americans lost their lives and many more were injured on April 19, 1995, when a bomb was detonated at the Alfred P. Murrah Federal Building in Oklahoma City, Oklahoma. This tragedy constitutes the worst domestic terrorist incident in American history.

This legislation would create a memorial at the site of the Murray Federal Building in Oklahoma City on 5th Street, Between Robinson and Harvey Streets and would also include the sites of the Water Resources Building and Journal Record Building.

Concepts for the memorial were solicited through a design competition that included 624 design submissions from all 50 states and 23 foreign countries. The design that was selected was created by Hans-Ekkehard Butzer, Torrey Butzer and Sven Berg, a German-based design team. The design includes 168 chairs in the Murrah Building footprint, a water element designed to reflect spirit of change, a survivor tree, envisioned to reflect hope and "gates of time" on each end of Fifth Street that focus the visitor's attention on memorial inscriptions and the other elements of the memorial. Torrey Butzer of the German team states, "We watched Oklahomans and the world respond to this terrible tragedy from afar. This is our way of giving something to honor the victims, survivors and the heros. This design will tell the story of all of us changed forever."

The memorial established pursuant to this Act would serve not only as a monument to those who died and were injured in the bombing on April 19th, but also as a symbol of the galvanization of 'assistance, courage and good will shown by local citizens and Americans across the country in their outpouring of aid following the incident.

The Oklahoma City National Memorial will be designated as a unit of the National Park System. It will be placed under the charge of a wholly-owned government corporation, to be known as the Oklahoma City National Trust (Trust). The Trust will be governed by a nine-member Board of Directors (Board) which will have the authority to appoint an executive director and other key staff. Interim staff are authorized for two years to assist in the development of the memorial. Permanent National Park service staff and the ability to retain staff from other Federal agencies are also provided for by this measure on a reimbursable basis.

S. 871 authorizes $5 million in Federal funds for construction and maintenance, but stipulates that any Federal expenditures must be matched by non-Federal funds, dollar for dollar. It is expected that matching fund sources will include the Oklahoma State legislature and private donations.

FIGURE 7-3 Sample Page from U.S.C.C.A.N.

LEGISLATIVE HISTORY

S. 871 was introduced June 10, 1997 by Senators Nickles and Inhofe and was referred to the Committee on Energy and Natural Resources. The Subcommittee on National Parks, Historic Preservation and Recreation held a hearing in Oklahoma City on July 3, 1997 and in Washington, D.C. on July 17, 1997.

COMMITTEE RECOMMENDATIONS AND TABULATION OF VOTES

The Committee on Energy and Natural Resources, in open business session on July 30, 1997, by a unanimous vote of a quorum present, recommends that the Senate pass S. 871 without amendment.

The rollcall vote on reporting the measure was 20 yeas, 0 nays, as follows:

YEAS	NAYS
Mr. Murkowski	
Mr. Domenici	
Mr. Nickles	
Mr. Craig	
Mr. Campbell[1]	
Mr. Thomas	
Mr. Kyl	
Mr. Grams	
Mr. Smith	
Mr. Gorton	
Mr. Burns[1]	
Mr. Bumpers	
Mr. Ford	
Mr. Bingaman[1]	
Mr. Akaka	
Mr. Dorgan	
Mr. Graham	
Mr. Wyden	
Mr. Johnson	
Ms. Landrieu[1]	

[1]Indicates voted by proxy.

SECTION-BY-SECTION ANALYSIS

Section 1 entitles the bill the "Oklahoma City National Memorial Act of 1997".

Section 2 sets forth Congressional findings and purpose. The purpose of the bill is to establish the Oklahoma City National Memorial as a unit of the National Park System and to further establish how the memorial will be developed and managed.

Section 3 defines certain terms in the bill.

Section 4(a) establishes the Oklahoma City National Memorial (Memorial) and further establishes the Memorial as a unit of the National Park System.

Subsection (b) references the official boundary map for the memorial and authorizes the Oklahoma City National Memorial Trust (the Trust) to make boundary revisions when necessary.

Section 5(a) establishes a wholly owned government corporation to be known as the Oklahoma City National Memorial Trust.

Section (b)(1) sets forth the membership of the Board of Directors (Board) for the Trust. The 9-member Board shall consist of the Secretary of the Interior (Secretary) or his designee and 8 additional members appointed by the President, but selected from lists of nominees submitted by the Governor of Oklahoma, the Mayor of Oklahoma City and the Oklahoma delegations from the United States House of Representatives and Senate. This section also directs that the President is to appoint the Board members within 90 days after the date of enactment.

Paragraph (b)(2) sets the terms of Board members at 4 years and limits consecutive terms to 8 years. The section also staggers the first series of appointments, with two members serving for 2 years and two members serving a term of 3 years.

Paragraph (b)(3) directs that 5 members shall constitute a quorum.

Paragraph (b)(4) directs that the Board shall organize itself in a manner it deems most appropriate and that members shall not receive compensation, but may be reimbursed for actual and necessary travel and subsistence associated with Trust duties.

Paragraph (b)(5) establishes that Board members will not be considered Federal employees except for the purposes of the Federal Tort Claims Act, the Ethics in Government Act and provisions of titles 11 and 18 of the United States Code.

FIGURE 7-3
(continued)

7-3 APPLYING STATUTORY LAW TO A FACT PATTERN

Statutory analysis is not complete until you *explain* how a particular code section controls your factual situation. When you explain a position you should use the general IRAC approach in much the same way you do in using case law. (Review Chapters 4 and 5.) The IRAC approach consists of the following:

1. stating your **I**ssue
2. stating the **R**ule of law that applies
3. **A**nalyzing the situation by applying the law to your facts, and
4. reaching a **C**onclusion.

The issue is the question you are researching. The rule of law is the relevant code section. The analysis consists of applying your facts to the language of the law. The conclusion is the answer to the question you research. Any factual situation may contain more than one issue. Each issue is analyzed separately using the IRAC approach. Consider the Rambeaux case and the memo at the beginning of the chapter. Assume you are working with the following facts.

Randy Rambeaux made a routine traffic stop on an automobile because the driver failed to signal when making a right-hand turn. The occupants of the vehicle were two Latino males in their late teens. According to the occupants, the following events occurred. Rambeaux approached the car and ordered the two out of the car. When the occupants asked why, Rambeaux opened the driver's door, and with his weapon drawn and pointed directly at the driver, again ordered them out of the car. After the driver exited the vehicle, Rambeaux struck him on the head with the gun and, according to the two occupants, said, "Why don't you guys go back where you belong? This country is for Americans." The driver maintains that he did nothing to provoke the attack.

One of the questions asked in the initial memorandum is whether Rambeaux is criminally responsible under 18 U.S.C. § 242. This is an issue. The rule of law in this case is the code section 18 U.S.C. § 242. The analysis is accomplished by breaking down the code section into its elements and then matching each element with the relevant facts. This should be done initially in an outline form. See Figure 7-4 for an example.

The conclusion should answer the question you are researching. In this case, the conclusion tells whether Rambeaux violated the statute. Figure 7-5 illustrates a written statutory analysis using the IRAC method, using only the statute as authority.

1. Someone must act under color of authority.	Rambeaux is a police officer, performing police function.
2. The action must be willful.	The incident was intentional, not accidental.
3. The action must either:	
Deprive a person of civil rights *or*	Rambeaux violated 4th Amendment to the Constitution: unreasonable arrest.
Impose different punishment, penalties, or pains because of race, etc.	Rambeaux beat the suspect; his comments about "going back" and "Americans" suggest racial bias.

FIGURE 7-4
Statutory Outline

Under the facts presented, Rambeaux probably violated one of the civil rights statutes found in the United States Code. Title 18 section 242 of the United States Code makes it a federal crime for anyone acting under color of authority to deprive any inhabitant of any state of any constitutional rights or subject a person to different punishments, pains or penalties because of that person's race or color.

> Whoever, under color of any law, statute, ordinance, regulation, or custom, willfully subjects any person . . . to the deprivation of any rights, privileges, or immunities secured or protected by the Constitution or laws of the United States or to different punishments, pains or penalties on account of such inhabitant being an alien, or by reason of his color, or race . . . shall be fined under this title or imprisoned not more than one year, or both. . . .

In order for Rambeaux to be guilty of the federal crime, the following elements must be shown:

1. That he acted under color of law;
2. That he acted willfully:
3. That he deprived someone of his constitutional rights: or
4. That he imposed different punishments, pains or penalties and that he did this because of the person's race or color.

In this case, when Rambeaux made the traffic stop and ordered the occupants out of the car, he was acting in his capacity as a police officer. He was in uniform and was doing what police officers routinely do—stopping traffic offenders. He is authorized by his state law to do this. Thus, Rambeaux was acting under color of law, meeting the first element of the statute.

All of the actions in this case were clearly willful. Rambeaux knew what he was doing and intended to do what he did. This was no accident. Thus, the second element is met.

In making this traffic stop, Rambeaux violated the constitutional rights of the driver. The Constitution guarantees that all persons have the right to be free from unreasonable searches and seizures. In this case, Rambeaux made a traffic stop and in doing this "seized" the persons in the vehicle, even if only temporarily. While Rambeaux may have been justified in making the stop, his conduct during this seizure was clearly unreasonable. The use of physical force, such as occurred here, is not allowed in simple traffic stops where the offender neither uses any force nor threatens the officer with the use of force. Thus, the third element of the statute is met.

In addition to violating the victim's constitutional rights, the evidence also suggests that Rambeaux subjected him to different punishment or pain because of the victim's race. Rambeaux used unnecessary force, subjecting the victim to pain. While it may be difficult to prove racial motivation, the facts do support its existence. According to the witnesses, Rambeaux made the statement, "Why don't you guys go back where you belong? This country is for Americans." This is strong evidence of the fact that Rambeaux's actions were racially motivated, fulfilling the final requirement of the statute.

In conclusion, the facts of this case support the fact that Rambeaux violated the federal law.

ISSUE
(At the beginning, describe the issue to be analyzed.)

RULE
(Here you set out the statutory requirements or the language of the statute.)

ANALYSIS
(Here you apply the language of the statute to your facts.)

CONCLUSION

FIGURE 7-5 Statutory Analysis

Whenever possible support statutory analysis with case law. If your research uncovers a case where 18 U.S.C. § 242 was applied to a factual situation that parallels or is analogous to the facts of the Rambeaux case, that case should be discussed following your statutory analysis. (Review Chapters 4 and 5 for how to use case law.) Compare your facts to the facts of any case you find to show that the code section should also apply to the Rambeaux case.

Sometimes in researching statutory law, you find that the language of the statute does not clearly apply to your factual situation. For example, suppose in the Rambeaux case that Rambeaux was off duty when the incident occurred. Under such circumstances, whether he was acting under color of authority is questionable and this becomes another issue. This issue is researched and analyzed just like your main issue (i.e., Rambeaux's liability under the statute). Further research into this issue might lead you to the case of *United States v. Tarpley*, 945 F.2d 806 (5th Cir. 1991), reprinted in Case 7-2. If you rely on this case to argue that Rambeaux is acting under color of authority, your written analysis incorporates a reference to this case and should resemble Figure 7-6. Be sure that you read the *Tarpley* case before you read the analysis.

CASE 7-2

United States v. Tarpley
945 F.2d 806 (5th Cir. 1991)

A deputy sheriff appeals his conviction for violations of 18 U.S.C. §§ 241 and 242, which prohibit the deprivation of rights secured by the Constitution and laws of the United States under color of law. We find sufficient evidence to show that the defendant acted under color of law and conspired with another in doing so, and affirm.

I.

This is what happened, in the light most fav-orable to the government. In 1988, William Tarpley, deputy, Collingsworth County Sheriff's police force, learned of a past affair of his wife, Kathryn and Kerry Lee Vestal. Tarpley devised a plan to lure Vestal to the Tarpley home for the purpose of assaulting him.

Tarpley had his wife call Vestal and tell him that she had separated from her husband and that she wanted him to come pick her up. On the day that Vestal was to arrive, Tarpley and another deputy, Michael Pena, made a pair of "sap gloves" in his office at the sheriff's station. These are gloves with rubber hosing filled with metal or lead shot attached to the fingers.

Tarpley told Pena that he planned to have his wife call her boyfriend over and then use the sap gloves on him.

That evening, Tarpley parked his patrol car behind the house of another deputy so as not to alert Vestal that he was at home. When Vestal arrived at the Tarpley residence, Mrs. Tarpley opened the door and pulled him into the house. Mr. Tarpley immediately tackled Vestal and hit him repeatedly in the head. He also inserted his service pistol in Vestal's mouth. He told Vestal that he was a sergeant on the police department, that he would and should kill Vestal, and that he could get away with it because he was a cop. He repeated "I'll kill you. I'm a cop. I can." As he continued to beat and threaten Vestal, Mrs. Tarpley may have been taking pictures of the encounter. Tarpley then had his wife telephone the sheriff's station and ask Pena to come to their house. She did, and when Pena arrived, Tarpley introduced him to Vestal as a fellow sergeant from the police department. Pena confirmed Tarpley's claims that Tarpley had shot people in the past.

Eventually, Tarpley let Vestal go, chasing him out of the house with threats to

kill him if he reported the incident. Pena then gave Vestal his keys, and Vestal drove away, but not before Tarpley smashed the headlights on Vestal's truck. Pena and the Tarpleys followed Vestal in Pena's squad car until Vestal had left town. Pena also apparently radioed for another officer to meet up with them and that police car also followed Vestal to the edge of town.

A federal grand jury indicted Tarpley and Pena and "another individual known to the grand jury" for conspiracy to injure and oppress Vestal in the exercise of his constitutional rights, as well as willfully subjecting Vestal to a deprivation of his constitutional rights, in violation of 18 U.S.C. §§ 241 and 242. Jointly tried, Pena was acquitted on both counts and Tarpley was convicted on both counts. Defense counsel later learned that during the trial one of the jurors spoke with the juror's daughter, a legal secretary, about the difficulty he had understanding the nature of a conspiracy charge. There was also evidence that the juror's daughter had in turn contacted a lawyer about the matter. The district court held a hearing concerning these events at which both the lawyer and the juror's daughter testified. The court determined that no extrinsic evidence had reached the jury and that further investigation was not required.

Tarpley now appeals his conviction to this court.

II.

Tarpley was convicted of violating two statutes, both of which require that an individual act "under color of law." 18 U.S.C. §§ 241 and 242. Tarpley argues that the jury's finding that he acted "under color of law" was insufficiently supported by the evidence produced at trial. In reviewing the sufficiency of the evidence, this court "must view the evidence in the light most favorable to the verdict to determine whether any rational trier of fact could have found each element of the crime beyond a reasonable doubt." *United States v. Berisha*, 925 F.2d 791, 795 (5th Cir. 1991).

The Supreme Court has in two famous cases explained the concept of "under color of law." In *United States v. Classic*, 313 U.S. 299, 326 (1941), the court stated that "misuse of power, possessed by virtue of state law and made possible only because the wrongdoer is clothed with the authority of

state law, is action taken 'under color of' state law." In *Screws v. United States*, 325 U.S. 91, 111 (1944), the court reaffirmed the classic formula and stated more simply that "under 'color' of law means under 'pretense' of law." The court in *Screws* also observed that "acts of officers who undertake to perform their official duties are included whether they hew to the line of their authority or overstep it." *Id.* However, "acts of officers in the ambit of their personal pursuits are plainly excluded."

This court and other courts of appeals have made clear that whether a police officer is acting under color of law does not depend on duty status at the time of the alleged violation. *Delcambre v. Delcambre*, 635 F.2d 407 (5th Cir. 1981) (*per curiam*); *Layne v. Sampley*, 627 F.2d 12, 13 (6th Cir. 1980). Nor does *Screws* mean that if officials act for purely personal reasons, they necessarily fail to act "under color of law." *Brown v. Miller*, 631 F.2d 408 (5th Cir. 1980); *United States v. Davila*, 704 F.2d 749 (5th Cir. 1983). Rather, *Screws* held simply that individuals pursuing private aims and not acting by virtue of state authority are not acting under color of law purely because they are state officers. *Brown*, 631 F.2d at 411. Tarpley argues that there is no evidence that he "misused power possessed by virtue of state law" or that his actions were "made possible only because" he was "clothed with state authority." According to Tarpley, he was acting as a jealous husband, not as a police officer. He assaulted Vestal in his own home under circumstances in which it was clear that the motive for his attack was the extra-marital affair. That he told Vestal that he was a police officer, the argument continues, does not suggest that he was purporting to act under official authority. He never threatened to arrest Vestal. Vestal already knew he was a cop.

We are not persuaded. There was sufficient evidence in the record from which a rational juror could conclude that Tarpley was acting under color of law. Tarpley did more than simply use his service weapon and identify himself as a police officer. At several points during his assault of Vestal, he claimed to have special authority for his actions by virtue of his official status. He claimed that he could kill Vestal because he was an officer of the law. Significantly, Tarpley summoned another police officer from the sheriff's station and identified him

as a fellow officer and ally. The men then proceeded to run Vestal out of town in their squad car. The presence of police and the air of official authority pervaded the entire incident. Under these circumstances, we are unwilling to say that no rational juror could find that Tarpley acted under color of law.

III.

The defendant also contends that he cannot be convicted on the conspiracy count after his alleged co-conspirator, Pena, was acquitted in the same proceeding. *The United States v. Klein,* 560 F.2d 1236, 1242 (5th Cir. 1977), *cert. denied,* 434 U.S. 1073 (1978), for the proposition that the conviction of only one defendant in a conspiracy prosecution will not be upheld if all other alleged co-conspirators are acquitted. Although this has long been the rule in this Circuit, *see, e.g., Herman v. United States,* 289 F.2d 362, 368 (5th Cir.1961); *United States v. Sheikh,* 654 F.2d 1057, 1062 (5th Cir. 1981), its continuing validity has recently come into question. We need not address this issue in this case, however, because there was a third potential co-conspirator not acquitted. The indictment alleged that "Tarpley and Pena, and another individual known to the grand jury, conspired to injure, threaten, oppress, and intimidate Kerry Vestal." The evidence is sufficient to support a conspiracy between Tarpley and this other individual, namely his wife. Mrs. Tarpley phoned Vestal and convinced him to come to the Tarpley home. She pulled Vestal into the house and apparently took pictures while her husband beat him. She contacted Pena at her husband's bidding and accompanied the two men as they followed Vestal out of town.

This court has held that even when named co-conspirators are acquitted, a person can be convicted of conspiring with unnamed individuals as long as the indictment refers to these individuals and the evidence supports their complicity. *United States v. Price,* 869 F.2d 801, 805 (5th Cir. 1989). It is also clear that "private persons, jointly engaged with state officials in the prohibited action, are acting 'under color' of law for purposes of the statute." *United States v. Price,* 383 U.S. 787, 794 (1996), *Adickes v. S.H. Kress & Co.,* 398 U.S. 144, 152 (1970).

IV.

The defendant argues next that the district court erred in its investigation of ju-

ror misconduct by failing to allow him to question the jurors or by failing to conduct its own voir dire. He relies on *United States v. Phillips,* 664 F.2d 971 (5th Cir.), *cert. denied,* 457 U.S. 1136 (1981), for the proposition that "any off-the-record contact with a jury is presumptively prejudicial and the Government bears a heavy burden of proving that such contact did not affect the jury; if the Government cannot meet this burden, a new trial is required." He argues that the government failed to carry its burden and that the district court effectively shifted the burden to him. We review the district court's decision not to grant a new trial for an abuse of discretion. *United States v. Sedigh,* 658 F.2d 1010, 1014 (5th Cir. 1981), *cert. denied,* 455 U.S. 921 (1982).

The defendant's argument is without merit. The district court here followed established procedure for addressing allegations of juror misconduct. This court has held that "the trial court should investigate the asserted impropriety to determine initially if and what extrinsic factual matter was disclosed to the jury." *Sedigh,* 658 F.2d at 1014. When the allegations remain speculative, the trial court need not inquire further. *Id.*

The district court in this case held a hearing at which the juror's daughter and the lawyer with whom she spoke testified. The juror's daughter testified that although her father had expressed uncertaintly as to whether the crime of conspiracy required that both co-conspirators be convicted, she did not express any opinion on the matter. When she asked a lawyer about it, he told her that any communication with a juror on such issues was improper, and the juror's daughter had no further contact with the juror until after the verdict was rendered. The district court found that this testimony indicated beyond a reasonable doubt that extrinsic evidence was not disclosed to the jury. Consequently, further investigation was not required. The district court acted in accordance with standard procedures and did not abuse its discretion.

It is true that if the defendant had been able to demonstrate as a threshold matter that improper communication of extrinsic information had likely occurred, further investigation might have been required. *See United States v. Forrest,* 620 F.2d 446, 457–58 (5th Cir. 1980) (describing

a two-part process under which voir dire is required upon a threshold showing of likely communication of extrinsic material). However in this case, the district court found that no extrinsic information had reached the jury. Contrary to defendant's assertions, it is not sufficient to trigger the requirement of further investigation that a juror have had contact with an outside source of information. Rather, the defendant must show "that extraneous prejudicial material had likely reached the jury." *Forrest*, 620 F.2d at 458. This showing was not made in the present case.

V.

Finally, the defendant argues that several sentences in the jury instructions were misleading. The standard for their review is " 'whether the court's charge, as a whole, is a correct statement of the law and whether it clearly instructs the jurors as to the principles of law applicable to the factual issues confronting them.' " *United States v. Stacey*, 896 F.2d 75, 77 (5th Cir. 1990) [citations omitted].

Defendant's objections to the length and repetition in the jury instructions are without merit. Evaluated as a whole, the court's instructions stated the law. AFFIRMED.

Under the facts presented, Rambeaux probably violated one of the civil rights statutes found in the United States Code. Title 18 Section 242 of the United States Code makes it a federal crime for anyone acting under color of authority to deprive any person of any constitutional rights or to subject a person to different punishments, pains or penalties because of that person's race or color.

> Whoever, under color of any law, statute, ordinance, regulation, or custom, willfully subjects any person . . . to the deprivation of any rights, privileges, or immunities secured or protected by the Constitution or laws of the United States or imposes different punishments, pains or penalties on account of such inhabitant being an alien, or by reason of his color, or race . . . shall be fined under this title or imprisoned not more than one year, or both. . . .

In order for Rambeaux to be guilty of the federal crime, the following elements must be shown:

1. That he acted under color of law;
2. That he acted willfully;
3. That he deprived someone of his constitutional rights or;
4. That he imposed different punishments, pains or penalties and that he did this because of the person's race or color.

In this case, when Rambeaux made the traffic stop and ordered the occupants out of the car, he was off duty. Therefore, a question arises as to whether he was acting under color of law. However, even off-duty police officers are considered to be under color of authority under certain situations. The case of *United States v. Tarpley*, 945 F.2d 806 (5th Cir. 1991) explains. In the *Tarpley* case, defendant Tarpley, a deputy sheriff, learned of a past affair between his wife and Vestal. He assaulted Vestal by inserting his service revolver in Vestal's mouth and told Vestal that he could get away with it because he was a cop. Tarpley also enlisted the aid of another sheriff's deputy to threaten Vestal. When they finally released Vestal, the officers followed him in a police vehicle. Tarpley was arrested and charged with violating 18 U.S.C. § 242. He was found guilty and appealed, claiming among other things that he was not acting under color of authority at the time because he was off duty. The court of appeals found that even though he was off duty, he was still acting under color of authority because "the air of official authority pervaded the entire incident." *United States v. Tarpley*, 945 F.2d 806, 809. In like manner, the air of official authority pervaded the

MAJOR ISSUE
(At the beginning, state the main issue to be analyzed.)

MAJOR RULE
(Here you set out the statutory requirements or the language of the statute.)

ANALYSIS
(Here you apply the language of the statute to your facts.)

SUB-ISSUE

RULE
(Here you give facts and holding from case.)

ANALYSIS
(Here you compare facts.)

FIGURE 7-6 Statutory Analysis Incorporating Case Law

CONCLUSION TO SUB-ISSUE

Rambeaux incident. Rambeaux was doing what police officers routinely do—stopping traffic offenders. He was acting on behalf of the state, attempting to enforce state laws. Thus, Rambeaux was acting under color of law, meeting the first element of the statute.

All of the actions in this case were clearly willful. Rambeaux knew what he was doing and intended to do what he did. This was no accident. Thus, the second element is met.

In making this traffic stop, Rambeaux violated the constitutional rights of the driver. The Constitution guarantees that all persons have the right to be free from unreasonable searches and seizures. In this case, Rambeaux made a traffic stop and in doing this "seized" the persons in the vehicle, even if only temporarily. While Rambeaux may have been justified in making the stop, his conduct during this seizure was clearly unreasonable. The use of physical force, such as occurred here, is not allowed in simple traffic stops where the offender neither uses any force nor threatens the officer with the use of force. Thus, the third element of the statute is met.

In addition to violating the victim's constitutional rights, the evidence also suggests that Rambeaux subjected him to different punishment or pain because of the victim's race. Rambeaux used unnecessary force, subjecting the victim to pain. While it may be difficult to prove racial motivation, the facts do support its existence. According to the witnesses, Rambeaux made the statement, "Why don't you guys go back where you belong? This country is for Americans." This is strong evidence of the fact that Rambeaux's actions were racially motivated, fulfilling the third requirement of the statute.

CONCLUSION

In conclusion, the facts of this case support the fact that Rambeaux violated the federal law.

FIGURE 7-6 (continued)

Box 7-2

STATUTORY ANALYSIS CHECKLIST

√ Outline statutory language, listing the elements or requirements of the law.

√ Note the meaning of connectors such as *and, or,* etc.

√ Determine meaning of statutory terms by referring to other code sections, case law, or legislative histories.

√ Apply statutory law to factual situation using IRAC method.

7-4 CONSTITUTIONAL ANALYSIS

Article VI of the U.S. Constitution states that the Constitution is the supreme law of this land. "This Constitution, and the Laws of the United States which shall be made in Pursuance thereof . . . shall be the supreme Law of the Land; and the Judges in

every State shall be bound thereby, any Thing in the Constitution or Laws of any State to the Contrary notwithstanding." It is therefore important to determine if a matter is controlled by any provision in the Constitution. Just as with statutory law, this determination usually requires that you understand what the relevant part of the Constitution means.

Many of the words and phrases found in the Constitution are not precise and are subject to various interpretations. For example, the Fourth Amendment prohibits "unreasonable searches and seizures," but fails to define *unreasonable.*

Whenever you are faced with a research problem requiring interpretation and analysis of the U.S. Constitution, you must research case law that applies to the Constitutional provision. The United States Supreme Court has the final say on what the U.S. Constitution means.

Once you determine that a specific constitutional provision applies to your research problem, and have researched all relevant case law, your analysis is similar to an analysis involving statutory law.

Constitutional research and analysis, however, sometimes presents an additional consideration. Many constitutional research problems deal with an individual's constitutional rights under the Bill of Rights (the first ten amendments) and under the Due Process and Equal Protection Clauses of the Fourteenth Amendment. Consider the following situation.

Smith is stopped for speeding by Officer Marlow. Marlow writes a speeding ticket and gives it to Smith. After giving Smith the ticket, Marlow asks Smith if he can search the car. Smith says "yes," thinking that the officer will probably search the car regardless of what he says. Illegal drugs are found in the vehicle. Smith is arrested and charged with possession of the drugs. Marlow is a state police officer, possession of drugs is a state crime, and Smith is prosecuted in a state court. Smith asks the court to dismiss the case because the officer conducted an unreasonable search and seizure.

You are faced with an important initial research question here. Should you begin your research in state sources or in federal sources? This is a state crime prosecuted in a state court. In all probability, this state has a state constitutional provision also regulating the area of search and seizure. However, the U.S. Constitution gives all individuals certain rights. Should your research focus on the state constitution and state cases or on the U.S. Constitution and Supreme Court cases? Your ability to research this type of issue properly requires that you understand the concept of **federalism** and the relationship between state and federal governments.

Federalism—The Relationship Between Federal and State Government

In the United States, government operates under a principle called **federalism.** Federalism means that citizens are regulated by two separate governments: federal and state. The federal government has *limited* power over all fifty states. State governments have power only within their state boundaries. These powers are also limited in the sense that states cannot make laws that conflict with the laws of the federal government.

Because there are areas of **concurrent jurisdiction,** conflicts exist between laws made by the federal government and laws made by states. Where a conflict exists, federal law controls. This is because of the **Supremacy Clause** of the Constitution mentioned above. When a state passes a law that conflicts with the Constitution, the

federalism. A system of government in which the people are regulated by both federal and state governments.

concurrent jurisdiction. Jurisdiction or power exercised by two different entities.

Supremacy Clause. Clause in the U.S. Constitution providing that the U.S. Constitution is the supreme law of the land.

United States Supreme Court has the power to declare the state law unconstitutional and unenforceable.

However, the fact that both state and federal governments regulate an area does not necessarily create a conflict. For example, if a defendant kidnaps a victim and takes the victim across state lines, both federal and state laws have been violated and the defendant could be tried in either the state or federal court (or both) for the crime. Furthermore, in this situation the federal court has no priority over the state court.

In determining if a conflict between state and federal law exists, a particular problem arises in the area of criminal procedure. If an individual is arrested for a state crime, such as murder, that individual is tried in the state courts. States are allowed to formulate their own procedural rules for this process. Furthermore, each state has a state constitution that, like the U.S. Constitution, affords certain rights to individuals within that state. On the other hand, the United States Constitution affords criminal defendants certain basic rights not only in federal cases but also in state cases. In federal cases those rights are specifically spelled out in the Bill of Rights (specifically the Fourth, Fifth, Sixth, and Eighth Amendments). These specific amendments apply only in federal cases.

In state criminal cases, each state must follow the Fourteenth Amendment to the Constitution, which provides in part, "nor shall any State deprive any person of life, liberty, or property, without due process of law." The United States Constitution does not set out specific rights that states must respect. Rather, it sets out a minimum standard that all states must follow, i.e., due process. The Supreme Court decides what *due process* means. But remember that it is a minimum standard. States can grant more rights to criminal defendants and not be in conflict with federal law because the federal government has not **preempted** this area of law. On the other hand, once the Supreme Court sets forth a specific minimum standard, states cannot take away a right. States may make laws in this area as long as those laws do not violate due process.

preempt. To assume sole authority to regulate.

A conflict does not necessarily exist just because the state and federal rules differ. When you research such a problem, you must read Supreme Court cases to determine the minimum standard. You must then review state cases to determine how the state constitution has been interpreted. If the state constitution affords more rights, it controls. If it affords fewer rights, then the United States Constitution and the cases decided by the U.S. Supreme Court control.

⇨ **A Point to Remember**   Where conflicts exist between federal and state laws, the federal law controls. However, not all differences result in a conflict. Do not assume that federal law always controls. In determining if a difference results in a conflict, first determine if the federal law has preempted the area of law. If it has, then the federal law controls. If the federal law has not preempted the area, then read the federal law carefully to determine its meaning. You must understand the federal law to determine if a conflict exists in the state law.

Reread the case of *Ohio v. Robinette,* found in Chapter 2. This case deals with a factual situation similar to the Smith hypothetical described above. Both the majority and concurring opinions explain the applicability of the federal and state constitutions to a situation. In this case, the Court discusses the Fourth and Fourteenth Amendments to the U.S. Constitution and a provision in the Ohio State Constitution that contains identical language. After reading the case, consider the following questions.

1. When the case is remanded to the Ohio court, what legal sources should Robinette ask the court to rely on?

2. The Ohio Constitution and the U.S. Constitution contain identical language regarding unreasonable search and seizure. Why is the Ohio court allowed to interpret the language differently than the U.S. Supreme Court?

3. If the Smith and Marlow hypothetical occured in your state, would you rely on the U.S. Constitution and the case of *Ohio v. Robinette?* Why or why not?

⇨ **A Point to Remember**   Before you complete an analysis of a problem involving constitutional questions, be sure to consider the relationship between the state and federal laws. Do not always assume that federal case law controls.

Box 7-3

CONSTITUTIONAL ANALYSIS

√ Determine if state or federal law governs your case.

√ If your case is governed by state law, then review the relationship between state and federal constitutional provisions.

√ Determine if state or federal constitutional provisions apply.

√ Proceed with analysis as you do with statutory law.

TECHNOLOGY CORNER

One good source for constitutional law is Findlaw. This Web site contains an annotated United States Consitution prepared by the Congressional Research Service, Library of Congress. In addition to the text of the Constitution, this reference provides an analysis and interpretation of the articles and amendments. To access the Constitution go to: http://www.findlaw.com/casecode/constitution/.

Legislative information is found at: //thomas.loc.gov or www.loc.gov

Additional sites on which you may perform Constitutional research are:

www.usscplus.com
www.lawguru.com

CHAPTER SUMMARY

Unlike case law, statutory law, administrative regulations, and constitutions contain general rules intended to apply to many different factual situations. Therefore, legal analysis based on these sources differs from analysis based on case law. Analyzing a legal question based on these sources requires that you determine the meaning of the law. You should outline relevant provisions of the law by breaking the law down into various parts or elements, sometimes referred to as *statutory requirements.* The various elements should then be applied to the facts of the case. Where the meaning of a word or phrase is unclear, you should review other statutory law, case law, or legislative history. A written analysis of a statute, administrative regulation, or constitution should follow the IRAC method. State the issue, give the rule, apply the rule to your facts, and reach a conclusion.

In addition, when researching constitutional law, you must further determine whether the situation is governed by the state constitution or the U.S. Constitution.

TERMS TO REMEMBER

stare decisis

mandatory authority

statutory requirements

federalism

concurrent jurisdiction

Supremacy Clause

preempt

QUESTIONS FOR REVIEW

1. How does statutory analysis differ from case law analysis?
2. What is meant by *statutory requirements?*
3. List the steps in analyzing a statute or administrative regulation.
4. What sources can you consult to determine the meaning of a statute, administrative regulation, or constitutional provision?
5. How do you determine whether the U.S. Constitution or a state constitution applies to a factual situation arising under state law?

CAN YOU FIGURE IT OUT?

1. The following abbreviations appear in the cases found in this chapter. What does each of them mean?

    Per curiam

    Slip op

    Id.

    Cert. Denied

    En banc

2. Refer to Figure 7-1. Can excessive force be the basis of an action under 18 U.S.C. § 242? Cite a case for your answer.
3. Refer to Figure 7-2. Richards dies and leaves a will in which he leaves all of his "property" to Westin. Richards has the following assets at his death: a home, a bank account with $100,000, furniture, and various stocks and bonds. What does Westin inherit?

RESEARCH ASSIGNMENTS AND ACTIVITIES

1. Read 42 U.S.C. § 1983 (found at the beginning of the chapter) and list the elements or requirements for finding a person liable for civil damages under this code section.
2. Read the following code section.

    Robbery defined: Robbery is the felonious taking of personal property in the possession of another, from his person or immediate presence, and against his will, accomplished by means of force or fear.

a. Complete the following list of the statutory elements.

1. felonious taking
2. personal property
3.
4.
5.
6.

b. Analyze the following factual situation and determine if the defendant committed a robbery.

Defendant points a gun at a victim and tells him to hand over his wallet. The victim does and defendant opens the wallet, looks inside, sees it is empty, and throws it on the ground.

Begin your analysis by completing the following chart.

Elements of Statute	Factual Application
1. Felonious taking →	1. D told V to "hand over" and V does
2. Personal Property →	2. A wallet is personal property
3.	
4.	
5.	
6.	

Reach a Conclusion: Did Defendant commit a robbery?

c. Using the same chart and the same statute, analyze the following facts.

1. X and Y were engaged. X gave Y his grandmother's ring as engagement ring. They break up and X wants the ring back. Y refuses. X threatens Y and Y gives back the ring.

2. X steals a saxophone from a store. A security guard from another establishment chases and is threatened.

3. D and V know each other. He drugs her coffee. When she passes out, he steals her jewelry.

3. Read the following code section.

Subject to this division, the father and mother of a minor child have an equal responsibility to support their child in the manner suitable to the child's circumstances.

The duty of support imposed herein continues as to an unmarried child who has attained the age of 18 years, is a full-time high school student, and who is not self-supporting, until the time the child completes the 12th grade or attains the age of 19 years, whichever occurs first.

a. Outline the statutory requirements for a parent to be responsible for supporting a child who is 18 years of age.

b. Consider the following facts: Jeffrey turned 18 four months ago. He is a senior in high school, living at home, and will graduate in two months. He has a part-time job at a local fast-food restaurant and earns approximately $400 per month, most of which he spends on his car and entertainment. He is not married. Apply the code section to these facts, using the outline format found in Figure 7-4. Are his parents obligated to support him? If so, for how long?

4. Read the following language from 18 U.S.C. § 115.

Whoever–

assaults, kidnaps, or murders, or attempts or conspires to kidnap or murder, or threatens to assault, kidnap or murder a member of the immediate family of a United States official, a United States judge, a Federal law enforcement officer, with intent to impede, intimidate, or interfere with such official, judge, or law enforcement officer while engaged in the performance of official duties, or with intent to retaliate against such official, judge, or law enforcement officer on account of the performance of official duties, shall be punished as provided in subsection (b).

As used in this section, the term

"immediate family member" of an individual means-

    a. his spouse, parent, brother or sister, child or person to whom he stands in loco parentis; or

    b. any other person living in his household and related to him by blood or marriage;

Now consider the following facts: Judge Thomas Merkins, a United States district court judge, sentenced James Oakley to a lengthy prison term for a drug-related offense. Oakley's father, John, outraged at the sentence, vowed to get even with the judge. He hired two thugs to attack the judge's son-in-law. Police officials learned of this before any attack occurred. The judge's daughter and son-in-law are temporarily living with the judge. Consider if John Oakley can be punished under 18 U.S.C. § 115. Before reaching your conclusion, do the following.

    a. Outline the statutory elements or requirements under 18 U.S.C. § 115 for any person to be punished under the section.

    b. Prepare a statutory analysis of the facts in outline form, relating appropriate statutory language to relevant facts. (See Figure 7-4.)

    c. Determine if there are any ambiguities or uncertainties that necessitate further research. If so, explain what research steps you would take.

5. Read the following amendments to the U.S. Constitution.

Amendment V:

No person shall be held to answer for a capital, or otherwise infamous crime, unless on a presentment or indictment of a Grand Jury, except in cases arising in the land or naval forces, or in the Militia, when in actual service in time of War or public danger; nor shall any person be subject for the same offence to be twice put in jeopardy of life or limb; nor shall be compelled in any criminal case to be a witness against himself, nor be deprived of life, liberty, or property, without due process of law; nor shall private property be taken for public use, without just compensation.

Amendment XIV:

All persons born or naturalized in the United States and subject to the jurisdiction thereof, are citizens of the United States and of the State wherein they reside. No State shall make or enforce any law which shall abridge the privileges or immunities of citizens of the United States; nor shall any State deprive any person of life, liberty, or property, without due process of law; nor deny to any person within its jurisdiction the equal protection of the laws.

    a. List all terms in these amendments that could be considered ambiguous.

    b. Keeping in mind that the Bill of Rights (the first ten amendments) applies only to the federal government, analyze the following factual situations in relation to the Fifth and Fourteenth Amendments. Pre-

pare an outline of the appropriate constitutional language related to the relevant facts (Figure 7-4) and answer the specific questions asked.

1. Financial support of elementary schools in Washington, D.C. that are predominantly composed of minority students is substantially less than the support given to elementary schools that are not minority-based.

   a. Is there a potential violation of the Fifth Amendment?

   b. Is there a potential violation of the Fourteenth Amendment?

   c. Are there any issues or questions you would want to research further? If so, list those questions and identify the sources you would consult.

2. A regional planning commission in the Lake Tahoe area imposed a three year moratorium on all building near the lake. Jones, who owned lake-view property, was unable to build and therefore unable to use his land. He claimed that the government should compensate him for his property.

   a. Does Jones have any potential claims under the Fifth Amendment?

   b. Does Jones have any potential claims under the Fourteenth Amendment?

   c. Are there any issues or questions you would want to research further? If so, list those questions and identify the sources you would consult.

6. Review the case of *Robinson v. Shell Oil* found in this chapter. What steps did the Court go through in interpreting the term *employee?*

7. Write an analysis of the Rambeaux situation regarding Rambeaux's civil liability under 42 U.S.C. § 1983.

CASE PROJECT

In the previous chapter, you researched one of the hypothetical situations in Appendix A to determine what statutory law applied. Taking your results

a. break each of the statutes into its elements,

b. write an outline of the statutory elements and the facts (see Figure 7-4), and

c. write a statutory analysis using the facts of the hypothetical situation.

SECONDARY SOURCES

C HAPTER OUTLINE

C HAPTER OBJECTIVES

When you complete this chapter you should be able to

- List the common features of secondary source materials.
- Explain the contents of legal encyclopedias.
- Explain how to use the *American Law Reports*.
- Compare and contrast treatises and periodicals.
- Explain how looseleaf services differ from other secondary sources.

CITATION MATTERS

SECONDARY RESOURCES

THE BLUEBOOK—RULES 15, 16, 17, AND 18

Books, Periodical Materials, and Other Secondary Sources

Rules 15 through 18 provide numerous examples for citation format for secondary sources. Set out below are common examples. If you cannot find an example of the exact source you need to cite, find a very similar resource and follow the general format for that citation.

Examples:

15 AM. JUR. 2D *Civil Rights* § 18 (1983) (legal encyclopedia)

23 C.J.S. *Contracts* § 33 (1977) (legal encyclopedia)

William B. Johnson, Annotation, *Use of Plea Bargain or Grant of Immunity as Improper Vouching for Credibility of Witness in Federal Cases,* 76 A.L.R. FED. 409 (1986). (*THE BLUEBOOK* example for the *American Law Reports* citation format.)

INTEROFFICE MEMORANDUM

TO: Research Associate

FROM: Supervising Attorney

RE: Rambeaux

We really need to get going on the Rambeaux cases. Criminal charges were filed against Rambeaux last week. Yesterday Rambeaux was served with a civil complaint. We are representing Rambeaux in both cases. Please research both cases and give me a memo containing an overview of all the law that might be relevant to each of these cases.

8-1 INTRODUCTION

Usually, the goal of legal research is to find primary law that controls a factual dispute or question. As you saw in previous chapters, if you use only the books that contain the primary law, finding the answer to a specific question can be difficult. In the Rambeaux matter, you already know that at least two code sections are relevant. But there may be other relevant statutory law. Furthermore, case law is obviously important. You have seen how to locate case law through the annotations following the code. However, there are other, and often easier, ways to find all the relevant law.

To facilitate the legal research process many publishers produce works generally known as *secondary sources*. A **secondary source of law** is not the law itself. It is someone's interpretation or explanation of the law. Most secondary sources provide references or citations to the **primary source of law.** Using secondary sources in the

secondary sources of law. Tools we use to help us understand the law; one such tool is a legal encyclopedia, which explains the law.

primary source of law. A work that contains the law itself.

initial research process is very helpful because it provides an overview of the area of law you are researching and enables you to identify the key facts and legal issues of the research problem. Once you identify the precise issue, a secondary source also provides a thorough discussion of the controlling legal principles, leading you to the relevant primary law. If both statutory law and case law apply to a situation, the secondary source refers you to each. Secondary sources include multivolume works, single books, and periodicals. Many are available on disk, CD-ROM, or through online services such as LEXIS or Westlaw. This chapter covers some of the more common types of secondary sources.

⇨ **A Point to Remember**   A secondary source is someone's interpretation of the primary law. It is not the law and you should never rely on a secondary source as authority. You should always read the primary law and cite to it.

8-2 FEATURES OF SECONDARY SOURCE MATERIALS

Finding specific information in secondary source materials is facilitated by several editorial features added to the text materials. Most secondary source materials have some, if not all, of the following features.

- **Descriptive Word Index**—An alphabetized list of words or phrases describing subjects discussed in the text. The index directs you to the page or section in the text where the material is covered; it is usually located at the end of the secondary source material. Multivolume works often contain separate volumes located at the end of the set containing the index. By identifying key words in your research problem, you are able to check these terms in an index and find the appropriate sections in the secondary source. See Figure 8-1.
- **Table of Contents**—A detailed list of topics covered in the text that precedes the text material. This is organized in the same order as the material appears in the text; similar and related topics are usually grouped together. A table of contents provides an overview of the material covered. See Figure 8-2.
- **Table of Statutes Cited**—A list of statutes or codes discussed in the text. This is usually arranged alphabetically by name of code and then numerically within each titled code. If the code has no name, then it is arranged numerically. The table of statutes tells you where in the text material the code section is discussed. If you know of a code section that applies to your research problem, you can check the table of statutes cited to find a discussion. See Figure 8-3.
- **Table of Cases Cited**—A list of cases cited in the text material, arranged alphabetically by plaintiff's name; sometimes also arranged alphabetically by defendant's name. This table normally provides the case citation as well as a reference to the page in the text material where the case appears; sometimes called "Plaintiff/Defendant Index" or "Defendant/Plaintiff Index." See Figure 8-4.
- **Table of Abbreviations**—A list of all abbreviations used in the text including those used for case reporters and other legal sources. This is an important feature to check because many secondary sources do not use standard or approved abbreviations for legal sources. See Figure 8-5.
- **Preface**—A description of the contents and purpose of the material; often contains an explanation of how to use the material.

- **Parallel Reference Tables**—Tables included in works that are published in more than one series or edition. These tables show the reader how to find in the new editions material contained in the original editions. See Figure 8-6.
- **Pocket Part Supplement**—Many secondary sources are supplemented in the way that codes are, i.e., with pocket part supplements.

AMERICAN JURISPRUDENCE 2d

SHERIFFS AND POLICE—Cont'd
Election—Cont'd
    omissions and delay, **Sheriffs** § 112
    removal from office, **Sheriffs** § 136
    sale under process, **Sheriffs** § 136
Election of remedies, **Sheriffs** § 112, 136
Elevators and escalators, status of person injured, **Elevators** § 30
Eligibility and qualification
    generally, **Sheriffs** § 10, 11, 15, 59, 150
    constables, **Sheriffs** § 54
    coroner acting as sheriff in event of disqualification, **Sheriffs** § 52
    holdovers, **Sheriffs** § 21, 22
    jury service, **Sheriffs** § 6, 59
    limitation on number of terms, **Sheriffs** § 20
    pardon for conviction, **Sheriffs** § 35
    previous or prior term of office, **Sheriffs** § 32
Elisor appointment on default or disqualification of sheriff, **Sheriffs** § 52
Embezzlement, **Sheriffs** § 198, 277
Emergencies
    generally, **Negligence** § 227
    vehicles. **Emergency Vehicles** (this index)
Emoluments. Compensation and wages, above
Encumbrances. Liens and encumbrances, below
Entrapment (this index)
Equity
    injunctions, **Sheriffs** § 45, 101, 135, 229
    redemption, **Sheriffs** § 85, 179, 198
    setting aside judgment based on false return, **Sheriffs** § 271
Error. Mistake or accident, below
Estoppel. Waiver and estoppel, below
Eviction. **Ejection, Eviction or Ouster** (this index)
Evidence
    generally, **Sheriffs** § 245-264
    admissibility, generally, **Sheriffs** § 245-255
    admissions and declarations, above
    burden of proof. Presumptions and burden of proof, below
    Confessions (this index)
    documentary evidence, **Evidence** § 1158, 1316, 1360-1362
    Expert and Opinion Evidence (this index)
    fines and penalties, **Sheriffs** § 249, 252
    judgments and decrees, **Sheriffs** § 248, 249, 254, 259, 262
    judicial sales, **Sheriffs** § 145, 246, 253
    justification and excuse, **Sheriffs** § 254, 259, 262, 263
    materiality and relevancy of evidence, **Sheriffs** § 254
    misconduct, effect of exclusionary rule in deterring, **Evidence** § 590
    money or cash, **Sheriffs** § 251, 263, 264
    obstruction of justice, **Obstruct** § 56, 60, 72, 108, 110
    official bond, actions on, **Sheriffs** § 247
    presumptions and burden of proof, below

SHERIFFS AND POLICE—Cont'd
Evidence—Cont'd
    prima facie evidence or case, below
    removal from office, **Sheriffs** § 43
    res ipsa loquitur, **Negligence** § 1859, 1902, 1908
    return of process, below
    routine of, habit or routine practice (rule 406), **Evidence** § 40
    search for defendant as showing flight, **Evidence** § 533
    seizures of property, actions relating to, generally, **Sheriffs** § 246
    third persons, below
    title and ownership, below
    trespass, **Sheriffs** § 255, 256
Exceptions. Exemptions, below.
Excessive authority, **Sheriffs** § 98, 164, 182, 199, 260
Excuse. Justification and excuse, below
Executions and Enforcement of Judgments (this index)
Executive officers, United States marshals as, **Sheriffs** § 53
Exemplary damages, **Sheriffs** § 265, 268, 270, 271, 273
Exemptions from claims of creditors
    bonds and undertakings, **Sheriffs** § 195, 216, 219
    commingling with exempt property, **Sheriffs** § 222
    defenses to omissions of duty as to levy, **Sheriffs** § 175
    demand as prerequisite to action for wrongful levy, **Sheriffs** § 222
    execution and levy, generally, **Sheriffs** § 107, 175
    homestead, damages for loss of, **Sheriffs** § 267
    presumptions and burden of proof, **Sheriffs** § 259, 260
    replevin of wrongfully seized property, **Sheriffs** § 231
Ex officio duties, additional compensation for, **Sheriffs** § 71
Exonerating writ upon expiration of term of office, **Sheriffs** § 58
Expenses. Costs and expenses, above
Expert and Opinion Evidence (this index)
Expiration. Termination and cancellation, below
Extension of time, **Sheriffs** § 20-22, 209
Extortion, blackmail, and threats, **Sheriffs** § 109, 227
Extraterritorial jurisdiction or power, **Sheriffs** § 57, 71, 78
Facial appearance, **Sheriffs** § 9
Fact, questions of, **Sheriffs** § 99, 117, 149, 265
Failure to act, malfeasance, or misfeasance, generally, **Sheriffs** § 30-32, 90-180, 280
Fair employment practices act, **Sheriffs** § 6, 10
False imprisonment, **Sheriffs** § 155, 199, 256
Falsity, generally. Fraud and deceit, below
Federal Bureau of Investigation (this index)
Federal conviction of crime, removal from

SHERIFFS AND POLICE—Cont'd
    office for, **Sheriffs** § 35
Federal Courts (this index)
Federal Employers' Liability and Compensation Act (FELCA) (this index)
Federal government
    Attorney General of United States, **Sheriffs** § 5, 53, 88, 89
    courts, **Sheriffs** § 53, 82, 134
    Federal Bureau of Investigation (this index)
    Marshals (this index)
    officers. Federal officers, below
    official bond, party aggrieved on, **Sheriffs** § 226
Federal marshals. **Marshals** (this index)
Federal officers
    Attorney General of United States, **Sheriffs** § 5, 53, 88, 89
    Federal Bureau of Investigation (this index)
    federal marshals. **Marshals** (this index)
    intent to obstruct justice, **Obstruct** § 95, 96
    jurisdiction, **Sheriffs** § 57, 232
    President of United States, **Sheriffs** § 37, 53
    replevin actions against federal officers, **Sheriffs** § 231
    United States marshals and deputies. **Marshals** (this index)
Federal Tort Claims Act (this index)
Fees
    generally, **Sheriffs** § 1, 67, 68, 75, 78-83
    amount of fees, **Sheriffs** § 82, 86
    attachment, **Sheriffs** § 78, 80, 82, 84, 86
    attorneys, **Sheriffs** § 86, 219, 267, 275
    care and custody of property, **Sheriffs** § 78, 86
    coercion or duress, payments to sheriff under, **Sheriffs** § 85
    constables, **Sheriffs** § 78, 86
    constitutional law, **Sheriffs** § 70, 82
    damages for wrongful sale, collection fees as, **Sheriffs** § 272
    execution and levy, **Sheriffs** § 78, 84, 85
    failure to levy based on absence of payment of fees, **Sheriffs** § 173
    failure to sell after levy based on absence of advancement of fees, **Sheriffs** § 180
    illegal fees, payments of, **Sheriffs** § 73
    increase or decrease in fees, entitlement to, **Sheriffs** § 70
    insufficient levy, nonpayment of fees as defense to, **Sheriffs** § 174
    judicial sales, **Sheriffs** § 80, 83-86
    misconduct in execution or levy to collect fees, **Sheriffs** § 30
    mistake of law, fees paid under, **Sheriffs** § 73
    parties liable for fees, **Sheriffs** § 86
    poundage, **Sheriffs** § 82, 83, 86
    sureties on official bonds, liability of, **Sheriffs** § 79, 86, 198
    travel and transportation fees and expenses, **Sheriffs** § 79, 83, 89
    unlawful collection of fees, liability of sureties on bond, **Sheriffs** § 198

Instead of looking under "SHERIFFS AND POLICE" go to "Marshals" in the index.

To find general information about fees charged by sheriffs, go to the topic "Sheriffs" in Am. Jr. 2d and read sections 1, 67, 68, etc.

350   For assistance using this index, call 1-800-328-4880

FIGURE 8-1
American Jurisprudence 2d, Index Page

GENERAL INDEX

FIGURE 8-1
(continued)

Reprinted with permission of Thomson/West

JOB DISCRIMINATION

> KeyCite : Cases and other legal materials listed in KeyCite Scope can be researched through West Group's KeyCite service on Westlaw®. Use KeyCite to check citations for form. parallel references, prior and later history, and comprehensive citator information, including citations to other decisions and secondary materials.

Volume 45A

I. GOVERNING LAWS, IN GENERAL (§§ 1 TO 35)

    A. TITLE VII OF THE CIVIL RIGHTS ACT OF 1964 (§§ 1 TO 5)

    B. EARLY CIVIL RIGHTS ACTS; SECTION 1981A (§§ 6 TO 15)

    C. LAWS COVERING AGE, DISABILITY, AND SEX DISCRIMINATION IN EMPLOYMENT (§§ 16 TO 20)

    D. LAWS OUTLAWING DISCRIMINATION ON FEDERAL PROJECTS (§§ 21 TO 26)

    E. OTHER FEDERAL LAWS REGULATING EMPLOYMENT DISCRIMINATION (§§ 27 TO 35)

II. SCOPE OF LAWS (§§ 36 TO 114)

    A. IN GENERAL (§§ 36 TO 39)

    B. WHO MUST COMPLY (§§ 40 TO 104)

        1. In General; Private Employers Under Federal Job Discrimination Laws (§§ 40 to 65)

            a. In General (§§ 40 to 57)

            b. Liability of Employers and Agents for Discriminatory Acts (§§ 58 to 65)

        2. Coverage of Public Employers Under Federal Job Discrimination Law (§§ 66 to 76)

        3. Employers Subject to Other Employment Laws (§§ 77 to 80)

        4. Labor Organizations (§§ 81 to 86)

        5. Employment Agencies; Labor-Management Training Committees (§§ 87 to 89)

        6. Government Contractors Subject to Job Discrimination Laws (§§ 90 to 97)

        7. Recipients of Government Funds (§§ 98 to 104)

5

FIGURE 8-2

American Jurisprudence 2d Table of Contents

FIGURE 8-2
(continued)   6

JOB DISCRIMINATION

        (1)   Requirement of Disability (§§ 183 to 193)

        (2)   Requirement of Qualification for Position (§§ 194 to 198)

    c.   Reasonable Accommodation and Undue Hardship (§§ 199 to 213)

        (1)   The Reasonable Accommodation Requirement (§§ 199 to 205)

        (2)   Types of Reasonable Accommodation (§§ 206 to 209)

        (3)   What Is "Undue Hardship" (§§ 210 to 213)

IV. OTHER PROHIBITED DISCRIMINATION-RELATED CONDUCT (§§ 214 TO 252)

  A. RETALIATION AGAINST OPPONENTS OF DISCRIMINATION (§§ 214 TO 251)

    1. In General (§§ 214 to 229)

      a. Provisions Prohibiting Retaliation (§§ 214 to 219)

      b. General Considerations in Retaliation Claims (§§ 220 to 223)

      c. Retaliation for Acts in Opposition to Unlawful Employment Practices (§§ 224 to 226)

      d. Retaliation for Participating in Administrative Process (§§ 227 to 229)

    2. Persons Protected From Retaliation (§§ 230 to 233)

    3. Particular Types of Retaliatory Acts (§§ 234 to 239)

    4. Proof of Retaliation (§§ 240 to 251)

      a. In general (§§ 240 to 244)

      b. Causation (§§ 245 to 248)

      c. Defending against a retaliation claim (§§ 249 to 251)

  B. OTHER PROHIBITED ACTS RELATING TO DISCRIMINATION (§ 252)

V. EXCEPTIONS TO PROHIBITIONS ON DISCRIMINATORY CONDUCT (§§ 253 TO 278)

  A. BUSINESS NECESSITY (§ 253)

7

FIGURE 8-2
(continued)

Reprinted with permission of Thomson/West

Section 34, under the topic "Civil Rights," contains a mention or discussion of 2 U.S.C.S § 2000 (a).

TABLE OF STATUTES CITED

This table shows, by reference to title and section, where provisions of the United States Code Service, the Federal Rules of Procedure, and the Uniform Laws are cited in this volume.

UNITED STATES CODE SERVICE

Title and section	Am Jur 2d title and section	Title and section	Am Jur 2d title and section
2 USCS		§§ 245 et seq.	CIVIL RIGHTS § 3
§ 2000a(a)	CIVIL RIGHTS § 34	§ 245	CIVIL RIGHTS §§ 22, 27, 55, 62, 256, 259, 272
5 USCS		§ 245(b)	CIVIL RIGHTS §§ 27, 256, 288
§ 102	CIVIL RIGHTS §§ 98, 295	§ 371	CIVIL RIGHTS § 15
§ 105	CIVIL RIGHTS §§ 98, 295	§ 1001	CIVIL RIGHTS §§ 299, 463
§§ 551–559	CIVIL RIGHTS § 291	§ 1509	CIVIL RIGHTS § 23
§ 552(b)(7)	CIVIL RIGHTS § 96	§ 3231	CIVIL RIGHTS §§ 12, 288
§§ 701 et seq.	CIVIL RIGHTS § 364	**20 USCS**	
§§ 701–706	CIVIL RIGHTS §§ 291, 476	§§ 401 et seq.	CIVIL RIGHTS § 61
§ 1305	CIVIL RIGHTS § 291	§§ 821 et seq.	CIVIL RIGHTS § 61
§§ 1501 et seq.	CIVIL RIGHTS § 243	§§ 880b et seq.	CIVIL RIGHTS § 79
§§ 1501–1503	CIVIL RIGHTS § 243	§ 880b(a)	CIVIL RIGHTS § 79
§ 2102	CIVIL RIGHTS § 98	§ 884	CIVIL RIGHTS § 61
§ 3105	CIVIL RIGHTS § 291	§§ 1601 et seq.	CIVIL RIGHTS §§ 61, 467
§ 3344	CIVIL RIGHTS § 291	§ 1617	CIVIL RIGHTS §§ 278, 472
§ 5362	CIVIL RIGHTS § 291	§§ 1651 et seq.	CIVIL RIGHTS §§ 61, 467
§ 7521	CIVIL RIGHTS § 291	§§ 1651–1658	CIVIL RIGHTS § 69
§ 8335	CIVIL RIGHTS § 247	§§ 1651–1656	CIVIL RIGHTS §§ 61, 69
8 USCS		§ 1651	CIVIL RIGHTS §§ 61, 69
§§ 1101 et seq.	CIVIL RIGHTS § 114	§ 1652	CIVIL RIGHTS §§ 69, 467
10 USCS		§ 1652(a)	CIVIL RIGHTS § 467
§ 6382(a)	CIVIL RIGHTS §§ 208, 220	§ 1652(b)	CIVIL RIGHTS § 466
§ 6401	CIVIL RIGHTS § 208	§ 1653	CIVIL RIGHTS § 69
§ 6401(a)	CIVIL RIGHTS § 220	§ 1654	CIVIL RIGHTS § 469
12 USCS		§ 1655	CIVIL RIGHTS § 465
§ 1715z-1	CIVIL RIGHTS § 97	§ 1656	CIVIL RIGHTS § 69
15 USCS		§§ 1681 et seq.	CIVIL RIGHTS §§ 84, 88, 91, 154
§§ 1671–1677	CIVIL RIGHTS § 149	§§ 1681–1686	CIVIL RIGHTS § 61
§ 1674	CIVIL RIGHTS § 149	§ 1681	CIVIL RIGHTS § 85
§§ 1681 et seq.	CIVIL RIGHTS § 111	§ 1681a(1)	CIVIL RIGHTS § 85
§ 1681a(f)	CIVIL RIGHTS § 111	§ 1681a(2)(A)	CIVIL RIGHTS § 84
§§ 1681–1681t	CIVIL RIGHTS § 111	§ 1681a(2)(B)	CIVIL RIGHTS § 84
18 USCS		§ 1681a(3)	CIVIL RIGHTS § 84
§ 1	CIVIL RIGHTS §§ 15, 22	§ 1681a(4)	CIVIL RIGHTS § 84
§ 241	CIVIL RIGHTS §§ 7, 22–25, 55, 263, 272, 288, 289, 462	§ 1681a(5)	CIVIL RIGHTS § 85
§ 241(2)	CIVIL RIGHTS § 22	§ 1681a(6)(A)	CIVIL RIGHTS § 84
§ 241(3)	CIVIL RIGHTS § 22	§ 1681a(6)(B)	CIVIL RIGHTS § 84
§ 242	CIVIL RIGHTS §§ 12, 15, 18, 20, 24, 25, 263, 272, 288, 289	§ 1684	CIVIL RIGHTS § 61
§ 243	CIVIL RIGHTS § 12	§§ 1701 et seq.	CIVIL RIGHTS § 61
		§§ 1701–1758	CIVIL RIGHTS § 69

xiii

FIGURE 8-3 Table of Statutes Cited

From *CURRENT LAW INDEX*, by Thomson Gale, © 1998, Thomson Gale. Reprinted by permission of The Gale Group.

CASES CITED IN ALR FEDERAL

Urquhart v Lockhart (1983, E.D.Ark) 557 F Supp 1334
75 ALR Fed 9, § 26

Urrutia, In re (1990, DC Puerto Rico) 137 BR 563
140 ALR Fed 1, § 43, 45

Urrutia v United States (1958, CA5 Fla) 253 F2d 501
38 ALR Fed 617, § 3, 4

Ursic v. Bethlehem Mines, 719 F.2d 670, 4 Employee Benefits Cas. (BNA) 2297, 14 Fed. R. Evid. Serv. 395 (3d Cir. 1983)
172 ALR Fed 571, § 4

Urtz v. Callahan, 965 F. Supp. 324, 53 Soc. Sec. Rep. Serv. 605, Unempl. Ins. Rep. (CCH) ¶ 15780B (N.D.N.Y. 1997)
165 ALR Fed 203, § 3-5, 9, 10, 20, 24, 25, 28, 31

Urwyler v Reece (1987, ED Cal) 87-1 USTC P 9298, 59 AFTR 2d 87-843
99 ALR Fed 700, § 4, 10

Urwyler v United States (1989, ED Cal) 90-1 USTC P 50016, 71A AFTR 2d 93-3338
117 ALR Fed 75, § 16, 18, 34

Ury v Santee (1969, ND Ill) 303 F Supp 119
66 ALR Fed 750, § 6, 12

U.S. v. 1,380.09 Acres of Land, More or Less, Situated In Caldwell Parish, State of La., 574 F.2d 238 (5th Cir. 1978)
172 ALR Fed 507, § 24

U.S. v. 2,116 Boxes of Boned Beef, Weighing Approximately 154,121 Pounds, 726 F.2d 1481 (10th Cir. 1984)
173 ALR Fed 465, § 7, 10

U.S. v. 2,200 Paper Back Books, 565 F.2d 566 (9th Cir. 1977)
172 ALR Fed 239, § 3

U.S. v. 4.18 Acres of Land, More or Less, in Idaho County, State of Idaho, 542 F.2d 786 (9th Cir. 1976)
172 ALR Fed 507, § 2, 4

U.S. v. 5,553.80 Acres of Land, More or Less, in Concordia Parish, State of La., 451 F. Supp. 220 (W.D. La. 1978)
172 ALR Fed 507, § 5

U.S. v. 12 200-Foot Reels of Super 8mm. Film, 413 U.S. 123, 93 S. Ct. 2665, 37 L. Ed. 2d 500 (1973)
172 ALR Fed 239, § 2

U.S. v. 25,000 Magazines, Entitled ""Revue", 254 F. Supp. 1014 (D. Md. 1966)
172 ALR Fed 239, § 3

U.S. v. 31 Photographs, 156 F. Supp. 350 (S.D.N.Y. 1957)
172 ALR Fed 239, § 3, 5

U.S. v. 35 MM. Motion Picture Film "Language of Love", 432 F.2d 705 (2d Cir. 1970)
172 ALR Fed 239, § 4

U.S. v. 40.00 Acres of Land, More or Less, in Henry County, Mo., 427 F. Supp. 434 (W.D. Mo. 1976)
172 ALR Fed 507, § 6

U.S. v. 122.00 Acres of Land, More or Less, Located in Koochiching County, Minn., 856 F.2d 56 (8th Cir. 1988)
172 ALR Fed 507, § 4, 10

U.S. v. 127,295 Copies of Magazines, More or Less, Entitled "Amor", 295 F. Supp. 1186 (D. Md. 1968)
172 ALR Fed 239, § 3

U.S. v. 243.538 Acres of Land, More or Less, In Maui County, State of Hawaii, 509 F. Supp. 981 (D. Haw. 1981)
172 ALR Fed 507, § 4, 10, 15, 16, 20, 21, 28

U.S. v. 329.73 Acres of Land, Situated in Grenada and Yalobusha Counties, State of Miss., 704 F.2d 800, 20 Env't. Rep. Cas. (BNA) 1025 (5th Cir. 1983)
172 ALR Fed 507, § 2

U.S. v. 341.45 Acres of Land, More or Less, Located in the County of St. Louis, State of Minn., 751 F.2d 924 (8th Cir. 1984)
172 ALR Fed 507, § 2

U.S. v. 410.69 Acres of Land, More or Less in Escambia County, State of Fla., 608 F.2d 1073 (5th Cir. 1979)
172 ALR Fed 507, § 4

U.S. v. 431.60 Acres of Land, More or Less, in Richmond County, State of Ga., 355 F. Supp. 1093 (S.D. Ga. 1973)
172 ALR Fed 507, § 2, 10, 15, 26, 28

U.S. v. 640.00 Acres of Land, More or Less, In Dade County, State of Fla., 756 F.2d 842 (11th Cir. 1985)
172 ALR Fed 507, § 2

U.S. v. 1500 Cases, More or Less, etc., 249 F.2d 382 (7th Cir. 1957)
173 ALR Fed 465, § 7, 10

U.S. v. A Motion Picture Film Entitled "I Am Curious-Yellow", 404 F.2d 196 (2d Cir. 1968)
172 ALR Fed 239, § 4

U.S. v. Abod, 770 F.2d 1293 (5th Cir. 1985)
173 ALR Fed 613, § 2, 4, 5, 9

U.S. v. ACB Sales & Service, Inc., 590 F. Supp. 561 (D. Ariz. 1984)
173 ALR Fed 223, § 7

U.S. v. Adler, 52 F.3d 20 (2d Cir. 1995)
173 ALR Fed 667, § 3

U.S. v. Ailsworth, 948 F. Supp. 1485 (D. Kan. 1996)
173 ALR Fed 1, § 61

U.S. v. Al-Cantara, 978 F.2d 1256 (4th Cir. 1992)
173 ALR Fed 613, § 9

U.S. v. Alessi, 638 F.2d 466, 7 Fed. R. Evid. Serv. 909 (2d Cir. 1980)
173 ALR Fed 613, § 9

U.S. v. Alexander, 48 F.3d 1477, 41 Fed. R. Evid. Serv. 774 (9th Cir. 1995)
173 ALR Fed 1, § 24

U.S. v. Alkins, 925 F.2d 541 (2d Cir. 1991)
172 ALR Fed 109, § 3-5, 18

U.S. v. American Cyanamid Co., 427 F. Supp. 859, 1 Fed. R. Evid. Serv. 672 (S.D.N.Y. 1977)
173 ALR Fed 1, § 28

U.S. v. American Tel. and Tel. Co., 516 F. Supp. 1237, 8 Fed. R. Evid. Serv. 893 (D.D.C. 1981)
173 ALR Fed 1, § 26, 28, 46, 95

U.S. v. American Tel. and Tel. Co., 1981-1 Trade Cas. (CCH) ¶ 63938, 1981 WL 2047 (D.D.C. 1981)
173 ALR Fed 1, § 7, 95

U.S. v. Ames Sintering Co., 927 F.2d 232 (6th Cir. 1990)
172 ALR Fed 109, § 3

U.S. v. Antelope, 430 U.S. 641, 97 S. Ct. 1395, 51 L. Ed. 2d 701 (1977)
172 ALR Fed 1, § 2, 23

U.S. v. Ardoin, 19 F.3d 177, 73 A.F.T.R.2d 94-1799, 73 A.F.T.R.2d 94-2432 (5th Cir. 1994)
173 ALR Fed 667, § 4

U.S. v. Armstrong, 517 U.S. 456, 116 S. Ct. 1480, 134 L. Ed. 2d 687 (1996)
172 ALR Fed 1, § 26

U.S. v. Articles of Food Clover Club Potato Chips, 67 F.R.D. 419 (D. Idaho 1975)
173 ALR Fed 465, § 10

U.S. v. Atkins, 558 F.2d 133, 2 Fed. R. Evid. Serv. 296 (3d Cir. 1977)
173 ALR Fed 1, § 6

U.S. v. Atkins, 618 F.2d 366, 6 Fed. R. Evid. Serv. 166 (5th Cir. 1980)
173 ALR Fed 1, § 57

U.S. v. Azure, 801 F.2d 336, 21 Fed. R. Evid. Serv. 801 (8th Cir. 1986)
173 ALR Fed 1, § 64

U.S. v. Azure, 845 F.2d 1503, 25 Fed. R. Evid. Serv. 1053 (8th Cir. 1988)
173 ALR Fed 1, § 64

U.S. v. Bachsian, 4 F.3d 796, 39 Fed. R. Evid. Serv. 1091 (9th Cir. 1993)
173 ALR Fed 1, § 3, 7, 22

U.S. v. Bailey, 581 F.2d 341, 3 Fed. R. Evid. Serv. 371 (3d Cir. 1978)
173 ALR Fed 1, § 5, 6

U.S. v. Bailin, 1990 WL 114741 (N.D. Ill. 1990)
172 ALR Fed 109, § 5

U.S. v. Bajakajian, 524 U.S. 321, 118 S. Ct. 2028, 141 L. Ed. 2d 314, 172 A.L.R. Fed. 705 (1998)
172 ALR Fed 389, § 3, 5-7, 12

U.S. v. Balfany, 965 F.2d 575, 35 Fed. R. Evid. Serv. 990 (8th Cir. 1992)
173 ALR Fed 1, § 64

U.S. v. Banner, 226 F. Supp. 904, 64-1 U.S. Tax Cas. (CCH) ¶ 9264, 13 A.F.T.R.2d 579 (N.D.N.Y. 1963)
173 ALR Fed 465, § 27, 28

U.S. v. Barnes, 12 M.J. 614 (N.M.C.M.R. 1981)
173 ALR Fed 1, § 71

U.S. v. Barnes, 586 F.2d 1052, 3 Fed. R. Evid. Serv. 1278 (5th Cir. 1978)
173 ALR Fed 1, § 57

U.S. v. Barrett, 8 F.3d 1296, 38 Fed. R. Evid. Serv. 398 (8th Cir. 1993)
173 ALR Fed 1, § 67

U.S. v. Barrett, 598 F. Supp. 469 (D. Me. 1984)
173 ALR Fed 1, § 4, 39

U.S. v. Barretto, 708 F. Supp. 577, 89-2 U.S. Tax Cas. (CCH) ¶ 9646, 64 A.F.T.R.2d 89-5623 (S.D.N.Y. 1989)
173 ALR Fed 465, § 26

U.S. v. Bell, 86 F.3d 1164 (9th Cir. 1996)
173 ALR Fed 1, § 60

U.S. v. Beltran, 761 F.2d 1, 18 Fed. R. Evid. Serv. 40 (1st Cir. 1985)
173 ALR Fed 1, § 83

For assistance, call 1-800-328-4880   **465**

U.S. v. Ames Sintering Co. is cited in section 3 of the article starting on page 109 in volume 172 of *A.L.R. Fed.*

FIGURE 8-4   Cases Cited in *A.L.R. Federal*

Reprinted with permission of Thomson/West

TABLES OF ABBREVIATIONS

A2d—Atlantic Reporter, Second Series
A2—American Law Reports, Second Series
A3—American Law Reports, Third Series
A4 or AR4th—American Law Reports, Fourth Series
A5 or AR5th—American Law Reports, Fifth Series
AR—American Law Reports
AR—American Law Reports, Federal
At—Atlantic Reporter
BRW—Bankruptcy Reporter
CaR—California Reporter
CaR2d—California Reporter, Second Series
ClC—Claims Court Reporter
F—Federal Reporter
F2d—Federal Reporter, Second Series
F3d—Federal Reporter, Third Series
FC—Federal Cases
FedCl—Federal Claims Reporter
FRD—Federal Rules Decisions
FS—Federal Supplement
FS2d—Federal Supplement, Second Series
Ga—Georgia Reports
GaA—Georgia Appeals Reports
IlA—Illinois Appellate Court Reports
LE—United States Supreme Court Reports, Lawyers' Edition
LE—United States Supreme Court Reports, Lawyers' Edition Second Series

MJ—Military Justice Reporter
NC—North Carolina Reports
NCA—North Carolina Court of Appeals Reports
NE—Northeastern Reporter
NE—Northeastern Reporter, Second Series
NW—Northwestern Reporter
NW—Northwestern Reporter, Second Series
NYS—New York Supplement
NYS2d—New York Supplement, Second Series
OA—Ohio Appellate Reports
P—Pacific Reporter
P2d—Pacific Reporter, Second Series
P3d—Pacific Reporter, Third Series
PaS—Pennsylvania Superior Court Reports
SC—Supreme Court Reporter
SE—Southeastern Reporter
SE—Southeastern Reporter, Second Series
So—Southern Reporter
So2d—Southern Reporter, Second Series
SoC—South Carolina Reports
SW—Southwestern Reporter
SW—Southwestern Reporter, Second Series
SW—Southwestern Reporter, Third Series
US—United State Reports
Va—Virginia Reports
VaA—Virginia Court of Appeals Reports
WV—West Virginia Reports

COURT ABBREVIATIONS

Cir. (number)—United States Court of Appeals, Circuit (number)
Cir. DC—United States Court of Appeals, DC Circuit
Cir. Fed.—United States Court of Appeals, Federal Circuit
CIT—United States Court of International Trade
CCPA—Court of Customs and Patent Appeals

Cl Ct—United States Claims Court
Ct Cl—United States Court of Claims
Cu Ct—United States Customs Court
ECA—Temporary Emergency Court of Appeals
ML—Judicial Panel on Multidistrict Litigation
RRR—Special Court Regional Rail Reorganization Act of 1973

FIGURE 8-5 Tables of Abbreviations

Reprinted with permission of LexisNexis

xii   TABLE OF PARALLEL REFERENCES

SHERIFFS, POLICE, AND CONSTABLES—Continued

Am Jur §§	Am Jur 2d §§	Am Jur §§	Am Jur 2d §§	Am Jur §§	Am Jur 2d §§
92	98	138	181	187	109, 173
93, 94	70	139	203	188	174
95	56, 70	140	204	189	206
96	36, 37	141	205	190	175
97	39	142	203	191	177
98	Deleted	143	149, 156	192	106
99	40	144	150	193	108
100	41	145	151	194, 195	109
101	41, 42	146	152	196	Deleted
102	43	147	153, 154	197	164
103	44	148	155	198, 199	110
104, 105	45	149	156	200	111
106	PUBLIC OFFICERS AND EMPLOYEES	150	157	201	112
107	46	151	158	202	113
108	10, 47	152	159	203	114
109	48	153	ATTACHMENT AND GARNISHMENT; EXECUTIONS	204	115
110	49	154	2, 6, 22, 50	205	116
111	Deleted	155	11	206	117
112	127	156	3	207	118
113	131	157	9	208	119
114	Deleted	158, 159	99	209	120
115	132	160	100	210	121
116	133	161	102	211	123
117	134	162	103	212	124
118	129, 138	163	Deleted	213	125
119	129, 135, 137, 138, 143, 147	164	103	214	178, 179, 186
120	135	165	104	215	180
121	137	166	202	216	182
122	138	167, 168	Deleted	217	183
123	140	169	101	218	184
124	136	170	128, 135	219	185
125	139	171	130	220	186
126	141	172	142	221	187
127	143	173	160, 169, 170	222	188, 191
128	141, 144	174	162	223	189
129	145	175	163	224	190
130	146	176	165	225	191
131	147	177	167	226	192
132	148	178	168	227	193, 194, 201
133	161, 166	179	169	228	194
134	166	180-183	Deleted	229	195, 196
135	176	184	170, 171	230	198
136	179	185	65, 198	231	199
137	107	186	172	232	200
				233, 234	201
				235-237	EXECUTIONS

Am Jur 2d to Am Jur 2d Revised

Am Jur 2d §§	Am Jur 2d (Rev) §§	Am Jur 2d §§	Am Jur 2d (Rev) §§	Am Jur 2d §§	Am Jur 2d (Rev) §§
1	1, 2, 5	9	16	17	23
2	6	10	17	18	25
3	18	11	20-22	19	24
4	10	12	26-28, 32	20	52
5	11	13	36	21	46, 48, 49, 61
6	12	14	37	22	9, 50, 63
7	14	15	38	23	53
8	15	16	42	24	54

FIGURE 8-6 Table of Parallel References

Reprinted with permission of Thomson/West

8-3 LEGAL ENCYCLOPEDIAS: *AMERICAN JURISPRUDENCE 2D* AND *CORPUS JURIS SECUNDUM*

legal encyclopedia.
A collection of legal information arranged alphabetically by topic; a secondary source of the law.

Non-legal encyclopedias are multivolume works containing thorough discussions of a variety of subjects arranged alphabetically. **Legal encyclopedias** follow the same general format. They are multivolume works containing comprehensive and thorough discussions of *legal* topics. For example, you might find such general topics as "bail," "civil rights," "contracts," "federal courts," "illegitimate children," "negligence," and "space law." There are hundreds of different topics.

Two major legal encyclopedias cover the entirety of U.S. law. These are *American Jurisprudence 2d (Am. Jur. 2d)* and *Corpus Juris Secundum (C.J.S.)*. These encyclopedias discuss legal topics of both state and federal law and are similar works. Some states also have their own encyclopedias covering the law of that particular state.

Topics are arranged alphabetically just as they are in a non-legal encyclopedia. Topics are often broken down into subtopics or sections. The topic begins with an outline of the subtopics that are discussed. This is followed by a discussion of the law that contains an explanation and reference to controlling primary law. Footnotes contain many citations to case law (from all jurisdictions) and other legal sources that pertain to the subject. Articles in both *American Jurisprudence 2d* and *Corpus Juris Secundum* are kept current with pocket part supplements.

Using Legal Encyclopedias

Using a legal encyclopedia can be as easy as using any encyclopedia. If you know your general topic, it is located by finding the volume that contains that part of the alphabet. However, you may not know the name of the topic covering your specific question. In this case, an index is available to help locate the appropriate section. For example, in the case of Rambeaux, suppose the question you are researching is as follows: "Is a police officer who uses excessive force in making an arrest guilty of any federal crime?" If you know nothing about the federal civil rights acts you might not know that the answer to your question is found in the general topic "civil rights." At this point you should proceed as follows.

1. Go to the index found at the end of the set of books.
2. Determine terms or words to check in the index. Do this by reviewing the known facts. For example, since Rambeaux is a police officer, you might check for the word *police*. *American Jurisprudence 2d* refers you to the phrase "Sheriffs and Police." (See Figure 8-1.)
3. Review the subtopics found under the main topic. As you can tell from Figure 8-1, the topic "Sheriffs and Police" contains numerous subtopics. Since you know that Rambeaux is accused of using excessive force, you can check for the term *force*. Again look at Figure 8-1 and find the subtopic "force and violence" under "Sheriffs and Police."
4. Note the topics and section numbers that follow your topics. "Force and violence" refers you to several sections in the encyclopedia, including "Sheriff" § 155.
5. Find the volume of the encyclopedia that contains the term *Sheriff*. (Remember the terms are listed alphabetically in the encyclopedia.) Then find the appropriate section number. See Figure 8-7 for sample pages from "Sheriff and Police" § 155.

70 Am Jur 2d   SHERIFFS, POLICE, AND CONSTABLES   § 155

Volume 70 of *American Jurisprudence Second*, page 343, section 155; the main topic here is "SHERIFF'S, POLICE AND CONSTABLES."

his deputy's failure to make return of an execution within the time required by statute.[64]

If a deputy is negligent in the performance of his duties in regard to the notification, the mode of conducting sale, the title to be given the purchaser, and the return of his precept, the principal is liable to persons injuriously affected.[65] Constables and sheriffs have also been held liable for false returns made by deputies,[66] but the plaintiffs alleging that a deputy sheriff had made a false return of service have the burden of establishing that service of civil process was within the deputy's authority.[67]

§ 155. Acts in connection with arrest or imprisonment

A sheriff may be liable for the wrongful acts of his deputy in making an arrest,[68] including alleged violations of the suspect's civil rights,[69] using excessive force to capture persons committing a crime,[70] and escaping prisoners,[71] or for false imprisonment,[72] where such acts are done by virtue of his office as deputy and within the scope of his authority. For the act to have that character, it must have been done under a warrant or under circumstances which authorized the deputy to make an arrest without warrant. If the deputy makes an arrest in any other way it is not authorized by law and is consequently his individual, and not his official, act. But where the deputy acts under a warrant and abuses that process in making the arrest, the sheriff will be liable.[73] An arrest made in any other way is not authorized by law and

Cases and other supporting authorities are cited in footnotes.

64. Rogers v Anderson (Tenn) 580 SW2d 782.

65. Sexton v Nevers, 37 Mass 451.

66. Houser v Hampton, 29 NC 333.

Under a statute providing that the official acts of a deputy sheriff shall be deemed to be those of the sheriff himself, the sheriff alone, and not the deputy, is liable for a deputy's failure to take bail from a person arrested on civil process or for his false return that he has taken bail. Liability may not exist, however, where the plaintiff has directed the deputy not to take bail. Ordway v Bacon, 14 Vt 378.

67. Karr v Dow (App) 84 NM 708, 507 P2d 455, cert den 84 NM 696, 507 P2d 443.

68. Miles v Wright, 22 Ariz 73, 194 P 88, 12 ALR 970.

Practice Aids.—Complaint in action against deputy, sheriff, and sheriff's surety for wounding by sheriff's deputy. 22 Am Jur Pl & Pr Forms (Rev) Sheriffs, Police, and Constables, Form 133.

Police Misconduct Litigation—Plaintiff's Remedies. 15 Am Jur Trials 555 §§ 21-25.

69. § 156.

70. Widow stated cause of action against sheriff for death of husband killed in exchange of gun fire between sheriff's deputies and fleeing felons who had taken husband as hostage where complaint alleged that sheriff's deputies were negligent in failing to engage in proper police practices. in engaging in close pursuit and thus placing husband's life in jeopardy, and in failing to retreat despite fact that husband's life was endangered. Michel v Hometown Super Markets, Inc. (La App 4th Cir) 352 So 2d 357.

71. Andry v Orleans (La App 4th Cir) 309 So 2d 814, later app (La App 4th Cir) 358 So 2d 334 (holding that under a statute providing that no sheriff nor his surety shall be liable for any act or tort committed by one of his deputies beyond the amount of the bond or limits of liability insurance furnished by the deputy sheriff, unless the deputy sheriff in the commission of the said tort acts in compliance with a direct order of, and in the personal presence of, the sheriff, at the time the act or tort is committed, a sheriff would not be liable individually for excessive force allegedly used by his deputy sheriff to apprehend a prisoner during an escape attempt. but a cause of action existed against the sheriff in his official capacity).

As to means permissible in recapturing prisoners, generally, see 27 Am Jur 2d, Escape. Prison Breaking, and Rescue § 26.

72. Abbott v Cooper. 218 Cal 425, 23 P2d 1027.

73. Miles v Wright, 22 Ariz 73, 194 P 88, 12 ALR 970; Ivy v Osborne, 152 Tenn 470, 279 SW 384.

FIGURE 8-7   Text Material, *Am. Jur. 2d*

consequently is not the deputy's official act, but his individual act, for which his superior is then not liable.[74]

A chief of police sued for false imprisonment for the acts of police officers in which he did not participate has been held entitled to the benefit of the general rule that with respect to governmental functions a municipal officer performing duties strictly public is not liable for negligent acts of misfeasance of persons employed by the municipality who are under his general direction and authority.[75] But if superior officers order that an arrest be made, their actions may be so intertwined with that of the officer making the arrest that the liability of all must be considered together.[76]

Although it is frequently held that where a superior officer has not authorized nor consented to the wrongful act of his deputy, no liability will attach,[77] lack of knowledge of the wrongful acts has also been held not to prevent a finding of liability.[78]

---

74. Where plaintiff was arrested without any process, warrant, or other legal authority, by one not a deputy sheriff, who turned him over to the deputy sheriff in charge of the jail, and the deputy then imprisoned the plaintiff, such imprisonment was a usurpation of power by the deputy, for which the sheriff could not be held liable. Swenson v Cahoon, 111 Fla 788, 152 So 203.

Where the petition and the evidence negate every state of facts under which the deputy constable might have made a lawful arrest, it follows that he was acting in his individual capacity, and not in his official capacity, and the surety on the bond of the constable is not liable under a statute providing that a constable and his sureties shall be liable on the bond for the acts and omissions of his deputy. Fidelity & Deposit Co. v Hall, 215 Ky 36, 284 SW 426.

Arrest by a deputy without a warrant for an alleged offense beyond the view of the deputy is without color of authority and is a personal wrong committed by the deputy for which he alone would be liable, in accordance with the general rule that public officers are not liable to third persons for the extraofficial acts of their deputies. Ivy v Osborne, 152 Tenn 470, 279 SW 384.

75. Wommack v Lesh, 180 Kan 548, 305 P2d 854.

Practice Aids.—Complaint in action against peace officers for assault and battery on prisoner. 22 Am Jur Pl & Pr Forms (Rev), Sheriffs, Police, and Constables, Form 132.

76. Nesmith v Alford (CA5 Ala) 318 F2d 110, reh den (CA5 Ala) 319 F2d 859, and cert den 375 US 975, 11 L Ed 2d 420, 84 S Ct 489.

77. Kangieser v Zink (1st Dist) 134 Cal App 2d 559, 285 P2d 950; Klam v Boehm, 72 Idaho 259, 240 P2d 484.

Where an arrest is made by a deputy sheriff without warrant and the prisoner is incarcerated in a jail for the management of which the sheriff was responsible without the knowledge of the sheriff, the sheriff would not be responsible for such arrest or imprisonment. McBeath v Campbell (Tex Com App) 12 SW2d 118.

A police captain who receives a call to the effect that trouble may be brewing and assigns an officer to investigate is not, without other evidence, liable for a false arrest by the investigating official. Nesmith v Alford (CA5 Ala) 318 F2d 110, reh den (CA5 Ala) 319 F2d 859, and cert den 375 US 975, 11 L Ed 2d 420, 84 S Ct 489.

A sheriff may be held liable for the brutality and mistakes of his deputies only if the sheriff knew of and participated in the torts, ratified the tortious conduct, or if the tortious conduct had persisted for such an extended period that the sheriff is, factually or legally, charged with knowledge. Dean v Gladney (SD Tex) 451 F Supp 1313, affd in part and revd in part (CA5 Tex) 621 F2d 1331, cert den 450 US 983, 67 L Ed 2d 819, 101 S Ct 1521.

78. A chief of police who was made keeper of the city prison by the city charter would be liable for the conduct of the persons immediately in charge of the prison, notwithstanding that he might not have participated in or known of such conduct. Ulvestad v Dolphin, 152 Wash 580, 278 P 681, distinguishing Pavish v Meyers, 129 Wash 605, 225 P 633, 34 ALR 561, on the ground that in the Ulvestad Case there was a city charter making the chief of police the keeper of the city prison.

If a deputy sheriff were acting in his capacity as deputy sheriff at the time of an alleged false arrest, he and a surety on his bond, and a sheriff and a surety on his bond, would be proper and necessary parties to the action based on the cause of action for the alleged false arrest. State ex rel. Cain v Corbett, 235 NC 33, 69 SE2d 20.

FIGURE 8-7
(continued)

70 Am Jur 2d   SHERIFFS, POLICE, AND CONSTABLES   § 156

The provisions of applicable statutes have also been determinative of liability.[79] The acts of deputy sheriffs in shooting a person while attempting to arrest him for an offense committed in their presence are "official acts" within a statute making a sheriff responsible for the official acts of his deputies.[80]

|||| *Practice guide:* In such a case, the plaintiff should allege that the deputy's act was done not in the lawful exercise of his authority, but while he was pretending or professing to act by virtue of his office, that is, under color of his office.[81] However, if the evidence fails to show that the offense for which the deputies were attempting to make an arrest was committed in their presence or that they were acting under a warrant, a case of "official acts" is not made out so as to render the sheriff liable.[82]

§ 156. Deprivation of civil rights

In general the federal courts have rejected the concept of imposing vicarious liability upon a public officer, such as a sheriff or police commissioner, for his deputy's civil rights violations[83] under the applicable federal statute.[84] Exceptions to the general rule rejecting vicarious liability for civil rights violations have been recognized where the sheriff participated directly in, was present at, or otherwise authorized the actions of his deputy;[85] absent such involvement, however, the sheriff escapes liability.[86] Some cases holding that absent overt

79. Under a statute making the sheriff and his surety liable for any misconduct of his deputy, they were held liable for his act in killing one arrested under a warrant for a misdemeanor, since he was acting by virtue of his office, and what he did was done as an official act. Brown v Weaver, 76 Miss 7, 23 So 388.

80. Brown v Wallis, 100 Tex 546, 101 SW 1070.

81. Harwell v Morris, 255 Ala 344, 51 So 2d 511.

82. Brown v Wallis, 100 Tex 546, 101 SW 1070.

83. Jennings v Davis (CA8 Mo) 476 F2d 1271 (neither chief of police nor board of police commissioners of a major city were to be liable under respondeat superior for civil rights violations of police officers); Kroes v Smith (ED Mich) 540 F Supp 1295 (deputy county sheriff charged with civil rights violations in beating plaintiff and subjecting him to strip search after stopping automobile following high speed chase by police; county could not be liable for acts of deputy sheriffs under respondeat superior); Painter v Baltimore County (DC Md) 535 F Supp 321 (dismissing action against chief of police for vicarious liability regarding assault by police officer); Dunkin v Lamb (DC Nev) 500 F Supp 184 (granting sheriff's motion for summary judgment since action attempting to make sheriff liable through agency theory and effect was not permissible under civil rights act); Schweiker v Gordon (ED Pa) 442 F Supp 1134 (police commissioner; no vicarious liability under respondeat superior for police offi-

cer's civil rights violations); Delaney v Dias (DC Mass) 415 F Supp 1351 (police commissioner not charged with personal involvement in the alleged civil rights violations of his subordinates; respondeat superior inapplicable to impose vicarious liability); Manfredonia v Barry (ED NY) 401 F Supp 762 (no vicarious liability; plaintiffs acknowledged that the police commissioner had neither ordered the offending acts nor participated in their execution, but sought to impose liability on the theory that the commissioner's failure to undo the acts thereafter should constitute ratification thereof); Runnels v Parker (CD Cal) 263 F Supp 271 (chief of police could not be liable for false arrest of plaintiffs by police officers because of departmental policy requiring arrests and transportation to the police station of suspects whose interrogation would take more than ½ hour; no liability for chief of police unless he was present, directed such acts, or personally cooperated in them).

Annotation: 51 ALR Fed 285 § 3; 61 ALR Fed 7.

84. 42 USCS § 1983.

85. Campbell v Buckles (DC Tenn) 448 F Supp 288.

86. Harris v Pirch (CA8 Mo) 677 F2d 681 (action under 42 USCS § 1983 will not lie against police supervisory officers for failure to prevent police misconduct absent a showing of direct responsibility therefor; Hopper v Hayes (DC Idaho) 573 F Supp 1368 (although a city police officer was deputized to act as a deputy sheriff, the county sheriff could not be held

345

FIGURE 8-7 (continued)

acts, the statute does not authorize recovery of monetary damages through respondeat superior, recognize other exceptions to the rule, and a sheriff may be held liable, without necessarily having participated therein or authorized such acts, for the actions of his appointed deputies, over whom he has control, in certain circumstances.[87]

A number of courts have held that regardless of whether concepts of vicarious liability may be inherently within the scope of the federal statute itself, superiors sued under that statute for civil rights violations committed by their subordinates may be vicariously liable where state law imposes liability without personal fault on the particular superior for the wrong of his subordinates in the scope of employment. Hence, state law may require that a sheriff be found liable for the civil rights violations committed by a deputy.[88] Conversely, in a state which absolves the sheriff from vicarious liability for the acts of his deputy, the state rule applies to bar liability for the deputy's civil rights violations.[89] Without precisely declaring that a state law imposing vicarious liability on a superior public official for wrongs committed by his subordinates in the course of their employment would serve to impose such liability for civil rights violations by such subordinates in an action under the federal civil rights acts, the courts of one circuit have supported such a view.[90] Other courts have specifically stated that liability of a superior for civil rights violations by his subordinates cognizable under the federal statute cannot be imposed by reference to state laws imposing vicarious liability on such superiors for subordinates' wrongs.[91]

§ 157.   Operation of motor vehicle

The liability of a sheriff or other peace officer for damages resulting to a third person from the operation of a motor vehicle by a deputy or other subordinate of the peace officer depends heavily upon the circumstances presented. Factors considered in determining such liability have included whether or not the subordinate was proceeding toward or returning from the spot where his actual official duty was performed,[92] whether or not the person

liable for the shooting of a plaintiff by the city police officer absent any specific request or authorization that the city police officer so act on the day in question or in relation to the incident).

87. Taylor v Gibson (CA5 Ala) 529 F2d 709 (recognizing rule; court did not specify circumstances, and declined to determine whether derivative liability would be supported under the broad allegations of the complaint).

88. Scott v Vandiver (CA4 SC) 476 F2d 238; Hesselgesser v Reilly (CA9 Wash) 440 F2d 901; Whited v Fields (WD Va) 581 F Supp 1444; Knipp v Weikle (ND Ohio) 405 F Supp 782.

The sheriff could be held liable for the alleged unlawful arrest and beating of the plaintiff by his deputies, on the basis of state law establishing such liability independent of 42 USCS § 1983. Brunson v Hyatt (DC SC) 409 F Supp 35.

346

Annotation: 51 ALR Fed 285 § 4.

89. Johnson v Duffy (CA9 Cal) 588 F2d 740; Dudley v Bell, 50 Mich App 678, 213 NW2d 805.

90. McDaniel v Carroll (CA6 Tenn) 457 F2d 968, cert den 409 US 1106, 34 L Ed 2d 687, 93 S Ct 897; Sandlin v Pearsall (ED Tenn) 427 F Supp 494.

91. Marks v Lyon County Bd. of County Comrs. (DC Kan) 590 F Supp 1129; Love v Davis (WD La) 353 F Supp 587 (notwithstanding the existence of a state law imposing liability on a sheriff for the wrongful acts of his deputy acting in the scope of employment, liability under the federal civil rights acts must be premised on personal culpability).

92. Usrey v Yarnell, 181 Ark 804, 27 SW2d 988.

Annotation: 15 ALR3d 1189 § 2[a].

A marshal is not liable for the negligence of his deputy where, having served a writ in a

FIGURE 8-7
(continued)

Reprinted with permission of Thomson/West

⇨ **A Point to Remember**   If you have trouble finding the right term in an index, go back to your problem and make a list of all key words. If necessary, use a legal thesaurus.

Even knowing the general topic, you may find it difficult or time-consuming to pinpoint a specific topic in the article. Some of the articles in the encyclopedias are very long. Pinpointing a specific topic can be done in two ways: reviewing the outline at the beginning of the article, or using the index.

Once you find the specific topic, you are given numerous citations to primary law. At this point, consider the issues of mandatory and persuasive authority discussed in earlier chapters. Both *Am. Jur. 2d* and *C.J.S.* provide cites to authorities in many different states. If the topic is one that is controlled by state law, first look for authorities from your state, as only these are binding. Other authorities are persuasive.

⇨ **A Point to Remember**   Regardless of how you find your topic and regardless of which encyclopedia you use, check the pocket part supplement for any changes or additions to the law. Also check the pocket part supplement to the index. Sometimes new topics or subtopics are added to reflect changes in the law. If the concept of pocket parts still confuses you, go to a code and check the date of publication of the hardbound book. Then check the date of the supplement.

BOX 8-1

USING ENCYCLOPEDIAS

(*AMERICAN JURISPRUDENCE 2d* AND *CORPUS JURIS SECUNDUM*)

√ Review your research question and identify:
  General legal topic
  Specific legal topic
  All descriptive words

√ Look up descriptive words in index and note cite to topic and section **or** go directly to the alphabetically arranged volume containing your general topic and review outline for specific topic section number.

√ Read article and make note of primary law from your jurisdiction.

√ Check pocket part supplement for updates.

8-4 *AMERICAN LAW REPORTS*

American Law Reports (A.L.R.) and *American Law Reports Federal (A.L.R. Fed.)*, published by West Group, are other important secondary sources used by legal researchers. *American Law Reports* covers American law as found in the various states, and *American Law Reports Federal* covers federal law. The publishers of *A.L.R.* look for recent case law that discusses important legal issues. These cases are then published along with an article, called an annotation, which discusses and analyzes the legal issue raised in the case. Figure 8-8 shows sample pages from *A.L.R.* illustrating a case and the annotation that follows.

Title of annotation.

ANNOTATION

WHEN DOES POLICE OFFICER'S USE OF FORCE DURING ARREST BECOME SO EXCESSIVE AS TO CONSTITUTE VIOLATION OF CONSTITUTIONAL RIGHTS, IMPOSING LIABILITY UNDER FEDERAL CIVIL RIGHTS ACT OF 1871 (42 USCS § 1983)

by

Richard P. Shafer, J.D.

TOTAL CLIENT-SERVICE LIBRARY® REFERENCES

5 Am Jur 2d, Arrest §§ 80–85, 114; 6 Am Jur 2d, Assault and Battery §§ 125, 148; 15 Am Jur 2d, Civil Rights §§ 11–21, 263–287; 40 Am Jur 2d, Homicide §§ 134–137

Annotations: See the related matters listed in the annotation, infra.

6 Federal Procedure L Ed, Civil Rights §§ 11:146–11:187

5 Federal Procedural Forms L Ed, Civil Rights §§ 10:41, 42, 47, 48, 50

5 Am Jur Pl & Pr Forms (Rev), Civil Rights, Form 2.4 (Supp); 22 Am Jur Pl & Pr Forms (Rev), Sheriffs, Police, and Constables, Forms 135–137

9 Am Jur Proof of Facts 2d 363, Police Officer's Use of Excessive Force in Making Arrest

15 Am Jur Trials 555, Police Misconduct Litigation—Plaintiff's Remedies

42 USCS § 1983

US L Ed Digest, Civil Rights § 12.5

L Ed Index to Annos, Arrest; Assault and Battery; Civil Rights; Police

ALR Quick Index, Arrest; Assault and Battery; Discrimination; Force and Violence; Police

Federal Quick Index, Arrest; Assault and Battery; Civil Rights; Force or Violence; Police

Consult POCKET PART in this volume for later cases

204

FIGURE 8-8 *A.L.R.*
Annotation

60 ALR Fed   ARREST—EXCESSIVE FORCE
60 ALR Fed 204

Outline of sections found
in annotations

205 | **FIGURE 8-8**
(continued)

[b] Force held not to violate constitutional rights

INDEX

These words or terms are found in the annotation in the section indicated.

FIGURE 8-8
(continued)

60 ALR Fed   ARREST—EXCESSIVE FORCE   § 1[a]
60 ALR Fed 204

TABLE OF COURTS AND CIRCUITS

Consult POCKET PART in this volume for later cases and statutory changes

I. Preliminary matters

§ 1. Introduction

[a] Scope

This annotation[1] discusses and analyzes the federal cases that have examined the question of when a police officer's use of force to effect an arrest[2] is so excessive as to violate the arrestee's constitutional rights and provide a basis for the imposition of civil liability upon the police officer under 42 USCS § 1983. Cases are included herein only if they pertain to or discuss force employed during an arrest and in order to effect an arrest. Thus, cases pertaining to or discussing the use of force by police officers at other times[3] are excluded from this annotation.

---

1. This annotation supercedes § 4 of the annotation at 1 ALR Fed 519.

2. This annotation includes cases relating to the use of force to prevent a suspected criminal from escaping an arrest, although at least one court has distinguished such cases from cases relating to the use of deadly force in effectuating an arrest in a nonescape situation. See Jones v Marshall (1975, **CA2 Conn**) 528 F2d 132.

3. For example, this annotation excludes cases that pertain to the assault of an individual without a subsequent arrest

The annotation starts here.

207

FIGURE 8-8
(continued)

Issues relating to color of law, immunity, vicarious liability, respondeat superior, and defenses based on an officer's good-faith belief in the propriety of his actions are outside the scope of this annotation.

[b] Related matters

Exhaustion of state administrative remedies as prerequisite to federal civil rights action based on 42 USCS § 1983. 47 ALR Fed 15.

Actionability, under 42 USCS § 1983, of claims for false arrest or false imprisonment. 44 ALR Fed 225.

Actions of off-duty policeman acting as private security guard as actions "under color of state law" actionable under Civil Rights Act of 1871 (42 USCS § 1983). 56 ALR Fed 895.

Vicarious liability of superior under 42 USCS § 1983 for subordinate's acts in deprivation of civil rights. 51 ALR Fed 285.

Survivability of actions against federal officials for damages based on alleged constitutional violation. 48 ALR Fed 587.

What statute of limitations is applicable to civil rights action brought under 42 USCS § 1983. 45 ALR Fed 548.

Actionability, under 42 USCS § 1983, of claims against persons other than police officers for false arrest or false imprisonment. 44 ALR Fed 225.

Survivability of civil rights cause of action based on 42 USCS § 1983. 42 ALR Fed 163.

Police action in connection with arrest as violation of Civil Rights Act, 42 USCS § 1983. 1 ALR Fed 519.

Civil liability of peace officer for death or personal injuries caused by intentional force in arresting misdemeanant. 83 ALR3d 238.

Right of peace officer to use deadly force in attempting to arrest fleeing felon. 83 ALR3d 174.

◆

Deadly force to arrest: triggering constitutional review. Harv. Civil Rights L Rev 11:361–389 (Spring, 1976).

[c] Statutory provision

The Civil Rights Act of 1871, 42 USCS § 1983, provides as follows:

§ 1983. Civil action for deprivation of rights

Every person who, under color of any statute, ordinance, regulation, custom, or usage, of any State or Territory, subjects, or causes to be subjected, any citizen of the United States or other person within the jurisdiction thereof to the deprivation of any rights, privileges, or immunities secured by the Constitution and laws, shall be liable to the party injured in an action at law, suit in equity, or other proper proceeding for redress.

§ 2. Summary, background, and comment

[a] In general

The use of force by police officers in effecting arrests has been a source of a substantial amount of litigation under 42 USCS § 1983. This statute, which was enacted as § 1 of the Ku Klux Act of April 20, 1871, was one of the means by which Congress exercised the power vested in it by § 5 of the Fourteenth Amendment to enforce the provisions of that Amend-

---

or with a subsequent arrest on fabricated charges to cover up the assault and the

beating of an individual after he has been secured.

FIGURE 8-8

(continued)

60 ALR Fed   ARREST—EXCESSIVE FORCE   **§ 2[a]**
60 ALR Fed 204

ment.[4] In enacting this statute, Congress intended to give a remedy to parties deprived of their constitutional rights, privileges, and immunities by an official's abuse of his position and intended to override certain kinds of state laws, to provide a remedy where state law is inadequate, to provide a federal remedy where a theoretically adequate state remedy is not practically available, and to provide a federal remedy supplemental to existing state remedies.[5]

One of the prerequisites for recovery under 42 USCS § 1983 by a plaintiff alleging that a police officer used excessive force during an arrest is that it must be shown that the force to which the plaintiff was subjected constituted a "deprivation of any rights, privileges, or immunities secured by the Constitution and laws." The courts that have ruled on such an allegation have enunciated several variant views of the test for determining whether a police officer's use of force during an arrest was so excessive as to violate one's constitutional rights, with the courts of some circuits having stated and applied more than one of these views in various cases. The courts' statements of the rule include the view that the use of unreasonable force during an arrest is a violation of constitutional rights, with the reasonableness of the force gauged by the ordinary, prudent man standard (§ 3, infra); the view that the use of unreasonable force during an arrest that also violates standards of decency that are generally accepted is a violation of constitutional rights (§ 3[c], infra); the view

that the infliction of injury as punishment during an arrest is a violation of constitutional rights (§ 4, infra); and the view that brutality or other action during an arrest that shocks the conscience is a violation of constitutional rights (§ 5, infra).

In cases involving the use of deadly force by a police officer in effecting an arrest, it has been held or recognized by some courts that federal law is supreme in the determination of when such force may be used, although other courts have applied state law to that determination without appearing to have considered the question of which law is supreme (§ 6, infra). It has generally been held that the use of deadly force by a police officer during the arrest of a misdemeanant is prohibited (§ 7, infra). However, the status of the privilege for use of deadly force during the arrest of a felon does not appear to be well-settled, with two differing rules having been applied by various courts. The first, and older, rule that has been applied is that a police officer may use deadly force during an arrest if he believes that a felony has been committed and that such force is necessary to effect the arrest (§ 8[a], infra). The second, and more modern, rule is a restriction of the older rule and prohibits the use of deadly force in the arrest of a non-violent felon (§ 8[b], infra).[6] The view has also been stated that a police officer has the right to employ deadly force in self-defense during the arrest of an individual (§ 9, infra). Various circumstances involving the use of deadly force by a police officer during

---

4. 15 Am Jur 2d, Civil Rights § 16.

5. 15 Am Jur 2d, Civil Rights § 16.

6. This rule is in accordance with the American Law Institute's Model Penal Code § 3.07(2)(b)(iv) (1962) which limits

the privilege to use deadly force to certain felonies that are deemed to represent some threat of harm to persons and are designated as forcible or serious crimes.

209   **FIGURE 8-8**
(continued)

an arrest have been examined by the courts and have been held either to have involved or not have involved a violation of the constitutional rights of the arrestee in cases brought under 42 USCS § 1983 for damages alleged to have resulted from a police officer's employment of excessive force during an arrest (§§ 10, 11, infra).

In relation to the use of other than deadly force in effecting an arrest, it has been held that police officers generally have the right to use such force as is necessary in self-defense (§ 12, infra). The use of various types of nondeadly force by a police officer during an arrest has also been examined by the courts and has been held either to have violated or not to have violated the constitutional rights of an arrestee in cases brought pursuant to 42 USCS § 1983 for damages alleged to have resulted from a police officer's employment of excessive force during an arrest (§§ 13–15, infra).

[b] Practice pointers

Counsel should be aware of various requirements relating to the preparation of a complaint in an action brought pursuant to 42 USCS § 1983.

A complaint based on 42 USCS § 1983 must allege (1) that the conduct complained of was engaged in under color of state law, and (2) that such conduct subjected the plaintiff to the deprivation of rights, privileges, and immunities secured by the Federal Constitution and laws.[7] Thus, an allegation that the defendant was authorized to act by state law is insufficient to assert that the defendant's conduct was engaged in under color of state law.[8] However, an allegation that the defendant acted under color and pretense of law while engaged in the complained of conduct is sufficient without the further allegation that the defendant was lawfully in office or setting forth a particular statute under which the defendant was purportedly acting.[9]

In preparation of the pleadings in an action brought pursuant to 42 USCS § 1983, counsel should be aware that in deliberating on a motion to dismiss a complaint based on § 1983, the court must take the facts alleged in the complaint to be true, no matter how rash and improbable they may appear, and should not dismiss the complaint unless it appears to a certainty that the plaintiff would not be entitled to relief under any set of facts that he might prove in support of his claim.[10] However, only material facts and not unsupported conclusions contained in the plaintiff's complaint will be considered in the light most favorable to the plaintiff on a motion to dismiss the complaint.[11]

Counsel should also note that a court may not dismiss a complaint based on 42 USCS § 1983 on the basis of affidavits submitted by the moving defendant without giving the plaintiff a chance to reply, and should, in such a situation, treat the motion to dismiss as a motion for summary judgment.[12] Summary judgment may be granted by a court in

7. 15 Am Jur 2d, Civil Rights § 286.

8. Miles v Armstrong (1953, **CA7 Ill**) 207 F2d 284.

15 Am Jur 2d, Civil Rights § 286.

9. 15 Am Jur 2d, Civil Rights § 286.

10. Wirth v Surles (1977, **CA4 SC**) 562 F2d 319, 45 ALR Fed 864, cert den 435 US 933, 55 L Ed 2d 531, 98 S Ct 1509.

15 Am Jur 2d, Civil Rights § 287.

11. 15 Am Jur 2d, Civil Rights § 287.

12. Cohen v Cahill (1960, **CA9 Cal**) 281 F2d 879, 3 FR Serv 2d 890.

15 Am Jur 2d, Civil Rights § 286.

FIGURE 8-8
(continued)

60 ALR Fed   ARREST—EXCESSIVE FORCE   § 3[a]

an action based on 42 USCS § 1983 where there are no substantial issues of facts.[13]

II. Factors in determination as to existence of violation of constitutional rights

§ 3. Use of unreasonable force

[a] Generally

In the following cases, the courts have held or recognized, without any further discussion of the standards to be used to determine reasonableness, that a police officer can be found liable for damages under 42 USCS § 1983 for the use of unreasonable force in effecting an arrest.

While concluding that the plaintiff's constitutional rights were not violated when he was shot and injured during his arrest, the court in Dolan v Golla (1979, **MD Pa)** 481 F Supp 475, affd without op (CA3 Pa) 633 F2d 209, held that a police officer may not use force which far exceeds that which is reasonable and necessary under the circumstances to make an arrest and that the use of such force imposes liability under 42 USCS § 1983.

In Samuel v Busnuck (1976, **DC Md)** 423 F Supp 99, the court held that the use of unreasonable force by police officers in making an arrest is actionable under 42 USCS § 1983. However, the court stated, police officers are entitled to use such force as is reasonably necessary to accomplish an arrest, and the reasonableness or excessiveness of the force necessary is a matter to be determined in the light of the circumstances as they appeared to the officer at the time of the arrest. Thus, the court stated, courts are not to substitute their own judgment for

the official discretion of the police officer in the front line, when such discretion is exercised reasonably and in good faith.

Reversing the District Court's grant of summary judgment to the defendants in an action brought under 42 USCS § 1983, the court in Courtney v Reeves (1981, **CA5 Tex)** 635 F2d 326, held that the accompaniment of a technically lawful arrest by unreasonable, unnecessary, or unprovoked force is actionable under § 1983 and found that the plaintiff's complaint properly stated a cause of action against the defendant officers for the use of such excessive force in effectuating his lawful arrest.

Finding that the force used to accomplish the arrest of the plaintiff was not disproportionate to the exigencies of the situation, the court in Melton v Shivers (1980, **MD Ala)** 496 F Supp 781, 60 ALR Fed 196, recognized that in the course of making a lawful arrest, police officers are entitled to use such force as is reasonably necessary to accomplish the task, and that force thus found to be reasonable or not excessive under the circumstances is deemed to be in conformity with, and not in contravention of, due process of law and hence does not create liability under 42 USCS § 1983. The reasonableness or excessiveness of the force necessary, the court stated, is a matter to be determined in the light of the circumstances as they appeared to the officer at the time of the arrest.

Concluding that the shooting and killing of the plaintiff's decedent was necessary in order to apprehend him and that no liability existed under 42 USCS § 1983, the court in Smith v Jones (1973, **MD Tenn)** 379 F Supp 201, affd without op (CA6 Tenn) 497

---

13. 15 Am Jur 2d, Civil Rights § 287.

FIGURE 8-8
(continued)

F2d 924, held that the use of unreasonable and unnecessary force by police officers making an otherwise lawful arrest violates the due process clause of the United States Constitution and imposes liability under § 1983, further stating that a law enforcement officer may shoot a person whom he is attempting to arrest only in certain aggravated circumstances.

Affirming a jury's verdict in favor of the plaintiff who alleged that the defendant police officers used excessive force while arresting him for disturbing the peace, the court in Morgan v Labiak (1966, **CA10 Colo**) 368 F2d 338, 1 ALR Fed 512, held that a person's constitutional rights are violated and liability exists under 42 USCS § 1983 where unnecessary, unreasonable, or violent force is used in the arrest of a person.

[b] Applicability of ordinary, prudent man standard

It has been held that the standard for determining whether a police officer used unreasonable and, therefore, excessive force in making an arrest is that of the conduct of ordinary, prudent men under the circumstances.

Affirming a judgment of dismissal with prejudice entered upon a jury verdict for the defendant police officers in an action under 42 USCS § 1983 for injuries to, and the wrongful death of, a 15-year-old boy, the court in Hamilton v Chaffin (1975, **CA5 Miss**) 506 F2d 904, held that the standard for determining whether excessive force was used in effecting an arrest is the conduct of ordinary, prudent men under the existing circumstances. The court explained that in determining whether the constitutional line between the proper and improper use of force has been crossed, a court must look to such

factors as the need for the application of force, the relationship between the need and the amount of force that was used, the extent of the injury inflicted, and whether force was applied in a good-faith effort to maintain or restore discipline or maliciously and sadistically for the very purpose of causing harm.

In Conklin v Barfield (1971, **WD Mo**) 334 F Supp 475, the court held that the applicable test of whether force used to effect an arrest was excessive and unlawful so as to impose liability under 42 USCS § 1983 is the conduct of ordinary, prudent men under the existing circumstances.

The court in Morgan v Labiak (1966, **CA10 Colo**) 368 F2d 338, 1 ALR Fed 512, held that the reasonableness of the force used by a police officer in making an arrest is a question of fact for the jury, and that the standard for determining whether the force employed was reasonable is the conduct of ordinary, prudent men under the existing circumstances.

[c] Together with violation of standards of decency

It was held in the following cases that a police officer can be found liable for damages under 42 USCS § 1983 for employing force during an arrest in excess of that which is reasonable and necessary in the circumstances and also violating standards of decency more or less universally accepted.

Finding that the defendant police officer used excessive force in making an arrest on numerous occasions, the court in Pennsylvania v Porter (1979, **WD Pa**) 480 F Supp 686, affd in part and revd in part on other grounds (CA3 Pa) 659 F2d 306, held that where the application of force by a

FIGURE 8-8
(continued)   **212**

police officer exceeds that which is reasonable and necessary under the circumstances and also violates standards of decency more or less universally accepted, it amounts to cruel and unusual punishment actionable under 42 USCS § 1983.

While concluding that the defendant police officer did not use excess force while attempting to arrest the plaintiff for underage drinking, the court in Hausman v Tredinnick (1977, **ED Pa**) 432 F Supp 1160, stated that a police officer who uses force which far exceeds that which is reasonable and necessary under the circumstances to make the arrest and which also violates standards of decency more or less universally accepted stands beyond the pale of permitted conduct and may be liable for damages to his arrestee under 42 USCS § 1983. The court further stated that when a police officer makes a lawful arrest but uses excessive force in making that arrest, the citizen being arrested has a right to resist that arrest and unlawful use of force, and if the citizen receives a beating due to his resisting the arrest, the police are liable for damages to that person under § 1983.

Although finding that the defendant police officer was not liable for damages under 42 USCS § 1983 for conducting a pat down search and handcuffing the plaintiff's decedent after he refused a traffic citation and resisted arrest, the court in Donaldson v Hovanec (1979, **ED Pa**) 473 F Supp 602, stated that excessive force is utilized, and that liability will be imposed under § 1983, when force is applied that exceeds that which is reasonable under the circumstances and also violates standards of decency more or less universally accepted.

In Lamb v Cartwright (1975, **ED**

Tex) 393 F Supp 1081, affd without op (CA5 Tex) 524 F2d 238, the court held that the application of force exceeding that which is reasonable and necessary under the circumstances and violating standards of decency more or less universally accepted constitutes the use of excessive force in the effecting of an arrest in violation of 42 USCS § 1983.

§ 4. Infliction of injury as punishment

It has been held or recognized that a police officer's infliction of corporal injury on a suspect during an arrest as punishment for supposed offenses may be the basis for the imposition of liability for damages under 42 USCS § 1983.

Of interest in this regard is Pennsylvania v Porter (1979, **WD Pa**) 480 F Supp 686, affd in part and revd in part on other grounds (CA3 Pa) 659 F2d 306, in which the court said that the application of force during an arrest by a police officer that exceeds that which is reasonable and necessary under the circumstances and also violates standards of decency more or less universally accepted amounts to cruel and unusual punishment actionable under 42 USCS § 1983.

While holding that the defendant police officer's striking of the plaintiff with his nightstick and handcuffs during the plaintiff's arrest did not constitute a violation of 42 USCS § 1983, the court in Samuel v Busnuck (1976, **DC Md**) 423 F Supp 99, recognized that if police officers act in excess of their lawful authority during an arrest and inflict corporal injury on suspects by way of punishment for supposed offenses, their action is not in conformity with due process of law and imposes liability under § 1983.

While concluding that the defen-

213

FIGURE 8-8
(continued)

dant police officers did not use excessive force in arresting a suspect in an attempted burglary who failed to obey instructions to remain at the scene and flagrantly, repeatedly, and dangerously refused to yield in the pursuit which followed, the court in Melton v Shivers (1980, **MD Ala**) 496 F Supp 781, 60 ALR Fed 196, stating that the function of police officers, preliminary to trial, is to arrest a suspect and present him before the proper authorities rather than to determine guilt and inflict punishment, recognized that police officers who beat or otherwise inflict corporal injury upon suspects by way of punishment for supposed offenses act in contravention of due process of law and may be held liable for damages under 42 USCS § 1983.

§ 5. Brutality or other action that shocks conscience

The following cases support the proposition that a police officer may be liable under 42 USCS § 1983 for brutality or the application of such undue force during an arrest that it shocks the conscience.

While concluding that a complete defense to the plaintiff's 42 USCS § 1983 action for deprivation of life without due process of law was afforded by a rule permitting the use of deadly force in certain situations, the court in Jones v Marshall (1975, **CA2 Conn**) 528 F2d 132, stated that the elementary requirements of a use of force rule under § 1983 must be that it neither permit brutal police conduct nor allow the application of

such undue force during an arrest that the police conduct shocks the conscience. The application of this rule, the court explained, requires the analysis of such factors as the need for the application of force, the relationship between the need and the amount of force that was used, the extent of the injury inflicted, and whether the force was applied in a good-faith effort or maliciously or sadistically.

While affirming a judgment in favor of the plaintiff in an action commenced pursuant to 42 USCS § 1983 for injuries caused to the plaintiff during his arrest, the court in Roberts v Marino (1981, **CA5 La**) 656 F2d 1112, stated that the reasonableness of force used in an arrest must be evaluated in light of the need, the motivation, and the extent of injury inflicted and held that a police officer's action will be redressed under § 1983 if that action amounted to an abuse of official power that shocks the conscience.

III. Use of deadly force as violation of constitutional rights

A. Generally

§ 6. Supremacy of federal law in determination of when deadly force may be used to effect arrest

The following cases have held or recognized that federal, rather than state, law is supreme in the determination of whether a police officer's use of deadly force in the effecting of an arrest imposes liability upon him under 42 USCS § 1983.[14]

---

14. However, attention is directed to numerous cases that have applied state law to such a determination without appearing to address the question whether federal or state law is supreme. For example, Love v Davis (1972, **WD La**) 353 F Supp 587, infra § 8[b]; Wiley v Memphis Police Dept. (1977, **CA6 Tenn**) 548 F2d 1247, cert den 434 US 822, 54 L Ed 2d 78, 98 S Ct 65, infra § 8[a]; Landrum v Moats (1978, **CA8 Neb**) 576 F2d 1320, cert den 439 US 912, 58 L Ed 2d 258, 99 S Ct 282, infra § 8[b].

FIGURE 8-8
(continued)

Observing that one of the principal purposes underlying the Civil Rights Act of 1871 was to protect individuals against misuse of power possessed by virtue of state law and made possible only because the wrongdoer is clothed with the authority of state law, the court in Jones v Marshall (1975, **CA2 Conn**) 528 F2d 132, held that in interpreting the scope of 42 USCS § 1983, the federal courts are not bound by the state law of torts or the defenses of privilege that state law provides, and that the applicable standards are those demanded by the Constitution of the United States. However, the court continued, a federal court is still by no means free to elevate whatever view of the privilege to use deadly force to effect an arrest it thinks to be preferable to the constitutional level envisaged by § 1983 and, rather, must make an attempt to weigh the competing interests in the light of historical and current cases and commentary to arrive at the proper scope of the privilege to use deadly force in particular instances. Thus, while stating that it thought the preferable rule would limit the privilege to the situation where the crime involved causes or threatens death or serious bodily harm, or where there is a substantial risk that the person to be arrested will cause death or serious bodily harm if his apprehension is delayed, the court concluded that the Connecticut rule allowing an officer to use deadly force against anyone who has committed a felony and is trying to escape arrest was not fundamentally unfair and, therefore, applied that rule in affirming a grant of summary judgment in favor of the defendant police officers in an action for damages under § 1983.

In Qualls v Parrish (1976, **CA6 Tenn**) 534 F2d 690, the court adopted and applied the Tennessee rule relating to the use of deadly force by a police officer in the effecting of an arrest, while noting that federal law applies and determines the adequacy of defenses asserted in a civil rights action under 42 USCS § 1983. The court stated that, although it is not bound by a state law privilege available to a police officer, nevertheless it still is by no means free to elevate whatever view of the privilege it thinks to be preferable to the constitutional level and explained that its principal reason for adopting the Tennessee rule, which allows a police officer to use deadly force only when he has reasonable grounds to believe that the person he is attempting to arrest has committed a felony, was that a decision to the contrary would be unfair to an officer who relied, in good faith, upon the settled law of his state that relieved him from liability for particular acts performed in his official capacity.

While recognizing the applicability of an Illinois statute directing that a police officer is justified in using force likely to cause death or great bodily harm during an arrest only when he reasonably believes that such force is necessary to prevent death or great bodily harm to himself, the court in Willis v Tillrock (1976, **ND Ill**) 421 F Supp 368, held that the test for determining whether an arrestee's constitutional rights have been violated is a federal one and stated that, therefore, state statutes are pertinent but not dispositive in such an inquiry.

See Clark v Ziedonis (1975, **CA7 Wis**) 513 F2d 79, where the court noted that federal law determines the adequacy of defenses asserted in a suit under 42 USCS § 1983 and discussed numerous rules relating to the use of deadly force in the arrest of a

215

Reprinted with permission of Thomson/West

FIGURE 8-8
(continued)

American Law Reports was first published in 1919 and is currently in its fifth edition or series. The various series are referred to as *A.L.R., A.L.R.2d, A.L.R.3d, A.L.R.4th,* and *A.L.R.5th.* The federal series is still in its first series and is known as *A.L.R. Fed.*

The legal topics that form the basis of each article in *American Law Reports* are much more specific than those found in encyclopedias. For example, look at the title of the annotation reprinted in Figure 8-8. This article deals entirely with the question of whether an off-duty police officer is acting under color of authority. Compare that with the articles found in Figure 8-7, which come from an encyclopedia. The encyclopedia articles deal with liability of police in general. The question of whether an off-duty police officer acted under color of authority and violated the Civil Rights Act is a small part of the article.

A second major difference between *A.L.R.* and encyclopedias is the arrangement of topics. *A.L.R.* does not arrange alphabetically. Rather, the arrangement is dependent on the date of the case law that leads to the article.

Using *A.L.R.*

The easiest way to find an article is to use the general *A.L.R. Index.* This is a descriptive word index that covers *A.L.R.2d* through *A.L.R.5th.* The first series of *A.L.R.* contains a separate index. A separate index also exists for *A.L.R. Fed.* The index refers you to specific articles. In addition to the index, *A.L.R.* contains a digest covering all of the topics found in *A.L.R.3d* through *5th.* The digest organizes all law into over 400 legal topics. The digest arranges these in alphabetical order. To use the digest, you must first identify the proper legal topic. One advantage of the digest over the index is that the digest refers to other secondary sources.

All *A.L.R.* articles have similar features. Each article contains the following.

1. **Table of Contents** describes what you will find in the annotation.
2. **Research References** refers you to other legal resources that are related to your topic.
3. **Research Sources** lists the sources used in compiling the article; *A.L.R.5th* includes the **electronic search query** used by authors of the article as well as West Digest Key Numbers; the electronic search query is used to find information on Westlaw and LEXIS. This is discussed in Chapter 11.
4. **Article Descriptive Word Index** helps you locate treatment of specific subjects within the article.
5. **Jurisdictional Table of Cited Statutes and Cases** lists by jurisdiction all cases and statutes cited in the article.
6. **Scope** states exactly what is covered in the article.
7. **Related Annotations** lists other *A.L.R.* articles that are closely related.
8. **Summary and Comment** summarizes the substantive part of the article.
9. **Practice Pointers** hints to the best way to handle a case within the scope of the article.
10. **Substantive Sections** discusses the legal topic thoroughly.

Identify each of these in Figure 8-8.

When you use an *A.L.R.* article check to see if the article was updated or **supplemented.** The publishers update the articles by providing references to new cases and statutes that deal with the topic. Later series of *A.L.R.* (3d, 4th, and 5th series) are updated by pocket part supplements. *A.L.R.* is supplemented by the *A.L.R. Blue Book of Supplemental Decisions. A.L.R.2d* is supplemented by *A.L.R.2d Later Case Service.*

electronic search query. Words that constitute a search request when using electronically stored data, i.e., information on the Internet or on a CD-ROM.

supplemented. Kept up-to-date.

BOX 8-2

USING *A.L.R.* OR *A.L.R. FED.*

√ Determine if research question is one of state law or federal law.

√ Review research question and identify descriptive words.

√ Check general *A.L.R. Index* or *Digest* for a cite to an article if question is one of state law.

√ Check *A.L.R. Fed. Index* or *Digest* for a cite to an article if question is one of federal law.

√ Find appropriate article(s).

√ Identify primary law from your jurisdiction.

√ Check pocket part supplement (or other supplement for early editions).

√ Check history of annotations table for superseded articles.

In addition to checking if your article was supplemented, check if the article was **superseded.** In some cases, the law changes so often that an older article is no longer valid or helpful. As a result, a new article is written, superseding the prior article. The last volume of the *A.L.R. Index* contains an annotation history table that provides this information.

superseded. Replaced.

⇨ **A Point to Remember** Remember that an *A.L.R.* article is a secondary source. Do not cite it to a court as your only authority. Always give the court references to primary law.

BOX 8-3

COMMON SECONDARY SOURCES

- *American Jurisprudence 2d*
- *Corpus Juris Secundum*
- *American Law Reports*
- Legal treatises
- Legal periodicals and law reviews

8-5 TREATISES

A **treatise** is a publication covering a single legal topic, usually written by a legal scholar or practicing attorney who specializes in that area of law. It contains a thorough discussion and explanation of the law and provides cites to primary authority. Treatises may be a single volume or a multivolume set. Some are updated regularly, while others may never be supplemented. A well-known class of treatises is published by West and known as the **hornbook** series. These books are written primarily for law students but are useful to anyone. Hornbook series books are also often published in a condensed version called the **Nutshell Series.**

treatise. Either one book or a multivolume series of books dealing with one legal topic.

hornbook. Name given to books published by West that are a type of treatise; commonly used by law students.

Nutshell Series. Condensed versions of hornbooks.

Using a Treatise

If a treatise has been written relating to your research question (and probably it has), you can locate it in a library by checking the library catalogue. The catalogue contains an alphabetical listing of legal topics and a list of all books relating to that topic that can be found in the library. Most treatises contain an index at the end of the book that is designed to help you locate your specific research issue. In using a treatise, be particularly careful to check the copyright date of the book, especially if there is no pocket part supplement. Some treatises found in law libraries are outdated.

BOX 8-4

USING A TREATISE

√ Identify legal topic.

√ Check library catalog.

√ Check copyright date on treatise.

√ Determine if treatise is supplemented.

√ Use index to find specific topic.

8-6 PERIODICALS

periodical. Legal material, published at regular inntervals, consisting of magazines, journals, and law reviews.

Numerous legal magazines and journals (**periodicals**) are published. Many professional associations publish magazines. For example, the American Bar Association publishes a monthly magazine, *The American Bar Journal,* for its members. See Figure 8-9 for a copy of the table of contents of one such magazine. The state bar asssociations also publish regular magazines or journals for their members. Magazines containing articles on legal topics are published for paralegals, for example, *Legal Assistant Today.* National and local paralegal associations may also publish regular newsletters. Often, these newsletters contain articles on current legal topics.

law review. A type of legal periodical published by law schools containing articles on different legal topics.

One very important type of periodical publication is a **law review.** A law review is a publication from a law school. It contains scholarly articles by noted legal authorities, usually on current legal issues. It may also contain shorter articles written by law students. Most law schools publish law reviews at regular intervals. A law review article can be an excellent research source. If your research issue is the subject of a law review article, you will find a thorough discussion of the law including references to numerous primary authorities. The major disadvantage of law review articles (or most periodical literature) is that they are not supplemented or updated.

Guides to Periodicals

Finding an article in a legal periodical is done in much the same way that you find an article in any periodical. Two indexes to legal periodicals are published: *Current Law Index* and *Index to Legal Periodicals and Books.* The publishers of *Current Law Index* also produce LegalTrac, an optical disk information system.

FIGURE 8-9 *Cover Page for California Lawyer*

CONTENTS

CALIFORNIA LAWYER   MARCH 2003

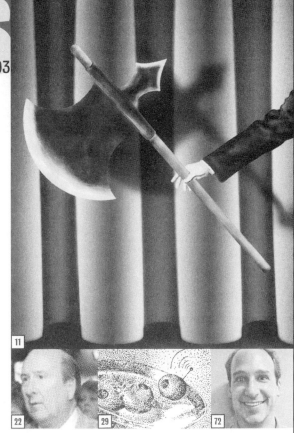

FEATURES

COVER:
THE CLAY AWARDS | 15
CALIFORNIA LAWYER honors 26 attorneys for their extraordinary achievements in 2002.

> by Lucia Hwang, Gwendolyn Mariano, and Deborah Rosenthal

DOUBLE CROSS TO BEAR | 22
After months of investigation, Dennis L. Stout, the district attorney of San Bernardino County, thought he was about to nail a corrupt supervisor. Then Stout suddenly became the target.

> by Matthew Heller

Cover photograph by Doug Workmaster

CALIFORNIA LAWYER (ISSN 0279-4063) Volume 23, Number 3, March 2003. Published monthly by Daily Journal Corporation, 915 E. First St., Los Angeles, CA 90012. Copyright ©2003 Daily Journal Corporation. All rights reserved. SUBSCRIPTIONS: $75 per year for subscriptions within the United States. Periodicals postage paid at Los Angeles, California, and at additional mailing offices. Subscription inquiries and changes of address should be sent to CALIFORNIA LAWYER Circulation, P.O. Box 54026, Los Angeles, CA 90054-0026. POSTMASTER: Please send address changes to CALIFORNIA LAWYER Circulation, P.O. Box 54026, Los Angeles, CA 90054-0026.

Reprinted with permission of *California Lawyer*

FIGURE 8-9   (continued) Table of Contents, *California Lawyer*

These indexes, which resemble the *Readers Guide to Periodical Literature,* allow you to find information by subject matter or by author. They contain references to more than 1,000 different sources from the United States and several foreign jurisdictions.

BOX 8-5

USING PERIODICALS

√ Identify legal topic or author.

√ Check *Index to Legal Periodicals* and/or *Current Law Index.*

√ Locate periodical.

√ Check current status of the law.

8-7 LOOSELEAF SERVICES

The term **looseleaf service** is used to describe a type of secondary research material that is published in a binder format rather than as a bound book. Material concerning an area of law is printed on unbound, or "loose," pages and assembled in a binder. The purpose of these services is to allow frequent supplementation of the material without the use of the traditional pocket part supplement. As changes occur in the law, subscribers to the looseleaf service are sent the changes. These are printed on replacement pages for the binder. The subscribers takes out the old page and replaces it with a new page reflecting the current law.

looseleaf service. Legal material published in a binder format, regularly supplemented with replacement pages.

Looseleaf services are commonly used for areas of law regulated by administrative rules or regulations. If you recall from Chapter 6, finding the latest updates for administrative regulations is a cumbersome process if you rely on the official publications. Looseleaf services are secondary sources that provide this information. Major publishers of looseleaf services are Commerce Clearing House (CCH), Prentice Hall, and Bureau of National Affairs (BNA).

⇨ **A Point to Remember**   When replacement pages are sent to a looseleaf service subscriber, a preface page is included indicating the date of the latest page revisions. If you are responsible for updating the books, always file this page. If you are using the book, always check the date to make sure the material is current.

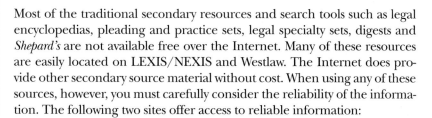ECHNOLOGY CORNER

Most of the traditional secondary resources and search tools such as legal encyclopedias, pleading and practice sets, legal specialty sets, digests and *Shepard's* are not available free over the Internet. Many of these resources are easily located on LEXIS/NEXIS and Westlaw. The Internet does provide other secondary source material without cost. When using any of these sources, however, you must carefully consider the reliability of the information. The following two sites offer access to reliable information:

http://tarlton.law.utexas.edu/vlibrary/

http://www.loc.gov/law/guide/lawreviews.html

CHAPTER SUMMARY

Secondary sources are research tools that contain discussions and explanations of the primary law. They refer the researcher to the primary law by providing citations to relevant cases, statutes, and constitutional provisions. There are different types of secondary sources, but many have some, if not all, of the following features: descriptive word indexes, tables of contents, tables of statutes cited, tables of cases cited, tables of abbreviations, prefaces, parallel reference tables, and pocket part supplements.

One important type of secondary source is the legal encyclopedia. *American Jurisprudence 2d* and *Corpus Juris Secundum* are two national legal encyclopedias. In these works, hundreds of legal topics are arranged alphabetically. The encyclopedias contain discussions and explanations of those topics with references to relevant primary law. These books are updated with pocket part supplements. Some states have specific encyclopedias for legal topics in their jurisdictions.

Another important type of secondary source is *American Law Reports (A.L.R.)*. The publishers of *American Law Reports* select important new cases, reprint the cases, and publish annotations dealing with the legal issues of the cases. The annotations contain extensive discussions of the issues as well as references to other relevant primary law. *A.L.R.* annotations are now supplemented with pocket part supplements. Occasionally, because of extensive changes in the law, an annotation is superseded rather than supplemented.

Secondary source material also includes treatises and a variety of legal periodicals, including law reviews. These materials often are not supplemented.

Looseleaf services consist of material found in binders. These materials are supplemented frequently by revised replacement pages.

TERMS TO REMEMBER

secondary source of law	treatise
primary source of law	hornbook
legal encyclopedia	Nutshell Series
electronic search query	periodical
supplemented	law review
superseded	looseleaf service

QUESTIONS FOR REVIEW

1. What is the purpose of a secondary source of law?
2. Describe some of the common features of secondary sources.
3. What is a legal encyclopedia?
4. How do you use a legal encyclopedia?
5. Describe the contents of *American Law Reports*.
6. How is *A.L.R.* kept up-to-date?
7. How does a treatise differ from a legal encyclopedia or *A.L.R.*?
8. What is a major disadvantage of a treatise?
9. What is a law review?
10. How would you find a specific topic in a legal periodical?

CAN YOU FIGURE IT OUT?

1. Refer to Figure 8-3. In which *Am. Jur. 2d* title and section will you find a discussion of 10 U.S.C.S. § 6401 (a)?

2. Refer to Figure 8-7. Cite a case for the proposition that a sheriff may be liable for the wrongful acts of his deputy in making an arrest of an escaping prisoner.

3. Refer to Figure 8-7. Where would you find a form for a complaint in an action against peace officers for wounding a prisoner?

4. Refer to Figure 8-8. Give the cites to provisions in *Am. Jur. 2d* that deal with the same topic that is the subject of this *A.L.R.* annotation.

5. Refer to Figure 8-8. Which sections of this annotation deal with patdown searches?

6. Refer to Figure 8-8. Cite the cases found in § 3 of the annotation dealing with liability of police officers for use of unreasonable force.

RESEARCH ASSIGNMENTS AND ACTIVITIES

Part One: Using Encyclopedias: *American Jurisprudence 2d*

For each of the following answer the questions and cite to the section in *Am. Jur. 2d* where you found the answer.

1. Can a state consider a lost animal to be abandoned? Cite case authority for your answer.

2. What is the monetary liability of credit card owners for unauthorized use of their credit card? Cite statutory authority for your answer.

3. Can a child who is born illegitimate, but later legitimized, inherit from the natural father?

4. What is the test to determine whether a game is one of chance or one of skill?

5. Is there a difference between a malicious prosecution and abuse of process?

6. Susan knowingly makes a false statement of fact under penalty of perjury. Later Susan changes the story to the truth. Does this excuse the prejury? What is the controlling federal statute?

7. Is it all right for a company that does interstate business to refuse to hire a woman as vice president of international operations where foreign clients might react negatively to a woman? Cite the controlling case.

8. John married his cousin but believed that the marriage was void. After separating from his cousin, John later married Jill without obtaining a divorce from his first wife. Is John guilty of bigamy? Cite the controlling case.

Part Two: Using *A.L.R.*

9. Cite an *A.L.R.* annotation dealing with liability of property owners for injury caused by failure of an elevator to level at the floor.

10. What is the subject of the annotation found at 6 *A.L.R. 2d* 391? What issue is discussed in § 2 of this article?

11. Find and cite an *A.L.R.* annotation in *A.L.R. 4th* dealing with state laws that require a person who requests a jury trial in a civil case to pay costs associated with the jury.

12. Find and cite an *A.L.R.* annotation in *A.L.R. Fed.* dealing with the complexity of civil action as affecting the Seventh Amendment right to trial by jury.

13. What is the purpose of the annotation found at 24 *A.L.R. Fed.* 940? What is meant by the phrase "comity of nation" as used in the article?

14. Find and cite an *A.L.R.* annotation involving undue influence and nontestamentary gifts to clergymen, spiritual advisors, or the church.

15. Find and cite an *A.L.R.* annotation dealing with injury or property damage caused by lightning as a basis of tort liability.

Part Three: Periodicals and Law Reviews

16. Find and cite a law review article comparing community property law reform in the United States and in Canada.

17. Find and cite a 1995 article in the *U.C.L.A. Law Review* dealing with lunar mining.

18. Find and cite an article in the *American Bar Association Journal* dealing with the legal aspects of artifical insemination.

Part Four: State Research

19. Find out if your state has a state-specific encyclopedia. If so, what is its title and who is the publisher?

20. Identify at least one secondary source in your state that covers state law in general.

21. Identify at least three law reviews in your state.

22. Find out if your state bar association publishes a journal. If so, what is its title?

CASE PROJECT

Using the same case that you researched in previous chapters, find and cite articles in appropriate encyclopedias, periodicals, and the *A.L.R.* that relate to the issue. Read the articles and note cases and statutes that might apply to these issues. Write a brief summary of the articles and list cases and statutes that you should read. Read the cases and statutes and take notes.

DIGESTS AND MISCELLANEOUS RESEARCH TOOLS

CHAPTER OUTLINE

CHAPTER OBJECTIVES

When you complete this chapter you should be able to

- Explain the purpose of a digest.
- Describe how a researcher uses headnotes.
- List some of the more popular legal digests.
- Explain how and when to use a digest.
- Discuss the purpose of the Restatements of Law.
- Explain why pattern jury instructions are a useful research tool.
- Describe when a researcher might use form books.

CITATION MATTERS

BOOKS

THE BLUEBOOK—RULE 15

Rule 15 states: "Cite books, pamphlets, and other nonperiodic materials by volume, if more than one (rule 3.2(a)); author, editor, and/or translator (rule 15.1); title (rule 15.2); serial number, if any (rule 15.3); page, section, or paragraph (rules 3.3 and 3.4), if only part of a volume is cited; edition, if more than one has appeared; publisher, if not the original one; and date (rule 15.4). Cite prefaces or forewords according to rule 15.6, supplements according to rule 3.2(c), and appendices according to rule 3.5."

THE BLUEBOOK provides the following examples:

full name of first author	ampersand	full name of second author	title of the book	section sign
FLEMING JAMES, JR.	&	GEOFFREY C. HAZARD, JR.,	CIVIL PROCEDURE	§ 2.35 (3d ed. 1985)

edition cited   date of edition cited   specific section

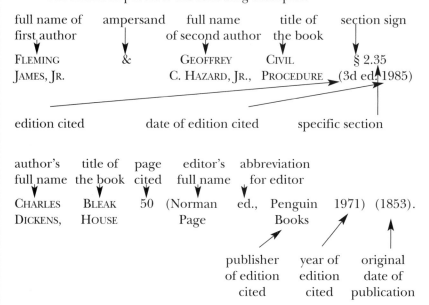

author's full name	title of the book	page cited	editor's full name	abbreviation for editor			
CHARLES DICKENS,	BLEAK HOUSE	50 Page	(Norman	ed.,	Penguin Books	1971)	(1853).

publisher of edition cited   year of edition cited   original date of publication

---

INTEROFFICE MEMORANDUM

TO: Research Associate

FROM: Supervising Attorney

RE: Rambeaux File

I finished reading your recent memo on the Rambeaux case. I think the *Tarpley* case that you mention in the memo is very helpful. Please keep looking and see if you can find any similar cases. Also, I previously mentioned that Rambeaux was served with a civil complaint. We need to file a responsive pleading soon. Find a form for this and check the time requirement for filing an answer.

9-1 INTRODUCTION

In addition to the secondary sources described in the previous chapter, many other materials help the researcher find and understand the primary law. An important legal resource that helps you find primary case law is a **digest.** Digests are multivolume works that function as indexes to case reporters.

> ➪ **A Point to Remember**   Remember that when case law is published, the case reporters do not contain a cumulative index. To find a case on a particular topic, you need to use another resource in addition to the case reporters.

In a digest, hundreds of legal topics are arranged alphabetically, just as they are in a **descriptive word index.** However, under each topic in a digest you find references to cases that involve the topic. In addition to digests, there are miscellaneous research tools, such as form books, pattern jury instructions, and the Restatement of Law. A legal dictionary and legal thesaurus are also essential research tools. All of these research materials help you understand the law and often lead to primary sources of law. Materials such as form books and pattern jury instructions are used by legal practitioners to help them draft legal documents. This chapter discusses digests and other miscellaneous research tools.

digest. An index to reported cases, arranged by subject; a short summary of cases is provided.

descriptive word index. An alphabetical listing of words describing the topics contained in a book or set of books; refers the researcher to the volume and page where the topic is discussed.

9-2 DIGESTS

Unlike legal encyclopedias, *American Law Reports,* and treatises, digests do not explain or discuss the law. Digests do not refer you to constitutional or statutory law. Digests are a special type of index to case reporters and are published by both West and LEXIS Law Publishing to accompany their case reporters. Digests are based on the headnotes that precede the cases.

Headnotes

Recall from Chapter 4 that when cases are published in case reporters, the publishers add many features including **headnotes.** Editors of the case reporters read each case and summarize the legal principles found in the case. Each legal principle is given a topic name and number. Headnotes found in West Reporters utilize the

headnotes. Editorial enhancement added to the front material of a case; useful summary of most of the legal topics addressed in the case.

topic and key number.
System used by West Group
to integrate its various primary and secondary
resource materials.

topic and key number system. See Figure 9-1 for the headnotes of a case printed in a West Reporter, the *Supreme Court Reporter.* Note the topics and key numbers for the headnote. Headnotes found in other reporters use similar systems, using a section sign (§) rather than the key symbol. Figure 9-2 is a reprint of the same case shown in Figure 9-1 found in a different reporter. Although the headnotes each have topics and numbers, note that the topics and numbers are different in the various reporters.

When editors read new cases and write headnotes, generally they assign an existing topic to each legal principle. These topics were developed over many years. Remember, however, that different publishers use different terms to describe various legal topics. In the examples found in Figures 9-1 and 9-2, note that one publisher uses the term "States," while the other uses the terms "States, Territories and Possessions." Because many cases deal with the same or similar subjects, several different cases found in the same reporter system often contain the same headnote topic and number. Also, because one case may contain a discussion of several legal topics, one case often has several different headnote topics and numbers. Review Figures 9-1 and 9-2 and note the different topics found in the headnotes.

It is important to remember that when the same case is reported in different reporters, the headnotes are different, even though the opinions are identical. Because the digests are based on the headnotes, different digests are thus published for different case reporters.

Digest Topics

In the digests, headnote topics are arranged alphabetically. Each topic is then broken down into many subtopics or sections. Under each topic and section are case citations to all cases containing that topic and section in a headnote. Refer to Figures 9-3 and 9-4 to see pages in different digests corresponding to the cases found in Figures 9-1 and 9-2. Examine Figure 9-4 closely and locate the reference to the name of the case whose headnotes are seen in Figure 9-2. Note how other cases involving the same topic are referenced. Compare this to Figure 9-3. In this digest, only one case is referenced.

▷ **A Point to Remember**   Remember: Each publisher uses topics that *it* selects. Thus, the same legal principle may be identified by different topic names in different publications.

West Digests

A major publisher of case reporters, West Group publishes numerous digests. Like other West Group publications, the West digests use the key number system. A comprehensive digest system, the American Digest System, covers annotations to *all* state and federal cases. Other West digests contain case annotations to United States Supreme Court cases, to selected state cases, to federal district court and appellate court cases, and to cases found in various specialty court reporters.

The American Digest System   The largest digest available to researchers is the American Digest System, published by West. This digest system, which is based on the headnotes found in case reporters in the West Reporter system, is a topical arrangement of all headnotes of *all* state and federal cases published in any of the national reporters. The American Digest System, first published at the end of the 1800s, includes case references to every state and dates back to 1658! When first

2302   **108 SUPREME COURT REPORTER**   **487 U.S. 130**

that the acceptance of employment should be deemed a waiver of a specific protection that is as basic a part of our constitutional heritage as is the privilege against self-incrimination.

The law is not captive to its own fictions. Yet, in the matter before us the Court employs the fiction that personal incrimination of the employee is neither sought by the Government nor cognizable by the law. That is a regrettable holding, for the conclusion is factually unsound, unnecessary for legitimate regulation, and a violation of the Self-Incrimination Clause of the Fifth Amendment of the Constitution. For these reasons, I dissent.

487 U.S. 131, 101 L.Ed.2d 123

131 Bobby FELDER, Petitioner

v.

Duane CASEY et al.

No. 87–526.

Argued March 28, 1988.

Decided June 22, 1988.

Wisconsin arrestee brought action against police officers, police chief, and city for violations of federal civil rights arising out of his arrest. The trial court denied motion to dismiss federal civil rights claim because of arrestee's failure to comply with that state's notice-of-claim statute and the Wisconsin Court of Appeals affirmed. The Wisconsin Supreme Court, Ceci, J., 139 Wis.2d 614, 408 N.W.2d 19, reversed and remanded. Certiorari was granted. The Supreme Court, Justice Brennan, held that Wisconsin notice-of-claim statute was

* The syllabus constitutes no part of the opinion of the Court but has been prepared by the Reporter of Decisions for the convenience of the

preempted with respect to federal civil rights actions brought in state court.

Reversed and remanded.

Justice White filed concurring opinion.

Justice O'Connor filed dissenting opinion in which Chief Justice Rehnquist joined.

Municipal Corporations ⟜741.1(4) ◄

States ⟜197

Wisconsin notice-of-claim statute, providing that no action may be brought or maintained against any state governmental subdivision, agency, or officer unless claimant either provides written notice of claim within 120 days of alleged injury or demonstrates that relevant defendant had actual notice of claim and was not prejudiced by lack of written notice, is preempted when federal civil rights action is brought in state court; state statute conflicts in its purpose and effects with remedial objectives of federal civil rights law, and its enforcement would produce different outcomes in § 1983 litigation based solely on whether claim was asserted in state or federal court. W.S.A. 893.80(1)(a); 42 U.S.C.A. § 1983.

Syllabus *

Nine months after being allegedly beaten by Milwaukee police officers who arrested him on a disorderly conduct charge that was later dropped, petitioner filed this state-court action against the city and certain of the officers under 42 U.S.C. § 1983, alleging that the beating and arrest were racially motivated and violated his rights under the Fourth and Fourteenth Amendments to the Federal Constitution. The officers (respondents) moved to dismiss the suit because of petitioner's failure to comply with Wisconsin's notice-of-claim statute, which provides, *inter alia*, that before suit may be brought in state court against a state or local governmental entity or officer, the plaintiff, within 120 days of

reader. See *United States v. Detroit Lumber Co.,* 200 U.S. 321, 337, 26 S.Ct. 282, 287, 50 L.Ed. 499.

Headnote from Supreme Court Reporter version of Felder v. Casey. See how this relates to Figure 9-3.

FIGURE 9-1
Supreme Court Reporter Headnote

Reprinted with permission of Thomson/West

Headnotes from *Lawyers Edition* version of *Felder v. Casey.*

See Figure 9-4. Headnotes 5a, 5b refer you to the *Lawyers Edition Digest* and the topic "Civil Rights." Sections 2 and 27 contain a reference to *Felder v. Casey* and other cases that deal with the same topic.

FIGURE 9-2
Lawyers' Edition Headnotes

FELDER v CASEY
(1988) 487 US 131, 101 L Ed 2d 123, 108 S Ct 2302

underlying a state rule of decision at the expense of the federal right. (O'Connor, J., and Rehnquist, Ch. J., dissented in part from this holding.)

States, Territories, and Possessions § 18 — subordination to federal power

4. Under the supremacy clause (Art VI, cl 2) of the Federal Constitution, the relative importance to the state of its own law is not material when there is a conflict with a valid federal law, for any state law, however clearly within a state's acknowledged power, which interferes with or is contrary to federal law, must yield.

Civil Rights §§ 2, 27 — civil liability — objective

5a, 5b. The central objective of the Reconstruction-era federal civil rights statutes, such as 42 USCS § 1983, is to insure that individuals whose federal constitutional or statutory rights are abridged may recover damages or secure injunctive relief; thus, § 1983 (1) creates a species of liability in favor of persons deprived of their federal civil rights by those wielding state authority, (2) provides a uniquely federal remedy against incursions upon rights secured by the Federal Constitution and laws of the nation, and (3) is to be accorded a sweep as broad as its language; § 1983 accomplishes its goal of providing compensatory relief to those deprived of their federal rights by state actions by creating a form of liability that, by its very nature, runs only against a specific class of defendants—government bodies and their officials.

Civil Rights § 19; Courts §§ 183, 892 — 42 USCS § 1983 action — applicability of state law — state courts — federal courts

6a, 6b. Any assessment of the ap-

plicability of state law to federal civil rights litigation, such as litigation under 42 USCS § 1983, must be made in light of the purpose and nature of the federal right, whether the question arises (1) in state-court § 1983 litigation, or (2) in federal-court § 1983 litigation—where, under 42 USCS § 1988, courts are occasionally called upon to borrow state law, because the federal civil rights laws fail to provide certain rules of decision thought essential to the orderly adjudication of rights; although a determination that a state law does not apply to a federal-court § 1983 action is not dispositive of whether the same law applies in a state-court § 1983 action, the federal-court determination can inform the analysis of the state-court question. (O'Connor, J., and Rehnquist, Ch. J., dissented in part from this holding.)

Courts § 711 — concurrent state and federal jurisdiction

7. State courts possess concurrent jurisdiction with federal courts over federal civil rights litigation under 42 USCS § 1983.

Civil Rights § 19; Courts §§ 892, 901; Statutes §§ 102, 103 — applicability of state laws in federal court — notice of claim — limitations

8a-8c. Under 42 USCS § 1988, state notice-of-claim statutes—such as one which provides that (1) no action may be brought against any state governmental subdivision or officer unless the claimant either (a) provides written notice of the claim within 120 days of the alleged injury, or (b) demonstrates that the subdivision or officer had actual notice of the claim and was not prejudiced by the lack of written notice, and (2) the claimant must refrain

127

Reprinted from *U.S. Supreme Court Reports, Lawyers' Edition* with permission. Copyright 1990 Matthew Bender & Company, Inc., a member of the LexisNexis Group. All Rights Reserved.

State of Nevada could not claim immunity from suit in action brought in California court by California residents to recover for injuries sustained in automobile collision on California highway involving vehicle owned by State of Nevada, and full faith and credit clause did not require California to limit recovery to the $25,000 maximum limitation in Nevada's statutory waiver of its immunity from suit in its own courts. U.S.C.A.Const. art. 4, § 1; Amend. 11; West's Ann.Cal. Vehicle Code, § 17451; N.R.S. 41.031, 41.035, subd. 1.—Id.

Constitutional limitations on sovereignty of the several states precluding the states from levying discriminatory taxes on goods of other nations or to bar their entry altogether, denying state's freedom to deny extradition of a fugitive when a proper demand is made by executive of another state and concerning privileges and immunities of citizens in the several states do not imply that any one state's immunity from suit in the courts of another state is anything other than a matter of comity. U.S.C.A.Const. art. 1, § 8, cl. 3; art. 4, § 2, cl. 2; Amend. 10.—Id.

U.S.W.Va. 1987. States retain no sovereign immunity as against the federal Government; calling into doubt *United States v. North Carolina,* 136 U.S. 211, 40 S.Ct. 920, 34 L.Ed. 336.—West Virginia v. U.S., 107 S.Ct. 702, 479 U.S. 305, 93 L.Ed.2d 639.

☜**191.6(1). In general.**
U.S.Alaska 1991. Statute authorizing district courts to exercise jurisdiction over civil actions brought by Indians under the Constitution, laws, or treaties of the United States is not a delegation to tribes of the federal Government's exemption from state sovereign immunity. 28 U.S.C.A. § 1362.—Blatchford v. Native Village of Noatak and Circle Village, 111 S.Ct. 2578, 501 U.S. 775, 115 L.Ed.2d 686, appeal after remand 38 F.3d 1505.

☜**191.8(1). In general.**
U.S.Alaska 1991. Fact that Congress grants jurisdiction to hear a claim does not suffice to show that Congress has abrogated all defenses to that claim.—Blatchford v. Native Village of Noatak and Circle Village, 111 S.Ct. 2578, 501 U.S. 775, 115 L.Ed.2d 686, appeal after remand 38 F.3d 1505.

☜**191.9(1). In general.**
U.S.Ill. 1992. Adoption Assistance and Child Welfare Act does not create implied private cause of action for alleged failure by State to make reasonable efforts to prevent removal of children from their homes and to facilitate reunification of families. Social Security Act, § 471(a)(15), as amended, 42 U.S.C.A. § 671(a)(15).—Suter v. Artist M., 112 S.Ct. 1360, 503 U.S. 347, 118 L.Ed.2d 1, on remand Artist M. v. Johnson, 968 F.2d 1218.

☜**191.9(7). Torts.**
U.S.S.C. 1991. Federal Employers' Liability Act (FELA) created cause of action by injured state railroad employee against state-owned railroad, enforceable in state court, pursuant to holding in *Parden* to effect that statutory phrase "[e]very common carrier by railroad" was intended to include state-owned railroads. Federal Employers' Liability Act, §§ 1–10, as amended, 45 U.S.C.A. §§ 51–60.—Hilton v. South Carolina Public Railways Com'n, 112 S.Ct. 560, 502 U.S. 197, 116 L.Ed.2d 560, on remand 413 S.E.2d 845, 307 S.C. 63.

☜**191.10. —— What are suits against state or state officers.**
U.S.Mich. 1989. Suit against state official in his or her official capacity is suit not against official, but rather against official's office; as such, suit is no different from one against state itself. 42 U.S.C.A. § 1983.—Will v. Michigan Dept. of State Police, 109 S.Ct. 2304, 491 U.S. 58, 105 L.Ed.2d 45.

U.S.Pa. 1984. Insofar as an injunctive relief is sought, an error of law by state officers acting in their official capacities will not suffice to override sovereign immunity of state where relief effectively is against it. U.S.C.A. Const.Amend. 11.—Pennhurst State School & Hosp. v. Halderman, 104 S.Ct. 900, 465 U.S. 89, 79 L.Ed.2d 67.

☜**193. Rights of action against state or state officers.**
U.S.N.J. 1994. Judgment against Port Authority Trans-Hudson Corporation (PATH), a wholly owned subsidiary of the Port Authority of New York and New Jersey, would not be enforceable against either New York or New Jersey. N.J.S.A. 32:1–18; N.Y.McK.Unconsol.Laws § 6418.—Hess v. Port Authority Trans-Hudson Corp., 115 S.Ct. 394, 513 U.S. 30, 130 L.Ed.2d 245.

☜**197. —— Presentation of claim.**
U.S.Wis. 1988. Wisconsin notice-of-claim statute, providing that no action may be brought or maintained against any state governmental subdivision, agency, or officer unless claimant either provides written notice of claim within 120 days of alleged injury or demonstrates that relevant defendant had actual notice of claim and was not prejudiced by lack of written notice, is preempted when federal civil rights action is brought in state court; state statute conflicts in its purpose and effects with remedial objectives of federal civil rights law, and its enforcement would produce different outcomes in § 1983 litigation based solely on whether claim was asserted in state or federal court. W.S.A. 893.80(1)(a); 42 U.S.C.A. § 1983.—Felder v. Casey, 108 S.Ct. 2302, 487 U.S. 131, 101 L.Ed.2d 123, on remand 427 N.W.2d 854, 145 Wis.2d 631, reconsideration granted, opinion withdrawn 431 N.W.2d 175, 146 Wis.2d 354, on reconsideration 441 N.W.2d 725, 150 Wis.2d 458.

☜**201. Time to sue, limitations, and laches.**
See also LIMITATION OF ACTIONS.
U.S. 1991. Doctrine of laches did not preclude State of Illinois from bringing original action in United States Supreme Court seeking determination that boundary with Commonwealth of Kentucky was the low-water mark of the northerly shore of the Ohio River as it existed in 1792; laches defense is generally inapplicable against a state. U.S.C.A. Const. Art. 3, § 2, cl. 2.—Illinois v. Kentucky, 111 S.Ct. 1877, 500 U.S. 380, 114 L.Ed.2d 420.

U.S.Ill. 1991. Doctrine of laches did not preclude State of Illinois from bringing original action in United States Supreme Court seeking determination that boundary with Commonwealth of Kentucky was the low-water mark of the northerly shore of the Ohio River as it existed in 1792; laches defense is generally inapplicable against a state. U.S.C.A. Const. Art. 3, § 2, cl. 2.—Illinois v. Kentucky, 111 S.Ct. 1877, 500 U.S. 380, 114 L.Ed.2d 420.

U.S.Ky. 1991. Doctrine of laches did not preclude State of Illinois from bringing original action in United States Supreme Court seeking determination that boundary with Commonwealth of Kentucky was the low-water mark of the northerly shore of the Ohio River as it existed in 1792; laches defense is generally inapplicable against a state. U.S.C.A. Const. Art. 3, § 2, cl. 2.—Illinois v. Kentucky, 111 S.Ct. 1877, 500 U.S. 380, 114 L.Ed.2d 420.

☜**215. Costs.**
U.S.Ark. 1978. Award of attorney fees against a state disregarding a federal order stands on the same footing as federal ruling requiring state to support programs that compensate for past misdeeds; like other enforcement powers, it is integral to court's grant of prospective relief.—Hutto v. Finney, 98 S.Ct. 2565, 437 U.S. 678, 57 L.Ed.2d

Note how topic (STATES) and key number (197) relate to headnote in Figure 9-1.

FIGURE 9-3 *Supreme Court Digest*

Reprinted with permission of Thomson/West

Note how topic (Civil Rights) and section (27) relate to headnote in Figure 9–2.

Civil Rights § 27

Municipal liability may be imposed in a civil rights action under 42 USCS § 1983 for a single decision by municipal policymakers under appropriate circumstances. Pembaur v Cincinnati, 475 US 469, 106 S Ct 1292,

89 L Ed 2d 452

A municipality is responsible under 42 USCS § 1983 for action directed by those who establish governmental policy, whether that action is to be taken only once or to be taken repeatedly. Pembaur v Cincinnati, 475 US 469, 106 S Ct 1292.

89 L Ed 2d 452

Municipal liability for damages under 42 USCS § 1983 attaches where—and only where—a deliberate choice to follow a course of action is made from among various alternatives by the official or officials responsible for establishing final policy with respect to the subject matter in question. [Per Brennan, White, Marshall, and Blackmun, JJ.: Pembaur v Cincinnati, 475 US 469, 106 S Ct 1292,

89 L Ed 2d 452

An award of damages under 42 USCS § 1983, for an arrest allegedly without probable cause and with excessive force, is not authorized against a municipal corporation based on the actions of one of its officers, when the jury has concluded that the officer inflicted no constitutional harm, and the fat that departmental regulations might have authorized the use of constitutionally excessive force is beside the point. (Stevens and Marshall, JJ., dissented from this holding). Los Angeles v Heller, 475 US 796, 106 S Ct 1571,

89 L Ed 2d 806

Congress intends courts to look to agency principles for guidance with regard to whether employers are liable under Title VII of the Civil Rights Act of 1964 (42 USCS §§ 2000e—2000e-17) for sexual harassment of employees by their superiors. Meritor Sav. Bank, FSB v Vinson, 477 US 57, 106 S Ct 2399,

91 L Ed 2d49

Distinguished in Gebser v Lago Vista Indep. Sch. Dist., 524 US 274, 141 L Ed 2d 277, 118 S Ct 1989, holding that in action under Title IX of Education Amendments of 1972 (20 USCS §§ 1681 et seq.). for teacher's sexual harassment of student, damages were not recoverable form school district absent official's actual notice and deliberate indifference.

Employers are not automatically liable under Title VII of the Civil Rights Act of 1964 (42 USCS §§ 2000e—2000e-17) for sexual harassment of employees by their supervisors, without regard to the circumstances of a particular case. Meritor Sav. Bank, FSB c Vinson, 477 US 57, 106 S Ct 2399,

91 L Ed 2d 49

Absence of notice to an employer does not necessarily insulate that employer from liability under Title VII of the Civil Rights Act of 1964 (42 USCS

§§ 2000e—2000e-17) for sexual harassment of its employees by their supervisors. Meritor Sav. Bank, FSB v Vinson, 477 US 57, 106 S Ct 2399,

91 L Ed 2d 49

The mere existence of a grievance procedure and a policy against discrimination, coupled with a complainant's failure to invoke that procedure, does not insulate an employer from liability under Title VII of the Civil Rights Act of 1964 (42 USCS §§ 2000e;mnd2000e-17) for sexual harassment of its employees by their supervisors. Meritor Sav. Bank, FSB v Vinson, 477 US 57, 106 S Ct 2399,

91 L Ed 2d 49

The United States Supreme Court will reverse a Federal Court of Appeals decision, which affirmed a Federal District Court judgment finding a city liable under 42 USCS § 1983 for the violation of a city employee's federal constitutional rights through retaliatory employee transfer and layoff actions taken by city agency supervisors in response to the employee's appeal of his suspension to the city's grievance review board, where (12) four Justices are of the opinion that the Federal Court of Appeals applied an incorrect legal standard in concluding that the supervisors were city "policymakers" whose actions could subject the city to liability under § 1983, in that (a) the identification of officials with such final policymaking authority is a question of state and local law, rather than a question of fact for the jury, and (b) the stated bases for the Court of Appeals' conclusion that the architect's supervisors had the requisite final policymaking authority, namely (i) that the supervisors' decisions were not individually reviewed by higher officials and (ii) that the city's employee grievance review board gave substantial deference to the supervisors' employment decisions, are insufficient to support such conclusion, and (2) three Justices are of the opinion (a) that the supervisor who transferred the employee did not possess the authority to establish final employment policy for the city such that the city could be held liable under § 1983 for the supervisor's retaliatory transfer decision, (b) that it is unnecessary to decide who the actual policymakers of the city are and (c) that while state law is the appropriate starting point in identifying policymaking officials for purposes of § 1983, the determination of where policymaking authority actually resides is ultimately a question for the factfinder, [Per O'Connor, J., Rehnquist, Ch. J., and White, Scalia, Brennan, Marshall, and Blackmun, JJ. Dissenting: Stevens, J.] St. Louis v Praprotnik, 495 US 112, S Ct 915,

99 L Ed 2d 107

Distinguished in Board of the County Comm'rs v Brown 520 US 397, 137 L Ed 2d 626, 117 S Ct 1382, holding that 42 USCS § 1983 case at hand did not present any difficult questions concerning whether county sheriff had final authority to act for county in hiring matters.

FIGURE 9-4 *Lawyers' Edition Digest*

§ 27 **Civil Rights**

It is incorrect to intimate that, because a 1976 United States Supreme Court decision benefited civil rights plaintiffs by expanding liability under 42 USCS § 1981, the statutory question involved in the 1976 decision should not be subject to the same principles of stare decisis as other Supreme Court decisions; the Supreme Court may not recognize any such exception to the abiding rule that the Supreme Court treat all litigants equally—that is, that the claim of any litigant for the application of a rule to the litigant's case should not be influenced by the court's view of the worthiness of the litigant in terms of extralegal criteria; such is what Congress meant when it, in 28 USCS § 453, required each Justice or judge of the United States to swear to administer justice without respect to persons, and do equal right to the poor and to the rich. Patterson v McLean Credit Union, 485 US 617, 108 S Ct 1419,

99 L Ed 2d 879

The central objective of the Reconstruction-era federal civil rights act statutes, such as 42 USCS § 1983, is to insure that individuals whose federal constitutional or statutory rights are abridged may recover damages or secure injunctive relief; thus, § 1983 (1) creates a species of liability in favor of persons deprived of their federal civil rights by those wielding state authority, (2) provides a uniquely federal remedy against incursions upon rights secured by the Federal Constitution and laws of the nation, and (3) is to be accorded a sweep as broad as its language; § 1983 accomplishes its goal of providing compensatory relief to those deprived of their federal rights by state actions by creating a form of liability that, by its very nature, runs only against a specific class of defendants—government bodies and their officials. Felder v Casey, 487 US 131, 108 S Ct 2302,

101 L Ed 2d 123

Where a plaintiff, in an action under 42 USCS § 1983, alleges that a beating and arrest by city police officers (1) were unprovoked and racially motivated, and (2) violated the plaintiff's rights under the Fourth and Fourteenth Amendments to the United States Constitution, the plaintiff's action has a common-law, intentional-tort analogue to an action for battery. Felder v Casey, 487 US 131, 108 S Ct 2302,

101 L Ed 2d 123

A municipality may be held liable under 42 USCS § 1983 for violations of rights guaranteed by the Federal Constitution, which violations result from the municipality's failure adequately to train its employees, only if that failure reflects a deliberate indifference on the part of the municipality to the constitutional rights of its inhabitants and thus constitutes a municipal "policy," that is, a deliberate or conscious choice by the municipality; a rule which allows a municipality to be held liable under § 1983 for failure to train its police force where it is shown

that the municipality acted recklessly, intentionally, or with gross negligence so that deprivations of constitutional rights were substantially certain to result, is overly broad; the requirement that constitutional deprivations be caused by a municipal "policy" will not be satisfied by merely alleging that the existing training program for a class of employees represents a policy for which the municipality is responsible, but failure to train may fairly be said to represent a policy for which the municipality is responsible, and for which it may be held liable where injury results, if, in the light of the duties assigned to specific officers or employees, the need for more or different training is so obvious, and the inadequacy so likely to result in the violation of constitutional rights, that municipal policymakers can reasonably be said to have been deliberately indifferent to the need—as, for example, the need to train police officers in the limitations imposed by the Federal Constitution on the use of deadly force can be said to be so obvious that failure to do so may properly be characterized as deliberate indifference to constitutional rights; this "deliberate indifference" standard does not turn upon the degree of fault, if any, that a plaintiff must show in order to make out an underlying claim of a constitutional violation. Canton v Harris, 489 US 378, 109 S Ct 1197,

103 L Ed 2d 412

Distinguished in Farmer v Brennan, 511 US 825, 129 L Ed 2d 811, 114 S Ct 1970, holding that showing of prison officials; subjective awareness of risk of harm was required in order for officials to be liable, under cruel and unusual punishments clause of Federal Constitution's Eighth Amendment, for failing to protect transsexual prisoner from assault, but that prisoner's failure to give advance notice to officials of risk of harm was not dispositive; Board of the County Comm'rs v Brown, 520 397, 137 L Ed 2d 626, 117 S Ct 1382, holding that Federal District Court erred in submitting to jury individual's claim that county, on basis of county sheriff's decision to hire deputy, ought to be held liable under 42 USCS § 1983 for deputy's alleged use of excessive force on individual.

A city is not automatically liable under 42 USCS § 1983, without more, if its policy regarding medical treatment for detainees of its police department—which policy states that a police officer assigned to act as "jailer" at a city police station shall, when a prisoner is fund to be unconscious or semiconscious, is unable to explain his or her condition, or complains of being ill, have such person taken to a hospital for medical treatment, with permission of the officer's supervisor—is applied by one of its employees in an unconstitutional manner, for liability would then rest improperly on respondeat superior. Canton v Harris, 489 US 378, 109 S Ct 1197,

103 L. Ed 2d 412

Respondeat superior or vicarious liability will not attach to a municipality in an action under 42 USCS § 1983; it is only when the execution of the

Note cases other than *Felder v. Casey.*

FIGURE 9-4 (continued)

municipal government's policy or custom inflicts the injury in question that the municipality may be held liable under § 1983; thus, the first inquiry in any case alleging municipal liability under § 1983 is whether there is a direct causal link between a municipal policy of custom and the alleged deprivation of rights guaranteed by the Federal Constitution. Canton v Harris, 489 US 378, 109 S Ct 1197,

103 L. Ed 2d 412

A municipality's liability under 42 USCS § 1983 for deprivations of rights guaranteed by the Federal Constitution, which deprivations are allegedly caused by a municipal policy, is not limited to the situation where the policy itself is unconstitutional. Canton V Harris, 489 US 378, 109 S Ct 1197,

103 L Ed 2d 412

The United States Supreme Court—in reviewing on certiorari a case in which a former detainee of the defendant city's police department alleges that her rights under the due process clause of the Federal Constitution's Fourteenth Amendment were violated as a result of the defendant city's failure to give its police adequate training in determining when detainees require medical attention—need not resolve the question whether something less than the "deliberate indifference" test established under the Federal Constitution's Eighth Amendment may be applicable to claims by detainees asserting violations of their due process right to medical car while in custody, given that (1) the former detainee concedes that, as the case comes to the Supreme Court, the court must assume that her right to receive medial care was denied by medical employees, whatever the nature of that right may be, and (2) theproper standard for determining whether a municipality will be liable under § 1983 for constitutional wrongs does not turn on any underlying culpability test that determines when such wrongs have occurred. Canton v Harris, 489 US 378, 109 S Ct 1197,

103 L Ed 2d 412

Municipal liability under 42 USCS § 1983 attaches only where a deliberate choice to follow a course of action is made from among several serious alternatives by city policy makers. Canton v Harris, 489 US 378, 109 S Ct 1197,

103 L Ed 2d 412

In resolving the issue of a municipality's liability under 42 USCS § 1983 for allegedly failing adequately to train its employees and for thereby causing

deprivations of rights guaranteed by the Federal Constitution, the focus must be on the adequacy of the training program in relation to the tasks which the particular municipal officers must perform; the fact that a particular municipal officer may be unsatisfactorily trained will not alone suffice to fasten liability on the municipality, since the officer's shortcomings may have resulted from factors other than a faulty training program, such as the negligent administration of an otherwise sound program; nor will it suffice to prove that an injury or accident could have been avoided if an officer had had better or more training sufficient to equip him or her to avoid the particular injury-causing conduct. Canton v Harris, 489 US 378, 109 S Ct 1197,

103 L Ed 2d 412

In order for a municipality to be held liable under 42 USCS § 1983 for failing adequately to train employees who violate an individual's right sunder the Federal Constitution, the identified deficiency in the municipality's training program must be closely related to the ultimate injury; thus—in a case in which (1) a city's police officers allegedly violated the rights, under the due process clause of the Federal Constitution's Fourteenth Amendment of a detainee who was subsequently diagnosed as suffering form emotional ailments, by failing to obtain medical assistance for her after she fell down repeatedly and responded incoherently to inquiries as to whether she required such assistance, and (2) there is evidence indicating that city regulations give police shift commanders sole discretion to determine whether a detainee required medical care, but that shift commanders do not receive any special training to make such determinations—the plaintiff detainee must prove that the deficiency in training actually caused the officers' indifference to her medical needs. Canton v Harris, 489 US 378, 109 S Ct 1197,

103 L Ed 2d 412

In an action under 42 USCS § 1983, whereby the relatives of an individual who fatally crashed into a police roadblock following a high-speed nighttime chase by county police seek to hold the county and other defendants liable on the ground that they unreasonably seized the individual in violation of his rights under the Federal Constitution's Fourth Amendment, a determination that the use of the roadblock constitutes a "seizure" is not enough for § 1983 liability, as the seizure must be "unreasonable"; the relatives can claim the right to recover for the individual's death only because the unreasonableness they allege con-

FIGURE 9-4
(continued)

Reprinted from *U.S. Supreme Court Digest, Lawyers' Edition 2d.* Copyright © 1998 Matthew Bender & Company, Inc., a member of the LexisNexis Group. All rights reserved. Reprinted with permission.

published, it consisted of 50 volumes and was called the **Century Digest.** The *Century Digest* contains case annotations for the years 1658 to 1896. After the publication of the *Century Digest,* West updated the set with the publication of **Decennial Digests.** As the name suggests, these digests were published every ten years, and are known as *First Decennial Digest, Second Decennial Digest,* and so on. These are now published every five years, and are referred to as Part I and Part 2 of that *Decennial Digest.* Each decennial digest contains case annotations for the ten-year period it serves and consists of many volumes.

Century Digest. Part of the American Digest System; contains case annotations for the years 1658 to 1896.

Decennial Digest. Updates to the Century Digest, published every five years.

⟳ **A Point to Remember**   Each decennial digest is not a cumulative supplement of case annotations. It covers only a ten-year period.

In addition to the *Century Digest* and the *Decennial Digests,* the American Digest system contains a set known as the **General Digest.** This set contains volumes that update the latest *Decennial Digest.*

General Digest. Updates to the *Decennial Digest.*

State Digests   West publishes digests for cases from most states. In addition, digests are available for the regional reporters, *Atlantic Reporter, Pacific Reporter, North Western Reporter,* and *South Western Reporter.*

Federal and Supreme Court Digests   West digests exist for cases published in federal reporters. The *United Supreme Court Digest* is tied to the *Supreme Court Reporter* and contains annotations to United States Supreme Court cases. West's *Federal Practice Digest* (now in its fourth series) contains references to published federal district court, court of appeals cases, and Supreme Court cases. Earlier editions of the *Federal Practice Digest* are known as the *Federal Digest* and *Modern Federal Practice Digest.*

Specialty Digests   Digests also exist for certain special case reporters. Examples include West's *Bankruptcy Digest* and *United States Court of Claims Digest.*

BOX 9-1

WEST DIGEST SYSTEM

The American Digest System
  Centennial Digest
  Decennial Digest
  General Digest
Supreme Court Digest
Federal Practice Digest
Atlantic Digest
North Western Digest
Pacific Digest
South Eastern Digest
State Digests
Specialty Digests

West Digest Topics   In selecting its digest topics, West uses seven main divisions of law: persons, property, contracts, torts, crimes, remedies, and government. These are subdivided into numerous other topics. See Figure 9-5 for a complete list of West digest topics.

DIGEST TOPICS

See, also, Outline of the Law by Seven Main Divisions of Law preceding this section.

The topic numbers shown below may be used in WESTLAW searches for cases within the topic and within specified key numbers.

1	Abandoned and Lost Property	42	Assumpsit, Action of	77	Citizens
2	Abatement and Revival	43	Asylums	78	Civil Rights
		44	Attachment	79	Clerks of Courts
4	Abortion and Birth Control	45	Attorney and Client	80	Clubs
		46	Attorney General	81	Colleges and Universities
5	Absentees	47	Auctions and Auctioneers·		
6	Abstracts of Title			82	Collision
7	Accession	48	Audita Querela	83	Commerce
8	Accord and Satisfaction	48A	Automobiles	83H	Commodity Futures Trading Regulation
		48B	Aviation		
9	Account	49	Bail		
10	Account, Action on	50	Bailment	84	Common Lands
11	Account Stated	51	Bankruptcy	85	Common Law
11A	Accountants	52	Banks and Banking	88	Compounding Offenses
12	Acknowledgment	54	Beneficial Associations		
13	Action			89	Compromise and Settlement
14	Action on the Case	55	Bigamy	89A	Condominium
15	Adjoining Landowners	56	Bills and Notes	90	Confusion of Goods
		58	Bonds	91	Conspiracy
15A	Administrative Law and Procedure	59	Boundaries	92	Constitutional Law
		60	Bounties	92B	Consumer Credit
16	Admiralty	61	Breach of Marriage Promise	92H	Consumer Protection
17	Adoption				
18	Adulteration	62	Breach of the Peace	93	Contempt
19	Adultery	63	Bribery	95	Contracts
20	Adverse Possession	64	Bridges	96	Contribution
21	Affidavits	65	Brokers	97	Conversion
23	Agriculture	66	Building and Loan Associations	98	Convicts
24	Aliens			99	Copyrights and Intellectual Property
25	Alteration of Instruments	67	Burglary		
		68	Canals		
26	Ambassadors and Consuls	69	Cancellation of Instruments	100	Coroners
				101	Corporations
27	Amicus Curiae	70	Carriers	102	Costs
28	Animals	71	Cemeteries	103	Counterfeiting
29	Annuities	72	Census	104	Counties
30	Appeal and Error	73	Certiorari	105	Court Commissioners
31	Appearance	74	Champerty and Maintenance		
33	Arbitration			106	Courts
34	Armed Services	75	Charities	107	Covenant, Action of
35	Arrest	76	Chattel Mortgages	108	Covenants
36	Arson	76A	Chemical Dependents	108A	Credit Reporting Agencies
37	Assault and Battery	76D	Child Custody		
38	Assignments	76E	Child Support	110	Criminal Law
40	Assistance, Writ of	76H	Children Out-of-Wedlock	111	Crops
41	Associations			113	Customs and Usages

XIII

FIGURE 9-5   West's Key Number System: Alphabetical List of Digest Topics

DIGEST TOPICS

114	Customs Duties	165	Extortion and Threats	212	Injunction
115	Damages	166	Extradition and Detainers	213	Innkeepers
116	Dead Bodies			216	Inspection
117	Death	167	Factors	217	Insurance
117G	Debt, Action of	168	False Imprisonment	218	Insurrection and Sedition
117T	Debtor and Creditor	169	False Personation		
118A	Declaratory Judgment	170	False Pretenses	219	Interest
		170A	Federal Civil Procedure	220	Internal Revenue
119	Dedication			221	International Law
120	Deeds	170B	Federal Courts	222	Interpleader
122A	Deposits and Escrows	171	Fences	223	Intoxicating Liquors
		172	Ferries	224	Joint Adventures
123	Deposits in Court	174	Fines	225	Joint-Stock Companies and Business Trusts
124	Descent and Distribution	175	Fires		
		176	Fish		
125	Detectives	177	Fixtures	226	Joint Tenancy
126	Detinue	178	Food	227	Judges
129	Disorderly Conduct	179	Forcible Entry and Detainer	228	Judgment
130	Disorderly House			229	Judicial Sales
131	District and Prosecuting Attorneys	180	Forfeitures	230	Jury
		181	Forgery	231	Justices of the Peace
		183	Franchises	232	Kidnapping
132	District of Columbia	184	Fraud	232A	Labor Relations
133	Disturbance of Public Assemblage	185	Frauds, Statute of	233	Landlord and Tenant
		186	Fraudulent Conveyances		
134	Divorce			234	Larceny
135	Domicile	187	Game	235	Levees and Flood Control
135H	Double Jeopardy	188	Gaming		
136	Dower and Curtesy	189	Garnishment	236	Lewdness
137	Drains	190	Gas	237	Libel and Slander
138	Drugs and Narcotics	191	Gifts	238	Licenses
141	Easements	192	Good Will	239	Liens
142	Ejectment	193	Grand Jury	240	Life Estates
143	Election of Remedies	195	Guaranty	241	Limitation of Actions
		196	Guardian and Ward	242	Lis Pendens
144	Elections	197	Habeas Corpus	245	Logs and Logging
145	Electricity	198	Hawkers and Peddlers	246	Lost Instruments
146	Embezzlement			247	Lotteries
148	Eminent Domain	199	Health and Environment	248	Malicious Mischief
148A	Employers' Liability			249	Malicious Prosecution
149	Entry, Writ of	200	Highways		
150	Equity	201	Holidays	250	Mandamus
151	Escape	202	Homestead	251	Manufactures
152	Escheat	203	Homicide	252	Maritime Liens
154	Estates in Property	204	Hospitals	253	Marriage
156	Estoppel	205	Husband and Wife	255	Master and Servant
157	Evidence	205H	Implied and Constructive Contracts	256	Mayhem
158	Exceptions, Bill of			257	Mechanics' Liens
159	Exchange of Property			257A	Mental Health
		206	Improvements	258A	Military Justice
160	Exchanges	207	Incest	259	Militia
161	Execution	208	Indemnity	260	Mines and Minerals
162	Executors and Administrators	209	Indians	265	Monopolies
		210	Indictment and Information	266	Mortgages
163	Exemptions			267	Motions
164	Explosives	211	Infants	268	Municipal Corporations

XIV

FIGURE 9-5
(continued)

DIGEST TOPICS

269	Names	320	Railroads	365	Submission of Controversy
270	Navigable Waters	321	Rape	366	Subrogation
271	Ne Exeat	322	Real Actions	367	Subscriptions
272	Negligence	323	Receivers	368	Suicide
273	Neutrality Laws	324	Receiving Stolen Goods	369	Sunday
274	Newspapers			370	Supersedeas
275	New Trial	325	Recognizances	371	Taxation
276	Notaries	326	Records	372	Telecommunications
277	Notice	327	Reference	373	Tenancy in Common
278	Novation	328	Reformation of Instruments	374	Tender
279	Nuisance			375	Territories
280	Oath	330	Registers of Deeds	376	Theaters and Shows
281	Obscenity	331	Release	378	Time
282	Obstructing Justice	332	Religious Societies	379	Torts
283	Officers and Public Employees	333	Remainders	380	Towage
		334	Removal of Cases	381	Towns
284	Pardon and Parole	335	Replevin	382	Trade Regulation
285	Parent and Child	336	Reports	384	Treason
286	Parliamentary Law	337	Rescue	385	Treaties
287	Parties	338	Reversions	386	Trespass
288	Partition	339	Review	387	Trespass to Try Title
289	Partnership	340	Rewards	388	Trial
290	Party Walls	341	Riot	389	Trover and Conversion
291	Patents	342	Robbery		
294	Payment	343	Sales	390	Trusts
295	Penalties	344	Salvage	391	Turnpikes and Toll Roads
296	Pensions	345	Schools		
297	Perjury	346	Scire Facias	392	Undertakings
298	Perpetuities	347	Seals	393	United States
299	Physicians and Surgeons	348	Seamen	394	United States Magistrates
		349	Searches and Seizures		
300	Pilots			395	United States Marshals
302	Pleading	349A	Secured Transactions		
303	Pledges			396	Unlawful Assembly
304	Poisons	349B	Securities Regulation	396A	Urban Railroads
305	Possessory Warrant			398	Usury
306	Postal Service	350	Seduction	399	Vagrancy
307	Powers	350H	Sentencing and Punishment	400	Vendor and Purchaser
307A	Pretrial Procedure				
308	Principal and Agent	351	Sequestration	401	Venue
309	Principal and Surety	352	Set-Off and Counterclaim	402	War and National Emergency
310	Prisons				
311	Private Roads	353	Sheriffs and Constables	403	Warehousemen
313	Process			404	Waste
313A	Products Liability	354	Shipping	405	Waters and Water Courses
314	Prohibition	355	Signatures		
315	Property	356	Slaves	406	Weapons
316	Prostitution	356A	Social Security and Public Welfare	407	Weights and Measures
316A	Public Contracts				
317	Public Lands	357	Sodomy	408	Wharves
317A	Public Utilities	358	Specific Performance	409	Wills
318	Quieting Title			410	Witnesses
319	Quo Warranto	359	Spendthrifts	411	Woods and Forests
319H	Racketeer Influenced and Corrupt Organizations	360	States	413	Workers' Compensation
		361	Statutes		
		362	Steam	414	Zoning and Planning
		363	Stipulations		

FIGURE 9-5
(continued)

Reprinted with permission of Thomson/West

LEXIS Law Publishing Digests

LEXIS Law Publishing produces a digest to accompany its case reporter, *United States Supreme Court Cases, Lawyers' Edition.* This is known as the *United States Supreme Court Reports Digest, Lawyers' Edition.* (Until recently, this case reporter and digest were published by Lawyers Cooperative Publishing Company.)

State Digests State-specific digests, accompanying state reporters, are also published.

BOX 9-2

If You Are Using This Case Reporter:	Then Use This Digest:
Lawyers' Edition	*Supreme Court Digest, Lawyers' Ed.*
Supreme Court Reporter	*Supreme Court Digest*
Federal Reporter	*Federal Practice Digest*
Atlantic Reporter	*Atlantic Digest*
North Western Reporter	*North Western Digest*
Pacific Reporter	*Pacific Digest*
South Eastern Reporter	*South Eastern Digest*
Any West Reporter	*American Digest*

Using Digests

A digest is most effectively used in legal research once you find a case (either through encyclopedias or other sources) dealing with your research issue. Once a case is found, identify the headnote or headnotes dealing with your issue. At this point, take the topic and number of the headnote, go to the appropriate digest, and find the topic and number. You will find references to other cases dealing with the same issue. Using a digest in this way, you must pay attention to a few matters. Be careful about which digest you use. If you have a topic and number from a West case reporter, you cannot locate that information in any digest not published by West. Be careful about relying on all cases you find in a digest. The American Digest System and the regional digests all contain case references from several states. When researching an issue of state law, remember that only cases from your state are binding authority. Using a digest that is specific to a state reporter (if available) is the way to begin. If you find cases dealing with the legal issue from your state, there is no need to use a larger digest.

Although not recommended, digests can be used as a starting point in your research. All digests contain descriptive word indexes just like other secondary sources. When using a digest, check the latest updates or supplements. Digests might be supplemented by bound volumes, by pocket part supplements, or by supplemental pamphlets. In addition, when using a digest, you must check to see what years are covered in the particular series you are using. Later series of digests are not usually cumulative. For example, if you use the *Federal Practice Digest 4th,* you will see that it does not contain references to cases that were summarized in *Federal Practice Digest 3d.* This information is found in the **prefatory material** and should always be checked.

prefatory material.
Material found in the front of a book or set of books describing such matters as the purpose of the book and directions for using the book.

One special and very helpful feature found in digests is the table of cases. This table alphabetically lists all cases found in the digest by both the plaintiff's name and the defendant's name. Thus, if you know only a case name, you can find the citation. This table provides not only the case cite but also the topic name and numbers where the case appears.

BOX 9-3

USING DIGESTS

Starting with a Known Case
- √ Identify headnotes relevant to your issue.
- √ Note topic and number of those headnotes.
- √ Find digest corresponding to case reporter.
- √ Locate topic and number in digest.
- √ Note citations to other cases under topic and number.
- √ Read other cases.

BOX 9-4

USING DIGESTS

Starting with Issue or Facts, but No Known Cases
- √ Identify key words in facts and issues.
- √ Locate key words in descriptive word index.
- √ Identify proper topic and numbers from index.
- √ Locate topic and number in digest.
- √ Note case citations under topic and number.
- √ Read cases.

BOX 9-5

CITING THE LAW

Restatement	RESTATMENT (SECOND) OF TORTS § 70 (year)
Dictionaries	BALLENTINE'S LAW DICTIONARY 361 (3d ed. 1969)
Digests	Do **not** cite a digest. Always refer to the actual case.

(*THE BLUEBOOK*, Rule 12.8.5, Rule 15.8)

9-3 RESTATEMENT OF LAW

In reading case law, you have undoubtedly come across references to the "Restatement." This is a multivolume work compiled by The American Law Institute, and is the result of the efforts of well-known and respected legal scholars. U.S. law

is largely the result of English Common Law. However, because of many court decisions and legislative changes, some of those principles have evolved and changed. The Restatement is a "statement" of the many principles of U.S. law as those principles exist today. The work is organized by legal topic and each is known accordingly, for example, the *Restatement of the Law of Torts* and the *Restatement of the Law of Contracts*. The principles of law found in the Restatement look very similar to code sections. They are often followed by comments and examples. It is important to remember that even though the statements of law look like code sections, the Restatement is not primary law. The statements of law found here may or may not reflect the law in your state. However, this is a well-respected source and it is often quoted by judges in written opinions. The Restatement and the comments are especially helpful when the law of your state is not clear. In such an instance, referring to the Restatement can help. Although, remember, this is only persuasive authority, not mandatory. See Figure 9-6 for sample pages from the *Restatement of Torts 2d.*

9-4 FORM BOOKS

Form books are another type of research tool that lawyers and their assistants frequently utilize. The main purpose of these books, of course, is to provide sample forms for lawyers to follow. However, form books are a valuable secondary source of the law. In addition to containing sample forms, many form books provide explanations of the law related to the use of the form, including references to the controlling primary law. Form books, which are often multivolume sets, are published for practice in the federal courts, as well as for practice in state courts. For an example of the type of material found in a form book see Figure 9-7, an excerpt from *American Jurisprudence Forms of Pleading and Practice.*

There are two major types of comprehensive form books: those that contain forms for use in connection with a lawsuit and those for use in connection with business or personal transactions. Forms for use in connection with lawsuits are often called **forms of pleading and practice.** In this type of work are such forms as sample complaints, responsive pleadings, and motions. Forms for use in business or personal transactions are often called **transaction forms.** In this type of work are forms such as sample articles of incorporation, partnership agreements, and wills.

In your state research material you may find **practice books.** These are usually single-volume books (although some may be many volumes) that deal with one legal topic and contain both explanations and discussions of the law and sample forms related to the practice of that area of law.

9-5 PATTERN JURY INSTRUCTIONS

At the end of any jury trial, the judge must tell the jury what law applies to the evidence presented during trial. These statements of law are called **jury instructions.** Judges do not create new instructions every time they preside over a trial. Instead, they consult books containing approved statements of law or jury instructions, referred to as *pattern jury instructions.* Using these books, the judge and the attorneys

forms of pleading and practice. Form books containing forms for use in connection with litigation.

transaction forms. Form books containing forms for use in connection with business and personal transactions.

practice books. Books for use in federal and state legal practice; these often contain discussions of an area of law and provide forms needed for practice in that legal area.

jury instructions. Statements of the law read to the jury at the end of trial.

§ 70   TORTS, SECOND   Ch. 4

to inflict, as where his assailant is standing on the brink of a cliff or on a girder of a steel building under construction so that the actor should realize that the other's instinctive reaction to his threatening gesture may cause a serious fall. If such is the case, the actor may not be privileged even to threaten to inflict a harm which under ordinary circumstances he would be privileged to inflict, and certainly is not privileged to threaten a greater harm. It is frequently a matter for the jury to to determine, under proper instructions, whether the privilege exists in such a case.

§ **71.** Force in Excess of Privilege

If the actor applies a force to or imposes a confinement upon another which is in excess of that which is privileged,

(a) the actor is liable for only so much of the force or confinement as is excessive;

(b) the other's liability for an invasion of any of the actor's interests of personality which the other may have caused is not affected;

(c) the other has the normal privilege stated in this Topic to defend himself against the actor's use or attempted use of excessive force or confinement.

See Reporter's Notes.

Comment on Clause (a):

a. While the actor is liable to another for any force or confinement which he applies or imposes upon the other which is in excess of that which he is privileged to impose, he is not liable for so much of the force or confinement as he is privileged to apply or impose, and so he does not become a "trespasser ab initio" by his abuse of his privilege.

b. While it is usually difficult to separate the harm done by the excess of force, it can sometimes be done, as where a confinement is continued longer than is necessary to prevent the commission of a battery. Where no such separation can be made, the actor is held liable for all of the harm inflicted by the use of the excessive force.

FIGURE 9-6

Restatement of Torts, Second

Ch. 4   SELF-DEFENSE   § 71

Illustrations:

1. A inflicts an offensive contact upon B, and threatens to continue it. Being stronger than A, B could easily prevent a continuance of the contact by seizing and holding A, and does so. B then unnecessarily strikes A in the face, breaking A's nose. B is not liable for holding A, but is subject to liability to A for the broken nose.

2. A inflicts an offensive contact upon B, and threatens to continue it. B could easily prevent the continuance of the contact by striking A a light blow. Instead he strikes a heavy blow, which breaks A's nose. B is subject to liability to A for the blow and the harm done.

Comment on Clause (b):

c. If the actor applies a force to or imposes a confinement upon another which is in excess of that which is privileged, the other's liability for an invasion of any of the actor's interests of personality which the other may have caused is not affected. In such a case, the actor and the other have cross actions against one another; the actor for the "assault," "battery," or "false imprisonment" which the other committed before the actor abused his privilege by using excessive force, the other for the excess of force used by the actor. The other's violation of the actor's right is entirely independent of the actor's abuse of his privilege. So far from being caused by the actor's misconduct, the violation of the actor's right gives the privilege which he abuses. There is, therefore, no reason why the actor's misconduct should exonerate the other's independent violation of his right, nor should the actor be penalized for his abuse of his privilege by a forfeiture of his right of action which preceded and was the occasion for his abuse. The liability to answer for his excess of force is both a sufficient punishment for the actor's abuse of his privilege and a sufficient deterrent to such misconduct.

Illustration:

3. Under the circumstances given in Illustration 1, while B is liable to A for the harm which he has caused to A by the excess of force which he used in self-defense, A is subject to liability to B for the offensive contact which he has inflicted upon B.

FIGURE 9-6
(continued)

§ **71**   TORTS, SECOND   Ch. 1

Comment on Clause (c):

d. If the actor applies a force to, or imposes a confinement upon another which is in excess of that which is privileged, the other has the normal privilege stated in this Topic to defend himself against the actor's use, or attempted use, of excessive force or confinement. One who intentionally invades or attempts to invade any of another's interests of personality, does not by his wrongdoing forfeit his privilege to defend himself by any means which would be privileged were he innocent of wrongdoing against any excess of force which the other uses in self-defense. A fortiori, mere provocation by words or conduct does not deprive a man of his privilege to defend himself against an attack which another is thereby provoked into making upon him.

Illustration:

4. A attempts to slap B's face. Although B can easily prevent A from so doing by pushing A away, he attempts to protect himself by striking A with a heavy stick. A is privileged to defend himself by using appropriate force against B.

e. Withdrawal from combat. The aggressor may withdraw from the combat which he has initiated. If he does so, and makes clear by words or conduct his intention to discontinue the encounter, he may thereafter be privileged to defend himself against the man he has attacked. His original aggression does not justify retaliation, or acts no longer necessary for defense against him. Allowance must, however, be made for the excitement of the fight and the absence of time for reflection, and if under the circumstances the defendant reasonably believes that he is still under attack, he may be privileged to continue to act in self-defense, although the attack has in fact terminated.

Illustration:

5. A insults B. B attacks A, knocks him down and jumps on him, and inflicts a severe beating. B then abandons his attack and starts to walk away. A arises, pursues B, and strikes him a heavy blow. Whether A is liable to B depends upon whether, making allowance for A's disturbed state of mind and the absence of time for reflection, A should know that B has abandoned the attack.

See Appendix for Reporter's Notes, Court Citations, and Cross References

FIGURE 9-6
(continued)

Reprinted with permission of American Law Institute

CIVIL RIGHTS

Scope of Topic

This topic contains discussion and forms for use in administrative proceedings and civil actions brought to enforce civil rights and remedies, including actions based on rights guaranteed by the United States Constitution and those created by statute. Included are forms relating to discrimination in public accommodations, transportation, education, and housing. Also included are forms relating to discrimination in employment, where the cause of action is based on job discrimination generally, or discrimination based on race, sex, age, religion and religious beliefs, or physical handicap.

Treated Elsewhere

Related subjects treated elsewhere in this work are Aliens and Citizens; Constitutional Law; Elections; Housing Laws and Urban Redevelopment; Indians; Privacy; Public Officers and Employees; Searches and Seizures.

Research References

Antieu, Federal Civil Rights Acts, Second Edition.
Danner, Pattern Discovery: Employment Discrimination.
Employment Coordinator.
Employment Discrimination Coordinator.
Guide to Employment Law and Regulation.
Modjeska, Handling Employment Discrimination Cases.
Richey, Manual on Employment Discrimination Law and Civil Rights Actions in the Federal Courts.
Rossein, Employment Discrimination, Law and Litigation.
Ruzicho & Jacobs, Employment Law Checklists and Forms.

Text References

15 Am Jur 2d, Civil Rights.
45A-C Am Jur 2d, Job Discrimination.

Tax References

Am Jur 2d, New Topic Service, Americans with Disabilities Act: Analysis and Implications.

Text References

6 Federal Procedure, L Ed, Civil Rights Ch 11.
21 Federal Procedure, L Ed, Job Discrimination Ch 50.
Americans With Disabilities, Practice and Compliance Manual.

West Digest References

Civil Rights ☜1 et seq.

Page 219

Many form books contain more than sample forms. Read "Scope of Topic."

References to research materials related to forms.

FIGURE 9-7

American Jurisprudence Forms of Pleading and Practice

AM JUR PLEADING AND PRACTICE FORMS

Annotation References

ALR Digest Civil Rights.

ALR Index Age Discrimination; Civil Rights and Discrimination; Civil Rights Attorney's Fees Awards Act; Disabled Persons; Discharge from Employment or Office; Equal Protection of Law; Segregation; Sex Discrimination; Sexual Harassment.

Tax References

RIA Federal Tax Coordinator ¶ J-5801 et seq. (taxability of award of backpay and damages under Title VII of the Civil Rights Act of 1964).

Forms References

5 Federal Procedural Forms, L Ed, Civil Rights (Ch 10).

12 Federal Procedural Forms, L Ed, Job Discrimination (Ch 45).

Trial Strategy References

65 Am Jur Trials 65, Taking the Deposition of the Sexual Harassment Plaintiff.

64 Am Jur Trials 425, Asserting Claims of Unconstitutional Prison Conditions.

63 Am Jur Trials 257, Defendant Class Actions Under Title VII.

62 Am Jur Trials 235, Workplace Sexual Harassment: Quid Pro Quo.

62 Am Jur Trials 547, Obtaining Damages in Federal Court for State and Local Police Misconduct.

53 Am Jur Trials 299, Sex Discrimination Based Upon Sexual Stereotyping.

49 Am Jur Trials 171, Defense of Claim Brought Under the Americans with Disabilities Act.

43 Am Jur Trials 1, Constitutional Employment Litigation: Political Discharge Case.

38 Am Jur Trials 493, Defense of a Police Misconduct Suit.

35 Am Jur Trials 505, Police Misconduct Litigation.

33 Am Jur Trials 257, Sexual Harassment in Employment.

29 Am Jur Trials 1, Age Discrimination in Employment under ADEA.

28 Am Jur Trials 1, Housing Discrimination Litigation.

22 Am Jur Trials 1, Prisoners' Rights Litigation.

21 Am Jur Trials 1, Employment Discrimination Action under Federal Civil Rights Acts.

21 Am Jur Trials 625, Preparation and Trial of Federal Class Action.

15 Am Jur Trials 555, Police Misconduct Litigation—Plaintiff's Remedies.

44 Am Jur Proof of Facts 3d 79, Proof of Discrimination Under Age Discrimination in Employment Act.

42 Am Jur Proof of Facts 3d 1, Defense of Claim Under the Americans with Disabilities Act.

42 Am Jur Proof of Facts 3d 85, Claims Under Gender Motivated Violence Against Women Act.

38 Am Jur Proof of Facts 3d 129, Proof of Employment Discrimination on Account of a Repetitive Strain Injury Under the Americans with Disabilities Act.

33 Am Jur Proof of Facts 3d 1, Proof of "Disability" Under the Americans with Disabilities Act.

26 Am Jur Proof of Facts 3d 269, Proof of Violation of Equal Pay Act.

26 Am Jur Proof of Facts 3d 341, Proof of Discriminatory Termination of HIV-Positive Employee.

25 Am Jur Proof of Facts 3d 415, Employment Handicap Discrimination Based on Gender Dysphoria (Transsexualism).

24 Am Jur Proof of Facts 3d 393, Proof of Damages for Sexual Harassment Under the Civil Rights Act of 1991.

23 Am Jur Proof of Facts 3d 499, Discrimination on the Basis of Handicap Under the Fair Housing Act.

FIGURE 9-7
(continued)

Page 220

Delaware Code title 6 § 4501 et seq.

Illinois Compiled Statutes Ch 775 §§ 5/1-101 et seq., 10/0.01 et seq., 15/1 et seq., 20/1 et seq., 25/0.01 et seq., 30/1 et seq.

Indiana Code § 22-9-1-1 et seq.

Iowa Code § 216.1 et seq.

Kansas Statutes § 44-1001 et seq.

Maryland Code Art 49B § 5 et seq.

Massachusetts General Laws Ch 272 §§ 92A, 98

Michigan Compiled Laws § 37.1101 et seq., 37.2101 et seq.

Minnesota Statutes § 363.12

Nebraska Revised Statutes § 20-302 et seq.

New Hampshire Revised Statutes § 354-A:1 et seq.

New Jersey Revised Statutes § 10:1-1 et seq.

New York Civil Rights Law § 40 et seq.

New York Executive Law § 290 et seq.

Ohio Revised Code § 2921.45

Oregon Revised Statutes § 30.670 et seq.

Wisconsin Statutes § 106.04

§ 4 Checklist—Matters that should be alleged in complaint in action arising from deprivation of individual's civil rights

Checklist for preparing form.

Checklist of matters, inter alia, that should be alleged in a complaint, petition, or declaration in an action arising from the deprivation of an individual's civil rights:

- Residence or other jurisdictional facts, if required.
  - Allegation of basis of jurisdiction, such as 28 USCA § 1343, if action is brought in federal court.
- Facts establishing venue, if required.
- Statute or other basis of federal jurisdiction, if complaint is to be filed in federal court.
- If action is to be brought as a class action:
  - Existence of multiple parties too numerous to be brought before the court.
  - Existence of a common question of law or fact.
  - Existence of a several right sought to be enforced for or against the parties.
- Plaintiff's standing and capacity to sue, if required.
- Acts of defendant resulting in violation of plaintiff's civil rights, and illegality of those acts.
- Allegation that the conduct alleged was engaged in under color of state law, and that such conduct subjected plaintiff to the deprivation of rights, privileges, and immunities secured by the Federal Constitution and laws, where complaint is based on 42 USCA § 1983.
- A conspiracy to interfere, in the manner proscribed by the statute, with the civil rights of another; and an overt act done in furtherance of the object of the conspiracy, whereby another is injured or is deprived of any right or privilege of a citizen of the United States; where complaint is based on 42 USCA § 1985(3).
- Citations and provisions of applicable statutes, ordinances, and regulations.

Page 232

FIGURE 9-7
(continued)

Sample form.

§ 13 Complaint in federal court—Civil Rights Act— Unlawful arrest, search, and incarceration—Abusive treatment—Personal injuries—Against police officers

[Caption, see § 11]

COMPLAINT

1. Plaintiff, _____ *[name]*, is a citizen of the United States of America and a resident of the City of _____, County of _____, State of _____.

2. Defendants, _____ *[list names]*, are police officers of the City of _____, County of _____, a municipal corporation and governmental subdivision of the State of _____; defendants are also residents of such city and county.

3. This action arises under the United States Constitution, particularly under the provisions of the Fourth, Sixth, and Fourteenth Amendments to the Constitution of the United States, and under federal law, particularly the Civil Rights Act, Title 42 of the United States Code, Section 1983.

4. This court has jurisdiction of this cause under Title 28 of the United States Code, Section 1343.

5. Each of the acts of defendants alleged in this complaint were done by defendants under the color and pretense of the statutes, ordinances, regulations, customs, and usages of the State of _____, the City of _____, and the County of _____, and under the authority of their office as police officers for such city and county.

6. On or about _____ *[date]*, at approximately _____ *[time]*, plaintiff was lawfully operating a _____ automobile in _____ *[city]*, on _____ *[street X]*, driving in a _____ direction, approaching the intersection of _____ *[street X]* and _____ *[street Y]*, at which time and place defendants were then, as a part of their regular and official employment as police officers for the City of _____, operating an automotive police patrol vehicle owned and maintained by such city for the use of its police department. Defendants then signaled plaintiff to stop _____ *[his or her]* vehicle, which plaintiff did, in response to the evident authority of defendants who were at all times mentioned wearing official uniforms, insignia, and badges of the police department of such city.

7. Defendants left their police vehicle and approached plaintiff in _____ *[his or her]* vehicle. At defendants' request, plaintiff displayed _____ *[his or her]* valid driver's license and certificate of automobile registration issued by the State of _____, when defendants, without any warrant or probable cause, ordered plaintiff to get out of _____ *[his or her]* car and submit to a search of _____ *[his or her]* person. This search was conducted in a violent and abusive manner, during the course of which defendants pulled, shoved, cuffed, and verbally assaulted and abused plaintiff with the intent of humiliating and embarrassing plaintiff in the presence of the public generally, and particularly the people present at the scene.

8. After searching plaintiff's person as described above, which search did not reveal any incriminatory or dangerous article, defendants required plaintiff to abandon _____ *[his or her]* vehicle and accompany them to the jail of the City of _____, State of _____, where, at the direction of defendants, plaintiff was unlawfully detained without bail for _____ *[number]* days, all without warrant, probable cause, or any lawful cause whatever.

Page 252

Reprinted with permission of Thomson/West

FIGURE 9-7
(continued)

17–3	**Civil Rights**	**§ 27**

Instruction 17–2
Purpose of the Statue

Congress enacted section 242 to provide for the imposition of criminal penalties on anyone who, under color of law, willfully deprives another of a right protected by the Constitution or the laws of the United States. The statute is directed only against the activities of the state or to its authorized agents; it does not create or add to the rights of one citizen as against another. Rather, it guarantees against the encroachment by the state and its authorized agents upon the rights of citizens under the Constitution or laws of the United States.

Judge reads this to jury.

Authority

United States Supreme Court: Screws v. United States, 325 U.S. 91, 65 S. Ct. 1031, 89 L. Ed. 1495 (1945).
Third Circuit: Sinchak v. Parente, 262 F. Supp. 79 (W.D. Pa. 1966).
Tenth Circuit: United States v. Cooney, 217 F. Supp. 417 (D. Colo. 1963).

Jury is not given this information.

Reprinted from *Modern Federal Jury Instructions.* Copyright © 1997 Matthew Bender & Company, Inc., a member of the LexisNexis Group. All Rights Reserved. Reprinted with permission.

FIGURE 9-8 Instruction 17–2: Purpose of the Statute

develop a set of instructions to give the jury. However, the court is not limited to these approved jury instructions, and sometimes the judge or the attorneys write specific instructions for a case.

Books containing jury instructions can be valuable research tools for two reasons. First, each jury instruction provides a reference to the primary law from which it is taken. Second, unlike many other sources, these statements of law are written in easy-to-understand language because they are written for jurors, not lawyers. See Figure 9-8 for an example.

Pattern jury instructions exist for practice in the state and federal courts.

9-6 THE LEGAL DICTIONARY AND LEGAL THESAURUS

A legal dictionary and a legal thesaurus are essential tools for any legal researcher. A legal dictionary contains definitions of legal words and phrases. Because legal vocabulary is often unique, a beginning researcher can be very confused without the help of a legal dictionary. There are many legal dictionaries available for researchers: The most famous, and probably the most comprehensive, is *Black's Law Dictionary.* A legal thesaurus provides synonyms and antonyms for legal words. This tool is invaluable in helping you use an index to legal source material. See Figure 9-9 for sample pages from both a legal thesaurus and a legal dictionary.

A work that is somewhat similar to a legal dictionary is *Words and Phrases.* This set, published by West, contains numerous legal terms as they are defined in court opinions. References to the cases defining the terms are also given. See Figure 9-10.

deadly - decrease

deadly [*ded* · lee] *adj.* dangerous, destructive, lethal, fatal, hazardous, grave, murderous, perfidious.

dealer [*deel* · er] *n.* wholesaler, merchant, broker, retailer, representative, vendor, middleman. *Ant.* consumer.

death *n.* end of life, expiration, annihilation, extinction, end, destruction. *Ant.* life, resurrection.

debar [dee · *bar*] *v.* exclude, bar, shut out ("debar the unethical lawyer").

debase [dee · *base*] *v.* adulterate, cheapen, belittle, reduce, dishonor, pollute, contaminate. *Ant.* upgrade, encourage.

D

debatable [dee · *bate* · uh · bul] *adj.* arguable, in question, open to doubt, unresolved, disputable, suspect, dubious, conjectural.

debate [de · *bate*] *v.* discuss, altercate, controvert, wrangle, confute, consider, ponder.

debauchery [de · *baw* · che · ree] *n.* self-indulgence, lust, excesses, seduction, vice, overindulgence.

debenture [de · *ben* · cher] *n.* unsecured bond, unsecured note.

debilitate [de · *bill* · ih · tayt] *v.* cripple, enervate, weaken, eviscerate, exhaust, devitalize.

debit [*deb* · it] *v.* charge, list, post.

debit [*deb* · it] *n.* debt, indebtedness, obligation, arrears, liability. *Ant.* credit.

debt *n.* obligation, liability, debit, dues, commitment, encumbrance.

debtee [*det* · ee] *n.* creditor, lender.

debtor [*det* · er] *n.* borrower, buyer, deadbeat.

deceased [de · *seessd*] *n.* dead person, departed, decedent.

decedent [de · *see* · dent] *n.* deceased, testator, intestate, dead individual, departed.

deceit [de · *seet*] *n.* fraud, misrepresentation, cheating, dishonesty, trickery, duplication, falsification.

deceive [de · *seev*] *v.* delude, mislead, swindle, scam, defraud, dupe, hoodwink, screw, trick, victimize.

decent [*dee* · sent] *adj.* proper, suitable, ethical, honorable, prudent, respectable, courteous, kind, thoughtful, obliging.

deception [de · *cep* · shun] *n.* fraud, betrayal, trickery, pretense, duplicity, cunning, insincerity.

decide [de · *side*] *v.* adjudge, conclude, hold, find, decree, determine, establish, resolve, rule.

decision [de · *sizh* · en] *n.* conclusion, resolution, agreement, judgment, adjudication, outcome, ruling.

declarant [de · *clare* · ent] *n.* speaker, affirmant, informer, deponent, witness.

declaration [dek · la · *ray* · shun] *n.* affirmation, statement, admission, profession, expression, proclamation, revelation.

declaratory [de · *klar* · uh · toh · ree] *adj.* elucidating, explanatory, clarifying, assertive ("declaratory judgment"). *Ant.* confusing.

declare [de · *klare*] *v.* allege, admit, convey, attest, feel, disclose, assert, state.

decline [de · *cline*] *v.* reject, renounce, repudiate, veto, spurn, repel ("decline representation"); fall, decay, drop, ebb, wane ("prices decline").

decrease [de · *kreese*] *v.* diminish, subside, curtail, abate, deduct, recede, taper, quell.

FIGURE 9-9 Legal Thesaurus

44

debar [dee · *bar*] To exclude; to bar; to shut out. USAGE: "Because he is financially irresponsible, he was debarred from the bidding." *Note* that "debar" is not **"disbar."**

debase [dee · *base*] To adulterate. *See* adulteration. 2. To cheapen; to belittle.

debauchery [de · *baw* · che · ree] Excessive indulgence, including drunkenness and similar habits, seduction, and sexual immorality generally.

D

debenture [de · *ben* · cher] An **unsecured, long-term corporate bond** or **note.** *See* long-term.

debit *noun* [*deb* · it] An **obligation** charged or assessed against a debtor by a creditor. 2. An accounting term for what appears to be owing by one person to another. *Compare* credit.
verb [*deb* · it] To charge. 2. To post or enter a charge upon a ledger. *Compare* credit.

debt An unconditional and legally enforceable **obligation** for the payment of money. 2. That which is owing under any form of promise, including obligations arising under contract (EXAMPLES: **a mortgage; an installment sale contract**) and obligations imposed by law without contract (EXAMPLES: **a judgment; unliquidated damages**). A debt not presently due is nonetheless a debt. *See* antecedent debt; bad debt; judgment debt; legal debt; secured debt.

debt limitation [lim · i · *tay* · shen] A provision in a state constitution that places a limit on the total amount of indebtedness which the state, or cities and towns within the state, can legally incur. 2. A similar limit placed upon a corporation by its **articles of incorporation.**

debtor [*det* · er] A person who owes another person money. 2. A person who owes another person anything. *See* debt.

debtor in possession [po · *zesh* · en] A debtor who continues to operate his business while undergoing a **business reorganization** under the **jurisdiction** of the **Bankruptcy Court.** *See* bankruptcy.

deceased [de · *seessd*] A dead person; a person who has died; a **decedent.**

decedent [de · *see* · dent] A legal term for a person who has died. *See* decedent's estate.

decedent's estate [es · *tate*] The total property, real and personal, that a decedent owns at the time of her death.

deceit [de · *seet*] Any **false representation** by means of which a person misleads another and causes him harm. Deceit is a form of **fraud.**

deception [de · *sep* · shen] The act of deceiving; deceit. *See* theft by deception.

decision [de · *sizh* · en] The conclusion of a court in the **adjudication** of a case, or by others who function in an adjudicatory capacity, for EXAMPLE, an **arbitrator** or an administrative agency. Although "decision" and **opinion** are often used interchangeably, the words are not usually synonymous, as an opinion is an expression of the court's reasoning for its decision. More nearly synonymous are "decision" and **judgment.** *See* memorandum decision.

decision on the merits [*merr* · its] *See* judgment on the merits.

declarant [de · *clar* · ent] A person who makes a **declaration;** a person who declares.

declaration [dek · le · *ray* · shen] An **unsworn statement,** whether written or oral, the significance of which lies in its **hearsay** character. EXAMPLES: a **declaration against interest;** a dying **declaration.** 2. A formal statement of fact made for an official purpose. EXAMPLE: a customs declaration, in which a person lists articles she has brought into the country. 3. In older legal practice, a plaintiff's initial **pleading,** known in modern practice as a **complaint** or **petition.** 4. A public pronouncement. 5. A pledge or promise. 6. Any statement or announcement. *See* declarant; declare.

declaration against interest [a · *genst in* · trest] A statement contrary to the financial or property interests of the declarant. Such a statement, made out of court, is admissible through a witness other than the declarant as an **exception to the hearsay rule.**

128

FIGURE 9-9
(continued)
Legal Dictionary

Copyright 1994 Matthew Bender & Company, Inc., a member of the LexisNexis Group. All Rights Reserved. Reprinted with permission.

ABSOLUTE CLAIM

ABSOLUTE AND UNDISTURBED USE AND OCCUPATION

Under a treaty setting apart a described area for the "absolute and undisturbed use and occupation" of the Shoshone Indians, the phrase "absolute and undisturbed use and occupation" was to be read with other parts of the document having regard to the purpose of the arrangement made, the relations between the parties, and the settled policy of the United States fairly to deal with Indian tribes. U. S. v. Shoshone Tribe of Indians of Wind River Reservation in Wyoming, Ct.Cl., 58 S.Ct. 794, 797, 798, 304 U.S. 111, 82 L.Ed. 1213.

Under a treaty setting apart a described area for the "absolute and undisturbed use and occupation" of the Shoshone Indians wherein the United States agreed to exclude strangers and granted the right to members of the tribe severally to select and hold tracts on which to establish homes and imposed restraint on cession of land held in common or individually, beneficial ownership of the land, including timber and minerals, was in the tribe rather than in the United States, especially in view of the tribe's cession to the United States of part of the land in trust for the sale of lands, timber, and other products, and making of leases for various purposes. U. S. v. Shoshone Tribe of Indians of Wind River Reservation in Wyoming, Ct.Cl., 58 S.Ct. 794, 304 U.S. 111, 82 L.Ed. 1213.

ABSOLUTE ASSIGNMENT

An instrument whereby authors sold, assigned, transferred, and delivered song to publisher, its successors and assigns, and right to secure copyright therein, and whereby publisher agreed to pay royalties to authors, and to publish song within one year, in default of which all rights should revert to authors, was an "absolute assignment", and hence, where publisher obtained copyright, author could not sue third party for infringement thereof. Kriger v. MacFadden Publications, D.C.N.Y., 43 F.Supp. 170, 172.

An assignment of a policy to secure a debt is not an "absolute assignment" where it is not clearly evidenced that it is so intended, especially where premiums are charged to debtor, and an assignment which limits extent of recovery and which is in effect one for security for advances will operate as a contract for security only, and although an assignment is absolute on its face, entire transaction must be inquired into by court and interest should be limited to sum or amount which it was intended should be secured. Mutual Life Ins. Co. of New York v. Illinois Nat. Bank of Springfield, Ill., D.C. Mich., 34 F.Supp. 206, 210.

ABSOLUTE BEQUEST

Under will bequeathing the residue of estate to the "Spiritualistic College to Educate Mediums" at named place in New York, the bequest was "absolute" and not "in trust", since the quoted phrase constituted a description of the legatee rather than a statement of a trust. In re Lockwood's Estate, 25 A.2d 168, 170, 344 Pa. 293.

Where testator bequeathed to his wife two horses and two cows and directed that she should select them, the bequest was "absolute" so that the legacy was not forfeited although the wife died two days after death of testator without making a selection, and the bequest inured to the administrator of the wife's estate. Snellings v. Downer, 18 S.E. 2d 531, 537, 193 Ga. 340, 139 A.L.R. 860.

ABSOLUTE CERTAINTY

In personal injury action, instruction that damages should include compensation for pain and suffering that plaintiff might with reasonable probability suffer in future held not error, since term "reasonable probability" is equivalent of "reasonable certainty" and does not mean "absolute certainty." Great Atlantic & Pacific Tea Co. v. Hughes, 4 N.E.2d 700, 705, 53 Ohio App. 255.

ABSOLUTE CLAIM

A contingent claim does not become "absolute," within the meaning of the decedent's act, until it becomes a claim proper to be presented to the county court for final adjudication as a claim against the estate. Hazlett v. Blakely's Estate, 97 N.W. 808, 811, 70 Neb. 613.

Where bank remained solvent for more than eight years after stockholder's death, action to enforce stockholders' constitutional liability held not barred by failure to file contingent claim against stockholder's es-

1 W. & P.—18   273

FIGURE 9-10
Words and Phrases

Reprinted with permission of Thomson/West

TECHNOLOGY CORNER

Legal Dictionaries

www.lectlaw.com/ref.html

http://dictionary.law.com/

http://dictionary.lp.findlaw.com/

Dictionaries

www.m-w.com/ (Webster)

www.onelook.com/ (links to dozens of dictionaries)

Thesaurus

www.thesaurus.com/

www.m-w.com/

Many Web sites provide legal forms. The following site contains legal documents, legal forms, contracts, leases, wills, and more. Most of the forms are explained and some general advice on filling out the form may also be provided.

www.legaldocs.com

Some of the Web pages offering forms allow you to fill out the forms online, but a fee is required. Be a cautious consumer.

CHAPTER SUMMARY

Several secondary sources are published to help legal practitioners. An important research tool used to find case law is the digest. A digest is an alphabetical arrangement of topics found in headnotes with references to the cases in which the headnotes are found. The publishers of the various case reporters publish digests corresponding to the case reporters. You can use a digest to find case law if you already have one case that relates to your issue or if you have identified key words from your facts and issues. If you have a known case, you note the appropriate headnotes, locate them in the digest that accompanies the case reporter you are using, and then find other cases on the same topic. If you do not have a known case, check the key terms in the descriptive word index. The index directs the researcher to various topics in the digest.

Form books are another valuable research tool for lawyers. Form books are found in comprehensive multivolume sets containing either forms for use in the courts (forms of pleading and practice) or for use in business or personal matters (transaction forms). Forms may be found in single-topic works, often referred to as *practice books*. Many form books provide not only sample forms, but explanations of the law related to the forms and reference the controlling primary law.

Also important are pattern jury instructions. These contain, short, concise statements of law written for non-lawyers. Books containing pattern jury instructions reference the primary law from which the instruction was taken.

A legal dictionary and a legal thesaurus are essential tools for researchers. Legal dictionaries explain legal words and phrases. A legal thesaurus provides synonyms and antonyms for legal words and phrases.

TERMS TO REMEMBER

digest

descriptive word index

headnotes

topic and key number

Century Digest

Decennial Digest

General Digest

prefatory material

forms of pleading and practice

transaction forms

practice books

jury instructions

QUESTIONS FOR REVIEW

1. What is a digest?
2. How do headnotes relate to a digest?
3. If you have a known case and are using a digest to find more cases, why is it important to use the digest published by the company that published the case reporter in which you found the case?
4. What types of cases are found in West's American Digest System?
5. What is a table of cases and why is it useful?
6. How do you use a digest if you do not have any case law related to your issue?
7. How are digests kept up-to-date?
8. What is the difference between pleading and practice forms and transaction forms?
9. Why are pattern jury instructions a useful research tool?
10. What is the Restatement?

CAN YOU FIGURE IT OUT?

1. List the legal topics and key number for the headnote found in Figure 9-1.
2. List the legal topics and section numbers for the headnotes found in Figure 9-2.
3. Refer to Figure 9-3. Find key number 201 under the general topic "States." Which other general topic should also be checked?
4. Refer to Figure 9-4. Cite cases other than *Felder* that deal with the topic and section number Civil Rights § 27.
5. Refer to Figure 9-5. Select one research problem from Appendix A and read it carefully. Find at least five topics in Figure 9-5 that apply to the situation.
6. Refer to Figure 9-6. What does *Restatement of Torts 2d* § 71 (a) provide?
7. Explain in your own words what Form § 13 found in Figure 9-7 is used for. The following terms are found in Figure 9-7: *standing to sue, caption,* and *jurisdiction.* Define each term.

RESEARCH ASSIGNMENTS AND ACTIVITIES

A. Using the *10th Decennial Digest—Part I,* answer the following.

    1. Cite a case in which Dannon Yogurt is a defendant.

    2. What is the specific topic of Patents 16.29?

        a. What is the name of a New York federal case, found in this section, dealing with a patent from the United Kingdom?

        b. Locate the case described in "a." What case headnote corresponds to this digest entry?

    3. Using the descriptive word index, which civil rights section deals with arrest as a deprivation of constitutional rights?

B. Using the Restatement, answer the following.

    4. Where in the *Restatement 2d* will you find a section dealing with undue influence by a third person rendering a transaction voidable at the request of the victim where the other contracting party knew of the undue influence?

    5. Where in the *Restatement 2d* is negligence defined? What does comment "d" provide?

CASE PROJECT

Using the same case that you researched in previous chapters, check the appropriate digest for topics relating to the issues. Begin by making a list of terms to check in the index to the digest. Make a list of relevant digest topics and cases. Read the cases and take notes.

VALIDATING YOUR RESEARCH: Using *Shepard's* and Other Citators

CHAPTER OBJECTIVES

When you complete this chapter you should be able to

- Explain the purpose of a citator.
- List the types of authorities that may be Shepardized.
- Describe the information found in *Shepard's* case citators.
- Explain the difference between the history of the case and the treatment of the case.
- Explain how *Shepard's* uses headnote numbers.
- Discuss the differences between *Shepard's* and other online citators.
- Explain what it means to "cite check" a document.

CITATION MATTERS

INTRODUCTORY SIGNALS

THE BLUEBOOK — RULE 1.2

The purpose of a signal is to alert the reader to something. Signals are used to show support, suggest a comparison, indicate a contradiction, and indicate background materials. These signals must be italicized. However, when a signal is used as a verb in a sentence, it is not italicized.

Examples of signals used to *show support:*

- **No signal**—indicates the cited authority (a) directly states the proposition, (b) shows the source of quoted language, or (c) identifies authority cited in the text.
- *E.g.,*—is used to show that the cited material states the proposition presented in the sentence; other materials also state the same proposition, but a citation to them is not helpful or is not necessary. This signal is often used in combination with other signals, for example: *See, e.g.,*
- *See*—is used instead of "no signal" when the proposition presented is not *exactly* stated by the authority cited, but it clearly follows from it. This signal alerts the reader that there is an *inferential step* between the proposition and the cited authority.
- *See Also*—is used to show that the cited authority is additional support for the proposition presented.
- *Cf.*—is used when the writer needs the reader to understand that the cited authority provides material that is analogous with the main proposition.

Example of a signal used to suggest a *comparison:*

- **Compare**—is used to show that comparison of the authorities offers support for the proposition presented. Parenthetical explanations often follow these authorities.

Examples of signals that indicate a *contradiction:*

- **Contra**—is used to show that the cited authority *states* the contrary of the proposition.
- **But see**—is used to show that the cited authority *supports* a position that is contrary to the writer's main position.

Example of a signal that indicates *background material:*

- **See generally**—is used to show that the cited authority offers background information related to the proposition.

Example of a signal used as a *verb:*

- *See Wisconsin v. Mitchell,* 508 U.S. 476 (1993). (*See* used as a signal.)
- See *Wisconsin v. Mitchell,* 508 U.S. 476 (1993) for an explanation of what made the statute at issue unconstitutionally overbroad. (*See* used as a verb.)

INTEROFFICE MEMORANDUM

TO: Research Associate

FROM: Supervising Attorney

RE: Hogan/Rider cases

I read the *Bramblett* case for the Hogan matter. It seems to be right on point. I assume that you Shepardized it and it is still good law. Perhaps you could go back to *Shepard's* and see if there are more recent similar cases. Also, I have attached a copy of a Memorandum of Points and Authorities to be filed in the *Rider* case. Please cite check it for me.

10-1 INTRODUCTION TO CITATORS

U.S. law is in a constant state of change. Although case law is founded on the concept of *stare decisis,* courts occasionally overrule or modify prior case law to meet the needs of justice in a changing society. Statutory law likewise undergoes changes. Statutes are commonly amended and repealed, or given new interpretations by

courts. Sometimes courts declare that statutes are unconstitutional and therefore unenforceable. Your research is never complete until you verify that your authorities are still **good law.**

 Determining that an authority is good law requires the use of special research material. Case reporters and code books do not provide totally up-to-date information on the cases and codes found in the books. When you read a case in a case reporter, you cannot tell whether that case was overruled or criticized in later cases. Published codes provide better information, but even they are not totally up-to-date. While most codes contain pocket part supplements, these supplements are replaced only once a year. Because most legislative changes take effect at the beginning of the year rather than when they are made, supplementing once a year is usually sufficient to provide the latest statutory language. However, some legislation is considered to be "emergency legislation" and takes effect immediately. This is not found in a supplement that is replaced only once a year. Furthermore, if you rely on case notes in an annotated code, you may miss important new relevant case law. The research materials used to update or **validate** legal authorities are known as **citators,** the most familiar of which is *Shepard's Citations. Shepard's* is available in print and online through LEXIS. LEXIS provides two other products, Auto-cite and Lexcite, which can be used to check citations. Another important citator is KeyCite, available online through Westlaw.

good law. Law that is still in effect or valid and can be cited as authority.

validate. To verify that an authority is still good law.

citator. Research materials used to update or "validate" legal authorities.

10-2 *SHEPARD'S CITATIONS*

Shepard's Citations is a popular collection that researchers use to validate their research. When you use any of the *Shepard's* citators to check a legal citation, you are said to be "**Shepardizing**" your authority. The legal citation you are Shepardizing is called the **cited authority.** New law found when Shepardizing is referred to as the **citing authority.** While *Shepard's* is most commonly used to check case law, it is also used to check other authorities, such as constitutions, statutory law, administrative regulations, selected law review articles, *A.L.R.* annotations, court rules, and approved jury instructions. *Shepard's* includes specialized citators for areas of law such as bankruptcy and patents.

 The primary reason for Shepardizing any authority is to verify that the law found is still good law. However, *Shepard's* provides much more information, depending on the type of authority Shepardized. For case law, *Shepard's* provides the following information about case citations:

Shepardize. To check the validity of a citation in one of the *Shepard's* citations.

cited authority. The authority you are Shepardizing.

citing authority. Authorities you are referred to when you Shepardize.

- Parallel cites
- Cites to the same case if it is the subject of published opinions from other courts
- Cites to all other cases discussing your citation
- Description of how other cases have considered your case citation
- Cites to selected secondary sources discussing your citation

 For statutory law, *Shepard's* provides the following information about the citation:

- Whether the statute has been amended or repealed
- Cites to case law discussing the statute

- Description of how case law considered the statute
- Cites to selected secondary sources discussing the citation

These features allow researchers to use *Shepard's* to find additional authorities, in addition to validating their research.

BOX 10-1

YOU CAN SHEPARDIZE THESE AUTHORITIES

Case law

Statutory law

Constitutions

Administrative regulations

Selected law reviews and *A.L.R.s*

Court rules

Approved jury instructions

Shepard's Case Citators in Print

Shepard's includes separate case citators for cases from different courts. For federal cases, *Shepard's* publishes the following:

- *Shepard's United States Citations* for Shepardizing United States Supreme Court cases
- *Shepard's Federal Citations* for Shepardizing federal district court and appellate court decisions (*Federal Supplement* and *Federal Reporters*)

Additionally, *Shepard's* publishes citators for each of the regional reporters as well as citators for state case reporters.

➪ **A Point to Remember** When you use a state-specific case citator, you can only Shepardize cases (cited authorities) from the selected jurisdiction. However, citing authorities may be from all jurisdictions.

Shepard's case citators are organized in a manner similar to case reporters. That is, cited cases or authorities are arranged numerically by volume and page number of the case. See Figure 10-1 for an example of a page from a *Shepard's* case citator in print. Because case citators are published for all major case reporters, researchers are able to Shepardize a case with either the official citation or with a parallel citation. It is advisable to Shepardize all citations to the same case, though, because cited authorities are different, especially secondary authorities. (This is not the case if you Shepardize online.) See Figures 10-2 and 10-3 for examples of pages from *Shepard's* showing the parallel cites for the same case as in Figure 10-1.

➪ **A Point to Remember** When you Shepardize a case, you must check all parallel cites to obtain references to all citing authorities.

Vol. 316 — UNITED STATES REPORTS

75McL527	400F2d823	12A2363n	q) 369US519	111FS418
65MnL80	270FS939	12A2368n	q) 369US520	123FS443
80MnL1451	Cir. 7	12A2370n	370US908	124FS37
83MnL1224	160FS328	12A2371n	372US337	141FS606
85MnL1437	Cir. 8	—455—	o) 372US339	332FS834
72NwL26	266F2d69	Betts v Brady	372US348	377FS1341
57TxL540	69F3d1407	1942	e) 372US349	432FS115
64TxL12	Cir. 9	(86LE1595)	372US478	q) 253FS2d33
77TxL167	172FS938	(62SC1252)	j) 375US3	Cir. 2
60VaL197	Cir. 10	s) 315US791	q) 378US6	e) 137F2d1010
83YLJ433	80FS344	317US24	j) 378US26	190F2d253
85YLJ45	Cir. DC	317US276	j) 378US407	221F2d629
94LE377n	707F2d561	321US115	q) 379US80	d) 250F2d354
94LE378n	Cir. Fed.	j) 322US495	q) 380US414	263F2d943
47LE851n	856F2d172	322US602	j) 381US512	292F2d323
171AR773n	CCPA	324US46	381US590	303F2d885
171AR788n	j) 359F2d885	324US764	j) 381US616	d) 313F2d460
16ARF429n	ClCt	324US768	384US469	315F2d866
—447—	36FedCl 33	325US95	e) 385US399	j) 319F2d318
National Broad-	38FedCl 667	325US97	385US564	330F2d304
casting Co. v	CtCl	326US326	q) 386US43	q) 330F2d310
United States	375F2d838	327US85	j) 388US172	j) 330F2d315
1942	530F2d869	329US665	q) 389US134	332F2d891
(86LE1586)	620F2d855	j) 332US83	395US794	q) 333F2d610
(62SC1214)	f) 47FS119	332US137	q) 395US795	398F2d985
s) 319US190	e) 48FS358	j) 332US140	c) 405US484	q) 465F2d121
s) 44FS688	55FS624	j) 332US141	j) 405US485	j) 611F2d421
s) 47FS940	60FS469	333US281	q) 407US31	694F2d22
cc) 316US407	f) 97CCL262	333US656	q) 407US65	e) 709F2d168
Cir. 7	e) 99CCL570	333US659	408US287	113FS920
95FS669	99CCL571	333US660	q) 411US788	171FS561
97CR840	101CCL743	333US666	j) 419US255	177FS507
80MnL1451	104CCL122	333US676	422US807	184FS282
94LE377n	179CCL610	j) 333US677	j) 422US844	184FS542
94LE378n	208CCL579	j) 333US679	q) 440US371	200FS907
47LE851n	223CCL430	334US684	j) 440US378	205FS514
171AR773n	4TCt216	j) 334US685	q) 452US25	209FS530
171AR788n	18TCt12	334US730	j) 452US35	210FS277
—450—	24TCt637	334US739	466US656	f) 210FS279
American	29TCt271	335US441	469US394	212FS880
Chicle Co. v	36TCt282	337US780	q) 492US12	212FS928
United States	58TCt911	c) 337US782	j) 492US21	214FS646
1942	59TCt74	339US661	499US34	219FS153
(86LE1591)	66TCt356	339US666	509US109	e) 219FS266
(62SC1144)	77TCt63	342US64	q) 510US273	q) 219FS268
s) 315US793	89TCt776	342US179	q) 511US493	261FS400
s) 41FS537	90TCt1306	d) 348US9	j) 511US738	q) 327FS546
s) 94CCL699	100TCt11	348US108	523US850	Cir. 3
493US140	103TCt470	349US391	j) 4LE292	130F2d657
505US73	104TCt729	350US118	q) 159LE507	175F2d254
Cir. 1	107TCt337	j) 351US36	j) 80SC315	203F2d426
61FS1016	Ala	354US77	q) 124SC2514	203F2d806
Cir. 2	503So2d303	355US159	9FRD348	224F2d508
158F2d161	Mass	j) 356US83	24FRD79	224F2d512
306F2d827	378Mas273	d) 357US441	33FRD424	f) 310F2d724
199FS458	391NE263	j) 357US442	33FRD438	j) 310F2d735
199FS466	Okla	358US636	33FRD454	e) 329F2d858
Cir. 3	780P2d668	361US246	38FRD463	q) 334F2d529
181F2d405	P R	j) 361US255	39FRD284	355F2d313
Cir. 4	74PRR922	j) 363US704	Cir. 1	j) 359F2d947
205F2d342	So C	j) 364US275	181F2d602	j) 430F2d469
Cir. 5	233SoC48	365US117	d) 191F2d965	752F2d921
562F2d978	103SE427	q) 365US119	203F2d935	j) 782F2d455
Cir. 6	78CR1659	j) 365US208	204F2d362	994F2d1016
151F2d1000	92HLR1646	j) 366US158	96FS707	74FS848
229F2d698	122PaL348	368US459	f) 101FS165	81FS870
	153AR1189n	369US517	f) 105FS529	81FS871

The reporter and volume number appear at the top of the page.

Here you find Shepard's analysis of *Betts v. Brady*, 316 U.S. 455 (1942) Parallel citations are found in other parts of *Shepard's*.

FIGURE 10-1

Shepard's United States Reports

22

Reprinted with the permission of LexisNexis

	UNITED STATES SUPREME COURT REPORTS, LAWYERS' EDITION			
Vol. 86				
38FedCl[1] 667	90LE[6]108	q) 17LE[7]721	q) 330F2d[7]310	130F2d[4]881
CtCl	90LE[2]548	j) 18LE[9]1121	j) 330F2d[7]315	133F2d477
375F2d[1]838	j) 91LE[4]1925	q) 19LE[8]340	332F2d[7]891	155F2d[4]5
530F2d869	91LE[4]1958	q) 23LE[6]716	q) 333F2d[4]610	198F2d[4]471
620F2d855	j) 91LE[4]1960	23LE[7]716	398F2d[7]985	280F2d[7]539
f) 47FS[1]119	92LE[4]698	c) 31LE[8]382	q) 465F2d[8]121	280F2d[9]539
e) 48FS[1]358	92LE[9]995	j) 31LE[4]383	j) 611F2d421	280F2d[6]541
55FS[1]624	92LE[7]997	j) 31LE[8]387	694F2d[8]22	294F2d[9]396
60FS[2]469	92LE[8]997	q) 32LE[6]535	e) 709F2d[9]168	294F2d[6]609
f) 97CCL262	92LE[6]1000	q) 32LE[8]554	113FS[6]920	297F2d853
e) 99CCL570	92LE[4]1001	33LE377	171FS[9]561	d) 299F2d[4]173
99CCL571	j) 92LE[4]1006	q) 36LE[7]665	177FS[2]507	j) 310F2d[6]917
101CCL743	j) 92LE[6]1006	j) 42LE[4]428	184FS[7]282	315F2d[7]644
104CCL122	j) 92LE[8]1006	j) 42LE[6]428	184FS[9]542	315F2d[8]644
179CCL610	j) 92LE[9]1006	45LE[5]566	200FS[7]907	q) 319F2d[9]2
208CCL579	j) 92LE[7]1007	j) 45LE587	205FS[9]514	q) 319F2d[9]4
223CCL430	92LE[4]1655	j) 45LE[4]587	209FS[4]530	q) 319F2d[8]772
4TCt216	j) 92LE[4]1655	q) 59LE[8]387	210FS[6]277	c) 368F2d298
18TCt12	92LE[4]1686	j) 59LE392	f) 210FS[6]279.	375F2d628
24TCt637	92LE[4]1692	q) 68LE[8]648	212FS[8]880	c) 381F2d[6]641
29TCt271	93LE[4]131	j) 68LE655	212FS[9]928	c) 415F2d1325
36TCt282	93LE[9]1691	80LE666	214FS[7]646	f) 443F2d[8]1095
58TCt911	c) 93LE1692	83LE828	219FS[7]153	j) 443F2d[4]1100
59TCt74	94LE1190	q) 106LE[9]12	e) 219FS[7]266	447F2d[4]57
66TCt356	94LE[7]1192	j) 106LE18	q) 219FS[9]268	483F2d[4]655
77TCt63	96LE[9]94	113LE[6]30	q) 220FS[9]892	j) 166F3d283
89TCt776	d) 99LE[4]9	125LE94	261FS[8]400	47FS[2]366
90TCt1306	99LE[6]138	q) 127LE123	q) 327FS[4]546	165FS[6]24
100TCt11	99LE[7]1174	q) 128LE[5]526	Cir. 3	176FS[4]954
103TCt470	100LE[9]130	j) 128LE762	130F2d[7]657	201FS[9]447
104TCt729	j) 100LE[6]908	140LE[7]1060	175F2d254	206FS[9]302
107TCt337	1LE[7]1197	q) 159LE507	203F2d[8]426	q) 216FS[8]290
Ala	2LE[9]171	9FRD348	203F2d[4]806	227FS[8]2
503So2d303	j) 2LE[9]627	24FRD79	224F2d[7]508	q) 227FS[8]3
Mass	d) 2LE[4]1455	33FRD424	224F2d[8]512	251FS[7]665
378Mas273	j) 2LE[4]1456	33FRD438	f) 310F2d[7]724	e) 257FS[4]808
391NE[2]263	3LE[4]560	33FRD454	j) 310F2d[7]735	q) 307FS[4]206
Okla	4LE[7]276	38FRD463	329F2d[7]858	j) 310FS[7]563
780P2d668	j) 4LE[4]292	39FRD284	e) 329F2d[8]858	q) 312FS[7]310
P R	j) 4LE[6]1505	Cir. 1	q) 334F2d[6]529	324FS[7]697
74PRR922	j) 4LE[8]1716	181F2d[6]602	355F2d[4]313	355FS[5]344
So C	5LE[6]451	d) 191F2d[9]965	j) 359F2d[4]947	Cir. 5
233SoC48	q) 5LE[6]452	203F2d[4]935	j) 430F2d469	158F2d[4]617
103SE[2]427	j) 5LE[6]517	204F2d[4]362	752F2d[4]921	194F2d[4]865
78CR1659	j) 6LE[6]182	96FS[7]707	j) 782F2d455	205F2d[6]668
92HLR1646	7LE[9]454	f) 101FS[7]165	994F2d1016	j) 205F2d[7]675
122PaL348	8LE[7]778	f) 105FS[9]529	74FS[2]848	224F2d[7]905
153ABR1189n	q) 8LE[7]779	111FS[6]418	74FS[6]848	228F2d[9]659
12A[2]363n	q) 8LE[7]780	123FS[6]443	74FS[8]848	228F2d[4]664
12A[2]368n	8LE[8]403	124FS[6]37	81FS[6]870	250F2d[6]647
12A[2]370n	9LE[9]801	141FS[7]606	81FS[9]871	258F2d[9]941
12A[2]371n	o) 9LE[9]802	332FS[8]834	84FS[6]940	j) 258F2d[4]944
—1595—	9LE[9]807	377FS[9]1341	85FS[6]787	261F2d[4]233
Betts v Brady	e) 9LE[9]808	432FS[7]115	88FS[6]780	j) 263F2d[7]44
1942	9LE[9]894	q) 253FS2d33	97FS[4]939	j) 263F2d[9]46
(316US455)	j) 11LE[9]42	Cir. 2	148FS[9]684	330F2d[7]525
(62SC1252)	q) 12LE[9]658	e) 137F2d[2]1010	187FS[6]715	341F2d[7]798
s) 86LE1194	j) 12LE[7]670	190F2d[9]253	196FS[6]53	c) 341F2d[9]776
87LE[2]10	j) 12LE[6]933	221F2d[7]629	208FS[9]639	341F2d[8]780
87LE[4]273	q) 13LE[7]136	d) 250F2d[4]354	226FS[6]420	e) 353F2d[6]107
j) 88LE[7]1415	q) 13LE[6]932	263F2d[6]943	q) 226FS[9]582	366F2d[7]727
88LE[7]1485	j) 14LE[7]532	292F2d[7]323	243FS[4]700	q) 400F2d[5]596
89LE[4]1352	14LE[6]585	303F2d[7]885	271FS[7]409	410F2d[9]335
89LE[2]1354	j) 14LE[6]600	d) 313F2d460	207FS2d347	j) 416F2d[5]1027
89LE[7]1499	16LE[7]720	315F2d[7]866	Cir. 4	422F2d[7]301
89LE[4]1500	e) 17LE[4]473	j) 319F2d[6]318	128F2d[4]1013	430F2d[8]1117
89LE[4]1742	17LE[7]614	330F2d[7]304	129F2d[4]110	496F2d[7]1058

1424

This page analyzes *Betts v. Brady*, if you have the *Lawyers' Edition* citation 86 L.Ed. 1595 (1942).

FIGURE 10-2

Shepard's United States Supreme Court Reports, Lawyers' Edition

Reprinted with the permission of LexisNexis

Vol. 62	SUPREME COURT REPORTER			
Ore	30LE835n	j) 80SC[10]315	Cir. 1	e) 329F2d[8]858
170Ore596	30LE839n	j) 80SC1319	181F2d602	q) 334F2d529
214Ore318	37LE1139n	j) 80SC[8]1470	d) 191F2d[7]965	355F2d[10]313
21OrA761	103LE966n	81SC418	203F2d[10]935	j) 359F2d[10]947
135P2d757	141AR1031n	q) 81SC419	204F2d[10]362	j) 430F2d[8]469
330P2d22	146AR109n	j) 81SC495	96FS[6]707	752F2d[10]921
537P2d125	147AR699n	j) 81SC977	f) 101FS[6]165	j) 782F2d455
Pa	93A2117n	82SC[7]507	f) 105FS[7]529	994F2d[9]1016
149PaS181	65A3514n	82SC[6]891	111FS418	74FS[2]848
153PaS434	**—1252—**	q) 82SC[6]892	123FS443	74FS[8]848
27A2d669	**Betts v Brady**	82SC1259	124FS37	81FS870
34A2d169	**1942**	83SC[7]770	141FS[6]606	81FS[7]871
R I	(316US455)	83SC[7]793	332FS[9]834	84FS940
121RI545	(86LE1595)	o) 83SC794	332FS[11]834	85FS787
401A2d445	s) 62SC639	83SC[7]799	377FS[11]1341	88FS780
So C	s) 62SC1252	e) 83SC[7]799	432FS[6]115	97FS[10]939
204SoC343	63SC[2]9	j) 84SC[7]81	Cir. 2	148FS[7]684
239SoC148	63SC[10]240	q) 84SC[7]1492	e) 137F2d[2]1010	187FS715
29SE541	64SC[10]449	j) 84SC[6]1503	190F2d[7]253	196FS53
122SE211	j) 64SC[6]1085	j) 84SC1797	221F2d[6]629	208FS[7]639
S D	64SC[6]1212	q) 85SC[4]218	d) 250F2d[10]354	226FS420
69SD471	65SC[10]520	q) 85SC1073	263F2d943	q) 226FS[7]582
11NW525	65SC[10]980	85SC1663	292F2d[6]323	243FS[10]700
Tenn	65SC[2]982	j) 85SC1677	303F2d[6]885	271FS[6]409
188Ten25	65SC[6]1032	j) 85SC[6]1697	d) 313F2d460	207FS2d347
216SW711	65SC[10]1033	86SC[6]1625	315F2d[6]866	Cir. 4
529SW58	66SC163	e) 87SC547	j) 319F2d318	128F2d[10]1013
Tex	66SC[2]453	87SC[6]653	330F2d[6]304	129F2d[10]110
j) 913SW502	67SC[7]597	q) 87SC[10]837	q) 330F2d[6]310	130F2d[10]881
j) 975SW584	j) 67SC[10]1692	j) 87SC[7]2000	j) 330F2d[6]315	133F2d[4]477
Va	67SC[10]1718	q) 88SC[7]256	332F2d[6]891	155F2d[10]5
186Va845	j) 67SC[10]1719	89SC[6]2062	q) 333F2d[10]610	198F2d[10]471
44SE412	j) 67SC[10]1720	q) 89SC[6]2063	398F2d[6]985	280F2d[6]539
Wash	68SC[10]511	c) 92SC[8]1020	q) 465F2d[10]121	280F2d[7]539
16Wsh2d380	68SC[7]771	j) 92SC[10]1020	j) 611F2d421	280F2d541
51Wsh2d770	68SC[6]773	j) 92SC[8]1023	694F2d[8]22	294F2d[7]396
6WAp98	68SC[8]773	q) 92SC[8]2009	e) 709F2d[8]168	294F2d609
133P2d807	68SC776	q) 92SC[6]2026	113FS920	297F2d853
322P2d848	68SC[10]781	92SC2751	171FS[7]561	d) 299F2d[10]173
492P2d241	j) 68SC782	q) 93SC[8]1763	177FS[2]507	j) 310F2d917
Wyo	j) 68SC[7]782	j) 95SC[8]471	184FS[6]282	315F2d[6]644
71Wyo94	j) 68SC[8]782	j) 95SC[10]471	184FS[7]542	315F2d[8]644
254P2d200	j) 68SC[10]782	95SC[5]2527	200FS[6]907	q) 319F2d[7]2
42CLA662	j) 68SC[6]783	j) 95SC2545	205FS[7]514	q) 319F2d[7]4
61Cor966	68SC[10]1254	j) 95SC[10]2546	209FS[10]530	q) 319F2d[8]772
74CR377	68SC[10]1257	q) 99SC[11]1161	210FS277	c) 368F2d298
82CR1099	68SC[10]1276	j) 99SC1164	f) 210FS279	375F2d628
99CR173	j) 68SC[10]1277	q) 101SC[8]2158	212FS[8]880	c) 381F2d[11]641
90McL225	69SC[10]186	j) 101SC2164	212FS[10]928	c) 415F2d1325
95McL334	69SC[7]1250	104SC2045	214FS[6]646	f) 443F2d[7]1095
67MnL545	c) 69SC1251	105SC835	219FS[6]153	f) 443F2d[8]1095
49NYL815	70SC911	q) 109SC[7]2772	e) 219FS[6]266	j) 443F2d[8]1100
150PaL119	70SC[6]913	j) 109SC2776	q) 219FS[7]268	447F2d[7]57
36StnL683	72SC[7]147	111SC1051	q) 220FS[7]892	447F2d[8]57
55TxL1160	72SC[7]213	113SC2524	261FS[8]400	483F2d[4]655
62TxL409	d) 75SC[10]4	q) 114SC813	q) 327FS[8]546	q) 561F2d[11]542
64TxL829	75SC147	q) 114SC[8]1737	Cir. 3	j) 166F3d283
64TxL831	75SC[6]823	j) 114SC1934	130F2d[6]657	47FS[2]366
74TxL1297	76SC[7]225	118SC[11]1719	175F2d[4]254	165FS24
77VaL749	j) 76SC599	q) 124SC2514	203F2d[8]426	176FS[10]954
87VaL781	77SC[6]1262	9FRD348	203F2d[10]806	201FS[7]447
88VaL485	78SC[7]194	24FRD79	224F2d[6]508	206FS[7]302
90YLJ745	j) 78SC[7]589	33FRD424	224F2d[8]512	q) 216FS[8]290
91YLJ1292	d) 78SC[7]1292	33FRD438	f) 310F2d[6]724	227FS[2]
93LE1160n	j) 78SC[10]1293	33FRD454	j) 310F2d[6]735	q) 227FS[8]3
93LE1182n	79SC[10]435	38FRD463	329F2d[6]858	251FS[6]665
96LE977n	80SC[6]303	39FRD284		e) 257FS[10]808

This page analyzes the *Supreme Court Reporter* version of *Betts v. Brady*, 62 S. Ct. 1252 (1942).

FIGURE 10-3
Supreme Court Reporter

Reprinted with the permission of LexisNexis

Analyzing Information   Once you find a case in *Shepard's*, you must analyze or interpret your findings. Shepardizing a case provides two types of information concerning your case (the cited case), the history of the case, and the treatment of the case. The history of the case provides the published background of the *same* case you are checking. If you are Shepardizing a U.S. Supreme Court case, *Shepard's* provides the cite to any published opinions of the same case from lower courts. If you are Shepardizing an appellate court case, *Shepard's* tells you if a higher court has granted a hearing. The treatment of the case provides citations to *other* authorities mentioning your case. In some instances, it tells you how these other authorities viewed your case. Some of the more important facts that *Shepard's* tells you are whether a case was:

- Overruled by a subsequent case
- Criticized by a subsequent case
- Approved by a subsequent case
- Questioned by a subsequent case
- Cited in the dissent of a subsequent case

Shepard's also tells you if a case has been cited in *A.L.R.* articles or law review articles. See Figure 10-4 for an illustrative page from *Shepard's* showing the various case treatments and corresponding abbreviations.

⇨ **A Point to Remember**   If you see the following abbreviations, stop:

"o" (*overruled*): If a case has been overruled, you cannot use the case as authority. This means it is no longer good law. However, sometimes only part of a case is overruled. You can use the case if your issue is not overruled.

"Grtd" (*hearing granted*): If a hearing has been granted in a higher court, you cannot use your citation as authority. It is not a final decision. If the higher court has issued a published opinion, you can use that cite.

"c" (*criticized*): If a case has been criticized, you can still use it as authority, but it would be better to find other authorities following your decision.

"q" (*questioned*): If a case has been questioned, you can still use it as authority, but it would be better to find other authorities following your decision.

"r" (*reversed*): If a case has been reversed by a higher court, you cannot cite it.

"S" (*superseded*): The decision in the case has been superseded or replaced by another decision. Do not cite it.

"v" (*vacated*): Your case is no longer law. Do not cite it.

When you Shepardize a case using *Shepard's* in print, you also find the following:

- The first time a case appears in *Shepard's*, you see the case name (for recent cases only).
- The first time a case appears in *Shepard's*, you find parallel citations in parentheses at the beginning of the citations.
- References to authorities are chronological (oldest cases first) within the following categories: U.S. Supreme Court cases, federal court cases, state court cases, and secondary sources. Citing references are not listed in order of importance.

See Figure 10-5 for an illustration from *Shepard's* case citations showing this.

⇨ **A Point to Remember**   When a case has been cited by numerous authorities, you must read the list of *all* of the citing authorities carefully. A citing authority overruling

CASE ANALYSIS–ABBREVIATIONS

HISTORY OF CASES

a	(affirmed)	On appeal, reconsideration or rehearing, the citing case affirms or adheres to the case you are *Shepardizing*.
cc	(connected case)	The citing case is related to the case you are *Shepardizing*, arising out of the same subject matter or involving the same parties.
D	(dismissed)	The citing case dismisses an appeal from the case you are *Shepardizing*.
De/ Cert den	(denied)	The citing case has denied further appeal in the case you are *Shepardizing*.
Gr	(granted)	The citing case has granted further appeal in the case you are *Shepardizing*.
m	(modified)	On appeal, reconsideration or rehearing, the citing case modifies or changes in some way, including affirmance in part and reversal in part, the case you are *Shepardizing*.
r	(reversed)	On appeal, reconsideration or rehearing, the citing case reverses the case you are *Shepardizing*.
ReD	(reh./recon. denied)	The citing order denies rehearing or reconsideration in the case you are *Shepardizing*.
ReG	(reh./recon. grated)	The citing order grants rehearing or reconsideration in the case you are *Shepardizing*.
s	(same case)	The citing case involves the same litigation as the case you are *Shepardizing*, but at a different stage of the proceedings.
S	(superseded)	On appeal, reconsideration or rehearing, the citing case supersedes or is substituted for the case you are *Shepardizing*.
US cert den		The citing order by the U. S. Supreme Court denies certiorari in the cases you are *Shepardizing*.
US cert dis		The citing order by the U. S. Supreme Court dismisses certiorari in the case you are *Shepardizing*.
US cert gran		The citing order by the U. S. Supreme Court grants certiorari in the case you are *Shepardizing*.
US reh den		The citing order by the U. S. Supreme Court denies rehearing in the case you are *Shepardizing*.
US reh dis		The citing order by the U. S. Supreme Court dismisses rehearing in the case you are *Shepardizing*.
v	(vacated)	The citing case vacates or withdraws the case you are *Shepardizing*.
W	(withdrawn)	The citing decision or opinion withdraws the decision or order you are *Shepardizing*.

FIGURE 10-4
Shepard's Case Analysis Abbreviations

your case may appear in the middle of several pages of citations. Other than the abbreviation "o," nothing distinguishes this cite. Examine Figures 10-1, 10-2, and 10-3. Note the placement of the overruling case.

Abbreviations *Shepard's* in print relies heavily on the use of abbreviations. The cited and citing references are abbreviated in a way that is unique to *Shepard's*. In describing the history and treatment of a particular case, one or two letter abbreviations are used. Often, although not always, the abbreviation for these is the first letter of the word. Each volume of *Shepard's* contains tables of abbreviations for cited cases, citing cases, history of the case, and treatment of the case. See Figure 10-4.

TREATMENT OF CASES

c	(criticized)	The citing opinion disagrees with the reasoning/result of the case you are *Shepardizing*, although the citing court may not have the authority to materially affect its precedential value.
ca	(conflicting authorities)	Among conflicting authorities as noted in cited case.
d	(distinguished)	The citing case differs from the case you are *Shepardizing*, either involving dissimilar facts or requiring a different application of the law.
e	(explained)	The citing opinion interprets or clarifies the case you are *Shepardizing* in a significant way.
f	(followed)	The citing opinion relies on the case you are *Shepardizing* as controlling or persuasive authority.
h	(harmonized)	The citing case differs from the case you are *Shepardizing*, but the citing court reconciles the difference or inconsistency in reaching its decision.
j	(dissenting opinion)	A dissenting opinion cites the case you are *Shepardizing*.
~	(concurring opinion)	A concurring opinion cites the case you are *Shepardizing*.
L	(limited)	The citing opinion restricts the application of the case you are *Shepardizing*, finding its reasoning applies only in specific limited circumstances.
o	(overruled)	The citing case expressly overrules or disapproves the case you are *Shepardizing*.
op	(overruled in part)	Ruling in the cited case overruled partially or on other grounds or with other qualifications.
q	(questioned)	The citing opinion questions the continuing validity or precedential value of the case you are *Shepardizing* because of intervening circumstances, including judicial or legislative overruling.
su	(superseded)	Superseded by statute as stated in cited case.

OTHER

#	The citing case is of questionable precedential value because review or rehearing has been granted by the California Supreme Court and/or the citing case has been ordered depublished pursuant to Rule 976 of the California Rules of Court. (Publication status should be verified before use of the citing case in California.)

FIGURE 10-4
(continued)

Reprinted with the permission of LexisNexis

Shepard's uses an unusual method of abbreviating the different series of case reporters. The series number is superimposed on the abbreviation for the case reporter. See Figure 10-2 and find the citing authority 1 L.Ed.2d 1197. (Look in the second and third columns.)

Headnotes   When an opinion in any case is written, the court often discusses different points of law within the opinion. For example, a court might discuss issues relating to the hearsay rule of evidence and the tort of strict liability in the same case. Cases that later cite to this case might be citing it because of what the court said about the hearsay rule or because of what it said about strict liability. When Shepardizing, your only concern might be to verify that what the court said about strict liability is still good law. How other courts have viewed this court's interpretation of

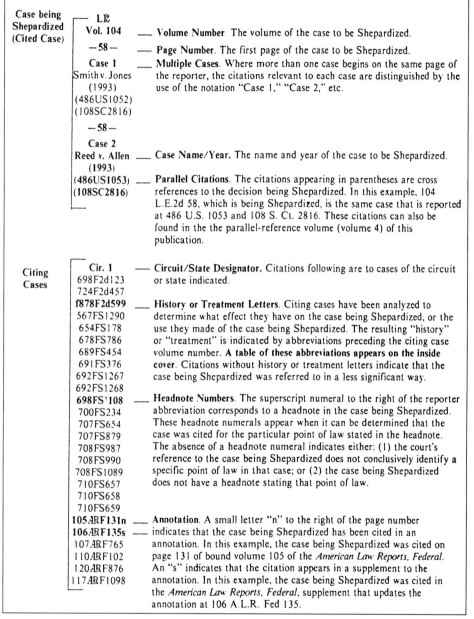

ILLUSTRATIVE CITATIONS

Various symbols and notations have been used to reflect Shepard's analysis of the cited authorities shown in *Shepard's United States Citations, Case Edition.* These symbols/notations are illustrated in the following diagram. The data contained in this diagram is provided solely for illustrative purposes, and should not be relied upon.

Case being Sheparized (Cited Case)

L.E.
Vol. 104 ___ **Volume Number.** The volume of the case to be Shepardized.

—58— ___ **Page Number.** The first page of the case to be Shepardized.

Case 1 ___ **Multiple Cases.** Where more than one case begins on the same page of
Smith v. Jones   the reporter, the citations relevant to each case are distinguished by the
(1993)   use of the notation "Case 1," "Case 2," etc.
(486US1052)
(108SC2816)

—58—
Case 2
Reed v. Allen ___ **Case Name/Year.** The name and year of the case to be Shepardized.
(1993)
(486US1053) ___ **Parallel Citations.** The citations appearing in parentheses are cross
(108SC2816)   references to the decision being Shepardized. In this example, 104
                        L.E.2d 58, which is being Shepardized, is the same case that is reported
                        at 486 U.S. 1053 and 108 S. Ct. 2816. These citations can also be
                        found in the the parallel-reference volume (volume 4) of this
                        publication.

Citing Cases

Cir. 1 ___ **Circuit/State Designator.** Citations following are to cases of the circuit
698F2d123   or state indicated.
724F2d457
f878F2d599 ___ **History or Treatment Letters.** Citing cases have been analyzed to
567FS1290   determine what effect they have on the case being Shepardized, or the
654FS178   use they made of the case being Shepardized. The resulting "history"
678FS786   or "treatment" is indicated by abbreviations preceding the citing case
689FS454   volume number. **A table of these abbreviations appears on the inside**
691FS376   **cover.** Citations without history or treatment letters indicate that the
692FS1267   case being Shepardized was referred to in a less significant way.
692FS1268
698FS'108 ___ **Headnote Numbers.** The superscript numeral to the right of the reporter
700FS234   abbreviation corresponds to a headnote in the case being Shepardized.
707FS654   These headnote numerals appear when it can be determined that the
707FS879   case was cited for the particular point of law stated in the headnote.
708FS987   The absence of a headnote numeral indicates either: (1) the court's
708FS990   reference to the case being Shepardized does not conclusively identify a
708FS1089   specific point of law in that case; or (2) the case being Shepardized
710FS657   does not have a headnote stating that point of law.
710FS658
710FS659
105ARF131n ___ **Annotation.** A small letter "n" to the right of the page number
106ARF135s ___ indicates that the case being Shepardized has been cited in an
107ARF765   annotation. In this example, the case being Shepardized was cited on
110ARF102   page 131 of bound volume 105 of the *American Law Reports, Federal.*
120ARF876   An "s" indicates that the citation appears in a supplement to the
117ARF1098   annotation. In this example, the case being Shepardized was cited in
                        the *American Law Reports, Federal,* supplement that updates the
                        annotation at 106 A.L.R. Fed 135.

FIGURE 10-5
Shepard's Illustrative
Citations

Reprinted with the permission of LexisNexis

hearsay might be irrelevant to you. *Shepard's* helps you to make this type of distinction by using the headnote numbers from your cited authority (the case you are Shepardizing). Review Figure 10-5 to see how this is done.

➪ **A Point to Remember** Each publisher of case reporters uses different headnotes and headnote numbers. The headnotes referred to when you Shepardize a *Lawyers'*

Edition cite relate only to those headnotes found in the *Lawyers' Edition* publication of the case. When you Shepardize parallel cites, be sure not to confuse headnote numbers.

Shepard's *Case Name Citators*   Using the case editions of *Shepard's* requires that you know at least one of the citations for your case. *Shepard's* publishes case name citators that are used to find a citation, if you know the name of one of the parties and you know the jurisdiction of the case. The case name citators give only the citation. You must then proceed to Shepardize the case in the appropriate *Shepard's* case edition. See Figure 10-6 for an example of pages from a case name citator.

Updating **Shepard's**   Legal researchers expect *Shepard's* to be as current as possible. In order to assure that this happens, *Shepard's* in print is continually supplemented. When you Shepardize, you must check all books containing references to your cited authority. Normally this includes the following:

1. The main citator. This volume indicates on the spine what years it covers. Sometimes there is more than one volume.
2. A cumulative supplement (a red-covered paperback).
3. An annual or semi-annual supplement (a gold-covered paperback).
4. White pamphlet-type supplements called Advance Sheets. (These are usually a few weeks old before they reach a library shelf.)

Shepard's helps you recognize what books and supplements you need to check, by printing on the cover "What your library should contain. . . ." Before you Shepardize any authority you must be sure that you have all the relevant books and supplements. (Most often the problem you will encounter in a library is that the librarians failed to remove a supplement that was replaced. This will not cause any serious research problems for you, although it might lead you to check more books than necessary.)

⇨ **A Point to Remember** If you are Shepardizing a relatively new case, it might not appear in the main citator. Always pay attention to the date of any case being Shepardized and start the Shepardizing process with the volume that first covers that time period. You can tell if you are in the right book if you see the case name and parallel cites for the case, as these only appear the first time the cite is mentioned.

If you use all of the *Shepard's* supplements that are in print, you are still missing recent case decisions. *Shepard's* therefore has a "Daily Update" service that provides you with information that is no more than 24 to 48 hours old. This service is accessed through the Internet, by fax, or by telephone.

Shepard's Case Citations Online

Shepard's is available through the online service LEXIS. *Shepard's* online is much easier to use than *Shepard's* in print and offers many advantages. Some of these advantages include the following:

*   Information is current so there is no need to check supplements or updates.
*   Information provided under all parallel citations is the same so a case must be checked only once.
*   Negative information, such as overruling, is highlighted at the beginning.
*   Citing information can be displayed selectively (i.e., only negative treatment).
*   Treatment of the case is explained in normal terminology rather than abbreviations.
*   Hyperlinks to citing authorities are provided.

UNITED STATES SUPREME COURT
CASE NAMES CITATOR   **Bet-Bil**

Beth Israel Hospital v National Labor Relations Board 437 US 483, 57 LE2d 370, 98 S Ct 2463 (1978)

Bethlehem Motors Corp. v Flynt 256 US 421, 65 LE 1029, 41 S Ct 571 (1921)

Bethlehem National Bank of Bethlehem, Pennsylvania, American Surety Co. of New York v 314 US 314, 86 LE 241, 62 S Ct 226 (1941)

Bethlehem Shipbuilding Corporation Ltd., Myers v 303 US 41, 82 LE 638, 58 S Ct 459 (1938)

Bethlehem Shipbuilding Corporation Ltd., Neirbo Co. v 308 US 165, 84 LE 167, 60 S Ct 153 (1939)

Bethlehem Shipbuilding Corporation Ltd., United States Shipping Board Merchant Fleet Corp. v 315 US 289, 86 LE 855, 62 S Ct 581 (1942)

Bethlehem Steel Co. v Anglo-Continentale Treuhand A. G. 307 US 265, 83 LE 1280, 59 S Ct 856 (1939)

Bethlehem Steel Co. v New York State Labor Relations Board 330 US 767, 91 LE 1234, 67 S Ct 1026 (1947)

Bethlehem Steel Co., Pocahontas Operators' Assoc. v 274 US 564, 71 LE 1204, 47 S Ct 727 (1927)

Bethlehem Steel Co., United States v 205 US 105, 51 LE 731, 27 S Ct 450 (1907)

Bethlehem Steel Co. v United States 246 US 523, 62 LE 866, 38 S Ct 347 (1918)

Bethlehem Steel Co., United States v 258 US 321, 66 LE 639, 42 S Ct 334 (1922)

Bethlehem Steel Co., United States v 274 US 564, 71 LE 1204, 47 S Ct 727 (1927)

Bethlehem Steel Co. v Zurich General Accident & Liability Insurance Co. Ltd. 307 US 265, 83 LE 1280, 59 S Ct 856 (1939)

Bethlehem Steel Corp., United States v 315 US 289, 86 LE 855, 62 S Ct 581 (1942)

Beto, Cruz v 405 US 319, 31 LE2d 263, 92 S Ct 1079 (1972)

Beto, Loper v 405 US 473, 31 LE2d 374, 92 S Ct 1014 (1972)

Beto, Reed v 385 US 554, 17 LE2d 606, 87 S Ct 648 (1967)

Better Business Bureau of Washington, D.C. Inc. v United States 326 US 279, 90 LE 67, 66 S Ct 112 (1945)

Bettman, Snyder v 190 US 249, 47 LE 1035, 23 S Ct 803 (1903)

Bettman, Unity Banking & Saving Co. v 217 US 127, 54 LE 695, 30 S Ct 488 (1910)

Betts v Brady 316 US 455, 86 LE 1595, 62 S Ct 1252 (1942)

Beutler v Grand Trunk Junction Railway Co. 224 US 85, 56 LE 679, 32 S Ct 402 (1912)

Beuttas, United States v 324 US 768, 89 LE 1354, 65 S Ct 1000 (1945)

Bevan v Krieger 289 US 459, 77 LE 1316, 53 S Ct 661 (1933)

Beyer v Le Fevre 186 US 114, 46 LE 1080, 22 S Ct 765 (1902)

Bezue, New York, New Haven & Hartford Railroad Co. v 284 US 415, 76 LE 370, 52 S Ct 205 (1932)

B. Fernandez & Bros. v Ayllon 266 US 144, 69 LE 209, 45 S Ct 52 (1924)

B. F. Goodrich Co. v United States 321 US 126, 88 LE 602, 64 S Ct 471 (1944)

B. F. Keith Vaudeville Exchange, Hart v 262 US 271, 67 LE 977, 43 S Ct 540 (1923)

Bhagat Singh Thind, United States v 261 US 204, 67 LE 616, 43 S Ct 338 (1923)

Bianc, New York Central Railroad Co. v 250 US 596, 63 LE 1161, 40 S Ct 44 (1919)

Bianchi v Morales 262 US 170, 62 LE 928, 43 S Ct 526 (1923)

Bibb v Navajo Freight Lines Inc. 359 US 520, 3 LE2d 1003, 79 S Ct 962 (1959)

Bica, De Canas v 424 US 351, 47 LE2d 43, 96 S Ct 933 (1976)

Bickell, Lee v 292 US 415, 78 LE 1337, 54 S Ct 727 (1934)

Bicknell, Herbert v 233 US 70, 58 LE 854, 34 S Ct 562 (1914)

Bicks, Idlewild Bon Voyage Liquor Corp. v 370 US 713, 8 LE2d 794, 82 S Ct 1294 (1962)

Bicron Corp., Kewanee Oil Co. v 416 US 470, 40 LE2d 315, 94 S Ct 1879 (1974)

Biddinger v Police of New York 245 US 128, 38 S Ct 41 (1917)

Biddle v Internal Revenue Commissioners 302 US 573, 82 LE 431, 58 S Ct 379 (1938)

Biddle v Luvisch 266 US 182, 69 LE 234, 45 S Ct 88 (1924)

Biddle v Perovich 274 US 480, 71 LE 1161, 47 S Ct 664 (1927)

Bidwell, Buttfield v 192 US 498, 48 LE 536, 24 S Ct 356 (1904)

Bidwell, Cruickshank v 176 US 73, 44 LE 377, 20 S Ct 280 (1900)

Bidwell, De Lima v 182 US 1, 45 LE 1041, 21 S Ct 743 (1901)

Bidwell, Downes v 182 US 244, 45 LE 1088, 21 S Ct 770 (1901)

Bien v Robinson 208 US 423, 52 LE 556, 28 S Ct 379 (1908)

Bienville Water Supply Co. v Mobile 186 US 212, 46 LE 1132, 22 S Ct 820 (1902)

Bifulco v United States 447 US 381, 65 LE2d 205, 100 S Ct 2247 (1980)

Bigby v United States 188 US 400, 47 LE 519, 23 S Ct 468 (1903)

Bigelow, Chapman & Dewey Land Co. v 206 US 41, 51 LE 953, 27 S Ct 679 (1907)

Bigelow v Old Dominion Copper Mining & Smelting Co. 225 US 111, 56 LE 1009, 32 S Ct 641 (1912)

Bigelow v RKO Radio Pictures Inc. 327 US 251, 90 LE 652, 66 S Ct 574 (1946)

Bigelow v Virginia 421 US 809, 44 LE2d 600, 95 S Ct 2222 (1975)

Bigger, Texas & Pacific Railway Co. v 239 US 330, 60 LE 310, 36 S Ct 127 (1915)

Biggers, Neil v 409 US 188, 34 LE2d 401, 93 S Ct 375 (1972)

Biggers v Tennessee 390 US 404, 19 LE2d 1267, 88 S Ct 979 (1968)

Biggs, United States v 211 US 507, 53 LE 305, 29 S Ct 181 (1909)

Big Vein Coal Company of West Virginia v Read 229 US 31, 57 LE 1053, 33 S Ct 694 (1913)

Bihn v United States 328 US 633, 90 LE 1484, 66 S Ct 1172 (1946)

Bilby v Stewart 245 US 255, 38 S Ct 264 (1918)

Bilder, Internal Revenue v 369 US 499, 8 LE2d 65, 82 S Ct 881 (1962)

Bildisco and Bildisco, National Labor Relations Board v 465 US 513, 79 LE2d 482, 104 S Ct 1188 (1984)

Billings v Illinois 188 US 97, 47 LE 400, 23 S Ct 272 (1903)

Reprinted with the permission of LexisNexis

If you know the name of a U.S. Supreme Court case, you can find the citation in this index.

FIGURE 10-6
Shepard's United States Supreme Court Case Names Citator

Because of the numerous advantages and greater reliability of information, *Shepard's* online is by far the preferred method of Shepardizing a case or other authority. See Figures 10-7 and 10-8 for examples of *Shepard's* Online.

Shepard's Statutory Citators

In addition to its case citators, *Shepard's* publishes citators that allow you to Shepardize constitutions, statutes or codes, and administrative rules or regulations, including the Code of Federal Regulations. These citators are similar to case citators in many respects. When you Shepardize this type of material, you find information about the history of the law, i.e., was it amended or repealed. You also find citations to cases that discuss the law. Again, in print *Shepard's* uses abbreviations and special terms to describe how cases have interpreted the written law. The terms and abbreviations *Shepard's* uses to describe the treatment of statutory law differ from the terms *Shepard's* uses to describe the treatment of cases. See Figure 10-9 for a list of these abbreviations and Figure 10-10 for an example of a page from a statutory citator. Like *Shepard's* case citators, statutory citators are available in print and online.

⇨ **A Point to Remember** *Shepard's* provides excellent explanations of how to use its resources along with complete tables of abbreviations. This is found in the preface if you are using *Shepard's* in print. This information is found in the "Help" menu on the online ser-vice. You can also find out more about *Shepard's* by visiting its Web site at www.shepards.com. This cite contains a good online tutorial.

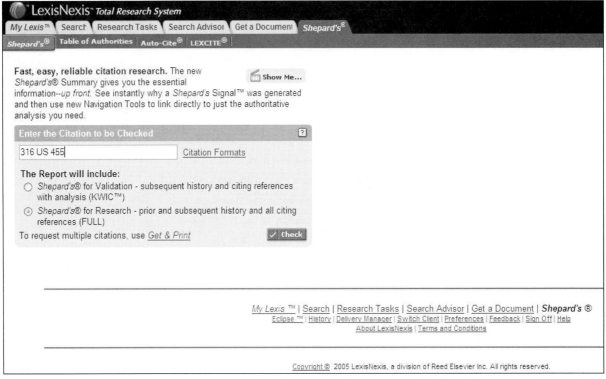

Reprinted with the permission of LexisNexis. LexisNexis and *Shepard's* are registered trademarks of Reed Elsevier Properties Inc. Used with the permission of LexisNexis.

FIGURE 10-7 *Shepard's* Online (LEXIS): Retrieving a Case

Signal: ● Warning: Negative treatment is indicated
Trail: **Unrestricted**

Betts v. Brady, 316 U.S. 455, 86 L. Ed. 1595, 62 S. Ct. 1252, 1942 U.S. LEXIS 489 (1942)

SHEPARD'S SUMMARY ◆ **Hide Summary**

Shepard's **FULL Summary:** ● **Warning** - Negative treatment is indicated

No negative case history.

Citing References:

Warning Analyses:	**Overruled (3)**
Questioned Analyses:	Questioned (55)
Cautionary Analyses:	Criticized (7), Distinguished (6)
Positive Analyses:	Followed (6)
Neutral Analyses:	Concurring Opinion (3), Dissenting Op. (61), Explained (10), Harmonized (1), Quest. Precedent (1)
Other Sources:	Law Reviews (442), Secondary Sources (15), Statutes (8), Treatises (16), American Law Rpts/Lawyers' Edition Annos (12)

CASE HISTORY (2 citing references) ◆ **Hide Case History**

↰ Select for Delivery

☐ 1. **Same case at:**
   Betts v. Brady, 315 U.S. 791, 86 L. Ed. 1194, 62 S. Ct. 639, 1942 U.S. LEXIS 919 (1942)

☐ 2. **Same case at:**
   Betts v. Brady, 316 U.S. 455, 86 L. Ed. 1595, 62 S. Ct. 1252, 1942 U.S. LEXIS 489 (1942)

CITING DECISIONS (777 citing decisions)

U.S. SUPREME COURT

☐ 3. **Questioned by:**
   Beard v. Banks, 159 L. Ed. 2d 494, 124 S. Ct. 2504, 2004 U.S. LEXIS 4572, 72 U.S.L.W. 4578, 17 Fla. L. Weekly Fed. S 442 (U.S. 2004)

   159 L. Ed. 2d 494 p.507
   124 S. Ct. 2504 p.2514

☐ 4. **Cited by:**
   County of Sacramento v. Lewis, 523 U.S. 833, 140 L. Ed. 2d 1043, 118 S. Ct. 1708, 1998 U.S. LEXIS 3404, 66 U.S.L.W. 4407, 11 Fla. L. Weekly Fed. S 555, 98 Cal. Daily Op. Service 3918, 1998 Colo. J. C.A.R. 2577, 98 D.A.R. 5389 (1998)

   140 L. Ed. 2d 1043 p.1060
   118 S. Ct. 1708 p.1719
   523 U.S. 833 p.850

☐ 5. **Cited in Dissenting Opinion at:**
   Nichols v. United States, 511 U.S. 738, 128 L. Ed. 2d 745, 114 S. Ct. 1921, 1994 U.S. LEXIS 4277, 62 U.S.L.W. 4421, 8 Fla. L. Weekly Fed. S 186, 94 Cal. Daily Op. Service 4114, 94 D.A.R. 7659 (1994)

   128 L. Ed. 2d 745 p.762
   114 S. Ct. 1921 p.1934
   511 U.S. 738 p.738

Reprinted with the permission of LexisNexis. LexisNexis and *Shepard's* are registered trademarks of Reed Elsevier Properties Inc. Used with the permission of LexisNexis.

FIGURE 10-8   *Shepard's* Online (LEXIS): History and Treatment

---

BOX 10-2

SHEPARDIZING IN PRINT

√ Note citation to be Shepardized.

√ Locate all relevant *Shepard's* volumes, including supplements and advance sheets.

√ Check "What your library should contain . . ." on cover of supplements.

√ Locate first appearance of your authority in *Shepard's*.

√ Check your citation in all supplements and advance sheets.

√ Interpret or analyze your findings.

√ Review tables of abbreviations in front of books, if necessary.

√ If Shepardizing case law, repeat process with all parallel cites.

√ Use Daily Update Service.

TABLES OF ABBREVIATIONS

A5—American Law Reports Fifth Series

ARF—American Law Reports Federal

BRW—Bankruptcy Reporter

F2d—Federal Reporter, Second Series

F3d—Federal Reporter, Third Series

FedCl—Federal Claims Reporter

FRD—Federal Rules Decisions

FS—Federal Supplement

FS2d—Federal Supplement, Second Series

LE— United States Supreme Court Reports, Lawyer's Edition, Second Series

MJ—Military Justice Reporter

SC—Supreme Court Reporter

TCt—Tax Court of the United States Reports; United States Tax Court Reports

US—United States Reports

COURT ABBREVIATIONS

Cir. (number)—United States Court of Appeals, United States District Court, Circuit

Cir. DC—United States Court of Appeals, United States District Court, DC Circuit

Cir. Fed.—United States Court of Appeals, Federal Circuit

ClCt—United States Claims Court and United States Court of Federal Claims

Cu Ct—United States Customs Court

CIT—United States Court of International Trade

CCPA—Court of Customs and Patent Appeals

ECA—Temporary Emergency Court of Appeals

ML—Judicial Panel on Multidistrict Litigation

RRR—Special Court Regional Rail Reorganization Act of 1973

STATUTE ABBREVIATIONS

Adj.—Adjourned Session

Amend.—Amendment

Appx.—Appendix

Art.—Article

Ch.—Chapter

Cl.—Clause

Div.—Division

Ex. Ord—Executive Order

Ex.—Extra Session

H.B.—House Bill

H.J.R.—House Joint Resolution

H.R.—House Resolution

J.R.—Joint Resolution

No.—Number

p—Page

¶—Paragraph

Pt—Part

P.A.—Public Act

P.L.—Public Law (United States)

Res.—Resolution

§—Section

S.B.—Senate Bill

S.J.R.—Senate Joint Resolution

Sp—Special Session

S.R.—Senate Resolution

St—Statutes at Large

Subch.—Subchapter

Subcl.—Subclause

Subd.—Subdivision

Sub.¶—Subparagraph

Subsec.—Subsection

T.—Title

FIGURE 10-9

Shepard's Tables of Abbreviations (Statutes)

Reprinted with the permission of LexisNexis

UNITED STATES CODE 1988 and 1994 Eds. **TITLE 18 § 700**

857F2d523
937F2d461
945F2d1075
969F2d775
9F3d68
11F3d120
22F3d942
C 40F3d1000
59F3d940
661FS723
789FS346
918FS1383

Cir. 10
799F2d619
53F3d1108
64F3d1515
79F3d994
814FS1528
149FRD647

Cir. 11
905F2d352
907FS402

§ 666 (a)

Cir. 2
4F3d108

Cir. 4
874F2d217

Cir. 5
841F2d575
930F2d1091
987F2d1136
659FS834
687FS1049
727FS1069
C 816FS1136

Cir. 6
63F3d463

Cir. 7
957F2d1393
982F2d1105

Cir. 10
53F3d1110

§ 666 (a) (1)

Cir. 6
63F3d462
66F3d129

§ 666 (a) (1) (A)

Cir. 2
979F2d936
55F3d723
784FS63

Cir. 5
987F2d1137
80F3d1055
C 816FS1134

Cir. 6
966F2d186

Cir. 9
11F3d121
40F3d1001

§ 666 (a) (1) (A) (1)

Cir. 3
990F2d101

Cir. 5
727FS1070

Cir. 6
63F3d462
66F3d127

§ 666 (a) (1) (A) (2)

Cir. 5
727FS1070

Cir. 6
63F3d462

Cir. 9
40F3d1001

§ 666 (a) (1) (B)

Cir. 2
996F2d18
4F3d104
37F3d849
57F3d172
73F3d485
795FS1268
809FS1002
809FS1010
833FS204

Cir. 3
938F2d443
10F3d981

Cir. 5
841F2d577
987F2d1137
80F3d1055

Cir. 6
966F2d188

Cir. 7
913F2d1259
46F3d27

Cir. 9
937F2d463

§ 666 (a) (2)

Cir. 1
983F2d1153

Cir. 2
909F2d63
996F2d19
4F3d104
42F3d99
57F3d169
57F3d172
784FS63

794FS530
842FS1535
913FS704

Cir. 4
11F3d430

Cir. 5
889F2d1369
687FS1048
781FS1183
C 816FS1134

Cir. 7
777FS1397

Cir. 10
36F3d946

Cir. 11
C 907FS402

§ 666 (b)

Cir. 2
986F2d33
4F3d104
55F3d729
784FS63
794FS530
913FS705

Cir. 3
874F2d180
938F2d443

Cir. 4
11F3d434

Cir. 5
841F2d574
846F2d968
889F2d1369
930F2d1091
987F2d1136
659FS834
687FS1048
727FS1070
C 816FS1137

Cir. 6
63F3d462

Cir. 8
977F2d1232

Cir. 9
857F2d521
937F2d463
11F3d121
40F3d1000

§ 666 (c)

Cir. 2
979F2d936
C 987F2d896
996F2d21
4F3d104
651FS1035
815FS619
913FS711

Cir. 5
987F2d1137

727FS1072
C 816FS1137

Cir. 6
63F3d465

Cir. 7
868F2d936

Cir. 8
915FS1477

Cir. 9
11F3d121
40F3d1000

Cir. 10
799F2d619

§ 666 (d)

Cir. 2
4F3d109

Cir. 9
857F2d523

Cir. 10
799F2d620

§ 666 (d) (1)

Cir. 2
851FS508

Cir. 3
990F2d101

Cir. 9
40F3d1001

§ 666 (d) (2)

Cir. 2
913FS707

Cir. 5
987F2d1137
727FS1070

Cir. 9
857F2d523

Cir. 10
799F2d620

§ 666 (d) (3)

Cir. 10
799F2d620

§ 666 (d) (4)

Cir. 2
851FS508

Cir. 4
11F3d434

Cir. 9
857F2d523
969F2d775

Cir. 10
799F2d620

§ 666 (d) (5)

Cir. 2
897FS113

Cir. 6
63F3d463

§ 667
Ad 98St2149

§ 687
487US255
101LE237
108SC2373

§ 688
122LE222
113SC865

§ 700 et seq.

Cir. 1
531F2d1087

§ 700
Ad 82St291
394US604
459US949
Up 496US312
22LE592
74LE207
U 110LE292
129LE520
89SC1372
103SC267
U 110SC2406
114SC2461
128FRD300
136FRD238

Cir. DC
445F2d226
511F2d1312
U 731FS1125

Cir. 1
343FS165
397FS263

Cir. 2
324FS1278

Cir. 3
765FS188

Cir. 4
313FS49
317FS138
322FS593

Cir. 5
479F2d1177

Cir. 8
C 897F2d918

Cir. 9
462F2d96
C 302FS1112
U 731FS416
790FS221

Cir. 11
758F2d1481
560FS546
105LE812n
105LE816n

41A3504n

§ 700 (a)
415US582
491US427
496US314
39LE617
105LE369
U 110LE293
94SC1251
109SC2551
U 110SC2407

Cir. DC
445F2d226
C 454F2d972

Cir. 2
324FS1278
385FS167

Cir. 5
479F2d1179
407FS497

Cir. 9
C 462F2d96

Cir. 11
739F2d571
571FS1025

§ 700 (a) (1)
496US317
U 110LE295
U 110SC2409

Cir. DC
U 731FS1125

Cir. 9
U 731FS417

§ 700 (a) (2)
496US317
U 110LE295
U 110SC2409

Cir. DC
U 731FS1125

Cir. 9
U 731FS417

§ 700 (b)
496US314
U 110LE294
U 110SC2407

Cir. DC
445F2d226
U 731FS1125

Cir. 9
C 462F2d96
U 731FS417

§ 700 (c)
394US598
22LE588
89SC1369

Cir. 4
322FS585

521

18 U.S.C. § 666(a) through 18 U.S.C. § 700 are Shepardized on this page. Cases citing these code sections are listed.

FIGURE 10-10
Shepard's United States Code 1988 and 1994 Eds.

Reprinted with the permission of LexisNexis

```
┌─────────────────────────────────────────────────────────────────┐
│ ┌───────────────────────────────────────────────────────────────┐ │
│ │                                                                 │ │
│ │   BOX 10-3                                                      │ │
│ │                                                                 │ │
│ │                     SHEPARDIZING ONLINE                         │ │
│ │                                                                 │ │
│ │   √ Note citation to be Shepardized.                           │ │
│ │   √ Access online service.                                     │ │
│ │   √ Access Shepard's online.                                   │ │
│ │   √ Enter citation.                                            │ │
│ │   √ Use "Help" feature, if necessary.                          │ │
│ │   √ Analyze or interpret results.                              │ │
│ │   √ Repeat process with parallel citations.                    │ │
│ │                                                                 │ │
│ └───────────────────────────────────────────────────────────────┘ │
└─────────────────────────────────────────────────────────────────┘
```

10-3 KEYCITE

KeyCite is an online citator available through Westlaw. Using KeyCite, a researcher can check a case, statute, administrative decision, or regulation to determine if it is still good law. As with *Shepard's,* the researcher also finds citing references to other authorities and again, as with *Shepard's,* using KeyCite with case law the researcher sees how the case was treated in subsequent cases. KeyCite also evaluates the importance of citing cases. This is reflected in the number of "depth of treatment stars" assigned to each of the citing cases. In this way, a researcher can tell if the cited case was merely mentioned in the citing authority or whether it was discussed and analyzed in great detail. Because KeyCite is part of the Westlaw database, the researcher can hyperlink to cited authorities through Westlaw. See Figures 10-11 and 10-12.

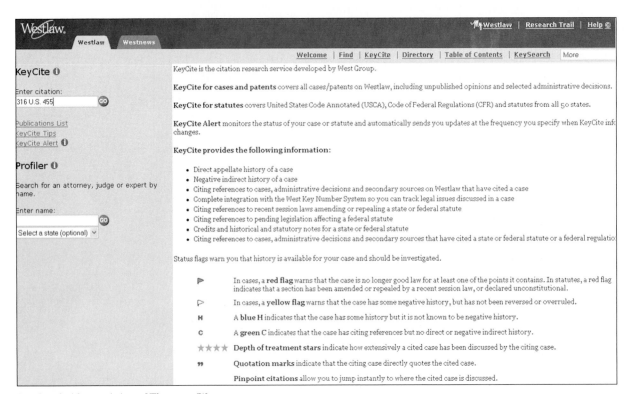

Reprinted with permission of Thomson/West

FIGURE 10-11   KeyCite

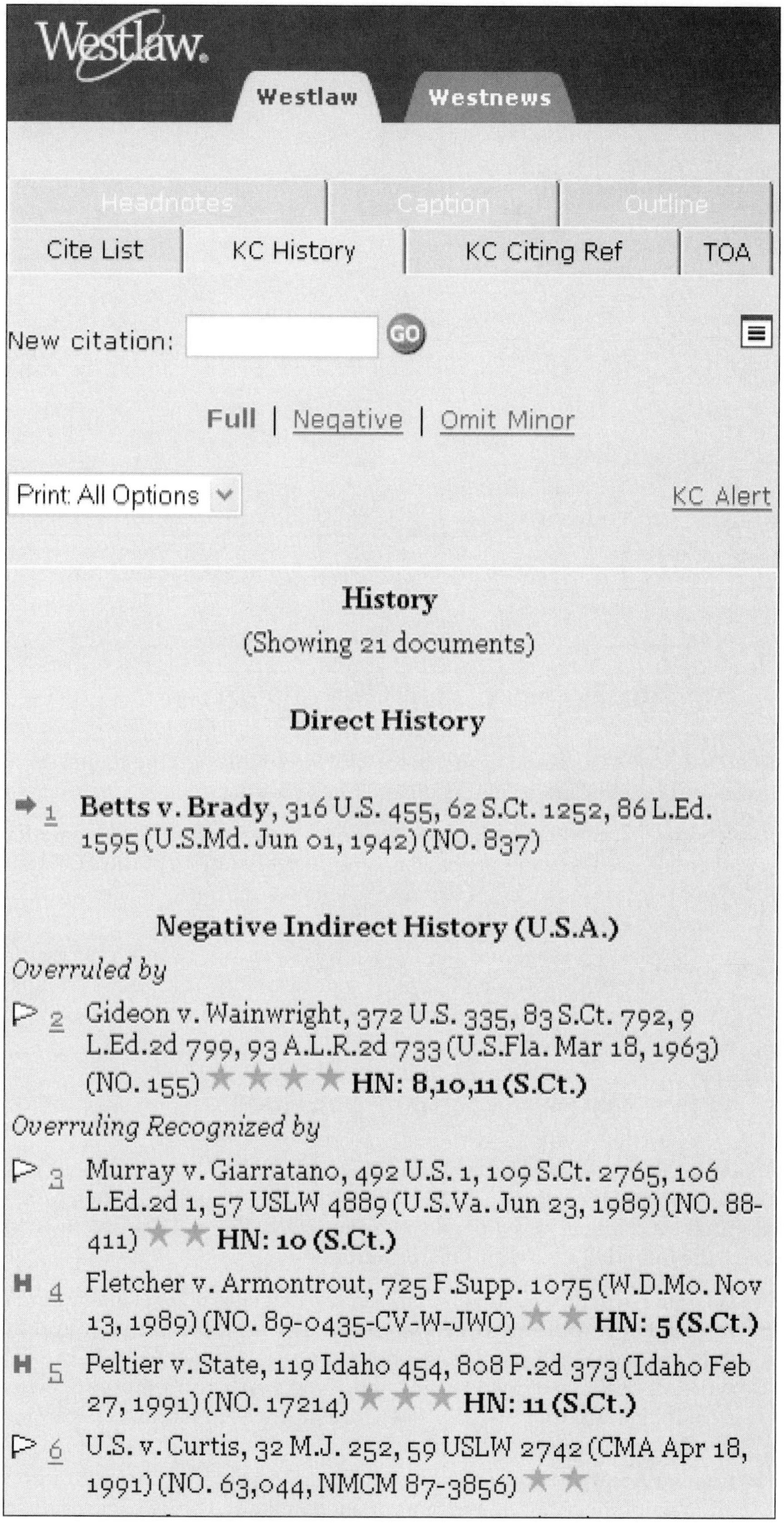

Westlaw.

Westlaw   Westnews

Headnotes   Caption   Outline

Cite List | KC History | KC Citing Ref | TOA

New citation: [_____] GO   [☰]

Full | Negative | Omit Minor

Print: All Options ⌄   KC Alert

History

(Showing 21 documents)

Direct History

➡ 1 **Betts v. Brady**, 316 U.S. 455, 62 S.Ct. 1252, 86 L.Ed.
1595 (U.S.Md. Jun 01, 1942) (NO. 837)

Negative Indirect History (U.S.A.)

Overruled by

▷ 2 Gideon v. Wainwright, 372 U.S. 335, 83 S.Ct. 792, 9
L.Ed.2d 799, 93 A.L.R.2d 733 (U.S.Fla. Mar 18, 1963)
(NO. 155) ★ ★ ★ ★ **HN: 8,10,11 (S.Ct.)**

Overruling Recognized by

▷ 3 Murray v. Giarratano, 492 U.S. 1, 109 S.Ct. 2765, 106
L.Ed.2d 1, 57 USLW 4889 (U.S.Va. Jun 23, 1989) (NO. 88-
411) ★ ★ **HN: 10 (S.Ct.)**

H 4 Fletcher v. Armontrout, 725 F.Supp. 1075 (W.D.Mo. Nov
13, 1989) (NO. 89-0435-CV-W-JWO) ★ ★ **HN: 5 (S.Ct.)**

H 5 Peltier v. State, 119 Idaho 454, 808 P.2d 373 (Idaho Feb
27, 1991) (NO. 17214) ★ ★ ★ **HN: 11 (S.Ct.)**

▷ 6 U.S. v. Curtis, 32 M.J. 252, 59 USLW 2742 (CMA Apr 18,
1991) (NO. 63,044, NMCM 87-3856) ★ ★

FIGURE 10-12
KeyCite (West)

Reprinted with permission of Thomson/West

Reprinted with the permission of LexisNexis

FIGURE 10-13 Auto-Cite Screen

10-4 OTHER ELECTRONIC CITATORS

In addition to *Shepard's,* several other citators are found through the online services of Westlaw and LEXIS. These citators include the following.

Auto-Cite: A case citator found on the LEXIS service; this citator provides parallel citations, the history of the case, and negative treatment of the case. It does not refer you to all cases that have cited your authority in a positive manner. See Figure 10-13 for an example.

Lexcite: Lexcite is a LEXIS feature that allows you to search the LEXIS case databanks for every case that has cited your authority. Your search results reveal those authorities without any editorial comment or evaluation.

10-5 CITE CHECKING A DOCUMENT

Before any legal memorandum or brief is filed with a court, the document is normally reviewed and all citations are checked. This task is one that is often assigned to a research assistant such as a paralegal or law clerk. When a document is "cite-checked," the following items must be verified.

1. **Citation Format:** Courts generally require that cites in legal memoranda or briefs comply with the format set out in *THE BLUEBOOK* or other approved style manual. Some states have adopted a style manual for use within the state. All citations in a document to be filed with a court must be reviewed to make certain they are in proper format. (See Appendix B for an introduction to the use of *THE BLUEBOOK.*)

2. **Citation Accuracy:** Obviously, attorneys and courts are concerned with the accuracy of the citation. A wrong volume number, a wrong page, or a wrong series in a case cite can make it impossible for a judge or other attorney to

find a case cited in a brief. Checking for citation accuracy requires that you physically check the primary source, either in print or online, to make sure that the cite is correct in all aspects.

3. **Validity of Authorities:** This involves Shepardizing or otherwise verifying the cited authority is still good law.

4. **Accuracy of Authority:** In addition to checking for the accuracy of the citation, cite checking sometimes requires that you check the accuracy of the authority itself. Does a case or code section really support the statements of law made in the brief? This requires that the person doing the cite checking actually read and analyze the law.

5. **Citation of Quotation:** Pages where quotations appear must be verified. If parallel citations are used, page numbers must be verified in those citations.

6. **Accuracy of Quotations:** Quotations must also be checked for accuracy. Any language quoted in a brief must match exactly the language found in a quoted case or statute.

It is a long and tedious job to cite check a memorandum or brief by referring to original sources entirely in print. The online services of Westlaw and LEXIS can make this a much easier and quicker task. In addition to Westlaw and LEXIS, there are some software packages that expedite the process. West produces software that will read all of the citations in your document. It will then verify the citations by using its citator (KeyCite). It will also verify the page and accuracy of any quotations. LEXIS provides access to similar software.

T ECHNOLOGY CORNER

Extensive information about *Shepard's* can be found at:

http://www.lexisnexis.com/shepards/

Information about KeyCite can be found at:

http://west.thomson.com/store/

On both sites look for user guides. Several are available for downloading without cost.

Both LEXIS and Westlaw have developed software to be used with their products, *Shepard's* and KeyCite, to automate the cite-checking process.

CHAPTER SUMMARY

Citators are a type of legal research material that allows the researcher to determine if certain legal authorities are still good law. Citators lead the researcher to additional authorities dealing with the same legal issues. The most well-known citators are published by *Shepard's*. *Shepard's* publishes citators for all jurisdictions and for many different types of legal authorities including cases, constitutions, statutes, and selected secondary sources. *Shepard's* is available in print and online. An alternative citator, KeyCite, is available online through Westlaw. KeyCite has many of the same features as *Shepard's*. Auto-Cite and Lexcite, features found on LEXIS, are sometimes used to determine if a case is still good law. Researchers often use citators to help cite check a memorandum or brief that is to be filed with the court. In addition to checking whether an authority is still good law, cite checking requires that one check citation format, citation accuracy, accuracy of the authority, and accuracy of quotations.

TERMS TO REMEMBER

good law	Shepardize
validate	cited authority
citator	citing authority

QUESTIONS FOR REVIEW

1. What is a citator?
2. What types of authorities can be Shepardized?
3. What information is found in *Shepard's* case citators?
4. What is the difference between cited authority and citing authority?
5. If a case has parallel cites, is it necessary to Shepardize all cites? Explain.
6. What is the difference between the history of the case and the treatment of the case?
7. How does *Shepard's* use headnote numbers in its case citators?
8. What is KeyCite?
9. What must a person do to cite check a document?
10. Explain how software can help cite check a document.

CAN YOU FIGURE IT OUT?

1. Refer to Figure 10-2.
    A. Find the case of *Betts v. Brady*.
        1. What is the citation for this case?
        2. This same case appears on a different page in the same volume. What is that cite?
        3. What are the parallel cites for the case?
        4. Give the *Lawyers' Edition* cite for the U.S. Supreme Court case that overruled *Betts v. Brady*.
        5. Give cites of all cases in the *Federal Reporter 2d* from the Third Circuit to discuss the issues found in headnote number 4 of *Betts v. Brady* (published in the *Lawyers' Edition*).
2. Refer to Figure 10-1.
    A. Find the case of *Betts v. Brady*.
        1. What is the cite for the U.S. Supreme Court case to overrule *Betts v. Brady*?
        2. Do any cases in the *Federal Reporter 2d* from the Third Circuit discuss headnote number 4?
3. Refer to Figure 10-3.
    A. Find the case of *Betts v. Brady*.
        1. What is the cite for the U.S. Supreme Court case to overrule *Betts v. Brady*?
        2. List the cites of all cases in the *Federal Reporter 2d* from the Third Circuit to discuss headnote number 4. Compare these cites with those found in Figure 10-2.
4. Refer to Figure 10-6.
    A. What is the cite for *Bethlehem Steel Co. v. Anglo-Continentale Treuhand A.G.*?
    B. What is the cite for *Buttfield v. Bidwell*?
    C. What are the cites for *U.S. v. Bethlehem Steel*?

    D. What is the cite for *Bethlehem Steel v. U.S.?*

    E. The citation for the first case in the second column is 250 U.S. 596. What is the name of this case?

5. Refer to Figure 10-10.

    A. Find 18 U.S.C. § 700.

    B. What has the U.S. Supreme Court said about this section?

    C. Give the *Lawyers' Edition* cite for a case to discuss 18 U.S.C. § 700 (c).

RESEARCH ASSIGNMENTS AND ACTIVITIES

1. Shepardize the *Bramblett* case mentioned in the memo at the beginning of the chapter. The cite is 348 U.S. 503. Answer the following questions.

    a. What are the parallel cites?

    b. What are the lower court citations for this case?

    c. Give all parallel cites for the case that overruled *Bramblett.*

    d. What is the full name of the *Bramblett* case?

    e. What is the citation for the case from the 8th Circuit that questioned *Bramblett?*

    f. What is the citation for an *A.L.R.* annotation in which the case is mentioned?

2. Shepardize the case at 279 U.S. 263.

    a. What is the case name?

    b. What are the parallel cites?

    c. Give all the parallel cites for the case that overruled it.

    d. Give the cite of a case from the 9th Circuit that harmonized with the cite.

    e. Give the cite to a *Stanford Law Review* that mentioned the case.

3. Shepardize 18 U.S.C. § 242.

    a. Give the citations for the *Statutes at Large* in which this section was amended.

    b. Give the citation for the U.S. Supreme Court case in volume 515 of the *U.S. Reports* that mentions this section.

    c. Give the cites for California cases that list this section as questionable precedent.

CASE PROJECTS

1. Shepardize any cases and statutes that you found previously. Have any cases been overruled? Make a list of any cases that question or criticize your cases. Read these.

2. Cite check the following Memorandum of Points and Authorities. Check each cite for format and accuracy. Also check each quotation for accuracy. Refer to Appendix B for proper citation format.

ATLAS INSURANCE COMPANY,	)	
A corporation,	)	
Plaintiff,	)	No. 12345
	)	
v.	)	MEMORANDUM OF POINTS &
	)	AUTHORITIES
SAVAGE RIDER, et al.	)	
Defendants	)	

Facts

The defendant was involved in a motor vehicle accident on June 23 of the previous year with an uninsured vehicle. Defendant Rider was operating a motorcycle owned by his roommate Motorcycle Murphy. This vehicle was not covered by insurance either. However, Rider did have a policy of automobile insurance, which policy is the subject of this lawsuit. The insurance policy in question covers Rider while he is operating another vehicle, as long as that vehicle is not owned by a "member of his household."

From the deposition testimony it is clear that Rider and Murphy had a typical roommate relationship. They shared rent on an apartment. However, they each led their own social lives and had their own friends. Murphy in fact had a girlfriend and spent much of his time with her, away from the apartment. Meals were seldom shared by the defendant and his roommate.

Issue

Are roommates, who are unrelated and live separate lives, "members of the same household" under the exclusion provision of an insurance policy?

Argument

1. A "HOUSEHOLD" REQUIRES A FAMILIAL BOND, NOT JUST A JOINT RESIDENCE

In their complaint, plaintiffs state that the basis of the controversy is the fact that Savage Rider was driving a vehicle owned by a member of his household. The courts in various jurisdictions, including California have clearly held that the mere fact that two persons reside under the same roof does not make them members of the same household. Rather a more familial or social bond is required. See *Island v. Fireman's Fund Indemnity Co.,* 30 C.2d 540 at 547-8. As the Supreme Court has stated, "Persons who dwell together as a family constitute a 'household.'" *Arthur v. Morton* 112 U.S. 495, 500.

A case on point with the one here is *Bartholet v. Berkness,* (Minn.) 189 N.W. 2d 410. In this case the court held that two unmarried and unrelated men, dwelling in the same living quarters and sharing expenses but having separate and independent social lives, were not members of the same household. And in a Texas case, the court stated:

> A rather unreasonable and ridiculous result follow from an attempt to ascribe to the term 'household' in the phrase under consideration the meaning of a building or structure, or to ascribe to the term resident a meaning which would embrace any and all persons who sleep within or take meals at such structure. . . .

> This court reached the conclusion that similar use of the term 'household' connoted a 'family' or a group of persons who habitually reside under one roof and form one domestic circle.

State Farm Mutual Automobile Insurance Company v. Walker et al., (1960, Tex. Civ. App.) 334 S.W.2d 458, 463-464. See also *Giakares v. Kincade* (1961. Mo.) 330 S.W.2d 633 wherein a grandmother was held not to be a member of the same household as her grandchildren even though living under the same roof.

2. ANY AMBIGUITY IN THE INSURANCE POLICY MUST BE INTERPRETED AGAINST THE INSURANCE COMPANY AND IN FAVOR OF THE INSURED

Clearly, in the common, ordinary meaning of the words, as well as by judicial interpretation of them, "members or residents of the same household" must have more than a relationship than just "roommates." At most in the case at hand plaintiffs could contend that there is some ambiguity as to the meaning of the words. However, even if that were true plaintiff could not prevail. It is a cardinal rule that where any ambiguity exists in an insurance policy it must be resolved in favor of the policy holder, not the insurance company. *Island v. Fireman's Fund Indemnity Co.,* 184 Pac. 153 at 159. See also *Juzefsky v. Western Cas. & Surety Co.,* 324 Pac. 2d 929.

Conclusion

In conclusion, clearly the purpose of an exclusionary provision in an insurance policy such as the one here is to avoid multiple coverage of several vehicles owned by members of the same family, who, by their close intimacy, might be expected to use each other's vehicles without hindrance and with or without the permission of another, thus increasing the liability of the insurer without benefit or added premium. The facts of this case show that the defendant, Rider, and his roommate, Murphy, led very separate and independent lives. Murphy's vehicle was not made freely available for Rider's use. In fact, Rider had only used it once, the day of the accident. Further, the motorcycle was generally kept at the house of Murphy's parents. In addition, there was no way that Rider could have obtained insurance for the motorcycle, as he had no insurable interest therein. Thus, it is clear that the objectives of the exclusionary provisions would not be properly served by applying the exclusion to the instant case.

COMPUTER ASSISTED LEGAL RESEARCH (CALR)

CHAPTER OUTLINE

CHAPTER OBJECTIVES

When you complete this chapter you should be able to

- List and describe the types of computer assisted legal research.
- Discuss the benefits of full-text searching.
- Explain the differences between Boolean searching and natural language searching.
- List the steps the researcher should follow when preparing to perform computer assisted legal research.

CITATION MATTERS

INTERNET CITATIONS

THE BLUEBOOK — RULE 18

Electronic Media and Other Nonprint Resources

Rule 18 covers a multitude of citation requirements. Legal researchers who use the Internet must pay close attention to the new rules associated with citing to the Internet. A short list of the rules and what each rule covers follows.

Rule 18.2:	information about the authority being cited
Rule 18.2.2:	explanatory phrase indicating which source was used
Rule 18.2.2:	provider responsible for the Internet site (if not clear from URL)
Rule 18.2.1(a):	the URL
Rule 18.2.3(e):	a date parenthetical
Rule 18.2.2(c):	order of authorities and parentheticals
Rule 18.2.3(d):	pinpoint citations to Internet sources

LEXIS, WESTLAW, AND OTHER ELECTRONIC DATABASES

THE BLUBOOK — RULE 18

Electronic Media and Other Nonprint Resources

LEXIS and Westlaw are large commercial electronic databases. There are other reliable and authoritative commercial databases as well. The rules covering citation to these resources are covered in the following rules.

INTEROFFICE MEMORANDUM

TO: Research Associate

FROM: Senior Attorney

RE: *Su v. KILR Radio Station*

We agreed to arbitrate the *Su v. KILR Radio Station* case and because there are so many issues in the case I want to start on our Arbitration Brief. Read the file for all of the facts (See Appendix A, Problem 6.) Our client, Su, made claims against Shriver, KILR Radio Station, and Metro City Police Department for her injuries. Our claim against Shriver was already settled. Our Arbitration Brief must address the liability of KILR and Metro City Police. Please research these issues and prepare a memorandum detailing your findings.

There is a second matter I also want you to research. We were given two names as potential arbitrators in the case, Susan Templeton and R. J. Guzman. Both individuals are retired appellate court judges in this state. Please see what you can find out about them. In particular, it would be nice to know if they favored plaintiffs or defendants in personal injury cases while they were on the bench.

11-1   INTRODUCTION

In previous chapters, you read about the various materials legal researchers use to find the law. For many years these materials were available only in print. As a result, if lawyers wanted quick and easy access to legal materials, they maintained substantial legal libraries in their offices. The alternative was to complete one's legal research at a law school or county law library. Today, legal researchers access many legal research materials with a computer. These materials are available on CD-ROM, on legal databases such as LEXIS and Westlaw, and on the Internet. Lawyers are no longer required to keep hundreds, or in some cases, thousands, of volumes of legal books in their offices. Nor are they limited to standard library hours in which to accomplish their research.

computer assisted legal research. Legal research done with the use of a computer; includes the use of CD-ROM, online services such as LEXIS and Westlaw, the Internet, and intranets.

Because CD-ROM and online databases are accessed with a computer, searching materials in these formats is often referred to as **computer assisted legal research.** In computer assisted legal research (or CALR), the legal researcher uses the computer to access and search various legal materials. The computer adds a great deal of flexibility and convenience to the research process. It gives the researcher access to many materials not otherwise available. On the other hand, computer

assisted legal research is not without its difficulties. This chapter covers the different types of computer assisted legal research, common search methodology, and some of the advantages and disadvantages of CALR.

11-2 TYPES OF COMPUTER ASSISTED LEGAL RESEARCH (CALR)

Computer assisted legal research involves the use of research materials found in electronic format rather than in print. This involves the use of CD-ROM, fee-based legal databases such as LEXIS and Westlaw, the Internet, and intranets.

CD-ROM

A CD-ROM is a compact disk that contains the equivalent of thousands of pages of written material. Today, most legal publishers provide their books and treatises in this format. Cases, codes, form books, encyclopedias, and many other secondary source materials are available on CD-ROM. The advantages to the use of CD-ROM are many. Much less physical space is needed to store volumes of materials. Materials that would normally fill all the shelves of a large library can be kept on a corner of an attorney's desk. Supplementing is much easier than it is with material in print. Pocket part supplements and separate supplement volumes are not necessary. Instead, the publishers supplement materials on CD-ROM with cumulative replacement CDs. See Figure 11-1 for a sample computer screen showing some available CD-ROMs.

LEXIS

LEXIS is a subscription online service providing access to several legal and non-legal resources. LEXIS is accessed through the Internet. The **database** includes primary and secondary sources of law as well as a variety of other important resources used in the legal profession. The following are examples of some of the material found through this database.

database. Compilation of electronically stored information.

Primary Law

United States Constitution
United States Code
Federal cases
Code of Federal Regulations
Federal Rules
State constitutions
State codes
State cases
State administrative regulations
Selected international laws

Statutory material on LEXIS is annotated and cases contain summaries and headnotes.

Secondary Sources

Encyclopedias
Treatises

Prev 1 | 2 | 3 Next

Format	Title
CD-ROM	**California Family Law Practice Library, LawDesk® CD-ROM ed.** Complete family law package combines treatises, forms, guides, codes, and effective family law software for a total "practice area" library on CD-ROM.
CD-ROM	**California Jurisprudence, 3d, LawDesk® CD-ROM ed.** Examination and analysis of constitutional, statutory, judicial, and administrative law devoted exclusively to the California jurisdiction, on LawDesk® CD-ROM.
CD-ROM	**California Jury Instructions Civil (BAJI), LawDesk® CD-ROM ed.** LawDesk® CD-ROM contains the complete text of *California Jury Instructions, Civil;* allows expedient search for jury instructions, use notes, and comments.
CD-ROM	**California Jury Instructions Criminal (CALJIC), LawDesk® CD-ROM ed.** Easily search for jury instructions, use notes and comments with this LawDesk® CD-ROM containing the complete text of *California Jury Instructions, Criminal.*
CD-ROM	**California Official Reports, 1st, LawDesk® CD-ROM ed.** Official compilation of California Supreme Court and Court of Appeal opinions from 1850 to 1934, on one LawDesk® CD-ROM.
CD-ROM	**California Official Reports, 2d, LawDesk® CD-ROM ed.** This LawDesk® format CD-ROM for Windows® includes the series that covers 1934–1969.
CD-ROM	**California Official Reports, 3d, LawDesk® CD-ROM ed.** CD-ROM version of the only official compilation of California Supreme Court and Courts of Appeal opinions.
CD-ROM	**California Official Reports, 4th, LawDesk® CD-ROM ed.** This LawDesk® CD-ROM is the only official compilation of California Supreme Court and Courts of Appeal opinions.
CD-ROM	**California Real Estate Practice Library, LawDesk® CD-ROM ed.** Complete library of California real estate titles from Miller & Star, The Rutter Group, and relevant codes on LawDesk® CD-ROM.
CD-ROM Archive	**California Style Manual 4th, LawDesk® CD-ROM ed.** The official, definitive handbook of legal style for the courts of California, on LawDesk® CD-ROM.
CD-ROM	**Callaghan's Michigan Civil Jurisprudence, LawDesk® CD-ROM ed.** An exhaustive reference on substantive civil law in Michigan, including full coverage of every important case and statute on a LawDesk®-format CD-ROM.
CD-ROM	**Callaghan's Michigan Pleading & Practice, LawDesk® CD-ROM ed.** Presents and analyzes all the requirements for case preparation, pleading, and practicing before any Michigan civil court on LawDesk®-format CD-ROM.
CD-ROM	**Carmody-Wait, 2d, LawDesk® CD-ROM ed.** Combines practice and procedure with forms, covering every type of civil and criminal proceeding before any New York state court on LawDesk®-format CD-ROM.
CD-ROM	**Causes of Action: Personal Injury Library, LawDesk® CD-ROM ed.** This LawDesk® format CD-ROM product contains articles on personal injury actions with advice and strategy for practice and procedure.
CD-ROM	**Civil Appeals and Writs, LawDesk® CD-ROM ed. (The Rutter Group California Practice Guides on CD-ROM)** Comprehensive LawDesk® CD-ROM provides practical and complete guidance through the entire writs and appeals process in California courts.
CD-ROM	**Civil Procedure Before Trial - LawDesk** Detailed CD-ROM practice guide through each stage of a lawsuit, from commencement of action, to the trial itself.
CD-ROM	**Civil Trials and Evidence, LawDesk® CD-ROM ed. (The Rutter Group California Practice Guides on CD-ROM)** From pretrial preparation to posttrial motions, this LawDesk ® CD-ROM delivers effective information and methodology for trying a civil lawsuit.
CD-ROM	**Code of Federal Regulations, LawDesk® CD-ROM ed.** Provides the full text of all *Code of Federal Regulations* titles on LawDesk®-format CD-ROM discs, with monthly updates.
CD-ROM	**Complete Texas Family Law, LawDesk® CD-ROM ed.** This LawDesk®-format CD-ROM edition includes the text of Sampson and Tindall's *Texas Family Code Annotated*, plus *Texas Family Law Service*—a comprehensive, how-to practice guide.
CD-ROM	**Corporations, LawDesk® CD-ROM ed. (The Rutter Group California Practice Guides on CD-ROM)** Delivers an integrated approach to corporate law, securities law and tax considerations on LawDesk® CD-ROM.

Reprinted with permission of Thomson/West

FIGURE 11-1 List of Resources on LawDesk CD

Practice books

Form books

Law reviews and journals

Restatement

***Shepard's* Citators**

Public Records

Business information

Real property information

Court records

News Sources

Legal news publications

Worldwide general news publications

LEXIS contains more material than any traditional legal library. In most cases, researchers have no need to search the entire database. For example, in the Su case described in the "Interoffice Memorandum," if the event occurred in California, a researcher would not be interested in New York law. Furthermore, a researcher might be interested in searching codes and cases, but not administrative regulations. So that researchers can focus their searches and retrieve only relevant documents, LEXIS organized its vast materials into smaller databases or sources. These are further subdivided into "files." In the Su case, the researcher could select a source containing only California case law. There are numerous sources that can be selected on LEXIS. For an example of some of the sources, see Figure 11-2.

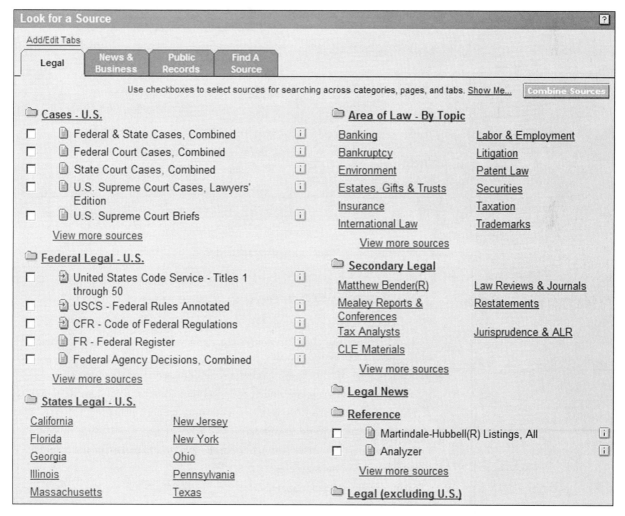

FIGURE 11-2 LEXIS Libraries (Databases)

| Look for a Source | ? |

Add/Edit Tabs

| **Legal** | News & Business | Public Records | Find A Source |

Legal > States Legal - U.S. > **Florida** (Add "Florida" as a tab)

Use checkboxes to select sources for searching across categories, pages, and tabs. Show Me...   [Combine Sources]

⚙ Florida Litigation Research Tasks

📁 **Cases**

☐ 📄 Federal & State Cases, Combined [i]
☐ 📄 FL Federal & State Cases, Combined [i]
☐ 📄 U.S. Supreme Court Cases, Lawyers' Edition [i]
☐ 📄 FL Cases, Administrative Decisions & Attorney General Opinions, Combined [i]
☐ 📄 FL State Cases, Combined [i]
   View more sources

📁 **Statutes & Regulations**

☐ 📄 FL - Florida Statutes, Constitution, Court Rules & ALS, Combined [i]
☐ 📄 FL - LexisNexis Florida Annotated Statutes [i]
☐ 📄 FL - Florida Administrative Code Annotated [i]
☐ 📄 FL - Florida Court Rules [i]
☐ 📄 USCS - United States Code Service: Code, Const, Rules, Conventions & Public Laws [i]
   View more sources

📁 **Agency & Administrative Materials**

☐ 📄 FL Agencies & Attorney General Opinions, Combined [i]

📁 **Forms & Agreements**

☐ 📄 LexisNexis(TM) Florida Forms, Combined [i]
☐ 📄 LexisNexis(TM) Florida Litigation Forms [i]
☐ 📄 LexisNexis(TM) Florida Transactions Forms [i]
   View more sources

📁 **Restatements & Jurisprudences**

☐ 📄 Florida Jurisprudence 2d [i]
   View more sources

📁 **CLE Course Materials & Publications**

☐ 📄 All Florida CLE Materials, Combined [i]
   View more sources

📁 **Legal News**

☐ 📄 Florida Daily Business Review [i]
☐ 📄 Florida: Mealey's Litigation NewsBriefs [i]
   View more sources

📁 **General News & Information**

☐ 📄 Florida News Publications [i]
   View more sources

Reprinted with the permission of LexisNexis

FIGURE 11-2 (continued)

BOX 11-1

COMPUTER ASSISTED LEGAL RESEARCH ALLOWS YOU TO

√ Search full text of case law and codes for specific words and phrases.

√ Search numerous secondary sources (e.g., encyclopedias, *A.L.R.,* law reviews) for specific words and phrases.

√ Search tables of contents for codes and numerous secondary sources.

√ Retrieve documents (cases, codes, and secondary sources) if you have a citation.

√ Search case opinions written by or mentioning specific justices.

√ Search for cases within certain dates.

√ Search numerous public documents (e.g., corporate and real estate documents).

√ Search general news articles.

√ Search selected foreign materials.

√ Validate your research findings (using *Shepard's,* KeyCite, and Auto-Cite).

LEXIS provides many "user guides" explaining its numerous features and offering research tips. Most of these can be downloaded without cost from the following site.

http://www.lexisnexis.com/custserv/Literature/.

Westlaw

Westlaw is an online subscription service similar to LEXIS in the type of material featured. Annotated constitutions, codes, and regulations can be searched. Case law contains case summaries and headnotes. International law is also accessible. Rather than *Shepard's*, Westlaw provides a service called KeyCite to check the validity of legal sources. As described in the previous chapter, KeyCite is similar to *Shepard's* in the information provided. In addition to primary law, numerous secondary sources, public records, and news sources are available through Westlaw. See Figure 11-3.

One of the unique features of West publications—key numbers—is found on Westlaw and can be used as a basis for searching. Westlaw has a feature titled Key-Search, which allows the researcher to browse the numerous topics and subtopics West has created in its key number system. The researcher can then search for primary law related to the topics. The researcher can also add other terms to the topics for a more specific search. Additionally, on Westlaw, just as with West case reporters, headnotes refer to topics and key numbers and allow the researcher to use the key number to do further searching.

West also publishes several short "user guides" to explain the various Westlaw features. These can be accessed online at http://west.thomson.com/westlaw/guides/.

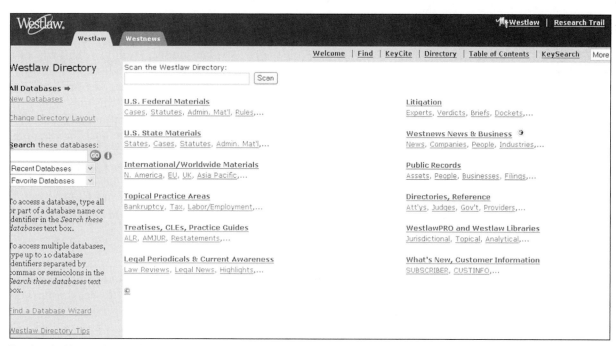

Reprinted with permission of Thomson/West

FIGURE 11-3 Westlaw Databases

Internet

Many legal resources are available for free on the Internet. However, extreme care must be taken before relying on information from any such source. The researcher must ask two critical questions: (1) Who is responsible for the Internet site? and (2) How current is the information on the site? Government sites, law school sites, and sites maintained by reputable legal publishers are the most reliable, provided that the information is current. Researchers must verify that the information is current, even with reputable sources. Additionally, although the researcher can generally locate primary law on the Internet, editorial enhancements found in books, such as case headnotes and cases summaries, are not included. Nor are the codes located on the Internet in an annotated format.

The following are some of the more popular and reputable general legal sites.

Findlaw (www.findlaw.com). This comprehensive site is now owned by West, the company that publishes Westlaw. On this site a researcher finds extensive primary law, including federal cases, the United States Code, the Code of Federal Regulations, and the U.S. Constitution. State law is also available, as are many sources of international law. Federal cases can be located with a citation, a party name, or through a full-text search. The United States Code can be searched by citation or by keywords. The Findlaw site also contains articles about the law. It does not contain traditional secondary sources described in earlier chapters of this text.

LexisOne (www.lexisone.com). This site is managed by LEXIS Law Publishing, the publishers of LEXIS. It provides access to all U.S. Supreme Court cases and to recent cases from other federal courts and state courts. It does not provide access to statutory law.

Cornell Law School's Legal Information Institute (http://www.law.cornell.edu/). Like Findlaw, this is a comprehensive site providing access to federal and state cases, codes, and constitutions, including the federal rules. Short explanations of various areas of law are also found here.

Law Library of Congress (http://www.loc.gov/law/public/law.html). This is a comprehensive site maintained by the Library of Congress. It provides access to international, federal, and state primary law. It also provides access to numerous law reviews. See Figure 11-4 for examples of the materials found on this site.

In addition to these general Internet sites, case law and statutory law can usually be accessed through a site maintained by the source of the law. For example, U.S. Supreme Court cases are found on the Web site for the Supreme Court (www.supremecourtus.gov). See Figure 11-5. The United States Codes can be accessed through the House of Representatives (http://uscode.house.gov/search/criteria.php). See Figure 11-6 to see some of the search options for codes through this site. State case law and statutory law is generally available through the individual state's home pages.

Discussion Groups   In addition to providing access to numerous databases of information, the Internet allows legal practitioners to set up "chat rooms" or discussion groups. In this way, attorneys from around the world can discuss legal issues and questions. If help is needed on a research question, it can usually be found.

intranet. A secure database set up and accessible by a specific group, such as a law firm.

Intranets

Intranets, as opposed to the *Internet,* are also tools for computer assisted legal research. **Intranets** are databases set up and accessible by a specific group, such as a

The Library of Congress >> Law Library of Congress Home

Law Library Pages

Guide to Law Online
Law Library of Congress

The *Guide to Law Online*, prepared by the Law Library of Congress Public Services Division, is an annotated guide to sources of information on government and law available online. It includes selected links to useful and reliable sites for legal information.

Select a Link:

- International and Multinational
- Nations of the World
- U.S. Federal - includes U.S. Code and Constitution links
- U.S. States and Territories
- Guide Index

Law Library Reading Room

Digital Legal Resources:

Global Legal Information Network (GLIN)

Courtesy of http://www.loc.gov/law/public/law.html

FIGURE 11-4 Law Library of Congress Web site

BOX 11-2

TYPES OF COMPUTER ASSISTED LEGAL RESEARCH

CD-ROM

LEXIS

WESTLAW

INTERNET

INTRANET

BOX 11-3

PROCEDURE FOR FULL-TEXT SEARCHING

√ Determine contents of available databases.

√ Select database(s) containing law of proper jurisdiction.

√ Select database(s) containing relevant source of law (i.e., case law, codes, etc.).

√ Identify relevant words and phrases.

√ Formulate search query.

√ Review results.

√ Validate results.

Courtesy of http://www.supremecourtus.gov/

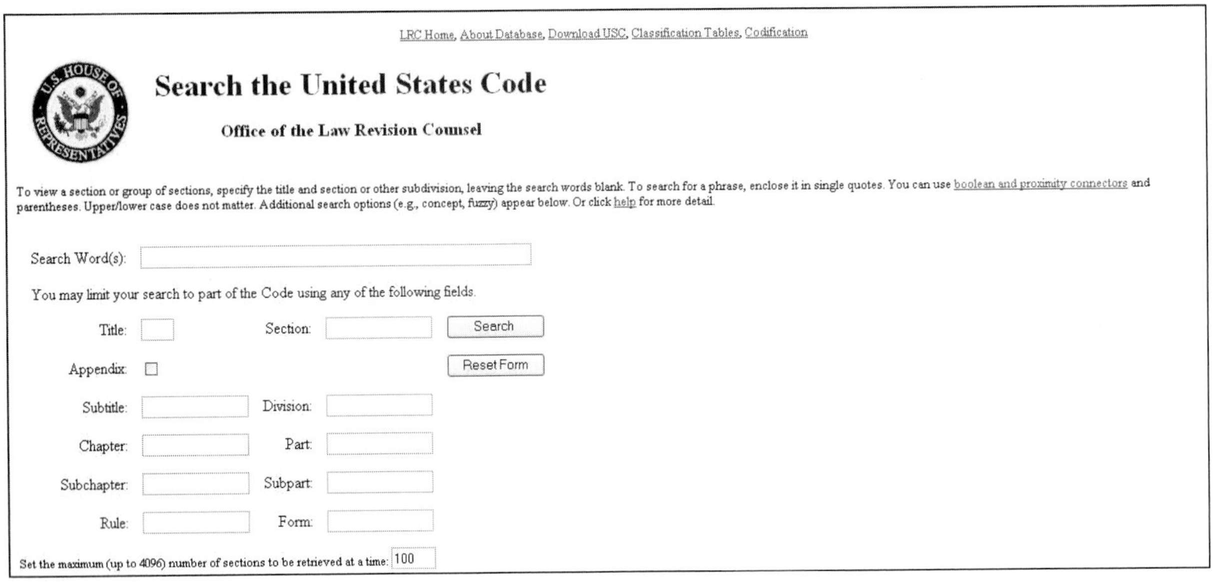

FIGURE 11-5 U.S. Supreme Court Web site

Courtesy of http://uscode.house.gov/search/criteria.php

FIGURE 11-6 U.S. Code from House of Representatives

law firm. All members of the firm can access it. If a law firm has several branches in different localities, information on an intranet can be accessed by all of them. Intranets also provide the mechanism for setting up e-mail among the various users. Because an intranet is not part of the Internet, some of the security concerns associated with the Internet do not exist. In terms of legal research, intranets

provide a vehicle for firms to index and maintain any legal memoranda they prepared. Before researching legal questions, lawyers can check this database to see if the research was done in connection with some other case in the office. Like the Internet, an intranet allows lawyers and their support staff to conduct online discussion groups.

11-3 SEARCH METHODS

Regardless of which form of electronic data you use, the search methods are similar. Before you can begin searching you must access the material. If you are using a CD-ROM, this is simple. You insert the CD into the CD drive on your computer. Accessing online services is different. LEXIS and Westlaw are commonly accessed through the Internet. And remember, even though you may be able to obtain legal materials on the Internet without cost, you may be paying for your use of the Internet.

Full-Text Searching

One of the advantages of computer assisted legal research is the ability to do a **full-text search.** Full-text searching involves searching the text of the legal material rather than an index. For example, full-text searching of case law means searching the actual opinions of all cases found in the database in which you are working. Consider the facts of the Su case mentioned at the beginning of this chapter. Suppose you wanted to search for all cases dealing with the potential liability of police departments for injuries occurring in high-speed chases. To do a full-text search of California cases for the legal issues in the Su case, you must read all California Supreme Court and Appellate Court cases! This is impossible if you are researching cases in print. However, it is not impossible if you are searching cases in an electronic format. Full-text searching works much like a "find" feature on your word processor. You tell the computer what words to look for and it finds those words. In order to conduct a full-text search, you must first formulate a **query.** A query consists of the words that you want the computer to find in a **document.** There are two different ways to formulate or phrase your search question. One is by using **Boolean** logic, often referred to as "terms and connectors." The other is by phrasing your question in a normal question format.

full-text search. Legal research method utilized in computer assisted legal research in which all documents in a database are searched for certain words.

query. Words that constitute a search request when using CD-ROM or online materials.

document. An identifiable item located in a database; can refer to a case or a single code section.

Boolean. A special logic used in computerized legal research; utilizes the use of connective words.

connectors. Words such as *and* or *or* used in a search query to show the relationship between key words or terms.

Boolean Searching

Boolean searching allows the researcher to search for certain combinations of words in a document. This is done by using connective words or **connectors.** The most common connectors are the words *and* and *or.* For example, review the case facts in the "Interoffice Memorandum." If you are researching the liability of the police department, you might be looking for cases dealing with the liability of police departments when innocent bystanders are hurt as a result of a car chase. Using a Boolean search method, you must formulate a query consisting of words you expect to see in cases dealing with this issue. You must join these words with the proper connectors. In this case, you might be looking for cases that contain all of the following terms: *police, liability, bystander, hurt, car,* and *chase.* Because you want to find cases containing all of these terms, you could connect them with *and.* On the other hand, you may not be sure if a case uses the term *hurt* instead of *injured* or *automobile* instead of *car.*

In that case, you could instruct the computer to search for hurt *or* injured, and car *or* automobile. In any one search query, you can combine different connectors. Thus, using only the *and* and *or* connectors, your search query in the Su case could read as follows.

Police and liability and bystander and hurt or injured and car or
automobile and chase

And and *or* are not the only connectors you can use. "Proximity connectors" allow you to search for words that appear in a certain proximity to one another. For example, you can search for words appearing in the same sentence, the same paragraph, or within a certain number of words of one another.

When using the various connectors, you often use abbreviated or shorthand ways of expressing them. Unfortunately, these abbreviations are different on LEXIS and Westlaw.

In addition to the use of connectors, formulating a Boolean search query also gives you the opportunity to search for variations of words without typing in each and every variation. Two characters, the asterisk (*) and the exclamation mark (!) allow you to do this. The asterisk is known as the "universal character" and is used in place of a specific letter in a word. For example, suppose you wanted to search for either the word *woman* or *women*. You could type the following: wom*n. The asterisk takes the place of any letter. The exclamation mark is known as a "root extender." It is used at the end of a word. When this is used, the computer searches for the root word (the letters that you have actually typed) with any ending. For example, using the term *liab!* retrieves documents containing the words *liable* or *liability*. Boolean searching is used to find documents on CD-ROM, LEXIS, Westlaw, and on the Internet. However, slight variations do exist. Both LEXIS and Westlaw provide online help explaining how Boolean searching works on their system. Often, on the Internet, you find information explaining how to conduct a Boolean search.

⇨ **A Point to Remember.** Developing effective Boolean search queries depends on intelligent use of connectors, the universal character, and the root extender. Commonly used connectors include the following:

- and
- or
- /n or w/n (proximity connectors)

The universal character (*) substitutes for any letter. The root extender (!) substitutes for all endings on the same root word.

Natural Language Searches

As an alternative to Boolean searches, both LEXIS and Westlaw (and some CD-ROMs) allow you to formulate a search using a normal question. This is usually known as a "natural language search." In a natural language search, a search query for the Su case might read as follows.

Is a police department liable for damages suffered by a bystander when police are
chasing a suspect in an automobile?

When you use natural language, the computer program converts your question into Boolean language.

Locating Known Citations

Boolean searches and natural language searches are used when the researcher is conducting a full-text search. Usually, this is done when you have a legal question and you are looking for authorities to answer the question. Sometimes, however, during the research process you know the citation for a specific legal authority and want to access or read that authority. Using the proper command, you can easily retrieve the known document by typing the citation.

Table of Contents

Searching codes and secondary sources is sometimes done by searching the table of contents. The researcher can either browse the full table of contents or do a word search within the table of contents. This method of searching often provides narrower results than a full-text search and is therefore more efficient.

11-4 PREPARING TO SEARCH

If you are engaged in computer assisted legal research, you must prepare to research just as you do when researching materials in print. This is even more important when researching on a fee-based service where you may be charged for the time you spend on the service. Your research process for using computer assisted legal research should include the following steps.

- Understand your research assignment.
- Review all available facts.
- Identify all key facts.
- Identify legal issues.
- List words describing your key facts and legal issues.
- Consider synonyms, antonyms, and variations of all words listed.
- Consider the relationship among the words (i.e., should two or more words appear in the same sentence, the same paragraph, etc.).
- Develop your search question.
- If you are using LEXIS or Westlaw, determine the controlling jurisdiction and the relevant types of legal materials; select the appropriate database(s) to search.

As with all legal research, adequate preparation will make your research much more efficient and successful.

11-5 SEARCH POSSIBILITIES AND PROBLEMS

Computer assisted legal research opens search possibilities that do not exist with materials in print. Full-text searching allows you to search for the presence of any word or combinations of words. This allows you to search not only for legal issues and facts, but for names of individuals appearing in cases. Thus, you can search for appellate cases written by certain judges or for cases dealing with lower court decisions by certain judges. If you are presented with a question about possible biases of a certain judge, you could search case law databases to see if his or her name appears.

Other advantages of computer assisted legal research include:

- Ability to restrict a full-text search by factors such as date, author, jurisdiction
- Ability to locate a case with the name of one party and no case citation
- Ability to hyperlink to an authority cited within the document you are reading
- Ability to instantly cite check a case you are reading by hyperlinking to *Shepard's* or KeyCite
- Ability to "copy and paste" language or citations into a word processing document
- Availability of popular materials (especially practice books) to more than one person at a time

On the other hand, computer assisted legal research is not without problems. Some of these include the following.

- Computers search literally; misspelled words or typographical errors will result in a failed search.
- Computers do not distinguish a different word usage; a search for RICO will produce references to the Rico Act as well as Puerto Rico.
- Computers do not automatically search for synonyms; a search for *vehicle* will not produce results containing the word *automobile*.
- A tendency to overuse hyperlinks can result in unorganized (and lost) research.
- The use of LEXIS and Westlaw can be costly.

Another potential problem with online services stems from the fact that the services contain some unpublished opinions and opinions that have been vacated because a higher court has granted a hearing. Most of these cases do not appear in printed case reporters. It is absolutely essential that any cite on these services be validated.

11-6   SOFTWARE ENHANCEMENTS

Computer assisted legal research is becoming essential to the practice of law. Its full potential, however, is still being explored. An example of what can be accomplished with the use of CALR is seen in some of the features and services used in conjunction with LEXIS and Westlaw. Both of these online services provide software that works with a legal memorandum or brief that has been written in either Microsoft Word or Corel's WordPerfect. This software will perform the following functions.

- Generate a table of authorities from those found within the document
- Check the format of all citations
- Utilize the online capabilities of Westlaw or LEXIS to check the accuracy of the citations
- Utilize the online capabilities of the service to check the accuracy of all quotations in the document
- Shepardize or otherwise validate legal authorities in the document

TECHNOLOGY CORNER

The two large computer assisted legal research online databases are LEXIS and Westlaw. These, of course, are not free resources. The Web sites for the databases are informative and some free materials are provided.

www.lexis.com

www.westlaw.com

In addition to Westlaw and LEXIS, several smaller fee-based services are available. These services do not offer the breadth of material available on Westlaw or LEXIS, but do offer basic research materials. One such service is Versus Law at www.versuslaw.com. This service offers special subscription rates to students.

Many CD-ROM products are available for legal research. They range in price from modest to very expensive. There are software products designed to assist the legal researcher. All of these are advertised in legal journals and newspapers. Watch for the ads offering a free demonstration CD or disk.

CHAPTER SUMMARY

Legal researchers today use legal resource material in electronic format in addition to material in print. This type of research is known as *computer assisted legal research.* Computer assisted legal research consists of the use of CD-ROMs, legal databases such as LEXIS and Westlaw, the Internet, and intranets.

Legal publishers produce many legal materials in CD-ROM format. A CD-ROM is a compact disk holding thousands of pages of material. A CD-ROM provides many benefits. Less space is needed to store material, supplementing is easier, and search possibilities are greater.

LEXIS and Westlaw are two online sources for legal researchers. These are fee-based services containing databases with extensive amounts of legal research material from the United States as well as from several foreign countries. In addition to legal research material, a researcher can also access public documents, records from popular current cases, and numerous news sources.

The Internet provides access to many free sources of legal research material. Federal and state governments publish many of their materials on the Internet. In addition, the Internet also provides access to many fee-based legal sites. An intranet, a database accessible only by a select group, is a popular complement to the Internet.

Conducting research with any method of computer assisted legal research often involves the use of Boolean logic to conduct full-text searches. A full-text search involves a search of the actual documents rather than a search of an index. Boolean logic involves the use of special connective words such as *and* and *or* to establish relationships between words. Natural language can also be used to formulate a search.

The use of computer assisted legal research offers search possibilities that do not exist otherwise. However, it is not without problems.

TERMS TO REMEMBER

computer assisted legal research (CALR)   query

database   document

intranet   Boolean

full-text search   connectors

QUESTIONS FOR REVIEW

1. What is computer assisted legal research?
2. List the different types of computer assisted legal research.
3. What are some of the advantages of a CD-ROM?
4. What types of materials can be found on LEXIS and Westlaw?
5. Explain the difference between the Internet and an intranet.
6. Explain full-text searching.
7. What is a Boolean search?
8. List the steps in preparing to search online.
9. What are some of the problems with computer assisted legal research?
10. How is software enhancing the use of online services such as LEXIS and Westlaw?

CAN YOU FIGURE IT OUT?

Refer to Figure 11-2.

1. Assume that the Su incident occurred in Florida. Which LEXIS sources contain applicable case law?
2. Which sources contain applicable statutory law?
3. Which sources contain annotations found in *American Law Reports?*
4. Which sources contain accounts of traffic accidents caused by the Metro Police Department?

Refer to Figure 11-3.

5. Answer questions 1 through 4 using Westlaw.

RESEARCH ASSIGNMENTS AND ACTIVITIES

1. Statutory Research on the Internet: Find answers to the following questions using the Internet. (Try www.findlaw.com and http://uscode.house.gov/usc.htm.)
   a. What does 28 U.S.C. §135 provide?
   b. What does 2 U.S.C. § 135 provide?
   c. Which section of the United States Code establishes the Department of Homeland Security?
   d. Where in the United States Code do you find the "Drive-by Shooting Prevention Act of 1994"?
   e. Which two constitutional amendments use the term *due process?*

2. Case Law Research on the Internet: Find answers to the following questions using the Internet. (Try www.findlaw.com and www.lexisone.com.)

   a. What U.S. Supreme Court cases prior to 2004 discuss the law regarding "enemy combatants"?

   b. Which 2003 U.S. Supreme Court case discusses the use of affirmative action in the admission process of a law school?

3. Using a general search engine such as www.google.com, search for information about employment discrimination. You should retrieve numerous sites. Would any of the first five sites help if you were doing legal research on this issue? Explain. Make a list of legal resources available through this site.

4. Review the problems in Appendix A.

   a. Draft queries for finding cases for each of the problems using Boolean logic. Use the LEXIS connectors.

   b. Do the same using the Westlaw connectors.

   c. Do the same using natural language.

CASE PROJECT

Use the Internet to do further research on your case. Do the following.

   a. Conduct a general search of the main issues in your case.

   b. See if any of the cases or statutes you have found can be located on the Internet.

   c. See if the local rules of court for your jurisdiction are on the Internet.

   d. See if your local court has a home page.

Summarize your results in writing.

HOW TO CREATE RESEARCH STRATEGIES

CHAPTER OUTLINE

CHAPTER OBJECTIVES

When you complete this chapter you should be able to

- Create a research vocabulary list from a factual situation.
- Write an issue for initial research purposes.
- Create a research plan.
- Explain the use of indexes in the legal research process.
- Explain when to begin research in primary sources.
- Explain when to begin research in secondary sources.
- Discuss the importance of updating and validating research results.

CITATION MATTERS

THE USE OF BRACKETS

THE BLUEBOOK — RULE 5.2

Brackets are used when a letter needs to be changed from lower to uppercase, or vice versa.

1. Substituted letters (possibly to change tense), or
2. words (possibly to correct agreement or provide clarification), and
3. other inserted material
4. should be enclosed in brackets.

> *THE BLUEBOOK* provides an excellent example:
>
> "[P]ublic confidence in the [adversary] system depend[s upon] full disclosure of all the facts, within the framework of the rules of evidence."

In this example, a lowercase *p* was capitalized and *adversary* and *s upon* were added to make the sentence read well.

When there is a significant error in the original quote, place *[sic]* directly following the mistake.

> "The Court noted that the judgment were [*sic*] not necessarily harsh, given the circumstances under which the crime was committed."

INTEROFFICE MEMORANDUM

TO: Research Associate

FROM: Supervising Attorney

RE: Research Assignment

The office has a new client, Ms. Grace Yoshida. Ms. Yoshida, a chemical engineer, was recently terminated from her job at RiteTech. RiteTech manufactures many chemical products. She believes she was fired because she made a report to the local office of the Environmental Protection Agency (EPA). After repeated attempts to get her company to properly dispose of its hazardous waste in the manner required by state and federal law, she reported the ongoing improper disposal of the toxic waste into the local sewers. She was fired the same day the EPA contacted RiteTech. RiteTech told her the company was downsizing. However, Ms. Yoshida still has many friends at RiteTech and they told her that she was replaced within a week. Your supervisor thinks this may be a case of retaliatory discharge. Please perform the initial research.

12-1 INTRODUCTION

This chapter provides a step-by-step overview of the research and initial analysis process. Before a researcher begins a research project, he or she must plan that process carefully. At first, doing so may appear overly burdensome; however, it is not as cumbersome as it looks on paper. Many of the steps take only moments to complete. These **strategies** save time and help to organize the researcher. The strategies begin by paying attention to terminology and the creation of a vocabulary list. From there, strategies move to issue formulation, use of dictionaries, creation of a research plan, use of indexes, determination of where to begin the research, the updating and validation of research results, the taking of purposeful notes, and the overall organization of the research results.

strategy. A well-thought-out plan or approach to a project.

12-2 CREATE THE VOCABULARY LIST

Every fact pattern provides an initial vocabulary or terminology list. Sort the terms into two lists: one factual and the other legal.

For example, your attorney gives you the assignment in the "Interoffice Memorandum" above. As you review what you know, some terms are easily placed into your vocabulary list. At this point, do not worry too much about which list a certain fact actually belongs on; just pull out the key terminology. Some terms or concepts may seem to be both legal and factual. Do not let that confuse you. Your research will help you separate the legal from the factual. You may even be able to add terms from your own experience or knowledge.

The important thing is that you have a list of words and phrases identified before you even consider using library resources. At this point, not every term from the fact pattern is included in the list. After researching case law other facts may become important. You now have a list of vocabulary terms to take to the index of the resource in which you choose to initiate research.

Factual Terms	**Legal Terms**
Environmental Protection Agency	Retaliatory discharge
Toxic waste	
Hazardous waste	
Disposal	
Employment termination	

12-3 FORMULATE THE ISSUE FOR INITIAL RESEARCH PURPOSES

If possible, attempt to articulate the **legal issue.** Remember, a well-written legal issue contains the cause of action (or legal problem) and the key facts. However, rather than attempt to write a formal issue statement at this early stage of research, you really just need to ask: Do the facts of the Yoshida case support a cause of action for retaliatory discharge?

   You may have no clue as to what the **elements** of the **cause of action** for retaliatory discharge are. That is not a problem. Your initial research will clarify the cause of action. Once the elements of the cause of action are known, you will be able to determine which of the facts are most important. This initial research also helps you articulate the issue in a more formal format, that is, a format acceptable to send to the court. But for now, keep it simple and remain focused on the research project.

legal issue. A question that must be decided by a court.

elements. The components of a cause of action or of a statute.

cause of action. The basis upon which a lawsuit may be brought to the court.

12-4 USE THE LEGAL DICTIONARY AND THESAURUS

Once your initial vocabulary list is complete, take a few moments to consult a legal dictionary and a legal thesaurus. These resources expand your research list. You will have a more complete list of vocabulary terms to take to the indexes of your legal research resources.

After reviewing these additional vocabulary-building resources, your list of terms might look something like this.

Factual Terms	**Legal Terms**
Environmental Protection Agency	Retaliatory discharge
Toxic waste	
Hazardous waste	
Disposal	
Terminated	

When you add additional terms from the dictionary and thesaurus, the list may grow.

Fire	Wrongful termination
Removal from employment	Employer/employee

> Get rid of   Relationship
>
> Dangerous situation/condition
>
> Public hazard
>
> Risk
>
> Dismiss

With this list of terms you are ready to begin work in legal indexes. The questions are, which set of books and which indexes?

12-5 CREATE A RESEARCH PLAN BEFORE GOING TO THE LAW LIBRARY

Before going to the law library, sit down and consider where to begin research. Make a list of books or sets of books you plan to review. Break that list into **primary sources** and **secondary sources.** For example:

primary sources. The resources that provide the actual law; laws are found in statutes, case law, the Constitution, and some administrative materials.

secondary sources. Tools used to understand the law; one such tool is a legal encyclopedia, which explains the law.

Primary Sources	Secondary Sources/Finding Tools
State statutes	Legal encyclopedias
Federal statutes	Speciality sets (on employment law)
Case law	Digests of case law
Ordinances	Pleading and practice guides
	Law review articles
	American Law Reports (A.L.R.)

legal encyclopedia. A collection of legal information; a secondary source of the law.

pleading and practice guide. A secondary source providing sample pleadings and general practice advice; available in most states and for some federal practice areas.

This list could go on and on. Many states have a state **legal encyclopedia.** This may be a good starting place when you know very little about the topic. **Pleading and practice guides** provide good examples. These secondary resources provide the researcher with a foundation to perform the research in primary sources. Once the vocabulary list and a list of library resources are prepared, you are ready to begin your initial research.

12-6 TAKE YOUR RESEARCH TERMS/ VOCABULARY TO THE INDEXES

Step One   Determine which resource to attack first. Take a moment to look over the set. Notice how much information is on the spine of every volume. Notice that some of the volumes say "Index" on them. This is a good sign. It means that in addition to a large comprehensive index at the end of the set, there is also a **topical index** for each topic.

topical index. An index arranged by subject matter topics.

Step Two   Locate the index for the set. The comprehensive index is usually at the end of the set of books. In most instances, the index is a large multivolume set. Sometimes these indexes are called "Descriptive Word Index" or "General Index." They are arranged alphabetically. Begin to methodically look up your vocabulary words and phrases. Consider beginning the Yoshida research with finding *retaliatory discharge.* You need to find out what elements make up this cause of

action. In other words, what facts must Ms. Yoshida prove in order to prevail on a cause of action for retaliatory discharge? An early understanding of the cause of action provides an overall understanding of the materials you locate.

⇨ **A Point to Remember**   If you begin this research by looking up *hazardous waste* and *toxic waste,* you will find a mountain of information. Think about this: Should *hazardous waste* be the topic of your research? What is Ms. Yoshida's case really about? It is about retaliatory discharge or maybe wrongful discharge. It is about employment termination. Try to remain *focused* on the cause of action. The actual facts surrounding her employment termination may play a role in your research, but leave them aside until you understand all potential causes of action. Remain open minded; try not to fixate on just one cause of

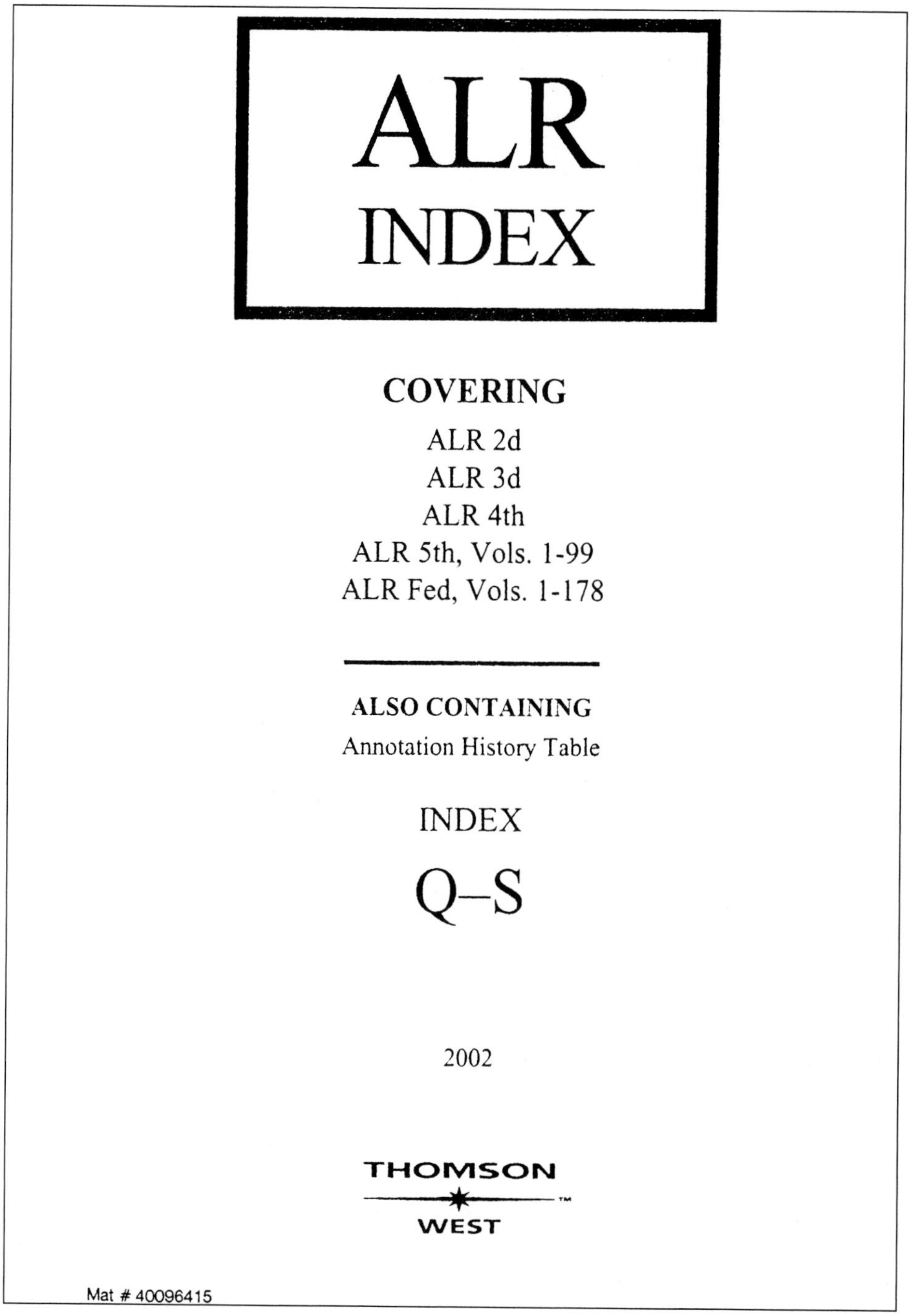

ALR
INDEX

COVERING

ALR 2d

ALR 3d

ALR 4th

ALR 5th, Vols. 1-99

ALR Fed, Vols. 1-178

ALSO CONTAINING

Annotation History Table

INDEX

Q–S

2002

THOMSON

WEST

Mat # 40096415

FIGURE 12-1
A.L.R. Cover Page for
Index *Q–S*

action, there may be others. Your supervisor will want to know all potential causes of action available to Ms. Yoshida.

The *American Law Reports* have an excellent topical index. In Figure 12-1 you see the cover page for the Index volume covering alphabet letters Q–S. When you

---

ALR INDEX

RETAIL BUSINESSES AND STORES —Cont'd
Taxes
excise tax, what constitutes a sale at retail within federal retailers' excise tax statute (26 U.S.C.A. (IRC 1954) chap 31), **93 ALR2d 1120**
intoxicating liquors, inspection, validity, construction, and application of provisions of Internal Revenue Code of 1954 authorizing entry and inspection of premises of retail liquor dealers (26 U.S.C.A. § 5146(b)) or premises where any articles or objects subject to tax are made, produced, or kept (26 U.S.C.A. § 7606), **25 ALR Fed 832**
larceny or embezzlement, retailer's failure to pay to government sales or use tax funds as constituting larceny or embezzlement, **8 ALR4th 1068**
sales and use taxes, see group Sales and use tax in this topic
Tenants, see group Landlord and tenant in this topic
Toilets and bathrooms, status of one who enters a store or other place of public resort solely for purpose of using facilities accessible to public, such as telephone, mailbox, lavatory, or the like, **93 ALR2d 784**
Trichinosis, liability of packer, food store, or restaurant for causing trichinosis, **96 ALR3d 451**
Uniform Commercial Code, who is person in business of selling goods of that kind within provision of UCC § 1-201(9) defining buyer in ordinary course of business for purposes of UCC § 9-307(1), **73 ALR3d 338**
Wholesale Businesses (this index)
Zoning
buffer provision in zoning ordinance as applicable to abutting land in adjoining municipality, **48 ALR3d 1303**
laundries, zoning regulation of self-service, **87 ALR2d 1009**

RETAINER
Attorneys
asset freeze, effect of asset freeze

RETAINER—Cont'd
Attorneys—Cont'd
obtained by Securities and Exchange Commission on attorneys' fees paid or owed by company subject to freeze, **161 ALR Fed 233**
construction and operation of attorney's general or periodic retainer fee or salary contract, **43 ALR2d 677**
Personal representative's right of retainer or setoff, against debtor's distributive share of estate, of debt barred by statute of limitations, **39 ALR2d 675**

RETAINING LIEN
Attorneys' Liens (this index)

RETAINING WALLS
Highway median barriers, governmental tort liability as to, **58 ALR4th 559, § 3(a)**
Post-transfer damage to property, vendor's liability to purchaser, **18 ALR4th 1168, § 4(b), 5, 9(b)**

RETAKING
Repossession (this index)

RETALIATION AND REVENGE
At-will employee
in-house complaints, liability under common law for wrongful or retaliatory discharge of at-will employee for in-house complaints or efforts relating to health or safety, **93 ALR5th 269**
public complaints, liability for retaliation against at-will employee for public complaints or efforts relating to health or safety, **75 ALR4th 13**
Banks, liability, under National Banking Act (12 U.S.C.A. § 93), of national bank directors for retaliation against officer or employee who discloses or refuses to commit banking irregularity, **101 ALR Fed 377**
Civil Service, prohibition, by Civil Service Reform Act of 1978, of reprisals against civil service whistleblowers (5 U.S.C.A. § 2302(b)(5)), **124 ALR Fed 381**

Consult POCKET PART for Later Annotations

283

Topic: Retaliation and Revenge

FIGURE 12-1
(continued) *A.L.R.* Index Page Showing *Retaliation.*

ALR INDEX

RETALIATION AND REVENGE
  —Cont'd
Communication between court officials or
  attendants and jurors in criminal trial as
  ground for mistrial or reversal—post-
  Parker cases, **35 ALR4th 890, § 12**
Discarge from employment or office ◄——————
  appropriate relief for retaliatory dis-
    charge under § 11(c) of
    Occupational Safety and Health Act
    (OSHA) (29 U.S.C.A. § 660(c)), **134
    ALR Fed 629**
  back pay, reductions to back pay
    awards under Title VII of Civil
    Rights Act of 1964 (42 U.S.C.A.
    § 2000e et seq.), **135 ALR Fed 1**
  excessiveness or adequacy of damages
    for wrongful termination of at will
    employee under state law, **86
    ALR5th 397**
  exhaustion of remedies, failure to
    pursue or exhaust remedies under
    union contract as affecting
    employee's right of state civil action
    for retaliatory discharge, **32 ALR4th
    350**
  garnishment order, employer's liability
    under state law for discharge of
    employee based on garnishment
    order against wages, **41 ALR5th 31**
  in-house complaints, liability under
    common law for wrongful or retalia-
    tory discharge of at-will employee
    for in-house complaints or efforts
    relating to health or safety, **93
    ALR5th 269**
  in-house counsel's right to maintain
    action for wrongful discharge, **16
    ALR5th 239**
  jury trial, right to jury trial in action for
    retaliatory discharge from employ-
    ment, **52 ALR4th 1141**
  liability, under National Banking Act
    (12 U.S.C.A. § 93), of national bank
    directors for retaliation against
    officer or employee who discloses or
    refuses to commit banking irregular-
    ity, **101 ALR Fed 377**
  limitation of actions, when statute of
    limitations commences to run as to
    cause of action for wrongful dis-

RETALIATION AND REVENGE
  —Cont'd
Discharge from employment or office
  —Cont'd
    charge, **19 ALR5th 439, § 3, 7, 8,
    10**
    maritime employees, recovery for
      retaliatory discharge of at-will mari-
      time employee, **62 ALR Fed 790**
    participant, who has "participated" in
      investigation, proceeding, or hearing
      and is thereby protected from retalia-
      tion under § 704(a) of Title VII of
      Civil Rights Act of 1964 (42
      U.S.C.A. § 2000e-3(a)), **149 ALR
      Fed 431**
    political views or conduct, liability for
      discharge of employee from private
      employment on ground of political
      views or conduct, **38 ALR5th 39**
    pre-emption of state-law wrongful dis-
      charge claim, not arising from
      whistleblowing, by § 541(a) of
      Employee Retirement Income Secu-
      rity Act of 1974 (29 U.S.C.A.
      § 1144(a)), **176 ALR Fed 433**
    professional ethics codes, wrongful
      discharge based on public policy
      derived from professional ethics
      codes, **52 ALR5th 405**
    punitive damages, availability of puni-
      tive damages in action for retaliatory
      discharge under § 16(b) of Fair
      Labor Standards Act (29 U.S.C.A.
      § 216(b)), **178 ALR Fed 15**
    Racketeer Influenced and Corrupt
      Organizations Act (RICO) (18
      U.S.C.A. § 1961-1968), liability for
      retaliation against employee for
      disclosing or refusing to commit
      wrongful act, **100 ALR Fed 667**
    same-sex sexual harassment under
      Title VII (42 U.S.C.A. § 2000e et
      seq.) of Civil Rights Act, **135 ALR
      Fed 307**
    union activities, discharge of employee
      as reprisal or retaliation for union
      organizational activities, **83 ALR2d
      532**
Whistleblowers (this index) ◄——————
  workers' compensation claim, recovery

Topic: Discharge from employment

Topic: Whistleblower

FIGURE 12-1
(continued) *A.L.R.* Index
Page Showing
Retaliation.

ALR INDEX

RETALIATION AND REVENGE
—Cont'd
Discharge from employment or office
—Cont'd
    for discharge from employment in
    retaliation for filing workers'
    compensation claim, **32 ALR4th**
    1221
Discrimination, construction and applica-
    tion of § 704(a) of Civil Rights Act of
    1964 (42 U.S.C.A. § 2000e-3(a)), mak-
    ing an unlawful employment practice to
    discriminate against individual for
    participation in equal opportunity
    proceedings or activities, **11 ALR Fed**
    316
Emotional distress, liability of employer,
    supervisor, or manager for intentionally
    or recklessly causing employee
    emotional distress, **52 ALR4th 853,**
    § 3(c, d), 8(b, c)
Eviction, retaliatory eviction of tenant for
    reporting landlord's violation of law, **23**
    ALR5th 140
Exhaustion of remedies, failure to pursue
    or exhaust remedies under union
    contract as affecting employee's right of
    state civil action for retaliatory dis-
    charge, **32 ALR4th 350**
Fair Labor Standards Act, see group Labor
    and employment in this topic
Frivolous action, bringing of frivolous civil
    claim or action as ground for discipline
    of attorney, **85 ALR4th 544, § 7**
Insurance, construction, complication, and
    operation of state retaliatory statutes
    imposing special taxes or fees on foreign
    insurers doing business within state, **30**
    ALR4th 873
Labor and employment
    at-will employee, liability for retalia-
      tion against at-will employee for
      public complaints or efforts relating
      to health or safety, **75 ALR4th 13**
    banks, liability, under National Bank-
      ing Act (12 U.S.C.A. § 93), of
      national bank directors for retaliation
      against officer or employee who
      discloses or refuses to commit bank-
      ing irregularity, **101 ALR Fed 377**
    discharge from employment or office,

RETALIATION AND REVENGE
—Cont'd
Labor and employment—Cont'd
    see group Discharge from employ-
      ment or office in this topic
    discrimination, construction and
      application of § 704(a) of Civil
      Rights Act of 1964 (42 U.S.C.A.
      § 2000e-3(a)), making an unlawful
      employment practice to discriminate
      against individual for participation in
      equal opportunity proceedings or
      activities, **11 ALR Fed 316**
    exhaustion of remedies, failure to
      pursue or exhaust remedies under
      union contract affecting employee's
      right of civil action for retaliatory
      discharge, **32 ALR4th 350**
    Fair Labor Standards Act
      complaint, Fair Labor Standards
        Act provision (29 U.S.C.A.
        § 215(a)(3)) forbidding reprisals
        against any employee who has
        filed complaint, or the like, under
        the act, **101 ALR Fed 220**
      employee's protection under
        § 15(a)(3) of Fair Labor Stan-
        dards Act (29 U.S.C.A.
        § 215(a)(3)), **101 ALR Fed 220**
    lockout of employees, or discontinu-
      ance or suspension by employer of
      all or part of his operations, as unfair
      labor practice, **20 ALR3d 403, § 4, 5**
    participant in investigation, who has
      "participated" in investigation,
      proceeding, or hearing and is thereby
      protected from retaliation under
      § 704(a) of Title VII of Civil Rights
      Act of 1964 (42 U.S.C.A. § 2000e-
      3(a)), **149 ALR Fed 431**
    RICO, liability, under Racketeer
      Influenced and Corrupt Organiza-
      tions Act (RICO) (18 U.S.C.A.
      § 1961-1968), for retaliation against
      employee for disclosing or refusing
      to commit wrongful act, **100 ALR**
      Fed 667
    sex discrimination, what constitutes
      sex discrimination in termination of
      employee so as to violate Title VII
      of Civil Rights Act of 1964 (42

Consult POCKET PART for Later Annotations

285

Topic: Labor and employment

FIGURE 12-1
(continued) *A.L.R.* Index
Page Showing
Retaliation.

Reprinted with permission of Thomson/West

look up *retaliatory discharge,* you locate the topical index references to "retaliation and revenge." Under this topic you have several good choices.

Many states have good state-specific secondary sources. Figure 12-2 shows a cover sheet from the *Summary of California Law* (a popular secondary source for California state law) and the index page where *wrongful termination* is listed. Under *wrongful termination,* the researcher is led to *whistleblowing.* This is a new term to add to the vocabulary list.

Supplement for Volume 13

SUMMARY OF CALIFORNIA LAW

Ninth Edition

---

by B. E. WITKIN

and members of the

Witkin Legal Institute

2002 SUPPLEMENT

ISSUED IN MAY, 2002

Table of Cases
Table of Code Citations
Table of Constitutions
Table of Rules, Forms, and Instructions
Index

WITKIN
LEGAL INSTITUTE

a West Group affiliate   IT- 13

FIGURE 12-2 Cover Page for Supplement for Vol. 13, *Summary of California Law*

Wrongful death
- domestic partner, **6** Torts §1209A
- killer of decedent, **6** Torts §1206
- one heir's abandonment of claim, **6** Torts §1203
- persons who may sue, statutory revision, **6** Torts §1209A
- survival of action, **12** Wills §493F
- workers' compensation remedy, **6** Torts §1197

Wrongful life
- proximate cause, **6** Torts §800A

Wrongful termination of private employment
- action for breach of covenant, **2** Agency §184G
- action on implied contract, **2** Agency §§184E, 184F
- administrative regulation in violation of public policy, effect of, **2** Agency §184K-3
- after-acquired evidence of employee's misconduct, **2** Agency §164A
- *Blom* case, **2** Agency §184J
- constructive discharge, **2** Agency §§184M, 184N, 184-O
- deceit, recovery for, **2** Agency §184D
- demotion, wrongful, **2** Agency §184F
- discipline, wrongful, **2** Agency §184F
- doctor advocating appropriate health care, **2** Agency §170D
- embezzler, recovery for employee's report of, **2** Agency §184-I
- employee participation in illegal scheme, **2** Agency.§184-I-1
- fraud, recovery for, **2** Agency §184D
- *Gantt* case, **2** Agency §184K
- illegality, employee participation in, **2** Agency §184-I-1
- independent contractors, application to, **2** Agency §184K-2
- instructions (BAJI), **2** Agency §184P
- literacy problem, employee disclosing, **2** Agency §170C

Wrongful termination of private employment—Cont'd
- misconduct, after-acquired evidence of, **2** Agency §164A
- nonemployers, actions for violation of public policy against, **2** Agency §184K-1
- regulation in violation of public policy, effect of, **2** Agency §184K-3
- retaliatory discharge of in-house counsel, **2** Agency §184L
- school, employee appearing at child's, **2** Agency §170B
- tort action repudiated, **2** Agency §§184A, 184B, 184C; **6** Torts §1357
- unclean hands doctrine, **2** Agency §184-I-1
- violation of law or public policy, **2** Agency §§184H, 184-I, 184J, 184K, 184K-1, 184K-3
- volunteer firefighter, **2** Agency §168
- whistleblowing, retaliation for, **2** Agency §§184-I, 187A

Topic: Whistleblowing, retaliation for

Y

Y2K Act, **5** Torts §§270A, 270B

Year 2000 problem, immunity from liability due to disclosures regarding, **5** Torts §303H

Youth Authority
- gang members, registration of, **10** P & C §829A
- registration of gang members, **10** P & C §829A

Z

Zoning
- interim ordinance, **8** Const Law §837
- local zoning: conditions must be reasonable, **8** Const Law §835
- local zoning: sexually oriented businesses, **8** Const Law §835
- nudist camps, **8** Const Law §824
- sexually oriented businesses, **8** Const Law §835
- transient commercial use of residential property, **8** Const Law §847A

References are to volume, chapter title, and section; see chapter abbreviations at beginning of Table of Cases

[667]

Reprinted from the *Summary of California Law, 9th edition,* with permission of the B.E. Witkin Article Sixth Testamentary Trust

FIGURE 12-2
(continued) *Summary of California Law*, Index Page, Showing *Whistleblowing.*

The Index to *Summary of California Law* directs the reader to Volume 2, Section 184-I. Figure 12-3 shows the cover page from Volume 2, Section 187A and the text of Section 187A. Notice Section (b) refers to a whistleblowing statute, refers to specific textual material, and refers to a case. This is a great deal of good information easily located in one resource.

Supplement for Volume 2

SUMMARY OF CALIFORNIA LAW

Ninth Edition

by B. E. WITKIN

and members of the

Witkin Legal Institute

2002 SUPPLEMENT

ISSUED IN MAY, 2002

See Vol. 13 Pamphlet for Supplement to
Table of Cases
Table of Code Citations
Table of Constitutions
Table of Rules, Forms, and Instructions
Index

WITKIN
LEGAL INSTITUTE

a West Group affiliate   IT- 2

FIGURE 12-3 Cover Page for *Summary of California Law,* a Secondary Resource

New York Times Co., Time, and Garrison cases:
Cross-Reference: 7 Summary (9th), *Constitutional Law,* §302 et seq.

[§187A]   (New)   Whistleblower Statutes.

(a) *False Claims Act.* The 1987 Legislature enacted Govt.C. 12650 et seq. to impose civil liability for presenting certain false claims to public entities in California. (See generally Cal. Civil Practice, 2 Torts, §§31:48, 31:49; C.E.B., 1 Wrongful Employment Termination Practice 2d, §4.10 et seq.) Govt.C. 12653(b) prohibits an employer from discharging or otherwise discriminating against an employee because of lawful acts done by the employee on behalf of himself or others (1) in disclosing information to a government or law enforcement agency, or (2) in furthering a false claims action under the statute.

In *Southern Calif. Rapid Transit Dist. v. Superior Court* (1994) 30 C.A.4th 713, 36 C.R.2d 665, plaintiffs, who were career investigators formerly employed by defendant public transit district, alleged they were wrongfully terminated in retaliation for reporting suspected forgery, fraud, mismanagement, and an official cover-up in connection with the certification of a minority contractor. The trial judge granted defendant's motion for summary judgment on plaintiffs' claim for wrongful termination in violation of their federal liberty interests under 42 U.S.C., §1983. However, the judge denied defendant's motion for summary judgment on plaintiffs' wrongful termination claims for violations of Govt.C. 12653(b) and their free speech rights under the federal civil rights statute, and defendant petitioned the Court of Appeal for mandamus relief. *Held,* petition denied.

(1) *False Claims Act claim.* Plaintiffs stated a valid claim for wrongful termination in violation of public policy:

(a) Plaintiffs' action involved a ''false claim'' within the meaning of Govt.C. 12653(b). A claim includes any request for ''money, property, or services'' from the state or any political subdivision. Plaintiffs alleged that the contractor provided false documentation to justify its claimed status as a minority contractor, entitling it to be considered for a special ''set aside'' contract, which, if received, would doubtless constitute property received from a state or a political subdivision. As a statute obviously designed to prevent fraud on the public treasury, Govt.C. 12653(b) should be given the broadest possible construction consistent with that purpose. (30 C.A.4th 724, 725.)

(b) A wrongful termination action is viable where the employee alleges that he was terminated for reporting illegal activity that could cause harm, not only to the interest of the employer, but also to the public; and an action brought under Govt.C. 12653(b) is inherently such an action. (30 C.A.4th 725.)

(c) That plaintiffs were at-will employees subject to termination without cause did not immunize defendant from liability under Govt.C.

[135]

FIGURE 12-3
(continued)   Text
Material (Section 187A)
from *Summary of
California Law*

820.2 (governmental tort immunity for injuries resulting from exercise of discretion; see 5 *Summary* (9th), *Torts,* §247). Finding that plaintiffs' discharge was simply a discretionary act to which qualified immunity applied, even though the discharge was a retaliatory act expressly prohibited by Govt.C. 12653(b), would emasculate the entire effect and purpose of the statute. (30 C.A.4th 725, 726.)

(2) *Federal civil rights claims.*

(a) There were triable issues of fact whether plaintiffs' termination violated their free speech rights. The content, form, and context of plaintiffs' accusations constituted matters of public, rather than personal, concern. No substantial issue arose as to workplace disruption. And triable issues whether the termination was retaliatory were presented by plaintiffs' exemplary employment records, the absence of any other cause for their termination, and the circumstances of the termination itself. (30 C.A.4th 729, 730.)

(b) However, there were no triable issues of fact whether plaintiffs' termination also violated their liberty interests. Their supervisor's act of having them escorted out of defendant's office was insufficient to show that some charge of misconduct had been asserted that caused such a stigma to their reputations that it impaired their ability to make a living. (30 C.A.4th 730.)

(c) Defendant had no qualified immunity under federal law, because its actions violated a clearly established statutory or constitutional right of which a reasonable person should have known. (30 C.A.4th 730, 731.)

See *LeVine v. Weis* (1998) 68 C.A.4th 758, 764, 80 C.R.2d 439 [teacher's complaint about understaffing was protected by Act, and school district was "person" subject to civil penalties under Act]; *LeVine v. Weis* (2001) 90 C.A.4th 201, 207, 108 C.R.2d 562 [appeal after remand, reaffirming original ruling, but holding that Act applies only to employers; thus, individuals, including defendant school district supervisors, are not subject to liability under Act]; 90 A.L.R.5th 687 ["public employers" or "public employees" under state whistleblower protection acts].

(b) *Whistleblowing by Employees and Job Applicants of Local Government Agencies.* No local government agency officer, manager, or supervisor may take a reprisal action against any local government agency employee or job applicant who files a complaint alleging gross mismanagement or significant waste of funds, an abuse of authority, or a substantial and specific danger to public health or safety. (Govt.C. 53298(a), amended in 1993.) A reprisal action includes any disciplinary action, including firing. (Govt.C. 53296(b), (j), amended in 1993.)

(c) *California Whistleblower Protection Act.* Under the California Whistleblower Protection Act (Govt.C. 8547 et seq.), enacted as the Reporting of Improper Governmental Activities Act in 1993 and renamed and amended in 1999, state employees are encouraged to disclose improper governmental activities to the State Auditor for investigation. No

[136]

FIGURE 12-3

(continued) Text Material (Section 187A) from *Summary of California Law.*

employee may use his official authority or influence to interfere, through acts of reprisal or coercion, with another employee's right to disclose these matters. (Govt.C. 8547.3(a).) A person who intentionally engages in acts of reprisal, coercion, or similar acts against a state employee or applicant for state employment for having disclosed improper governmental activities is subject to fines, imprisonment, and a civil action for damages, including punitive damages, by the injured party. (Govt.C. 8547.8(b), (c); see *Hood v. Hacienda La Puente Unified School Dist.* (1998) 65 C.A.4th 435, 439, 76 C.R.2d 448 [failure of dismissed teacher to pursue administrative remedies under Govt.C. 8547.3(c) precluded civil action for violation of statute].) (On employee's right to disclose information to government or law enforcement agency, see text, §313.)

Statements contained in the State Auditor's investigative audit and report, including those of whistleblowers, are subject to the absolute privilege for publications in official proceedings authorized by law (C.C. 47(b); see 5 *Summary* (9th), *Torts,* §512 et seq.). (*Braun v. Bureau of State Audits* (1998) 67 C.A.4th 1382, 1388, 79 C.R.2d 791.)

(d) *Whistleblower Protection Act.* The Whistleblower Protection Act (Govt.C. 9149.20 et seq.), enacted in 1999 and similar in name and substance to Govt.C. 8547 et seq., supra, also prohibits state or local governmental employees from using official authority or influence to interfere with a person's right to disclose improper governmental activities to an investigating committee of the Legislature. (Govt.C. 9149.23(a).) An employee violating this prohibition is liable to the offended party for civil damages. (Govt.C. 9149.23(b).)

The prohibited interference includes ''intimidating, threatening, coercing, commanding, or attempting to intimidate, threaten, coerce, or command'' the person for the purpose of interfering with the person's right to disclose the information. (Govt.C. 9149.23(a).)

''Use of official authority or influence'' means promising to confer, or conferring, any benefit; effecting, or threatening to effect, any reprisal; or taking, or directing others to take, or recommending, processing, or approving, any personnel action, including, but not limited to, appointment, promotion, transfer, assignment, performance evaluation, suspension, or other disciplinary action. (Govt.C. 9149.22(e).)

''Improper governmental activity'' means any activity by a governmental agency or by an employee that is undertaken in the performance of the employee's official duties, whether or not that action is within the scope of employment, and that (1) is in violation of any state or federal law or regulation, including, but not limited to, corruption, malfeasance, bribery, theft of government property, fraudulent claims, fraud, coercion, conversion, malicious prosecution, misuse of government property, or wilful omission to perform duty, or (2) is economically wasteful, or involves gross misconduct, incompetency, or inefficiency. (Govt.C. 9149.22(c).)

[137]

FIGURE 12-3 (continued) Text Material (Section 187A) from *Summary of California Law*

Reprinted from the *Summary of California Law, 9ᵗʰ edition,* with permission of the B.E. Witkin Article Sixth Testamentary Trust

12-7 EFFECTIVE USE OF THE INDEX VOLUMES ENABLES YOU TO ADD TERMS TO YOUR RESEARCH VOCABULARY LIST

As you look at the index pages, you may locate terms that are not on your initial list, but look interesting. Add them to your list and pursue them.

Sample pages from the Index to *Corpus Juris Secundum* appear in Figures 12-4 and 12-5. Notice that the same general topic is covered differently in each index.

CORPUS JURIS SECUNDUM

A CONTEMPORARY STATEMENT OF
AMERICAN LAW
AS DERIVED FROM
REPORTED CASES AND LEGISLATION

2002
General Index

R to Z

THOMSON

WEST

40034423

FIGURE 12-4 *C.J.S.*
General Index Cover
Page (*R to Z*)

Topic: Wrongful Discharge

Consult Correlation Tables in text volumes for references to materials published after this index.

757

FIGURE 12-4
(continued) *C.J.S.*
Index Page Showing
Wrongful Discharge

Reprinted with permission of Thomson/West

CORPUS JURIS SECUNDUM

A CONTEMPORARY STATEMENT OF
AMERICAN LAW
AS DERIVED FROM
REPORTED CASES AND LEGISLATION

2002
General Index

D to F

THOMSON
WEST

FIGURE 12-5   *C.J.S.*
General Index Cover
Page (*D* to *F*)

Figure 12-4 is a page from the General Index to *Corpus Juris Secundum* and the page in the Index where *Wrongful Discharge* is located. The terms *retaliation* and *retaliatory* are not in the Index. This is when the vocabulary list becomes important. Legal researchers must be armed with as many vocabulary terms as possible.

Figure 12-5 shows the cover page to the General Index for alphabet letters *D* to *F* and an index page. As you noticed in Figure 12-4, *Wrongful Discharge* refers the

EMP

EMPLOYER-EMPLOYEE RELATIONSHIP—Cont'd
Wages and other remuneration—Cont'd
temporary reduction, restoration to old wages. **Employer § 164**
termination of employment or relation
consent, termination by, as affecting right. **Employer § 172**
profits, computation. **Employer § 171**
recovery in case of. **Employer § 172**
time
computation of profits on which based. **Employer § 167**
payment, **Employer § 177**
unit of time basis. **Employer § 164**
time laborers, presumption of payment, **Employer § 180**
tips, compensation consisting of including, **Employer § 132**
traveling to and from work, right to recover compensation for time spent in. **Employer § 153**
unions, organization for purpose of, fixing rate, **Employer § 164**
unit of time
contractor fixing amount, **Employer § 164**
salary proportionate to. **Employer § 27**
vacation and pay, unused vacation time, **Employer § 151**
waiver
breach of employment, right to sue for, **Employer § 30**
claim for commissions, **Employer § 161**
deductions or forfeitures, **Employer § 161, 162**
discharge of employee, right of employer to for breach of contract or duty, **Employer § 57**
lie detector tests, **Employer § 5**
weekly employment
recovery for days of actual services. **Employer § 164**
reduction within term. **Employer § 164**
work and rate scale, **Employer § 161**
Waiver
nonperformance of contract by employee. **Employer § 127**
wages and other remuneration, above
Warning and instructing servant, independent contractors, latent dangers. **Employer § 251**
Whistle-blowing, discharge of employees, public policy considerations. **Employer § 69**
Workers' Compensation (this index)
Writing, contract of employment, **Employer § 28**
Written addition of contract, **Employer § 24**
Wrongful act, refusal to perform, discharge of employee, public policy considerations. **Employer § 77**
Wrongful discharge
see also, Title Index to Labor Relations
actions and remedies. **Employer § 80** et seq.
administrative remedies
exclusive, **Employer § 80**
exhaustion of, conditions precedents, **Employer § 84**
admissibility of evidence, **Employer § 90**
attorney fees. **Employer § 97**
burden of proof, **Employer § 89**
conditions precedent, **Employer § 82** et seq.
considerations, general considerations, **Employer § 80**
contract remedies, exhaustion of, conditions precedent, **Employer § 83**
contractual relationship. **Employer § 81**
damages, **Employer § 90, 98** et seq.
elements of damages, **Employer § 100**
equitable relief in general, **Employer § 94**
evidence, **Employer § 90, 91**
admissibility under pleading, **Employer § 90**

EMPLOYER-EMPLOYEE RELATIONSHIP—Cont'd
Wrongful discharge—Cont'd
actions and remedies—Cont'd
exhaustion
administrative remedies, conditions precedent, **Employer § 84**
contract remedies, conditions precedent, **Employer § 83**
fraud or deceit, wrongful termination, **Employer § 80**
instructions, **Employer § 93**
National Labor Relations Act, preemption, **Employer § 37**
nature of action, **Employer § 81**
nominal damages, **Employer § 102**
other employment as ground for mitigation of damages, **Employer § 105**
parties, **Employer § 85**
pleading, **Employer § 88**
presumptions, **Employer § 89**
questions of law and fact, **Employer § 92**
random drug test, **Employer § 78**
reinstatement, **Employer § 94**
rescission of contract, **Employer § 95**
review, general considerations, **Employer § 80**
time to sue, **Employer § 87**
weight and sufficiency of evidence, **Employer § 91**
after-acquired evidence
employee's misconduct, as bar to recovery, **Employer § 86**
retaliatory discharge actions, **Employer § 86**
attorney fees and actions for, **Employer § 97**
burden of proof, action for wrongful discharge, **Employer § 89**
damages, **Employer § 90, 98** et seq.
commencement of suit before expiration of term, **Employer § 101**
elements of damages, **Employer § 100**
jury question, **Employer § 93**
mitigation of damages in general. **Employer § 104**
nominal damages, **Employer § 102**
other employment as ground for reduction of damages, **Employer § 105**
pleading, matters and mitigation of damages, **Employer § 92**
procedural requirements for discharge, violation, **Employer § 98**
public policy considerations in general. **Employer § 99**
punitive damages. **Employer § 103**
reduction of damages, other employment as ground for, **Employer § 105**
defenses arising after discharge. **Employer § 86**
elements of damages and action for. **Employer § 100**
expiration of term, commencement of suit before. **Employer § 101**
federal preemption in general. **Employer § 37**
governing law. **Employer § 36**
instructions and action for. **Employer § 93**
justification, burden of proof, wrongful discharge, **Employer § 89**
mitigation of damages, **Employer § 104**
nominal damages, **Employer § 102**
performance, rescission, partial performance. **Employer § 95**
pleading in action for. **Employer § 88**
police officers, **MuncCorp § 523**
presumptions and actions for, **Employer § 89**
public policy considerations, actions, **Employer § 89**
punitive damages. **Employer § 103**
questions of law and fact in actions for. **Employer § 92**

Consult Correlation Tables in text volumes for references to materials published after this index.

243

Topic: retaliatory discharge actions

Topic: Wrongful Discharge

FIGURE 12-5
(continued) *C.J.S.*
Index Page

EMP

EMPLOYER-EMPLOYEE RELATIONSHIP—Cont'd
Wrongful discharge—Cont'd
    reinstatement of employee wrongfully discharged. **Employer § 94**
    review in actions for. **Employer § 96**
    summary judgment, affidavits and proof in actions for. **Judgments § 260-267**
    tender of performances conditions precedent to action for. **Employer § 82**
    unemployment compensation, see. **Title Index to Social Security and Public Welfare**
    weight of evidence and action, weight and sufficiency of action for. **Employer § 91**

EMPLOYER ORGANIZATIONS
Assessments, dues, fines. **Labor § 18**

EMPLOYERS AND EMPLOYEES
Employment (this index)

EMPLOYERS' LIABILITY FOR INJURIES TO EMPLOYEES
Generally. **EmployInj § 1 et seq.**
Accidental injuries
    nature and cause of injury. **EmployInj § 38**
Actions and remedies. **EmployInj § 312 et seq.**
    considerations, general considerations. **EmployInj § 312 et seq.**
    Federal Employers' Liability Act, governing law. **EmployInj § 9**
    fellow employees, liability of master for injuries by. **EmployInj § 167 et seq.**
    governing law. **EmployInj § 3**
    injuries to servant. **EmployInj § 312 et seq.**
    injury in unlawful act or employment. **EmployInj § 43 et seq.**
    misidentification as perpetrator of crime, cognizable cause of action. **EmployInj § 312**
    negligence, requisite, statutes. **EmployInj § 5**
    relationship, necessity for relation of employer and employee. **EmployInj § 13**
Acts or omissions
    persons compulsorily employed, nature and cause of injury. **EmployInj § 40**
    third persons, nature and cause of injury. **EmployInj § 39**
Age. **EmployInj § 152 et seq.**
Agreement of master to give warning. **EmployInj § 141**
Agricultural labors, safe place to work, statute requiring employer to furnish as applicable. **EmployInj § 66**
Aliens, actions and remedies. **Aliens § 48**
Animals, assumption of risk, knowledge of vicious propensity. **EmployInj § 97**
Assault and battery, fellow employees, liability of master. **EmployInj § 170**
Assumption of risk. **EmployInj § 210 et seq.**
    abrogation of defense
        Federal Employers' Liability Act. **EmployInj § 212**
        state employers' liability act. **EmployInj § 213**
    alteration of place of work, employee engaged in. **EmployInj § 225**
    appliances. Tools, machinery and appliances, below
    assurances of master. **EmployInj § 257**
        contributory negligence, reliance on. **EmployInj § 279**

EMPLOYERS' LIABILITY FOR INJURIES TO EMPLOYEES—Cont'd
Assumption of risk—Cont'd
    assurances or representations of employer. **EmployInj § 257 et seq.**
    attempt to save employer's property, knowledge of danger as affecting. **EmployInj § 235**
    basis of doctrine. **EmployInj § 210**
    changing condition of place as work progresses. **EmployInj § 225**
    commands or threats
        compliance with. **EmployInj § 253 et seq.**
        absence of knowledge and appreciation of danger. **EmployInj § 253 et seq.**
        appreciation of danger. **EmployInj § 255**
        effect of knowledge and appreciation of danger. **EmployInj § 255, 256**
        equal or superior knowledge of danger. **EmployInj § 255**
        jury questions. **EmployInj § 339**
        knowledge of danger, effect of. **EmployInj § 255**
        remaining in service after notice or complaint. **EmployInj § 256**
        requisite and sufficiency of command. **EmployInj § 254**
        risk outside scope of employment. **EmployInj § 260**
        remaining in service after notice of complaint. **EmployInj § 256**
    complaint, knowledge of danger, continuing to work after. **EmployInj § 251, 252**
    complaint by servant of defect or danger, instructions on law applicable. **EmployInj § 346**
    compliance with commands or threats. **EmployInj § 253 et seq.**
    compliance with negligent order, jury questions. **EmployInj § 339**
    concurrent negligence
        employers' negligence. **EmployInj § 215**
        master, instructions of jury on. **EmployInj § 346**
    considerations, general considerations. **EmployInj § 210**
    constitutional provisions, actions for injuries to servant. **EmployInj § 339**
    construction work, ordinary risk incident to. **EmployInj § 225**
    continuing to work after knowledge of danger. **EmployInj § 250 et seq.**
        burden of proof. **EmployInj § 327**
        jury question. **EmployInj § 339**
        notice of complaint. **EmployInj § 251**
        promise to remedy defect or remove danger. **EmployInj § 252**
    continuing to work on promise to repair defect, presumptions. **EmployInj § 328**
    contract, doctrine as based on. **EmployInj § 210**
    contributory negligence. **EmployInj § 340**
        distinguished. **EmployInj § 210**
        instructions to jury. **EmployInj § 346**
    dangerous machinery
        occupational places, knowledge of danger, continuing work after. **EmployInj § 250 et seq.**
        occupations or places
        instructions to jury. **EmployInj § 346**
        jury questions. **EmployInj § 339**
        knowledge of danger. **EmployInj § 238 et seq.**
            continuing work after, compliance with command. **EmployInj § 255**
            jury questions. **EmployInj § 339**

Consult Correlation Tables in text volumes for references to materials published after this index.

244

FIGURE 12-5
(continued) *C.J.S.* Index Page

Reprinted with permission of Thomson/West

researcher to *Employer-Employee Relationship*. When this new topic is located, you see that retaliatory discharge actions are covered under *Employer § 86*.

Figure 12-6 is taken from Volume 30 of *Corpus Juris Secundum*. As you may remember, this general encyclopedia set is arranged alphabetically by topic. *Employer-Employee Section 68* is located in Volume 30. Figure 12-6 is the first page of the entry on "Whistle blowing in general."

Topic: Whistle blowing in general →

| § 68 | CORPUS JURIS SECUNDUM |

the Commonwealth that is threatened for purposes of the public policy exception to the at-will employment doctrine. McLaughlin v. Gastrointestinal Specialists, Inc., 561 Pa. 307, 750 A.2d 283 (2000).

Car dealership's demand that employee, on pain of dismissal, pay fine as restitution for bad loans, even if unfair, did not rise to level of public policy violation which could form exception to employment at-will doctrine. Reese v. Tom Hesser Chevrolet-BMW, 413 Pa. Super. 168, 604 A.2d 1072 (1992).

Burton v. Exam Center Indus. & General Medical Clinic, Inc., 2000 UT 18, 994 P.2d 1261 (Utah 2000).

Roberts v. Dudley, 140 Wash. 2d 58, 993 P.2d 901 (2000).

Smith v. Bates Technical College, 139 Wash. 2d 793, 991 P.2d 1135 (2000).

Warnek v. ABB Combustion Engineering Services, Inc., 137 Wash. 2d 450, 972 P.2d 453 (1999).

Reninger v. State Dept. of Corrections, 134 Wash. 2d 437, 951 P.2d 782 (1998).

Selix v. Boeing Co., 82 Wash. App. 736, 919 P.2d 620 (Div. 1 1996).

§ 69 Whistle blowing in general

In some jurisdictions, no cause of action exists for "private whistleblowing," whistleblowing in a private work environment.[54.5]

Some statutes which prohibit the discharge of an employee for whistle blowing provide that the employee's participation in the wrongdoing is a defense to a retaliation claim, rather than an exception to the statute's protection.[54.5]

A whistle-blower's act is a remedial statute which may be applied retroactively.[64.10]

In order for an employee to be afforded protection as a whistleblower, he or she must strictly comply with the dictates of the whistleblower statute.[64.15]

Some whistleblowing statutes prohibiting the discharge of an employee because the employee refuses to carry out a directive are limited to situations involving a physically dangerous condition.[64.17]

An absentee employer may not avoid liability under a whistleblower statute by delegating to its employee responsibility for enforcement of safety laws.[64.20]

A whistleblower statute does not protect an employee who has been discharged because of an erroneous perception that he or she has reported a violation of law, regulations, or rules to a public body.[64.25]

Protections for contractor employees.

An employee of a contractor may not be discharged, demoted, or otherwise discriminated against as a reprisal for disclosing to a Member of Congress or an authorized official of an agency of the Department of Justice information relating to a substantial violation of law related to a contract, including the competition for or negotiation of a contract.[88.1]

False Claims Act.

Under the False Claims Act,[88.5] no employer may discriminate against any employee who makes a complaint of fraud to the government, in the terms and conditions of employment, because of such lawful acts done in furtherance of an action filed or to be filed pursuant to the Act.[88.10]

[54.5]Tex.—Thompson v. El Centro Del Barrio, App.-San Antonio, 905 S.W.2d 356, reh. over., err. den., reh. of writ of err. over.

[54.5]Fla.—Martin County v. Edenfield, 609 So.2d 27.

[64.10]Mich.—Chandler v. Dowell Schlumberger Inc., 456 Mich. 395, 572 N.W.2d 210, 13 I.E.R. Cas. (BNA) 1059, 135 Lab. Cas. (CCH) ¶ 58385 (1998).

To case pending on appeal
Fla.—Walsh v. Arrow Air, Inc., App. 3 Dist., 629 So.2d 144, quashed on oth. grds. 645 So.2d 422.

[64.15]Ohio—Contreras v. Ferro Corp., 652 N.E.2d 940, 73 Ohio St.3d 244.

[64.17]**Refusal to issue check not protected**
Me.—Devoid v. Clair Buick Cadillac, Inc., 669 A.2d 749.

[64.20]N.Y.—Granser v. Box Tree South Ltd., 623 N.Y.S.2d 977, 164 Misc.2d 191.

[64.25]Mich.—Chandler v. Schlumberger, 542 N.W.2d 310, 214 Mich.App. 111.

[88.1]10 U.S.C.A. § 2409, as amended in 1994, whistleblower protections for contractor employees of Department of Defense, Coast Guard, and National Aeronautics and Space Administration.

41 U.S.C.A. § 265, added in 1994, whistleblower protections for contractor employees of civilian agencies.

[88.5]31 U.S.C.A. § 3730(h).

[88.10]**Protection for intracorporate complaint**
U.S.—Neal v. Honeywell, Inc., N.D.Ill., 826 F.Supp. 266, affd. 33 F.3d 860.

Company president not "employer"
U.S.—U.S. ex rel. Lamar v. Burke, E.D.Mo., 894 F.Supp. 1345.

Elements of prima facie case of retaliation
U.S.—Eberhardt v. Integrated Design & Const., Inc., 167 F.3d 861, 15 I.E.R. Cas. (BNA) 687 (4th Cir. 1999).

What constitutes "protected activity"
(1) An employee engaged in a protected activity, as required for a prima facie case of retaliation under the False Claims Act, when he made clear to the employer prior to his termination that he intended to bring a qui tam action under the Act and that the Act protected him from retaliation.
U.S.—Eberhardt v. Integrated Design & Const., Inc., 167 F.3d 861, 15 I.E.R. Cas. (BNA) 687 (4th Cir. 1999).

8

2002 Cumulative Supplement

FIGURE 12-6 *C.J.S.*
Text

Reprinted with permission of Thomson/West

Figure 12-7 shows the cover page for the Cumulative Annual Pocket Part for Volume 30 and pages from the supplement. Remember to go to this pocket part to locate the most current information.

Figure 12-4 through Figure 12-7 are all from one resource: *Corpus Juris Secundum.* The next series of figures are from *American Jurisprudence 2d.* Notice the differences in the Index pages and the general vocabulary.

CORPUS JURIS SECUNDUM™

1998
Cumulative
Annual Pocket Part

Volume 30

NOTICE

**Index for titles contained in this
Pocket Part consult General Index.**

Insert this Pocket Part in back of volume
It replaces prior pocket part

ST. PAUL, MINN.
WEST GROUP

FIGURE 12-7 *C.J.S.*
Cover Page for 1998
Pocket Part
Supplement
Containing Text of
Volume 30

Topic: Whistle Blowing in General

4. Free access to courts not valid public policy

Ill.—Paris v. Cherry Payment Systems, Inc., 1 Dist., 638 N.E.2d 351, 202 Ill.Dec. 705, 265 Ill.App.3d 383.

page 113

Thus, where a public policy is sufficiently clear and compelling, the doctrine of employment at will can be overriden.[5.5]

5.5 Removing drunk drivers from road

Public policy in favor of removing drunk drivers from the roads is sufficiently clear and compelling to override doctrine of employment at will when employee is discharged because, she has informed police of likelihood that her superior at work is going to be driving while intoxicated.

Ohio—Stephenson v. Litton Sys., Inc., 2 Dist., 646 N.E.2d 259, 97 Ohio App.3d 125.

Encouraging citizens to save persons from serious bodily injury or death

Discharge of at-will employee for leaving armored truck unattended in violation of company rule in order to save woman from life-threatening hostage situation violated public policy of encouraging citizens to save persons from serious bodily injury or death.

Wash.—Gardner v. Loomis Armored Inc., 913 P.2d 377, 128 Wash.2d 931.

6. Fla.—Jarvinen v. HCA Allied Clinical Laboratories, Inc., App. 4 Dist., 552 So.2d 241.

7. Ohio—Greeley v. Miami Valley Maintenance Contractors, Inc., 551 N.E.2d 981, 49 Ohio St.3d 228.

The discharge of employees for violating an employer's no-dating policy has been held not to violate a statute forbidding employer discrimination against employees because of participation in legal recreational activities pursued outside of work hours.[7.5]

7.5 N.Y.—State v. Wal-Mart Stores Inc., 3 Dept., 621 N.Y.S.2d 158, 207 A.D.2d 150.

page 114

15. Wash.—Selix v. Boeing Co., Div. 1, 919 P.2d 620, 82 Wash.App. 736, review den. 930 P.2d 1230, 130 Wash.2d 1024.

Unreasonable searches and seizures

For purposes of public policy exception to at-will employment doctrine, state and federal constitutional safeguards against unreasonable searches and seizures do not constitute clear mandate of public policy, in private employment context and privacy, though important value of society, is too amorphous standard to qualify as clear mandate of public policy.

N.J.—Hennessey v. Coastal Eagle Point Oil Co., A.D., 589 A.2d 170, 247 N.J.Super. 297, affd. 609 A.2d 11, 129 N.J. 81.

Sufficient description required

Constitutional or statutory provision must sufficiently describe type of prohibited conduct to enable employer to know fundamental public policies that are expressed in that law in order for there to be claim for wrongful termination in violation of public policy.

Cal.—Sequoia Ins. Co. v. Superior Court (Norden), 6 Dist., 16 Cal.Rptr.2d 888, 13 C.A.4th 1472, review den.

The conduct of the employee, not the employer, must be evaluated in assessing the public policy component of a wrongful termination claim.[17.5]

17.5 U.S.—Frechette v. Wal-Mart Stores, Inc., D.N.H., 925 F.Supp. 95.

---

22. Unfair action

Car dealership's demand that employee, on pain of dismissal, pay fine as restitution for bad loans, even if unfair, did not rise to level of public policy violation which could form exception to employment at-will doctrine.

Pa.—Reese v. Tom Hesser Chevrolet-BMW, 604 A.2d 1072, 413 Pa.Super. 168.

In determining whether a discharge of an at-will employee is in violation of public policy so as to allow an employee to recover for wrongful discharge, courts must find and not create public policy.[25.5]

25.5 Wash.—Selix v. Boeing Co., Div. 1, 919 P.2d 620, 82 Wash.App. 736, review den. 930 P.2d 1230, 130 Wash.2d 1024.

26. U.S.—Johnson v. Baxter Healthcare Corp., N.D.Ill., 907 F.Supp. 271.

page 115

27. Despite availability of other remedies

U.S.—Davies v. American Airlines, Inc., C.A.10(Okl.), 971 F.2d 463, cert. den. 113 S.Ct. 2439, 508 U.S. 950, 124 L.Ed.2d 657.

29. U.S.—Cullen v. E.H. Friedrich Co., Inc., D.Mass., 910 F.Supp. 815.

Demotion.

An employer's implied-in-fact agreement to demote only for good cause does not violate public policy.[35.5]

35.5 Cal.—Scott v. Pacific Gas and Elec. Co., 46 Cal.Rptr.2d 427, 904 P.2d 834, 11 C. 4th 454.

37. Cal.—Sequoia Ins. Co. v. Superior Court (Norden), 6 Dist., 16 Cal.Rptr.2d 888, 13 C.A.4th 1472, review den.

page 116

39. Common law

(1)Pennsylvania common law regarding tortious invasion of privacy was source of Pennsylvania public policy for private employee's action to recover for wrongful discharge for refusing to consent to urinalysis screening for drug use and searches of personal property pursuant to employer's drug and alcohol policy.

U.S.—Borse v. Piece Goods Shop, Inc., C.A.3(Pa.), 963 F.2d 611, am., reh. den.

(2) Other cases.

Ohio—Painter v. Graley, 639 N.E.2d 51, 70 Ohio St.3d 377, reconsideration den. 640 N.E.2d 849, 70 Ohio St.3d 1477, reconsideration stricken 658 N.E.2d 1063, 74 Ohio St.3d 1493 (per A. William Sweeney, J. with one Justice concurring, one Justice concurring in judgment, and two Justices concurring in part and dissenting in part), overruling Tulloh v. Goodyear Atomic Corp., 584 N.E.2d 729, 62 Ohio St.3d 531.

Various sources

Ohio—Painter v. Graley, 639 N.E.2d 51, 70 Ohio St.3d 377, reconsideration den. 640 N.E.2d 849, 70 Ohio St.3d 1477, reconsideration stricken 658 N.E.2d 1063, 74 Ohio St.3d 1493 (per A. William Sweeney, J. with one Justice concurring, and two Justices concurring in part and dissenting in part), overruling Tulloh v. Goodyear Atomic Corp., 584 N.E.2d 729, 62 Ohio St.3d 531.

41. Ohio—Painter v. Graley, 639 N.E.2d 51, 70 Ohio St.3d 377, reconsideration den. 640 N.E.2d 849, 70 Ohio St.3d 1477, reconsideration stricken 658 N.E.2d 1063, 74 Ohio St.3d 1493 (per A. William Sweeney, J., with one Justice concurring, one Justice concurring in part and dissenting in part), overruling Tulloh v. Goodyear Atomic Corp., 584 N.E.2d 729, 62 Ohio St.3d 531.

46. U.S.—Adler v. American Standard Corp., D.C.Md., 538 F.Supp. 572, on subs. app. 830 F.2d 1303.

---

§ 69. Whistle Blowing in General

48. Report of abuse after discharge sufficient

Mich.—Lynd v. Adapt, Inc., 503 N.W.2d 766, 200 Mich.App. 305.

50. No established public policy exception

Pa.—Holewinski v. Children's Hosp. of Pittsburgh, 649 A.2d 712, 437 Pa.Super. 174, app. den. 659 A.2d 560, 540 Pa. 641.

page 117

52. Partner in partnership that has business relationship with employee's employer

N.J.—Barratt v. Cushman & Wakefield of New Jersey, Inc., 675 A.2d 1094, 144 N.J. 120.

53. Mich.—Covell v. Spengler, 366 N.W.2d 76, 141 Mich.App. 76, remd. 374 N.W.2d 420, 422 Mich. 977, on remand 396 N.W.2d 473, 153 Mich.App. 536, app. den.

Public policy claim preempted

Mich.—Dudewicz v. Norris-Schmid, Inc., 503 N.W.2d 645, 443 Mich. 68.

In some jurisdictions, no cause of action exists for "private whistleblowing." whistleblowing in a private work environment.[54.5]

54.5 Tex.—Thompson v. El Centro Del Barrio, App.—San Antonio, 905 S.W.2d 356, reh. over., err. den., reh. of writ of err. over.

59. Ohio—Phung v. Waste Management, Inc., 491 N.E.2d 1114, 23 Ohio St.3d 100, 23 O.B.R. 260, app. after remand 532 N.E.2d 195, 40 Ohio App.3d 130, cause dism. 532 N.E.2d 1317, 38 Ohio St.3d 702, app. after remand 1993 WL 325494, motion den. 617 N.E.2d 684, 67 Ohio St.3d 1434, motion all. on reh. 619 N.E.2d 425, 67 Ohio St.3d 1457.

Report to third party not required

N.H.—Appeal of Bio Energy Corp., 607 A.2d 606, 135 N.H. 517.

63. Reasonable belief

U.S.—Cucchi v. New York City Off-Track Betting Corp., S.D.N.Y., 818 F.Supp. 647.

Ohio—Fox v. Bowling Green, 668 N.E.2d 898, 76 Ohio St.3d 534.

64. N.Y.—Bordell v. General Elec. Co., 667 N.E.2d 922, 88 N.Y.2d 869, 644 N.Y.S.2d 912

Some statutes which prohibit the discharge of an employee for whistle blowing provide that the employee's participation in the wrongdoing is a defense to a retaliation claim, rather than an exception to the statute's protection.[64.5]

64.5 Fla.—Martin County v. Edenfield, 609 So.2d 27.

A whistle-blower's act is a remedial statute which may be applied retroactively.[64.10]

64.10 To case pending on appeal

Fla.—Walsh v. Arrow Air, Inc., App. 3 Dist., 629 So.2d 144, quashed on oth. grds 645 So.2d 422.

In order for an employee to be afforded protection as a whistleblower, he or she must strictly comply with the dictates of the whistleblower statute.[64.15]

64.15 Ohio—Contreras v. Ferro Corp., 652 N.E.2d 940, 73 Ohio St.3d 244.

Some whistleblowing statutes prohibiting the discharge of an employee because the employee refuses to carry out a directive are limited to situations in-

---

FIGURE 12-7
(continued) *C.J.S.*
Pocket Part
Supplement Covering
Recent Changes to
Volume 30, §69

§ 69　EMPLOYER—EMPLOYEE

Page 117

volving a physically dangerous condition.[64.17]

64.17　Refusal to issue check not protected
Me.—Devoid v. Clair Buick Cadillac, Inc., 669 A.2d 749.

An absentee employer may not avoid liability under a whistleblower statute by delegating to its employee responsibility for enforcement of safety laws.[64.20]

64.20　N.Y.—Granser v. Box Tree South Ltd., 623 N.Y.S.2d 977, 164 Misc.2d 191.

A whistleblower statute does not protect an employee who has been discharged because of an erroneous perception that he or she has reported a violation of law, regulations, or rules to a public body.[64.25]

64.25　Mich.—Chandler v. Schlumberger, 542 N.W.2d 310, 214 Mich.App. 111.

65.　Ill.—Martin v. Federal Life Ins. Co., 440 N.E.2d 998, 65 Ill.Dec. 143, 109 Ill.App.3d 596, app. after remand 518 N.E.2d 306, 115 Ill.Dec. 781, 164 Ill.App.3d 820, app. den. 526 N.E.2d 832, 122 Ill.Dec. 439, 121 Ill.2d 572, app. after remand 644 N.E.2d 42, 205 Ill.Dec. 826, 268 Ill.App.3d 698, app. den. 649 N.E.2d 417, 208 Ill.Dec. 361, 161 Ill.2d 528.

66.　Reporting possible environmental violations
La.—Cheramie v. J. Wayne Plaisance, Inc., 595 So.2d 619.

68.　U.S.—Adler v. American Standard Corp., D.C.Md., 538 F.Supp. 572, on subs. app. 830 F.2d 1303.

page 118

72.　Failure to maintain smoke-free work area
N.Y.—Bompane v. Enzolabs, Inc., 608 N.Y.S.2d 989, 160 Misc.2d 315.

73.　Tax law violation
U.S.—Adler v. American Standard Corp., D.C.Md., 538 F.Supp. 572, on subs. app. 830 F.2d 1303.

Refusal to participate in environmentally damaging work
La.—Cheramie v. J. Wayne Plaisance, Inc., 595 So.2d 619.

74.　Attorney discipline
N.Y.—Wieder v. Skala, 544 N.Y.S.2d 971, 144 Misc.2d 346, affd. 562 N.Y.S.2d 930, 167 A.D.2d 265, app. dism 575 N.E.2d 401, 77 N.Y.2d 989, 571 N.Y.S.2d 915, rearg. den. 578 N.E.2d 445, 78 N.Y.2d 952, 573 N.Y.S.2d 647, affd. as mod. on oth. grds. 609 N.E.2d 105, 80 N.Y.2d 628, 593 N.Y.S.2d 752.

Mistreatment of patients
Mo.—Clark v. Beverly Enterprises-Missouri, Inc., App. W.D., 872 S.W.2d 522, reh. and/or transf. den., transf. den.
N.C.—Lenzer v. Flaherty, 418 S.E.2d 276, 106 N.C.App. 496, review den. 421 S.E.2d 348, 332 N.C. 345.

75.　U.S.—English v. General Elec. Co., N.C., 110 S.Ct. 2270, 496 U.S. 72, 110 L.Ed.2d 65, on remand 765 F.Supp. 293, affd. 977 F.2d 572.

Banking Whistleblower Act only applicable to listed actors
Banking Whistleblower Act does not apply to Resolution Trust Corporation (RTC) or its personnel contractors; Act applies only to listed actors, and neither RTC nor its contractors fall within categories of actors listed in Act.
U.S.—Nowlin v. Resolution Trust Corp., C.A.5(Tex.), 33 F.3d 498.

page 119

76.　Employees not protected
"Whistle-blower" provision of Energy Reorganization Act (ERA) did not protect employees of contractors operating nuclear facilities owned by Department of Energy; provision protected only employees of licensees of Nuclear Regulatory Commission and their contractors.
U.S.—Adams v. Dole, C.A.4, 927 F.2d 771, cert. den. 112 S.Ct. 122, 502 U.S. 837, 116 L.Ed.2d 90.

78.　U.S.—English v. General Elec. Co., N.C., 110 S.Ct. 2270, 496 U.S. 72, 110 L.Ed.2d 65, on remand 765 F.Supp. 293, affd. 977 F.2d 572.

82.　49 App. U.S.C.A. § 1301 et seq., was repealed in 1994. See now, 49 U.S.C.A. § 40101 et seq., added in 1994.

84.　45 U.S.C.A. § 431 et seq., was repealed in 1994. See now 49 U.S.C.A. § 20103 et seq., added in 1994.

85.　45 U.S.C.A. § 441(a), was repealed in 1994. See now 49 U.S.C.A. § 20109(a), added in 1994.

Protections for contractor employees.

An employee of a contractor may not be discharged, demoted, or otherwise discriminated against as a reprisal for disclosing to a Member of Congress or an authorized official of an agency of the Department of Justice information relating to a substantial violation of law related to a contract, including the competition for or negotiation of a contract.[88.1]

88.1　10 U.S.C.A. § 2409, as amended in 1994, whistleblower protections for contractor employees of Department of Defense, Coast Guard, and National Aeronautics and Space Administration.
41 U.S.C.A. § 265, added in 1994, whistleblower protections for contractor employees of civilian agencies.

False Claims Act.

Under the False Claims Act,[88.5] no employer may discriminate against any employee who makes a complaint of fraud to the government, in the terms and conditions of employment, because of such lawful acts done in furtherance of an action filed or to be filed pursuant to the Act.[88.10]

88.5　31 U.S.C.A. § 3730(h).

88.10　Protection for intracorporate complaint
U.S.—Neal v. Honeywell, Inc., N.D.Ill., 826 F.Supp. 266, affd. 33 F.3d 860.

Company president not "employer"
U.S.—U.S. ex rel. Lamar v. Burke, E.D.Mo., 894 F.Supp. 1345.

§ 70.　Discrimination

89.　Gender-motivated discharge
U.S.—Kerrigan v. Magnum Entertainment, Inc., D.Md., 804 F.Supp. 733.

90.　Okl.—Tate v. Browning-Ferris, Inc., 833 P.2d 1218, 21 A.L.R.5th 831.

93.　Discrimination on basis of pregnancy
U.S.—Hughes v. Matthews, C.A.(Ark.), 986 F.2d 1168.

94.　U.S.—Revis v. Slocomb Industries, Inc., D.Del., 765 F.Supp. 1212.

page 120

1.　U.S.—Kelly v. National R.R. Passenger Corp., E.D.Pa., 731 F.Supp. 698.

3.　Or.—Goodlette v. LTM, Inc., 874 P.2d 1354, 128 Or.App. 62.

Under a statute, "retaliation" includes the refusal to hire or the discharge of a person because that person had filed a discrimination charge against another entity.[6.5]

6.5　Former employer
Ill.—Carter Coal Co. v. Human Rights Com'n, 5 Dist. 633 N.E.2d 202, 198 Ill.Dec. 740, 261 Ill.App.3d 1, app. den. 642 N.E.2d 1275, 205 Ill.Dec. 158, 157 Ill.2d 496.

§ 71.　Lie Detector Tests

page 121

12.　Okl.—Pearson v. Hope Lumber & Supply Co. Inc., 820 P.2d 443.

13.　Okl.—Pearson v. Hope Lumber & Supply Co. Inc., 820 P.2d 443.

page 123

§ 74.　Federal Employers' Liability Act

62.　U.S.—Shrader v. CSX Transp., Inc., C.A.2(N.Y.), 70 F.3d 255.

The Act does not cover the situation in which an employee tells an employer about his or her own accident.[62.5]

62.5　U.S.—Shrader v. CSX Transp., Inc., C.A.2(N.Y.), 70 F.3d 255.

page 124

§ 75.　Workers' Compensation

65.　Iowa—Smith v. Smithway Motor Xpress, Inc., 464 N.W.2d 682.

"Action"
Word "action" within meaning of statute prohibiting termination of employee for instituting action against employer for workers' compensation benefits, as exception to employment at will doctrine, includes filing claim for workers' compensation benefits as well as instituting judicial proceedings.
Ala.—McClain v. Birmingham Coca-Cola Bottling Co., 578 So.2d 1299.

Spouse
(2) When married couple both work for same employer, and one exercises his or her rights under Workers' Compensation Act following on-the-job injury, employer may not retaliate against noninjured spouse by terminating him or her from employment any more than employer can retaliate against injured spouse.
Kan.—Marinhagen v. Boster, Inc., 840 P.2d 534, 17 Kan.App.2d 532, review den.

66.　Since the publication of the bound volume, the case of Williams v. Amax Chemical Corp., 720 P.2d 1234, 104 N.M. 293, has been overruled by the Court holding that a statute pursuant to which an employer may not retaliate against an employee for seeking workers' compensation benefits does not provide an exclusive remedy for retaliatory discharge.
N.M.—Michaels v. Anglo American Auto Auctions, Inc., 869 P.2d 279, 117 N.M. 91, app. after remand 930 P.2d 783.

Retaliatory demotion
Kan.—Brigham v. Dillon Companies, Inc., 921 P.2d 837, 22 Kan.App.2d 717, review gr.

Retaliation against an employee for exercising his rights under workers' compensation laws need not result in termination of employment in order to state a cause of action.[66.5]

FIGURE 12-7
(continued)

Reprinted with permission of Thomson/West

Figure 12-8 is from the General Index to *American Jurisprudence 2d*. The heading *Retaliation* directs the researcher to *Job Discrimination*.

Topic: Retaliation or Revenge →

GENERAL INDEX

RETALIATION OR REVENGE —Cont'd
Americans with Disabilities Act (this index)
Arguments of counsel. **Trial § 564, 569, 665**
Contempt, **Contempt § 107, 111, 112**
Damages, **Damages § 769**
Disabled persons. **Americans with Disabilities Act** (this index)
Eviction, mobile homes, trailer parks, and tourist camps, **MobileHome § 36**
Handicapped persons. **Americans with Disabilities Act** (this index)
Job Discrimination (this index)
Labor and Labor Relations (this index)
Landlord and tenant
  eviction as retaliatory. **Landlord § 610, 649**
  mobile homes, trailer parks. and tourist camps, retaliatory eviction. **MobileHome § 36**
  summary possessory actions. retaliatory conduct of landlord, **Landlord § 1030**
Longshore and Harbor Workers' Compensation Act, retaliatory discharge for claim under, **FELCA § 112**
Mobile homes, trailer parks, and tourist camps, retaliatory eviction. **MobileHome § 36**
New trial, **NewTrial § 165**
Obstruction of justice. **Obstruct § 58, 68**
Penal and correctional institutions. **Penal § 27, 123, 132, 138**
Search and seizure, vengeful motive of informers, **Searches § 187**
Ships and shipping, **Shipping § 81**
Statutes. **Retaliatory Statutes** (this index)
Uniform Residential Landlord and Tenant Act, retaliatory eviction, **Landlord § 649**
Workers' compensation, retaliation for filing claim, **Workers § 39, 474**
Wrongful Discharge (this index)

RETALIATORY STATUTES
Foreign corporations, **ForeignCrp § 224**
Foreign Corporations (this index)
Insurance. **Insurance § 51, 52**
State and local taxes, foreign corporations, **StateLocl § 215**
Taxes (this index)

RETARDATION
Mentally Impaired Persons (this index)

RETAXATION OF COSTS
Costs of action, **Costs § 95**

RETENTION
Accord and satisfaction, retention of check, **Accord § 18, 19**
Accountants, right of retention of data, **Accountnt § 14**
Agency (this index)
Aliens, citizenship, **Aliens § 2713-2720, 2726**
Appeal and Review (this index)
Auctions, **Auctions § 78**

RETENTION—Cont'd
Bills and notes, retention of old instrument after execution of new, **BillsNotes § 170**
Contracts (this index)
Copyright and literary property. **Copyright § 139**
Corporations, **Corporatns § 39, 423, 425, 767, 1293**
Damages, **Damages § 716, 787, 791, 796**
Dead bodies. **DeadBodies § 42, 61**
Employment (this index)
Equity jurisdiction, **Equity § 103-107**
Estoppel. Waiver and estoppel. below
False imprisonment. liability of principal for retention of agent or employee. **FalseImp § 156**
Husband and Wife (this index)
Insurance (this index)
Inverse order of alienation. retained parcel as primarily liable to discharge paramount encumbrance, **Marshal § 37**
Landlord and Tenant (this index)
Liens, retention of title to items furnished, **Mechanics § 301**
Mechanic's liens, retention of title to items furnished, **Mechanics § 301**
Payment of lien for storage, retention of goods or vessel for, **Wharves § 37**
Public Works and Contracts (this index)
Remand, retained jurisdiction of appellate court, **Appellate § 806**
Reservations (this index)
Robbery. **Robbery § 13, 28**
Sale or Transfer of Personal Property (this index)
Secured Transactions (this index)
Speedy trial, **CrimLaw § 1039**
Trust funds and deposits. retention of control, **Banks § 697, 698**
Trusts (this index)
Veterans and veterans' laws, retention preferences, **Veterans § 104, 105**
Waiver and estoppel
  insurance, **Insurance § 1390, 1667**
Wharves, retention of goods or vessel for payment of lien for storage. **Wharves § 37**

RETIREMENT
Pensions and Retirement (this index)

RETIREMENT EQUITY ACT
Pensions and retirement funds, **Pensions § 239, 389, 410**

RETIREMENT HOME OR COMMUNITY
Secured transactions, **SecureTran § 69, 124**
Zoning and planning, **Zoning § 153, 245**

RETIREMENT HOMES
Supplemental Security Income (SSI) (this index)

RETIREMENT OF JURY
Jury Trials (this index)

RETIREMENT OF PARTNERS
Partnerships (this index)

RETIREMENT OF SECURITIES
Cooperative associations. **CoopAsso § 19**
Corporations (this index)
Federal deposit insurance corporation. **Banks § 63**
National banks. capital and capital stock. **Banks § 247**

RETRACING
Wills, effect of retracing of attesting witnesses signatures following execution of instrument by testator. **Wills § 314**

RETRACTION
Credit reporting agencies, **Collection § 32**

RETRACTION OR RECANTATION
Assignments. **Sales § 355**
Attorneys. disciplinary proceedings. **Attnys § 54**
Comment by counsel, **Trial § 710**
Contempt, **Contempt § 229**
Libel and Slander (this index)
New evidence. **NewTrial § 440-443, 466, 467**
New trial, **NewTrial § 421, 440-443, 457, 466, 467**
Obstruction of justice. **Obstruct § 42**
Payment, **Payment § 43**
Perjury, **Perjury § 107-109**
Privacy (this index)
Sale or transfer of personal property, generally, **Sales § 352, 353, 355, 882-887, 1080**

RETRANSFER
Transfer (this index)

RETRAXIT
Definitions and distinctions, **Dismissal § 6**
Judgments and Decrees (this index)

RETREADED TIRES
Generally, **Sales § 767**

RETREAT
Assault and Battery (this index)
Homicide (this index)

RETRIAL
New Trial or Proceeding (this index)
New Trial (this index)
Relitigation (this index)

RETRIBUTION
Retaliation or Revenge (this index)

RETROACTIVE LAWS
Children and Minors (this index)
Exemptions from claims of creditors. **Exemptions § 19-21**
Fraudulent conveyances, **FrauduConv § 5**
Public Utilities (this index)

For assistance using this index. call 1-800-328-4880   111

FIGURE 12-8
General Index Page for
Am. Jur. 2d Showing
Retaliation

Reprinted with permission of Thomson/West

The heading *Job Discrimination* is then located in the index volume covering the alphabet letter *J*. Figure 12-9 shows two pages from the index under the heading *Job Discrimination*. There are many references to *Retaliation*.

GENERAL INDEX

JOB DISCRIMINATION—Cont'd
Res judicata and other preclusions—Cont'd
　settlements previously
　　privity requirements, JobDiscrim
　　　§ 2320
　　voluntary and knowing waiver of
　　　rights, JobDiscrim § 2319
　Seventh Amendment implications of
　　erroneous dismissal, JobDiscrim
　　§ 2339
　state court decisions
　　ADEA, JobDiscrim § 2336
　　early Civil Rights Acts, JobDiscrim
　　　§ 2334, 2335
　　Title VII, below
　Title VII, below
　voluntary and knowing waiver of rights
　　in previous settlement, JobDiscrim
　　§ 2319
Rest and meal breaks
　generally, JobDiscrim § 890
　state protective laws for women under
　　Title VII, JobDiscrim § 891
Restrooms, terms and conditions of employ-
　ment, JobDiscrim § 989, 990
Retaliation
　generally, JobDiscrim § 228-260
　absence of good faith requirement,
　　participation in administrative pro-
　　cess, JobDiscrim § 241
　ADA prohibition, JobDiscrim § 228
　ADEA prohibition, JobDiscrim § 228
　administrative charge, subject matter
　　jurisdiction, postcharge retaliation
　　claims, JobDiscrim § 2315.7
　administrative process participant.
　　Participation in administrative pro-
　　cess, below in this group
　adverse actions
　　generally, JobDiscrim § 248
　　evidence, JobDiscrim § 253
　　lie detector testing, restrictions on
　　　adverse actions against test
　　　subjects, JobDiscrim § 1022
　　timing of employer's activity with,
　　　effect on showing of causation,
　　　JobDiscrim § 256
　applicants, protected persons,
　　JobDiscrim § 244, 1006
　causation, proof of
　　generally, JobDiscrim § 254
　　consistency of employer's actions,
　　　effect, JobDiscrim § 257
　　degree necessary, JobDiscrim § 258
　　employer's knowledge of employee's
　　　protected activity, JobDiscrim
　　　§ 255
　　timing of employer's activity with
　　　adverse action, effect, JobDiscrim
　　　§ 256
　charges, special processing, JobDiscrim
　　§ 232
　claims of
　　defending against, JobDiscrim § 259
　　settlement, JobDiscrim § 233
　complaining persons, suits against,
　　JobDiscrim § 250
　consistency of employer's actions, effect
　　on showing of causation, JobDiscrim
　　§ 257

JOB DISCRIMINATION—Cont'd
Retaliation—Cont'd
　defending against retaliation claim,
　　JobDiscrim § 259
　degree of causation to be shown,
　　JobDiscrim § 258
　demonstrating pretext, JobDiscrim
　　§ 260
　discipline for oppositional or participa-
　　tory acts, JobDiscrim § 236
　distinction between oppositional and
　　participatory actions, JobDiscrim
　　§ 234
　early Civil Rights Acts prohibition,
　　JobDiscrim § 230
　employees, protected persons,
　　JobDiscrim § 243, 1006
　employer's knowledge of employee's
　　protected activity, to prove causation,
　　JobDiscrim § 255
　employment relationship required, when
　　retaliation for participation in
　　administrative process, JobDiscrim
　　§ 242
　enforcement proceedings, above
　Equal Pay Act prohibition, JobDiscrim
　　§ 229
　evidence
　　adverse actions, defined, JobDiscrim
　　　§ 253
　　causation
　　　generally, JobDiscrim § 254
　　　consistency of employer's actions,
　　　　effect, JobDiscrim § 257
　　　degree necessary, JobDiscrim
　　　　§ 258
　　　employer's knowledge of
　　　　employee's protected activity,
　　　　JobDiscrim § 255
　　　timing of employer's activity with
　　　　adverse action, effect,
　　　　JobDiscrim § 256
　　defending against retaliation claim,
　　　JobDiscrim § 259
　　demonstrating pretext, JobDiscrim
　　　§ 260
　　pretext, JobDiscrim § 260
　　prima facie case, establishing,
　　　JobDiscrim § 251
　　underlying discrimination claim or
　　　activity, JobDiscrim § 252
　farm labor contractors, above
　former employees, protected persons,
　　JobDiscrim § 245
　good faith requirement
　　oppositional acts, JobDiscrim § 238
　　participation in administrative pro-
　　　cess, JobDiscrim § 241
　handling discrimination claims,
　　JobDiscrim § 249
　lawful employment practices,
　　oppositional acts to, JobDiscrim
　　§ 239
　lie detector testing, retaliation against
　　test subject, JobDiscrim § 1006, 1022
　oppositional acts
　　discipline for, JobDiscrim § 236
　　good faith requirement, JobDiscrim
　　　§ 238
　　lawful employment practices, to,
　　　JobDiscrim § 239

JOB DISCRIMINATION—Cont'd
Retaliation—Cont'd
　oppositional acts—Cont'd
　　participatory acts, distinguished,
　　　JobDiscrim § 234
　　unlawful employment practices, to
　　　good faith requirement,
　　　JobDiscrim § 238
　　unrelated acts to discrimination
　　　proceedings, JobDiscrim § 237
　　unrelated acts to discrimination
　　　proceedings, JobDiscrim § 237
　other federal prohibitions, JobDiscrim
　　§ 231
　participation in administrative process
　　absence of good faith requirement,
　　　JobDiscrim § 241
　　definition of participation,
　　　JobDiscrim § 240
　　employment relationship required,
　　　JobDiscrim § 242
　　good faith requirement not present,
　　　JobDiscrim § 241
　participatory acts
　　discipline for, JobDiscrim § 236
　　oppositional acts, distinguished,
　　　JobDiscrim § 234
　persons protected. Protected persons,
　　below in this group
　polygraph testing, retaliation against test
　　subject, JobDiscrim § 1006, 1022
　pretext, evidence, JobDiscrim § 260
　prima facie case, establishing,
　　JobDiscrim § 251
　processing of charges, JobDiscrim
　　§ 232
　prohibition
　　ADA, JobDiscrim § 228
　　ADEA, JobDiscrim § 228
　　Civil Rights Acts, early, JobDiscrim
　　　§ 230
　　early Civil Rights Acts, JobDiscrim
　　　§ 230
　　Equal Pay Act, JobDiscrim § 229
　　farm labor contractors, JobDiscrim
　　　§ 1204
　　lie detector testing, retaliation against
　　　employees and job applicants,
　　　JobDiscrim § 1006
　　other federal prohibitions,
　　　JobDiscrim § 231
　　Title VII, JobDiscrim § 228
　proof. Evidence, above in this group
　protected persons
　　applicants, JobDiscrim § 244, 1006
　　employment, JobDiscrim § 243, 1006
　　former employees, JobDiscrim § 245
　　lie detector testing, retaliation against
　　　test subject, JobDiscrim § 1006,
　　　1022
　　union members, JobDiscrim § 246
　relationship between retaliation and type
　　of discrimination, JobDiscrim § 235
　settlement of claims, JobDiscrim § 233
　special processing of charges,
　　JobDiscrim § 232
　subject matter jurisdiction, postcharge
　　retaliation claims, JobDiscrim
　　§ 2315.7
　suits against complaining persons,
　　JobDiscrim § 250

Topic: Retaliation

For assistance using this index, call 1-800-328-4880　　　　　　71

FIGURE 12-9
General Index Page for
Am. Jur. 2d Showing
Retaliation Under the
Broader Topic of Job
Discrimination

AMERICAN JURISPRUDENCE 2d

JOB DISCRIMINATION—Cont'd
Retaliation—Cont'd
timing of employer's activity with
adverse action, effect on showing of
causation, **JobDiscrim § 256**
Title VII prohibition, **JobDiscrim § 228**
type of discrimination, relationship to
retaliation, **JobDiscrim § 235**
types of retaliatory acts
handling discrimination claims,
JobDiscrim § 249
other adverse employment actions,
JobDiscrim § 248
suits against complaining persons,
JobDiscrim § 250
withholding wages, **JobDiscrim
§ 247**
underlying discrimination claim or activity, evidence, **JobDiscrim § 252**
union members, protected persons,
JobDiscrim § 246
unrelated acts to discrimination proceedings, **JobDiscrim § 237**
withholding wages, **JobDiscrim § 247**
Retirement. **Pensions and Retirement** (this
index)
Reverse discrimination
definition, **JobDiscrim § 129**
proof, **JobDiscrim § 130**
Right-to-sue notice
Age Discrimination in Employment Act,
right to sue notices not required,
JobDiscrim § 1409
enforcement proceedings, above
judicial proceedings, right-to-sue notice,
filed as complaint, **JobDiscrim
§ 2235, 2511, 2512**
pretrial pleadings and motions, above
Title VII, below
Ripeness for resolution, drug testing challenge of employee, **JobDiscrim § 481**
Safety. Health and safety, above
Salaries
Equal Pay Act, above
wages and salaries, below
Sanctions
administrative sanctions and remedies,
above
criminal sanctions, above
discovery, above
Schools and education
apprenticeships, above
college education, selection and screening practices, **JobDiscrim § 435**
content validation of tests applicable to
selection practices, **JobDiscrim § 386**
guidelines used in selection procedure,
JobDiscrim § 431
high school education, selection practices, **JobDiscrim § 436**
job skills, selection practices,
JobDiscrim § 438
justification of selection requirements
overcoming employer's justification,
JobDiscrim § 433
testimony, **JobDiscrim § 432**
language skills, selection practices,
JobDiscrim § 438
prima facie case, overcoming,
JobDiscrim § 430

JOB DISCRIMINATION—Cont'd
Schools and education—Cont'd
proving employee's case, selection practices, **JobDiscrim § 429**
relevance of charge drafter's education,
subject matter jurisdiction,
JobDiscrim § 2314.2
selection, screening and evaluation practices, generally, **JobDiscrim § 428-
439**
sex discrimination
generally, **CivilRghts § 333-337**
advertising, **CivilRghts § 336**
age discrimination, **CivilRghts § 371**
bona fide occupational qualification,
CivilRghts § 337
compensation, **CivilRghts § 334**
job classification and structure,
CivilRghts § 334
marital status, **CivilRghts § 335, 336,
342**
parental status, **CivilRghts § 335,
336, 342**
tenure, **JobDiscrim § 920, 921, 923**
testimony to justify requirements, selection practices, **JobDiscrim § 432**
Title IX, below
Title VII, below
training, below
validity determinations in particular
cases, selection practices, **JobDiscrim
§ 434**
work experience, selection practices,
JobDiscrim § 437
Scope of laws. Employment discrimination
laws, above
Screening of applicants. Selection, screening,
and evaluation practices, below
Seasonal agricultural workers. Farm labor
contractors, above
Security firms, lie detector testing,
JobDiscrim § 1004
Selection, screening, and evaluation practices
generally, **JobDiscrim § 316-556**
abortions, prohibiting use as selection
criterion, **JobDiscrim § 423**
abstention, advance notice of testing for
substance abuse, **JobDiscrim § 485**
accommodation. Reasonable accommodation of religious conflicts with
work time, below in this group
accuracy of proof of job-relatedness as
factor in choosing method of test
validation, **JobDiscrim § 361**
ADA
direct threat to health or safety,
qualifications avoiding,
JobDiscrim § 334
drug testing, policies permissible,
JobDiscrim § 471
health and physical fitness as
qualifications, validity, **JobDiscrim
§ 442**
health or safety threat, qualifications
avoiding, **JobDiscrim § 334**
qualification standards avoiding direct
threat to health or safety,
JobDiscrim § 334
safety threat, qualifications avoiding,
JobDiscrim § 334

JOB DISCRIMINATION—Cont'd
Selection, screening, and evaluation practices
—Cont'd
ADA—Cont'd
substance abuse policies permissible
under
generally, **JobDiscrim § 470**
testing, **JobDiscrim § 471**
testing requirements. ADA testing
requirements, below in this group
threat to health or safety, qualifications avoiding, **JobDiscrim § 334**
ADA testing requirements
administration
generally, **JobDiscrim § 335**
methods, prohibitions, **JobDiscrim
§ 332**
criteria, prohibitions, **JobDiscrim
§ 332**
employment tests, prohibitions,
JobDiscrim § 333
job qualifications and employment
tests, prohibitions, **JobDiscrim
§ 333**
prohibitions
job qualifications and employment
tests, **JobDiscrim § 333**
standards, criteria, and methods of
administration, **JobDiscrim
§ 332**
standards, prohibitions, **JobDiscrim
§ 332**
ADEA, health and physical fitness as
qualifications, validity, **JobDiscrim
§ 441**
administration of tests
ADA testing requirements,
JobDiscrim § 332, 335
employees, by, **JobDiscrim § 325**
experts, by, **JobDiscrim § 324**
adverse impact. Disparate impact, below
in this group
Affirmative Action (this index)
AIDS policies and testing
generally, **JobDiscrim § 463**
constitutionality of testing,
JobDiscrim § 464
alcohol use. Substance abuse, below in
this group
alternative selection procedures, duty to
consider, **JobDiscrim § 356**
alternatives to validation of tests,
JobDiscrim § 359
antinepotism rules, **JobDiscrim § 536**
appearance and grooming
generally, **JobDiscrim § 496-505**
beard rule as sex discrimination,
JobDiscrim § 502
dress codes
religious discrimination,
JobDiscrim § 505
sex discrimination, **JobDiscrim
§ 504**
EEOC processing of weight charges,
JobDiscrim § 499
ethnic characteristics, **JobDiscrim
§ 496**
hair rules
national origin discrimination,
JobDiscrim § 501

72   **For assistance using this index, call 1-800-328-4880**

Reprinted with permission of Thomson/West

FIGURE 12-9
(continued)

The number of references is almost overwhelming. At this point, the researcher may choose to begin with the very first reference under *Retaliation*. This directs the reader to sections 228–260. A quick look at the outline for the broad topic
Job Discrimination shows that sections 228–260 cover the topics "Retaliation Against

Opponents of Discrimination" and "Other Prohibited Acts Relating to Discrimination." Figure 12-10 shows the outline from *American Jurisprudence* for the general topic *Job Discrimination*.

45A Am Jur 2d JOB DISCRIMINATION

29 USCS § 2001 et seq. (Employee Polygraph Protection Act)
29 USCS § 2601 et seq. (Family and Medical Leave Act of 1993)
42 USCS §§ 1885 et seq. (Science and Technology Equal Opportunities Act)
42 USCS §§ 1981 et seq. (1866 and 1871 Civil Rights Acts)
42 USCS §§ 2000e et seq. (Title VII of Civil Rights Act of 1964)
42 USCS §§ 12111 et seq. (Americans With Disabilities Act)
P.L. 102-166, § 105 (Civil Rights Act of 1991)

Administrative Rules and Regulations:
5 CFR Part 1201 (Merit Systems Protection Board)
29 CFR Part 1600 et seq. (Equal Employment Opportunity Commission)
41 CFR Chapter 60 (Office of Federal Contract Compliance Programs)

Tax References:
RIA Federal Tax Coordinator 2d ¶ J-5801 et seq. (taxability of award of backpay and damages under Title VII and similar laws)
Auto-Cite®: Cases and annotations referred to herein can be further researched through the Auto-Cite® computer-assisted research service. Use Auto-Cite to check citations for form, parallel references, prior and later history, and annotation references.

Table of Parallel References
To convert General Index references to section references in this volume, or to ascertain the disposition (or current equivalent) of sections of articles in the prior edition of this publication, see the Table of References beginning at p ix.

Outline   ◄———

I. GOVERNING LAWS, IN GENERAL [§§ 1–35.1]
   A. TITLE VII [§§ 1–5]
   B. EARLY CIVIL RIGHTS ACTS [§§ 6–15]
   C. AGE DISCRIMINATION IN EMPLOYMENT ACT [§§ 16, 17]
   D. AMERICANS WITH DISABILITIES ACT [§§ 18, 19]
   E. EQUAL PAY ACT [§ 20]
   F. LAWS OUTLAWING DISCRIMINATION ON FEDERAL PROJECTS [§§ 21–27]
   G. OTHER FEDERAL LAWS REGULATING EMPLOYMENT DISCRIMINATION [§§ 28–35.1]

II. SCOPE OF LAWS [§§ 36–122]
   A. IN GENERAL [§§ 36–38.1]
   B. WHO MUST COMPLY [§§ 39–109]
   C. PERSONS PROTECTED UNDER FEDERAL LAWS [§§ 110–122]

III. TYPES OF PROHIBITED DISCRIMINATION: RACE, RELIGION, SEX, NATIONAL ORIGIN, AGE, DISABILITY [§§ 123–227]
   A. RACE OR COLOR [§§ 123–131]
   B. RELIGION OR CREED [§§ 132–145]
   C. SEX OR PREGNANCY [§§ 146–155]
   D. NATIONAL ORIGIN, ANCESTRY, OR CITIZENSHIP [§§ 156–167]
   E. AGE [§§ 168–172]
   F. DISABILITY [§§ 173–227]

3

———This is the general outline for the broad topic of *Job Discrimination*.

FIGURE 12-10 *Am. Jur. 2d* Outline

JOB DISCRIMINATION   45A Am Jur 2d

IV. OTHER PROHIBITED DISCRIMINATION-RELATED CON-
DUCT [§§ 228–267]
  A. RETALIATION AGAINST OPPONENTS OF DISCRIMINATION [§§ 228–260]
  B. OTHER PROHIBITED ACTS RELATING TO DISCRIMINATION [§§ 261–267]

V. EXCEPTIONS TO PROHIBITIONS ON DISCRIMINATORY CONDUCT [§§ 268–303]
  A. BUSINESS NECESSITY [§ 268]
  B. BONA FIDE OCCUPATIONAL QUALIFICATIONS [§§ 269–286]
  C. PERFORMANCE AND OTHER EXCEPTIONS RELATED TO JOB QUALIFICATIONS [§§ 287–290]
  D. NONDISCRIMINATORY PREFERENCES AND CONDUCT [§§ 291–296]
  E. RELIANCE ON ADMINISTRATIVE GUIDANCE [§§ 297–303]

VI. REGULATED EMPLOYER PRACTICES, GENERALLY; TESTING, EVALUATION AND SELECTION OF JOB APPLICANTS AND EMPLOYEES [§§ 304–700]
  A. OVERVIEW OF EMPLOYER LIABILITY [§§ 304–315]
  B. SELECTION, SCREENING, AND EVALUATION PRACTICES [§§ 316–556]
  C. RECRUITING AND HIRING PRACTICES [§§ 557–599]
  D. AFFIRMATIVE ACTION [§§ 600–700]

VII. EMPLOYMENT TERMS AND CONDITIONS [§§ 701–1054]
  A. IN GENERAL [§§ 701–724]
  B. COMPENSATION PACKAGES [§§ 725–868]
  C. TIME OFF BENEFITS [§§ 869–891]
  D. OTHER TERMS AND CONDITIONS OF EMPLOYMENT [§§ 892–1054]

VIII. DISCHARGE, DISCIPLINE AND OTHER PRACTICES [§§ 1055–1112]
  A. DISCHARGE AND DISCIPLINE [§§ 1055–1104]
  B. EMPLOYER'S ACTIONS UNDER LABOR RELATIONS LAW [§§ 1105–1108]
  C. OTHER PRACTICES [§§ 1109–1112]

IX. UNIONS', EMPLOYMENT AGENCIES', AND OTHER ENTITIES' PRACTICES [§§ 1113–1204]
  A. UNION PRACTICES [§§ 1113–1177]
  B. EMPLOYMENT AGENCY PRACTICES [§§ 1178–1192]
  C. TRAINING COMMITTEE PRACTICES [§§ 1193–1197]
  D. FARM LABOR CONTRACTOR PRACTICES [§§ 1198–1204]

X. ADMINISTRATIVE PROCEEDINGS [§§ 1205–2014]
  A. OVERVIEW OF THE AGENCIES [§§ 1205–1231]
  B. ENFORCEMENT PROCEEDINGS [§§ 1232–1895.2]
  C. ADMINISTRATIVE EXEMPTIONS [§§ 1896–1908]
  D. RECORDKEEPING AND REPORTING [§§ 1909–1948]

FIGURE 12-10
(continued)

Reprinted with permission of Thomson/West

Notice that the same approach was taken with *Corpus Juris Secundum* and *American Jurisprudence 2d*. However, the research results are not identical.
The following terms might be added to the list of vocabulary.

Factual Terms	Legal Terms
Terms Taken from the Initial Fact Pattern	
Environmental Protection Agency	Retaliatory discharge
Toxic waste	
Hazardous waste	
Disposal	
Terminated	
Additional Vocabulary from Dictionary and Thesaurus	
Fire	Wrongful termination
Removal from employment	Employer/employee
Get rid of	Relationship
Dangerous situation/condition	
Public hazard	
Risk	
Dismiss	

Additional Vocabulary from *American Law Reports, Summary of California Law, Corpus Juris Secundum* and *American Jurisprudence*

Whistleblower

Job discrimination

Unlawful employment practices

With this expanded vocabulary list you are ready to begin the actual research in the sources you chose.

12-8 WHEN TO BEGIN RESEARCH IN PRIMARY SOURCES

Although your first inclination may be to begin all research in primary sources, this may not always be the best initial choice. Remember, primary sources *contain* the law, not a *discussion* or *explanation* of the law. The primary sources are often annotated, but this information usually consists of a brief summary of case law, not an explanation or discussion written to educate or inform the reader.

Primary sources are a good place to begin research when you are familiar with the area of law to be researched and you are familiar with the vocabulary involved in the factual situation. In such cases, you may not need to perform foundation research.

Remember, you begin with the terms directly produced by the initial fact pattern. You may need to expand the list of terms through a dictionary, thesaurus, and various indexes. Good legal researchers work to expand their vocabulary. Take the time to understand all terminology before beginning the research.

With a good foundation of basic vocabulary and a clear legal issue, you are prepared to begin research in the statutes. You have already used the index to look for terms. While searching for terms, you must begin to make a list of codes that may be applicable to your fact pattern. Methodically list the code section names and numbers. When your initial list is complete, begin to locate and read the statutes you identified from the index.

Your vocabulary list, used to search in the general index to a code, leads to a statute similar to this:

Section 1102.5 Employer prohibition of disclosure of information by employee to government or law enforcement agency; suspected violation or noncompliance to federal or state law; employer retaliation

(a.) No employer shall make, adopt, or enforce any rule, regulation, or policy preventing an employee from disclosing information to a government or law enforcement agency, where the employee has reasonable cause to believe that the information discloses a violation of state or federal statute, or violation or noncompliance with a state or federal regulation.

(b.) No employer shall retaliate against an employee for disclosing information to a government or law enforcement agency, where the employee has reasonable cause to believe that the information discloses a violation of state or federal statute, or violation or noncompliance with a state or federal regulation.

In adddition to a general index, usually a multivolume set located at the end of the set of books you are researching in, there may be an index located at the end of the specific subject within the set of books. For example, if you know your topic is summary judgment motions, and you know that the general information on these motions is found in the Civil Procedure section of the state code, you could go to the last volume of the Civil Procedure sections of the state code where there is an index to the Civil Procedure statutes. This allows the researchers to limit or pinpoint the research. Think of this as a way to filter out other references that may be irrelevant.

12-9 WHEN TO BEGIN RESEARCH IN SECONDARY SOURCES

The set you choose to work in reflects how much prior knowledge you bring to the research situation. Legal encyclopedias, *American Law Reports,* and law review articles often provide a great deal of basic information. When a researcher knows very little about the topic, this is a good place to begin building a research foundation. *Caution:* When performing state-specific research, if possible use your state's legal encyclopedia and try to find law review articles and *American Law Report* annotations that include your state. If your issue is federal, you may need to look at *American Law Reports Federal* and search out law review articles focusing on federal issues.

digest. An index to reported cases arranged by subject; a very short summary of the case is provided.

If your topic is somewhat narrow and you need to search for case law, consider using the appropriate **digest.** The digest provides narrow topics, listed in alphabetical order. Following each topic are references to specific cases. These references are often referred to as annotations.

The specialty sets and pleading and practice sets work well when the researcher is focused and understands the basic vocabulary associated with the research topic.

Make a list of potential resources to be reviewed. Prioritize the list. Start with the set you feel will provide the most efficient path to your answers. Make sure you have thought about what you already know and what you need to know. Remember, your goal is to locate relevant primary law.

Let's reconsider the Yoshida retaliatory discharge case. If you know little or nothing about this topic, prepare your vocabulary, check your dictionary and thesaurus, state the basic issues, and create a list of primary and secondary sources to research. If you choose to begin your research in the secondary sources, you might decide to acquire background information or retaliatory discharge through the use of the *Current Law Index.* This is one of the indexes to legal periodicals. Figure 12-11 is a page from the Subject Index to the *Current Law Index. Retaliatory discharge of employees* is listed. The reseacher is directed to look up *Employee dismissals.*

Figure 12-12 is the first of several pages from the subject index under the heading *Employee dismissals.*

SUBJECT INDEX · RETIREES

What shall we do on Sunday? (shop closings on Sunday) (European Community) by Anthony Arnull
16 European Law Review 112-124 April '91

-Management
Industrial relations on the shop floor: the retail sector in perspective. (United Kingdom)
IRS Employment Trends 6-11 July 15 '94
Productivity and efficiency in the Japanese distribution system. by Syed Tariq Anwar and Michael A. Taku
27 Journal of World Trade (Law-Economics-Public Policy) 83-110 Oct '93
Retailers to shoplifters: let's make a deal. (New York) by Donald C. Dilworth *27 Trial 93(2) Nov '91*

-Officials and employees
Shopping around for effective training. (United Kingdom) *Employee Development Bulletin 8(9) Feb 15 '95*

-Personnel management
Dualism in part-time employment. by Chris Tilly
31 Industrial Relations 330-347 Spring '92

-Research
Fair driving: gender and race discrimination in retail car negotiations. by Ian Ayres
104 Harvard Law Review 817-872 Feb '91

-Salaries, benefits, etc.
The 1995 retail pay round.
Pay and Benefits Bulletin 2-8 Sept 15 '95
Sunday working in retail - drifting away from double-time. (includes related articles) (United Kingdom)
Pay and Benefits Bulletin 2-6 March 15 '95
The 1994 retail pay round. (United Kingdom)
Pay and Benefits Bulletin 2-6 August 15 '94
Retail pay awards below 3%. (United Kingdom)
Pay and Benefits Bulletin 2-9 July 15 '93
Retail pay deals hit by poor sales. (Great Britain)
Pay and Benefits Bulletin 5-11 July '92
Retail awards climb in spite of recession. (Great Britain) *Pay and Benefits Bulletin 7(5) June 7 '91*

-Statistics
Economic reports.
11 Tax Management Financial Planning Journal 260-261 Nov 21 '95

-Taxation
The Kansas retailers' sales tax: an overview. by Michael Lennen *62 The Journal of the Kansas Bar Association 24(9) Dec '93*
Operating retail clothing and optical goods businesses in same shopping mall not a single line of business for purposes of qualified employee discount rules.
21 Tax Management Compensation Planning Journal 234(1) Sept 3 '93
New tax rules for service warranty contracts. by Michael Lynch and Larry Witner
175 Journal of Accountancy 39(3) May '93
More special offers. (value added tax retail schemes) (United Kingdom) by Richard A. Pepper
130 Taxation 382-386 Jan 28 '93
Customs' special offers. (various value-added tax schemes) (Great Britain) by Richard A. Pepper
129 Taxation 510-515 August 20 '92
Another look at simplified LIFO for retailers. by Jeremy K. Holt *23 The Tax Adviser 37(2) Jan '92*
Taxpayers must accrue anticipated reimbursements under cooperative advertising programs when advertisements are placed.
32 Tax Management Memorandum 364-365 Dec 2 '91
The new Texas franchise tax. by Brandon Janes and Steve Moore *54 Texas Bar Journal 1108(4) Nov '91*
RETAIL inventories
Benefits available under the retail dollar-value LIFO method despite many obstacles. by W. Eugene Seago and Richard O. Davis
80 The Journal of Taxation 346(7) June '94
Regs. do not bar estimate of inventory shrinkage.
80 The Journal of Taxation 79(2) Feb '94
Another look at simplified LIFO for retailers. by Jeremy K. Holt *23 The Tax Adviser 37(2) Jan '92*
see also
Quick response inventory system
RETAIL price indexes *see*
 Consumer price indexes
RETAIL pricing *see*
 Pricing
RETAIL sales tax *see*
 Sales tax
RETAIL stores *see*
 Stores

RETAINED earnings tax *see*
 Accumulated earnings tax
RETALIATION (Law) *see*
 Lex talionis
RETALIATORY discharge of employees *see*
 Employee dismissals
RETARDATION, Mental *see*
 Mental retardation
RETARDED children *see*
 Mentally handicapped children
RETENTION basins, Storm water *see*
 Storm water retention basins
RETENTION of employees *see*
 Employee retention
RETENTION of title

-Analysis
Retention of title clauses: recent developments and current issues. (Australia) by Berna Collier
32 Law Society Journal 50(4) Oct '94
The financing of commercial international transactions and the rights of secured parties in Mexico. by Robert G. Gilbert and Carlos Angulo Parra
6 International Law Practicum 9(4) Spring '93
Retention of title - latest developments. (Great Britain) by Andrew Hicks
Journal of Business Law 398-415 July '92
Retention of title revisited. (European Community) (Great Britain) by Belinda Avery
141 New Law Journal 537(2) April 19 '91

-Laws, regulations, etc.
Romalpa theory and practice under retention of title in the sale of goods. (United Kingdom) by John De Lacy
24 Anglo-American Law Review 327-368 July-Sep '95
Debtor-to-creditor sales and the Sale of Goods Act 1979. (United Kingdom) by Scott Crichton Styles
Juridical Review 365-376 June '95
Retention of title: how to get value from a bad penny. (United Kingdom) by Dermot Turing
16 The Company Lawyer 119-122 April '95
Retention of title in German law. by K. von Metzler
22 International Business Lawyer 421(2) Oct '94
Reservation of title - past, present and future. (United Kingdom) by Gerard McCormack
Conveyancer and Property Lawyer 129-139 March-April '94
Retention of title: divining the principles, drafting a clause and some practical matters. (Victoria) by Matthew N. Connock *22 Australian Business Law Review 37-57 Feb '94*
A uniform solution to common law confusion: retention of title under English and U.S. law. by Rolf B. Johnson
12 International Tax & Business Lawyer 99-129 Wntr '94
Retention of title in English private international law. by C.G.J. Morse
Journal of Business Law 168-184 March '93
Reservation of title - an overview. (Great Britain) by Gerard McCormack
7 Insolvency Law & Practice 102-105 May-June '91

-Litigation
Retention of title, company charges and the scintilla temporis doctrine. (Stroud Architectural Systems Ltd. v. John Laing Construction Ltd.) (United Kingdom) by John de Lacy *Conveyancer and Property Lawyer 242-247 May-June '94*
Retention of title - the Leyland and DAF cases. (United Kingdom) by Laurence Elks
v9 Insolvency Law & Practice 171-175 Jan-Feb '94
Retention of title - fiduciary relationships and manufactured products. (United Kingdom) by John de Lacy *9 Insolvency Law & Practice 82-83 Nov-Dec '93*
When goods sold become a new species. (New Zealand) by Andrew Hicks
Journal of Business Law 485-490 Sept '93
Romalpa clauses. (United Kingdom) by D.S.K. Ong
4 Bond Law Review 186-197 Dec '92
Romalpa is dead. (United Kingdom) by Andrew Hicks
13 The Company Lawyer 217-218 Nov '92
Time for rejection of defective goods. (Great Britain) by Michael Hwang
Lloyds Maritime and Commercial Law Quarterly 334-350 August '92
Retention of title - rule in Dearle v. Hall. (Great Britain) by Sealy. L.S.
51 Cambridge Law Journal 19-21 March '92
The 'current account Romalpa clause' held to effectively retain title and permit tracing. (Australia) by Gregory Harris *9 Company and Securities Law Journal 390-394 Dec '91*

Romalpa clauses: the next step. (Great Britain) by Isla Davie and Alexandra McConnell
36 Journal of the Law Society of Scotland 384(2) Oct '91
A debate concluded! (retention of title under the Sale of Goods Act) (Great Britain) (Scotland) by William J. Stewart *Juridical Review 256-259 Oct '91*
All-sums retention of title: a comment. (Great Britain) by Alistair M. Clark
Scots Law Times 155-160 May 3 '91
Reservation of title - the House of Lords speaks with a Scottish accent. (Great Britain) by Gerard McCormack
Lloyds Maritime and Commercial Law Quarterly 154-162 May '91
Retention of title in mixed and processed goods. (New Zealand) (Great Britain) by A.H. Hudson
Lloyds Maritime and Commercial Law Quarterly 23-26 Feb '91
RETENTION (Psychology) *see*
 Memory
RETIN-A (Medication)
Ortho sentenced for obstruction of justice. (Ortho Pharmaceutical Corp.) United States v. Ortho Pharmaceutical Corp. Crim. No. 95-12 (WGB) (D.N.J. Jan. 11, 1995) by Jean Hellwege
31 Trial 17(2) May '95
Consumers at risk: off-label uses of medical drugs and devices. by Donald Payne *29 Trial 26(3) August '93*
RETINA
Systemic and ocular findings in 169 prospectively studied child deaths: retinal hemorrhages usually mean child abuse. by M.G.F. Gilliland, Martha W. Luckenbach and Thomas C. Chenier
68 Forensic Science International 117-132 Sept 16 '94
Retinal hemorrhages: replicating the clinician's view of the eye. by M.G.F. Gilliland and Robert Folberg
56 Forensic Science International 77-80 Sept '92
The eyes of child abuse victims: autopsy findings. by Ralph S. Riffenburgh and Lakshmanan Sathyavagiswaran
36 Journal of Forensic Sciences 741-747 May '91
RETINAL diseases *see also*
 Retrolental fibroplasia
RETINOPATHY of prematurity *see*
 Retrolental fibroplasia
RETIRED attorneys
Senior attorney volunteers: a resource for legal services programs. by Stephanie Edelstein and Jan May
27 Clearinghouse Review 619-621 Oct '93
RETIRED executives
Separate coverage election lowers cost of group-term life benefits for employees; reinstatement of retired executives in insured s. 79 plan does not affect 1984 TRA grandfather. (Tax Reform Act)
20 Tax Management Compensation Planning Journal 46-47 Feb 7 '92
RETIRED government officials and employees *see*
 Civil service pensioners
RETIRED judges
Judicial recantation. by Mark A. Graber
45 Syracuse Law Review 807-814 Summer '94
God speed and God bless. (The Dickson Legacy: L'heritage Dickson) (Transcript)
20 Manitoba Law Journal 557-561 Wntr '91
A tribute of affection and admiration. (Chief Justice Brian Dickson; Canada) (The Dickson Legacy: L'heritage Dickson) by Trevor Anderson
20 Manitoba Law Journal 546-556 Wntr '91
see also
Judges
RETIRED military personnel
Veterans Reemployment Rights out, Uniformed Service Reemployment Rights Act in. by Michael G. Tobin
68 The Wisconsin Lawyer 9(1) April '95
New procedures make collection more fair for military, federal pensioners. (Brief Article) by Rita L. Zeidner
57 Tax Notes 1403(1) Dec 7 '92
Payments beyond the grave: the military survivor benefit plan. by Edwin C. Schilling III
21 Colorado Lawyer 2571(3) Dec '92
Postemployment restrictions on former military officers. by Lisa B. Horowitz and Vernon L. Strickland
20 Public Contract Law Journal 632-642 Summer '91
United States v. Hedges: pitfalls in counseling prospective retirees regarding negotiating for employment. by Alan K. Hahn
Army Lawyer 16-21 May '91
see also
Veterans
RETIREES *see also*
 Civil service pensioners
 Social security beneficiaries

4091

Topic: Retaliatory discharge of employees.

From the CURRENT LAW INDEX, © 1998, Thomson Gale. Reprinted by permission of the Gale Group.

FIGURE 12-11 Subject Index to *Current Law Index*

-Surveys

The procedures. (Discipline at Work, part 2) (United Kingdom) *IRS Employment Trends 5-16 Sept 15 '95*

Discipline at Work - the practice. (part 1) (United Kingdom) *IRS Employment Trends 4-11 Sept '95*

EMPLOYEE dismissals *see also*
Downsizing (Management)
Executive dismissals
Layoffs

-Accounting and auditing

Accounting for certain restructuring charges. *179 Journal of Accountancy 89(5) March '95*

-Analysis

Prima facie tort and the employment-at-will doctrine in Florida. by Thomas G. Norsworthy *46 Florida Law Review 635-660 Sept '95*

Wieder v. Skala: a chink in the armor of the at-will doctrine or a lance for law firm associates? (New York) by Sandra J. Mullings *45 Syracuse Law Review 963-997 Spring '95*

Justice in dismissal: a reply to Hugh Collins. (response to book 'Justice in Dismissal') (United Kingdom) by Gwyneth Pitt *22 Industrial Law Journal 251-268 Dec '93*

The demise of breach of employment contracts and wrongful discharge cases. (Maine) by Elliott L. Epstein *8 Maine Bar Journal 242(5) July '93*

Representing the employer in the unemployment compensation appeals process. (Florida) by F. Damon Kitchen *67 Florida Bar Journal 53(5) July-August '93*

In-house counsel as whistle-blower: at-will employment on trial. by William L. Kandel and Kearney W. Kilens *19 Employee Relations Law Journal 91-102 Summer '93*

Natural selection: BT's programme of voluntary redundancy. (United Kingdom) *IRS Employment Trends 11-15 April '93*

A fair dismissal law is good public policy. (Massachusetts) by Ann Clarke *37 Boston Bar Journal 26(1) March-April '93*

Tenure: a system in need of reform. (Massachusetts) by Peter B. Finn *37 Boston Bar Journal 27(1) March-April '93*

Wrongful discharge and the California right of privacy: the drug testing of the California work force. by Elizabeth A. Harward *1 San Diego Justice Journal 227-252 Wntr '93*

The meaning of just cause for termination when an employer alleges misconduct and the employee denies it. by Michael D. Fabiano *44 Hastings Law Journal 399-420 Jan '93*

The continuing availability of retaliatory discharge and other state tort causes of action to employees covered by collective bargaining agreements. by Peter Zablotsky *56 Albany Law Review 371-402 Winter '92*

Disclaimers of wrongful discharge liability: time for a crackdown? by Michael J. Phillips *70 Washington University Law Quarterly 1131-1178 Winter '92*

Dealing with the disloyal employee. (United Kingdom) by Ian Smith *142 New Law Journal 1644(3) Nov 27 '92*

Employers beware! (employee dismissal) (Victoria) by Jay V. Pilai *66 Law Institute Journal 918-919 Oct '92*

Harsh, unjust or unreasonable dismissals. (Victoria) by John Bailey *66 Law Institute Journal 916-917 Oct '92*

Unfair and wrongful dismissal: recent developments. (Victoria) by Ian Grubb and Richard Naughton *66 Law Institute Journal 912-915 Oct '92*

Recent developments in unfair dismissal. (Great Britain) by Alan C. Neal *142 New Law Journal 1101(2) July 31 '92*

The work place rights of public employees in Delaware. by Mark H. Conner *10 Delaware Lawyer 44(4) Summer '92*

The neutral and public interests in resolving disputes in France. (The Neutral and Public Interests in Resolving Disputes) by Jacques Rojot *13 Comparative Labor Law Journal 438-448 Summer '92*

Wrongful discharge: the public policy exception, and public concern requirement, and employees' private lives. by Cynthia G. Dooley *11 Review of Litigation 387-414 Spring '92*

A quiet revolution: unfair dismissal in New South Wales. by Andrew Stewart *5 Australian Journal of Labour Law 69-83 March '92*

Don't just look at redundancy - look at the terms of employment. (Great Britain) by Richard de Metz *13 Business Law Review (UK) 51(2) Feb '92*

Employment at will and public policy. by Frank J. Cavico *25 Akron Law Review 497-546 Wntr-Spring '92*

Discrimination vignettes: age discrimination and retirement. by James P. Denardo *1989 Annual Labor and Employment Law Institute 85-92 Annual '92*

Employee manuals as implied contracts: the guidelines that bind. by Michael Rhodes Wallace *27 Tulsa Law Journal 263-282 Winter '91*

Dismissal: employee rights and procedural fairness. (Victoria) by Roy Kriegler *65 Law Institute Journal 1158(3) Dec '91*

The meaning of job security. (Great Britain) by Hugh Collins *20 Industrial Law Journal 227-239 Dec '91*

Procedural justification of dismissals: some recent developments. (New Zealand) by Isaacus K. Adzoxornu *New Zealand Law Journal 288-292 August '91*

'Taking part' question to be determined objectively. (Manifold Industries Ltd. v. Sims, EAT case) (Great Britain) *Industrial Relations Legal Information Bulletin 9(3) June 7 '91*

How the chief justice cut off his right hand; William Davis's departure leaves a host of unanswered questions. (California) by Peter Allen and Robert Egelko *11 California Lawyer 17(3) June '91*

A technical hitch. (Great Britain) by John E. McGlyne *141 New Law Journal 705(2) May 24 '91*

Reversing the presumption of employment at will. (Special Project: Civil Rights in the Workplace of the 1990s.) by Peter Stone Partee *44 Vanderbilt Law Review 689-712 April '91*

Do state fair employment statutes by 'negative implication' preclude common-law wrongful discharge claims based on the public policy exception? by M.E. Knack *21 Memphis State University Law Review 527-550 Spring '91*

The legal chokehold: professional employment in Ohio under the employment-at-will doctrine. (Ohio) by Lorraine K. Phillips *24 Akron Law Review 581-622 Spring '91*

Older workers face age-old problem. by Irene Pave *Business and Society Review 26-30 Spring '91*

Unfair dismissal. (Redundancy, part 5) (Great Britain) *Industrial Relations Legal Information Bulletin 2(8) March 8 '91*

Presidential address: toward a 'kinder and gentler' society. (at-will employment) *44 Proceedings of the annual meeting of the National Academy of Arbitrators 12-25 Annual '91*

Dismissal procedures and termination benefits in Japan. by Fumito Komiya *12 Comparative Labor Law Journal 151-164 Wntr '91*

Self-insurers and risk managers: annual survey. by Douglas H. Rand *26 Tort & Insurance Law Journal 389-401 Wntr '91*

-Cases

The impact of General Dynamics Corp. v. Superior Court on the evolving tort of retaliatory discharge for in-house attorneys.(Case Note) General Dynamics Corp. v. Superior Court 876 P.2d 487 (Cal. 1994) by Chanda R. Coblentz *52 Washington and Lee Law Review 991-1063 Summer '95*

Preemption, interpretation, and older employees under Montana's Wrongful Discharge from Employment Act.(Case Note) Tonack v. Montana Bank 854 P.2d 326 (Mont. 1993) by M. Scott Regan *56 Montana Law Review 585-602 Summer '95*

Two wrongs can make a right: McKennon v. Nashville Banner Publishing Co. and the after-acquired evidence doctrine.(Case Note) McKennon v. Nashville Banner Publishing Co. 115 S. Ct. 879 (1995) by Tricia Lynne Landthorn *56 Ohio State Law Journal 1019-1035 June '95*

'The last temptation if the greatest treason: to do the right deed for the wrong reason': after-acquired evidence in employment discrimination claims.(Issues in Discrimination)(Case Note) McKennon v. Nashville Banner Publishing Co. 115 S. Ct. 879 (1995) by Pamela M. Martey *28 Creighton Law Review 1031-1060 June '95*

A 'narrow' decision?(Case Note) NLRB v. Health Care & Retirement Corp. of America 114 S. Ct. 1778 (1994) by Kathryn L. Hays *55 Louisiana Law Review 987-1008 May '95*

One giant step forward for in-house counsel or one small step back to the status quo?(Case Note) General Dynamics Corp. v. Superior Court 876 P.2d 487 (Cal. 1994) by Elliot M. Lonker *31 California Western Law Review 277-315 Spring '95*

Expansion of Oklahoma's public policy exception to the employment-at-will doctrine.(Case Note) Groce v. Foster 880 P.2d 902 (Okla. 1994) by Jennifer L. Holland *30 Tulsa Law Journal 525-538 Spring '95*

Shoring up employer bargaining power by sandbagging nonunion workers.(Case Note) Bravo v. Dolsen Cos. 862 P.2d 623 (Wash. Ct. App. 1993) by Peter B. Gonick *70 Washington Law Review 203-225 Jan '95*

Employment law.(California Supreme Court Survey: March 1993 - May 1994)(Case Note) Hunter v. Up-Right, Inc. 864 P.2d 88 (Cal. 1993) by Marjorie Ann Waltrip *22 Pepperdine Law Review 839-844 Jan '95*

The Title VII pretext question: resolved in light of St. Mary's Honor Center v. Hicks. (Case Note) St. Mary's Honor Center v. Hicks 113 S. Ct. 2742 (1993) by Robert J. Smith *70 Indiana Law Journal 281-304 Winter '94*

Why is the Idaho Supreme Court providing no recourse to independent contractors discharged in bad faith.(Case Note) Ostrander v. Farm Bureau Mutual Insurance Co. 851 P.2d 946 (Idaho 1993) by Donald R. Mouton *31 Idaho Law Review 353-369 Winter '94*

Who your friends are could get you fired! The Connick 'public concern' test unjustifiably restricts public employees' associational rights. (Case Note) Connick v. Meyers 461 U.S. 138 (1983) by Paul Cerkvenik *79 Minnesota Law Review 425-453 Dec '94*

Employment law - exceptions to the at-will doctrine - the adoption of the public policy exception in two specific situations could signal the adoption of additional exceptions to the doctrine. (Case Note) McArn v. Allied Bruce-Terminix Co. 626 So. 2d 603 (Miss. 1993) by Debbie Ho *64 Mississippi Law Journal 257-273 Fall '94*

The court's reinterpretation of the McDonnell Douglas framework in a Title VII case - can the plaintiff win without a 'smoking gun'?(Case Note) St. Mary's Honor Center v. Hicks 113 S. Ct. 2742 (1993) by Glenn H. Egor *12 Hofstra Labor Law Journal 163-186 Fall '94*

Call off the funeral: Toussaint v. Blue Cross & Blue Shield of Michigan is alive under Rood v. General Dynamics Corp. (Case Note) Rood v. General Dynamics Corp. 507 N.W.2d 591 (Mich. 1993) by Gregory A. Przybylo *11 Thomas M. Cooley Law Review 947-967 Sept '94*

Making the government pay: the application of the Equal Access to Justice Act. (Survey of Developments in North Carolina and the Fourth Circuit, 1993) (Case Note) EEOC v Clay Printing Co. 955 F.2d 936 (4th Cir. 1992) by Mary Evelyn Thornton *72 North Carolina Law Review 1575-1607 Sept '94*

Labor law - Michigan's Whistleblowers' Protection Act - WPA protects from retaliatory discharge employees who report the crimes of co-workers arising out of workplace disputes over the handling of the employer's business.(Case Note) Dudewicz v. Norris-Schmid, Inc. 503 N.W.2d 645 (Mich. 1993) by Brendan J. Atkins *71 University of Detroit Mercy Law Review 1081-1093 Summer '94*

Workers' compensation - Tennessee Supreme Court specifies elements required to establish a cause of action for retaliatory discharge in workers' compensation cases. (Case Note) Anderson v. Standard Register Co. 857 S.W.2d 555 (Tenn. 1993) by Amanda C. Kaiser *24 Memphis State University Law Review 825-838 Summer '94*

RICO law - wrongful discharge and RICO conspiracy standing: direct-injury test resolves the standing issue. (Case Note) Holmes v. Securities Investor Protection Corp 112 S. Ct. 1311 (1992) by Keith S. Marks *16 Western New England Law Review 365-395 Spring '94*

Beyond Crosby v. Beam: Ohio courts extend protection of minority stockholders of close corporations. (Case Note) Crosby v. Beam 548 N.E.2d 217 (Ohio 1989) by Kathleen L. Kuhlman *27 Akron Law Review 477-500 Wntr-Spring '94*

When can an employee be discharged? Ask the Legislature. (California) (Case Note) Gantt v. Sentry Insurance 824 P.2d 680 (Cal. 1992) by Laurie A. Erdman *25 Pacific Law Journal 107-156 Oct '93*

Expanding the public policy exception to the employment-at-will doctrine. (Case Note) Borse v. Piece Goods Shop, Inc. 963 F.2d 611 (3d Cir. 1992) by David G. Gibson *38 Villanova Law Review 1527-1577 Oct '93*

From the CURRENT LAW INDEX, © 1998, Thomson Gale. Reprinted by permission of the Gale Group.

FIGURE 12-12 Subject Index, *Employee Dismissals, Current Law Index*

Another approach to locating background information is to locate and read *American Law Reports* annotations. Figure 12-1 shows an index page from the *American Law Reports*. Consultation of the pocket part of that index locates the article shown in Figure 12-13. Notice the detailed article outline, Research References, and the Jurisdictional Table of Cited Statutes and Cases.

---

52 ALR5th 405

WRONGFUL DISCHARGE BASED ON PUBLIC POLICY DERIVED FROM PROFESSIONAL ETHICS CODES

by
Genna H. Rosten, J.D.

A majority of states have adopted a public-policy exception to the employment-at-will rule. The public-policy exception states that an employee will have a claim for wrongful discharge if the discharge contradicts public policy. Courts have had difficulty in deciding which sources of public policy can validly sustain a cause of action for wrongful discharge. For example, in Rocky Mt. Hosp. & Medical Serv. v Mariani (1996, Colo) 916 P2d 519, 11 BNA IER Cas 1153, 52 ALR5th 857, the court held that in certain circumstances, a professional ethical code may be a source of public policy. The court stated that in order for the ethical code to qualify as public policy, it must serve the interests of the public rather than the interests of the profession, and it must provide a clear mandate to act or not act in a certain way. Lastly, it was said, the court must balance the public interest served by the ethical code and the need of an employer to make a business decision. The court in Rocky Mountain Hospital decided that a provision of the Colorado State Board of Accountancy Rules of Professional Conduct met this criteria and therefore constituted public policy. Other cases have reached contrary results depending on the particular facts presented and the ethical code in question. This annotation collects and analyzes those cases in which the courts have considered the issue whether a professional ethical code is recognized as a statement of public policy that will support a cause of action for wrongful discharge.

Rocky Mt. Hosp. & Medical Serv. v Mariani, is fully reported at page 857, infra.

405

FIGURE 12-13 *A.L.R.*
Annotation

TABLE OF CONTENTS

Research References

Index

Jurisdictional Table of Cited Statutes and Cases

ARTICLE OUTLINE

I. PRELIMINARY MATTERS

§   1. Introduction
   [a] Scope
   [b] Related annotations

§   2. Summary and comment
   [a] Generally
   [b] Practice pointers

II. GENERAL VIEWS

§   3. View that professional ethics code serving public interest may be source of public policy
   [a] In general
   [b] Code applicable to attorneys

§   4. View that professional ethics code is not source of public policy
   [a] In general
   [b] Code promulgated by private group

III. CODES OF ETHICS APPLICABLE TO PARTICULAR PROFESSIONS

§   5. Accountants
   [a] Claim sufficiently stated or proved
   [b] Claim not sufficiently stated or proved

§   6. Attorneys
   [a] Claim sufficiently stated or proved
   [b] Claim not sufficiently stated or proved

§   7. Municipal employees
§   8. Physicians
§   9. Nurses
§ 10. Pharmacists
§ 11. Social workers
§ 12. Pilots
§ 13. Securities brokers

FIGURE 12-13
(continued)

52 ALR5th　　　WRONGFUL DISCHARGE—ETHICS CODES
52 ALR5th 405

§ 14.　Defense contractors
§ 15.　Polygraph examiners

Research References

TOTAL CLIENT-SERVICE LIBRARY® REFERENCES

The following references may be of related or collateral interest to a user of this annotation.

Annotations

See the related annotations listed in the body of the annotation.

Encyclopedias and Texts

82 Am Jur 2d, Wrongful Discharge §§ 9, 11–22

Practice Aids

7A Am Jur Legal Forms 2d, Employment Contracts §§ 99:183, 99:185

12 Am Jur Legal Forms 2d, Master and Servant § 172:21

48 Am Jur Proof of Facts 2d 183, Wrongful Discharge—Bad Faith Dismissal of At-Will Employee

31 Am Jur Trials 317, Wrongful Discharge of At-Will Employee

Digests and Indexes

ALR Digest, Master and Servant §§ 51–55

ALR Index, Discharge from Employment or Office; Ethics and Ethical Matters; Professional Persons; Public Policy

Insta-Cite®

Cases referred to herein can be further researched through the Insta-Cite® computer-assisted research service. Use Insta-Cite to check citations for form, parallel references, and prior and later history.

RESEARCH SOURCES

The following are the research sources that were found to be helpful in compiling this annotation.

Encyclopedias

30 CJS, Employer-Employee Relationships § 68

Law Review Articles

Clements, The Public Policy Exception to the At-Will Employment Rule, 78 Massachusetts Law Review 88 (Spring 1993)

Moskowitz, Employment-At-Will & Codes of Ethics: The Professional's Dilemma, 23 Valparaiso University Law Review 33 (Fall 1988)

407

FIGURE 12-13
(continued)

WRONGFUL DISCHARGE—ETHICS CODES   52 ALR5th
52 ALR5th 405

Understaffing, physician's complaints   Weather conditions, pilot's refusal to
about, § 8   fly, § 12

Jurisdictional Table of Cited Statutes and Cases*

UNITED STATES

18 USCS § 3551. See § 14

Thompto v Coborn's Inc. (1994, ND Iowa) 871 F Supp 1097, 10 BNA
    IER Cas 263—§§ 3[b], 6[a]

CALIFORNIA

Cal Bus & Prof Code §§ 6101, 6106. See § 3[b]
Cal Evid Code §§ 956-958. See § 3[b]

Gantt v Sentry Ins. (1992) 1 Cal 4th 1083, 4 Cal Rptr 2d 874, 824 P2d
    680, 57 Cal Comp Cas 192, 92 Daily Journal DAR 2803, 7 BNA IER
    Cas 289, 59 CCH EPD ¶ 41597, 121 CCH LC ¶ 56853—§ 3[b]
General Dynamics Corp. v Superior Court (1994) 7 Cal 4th 1164, 32 Cal
    Rptr 2d 1, 876 P2d 487, 94 CDOS 5501, 94 Daily Journal DAR 10068,
    9 BNA IER Cas 1089, 128 CCH LC ¶ 57741—§ 3[b]

COLORADO

Crawford Rehabilitation Services, Inc. v Weissman (1997, Colo) 938 P2d
    540, 12 IER Cases 1671, 21 Colorado Journal 799—§ 3[a]
Rocky Mt. Hosp. & Medical Serv. v Mariani (1996, Colo) 916 P2d 519, 11
    BNA IER Cas 1153, 52 ALR5th 857—§§ 3[a], 5[a]

CONNECTICUT

Emerick v Kuhn (Conn Super, June 14, 1995) 1995 WL 405678—§§ 4[a],
    14

DELAWARE

Rule 1.2 of the Delaware Rules of Professional Conduct. See § 6[a]

Shearin v E.F. Hutton Group (1994, Del Ch Ct) 652 A2d 578, 9 BNA IER
    Cas 1317—§§ 2[b], 4[b], 6[a]

---

* Statutes, rules, regulations, and constitutional provisions bearing on the subject of
the annotation are included in this table only to the extent, and in the form, that they
are reflected in the court opinions discussed in this annotation. The reader should
consult the appropriate statutory or regulatory compilations to ascertain the current
status of relevant statutes, rules, regulations, and constitutional provisions.
    For federal cases involving state law, see state headings.

410

FIGURE 12-13
(continued)

Reprinted with permission of Thomson/West

There may be a specialty set appropriate to your research situation. Figure 12-14 shows the index to an *Employment Law* reference set. The index leads the reseacher to the subtopic *Governing law.* Figure 12-15 shows the first page of the information located under the subtopic *Governing law.*

I–157 **INDEX** **ROYALT**

[References are to text sections.]

RESTRAINT OF TRADE
Contracts restraining trade, prohibitions against . . . 70.07[1]
Covenants not to compete (See COVENANTS NOT TO COMPETE)

RESUME FRAUD
After-acquired evidence as employer defense (See HIRING AND RECRUITMENT)

RETAIL ESTABLISHMENTS
Minimum wages (See MINIMUM WAGES)
Overtime compensation (See OVERTIME COMPENSATION)

RETALIATION OR DISCRIMINATION AGAINST EMPLOYEE
Generally . . . 41.130[1]
California Fair Employment and Housing Act (See CALIFORNIA FAIR EMPLOYMENT AND HOUSING ACT (FEHA))
Defenses . . . 41.132
Family care and medical under CFRA and FMLA, retaliation for prosecuting rights under . . . 8.32
Former employees, protection for . . . . . . 41.130[4]
Governing law . . . 41.130
Medical information, discrimination against employees for refusal to sign authorization for release of . . . 50.42[2][b]
Occupational safety and health provisions (See OCCUPATIONAL SAFETY AND HEALTH)
Opposition to employment discrimination
Scope of protection . . . 41.130[2][a]
Unlawful practices, opposition to . . . 41.130[2][b]
Overtime compensation claim or testimony in overtime compensation claim, federal protection of employee from retaliation or discrimination resulting from . . . 5.83
Post-employment retaliation . . . 41.130[4]
Proceedings, participation in employment discrimination . . . 41.130[3]
Proof of retaliation
Generally . . . 41.131[1]
Pretext by employer, proof of . . . . . 41.131[4]
Prima facie case . . . 41.131[2]
Rebuttal by employer . . . 41.131[3]

RETALIATION OR DISCRIMINATION AGAINST EMPLOYEE—Cont.
Proof of retaliation—Cont.
Title VII of Civil Rights Act of 1964, proof of retaliation under . . . 43.10[2][d]
Sexual harassment, retaliation as . . . . . . 41.81[1][a][ii], [2]
Supervisor liability . . . 41.130[5]; 43.01[3A]
Wage claim, state remedy protecting employee or claimant against retaliation for filing (See WAGE AND HOUR LAWS—ADMINISTRATIVE AND JUDICIAL REMEDIES   )
Workers' compensation, retaliatory conduct by employer against employee seeking (See WORKERS' COMPENSATION, subhead: Retaliation against claimants)
Wrongful termination (See WRONGFUL TERMINATION AND DISCIPLINE)

RETIREMENT
California Fair Employment and Housing Act (See CALIFORNIA FAIR EMPLOYMENT AND HOUSING ACT (FEHA))
Pension and profit-sharing plans (See PENSION AND PROFIT-SHARING PLANS)
Unemployment compensation benefits (See UNEMPLOYMENT AND STATE DISABILITY INSURANCE)
Wrongful termination (See WRONGFUL TERMINATION AND DISCIPLINE)

REVENUE SHARING ACT
Repeal of . . . 40.29[2]; 40.31[4]

RIGHT-TO-SUE LETTER
Administrative remedies (See EQUAL EMPLOYMENT OPPORTUNITY—ADMINISTRATIVE ENFORCEMENT)
Americans with Disabilities Act of 1990 (See AMERICANS WITH DISABILITIES ACT OF 1990 (ADA))
California Fair Employment and Housing Act (See CALIFORNIA FAIR EMPLOYMENT AND HOUSING ACT (FEHA))
Equal Employment Opportunity Commission (See EQUAL EMPLOYMENT OPPORTUNITY COMMISSION)
Time limitations for requesting . . . 40.20[3]

ROYALTIES
Trade secret misappropriation remedy . . . 70.02[3][c]

(Rel.30–9.04   Pub. 282)

FIGURE 12-14
Index to *Employment Law* Reference Set

Reprinted from *California Employment Law.* Copyright 2004 Matthew Bender & Company, Inc., a member of the LexisNexis Group. All Rights Reserved. Reprinted with permission.

PART G. RETALIATION

§ 41.130 Governing Law

[1] Generally

Title VII, the ADEA, the ADA, and the FEHA contain substantially similar provisions making it an unlawful employment practice for an employer to discriminate against any person for (1) opposing any practice forbidden or made unlawful under those laws,[1] or (2) filing a complaint, making a charge, testifying, assisting, or participating in any investigation, proceeding, hearing, or litigation under those laws.[2] Effective January 1, 1988, former Gov. Code § 12940(f)[3] was amended to apply to *any person* who retaliates for engaging in protected activities.[4] The ADA also provides that it is unlawful to coerce, intimidate, threaten, or interfere with any individual in the exercise or enjoyment of his or her ADA rights, or because he or she exercised or enjoyed those rights, or because he or she aided or encouraged someone else in the exercise or enjoyment of ADA rights.[5] The United States Constitution,[6] Title 42 United States Code, section 1981,[7] section 1983,[8] the EPA,[9] and Executive Order No. 11246[10]may also provide a basis for attacking such "retaliation."

---

[1] *See* discussion in Parts A through F of this chapter.

[2] *See* 29 U.S.C. § 623(d)(ADEA); 42 U.S.C. § 2000e-3(a) (Title VII); Gov. Code § 12940(h) (FEHA); *see* Strother v. S. Cal. Permanente Medical Group (9th Circ. 1996) 79 F.3d 859, 865 (medical partner with reasonable belief she was an employee allowed to proceed with retaliation claim arising from having filed DFEH); 42 U.S.C. § 12203(a)(ADA; operative July 26, 1992).

[3] *Now see* Gov. Code § 12940(h).

[4] This amendment, however, has been held not to be retroactive. *See* Fisher v. San Pedro Peninsula Hospital (1989) 214 Cal. App. 3d 590, 615–616, 262 Cal. Rprt. 842 (holding that pre-1988 retaliation by coworker was not actionable under FEHA). For discussion of administrative enforcement proceedings under equal employment opportunity laws, *see* ch. 42. For discussion of civil actions under those laws, *see* ch. 43.

[5] *See* 42 U.S.C. § 12203(b).

[6] *See* Ramirez v. San Mateo County, Etc. (9th Cir. [Cal.] 1981) 639 F.2d 509, 515 42 U.S.C. § 1983 ("retaliation" question properly submitted to jury as First Amendment claim). For a general discussion of the United States Constitution as an equal employment opportunity source, *see* Chapter 40, Part C.

[7] *See* Manatt v. Bank of America, NA (9th Cir. 2003) 339 F.3d 792, 801–804 (although 42 U.S.C. § 1981 encompasses retaliation and hostile work environment claims, using Title VII framework for analyzing retaliation claims under § 1981, trial court properly granted employer summary judgment, where Chinese-American employee's myriad allegations of retaliation, as well as her constructive discharge claim, were without merit); London v. Coopers & Lybrand (9th Cir. 1981) 644 F.2d 811, 819. *See* Miller v. Fairchild Industries, Inc. (9th Cir. 1989) 885 F.2d 498, 503.

[8] *See* Title 42 U.S.C. § 1983; *see* Allen v. Iranon (9th Cir. 2002) 283 F.3d 1070, 1077 (action by prison doctor under 42 U.S.C. § 1983 alleging defendants retaliated against him for exercising his First Amendment right to free speech).

(Rel. 29–03.04 Pub282)

FIGURE 12-15   Text from *Employment Law* Reference Set

Reprinted from *California Employment Law.* Copyright 2004 Matthew Bender & Company, Inc., a member of the LexisNexis Group. All Rights Reserved. Reprinted with permission.

As you can see, there are several places to begin your research. With practice you will develop preferences for certain resources over other less user-friendly resources. Do not lose sight of the research plan. Create a plan and follow it until you have good reason to believe that the initial plan is not producing reliable results.

Primary sources include the following:

```
Federal Constitution
State constitutions
Federal statutes
State statutes
Federal case law
State case law
Administrative rules and regulations
```

Secondary sources include the following:

```
Legal encyclopedias
Specialty sets
Digests of case law
Pleading and practice guides
Law review articles
American Law Reports (A.L.R.)
```

12-10 UPDATE AND VALIDATE YOUR RESEARCH RESULTS

Finding the law is a good starting point. Try not to go too far into the research without slowing down and checking the validity of your research results. In addition, you must make sure you have the most current information available.

Use *Shepard's* to update and validate your research. *Shepard's* is available in print, and in several online databases, including the Internet. Shepardize any case or statute you feel you can rely on. Do not forget that you can Shepardize law review articles and *A.L.R.* annotations.

In addition to *Shepard's* you should consider using some of the features available through **LEXIS** and **Westlaw.** In LEXIS you may use the Auto-Cite feature, discussed in Chapters 10 and 11. Westlaw offers the service KeyCite, introduced in Chapters 10 and 11.

Shepard's. System used to update, validate, and expand research results.

LEXIS. A computer assisted legal research service.

Westlaw. A computer assisted legal research service.

12-11 TAKE NOTES WHEN WORKING WITH PRINTED MATERIALS

Loose leaf paper is easy to shuffle and organize later. It is also easy to misplace. These pages may look a lot like the other notes in your notebooks.

A bound tablet will keep everything in one place, but does not provide much flexibility when shuffling becomes necessary. At some point, it will become necessary to organize the notes in a logical order. Remember, your research results may not proceed in the same order that you will eventually use in writing up your memorandum or brief.

Large index cards, sometimes color coded, prove useful because of their versatility. Many researchers color code their issues. All research on a specific issue is placed, for example, on blue 5 × 7 index cards. On the back of each card the

---

ORGANIZATION AND ATTENTION TO DETAIL

Get ready to take notes.	You need pencils, pens, highlighters, self-adhesive notes, paperclips.
Be prepared to take notes.	Get your materials out and ready; be organized at each step of the research process.
Think about the paper you will use.	Loose leaf paper?
	Bound tablet?
	Large index cards?
	Adhesive notes?

---

researcher notes the date the research is performed, the source of the data, and any personal notes. It is easy to later shuffle and organize by color. Sometimes a researcher will place each case reviewed on a separate card. The notes on each statute will also be on separate cards. This makes organization much easier later.

Self-adhesive notes are small, come unstuck, and are easily misplaced. Consider using them only in addition to other resources.

Work toward establishing a personal preference. Consider the nature of your research. If you plan to take a good number of written notes, maybe index cards or loose leaf paper will provide you with the ability to easily organize and rearrange your results. Try several approaches and work toward finding a note-taking process that is comfortable and reliable. Always organize after each research session.

12-12 TAKE NOTES AND RECORD RESULTS WHEN WORKING WITH ONLINE OR CD-ROM MATERIALS

Instead of making handwritten notes from the screen during online research, consider cutting and pasting, printing, or downloading the relevant information. Some

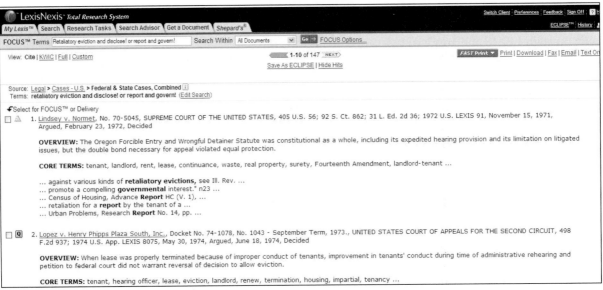

Reprinted with the permission of LexisNexis

FIGURE 12-16 LEXIS Screen

handwritten notes may be necessary. However, keep in mind that the database you are researching may be quite expensive and note taking is time consuming.

Keep track of the searches you run and the databases in which you run them. For example, the screen shown in Figure 12-16 is from LEXIS. Notice how the search and the library and file are clearly noted for the researcher.

When working with CD-ROM products, the time element is not so critical. Still, you may want to take minimal notes while you print and download the most useful data. Be sure to note why you printed the material and how you plan to use it.

⇨ **A Point to Remember**   It is easy to get carried away with the ease of printing and downloading. Be selective. Gathering hundreds of pages just because you can and doing so is easy is not good research practice.

12-13 ORGANIZATION OF PHOTOCOPIED OR DOWNLOADED MATERIALS

In the process of legal research, you will photocopy and download many documents—probably too many. It is critical that you organize these documents *as you acquire them*. Staple pages that belong together; do not paperclip them. On the reverse side of every document copied or printed note the date you acquired the material, the reason you copied it, the source, and the issue(s) it pertains to. Over days or weeks of research, you *will* forget why you copied materials and where they originated. You may also find that some of the documents you copy in the early stages of the research may not be as relevant as they seemed at the time you copied them. The date notation may help you place perspective on the data.

Create folders or files. Organize the materials issue-by-issue or separate the documents into groups of case law and statutes. If you organize from the very beginning, the process of creating the written document is much easier.

⇨ **A Point to Remember**   When you find yourself lugging around stacks (hundreds of pages) of printed material with no organization, stop and get organized. All of those pages are useless unless you impose order on your research findings. Eventually, all of that material will be converted into a memorandum or other written document. Organization saves time.

TECHNOLOGY CORNER

Research Guide:	www.llrx.com/guide
Virtual Law Library:	www.law.indiana.edu/
Internet Legal Resource Guide:	www.ilrg.com
Index for U.S. Legal Research:	www.catalaw.com

CHAPTER SUMMARY

Legal research is complicated and often frustrating. When the researcher is fully prepared and organized, the process of research becomes manageable, effective, and productive. Learning to slow down and think before beginning to research is essential. Getting ready to research is one step in the research process. A trip to the law library before you are fully prepared is time-consuming and probably unproductive. The strategies presented in this chapter lead to complete and effective legal research.

TERMS TO REMEMBER

strategy

legal issue

elements

cause of action

primary sources

secondary sources

legal encyclopedia

pleading and practice guide

topical index

digest

Shepard's

LEXIS

Westlaw

QUESTIONS FOR REVIEW

1. Why is the early formation of a vocabulary list helpful?
2. What does a well-written legal issue contain?
3. How do legal dictionaries help the legal researcher?
4. What is a research plan?
5. What is the purpose of an index?
6. When should research begin in primary sources?
7. When should research begin in secondary sources?
8. Identify three sources that help the researcher update and validate research results.
9. What should the researcher consider when getting ready to take notes?
10. When does downloading information work better than taking notes while working with an online database or a CD-ROM research product?

RESEARCH ASSIGNMENTS AND ACTIVITIES

1. Create a research plan for the assignment given in the "Interoffice Memorandum" presented at the beginning of this chapter.
2. Use a legal dictionary and expand the list of terms for the Yoshida research fact pattern. Begin with the list in section 12-4.
3. Where would you begin the research needed in the Yoshida case? Explain *why* you chose this source.

CASE PROJECT

Review the hypothetical case you selected in Chapter 1. Prepare an outline for a research strategy to be used in researching the issues in the case.

BASIC LEGAL WRITING TOOLS

CHAPTER OUTLINE

CHAPTER OBJECTIVES

When you complete this chapter you should be able to

- Discuss a researcher's initial consideration after completion of the research.
- Explain the purpose of a thesis paragraph.
- Describe how to arrange a thesis paragraph.
- Explain the role of topic sentences.
- Describe the editing and revision processes.

CITATION MATTERS

USE OF THE ELLIPSIS

THE BLUEBOOK — RULE 5.3

Legal writers often find it useful to use quoted language, but may not need all of the sentence or paragraph. The omission of a word or many words is indicated by inserting an ellipsis in place of the omitted word or words. An ellipsis consists of three periods separated by spaces and set off by a space before the first period and after the last period.

For example:

The "core of the judicial system . . . relies on early disclosure of all the facts."

Omission of words at the end of a quoted sentence is shown by an ellipsis between the last word of the quote and the final punctuation of the quoted sentence.

For example:

The "core of the judicial system . . . relies on early disclosure. . . ."

Never use an ellipsis to begin a quotation. When language at the beginning of a sentence is deleted, capitalize the first letter of the first word used and place it in brackets (unless that word is already capitalized).

For example:

"[T]he statute imposes special prohibitions on those speakers who express views on the disfavored subject of race, color, creed, religion or gender."

This is a simple way to alert the reader that the word *The* was not the first word in the quoted sentence. The use of brackets indicates that the writer only changed the case of the letter. This same tool (the bracket) is used to change a capital letter to lowercase when the writer needs to incorporate a phrase from the beginning of a quoted sentence into one of the writer's own sentences.

For example:

It is true that "[t]he ordinance, even as narrowly construed by the State Supreme Court, is facially unconstitutional. . . ."

In this example, *The* was the first word in the quoted sentence. But the writer needed to incorporate the quoted sentence into a new sentence. By placing the lowercase *t* in brackets, the writer signals the reader that he or she has changed the case of the letter.

INTEROFFICE MEMORANDUM

TO: Research Associate

FROM: Supervising Attorney

RE: Yoshida Case (from Chapter 12)

Use the facts we have on file in the Yoshida case. See the "Interoffice Memorandum" from Chapter 12 to write a fact statement to be used in a trial brief. Be sure to be as persuasive as possible.

13-1 INITIAL CONSIDERATIONS AFTER COMPLETION OF THE RESEARCH

- Before you begin to write, go back to your initial instructions. Did you follow them?
- Did you answer the questions clearly and concisely?
- Did you respond to *all* of the questions?
- Can you honestly tell your supervisor that your research results are accurate, current, and valid?
- Were you as thorough as possible?

If your response to each of these questions is "yes," you are ready to begin the drafting process. After the research is complete, the note taking and copying are replaced with analysis and writing. The following questions will help you organize your writing.

13-2 OVERVIEW OF A LEGAL RESEARCH AND WRITING PROJECT

These questions or considerations help the legal writer focus on the project and recognize problem areas.

1. What exactly is the research project or what is your goal?
2. Who is the reading audience?
3. What legal issues does the research explore?
4. How will the reading audience benefit from the results of the research?
5. List the most important points you must get across to your audience.
6. List the legal authority that supports each point listed in number 5 above.
7. Which citation manual must be followed?
   (*The Bluebook, A.L.W.D. Citation Manual*)
8. Is there a length restriction? If so, what is it?
9. What is the length of your current draft?
10. When must this project be completed?

These questions help the writer focus and provide structure to the process of research and writing.

13-3 THE THESIS PARAGRAPH

A well-written legal discussion lays a solid foundation for the reader. Before you begin to write, slow down and consider what your reader knows about the problem. You may have worked for many hours and become extremely familiar with all aspects of the problem, but the reader may have little or no knowledge.

A legal discussion or argument should begin with a **thesis paragraph** to introduce readers to your client's problem, the legal issues arising from the facts, the rules that govern the issues, and a legal conclusion. This paragraph sets the scene for the reader and provides a short overview of the interal organization of the argument section of a trial brief or the discussion section of a memorandum.

> **thesis paragraph.** The thesis paragraph lays a solid foundation for the reader. This paragraph sets forth the client's problem, states the legal issue, briefly explains the legal rules governing the issues, and states the legal conclusion.

How to Arrange a Thesis Paragraph

1. Set forth the client's problem.
2. State the legal issue.
3. Briefly explain the legal rules governing the issues.
4. State the legal conclusion (the thesis).

The thesis paragraph represents the writer's first chance to set the tone and educate the reader and is, therefore, very important. It also outlines the overall organization of the information. Clearly, the thesis paragraph cannot be written until the research is complete and the final analysis is performed.

The following paragraphs are taken from the Argument section of the Brief for the United States as Amicus Curiae Supporting Petitioner in *Minnesota v. Dickerson,* 508 U.S. 366 (1993). Notice that each paragraph follows the format set out above.

I. The Minnesota Supreme Court erred in holding that the police officer who searched respondent exceeded the scope of the protective pat-down search authorized under *Terry v. Ohio. Terry* authorizes a "careful exploration" of a suspect's outer clothing for weapons. 392 U.S. at 16. Officer Rose's brief and limited touching of the pocket of respondent's jacket was an appropriate part of the "careful" examination permitted under *Terry.* Officer Rose did not engage in the sort of prolonged and intrusive manipulation of clothing about which the state supreme court expressed concern. Nor does the record support the suggestion of the state supreme court that Rose made a discrete, conscious, decision to continue handling the object in respondent's pocket after concluding that the object was not a weapon. Instead, the officer's act of feeling the object was merely a continuation of a pat-down search indisputably justified at its inception. For that reason the officer's actions are distinguishable from the conduct found to constitute a separate, unauthorized search in *Arizona v. Hicks,* 480 U.S. 321 (1987).

II. The Minnesota Supreme Court also erred in holding that the sense of touch can never provide probable cause to believe that the object felt is contraband. This Court has recognized that probable cause can be acquired through senses other than the sense of sight. For example, in *United States v. Johns,* 469 U.S. 478 (1985), the Court held that the "distinct odor of marijuana" provided probable cause to believe that the vehicles from which the odor emanated contained contraband. Moreover, this Court's decision in *Terry* is premised on the ability of police officers to detect concealed firearms by touching the outside of a suspect's clothing. Many lower federal courts have held that the sense of

touch may provide probable cause to believe that an item is contraband. In holding to the contrary, the court below mistakenly relied on the differences it perceived between the sense of sight and the sense of touch. Those differences do not warrant a categorical prohibition of the use of the sense of touch to acquire probable cause.

Paragraphs in General

An effective paragraph is a grouping of related sentences that flow logically and that address one idea. It should be clear to the reader why a certain sentence is in a certain paragraph. Good paragraph construction takes time and patience. For each sentence, the writer must ultimately answer the question: Why is *this sentence* in *this paragraph?*

⇨ **A Point to Remember**   While drafting, try not to slow yourself down worrying about small writing errors. Get your ideas on the screen or page. You will have time to go back and edit your work. Sometimes valuable ideas are lost because we try to make our first draft absolutely perfect. Draft the document. Go back to edit.

The Role of Topic Sentences

Most paragraphs begin with a special type of sentence, a **topic sentence.** A good topic sentence introduces issues or subissues and connects back to the thesis paragraph. It creates unity within the paragraph by summarizing the point made in the paragraph. It forces the writer to articulate clearly. Its function is to set forth the relationship at the very beginning of the paragraph.

> **topic sentence.** A topic sentence introduces the issues or subissues and connects back to the thesis paragraph.

⇨ **A Point to Remember**   Topic sentences may be added after the paragraph is drafted in rough format. If you find that writing good topic sentences slows you down or even stops the flow of your writing, add them during the revision process.

Try to avoid placing a citation in the topic sentence. Readers are distracted by citations, and may miss the actual emphasis of the sentence.

During the revision process, make an outline using only the first sentences, the topic and transition sentences of each paragraph. Review this outline; does it flow? Can you easily follow the information? Topic sentences are a good way to check the internal organization of most legal documents.

These are the topic sentences from the two paragraphs taken from one of the briefs filed in the *Minnesota v. Dickerson* case.

The Minnesota Supreme Court erred in holding that the police officer who searched respondent exceeded the scope of the protective pat-down search authorized under *Terry v. Ohio.*

The Minnesota Supreme Court also erred in holding that the sense of touch can never provide probable cause to believe that the object felt is contraband.

Both sentences introduce the topic of the paragraph. Each topic sentence is clear and concise.

Construction of a Well-Written Paragraph

Consider the type of analysis to be used in the paragraph before drafting the body of the paragraph. A good paragraph does not assume too much knowledge on the reader's part; it is self-explanatory. There are various analytical tools available to the legal writer. A well-constructed paragraph may use a chronological narration of the facts, or comparison and contrast, or cause and effect to present the information.

The following paragraphs are from the *Minnesota v. Dickerson* decision. Notice the Court's use of detail and simple chronology. Each paragraph opens with a simple topic sentence that sets the scene for the information in the reminder of the paragraph.

On the evening of November 9, 1989, two Minneapolis police officers were patrolling an area on the city's north side in a marked squad car. At about 8:15 p.m., one of the officers observed respondent leaving a 12-unit apartment building on Morgan Avenue North. The officer, having previously responded to complaints of drug sales in the building's hallways and having executed several search warrants on the premises, considered the building to be a notorious "crack house." According to testimony credited by the trial court, respondent began walking toward the police but, upon spotting the squad car and making eye contact with one of the officers, abruptly halted and began walking in the opposite direction. His suspicion aroused, this officer watched as respondent turned and entered an alley on the other side of the apartment building. Based upon respondent's seemingly evasive actions and the fact that he had just left a building known for cocaine traffic, the officers decided to stop respondent and investigate further.

The officers pulled their squad car into the alley and ordered respondent to stop and submit to a pat-down search. The search revealed no weapons, but the officer conducting the search did take an interest in a small lump in respondent's nylon jacket. The officer later testified: "As I pat-searched the front of his body, I felt a lump, a small lump, in the front pocket. I examined it with my fingers and it slid and it felt to be a lump of crack cocaine in cellophane." The officer then reached into repsondent's pocket and retrieved a small plastic bag containing one-fifth of one gram of crack cocaine. Respondent was arrested and charged in Hennepin County District Court with possession of a controlled substance.

13-4 SENTENCES

Sentences are groups of words expressing a complete thought. This grouping of words must have a noun and a verb. In legal writing, it is best to keep your sentences short and direct. A concise, well-thought-out sentence is easy to read and understand. Long convoluted sentences are hard to follow and may actually present unwanted ambiguities.

⇨ **A Point to Remember**   Students are sometimes confused by what might be called the legal "Do as I say, not as I do" approach. Much of what students of the law read is law rather than summaries, discussions, explanations, and factual characterizations written for the court or for clients by legal professionals. Courts structure case opinions such that the opinion serves the purpose of educating the legal community. Legislatures create statutes to inform all of us as to the status of the law. Statutes are often very long and written in a complex format. This is not a signal to you that you should write in this fashion. Similarly, case opinions may not always offer great examples of clear and concise legal writing.

We can learn from case law and statutes, but using their organization and general format may not be the best approcah for the legal researcher who is writing to inform (predict) or convince (persuade).

Use Topic Sentences

The topic sentence is the writer's initial tool. Even thesis paragraphs need topic sentences. Some sentences serve as transitions from one topic to another or one paragraph to another.

Use Active Voice

Use **active voice** whenever possible. Sentences written in active voice usually follow this pattern of construction: subject–verb–object. In other words, open with the actor, move to the action, and then on to the object of the action. These active voice sentences are very easy to read because they open with a specific actor who then does something to someone.

Examples:

Active voice:	It was not long before she regretted her actions.
Passive voice:	It was not long before her actions made her sorry that she had done what she had.
Active voice:	Victor kicked the ball.
Passive voice:	The ball was kicked by Victor.
Active voice:	Susan drove the vehicle.
Passive voice:	The vehicle was driven by Susan.

Notice that the active voice sentences are shorter than the passive voice sentences. Check for passive voice while you edit your writing. If you think about it while you are drafting, it will slow you down and you may even lose your thoughts. Most word processing grammar-check programs help with identifying and correcting passive voice.

active voice. Active voice is a tool used by writers to shorten sentences. A sentence written in active voice uses the simple subject–verb–object approach.

13-5 KEEP LEGAL WRITING SIMPLE

Use Short Sentences

Keep sentences short. Use twenty-five words or less as the benchmark of an easily readable sentence. Long sentences become hard to read or even unreadable. As you review your written work, look for sentences that are longer than three lines. Edit these; in most cases they are too long for your reader to easily follow. Editing may involve cutting the sentence down in size or rewriting it as more than one sentence.

➡ **A Point to Remember**   Your legal writing is not meant to entertain the reader, but rather to inform or convince. Many of the tools writers of fiction use to entertain—for example, varying sentence length, creative use of adjectives and unnecessary words—must be avoided in legal writing. You are writing with a very specific purpose. Stay focused on the purpose of the document and the audience who will ultimately read it.

Avoid Unnecessary Words

Keep your legal writing simple. Get to the point, rather than introduce the point. Over the years, somewhere in an English course, we were told to introduce the topic. So we learned to open our sentences with a phrase intended to tell the reader what we were about to do. Edit those phrases and words out of your legal writing.

Use Specific, Concrete Terms

The use of specific terminology is essential. Ambiguity arises when vague words invade the legal writing. Be as specific as the facts of your situation allow. Use the most

important facts to tell a clear stroy about people. For example, if it was "cold," tell the reader how cold. If the tree was "big," tell the reader it was 50 feet high. If the officer "demanded" something, do not say he "asked" for something.

13-6 PERSUASIVE WRITING

Some documents must be persuasive. That is, the document is written so that the reader is persuaded to adopt the writer's point of view. Examples of such documents are trial briefs, points and authorities in support of motions, declarations, and demand letters. In persuasive writing, every word, phrase, and sentence must be carefully drafted. The writer must consider the impact the document will have on the reader. This goes beyond informative writing.

Set forth below are excerpts from briefs filed with the United States Supreme Court in the *Minnesota v. Dickerson* case.

This excerpt is from the opening argument section of the Brief for the United States as Amicus Curiae Supporting Petitioner.

ARGUMENT

I. OFFICER ROSE WAS CONDUCTING A LAWFUL PAT-DOWN SEARCH WHEN HE ACQUIRED PROBABLE CAUSE TO BELIEVE THAT RESPONDENT POSSESSED CONTRABAND.

The Minnesota Supreme Court not only declined as a general matter to recognize a "plain feel" corollary to the "plain view" doctrine; it also held that the crack seized from respondent's pocket would not be admissible under a "plain feel" analysis in any event. The latter holding was based on the court's view that, in the course of determining that the object in respondent's pocket was crack, Officer Rose exceeded the scope of the protective pat-down search authorized under *Terry v. Ohio.* To the contrary, we submit that Officer Rose was acting within the scope of *Terry* when he developed probable cause to believe that respondent was in possession of contraband.

At the outset, we agree with the premise underlying the state court's *Terry* holding: a "plain feel" corollary to the "plain view" doctrine would not authorize a police officer to seize evidence without a warrant if the police officer violated the Fourth Amendment in the course of developing probable cause to support the seizure. An "essential predicate" of a seizure based on "plain feel," like one based on "plain view," is that "the officer did not violate the Fourth Amendment in arriving at the place from which the evidence could be plainly [felt]." *Horton v. California* 469 U.S. 128, 136 (1990). Thus, if a police officer reaches into a suspect's pocket without reasonable suspicion or probable cause and feels an object that the officer knows to be contraband, the seizure of that object cannot be justified on the ground that the seizure was the product of a "plain feel" of the object. In *Sibron v. New York,* 392 U.S. 40, 65 (1968), this Court held that such an intrusion was unlawful, because the intrusion was not justified by reasonable suspicion or probable cause to believe that the suspect had contraband or a weapon in his pocket. The Court therefore ordered suppression of the contraband found in the course of that search.

Officer Rose's conduct, however, was a far cry from the sort of intrusion held to violate the Fourth Amendment in *Sibron.* This was not a case of retroactively justifying a search by what it turned up; rather, because the pat-down search was lawful, the fruits of that search could be considered in determining the lawfulness of Officer Rose's further investigative steps.

This next excerpt is from the opening argument section of the Brief filed for the American Civil Liberties Union and the Minnesota Civil Liberties Union as Amici Curiae in Support of Respondent.

ARGUMENT

I. THE WARRANTLESS SEARCH OF RESPONDENT'S POCKET CONTRAVENED THE FOURTH AMENDMENT BY EXCEEDING THE SCOPE OF *TERRY*.

A. A *Terry* frisk is limited solely to a narrowly-tailored search for weapons.

In *Terry v. Ohio*, this Court set forth the standard governing pat-downs of temporarily detailed suspects: an officer can only conduct a limited protective search for weapons (a "frisk") when there is "reason to believe that he is dealing with an armed and dangerous individual . . ." 392 U.S. at 27. Although subsequent cases have extended *Terry's* reach to other contexts, this Court has never deviated from the fundamental rule that a frisk is singularly limited to weapon searches, and thus cannot be conducted simply to locate contraband or evidence of crime.

These principles were reaffirmed in *Ybarra v. Illinois*: "The *Terry* case created an exception to the requirement of probable cause, an exception whose "narrow scope" this Court "has been careful to maintain." Under that doctrine a law enforcement officer, for his own protection and safety, may conduct a pat-down to find weapons that he reasonably believes or suspects are then in the possession of the person he has accosted. . . . Nothing in *Terry* can be understood to allow a generalized "cursory search for weapons" or, indeed, any search whatever for anything but weapons.

Both briefs go on for many pages. Both are convincing. Compare and contrast these two opening arguments.

13-7 OVERVIEW OF THE EDITING AND REVISION PROCESS

1. Print the document. If time permits, let it sit for a day before you look at it again. Reread your instructions. Have you adequately responded to the initial questions?

2. Look over the document; do not read it, just glance through it.

3. Is the organization of the document readily apparent, without actually reading it? If not, go back and work in appropriate point headings.

4. Check to see that each paragraph contains a topic sentence or a sentence that serves as a transition from the previous paragraph.

5. Does the discussion or argument section begin with a thesis paragraph? If not, insert a thesis paragraph now.

6. Make sure each paragraph contains facts or law to support your position.

7. Identify the verbs. Highlight the following: *was, were, is, are, has been, have been, had been, becomes, became, went, did,* and *came*. Where possible, replace these with active verbs. Active verbs create a mental picture of a specific sensation, activity, or sound in the reader's imagination.

8. Place transition words or phrases between sentences and paragraphs where appropriate.

9. Reread the opening of your document. Does it clearly and concisely introduce the topic of your writing? If not, revise or rewrite.

10. Reread the conclusion. Does it clearly and concisely conclude your document? If not, edit or rewrite. When you complete the conclusion ask yourself if you have created a tone of finality.

TECHNOLOGY CORNER

Basic Legal Citation: www.law.cornell.edu/citation/

CHAPTER SUMMARY

Keep your legal writing clear and concise. Strive to communicate in a straightforward manner. Before you begin to write, go back and check your instructions; have you followed them? Have you responded to all of the questions? Are your answers clear and concise? Is your research accurate, current, and validated? Have you been thorough? Be sure you understand the parameters of your project. Good legal writing will open with a thesis paragraph. Good paragraphs open with topic sentences. Use active voice when possible. Keep your sentences short and avoid the use of unnecessary words. Be specific and always edit your work before passing it along to anyone to review.

TERMS TO REMEMBER

thesis paragraph   active voice
topic sentence

QUESTIONS FOR REVIEW

1. Why should a writer use the Overview of a Legal Research and Writing Project form set forth in Section 13-2?
2. Discuss the purpose and importance of a thesis paragraph.
3. How should a thesis paragraph be arranged?
4. What is the role of the topic sentence?
5. Why should you use active voice whenever possible?

RESEARCH ASSIGNMENTS AND ACTIVITIES

1. Write the fact pattern requested in the "Interoffice Memorandum" at the beginning of this chapter.
2. Write a thesis paragraph for the Argument section of a trial brief in the Yoshida case. Use the information in Chapter 12 as the basis of your argument.
3. Compare and contrast the arguments set forth in the briefs filed with the United States Supreme Court in the *Minnesota v. Dickerson* case located in Section 13-6.

LEGAL WRITING: WRITING TO INFORM

CHAPTER OBJECTIVES

When you complete this chapter you should be able to

- Explain the purpose of a legal memorandum.
- Describe the format for a memorandum of law.
- List the components of a memorandum of law.
- Compare and contrast how to write about situations controlled by statutory law and those controlled by case law.
- Explain the purpose of each component of a memorandum of law.
- Explain the purpose of an opinion letter.

CITATION MATTERS

SHORT CITATION FORMAT

THE BLUEBOOK — RULE 4

Legal writing often contains a large number of citations. The "short citation formats" help the reader sort through the citations. The amount of repetition is cut down for both the writer and the reader.

Probably the most common short citation form is *Id.* Use *id.* when citing the immediately preceding legal authority. This tells the reader that the material originated in the same location as the material cited immediately preceding it.

For example:

> The *Ferber* case upheld a prohibition on the distribution and sale of child pornography, as well as its production, because these acts were 'intrinsically related' to the sexual abuse of children in two ways. *New York v. Ferber*, 458 U.S. 747, 759 (1982). First as a permanent record of a child's abuse, the continued circulation itself would harm the child who had participated. *See id.* Second, because the traffic in child pornography was an economic motive for its production, the State had an interest in closing the distribution network.
>
> *Id.* at 760.

In this example of a blocked quote, the reader is alerted that the material in the first sentence is found in the *Ferber* case. The entire citation is provided because this is the first time the case is used. The second sentence is followed by a short format citation. The "signal" *see* is followed by *id.*, meaning that the writer is asking the reader to look at page 759 in the case (page 759 is listed as the "pinpoint" page in the *Ferber* citation sentence). The *i* in *id.* is lowercase because *id* is not the first word in the citation sentence. The third sentence is followed simply by "*Id.* at 760." This tells the reader that this information is found on page 760 of the *Ferber* case.

The Bluebook — **THE BLUEPAGES —B5.2**

Short Forms in Court Documents and Legal Memoranda

The Bluepages at B5.2 offers a good list of short forms for cases, consitutions, statutes and regulations, and books, pamphlets, and other nonperiodic materials. For example, acceptable short form citations for *Ashcroft v. Free Speech Coalition,* 535 U.S. 234, 245 (2002) are the following:

> *Free Speech Coalition,* 535 U.S. at 245.
>
> 535 U.S. at 245.
>
> *Id.* at 245.

INTEROFFICE MEMORANDUM

TO: Research Associate

FROM: Senior Attorney

RE: Research Projects

There are several projects pending and I need your help. The Rambeaux criminal matter is set for a pretrial hearing and I need to review the facts and the law with Rambeaux before that time so that we can make a realistic appraisal of his chances should the case go to trial. I know you have done quite a bit of research on this case. Please put all of your findings in a memorandum of law so that I will be ready for my meeting with Rambeaux.

    As soon as you finish that, I need your help on a new case. This case involves a potential civil lawsuit against a shopping center by our client, who was assaulted in the parking lot of the center. Please let me know as soon as you finish the Rambeaux memo, and I will brief you on all the facts of the second case.

14-1 INTRODUCTION

As a legal researcher, you understand the importance of locating the cases or codes that answer your legal questions. However, your job as a researcher is not complete until you communicate your findings in an appropriate manner. In Chapter 1 you learned that legal research is performed for different reasons and the results are conveyed to different types of audiences. The result of your research may be conveyed to a lay person or an attorney in an *objective* manner. An objective evaluation or analysis of the case often includes a *prediction* of how a court would rule on the issues of the case. In other cases, it may be conveyed to an attorney or judge, not in an objective manner, but in an *argumentative* or *persuasive* fashion.

    A research assistant such as a paralegal or law clerk, does research for a supervising attorney that, initially, is communicated in an objective manner. Ultimately, the attorney might use the research to form the basis of advice given to a client or to form the basis of a formal legal document sent to another attorney and to the court.

memorandum of law. An objectively written document in which the researcher informs another of the law governing a specific situation.

opinion letter. Formal correspondence from an attorney to a client or other attorney explaining an attorney's interpretation of the law as applied to a factual situation.

memorandum of points and authorities. A formal document, written in an argumentative or persuasive manner, filed with the court, and advocating a certain position.

trial brief. A document filed with the court at the beginning of the trial in which the author is trying to persuade the trial judge to interpret the law in a way that is favorable to the author's client.

appellate brief. A document filed in support of or in opposition to an appeal, containing arguments related to legal errors that may have occurred at trial.

Documents conveying the results of legal research are known by various names. A **memorandum of law** is a document written in an objective manner in which the researcher explains the law governing a specific situation. An **opinion letter** is formal correspondence from an attorney to a client or other attorney explaining an attorney's interpretation of the law as applied to a factual situation. Usually, it contains an objective evaluation of the law and the facts. A **memorandum of points and authorities** is a more formal document, filed with the court, and advocating the client's position. In such a document, the author attempts to persuade the court to follow an interpretation of the law that favors the author's client. A memorandum of points and authorities is often used to support or oppose a motion made in court in connection with a civil or criminal case that was filed with the court. A **trial brief** is a formal document, filed with the court at the beginning of the trial, in which the author tries to persuade the trial judge to interpret the law in a way that is favorable to the author's client. An **appellate brief** is a document filed in support of or in opposition to an appeal. It contains arguments related to legal errors that may have occurred at trial. This chapter deals with writing in an objective manner for attorneys and clients. The following chapter deals with persuasive documents.

14-2 MEMORANDUM OF LAW

A researcher's initial findings and analysis are often written in a document called a memorandum of law. This document is included in the client file and is relied upon by the author or by other attorneys. It may form the basis for advice to the client or it may serve as the starting point for drafting persuasive documents filed with the court. It is important that a memorandum of law be complete and thorough. A memorandum of law is often written by a research assistant, such as a law clerk or paralegal. (The term *memorandum of law* is most commonly used to describe this type of document, but not always. Lawyers sometimes call this a *memo,* a *legal memorandum,* or even an *interoffice memo.*) It is intended to inform the reader, usually an attorney, of the state of the law concerning a certain issue. It contains a legal analysis of the facts and the law and should contain *all* relevant law, even law that does not support your client's position. The analysis in this type of document should include all reasonable arguments and inferences that can be drawn from the law, whether they support your client or not. The researcher, however, often gives an opinion as to what law and what arguments seem to be the strongest. The opinion must be supported by authority. Such a memorandum is sometimes referred to as a *predictive* memorandum because it strives to predict how a court will rule on the issue.

Attorneys who rely on research assistants depend a great deal on a memorandum of law. A properly researched and written memorandum saves an attorney a great deal of time. Instead of spending hours researching, reading, and analyzing cases and statutes, the attorney can read a memorandum of law summarizing relevant law. Because an attorney may rely exclusively on such a memorandum, it is essential that this document be complete and accurate.

➪ **A Point to Remember** If you rely on a memorandum of law found in an office file, always check the date that the memo was written. Many cases take years before they are completed; a memo found in a file might have been researched years ago. Remember that laws change; if any amount of time has lapsed since the memo was written, you should be sure to validate and update the research.

Although a memorandum of law is not filed with the court, it may later form the basis of an opinion letter to a client, or a more formal legal memorandum or brief

used to convince another attorney or the court of your client's legal position. Read Appendix D. See how the memoranda of law on pages 458 and 460 (in Appendix D) were used to prepare the formal memorandum of points and authorities.

14-3 FORMAT FOR A MEMORANDUM OF LAW

There are no absolute formalities for a memorandum of law, although most do follow similar formats. Because this document is likely to be included in a client file, it should contain basic information found in all office memoranda. It should identify the author of the document, the person for whom it is prepared, the date, and the subject matter. The subject matter must always identify the office client so that if the document is separated from the file, it can be properly identified. The beginning of a memorandum should look as follows.

MEMORANDUM OF LAW

To:

From:

Date:

Subject:

The memorandum itself should contain the following components: a concise statement of relevant facts, a statement of the issue(s) or question(s) forming the basis of the research, and a discussion of the law and the facts. Each component part should be clearly labeled with a heading. For example, a basic template for a memorandum looks like this.

Facts

[State the facts that are relevant to your research problem. Review Chapter 3 for identifying and writing a concise statement of facts. Remember, you identified these facts before you started your research.]

Issue(s)

[List the legal questions or issues you researched. If you are writing an objective memorandum of law, these questions were probably given to you by the supervising attorney. Refer to Chapter 3 for a review of writing issue statements.]

Discussion

[This is the most important part of the memorandum. In this section, you discuss each of the issues, present the authorities you found in your research, and explain or discuss why and how these authorities apply to your factual situation. In discussing your research, you should use the IRAC method. Review Chapters 5 and 7 on using the IRAC method with cases and statutes. Also, do not forget the basic writing techniques discussed in the prior chapter.]

Conclusion

[Although you give a conclusion to each issue you discuss, you should give a general conclusion summarizing all of your main points. Sometimes, in lieu of a conclusion or in addition to a conclusion, a memorandum contains a section titled "Brief Answer." This is usually placed at the beginning of the memo, immediately following the statement of issues.]

Some attorneys prefer a different order, such as the following:

- **Issue**
- **Brief Answer** (This is similar to the conclusion.)
- **Facts**
- **Discussion**

14-4 PREPARING TO WRITE THE MEMORANDUM OF LAW

Whether you realize it or not, you begin preparing to write a memorandum of law the moment you analyze the factual dispute and identify the legal issues. (Recall how and why you do this from Chapter 3.) In doing legal research, you look for relevant law. Your determination that law is relevant requires you to analyze the law you find and determine if and how it applies to your factual situation. You should recall from earlier chapters that this analysis is really a part of the research process. The memorandum of law *communicates* your analysis to the reader in an organized and logical manner.

Prior to writing the "Discussion," it is imperative that you organize your ideas and findings. Making an outline is a good way to do this. An outline for your discussion in a memorandum of law should contain the main points and the law that support each point in some logical order. Within the memorandum, the main points are usually stated in the topic sentences for each of your paragraphs.

In preparing an outline, remember that legal analysis usually follows the IRAC rule. Any legal analysis requires that you first identify the **I**ssue or question. That is followed by the rules of law that apply. These **R**ules of law are found in cases, codes, and constitutions. You then **A**pply the law to your facts. Finally, you reach a **C**onclusion. One of the most important results of making an outline before you begin to write is that you are forced to organize your ideas. Sticking to your outline while you are writing forces you to stay organized. There are, of course, different ways to organize the discussion in a memorandum. The following suggestions provide some assistance, but remember, they are not the only ways to organize your ideas.

Organizing a Memorandum

The organization of a memorandum of law often depends on the type of legal authorities controlling your case.

Situations Controlled by Statutory Law

Probably the easiest memorandum to write is one where you are asked to analyze a factual situation and determine whether a particular code section controls the facts. Review the Rambeaux hypothetical discussed in previous chapters in this text. Suppose you are asked to write a memorandum addressing the following question: Is Rambeaux criminally responsible for his acts under the Federal Civil Rights Act?

A written memorandum answering this question is easily organized around the relevant code section, which provides the following:

Whoever, under color of any law, statute, ordinance, regulation, or custom, willfully subjects any person in any State, Territory, Commonwealth, Possession, or District to the

deprivation of any rights, privileges, or immunities secured or protected by the Constitution or laws of the United States, or to different punishments, pains, or penalties, on account of such person being an alien, or by reason of his color, or race, than are prescribed for the punishment of citizens, shall be fined under this title or imprisoned not more than one year, or both; and if bodily injury results from the acts committed in violation of this section or if such acts include the use, attempted use, or threatened use of a dangerous weapon, explosive, or fire, shall be fined under this title or imprisoned not more than ten years, or both; and if death results from the acts committed in violation of this section or if such acts include kidnapping or an attempt to kidnap, aggravated sexual abuse or an attempt to commit aggravated sexual abuse, or an attempt to kill, shall be fined under this title, or imprisoned for any term of years or for life, or both, or may be sentenced to death. 18 U.S.C. § 242

In this situation, break down the relevant code section into the various elements and then discuss each separately. (Keep in mind that you have already done this type of analysis. As part of the research process, you analyzed the statute to determine if it applied. At this point, you are communicating this analysis in written form. Refer to Chapter 7.)

In the discussion section, you may need to refer to case law interpreting some or all of the elements of the code. In discussing these elements, you can arrange them in the same order that they appear in the code. Alternatively, you can first discuss elements that are fairly obvious and then discuss those that present problems and require a more detailed analysis.

One question that arises occasionally with this type of memorandum is whether you need to discuss every element of the code section. If the code section applies to your facts, then you do need to discuss each element (assuming, of course, that this is what you were asked to research). If, on the other hand, it is clear to you that the statute does *not* apply, you may only need to discuss those elements that make the statute nonapplicable. For example, in the Rambeaux case, suppose that Rambeaux is a private security guard rather than a police officer. The Federal Civil Rights Act requires that one be "acting under color of law." Because a private security guard does not act under color of authority, the section is clearly not applicable and it would not be necessary to discuss all the other elements of the code section.

An outline of a memo to be written in the Rambeaux case might look as follows.

Sample Outline

I. Introduction
   A. A violation of 18 U.S.C. § 242 requires that a person acting under color of law willfully deprive another of a constitutional right or subject another to different punishments or penalties because of color or race.
   B. Facts indicate Rambeaux's actions meet each of the elements.
II. Were Rambeaux's Actions Under Color of Law? *(This is a statement of the issue.)*
   A. 18 U.S.C. § 242 requires that action be under color of law. *(This is the rule of law.)*
   B. Rambeaux was in uniform.
   C. Rambeaux was performing a normal police function—a traffic stop. *(B. and C. constitute the analysis. Here you apply the facts to the language of the code.)*
III. Was Rambeaux's Conduct Willful?
   A. Code requires that conduct be willful.
   B. Rambeaux's actions were intentional.

    IV. Did Rambeaux Deprive Another of Constitutional Rights?

        A. Code requires a deprivation of constitutional rights.

        B. A traffic stop is a seizure under the Fourth Amendment to the U.S. Constitution.

        C. Rambeaux's actions were not reasonable as required by the Constitution.

    V. Did Rambeaux Inflict Different Punishment Due to Color or Race?

        A. As an alternative to a deprivation of constitutional rights, a violation of 18 U.S.C. § 242 can be based on infliction of different punishments due to color or race.

        B. Rambeaux inflicted extraordinary injury or punishment to victim.

        C. Rambeaux's statements indicate racial bias.

    VI. Conclusion

⇨ **A Point to Remember**   During the research process, if you take notes on index cards, using a separate card for each authority, you can arrange these cards according to your outline. Writing your memorandum is much easier.

Situations Controlled by Case Law

A legal memorandum based on a situation controlled entirely by case law is often more difficult to organize. The organization depends on the research question. One common research task is to determine whether a party has a certain **cause of action,** entitling that party to some sort of relief (most often money). A cause of action is a set of facts that the law recognizes as entitling a person to relief from the courts. Whether a cause of action exists or not is dependent on the substantive law. Like many code sections, causes of action can be broken down into elements that are almost always listed in relevant case law. Organizing this type of memorandum is thus very similar to organizing a memorandum based on statutory law. You begin by setting out the elements of the cause of action as described in case law. You then discuss each of the elements, bringing in additional case law where needed. If there are affirmative defenses, they must also be discussed. For example, consider the case described below.

    In this case, the relevant law is the law of negligence. Assume that this situation is controlled by the law of the state of California and your research uncovered the case of *Ann M. v. Pacific Plaza,* on the next page. In this opinion, the court states what must be shown for a cause of negligence to exist. The court states: "An action in negligence requires a showing that the defendant owed the plaintiff a legal duty, that the defendant breached the duty, and that the breach was a proximate or legal cause of injuries suffered by the plaintiff."

    In organizing your research for the memorandum of law regarding the *Victoria V.* case, you could take each of the factors mentioned by the court and discuss them separately, either in the order listed by the court or in any other logical order. Before going on, read the *Ann M.* case found later in this chapter.

cause of action. The basis upon which a lawsuit may be brought to the court.

VICTORIA V. v. U SHOP MALL

Victoria V. was sexually assaulted in the parking lot of U Shop Mall one evening about 9 p.m. Victoria had shopped for several hours. When she entered the shopping center it was still light outside but Victoria knew that she would be shopping for several hours and it would probably be dark when she left. Therefore, she parked under a light. Unknown to her, the light was not working.

The shopping center also employs a security guard to patrol its two parking areas, one in front and one in back. It takes the security guard about 30 minutes to patrol each of these. Incidentally, the security guard reported that the parking light was out about 24 hours prior to the assault on Victoria. However, the shopping center did not have any replacement bulbs on hand. Records also indicate that in the past month (before the assault) there were three reports of cars being broken into and items stolen. There was also one report of a mugging of an elderly gentleman that took place in the parking area. Finally, a report of a sexual assault that took place in a shopping center about two miles away was received by the U Shop Mall about two weeks prior to the assault on Victoria. No sexual assault had ever been reported in the U Shop Mall itself.

Your law firm represents Victoria and wants to file a civil lawsuit against U Shop Mall for its negligence. You are asked to research whether such a claim has any merit.

The first part of an outline for your memorandum might look something like this.

Sample Outline

I. Introduction
  A. Any action by Victoria must be based on the tort of negligence.
  B. An action for negligence requires the existence of a legal duty, breach of the duty, and the proximate or legal cause of injuries.

II. Does a landowner have a duty to protect others from criminal attack by third parties? *(This is a statement of the* **issue***. Note that it corresponds to the first element of the cause of action described in B above, i.e., the existence of a legal duty.)*

  A. Before a landowner owes a duty to protect a person from criminal attack, the harm must be foreseeable. This requires other similar incidents. *(State the rule of law or holding from the* Ann M. *case and from any other authorities that might relate to this issue. At this point, you give the proper cite for your authorities.)*

  B. Comparison of facts of *Ann M.* with facts of *Victoria V. (This is the* **analysis***. Because your authorities for this issue consist of case law, your analysis requires that you compare facts of the case law to facts of* Victoria. *Your outline should list the facts of* Ann M. *that you want to discuss with the facts of the* Victoria V. *case.)*

  C. Conclusion. *(Discuss your conclusion on this issue. An objective memorandum may not reach a definitive answer to the issue or question. You might be summarizing the various possibilities.)*

III. *(Continue with each element of the cause of action and any defenses that may exist.)*

CASE 14-1

Ann M. v. Pacific Plaza Shopping Center

6 Cal. 4th 666, 863 P.2d 207, 25 Cal.Rptr. 2d 137 (1993)

OPINION:
We granted review in this case to determine whether the scope of the duty owed by the owner of a shopping center to maintain common areas within its possession and control in a reasonably safe condition includes providing security guards in those areas. We conclude that, under the facts of this case, the owner did not owe a duty to provide security guards.

I. BACKGROUND

This case arises out of a civil complaint filed by Ann M. after she was raped at her place of employment. Unless otherwise indicated, the facts as stated herein are not in dispute.

On June 17, 1985, Ann M. was employed by the Original 60 Minute Photo Company, a photo processing service located in a secluded area of the Pacific Plaza Shopping Center (hereafter shopping center). The shopping center, owned and operated by defendants (hereafter sometimes collectively referred to as Pacific Plaza), is a strip mall located on Garnet Avenue in the Pacific Beach area of San Diego. Approximately 25 commercial tenants occupy the shopping center at any one time.

The lease between the photo store and the shopping center granted the owners of the shopping center the exclusive right to control the common areas. Although the lease gave Pacific Plaza the right to police the common areas, the lease did not purport to impose an obligation to police either common areas or those areas under the exclusive control and management of the tenants. In fact, Pacific Plaza hired no security guards.

At approximately 8 a.m. on June 17, Ann M. opened the photo store for business. She was the only employee on duty. The door was closed but unlocked. The store was equipped with a "drop gate" that was designed to prevent customer access behind the counter but it had been broken for some period of time. Shortly after Ann M. opened the store, a man she had never seen before walked in "just like a customer." Ann M. greeted the man, told him that she would assist him shortly, and turned her back to the counter. The man, who was armed with a knife, went behind the counter, raped Ann M., robbed the store, and fled. The rapist was not apprehended.

In 1984 and 1985 violent crimes occurred in the census tract in which the shopping center is located. While the record includes some evidence of criminal activity on the shopping center's premises prior to Ann M.'s rape—bank robberies, purse snatchings, and a man pulling down women's pants—there is no evidence that Pacific Plaza had knowledge of these alleged criminal acts. In fact, Pacific Plaza offers uncontroverted evidence that it "is the standard practice of [Pacific Plaza] to note or record instances of violent crime" and that Pacific Plaza's records contain no reference to violent criminal acts in the shopping center prior to Ann M.'s rape.

Ann M. presented evidence that the employees and tenants were concerned about their safety prior to her rape. These concerns centered around the presence of persons described as transients, who loitered in the common areas. One of the employees of the photo store called the police on two different occasions prior to the incident involved herein to complain that she felt threatened by persons loitering outside her employer's store. The photo store ultimately granted this employee permission to bring her dog to work for protection. This employee worked a late night shift, while Ann M. worked during the day. During periodic meetings of the merchants' association, an organization to which all tenants belonged, the tenants voiced complaints about a lack of security in the shopping center and the presence of transients. There is no evidence to indicate, however, that Ann M.'s rapist was one of the loitering transients or that the presence of the transients contributed in any way to Ann M.'s attack.

According to Ann M.'s deposition testimony, the merchants' association invited a security company to address the tenants' concerns at one of its meetings. During that meeting, the security company informed the tenants of different security options and recommended that regular walking patrols be instituted. Ann M. stated in her deposition that she was told that the merchants' association decided not to hire the security patrols, because the cost would be prohibitive. Ann M. further testified that she was told at these meetings that the merchants' association requested that the shopping center provide such patrols. No such patrols were provided. According to the lease, if the shopping center had provided the requested patrols, the tenants would have borne the cost in the form of additional rent. Ultimately, the merchants' association hired a security company to drive by the area three or four times a day instead of arranging for foot patrols. Ann M. was raped sometime thereafter.

After the rape, Ann M. filed a civil complaint for damages in the superior court, alleging causes of action for negligence against Amapho Corp. (the owner

and operator of the photo store), Glen Hutchinson (the president of Amapho Corp.), the shopping center, and La Jolla Development Co. (the corporation employed to manage the shopping center at the time of the rape). Ann M. alleged that the defendants were negligent in failing to provide adequate security to protect her from an unreasonable risk of harm. This risk specifically was alleged to be the presence of transients and the potential for violent confrontation between transients and employees of the shopping center.

Pacific Plaza filed a motion for summary judgment or summary adjudication of issues, claiming that it owed no legal duty to Ann M., primarily because Ann M.'s attack was unforeseeable. Ann M. countered that a duty was owed: the attack was foreseeable because Pacific Plaza permitted transients to congregate in the common areas of the shopping center. Ann M. contended that "[s]ecurity patrols to roust the center's transient population would have provided the [necessary] 'first line of defense'" that Pacific Plaza allegedly had a duty to provide. The trial court granted the motion, finding that Pacific Plaza owed Ann M. no duty of care, and entered judgment in favor of Pacific Plaza.

Ann M. appealed. Following rehearing, the Court of Appeal affirmed the judgment of the trial court, but on different grounds. The Court of Appeal held that Pacific Plaza owed a duty to tenants and their employees to maintain the common areas and leased premises in a reasonably safe condition, including the duty to take reasonable precautions against foreseeable criminal activity by their persons; however, based on the evidence presented, the Court of Appeal held that no reasonable jury could have concluded that Pacific Plaza acted unreasonably in failing to provide the security patrols that Ann M. claims were necessary.

We granted Ann M.'s petition for review.

II. DISCUSSION

A. Standard of review

Although Ann M.'s complaint is phrased in broader terms, Ann M. concedes that the gravamen of her complaint is that Pacific Plaza's failure to provide security patrols in the common areas consti-

tuted negligence. We therefore confine our review to this issue (*Cf. Chern v. Bank of America* (1976) 15 Cal.3d 866, 873 ["purpose of summary procedure is to penetrate through evasive language and adept pleading and ascertain the existence or absence of triable issues"]; *FPI Development, Inc. v. Nakashima* (1991) 231 Cal.App.3d 367, 381–382 [pleadings serve as the outer measure of materiality in a summary judgment proceeding].)

An action in negligence requires a showing that the defendant owed the plaintiff a legal duty, that the defendant breached the duty, and that the breach was a proximate or legal cause of injuries suffered by the plaintiff. [emphasis added] (*United States Liab. Ins. Co. v. Haidinger-Hayes, Inc.* (1970) 1 Cal.3d 586, 594; 6 Witkin, *Summary of Cal. Law* (9th ed. 1988) Torts, § 732, p. 60.) On review of a summary judgement in favor of the defendant, we review the record de novo to determine whether the defendant has conclusively negated a necessary element of the plaintiff's case or demonstrated that under no hypothesis is there a material issue of fact that requires the process of trial. (*Molko v. Holy Spirit Assn.* (1988) 46 Cal.3d 1092, 1107.)

For the reasons discussed below, we conclude that, under the facts of this case, the scope of any duty owed by Pacific Plaza to Ann M. did not include providing security guards in the common areas. Accordingly, we do not address whether Pacific Plaza's failure to provide security guards was a proximate cause of Ann M.'s injuries (*See Nola M. v. University of Southern California* (1993) 16 Cal.App.4th 421 [hereafter *Nola M.*].)

B. DUTY

The existence of a duty is a question of law for the court. (*Isaacs v. Huntington Memorial Hospital* (1985) 38 Cal.3d 112, 124 [hereafter *Isaacs*]; *Southland Corp. v. Superior Court* (1988) 203 Cal.App.3d 656, 663.) Accordingly, we determine de novo the existence and scope of the duty owed by Pacific Plaza to Ann M.

It is now well established that California law requires landowners to maintain land in their possession and control in a reasonably safe condition. (Civ. Code, § 1714; *Rowland v. Christian* (1968) 69 Cal.2d 108.)

In the case of a landlord, this general duty of maintenance, which is owed to tenants and patrons, has been held to include the duty to take reasonable steps to secure common areas against foreseeable criminal acts of third parties that are likely to occur in the absence of such precautionary measures. (*Frances T. v. Village Green Owners Assn.* (1986) 42 Cal.3d 490, 499–501 [hereafter *Frances T.*]; *O'Hara v. Western Seven Trees Corp.* (1977) 75 Cal.App.3d 798, 802–803 [hereafter *O'Hara*]; *Isaacs, supra,* 38 Cal.3d at pp. 123-124.)

Pacific Plaza argues that its relationship with Ann M. is insufficient to support the extension to Ann M. of the duty that it owes to its patrons and tenants to take reasonable steps to secure the common areas of its land. Ann M. counters that she is, in effect, Pacific Plaza's invitee and that this status creates a "special relationship" sufficient to support the imposition on Pacific Plaza of a duty to her.

In this state, duties are no longer imposed on an occupier of land solely on the basis of rigid clasifications of trespasser, licensee, and invitee. (*Peterson v. San Francisco Community College Dist.* (1984) 36 Cal.3d 799, 808, fn. 5; *Rowland v. Christian, supra,* 69 Cal.2d at p. 119.) The purpose of plaintiff's presence on the land is not determinative. We have recognized, however, that this purpose may have some bearing upon the liability issue. (*Rowland v. Christian, supra,* 69 Cal.2d at p. 119.) This purpose therefore must be considered along with other factors weighing for and against the imposition of a duty on the landowner.

We conclude that it is appropriate in this case to apply the rules specifying the duty of a landowner to its tenants and patrons. Ann M.'s reason for being upon Pacific Plaza's land at the time of her attack fully supports this conclusion. As stated above, it is established that a landlord owes a duty of care to its tenants to take reasonable steps to secure the common areas under its control. In this case, Ann M. admittedly was not Pacific Plaza's tenant; her employer was. Nevertheless, in "the commercial context where the tenant generally is not a natural person and must, therefore, act through its employees, it cannot be seriously asserted that a tort duty that a landlord owes to protect the personal safety of its tenant should not extend to its tenant's employees. (*Cf. DeGraf v. Anglo Cal-*

ifornia Nat. Bank (1939) 14 Cal.2d 87, 93 ["plaintiff, as manager of the business of a tenant of the building, stood in a position equal to that of an actual tenant thereof"].) Therefore, the issue of the existence and scope of Pacific Plaza's duty to Ann M. is not resolved by the fact that Ann M.'s employer, rather than Ann M. herself, was Pacific Plaza's tenant.

Pacific Plaza next contends that it owed no duty to Ann M. in this case because the crime occurred on property not within its possession and control. While it is true that Ann M. was raped within the tenant's premises, Ann M. alleges that it was Pacific Plaza's failure to adequately maintain the common areas that caused her injury. As a result, she contends that the location of the crime does not necessarily determine the landowner's liability for injuries resulting from criminal acts. (*Frances T., supra,* 42 Cal.3d at p. 503; *O'Hara, supra,* 75 Cal. App.3d at p. 803.)

In *O'Hara, supra,* 75, Cal.App.3d 798, a tenant sued her landlord, alleging that it was liable for injuries resulting from her rape inside her apartment. Knowing of several previous rapes of tenants and of conditions indicating a likelihood that the rapist would repeat his attacks, the landlord induced the plaintiff to rent an apartment in the complex without disclosing any of the above information, and by falsely assuring her that the premises were safe and patrolled at all times by professional guards. (at p. 802.) The landlord also failed to share with the plaintiff knowledge of the suspect's mode of operation and composite drawings of the suspect. (*Ibid.*) The Court of Appeal held that the landlord had a duty to take reasonable precautions to safeguard the common areas against the types of crimes of which it had notice and which were likely to recur if the common areas were not secure. (at pp. 803–804.) Because the landlord's failure to take "reasonable precautions to safeguard the common areas under [its] control could have contributed substantially, as alleged, to [the tenant's] injuries" (at p. 803), the Court of Appeal reversed the judgment of the trial court with directions to overrule the general demurrer (at p. 806).

In *Frances T., supra,* 42 Cal.3d 490, this court adopted the reasoning of the *O'Hara* court and extended it to the context of residential condominiums. We reasoned

that a condominium association functions as a landlord in maintaining the common areas of a large condominium complex and, thus, has a duty to exercise care for the residents' safety in those areas under its control. (at p. 499.) In *Frances T.*, the trial court had sustained the condominium association's demurrer to a unit owner's allegations that it had negligently failed to install adequate lighting in the common areas and was therefore liable for injuries she sustained from a rape that occurred inside her unit. (at pp. 495, 498.) We reversed. Although the rape occurred within the unit and not in a common area, we held that the association owed a duty to the plaintiff on the theory that an exterior condition over which the association had control contributed to the rape. (at pp. 498–503.)

Since the existence of a duty on the part of Pacific Plaza to Ann M. is not precluded in this case either by the lack of a direct landlord-tenant relationship or by the lack of control over the premises where the crime occurred, we turn to the heart of the case: whether Pacific Plaza had reasonable cause to anticipate that criminal conduct such as rape would occur in the shopping center premises unless it provided security patrols in the common areas. For, as frequently recognized, a duty to take affirmative action to control the wrongful acts of a third party will be imposed only where such conduct can be reasonably anticipated. (*E.g., Frances T., supra,* 42 Cal.3d at p. 501; *Isaacs, supra,* 38 Cal.3d at pp. 123–124; *Peterson v. San Francisco Community College Dist., supra,* 36 Cal.3d at p. 807.)

In this, as in other areas of tort law, foreseeability is a crucial factor in determining the existence of duty. (*Isaacs, supra,* 38 Cal.3d at p. 123; *Lopez v. McDonald's Corp.* (1987) 193 Cal.App.3d 495, 506.) Our most comprehensive analysis to date of the foreseeability required to establish the existence of a business landowner's duty to take reasonable steps to protect its tenants and patrons from third party crime is found in *Isaacs, supra,* 38 Cal.3d 112.

In *Isaacs*, a doctor affiliated with a private hospital was shot while in one of the hospital's parking lots. The doctor sued the hospital for failure to take reasonable security measures. Although the plaintiff presented evidence of several prior threatened assaults at the nearby hospital emergency room, he presented no evidence of prior assaults in the parking lot where he was shot. The trial court granted the defendant's motion for nonsuit because the plaintiff failed to show that prior similar incidents had occurred on the premises. We granted the petition for review to decide whether the plaintiff might "establish foreseeability other than by evidence of prior similar incidents on [the] premises." (*Isaacs, supra,* 38 Cal.3d at p. 120.)

We held that foreseeability, for tort liability purposes, could be established despite the absence of prior similar incidents on the premises. We explained that "foreseeability is determined in light of all the circumstances and not by a rigid application of a mechanical 'prior similars' rule." (*Isaacs, supra,* 38 Cal.3d at p. 126.) We also explained that prior similar incidents are "helpful to determine foreseeability but they are not necessary." (at p. 127.) We further explained that foreseeability should be assessed in light of the "totality of the circumstances," including such factors as the nature, condition and location of the premises. (at pp. 127–129.) We concluded that the totality of the circumstances in *Isaacs* strongly suggested that the foreseeability of an assault in the parking lot should have been presented to the jury. (at p. 130)

Since *Issacs* was decided, lower court opinions have questioned the wisdom of our apparent abandonment of the "prior similar incidents" rule. (*See Nola M., supra,* 16 Cal.App.4th at pp. 438–439 ["If there is a flaw in our analysis [finding the landowner not liable due to lack of causation between alleged security deficiencies and injury], we suggest it may be time for the Supreme Court to reexamine the concept of duty it articulated in [*Isaacs*] in the context of a society which appears unable to effectively stem the tide of violent crime."]; *Onciano v. Golden Palace Restaurant, Inc.* (1990) 219 Cal.App.3d 385, 396 [conc. & dis. opn. of Woods (Fred), J., following *Isaacs,* but observing that its holding leads to inequity].) In addition to judicial criticism, at least one commentator has noted that California is the only jurisdiction to adopt a "totality of the circumstances" rule in the business landowner context. (Kaufman, *When Crime Pays: Business Landlords' Duty to Protect Customers from Criminal Acts Committed on the Premises* (1990) 31 S. Tex. L.Rev. 89, 97 [hereafter Kaufman, *When Crime Pays*].)

Unfortunately, random, violent crime is endemic in today's society. It is difficult, if not impossible, to envision any locale open to the public where the occurrence of violent crime seems improbable. Upon further reflection and in light of the increase in violent crime, refinement of the rule enunciated in *Isaacs, supra,* 38 Cal.3d 112, is required. We are not reluctant to revisit the rule announced in *Isaacs* because it was unnecessary for this court to consider the viability of the "prior similar incidents" rule in order to decide the *Isaacs* case: the record contained evidence of prior, violent, third party attacks on persons on the hospital's premises in close proximity to where the attack at issue in that case occurred. (*Isaacs, supra,* 38 Cal.3d at p. 121.)

Moreover, broad language used in *Isaacs* has tended to confuse duty analysis generally in that the opinion can be read to hold that foreseeability in the context of determining duty is normally a question of fact reserved for the jury. (*Isaacs, supra,* 38 Cal.3d at pp. 126, 127, 130.) Any such reading of *Isaacs* is in error. Foreseeability, when analyzed to determine the existence or scope of a duty, is a question of law to be decided by the court. (*Ballard v. Uribe* (1986) 41 Cal.3d 564, 572-573, fn. 6; *Lopez v. McDonald's Corp., supra,* 193 Cal.App.3d at p. 507, fn. 6.)

Turning to the question of the scope of a landlord's duty to provide protection from foreseeable third party crime, we observe that, before and after our decision in *Isaacs,* we have recognized that the scope of the duty is determined in part by balancing the foreseeability of the harm against the burden of the duty to be imposed. (*Isaacs, supra,* 38 Cal.3d at p. 125.) "'[I]n cases where the burden of preventing future harm is great, a high degree of foreseeability may be required. [Citation.] On the other hand, in cases where there are strong policy reasons for preventing the harm, or the harm can be prevented by simple means, a lesser degree of foreseeability may be required.' [Citation.]" (*Ibid.*) Or, as one appellate court has accurately explained, duty in such circumstances is determined by a balancing of "foreseeability" of the criminal acts against the "burdensomeness, vagueness, and efficacy" of the proposed security measures. (*Gomez v. Ticor, supra,* 145 Cal.App.3d at p. 631.)

While there may be circumstances where the hiring of security guards will be required to satisfy a landowner's duty of care, such action will rarely, if ever, be found to be a "minimal burden." The monetary costs of security guards is not insignificant. Moreover, the obligation to provide patrols adequate to deter criminal conduct is not well defined. "No one really knows why people commit crime, hence no one really knows what is 'adequate' deterrence in any given situation." (*7735 Hollywood Blvd. Venture v. Superior Court* (1981) 116 Cal.App.3d 901, 905.) Finally, the social costs of imposing a duty on landowners to hire private police forces are also not insignificant. (*See Nola M., supra,* 16 Cal.App.4th at pp. 437–438.) For these reasons, we conclude that a high degree of foreseeability is required in order to find that the scope of a landlord's duty of care includes the hiring of security guards. We further conclude that the requisite degree of foreseeability rarely, if ever, can be proven in the absence of prior similar incidents of violent crime on the landowner's premises. To hold otherwise would be to impose an unfair burden upon landlords and, in effect, would force landlords to become the insurers of public safety, contrary to well-established policy in this state. (*See Riley v. Marcus* (1981) 125 Cal.App.3d 103, 109; *7735 Hollywood Blvd. Venture v. Superior Court, supra,* 116 Cal.App.3d at p. 905.)

Turning to the facts of the case before us, we conclude that violent criminal assaults were not sufficiently foreseeable to impose a duty upon Pacific Plaza to provide security guards in the common areas. (*Cf. Ballard v. Uribe, supra,* 41 Cal.3d 564, 572-573, fn. 6.) First, Pacific Plaza did not have notice of prior similar incidents occurring on the premises. Ann M. alleges that previous assaults and robberies had occurred in the shopping center, but she offers no evidence that Pacific Plaza had notice of these incidents. While a landowner's duty includes the duty to exercise reasonable care to discover that criminal acts are being or are likely to be committed on its land (*Peterson v. San Francisco Community College Dist., supra,* 36 Cal.3d at p. 807), Pacific Plaza presented uncontroverted evidence that it had implemented "a standard practice . . . to note or record instances of violent crime" and that Pacific Plaza's records contain no reference to violent criminal acts prior to Ann M.'s rape. Moreover, even assuming that Pacific Plaza had notice of these incidents, Ann M. concedes that they were not similar in nature to the violent

assault that she suffered. Similarly, none of the remaining evidence presented by Ann M. is sufficiently compelling to establish the high degree of foreseeability necessary to impose upon Pacific Plaza a duty to provide security guards in the common areas. Neither the evidence regarding the presence of transients nor the evidence of the statistical crime rate of the surrounding area is of a type sufficient to satisfy this burden.

We, therefore, conclude that Pacific Plaza was entitled to summary judgment on the ground that it owed no duty to Ann M. to provide security guards in the common areas.

III. DISPOSITION

The judgment of the Court of Appeal is affirmed.

Lucas, C. J., Kennard, J., Arabian, J., Baxter, J., and George, J., concurred.

14-5 WRITING THE MEMORANDUM OF LAW

Statement of Facts

The statement of facts should be a concise statement of all relevant and explanatory facts. The information for this statement comes from the client or from documents found in the client file. You identified key facts before you started the research. However, what is or is not a key fact is often affected by the results of your research. Therefore, the statement of facts for a memorandum should not be written until your research is complete.

Facts are generally presented in one of the following ways.

1. *Chronologically.* A common and easy way of organizing facts in a memorandum of law is in the order in which they occurred chronologically.

2. *By party.* Another way of organizing the facts is by party. Where multiple parties exist, they may all have their own version of the facts. State each version separately.

3. *According to the elements of a cause of action.* When your memorandum concerns whether a cause of action exists, the facts can be presented in the same order in which you discuss the elements of the cause of action.

Issue Statement

The issue statement is the question you research. Sometimes start with a very general research question and after doing your research you determine that other questions or issues must also be addressed. Many research problems have more than one issue. These questions should also be included in the issue statements of your memorandum. The issue part of a memorandum should be phrased as a question or questions. Review Chapter 3 for a more thorough discussion of identifying and stating the issues.

Discussion

The discussion section in a memorandum is where you explain the results of the research. In this section, you answer the question or questions stated in the issue section. You provide the reasons for your answers. This is called *legal analysis.*

Within the discussion, there will probably be several "issues" which are often subissues raised by the general issue. For example, the main issue in the Rambeaux case is whether Rambeaux faces criminal responsibility under 18 U.S.C. § 242. In researching this, you discover that you must also answer other questions, such as "Is an off-duty police officer acting under color of authority?" or "Were the victims

deprived of any constitutional rights?" In writing the discussion or analysis, you should discuss each issue separately.

Within the memorandum you can also use **point headings** to separate the discussion of different issues. Point headings, which are required in more formal argumentative writing, are similar to chapter titles or titles of various sections within a chapter. Headings not only help the reader stay focused on your ideas, but also help you, the writer, stay focused. See Figure 14-1 and note the use of headings in the discussion.

In discussing or analyzing each of your issues, you should follow the IRAC approach discussed in earlier chapters. There are, however, a few additional pointers for using the IRAC approach within a memorandum.

point headings. Phrases or sentences found in the discussion or argument sections of memoranda or briefs, identifying the topic of the following discussion or argument. These are set apart from the text by bolding and/or capitalization and are usually numbered.

Issue   State the issues in your case in the "Issue" section of the memorandum. It is not necessary to restate the question in your analysis. Where there is more than one issue, it is, however, necessary to let the reader know what issue you are discussing. This can be done with the use of a point heading or by the use of a **topic sentence** that lets the reader know the subject of the following paragraph.

topic sentence. A topic sentence introduces the issues or subissues and connects back to the thesis paragraph.

Stating the Rule of Law   The rule of law is taken from one or more of the primary sources of law (constitution, statutes, rules and regulations, or case law). In stating the rule of law, state the rule and then give the proper citation for the source. (For a review of citation format, see Appendix B.) At times, the rule of law may be a composite of law from several sources.

The following are examples of the different ways you can state a rule of law.

Case Law

- An off-duty police officer acts under color of authority when the air of official authority pervades the incident. *United States v. Tarpley*, 945 F.2d 806 (1991).
- In the case of *United States v. Tarpley* 945 F.2d 806 (1991), the appellate court held that an off-duty police officer acts under color of authority when the air of official authority pervades the incident.

Statutory Law

- Federal law makes it a crime for anyone acting under color of authority to deprive any person of any constitutional right or to subject that person to different punishments, pains, or penalties, because of that person's race or color. 18 U.S.C. § 242.
- Title 18 section 242 of the United States Code makes it a crime for anyone acting under color of authority to deprive any person of any constitutional rights or to subject any person to different punishments, pains, or penalties, because of that person's race or color.

This is not an exhaustive list. You may also use direct quotations from the case or statute to confirm the statement of the rule of law. In most cases, state the rule of law in your own words and then use a quotation to verify your statement. You should not use only a quotation.

Analysis

The analysis varies depending on whether the rule of law is based on statutory law or on case law. If it is statutory law, your analysis involves breaking the statute down into its elements and applying the language of the law to the facts of your case. If the rule of law comes from case law, analysis involves comparing the facts of the case law

Memorandum of Law

To: Attorney Smith
From: Research Associate/ T. Jacobs
Date: 4/7/XXXX

Subject: Criminal liability of R. Rambeaux under federal rules

FACTS

Our client, police officer Randy Rambeaux, made a traffic stop on an automobile because the driver failed to signal when making a right hand turn. The occupants of the vehicle were two young Latino males. According to one of the occupants and an independent witness the following events occurred. Rambeaux approached the car and ordered the two out of the car. When the occupants did not respond, Rambeaux opened the driver's door, grabbed the driver and pulled him out of the car. After the driver exited the vehicle, Rambeaux struck him on the head with his baton and said, "Why don't you guys go back where you belong. This country is for Americans." Rambeaux disputes that version of the facts. He states that as he was approaching the suspects' vehicle he noticed several passengers in the vehicle. Because of the location of the passenger he was unable to watch the driver and passengers at all times. Fearing for his safety, he requested that the driver and passengers exit the vehicle. Since they refused to follow his request, Rambeaux opened the driver's door and signalled for the driver to exit. As the driver exited the vehicle, he slipped and fell, hitting his head on the sidewalk. Rambeaux denies hitting anyone with the baton. He also denies making the statement. At the time of the incident, Rambeaux was off duty and was driving his own motorcycle. Since he had just gone off duty, he was still in uniform.

ISSUE

Assuming that the prosecutor can prove the allegations against Rambeaux, does Rambeaux face potential criminal liability under federal law?

DISCUSSION

I. INTRODUCTION

Assuming that the suspects' version of the facts can be proven, Title 18 § 242 of the United States Code may create criminal liability for Rambeaux. This section makes it a federal crime for anyone acting under color of authority to deprive any person of any Constitutional rights or subject that person to different punishments or penalties because of that person's race or color:

> Whoever, under color of any law, statute, ordinance, regulation, or custom, willfully subjects any person to the deprivation of any rights, privileges, or immunities secured or protected by the Constitution or laws of the United States or to different punishments, pains or penalties on account of such inhabitant being an alien, or by reason of his color, or race . . . shall be fined not more than $1000 or imprisoned not more than one year, or both. . . .

18 U.S.C. § 242.

In order for Rambeaux to be guilty of the federal crime, the following elements must be shown:

1. That he acted under color of law;
2. That he acted willfully;
3. That he deprived someone of his Constitutional rights, *or*
4. That he inflicted a different punishment because of the person's race or color.

A memorandum of law should always indicate who wrote it and the date.

The essential facts should be stated in an objective, unbiased manner.

Where factual disputes exist, this should be pointed out.

This question is the basis of your research assignment.

FIGURE 14-1 Sample Memorandum of Law

Note the use of the IRAC method in section II.

The ISSUE is identified in the point heading.

RULE OF LAW, found in statutory and case law, is stated in the first few sentences of this paragraph. Note how each rule is followed by a citation.

[*Tarpley* is italicized when referring to a case name, but not italicized when referring to the individual.]

ANALYSIS is found in this part of section II. In this instance, the analysis consists of comparing the facts of Rambeaux to the facts in the *Tarpley* case.

[Because *United States v. Tarpley* has already been cited, an abbreviated citation is used. *Id.* cannot be used because the case was not the immediately preceding cite. 18 U.S.C. § 242 intervened. Had there been no intervening cite, *Id.* would be used instead of *supra.*]

The final sentence of this section provides a CONCLUSION to *this* issue.

In a complete memorandum, sections III, IV, and V would also include legal authorities and more in-depth analysis.

II. ACTIONS UNDER COLOR OF LAW

The courts have often held that police officers acting in their capacity as law enforcement are acting under color of law and therefore are controlled by 18 U.S.C. § 242. *United States v. Reese*, 2 F.2d 870 (9th Cir. 1993). In this case, when Rambeaux made the traffic stop and ordered the occupants out of the car he was off duty. Therefore, a question arises as to whether he was acting under color of law. However, even off-duty police officers are considered to be acting under color of authority under certain situations. The case of *United States v. Tarpley*, 945 F.2d 806 (1991) explains. In the *Tarpley* case, defendant Tarpley, a deputy sheriff, learned of a past affair between his wife and Kerry Vestal. He assaulted Vestal by inserting his service revolver in Vestal's mouth and told Vestal that he could get away with it because he was a cop. Tarpley also enlisted the aid of another sheriff's deputy to threaten Vestal. When they finally released Vestal, the officers followed him in a police vehicle. Tarpley was arrested and charged with violating 18 U.S.C. § 242. He was found guilty and appealed, claiming among other things, that he was not acting under color of authority at the time because he was off duty. The court of appeals found that even though he was off duty, he was still acting under color of authority because "the air of official authority pervaded the entire incident." *Tarpley*, 945 F.2d at 809. In like manner, the air of official authority pervaded the Rambeaux incident. Rambeaux was doing what police officers routinely do, stopping traffic offenders. He was acting on behalf of the state, attempting to enforce state laws. Thus, Rambeaux was acting under color of law, meeting the first element of the statute.

III. WILLFUL ACTIONS

The second requirement of 18 U.S.C. § 242 is that the actions of the defendant be willful. According to witnesses, all of the actions in this case were clearly willful. Rambeaux knew what he was doing and intended to do what he did. This was no accident. Thus, the second element is met.

IV. DEPRIVATION OF CONSTITUTIONAL RIGHTS

In making this traffic stop, Rambeaux violated the Constitutional rights of the driver. The Constitution guarantees that all persons have the right to be free from unreasonable searches and seizures. In this case, Rambeaux made a traffic stop and in doing this "seized" the persons in the vehicle, even if only temporarily. While Rambeaux may have been justified in making the stop, his conduct, as described by witnesses, during this seizure was clearly unreasonable. The use of physical force, such as occurred here, is not allowed in simple traffic stops where the offender neither uses any force nor threatens the officer with the use of force. Thus, if the witnesses are believed, the third element of the statute is met.

V. DIFFERENT PUNISHMENT, PAINS OR PENALTIES IMPOSED BECAUSE OF COLOR OR RACE

In addition to depriving another of Constitutional rights, the facts also suggest that Rambeaux used force on the victims because of their race. In doing this it could be argued that he inflicted punishment, pain or penalties because of color or race, providing an alternative basis for criminal responsibility. According to the witnesses, Rambeaux made the statement, "Why don't you guys go back where you belong. This country is for Americans." This is strong evidence of the fact that Rambeaux's actions were racially motivated.

CONCLUSION

In conclusion, if the witnesses in this case are believed, the facts support a finding of criminal responsibility on the part of Rambeaux. Even though he was off-duty, he was still in uniform and performing a routine police task. He was clearly acting under color of law. His actions were willful and constituted both a deprivation of a Constitutional right and an infliction of punishment, pain or penalty because of race or color.

FIGURE 14-1
(continued)

to your facts. It may also involve applying the reasoning of the case to your facts. In many situations, the analysis involves both statutory and case law.

Conclusion The conclusion is usually the answer to the questions you raised in your statement of the issues. The conclusion should always be stated, even if you think it is obvious.

Citing Authorities

Format Citation of legal authorities in any type of legal writing should be in acceptable format. Often this means complying with the rules set out in a citation manual. Your state may have its own style manual. If so, you should follow those rules. An attorney may use your memorandum as the basis for the more formal memorandum of points and authorities or trial or appellate brief. If you follow the proper citation rules or your state's style manual, you may find that when you cite a case, it is only necessary to give the official cite. Parallel cites are not needed. However, your decision to use parallel cites in a memorandum of law should also be based on some practical considerations, specifically, the type of legal authority found in your office. If your law firm has an unofficial case reporter in print, it is necessary to cite to it in any office memorandum.

⇨ **A Point to Remember** If you have photocopied or downloaded important cases or statutes for your research, you might want to attach them to your memorandum. The attorney may want to read important legal authority. Attaching it to your memorandum saves time.

Using Id. and Supra In writing any type of legal memorandum, you occasionally use a shorthand or abbreviated way of citing cases. Once a case is fully cited within the memorandum, it is not necessary to use a complete citation each time you refer to it. If the case was the immediately preceding citation, the term *Id.* is substituted for the case name and citation. Thus, the case *United States v. Tarpley*, 945 F.2d 806 (1991) becomes *Id.* If the citation is used to support a quotation, it then becomes, *Id.* at 807. *Id.* is only used when the citation is the immediately preceding citation. If citations to any legal authorities (not just cases) intervene, you cannot use *Id.* The following are accepted shorthand ways of abbreviating this case.

Tarpley, 945 F.2d 806

Tarpley, 945 F.2d at 807

945 F.2d at 807

Normally when using a shorthand abbreviation you use the first name of the parties rather than the second name. Thus, in abbreviating the case name *Smith v. Jones*, you would use *Smith*. However, where the first name is a common one, such as *People* or *U.S.*, you must use the second name to avoid confusion.

Supra is used for authorities other than cases and statutes. (Although not approved by THE BLUEBOOK, you see *supra* used with cases by attorneys and judges.) Review Figure 14-1 to see how these terms are used.

Using Quotations Using quotations to emphasize your point can be an effective writing tool. Overuse, on the other hand, distracts the reader. You should keep quotations to a minimum. If your quotation is longer than three or four lines, read it to see if you really need all of it. Also, remember that quotations of less than three lines or less than 50 words are incorporated into the text with quotation marks. Longer quotations are indented on both right and left margins, are single spaced, and quotation marks are not used. In any cases, all quotations must provide the cite, including the page.

Conclusion

Every memorandum should have either a conclusion or a brief answer section. Some have both. This is a short summary of your findings. Often it contains a short and concise answer to the questions raised in your issue statement.

⇨ **A Point to Remember** When you write a memorandum of law, follow the directions of any supervising attorney. If you are asked to research an issue, research that issue in a complete and objective manner. Do not research an issue that you think is more interesting or you think is more important. If you are not sure what your supervising attorney wants, be sure to ask before you spend hours researching and writing.

Also review Figures 14-2 and 14-3 for samples of interoffice memoranda.

A BRIEF SUMMARY OF THE LAW REGARDING COMMERCIAL TRANSACTIONS INVOLVING MOTOR VEHICLES

By: Delene Waltrip, Senior Paralegal

I.

STATEMENT OF THE FACTS

The original owners of certain motor vehicles sold said vehicles to an auction dealer ("Dealer No. 1"), which then sold the same vehicles to an Auto Auction ("Dealer No. 2"), which is now defunct, and which ultimately sold the vehicles to bona fide purchasers. The bona fide purchasers paid the Auto Auction (Dealer No. 2) for the vehicles, sometimes financing the vehicles through a bank or finance company working in conjunction with the Auto Auction. The Auto Auction did not pay Dealer No. 1 for these vehicles. Dealer No. 1 retained the certificates of ownership (commonly called "pink slips") to the vehicles for which it had not been paid.

II.

ISSUE

IS DEALER NO. 1, AS AN UNPAID DEALER/SELLER, ENTITLED TO RETAIN THE CERTIFICATES OF TITLE TO THE CARS SOLD BY DEALER NO. 2 TO BONA FIDE PURCHASERS?

III.

LEGAL ANALYSIS AND DISCUSSION

A. DEALER NO. 1 DOES NOT HAVE THE RIGHT TO RETAIN THE CERTIFICATES OF TITLE TO THE VEHICLES SOLD BY DEALER NO. 2 TO BONA FIDE PURCHASERS.

This issue is governed by both the California Commercial Code[1] and California Vehicle Code. Although the Vehicle Code does govern most aspects of transactions involving vehicles, the Commercial Code has been held to cover the transfer and good faith purchase of vehicles. A key case, with similar facts to those in our situation, discusses how these code sections should be interpreted and applied.

In the case of *English v. Ralph Williams Ford*, 17 Cal. App. 3d 1038; 95 Cal. Rptr. 501 (1971), Ralph Williams Ford, a car dealership, sold a car to Intercontinental; Intercontinental then

---

[1] For purposes of simplicity and consistency, the California Commercial Code may sometimes be referred to as "UCC" as the cases reviewed often refer to these statutes in this manner.

FIGURE 14-2
Memorandum of Law

1

sold the same car to the Englishes. The Englishes obtained a bank loan on the car and executed a security agreement with the bank. Intercontinental's check to Ralph Williams Ford bounced before Ford had sent in the registration application. Ford then changed the designation of legal owner to itself, since it had not been paid, and sent the application to the DMV. Accordingly, the bank never received a pink slip. The bank discovered that Ford had the title and was the legal owner, but did nothing about it. Ford ultimately repossessed the car from the Englishes, claiming entitlement because it was never paid for the car by Intercontinental. Then, Ford re-sold the car to another purchaser. Questions of title, ownership and security interests arose from this situation.

In its analysis, the court first addressed the issue of the applicability of the Commercial Code to the transfer of automobiles vs. the title transfer statutes contained in the Vehicle Code. The court stated that Commercial Code Section 2105 (1) defines "goods" as "generally meaning all movable things other than the money in which the price is to be paid, investment securities and things in action." Furthermore, the court concluded that "sales of automobiles are clearly subject to the sales division of the UCC unless the remaining language in section 2102 excludes them." (*English*, 17 Cal. App. 3d at 1046).) Section 2102 excludes transactions, which are in the form of unconditional sales contracts or intended to operate only as a security transaction. Therefore, section 2102 does not exclude these types of automobile sales transactions, since they are not unconditional sales or solely security transactions.

Furthermore, the court determined that Ford did not have a security interest in the vehicle because Ford had not retained a reservation of title as part of the sale to Intercontinental, pursuant to UCC section 2401[2]. Therefore, Ford had only the rights of an unpaid seller and its right to reclaim the car was subject to the rights of a buyer/good faith purchaser, pursuant to UCC section 2702, which addresses a seller's rights on discovery of a buyer's insolvency and states that such rights are subject to the rights of the buyer.

In connecting these statutes for its analysis, this court ultimately relied upon UCC section 2403(1), which is the key statute applicable to our current situation. This statute states:

> (1) A purchaser of goods acquires all title which his transferor had or had power to transfer except that a purchaser of a limited interest acquires rights only to the extent of the interest purchased. A person with voidable title has power to transfer a good title to a good faith purchaser for value. When goods have been delivered under a transaction of purchase the purchaser has such power even though
>
> > (a)   The transferor was deceived as to the identity of his purchaser; or

---

[2]   UCC Section 2401(1) states that "Any retention or reservation by the seller of the title (property) in goods... delivered to the buyer is limited in effect to a reservation of a security interest."

2

FIGURE 14-2
(continued)

        (b)   The delivery was in exchange for a check which is later dishonored, or

        (c)   It was agreed that the transaction was to be a "cash sale"; or

        (d)   The delivery was procured through fraud punishable as larcenous under the criminal law.

(2) Any entrusting of possession of goods to a merchant who deals in goods of that kind gives him power to transfer all rights of the entruster to a buyer in ordinary course of business.

(3) "Entrusting" includes any delivery and any acquiescence in retention of possession for the purpose of sale, obtaining offers to purchase, locating a buyer, or the like; regardless of any condition expressed between the parties to the delivery or acquiescence and regardless of whether the procurement of the entrusting or the possessor's disposition of the goods have been such as to be larcenous under the criminal law.

Since the car was sold to a good faith purchaser by Intercontinental, which had the right to transfer title, Ford's repossession of the car constituted a conversion, even though Intercontinental may have had voidable title because of its failure to pay Ford for the cars. Nevertheless, this did not affect the good title, which the Englishes had purchased.

In the situation before us, similar facts exist. In applying UCC Section 2403(1)(b), it becomes clear that Dealer No. 2, by not paying Dealer No. 1, had potentially voidable title. However, since Dealer No. 2 sold the vehicles to bona fide purchasers, who purchased the cars in good faith and for valuable consideration, the bona fide purchasers purchased "good title" and are entitled to receive the certificates of title to the cars.

Additionally, as in the *Ford* case above, Dealer No. 1 did not retain a security interest in the vehicles, because it did not enter into a security agreement with Dealer No. 2 as part of the sales transaction. Therefore, since Dealer No. 1 did not have a security interest in the vehicles, it could not retain a "reservation of title" and must stand in the shoes of an unpaid seller pursuant to UCC Section 2702, subject to the bona fide purchaser's rights.

B.   THE BONA FIDE PURCHASERS HAVE EQUITABLE TITLE EVEN THOUGH LEGAL TITLE IS STILL HELD BY DEALER NO. 1

Vehicle Code section 5600 sets forth the law regarding transfer of title to motor vehicles:

FIGURE 14-2
(continued)

3

No transfer of the title or any interest in or to a vehicle registered under this code shall pass, and any attempted transfer shall not be effective, until the parties thereto have fulfilled either of the following requirements:

(a) The transferor has made proper endorsement and delivery of the certificate of ownership to the transferee as provided in this code and the transferee has delivered to the department or has placed the certificate in the United States mail addressed to the department when and as required under this code with the proper transfer fee, together with the amount required to be paid under . . . the Revenue and Taxation Code . . . .

(b) The transferor has delivered to the department or has placed in the United States mail addressed to the department the appropriate documents for the registration or transfer of registration of the vehicle pursuant to the sale or transfer . . . .

The cases interpreting this statute have long held that the meaning of this statute is to be taken liberally, not literally. The most recent California case dealing with this issue was a 9th Circuit Bankruptcy Appellate case entitled *In re Cohen.* In this case, the Bankruptcy Court addressed title and transfer issues involving vehicles sold prior to the filing of a bankruptcy by a party who was conducting a Ponzi scheme selling Mercedes Benz vehicles. The facts of this case are different; yet, the core issues which the court considered are very much the same as in our situation.

In the *Cohen* case, the Court stated that "California courts have long construed Vehicle Code section 5600 to refer to legal title but not equitable title and have held that equitable title does pass at the time of delivery." *Cohen*, at p. 714, citing *Stoddart v. Pierce*, 53 Cal.2d 105, 346 P.2d 774 (1959); *People v. Aiken*, 222 Cal. App. 2d 45, 34 Cal. Rptr. 828 (1963).

The Bankruptcy Court further quoted the 1972 case of *Security Pac. Nat'l Bank v. Goodman*, 24 Cal. App. 3d 131, 100 Cal. Rptr. 763 which states that a "transfer of the property interest in a motor vehicle is effective as between the immediate parties even though they have not complied with the registration statute." *Security* at 136.

Furthermore, cases dating back to 1927, and earlier, have generally held that a seller, who has not been paid by the secondary seller, cannot prevail in an action for claim and delivery against a bona fide purchaser who purchased from the secondary seller and paid him, even when there has been a failure to comply with the registration statutes. In citing an earlier case entitled *Parke v. Franciscus*, 194 Cal. 284, 228 P. 435, the court in *Kenny v. Christianson*, 200 Cal. 419, at 423–424 (1927) stated that it had held that:

while a compliance with said section and subdivision was essential

4

FIGURE 14-2
(continued)

to complete the transfer of title to the motor vehicle sought to be transferred and delivered to a purchaser, the failure of the transferee of the ownership of such car to procure the registration certificate required by the terms of said act did not render his right to the possession thereof so incomplete as to make the assertion thereof unavailing to him in an action against him by the vendor of the automobile thus actually sold and delivered to a purchaser in good faith and for a full consideration.

Subsequent cases cite the *Kenny* case to establish the issue of non payment from a second seller to the first seller, and the inability of the original seller to seek satisfaction through the bona fide purchaser. See *Security Pacific, supra.* Also, *see, In re Marriage of Finnell*, 182 Cal. App. 3d 52, 227 Cal. Rptr. 38 (1986), which held that an ex-wife with a judgment against ex-husband (who was still on title to a car he had sold) could not levy on said car now owned by a third party, even though registration was not in compliance with statute.   The court stated in *Finnell*, that "The law is well-settled that a 'transfer of the property interest in a motor vehicle is effective as between the immediate parties even though they have not complied with the registration statute." *Id*. at 56. This 1986 case also refers to both the *Security Pacific* and *Kenny* cases.

Accordingly, in our current situation, although Dealer No. 1 may be a creditor of Dealer No. 2, again, Dealer No. 1 does not have any rights as against the bona fide purchasers, even though Dealer No. 1 technically still holds the legal title.

IV.

CONCLUSION

The California courts have long favored the rights of an innocent bona fide purchaser in the purchase of goods, pursuant to the UCC. The bona fide purchasers of Dealer No. 2's cars therefore do have good title, pursuant to UCC 2403 and Dealer No. 1 should immediately turn over the certificates of title to these cars to the bona fide purchasers. Dealer No. 1 may have rights against Dealer No. 2 for money damages, but Dealer No. 1 does not have rights as against the bona fide purchasers. Non-compliance with the registration statute does not change this fact. The bona fide purchasers hold equitable, good title and Dealer No. 1 holds a piece of paper which is of no value to it and which cannot be used to effect any change in its predicament.

5

FIGURE 14-2
(continued)

Reprinted with permission of the author, Delene Waltrip

Memorandum

To: Supervising Deputy District Attorney in Charge,
Consumer Protection Unit

From: Delene Waltrip, Senior Paralegal

Date: June 11, XXXX

Subject Prepayment Penalties on R.E. Loans

      RE: **Advertisement -Mortgage Broker**

<u>Issue No. 1</u>:   Is there a disclosure requirement regarding prepayment penalties?

<u>Answer</u>: Yes.

<u>Discussion</u>:

Regulation Z of the Federal Truth in Lending Act, § 226.18(k) provides that a disclosure statement as to whether or not a prepayment penalty will be charged if the obligation is prepaid in full must be made in accordance with the form and time requirements of § 226.17(a).

Section 226.17(a) states that the creditor must make these disclosures "clearly and conspicuously in writing, in a form that the consumer may keep." Such disclosures must be made prior to consummation of the transaction. Pursuant to § 226.2 - Definitions and Rules of Construction, the term "Consummation means the time that a consumer becomes contractually obligated on a credit transaction." Additionally, pursuant to § 226.19(a)(1), in residential mortgage transactions subject to RESPA, the creditor must make good faith estimates of the disclosures required under § 226.18 before consummation of the transaction, or the creditor shall mail these disclosures to the consumer no later than 3 days after the creditor receives the consumer's written application, whichever is earlier.

Additionally, California law requires prepayment penalties to be stated in writing as well:

In the instance of a residential loan on property of four units or less, California Civil Code §2954.9(a)(2) provides that a borrower may be subject to a prepayment penalty <u>if he agrees in writing</u> to pay a prepayment charge. (emphasis added.)

Additionally, Civil Code § 2963 discusses disclosures required on purchase money liens on residential property. Although the term "prepayment penalty" is not specifically listed as a

1

FIGURE 14-3
Memorandum of Law

required disclosure, this section could be interpreted to include a prepayment penalty within the meaning of § 2963(b) which states that the following must be disclosed:

(b) A description of the terms of the promissory note . . .

(c) the principal terms and conditions of each recorded encumbrance . . . including the original balance, the current balance, the periodic payment, any balloon payment, the interest rate . . ., the maturity date, . . .

It would seem that a prepayment penalty could be construed to be a "term of the promissory note" and a "principal term and condition" of the encumbrance, just as is a balloon payment.

Further, Civil Code § 2964 states that the specification of items required to be disclosed (as cited above) "does not limit any obligation for disclosure created by any other provision of law or which may exist in order to avoid fraud, misrepresentation, or deceit in the transaction."

According to Miller & Starr, *California Real Estate Law 2d*, § 9:78, citing *Donahue v. Le Vesque* (1985) 169 Cal. App. 3d 620, 628-629, 215 Cal. Rptr. 388, the court has interpreted the law as follows:

When the secured obligation permits prepayment but there is no express provision for a prepayment fee, the trustor can prepay the debt at any time, and the beneficiary cannot charge any prepayment fee or penalty because of the prepayment.

Therefore, based upon this research, it seems clear that a prepayment penalty must be clearly and conspicuously disclosed under both state and federal law and could not be "buried" in the document as suggested in this mortgage broker's advertisements.

Issue No. 2: Are there any limits on prepayment penalties?

Answer: Yes, in some instances.

Discussion:

When a loan is negotiated by a real estate broker, California Business & Professions Code § 10242.6(a) states that prepayment of principal and interest on any loan secured by a mortgage or deed of trust on owner-occupied real property may be repaid at any time. A prepayment penalty may only be charged on such loans if prepayment is made within 7 years of the date of execution of the deed of trust. However, an amount up to 20% of the unpaid balance may be prepaid in any 12 month period without penalty. A prepayment charge may be imposed on any amount prepaid in any 12 month period in excess of 20% of the unpaid balance, which charge shall not exceed an amount equal to 6 months' advance interest on the amount prepaid in excess of 20% of the unpaid balance.

Further, § 10242.6(b) states that there shall be no prepayment penalty charged to a borrower if the dwelling securing the loan has been damaged to such an extent by a natural disaster for

FIGURE 14-3
(continued)

which a state of emergency is declared by the Governor if the dwelling cannot be occupied and the prepayment is causally related thereto.

When a loan securing an owner-occupied property of four units or less has not been negotiated (arranged) by a real estate broker, similar rules apply; however, instead of a 7 year time period for a prepayment penalty to apply, only loans paid off within 5 years of making are subject to a prepayment charge. Civil Code § 2954.9(b). (The same 20% rules apply.)

Also, loans with variable interest rates must provide for a right of prepayment of the debt without prepayment penalty within 90 days after the borrower receives notice of an increase in the interest rate. Civil Code § 1916.5(a)(5).

With regard to loans made by federally chartered banks or savings associations, I have inquired with the Office of Thrift Supervision (formerly the Federal Home Loan Bank Board) which informs me that there are no prepayment penalty limits. They take the position that their banks can charge prepayment penalties in accordance with the loan agreement. 12 CFR § 560.34 seems to agree: "Subject to the terms of the loan contract, a federal savings association may impose a fee for any prepayment of a loan."

Further, banks governed by the federal agencies are under federal law and, therefore, state law is preempted as to any inconsistency. 12 CFR § 560.2(a) and (b)(5).

(The term "federal savings association" applies to any federal savings bank or federal savings association.)

Further, pursuant to 12 CFR 560.2(a), "federal savings associations may extend credit as authorized under federal law, . . . , without regard to state laws purporting to regulate . . . their credit activities." However, "A national bank offering or purchasing ARM loans may impose fees for prepayment notwithstanding any State law limitations to the contrary." 12 CFR § 34.23.

One exception lies in the area of "High Rate Home Equity Loans" as defined by the Home Ownership and Equity Protection Act of 1994. These loans, with the exception of a "complex five-part exception," are exempt from any prepayment penalty. National Consumer Law Center "Truth in Lending" § 10.4.2. Loans covered by this Act are home equity loans, not purchase money loans, which have interest rates at the consummation of the loan, which exceed 10% above the current treasury bond rate. (Example: 30 yr. T-Bond Rate: 7.5%; Loan amount to trigger coverage: 17.5%.)

Finally, there are other specific rules governing GI, Cal-Vet and FHA loans. For example, FHA insured loans can be prepaid with a maximum penalty of 1% of the outstanding principal balance. 25 CFR §§ 207, 253 and GI loans can be prepaid at any time without a fee. 38 CFR § 36.4310.

An example of a prepayment penalty charged on a non-broker arranged loan, paid off within 5 years of its making, is as follows:

3

FIGURE 14-3
(continued)

Original Loan at 8%: $300,000

Balance at 5 years: $285,210

20% prepay w/o penalty: $(57,042)

Balance subject to penalty: $228,168

6 months interest on $228,168 = approximately $9,000.00

Therefore, the defendant mortgage broker's claim that a prepayment penalty could cost "several thousand dollars" could indeed be true, if the prepayment is made within 5 or 7 years (as specified above) of the date the loan is made. However, if the loan is paid off after 5 or 7 years, no prepayment penalty can be charged.

An example of an FHA insured loan is as follows:

Original Loan at 8%: $300,000.00

Balance at 5 years: $285,210.00

1% prepayment penalty: $ 2,852.10

A smaller loan paid off later in the life of the loan would yield a much lower prepayment penalty.

Based upon the above calculations, this mortgage broker's ad could be misleading. By stating that "these penalties cost several thousand dollars and make it too expensive to refinance," this mortgage broker is ignoring the fact that there is no prepayment penalty for loans governed by California law which are paid in full after 5 or 7 years of their making (depending on the loan), or that an FHA loan of a smaller amount, paid after, say 10 years or so, might only be a few hundred dollars.

Please let me know if you desire further research on these topics.

4

FIGURE 14-3
(continued)

Reprinted with permission of the author, Delene Waltrip

OPINION LETTERS

An opinion letter is a letter to a client or other attorney explaining a client's legal position in a matter. It takes the form of a typical business letter. Because it contains legal advice, it must be signed by an attorney rather than a paralegal or law clerk. The content of an opinion letter is not dissimilar from the discussion section in a memorandum. When you write an opinion letter to a client, you explain the law and how it applies to the client's factual situation. You should remember, however, that it is sometimes not directed to an attorney. Therefore, avoid legal jargon. (It should also be avoided in any legal writing, but it is particularly important to do so here.) One common question is whether you should give citations for any law that you mention in the letter. Some attorneys believe that clients do not understand citations, so including them in a letter is unnecessary. However, other attorneys are so used to citing law that they automatically include citations. There is an additional consideration. A copy of an opinion letter is included in the office client file. Should an attorney or other legal professional review the file and read the opinion letter, it is very helpful to have citations for authorities mentioned in the letter. See Figure 14-4 for an example of an opinion letter.

JANET BIRK-RAMIREZ
Attorney at Law

573 Second Ave.   (408)555-1111
San Jose, CA 95110

January 18, XXXX

Frank Bennett
3985 Monteverde Dr.
Cupertino, CA 94123

Re: Fence Dispute

Dear Mr. Bennett,

This letter is in response to your recent inquiry regarding a dispute you have with your neighbor over a fence. The facts you related to me are as follows. Your neighbor recently tore down a six-foot-high split rail fence located on the boundary between your two homes, and erected a brick fence measuring 10 feet high in its place. This new fence blocks your view of neighboring hills. You also informed me that you have a history of problems with your neighbor, dating back over 10 years. In the past, your neighbor has trampled on your flowers, thrown garbage in your yard and on several occasions shouted loud obscenities to you and your wife. Last summer, while you were on a two-week vacation, evidently your neighbor called the police complaining about the fact that your car was parked on the street where it remained during your vacation. You now want to know if you can force your neighbor to tear down the brick fence and if you are entitled to any monetary damages because of your neighbor's conduct. Pursuant to your request I have researched the matter. My findings are dependent on the facts you presented being complete and accurate.

California law contains a specific provision regarding "spite fences." This provision, section 841.1 of the California Civil Code, provides as follows:

> Any fence or other structure in the nature of a fence unnecessarily exceeding 10 feet in height maliciously erected or maintained for the purpose of annoying the owner or occupant of adjoining property is a private nuisance. Any owner or occupant of adjoining property injured either in his comfort or the enjoyment of his estate by such nuisance may enforce the remedies against its continuance prescribed in Title 3, Part 3, Division 4 of this code.

Under this section you must show that the fence exceeds 10 feet in height, that the height is unnecessary and that it was maliciously erected. The facts related to me indicate that the fence is 10 feet high. The code section applies to fences that *exceed* 10 feet. You must obtain exact measurements of the height of the fence. Even if the fence does not exceed 10 feet, it is still possible that other legal theories may apply to your case. Before spending time researching this, however, I advise that you obtain correct measurements. Assuming that the fence exceeds 10 feet, I believe you have strong evidence of a malicious motive on the part of your neighbor. Your neighbor's past conduct provides a history of ill will and bad feelings and is strong evidence of his intent in building this fence. In fact, there is a California case from the court of appeal, *Griffin v. Northridge* (1944) 67 Cal.App.2d 69, that closely parallels your situation. The court held that conduct such as has occurred in your case, is strong evidence of malicious intent.

If your neighbor will not voluntarily remove the fence, you can file a lawsuit and ask the court to order the removal of the fence. Alternatively, you may ask for money damages.

At this point, if you wish to proceed further, I suggest that you call me so that we can set up an appointment to discuss the next action to take.

Sincerely,

Janet Birk-Ramirez
Attorney at Law

FIGURE 14-4
Opinion Letter

TECHNOLOGY CORNER

The following legal writing sites provide a great deal of good information:

http://bartleby.com/141/

www.wilbers.com

www.drgrammar.org/

CHAPTER SUMMARY

The legal research process is usually not complete until the results are communicated to another person in either an objective or persuasive way, depending on the situation. Documents objectively conveying research findings are generally memoranda of law and opinion letters. Documents utilizing a persuasive approach include memoranda of points and authorities, trial briefs, and appellate briefs.

A memorandum of law, which is usually prepared for an attorney, contains an overview of all of the law related to the question that was researched. It must be accurate and complete. While there are no required formalities for such a document, a memorandum of law should identify the author, the recipient, the date, the subject matter, a statement of the facts, a statement of the issue or issues, a discussion of the relevant law, and a conclusion. Within the discussion, it is common to use the IRAC method of analysis. This includes stating the issue, stating the applicable rule of law (case law, statutory law, or consitutional law), applying the law to the facts, and reaching a conclusion.

An opinion letter is a letter to a client or an attorney explaining a legal position in a matter. It takes the form of a normal business letter. Because it contains legal advice, it must be signed by an attorney.

TERMS TO REMEMBER

memorandum of law	appellate brief
opinion letter	cause of action
memorandum of points and authorities	point headings
trial brief	topic sentence

QUESTIONS FOR REVIEW

1. Identify and describe the different types of documents used to convey the results of legal research.
2. List other names used to refer to a memorandum of law.
3. What is the purpose of a memorandum of law?
4. Why is it important that a memorandum of law include all law, even that which may be contrary to your client's position?
5. Describe the general format of a memorandum of law.
6. What steps should you follow in preparing to write a memorandum of law?

7. Describe one way of organizing a memorandum where the controlling law is found primarily in statutory law.

8. Describe one way of organizing a memorandum where the controlling law is found primarily in case law.

9. What is an opinion letter?

10. Why must an opinion letter be signed by an attorney and not a paralegal or law clerk?

CAN YOU FIGURE IT OUT?

Refer to the case of *Ann M.* found in this chapter.

1. The court uses several abbreviations in its opinion. Explain what each of the following means: *cf., de novo, fn., Ibid., conc. & dis. opn.*

2. The court uses the term *supra* frequently in its opinion. Give three examples from the case. Is the California court using *supra* in accordance with THE BLUEBOOK? Cite to the THE BLUEBOOK rule.

RESEARCH ASSIGNMENTS AND ACTIVITIES

1. Write an objective memorandum of law based solely on the *Victoria V.* facts and the *Ann M.* case found in this chapter.

2. Write a letter to Victoria V. explaining her possible rights under the *Ann M.* case found in this chapter.

3. Review sections III, IV and V of the memorandum in Figure 14-1. As indicated in the margin, these sections are incomplete and contain various rules of law that are not supported by legal authorities. Identify each statement that requires a citation to a legal authority and describe the type of authority you would expect to find.

CASE PROJECT

Write an objective memorandum of law detailing the rights of the parties in the Appendix A hypothetical researched in the previous chapter.

WRITING TO THE COURT

CHAPTER OBJECTIVES

When you complete this chapter you should be able to

- Explain rules of court.
- List and describe common features found in legal memoranda and briefs.
- Discuss the purpose of a memorandum of points and authorities.
- Explain how and why declarations are used.
- Discuss the purpose of a trial brief.
- Discuss the purpose of an appellate brief.

CITATION MATTERS

USE OF PINPOINT CITATIONS

THE BLUEBOOK — RULE 3.2

Legal writers use pinpoint citations to direct the reader to the exact page where the information cited to is located. This allows a reader to go directly to the relevant portion of a case, book, article, or periodical. Pinpoint citations also direct readers to specific subdivisions of a document or a statute. These pinpoint citations are widely used by good legal writers.

For example:

> *Ashcroft v. Free Speech Coalition*, 535 U.S. 234, 241 (2002). This citation includes the pinpoint to page 241 of the *Ashcroft* decision. This citation follows material taken from page 241. All quotes must be followed by a citation that includes a pinpoint cite, unless the material quoted from is not paginated. This is probably the most widely used type of pinpoint citation. Rule 3.2 illustrates how to use pinpoint citations for books, law review articles, the *Congressional Record*, the *United States Code*, and more.

The use of *id.* is not limited to quotations. Any time material is borrowed, even general ideas, citations must be used. The audience of a legal document expects to see well chosen and properly cited law.

INTEROFFICE MEMORANDUM

TO: Research Associate

FROM: Senior Attorney

RE: Rambeaux Case

On April 4, a preliminary examination in this case was assigned to Judge Phillips and the prelim took place on May 2. The defendant was held to answer and now faces trial. I filed a motion to dismiss the case on the basis that the judge should have disqualified himself because (1) prior to the preliminary examination, he erroneously reviewed the court file, and (2) because of a conflict of interest. It appears that the judge actually represented Rambeaux in a similar case 15 years ago. The prosecutor filed a memorandum of points and authorities in opposition to our motion. Please review this memorandum. Read the cases cited in the memo and prepare a draft of a reply memo for me to review. (See Figure 15-5 for the Memorandum of Points and Authorities in Opposition to the Motion.)

---

advocate. Arguing one side of an issue.

memorandum of points and authorities. Research document filed with the court containing legal analysis of disputed issues occuring in a case pending in court; often used to support or oppose motions.

trial brief. Research document filed with the court prior to trial addressing legal issues in the case.

appellate brief. Research document filed in an appeal addressing the legal issues forming the basis of the appeal.

motion. A request for a court order in connection with a case that is pending in court.

15-1 INTRODUCTION

In the previous chapter you saw how the results of legal research are objectively communicated in a memorandum of law. However, when research findings are communicated to a court, they are not presented in an objective manner but rather in a persuasive or argumentative way. The researcher **advocates** a position that is most favorable to his or her client. In advocating a position, the researcher tries to convince the court that the law supports the client's position.

When a researcher writes to the court, formal documents are used and technical rules must be followed. The documents used to present a legal argument to the court are **memoranda of points and authorities, trial briefs,** and **appellate briefs.** A memorandum of points and authorities is filed when a legal question arises in a case that is pending in court. Often it is used to support or oppose a **motion** in a case. A trial brief is a document filed at the beginning of a trial. In this document, the attorney often presents legal authorities and arguments showing that his or her client should prevail at trial. Trial briefs might also contain legal arguments regarding evidentiary issues that are expected to arise at trial. Appellate briefs are prepared and filed after a case is decided in the trial court. These briefs contain arguments regarding the validity of the trial court judgment.

rules of court. Rules regulating practice in a particular court or courts.

local rules of court. Procedural rules adopted by an individual court for practice in that specific court.

15-2 RULES OF COURT

Documents filed in a court must comply with rules regarding form and content. Most courts have these rules, which are part of their **rules of court,** sometimes called **local rules of court.** These rules usually cover such things as acceptable length, citation format, content requirements, and the number of copies that must be submitted. If the rules regarding form and content of a memorandum or brief are not followed, a court could refuse to consider the document.

Figure 15-1 contains a copy of one rule from the U.S. Supreme Court regarding briefs that are to be field in that Court.

RULE OF COURT FOR SUPREME COURT

Rule 24. Briefs on the Merits: In General

1. A brief on the merits for a petitioner or an appellant shall comply in all respects with Rules 33.1 and 34 and shall contain in the order here indicated:

(a) The questions presented for review under Rule 14.1(a). The questions shall be set out on the first page following the cover, and no other information may appear on that page. The phrasing of the questions presented need not be identical with that in the petition for a writ of certiorari or the jurisdictional statement, but the brief may not raise additional questions or change the substance of the questions already presented in those documents. At its option, however, the Court may consider a plain error not among the questions presented but evident from the record and otherwise within its jurisdiction to decide.

(b) A list of all parties to the proceeding in the court whose judgment is under review (unless the caption of the case in this Court contains the names of all parties). Any amended list of parent companies and nonwholly owned subsidiaries as required by Rule 29.6 shall be placed here.

(c) If the brief exceeds five pages, a table of contents and a table of cited authorities is needed.

(d) Citations of the official and unofficial reports of the opinions and orders entered in the case by courts and administrative agencies.

(e) A concise statement of the basis for jurisdiction in this Court, including the statutory provisions and time factors on which jurisdiction rests.

(f) The constitutional provisions, treaties, statutes, ordinances, and regulations involved in the case, set out verbatim with appropriate citation. If the provisions involved are lengthy, their citation alone suffices at this point, and their pertinent text, if not already set out in the petition for a writ of certiorari, jurisdictional statement, or an appendix to either document, shall be set out in an appendix to the brief.

(g) A concise statement of the case, setting out the facts material to the consideration of the questions presented, with appropriate references to the joint appendix, e. g., App. 12, or to the record, e. g., Record 12.

(h) A summary of the argument, suitably paragraphed. The summary should be a clear and concise condensation of the argument made in the body of the brief; mere repetition of the headings under which the argument is arranged is not sufficient.

(i) The argument, exhibiting clearly the points of fact and of law presented and citing the authorities and statutes relied on.

(j) A conclusion specifying with particularity the relief the party seeks.

2. A brief on the merits for a respondent or an appellee shall conform to the foregoing requirements, except that items required by subparagraphs 1(a), (b), (d), (e), (f), and (g) of this Rule need not be included unless the respondent or appellee is dissatisfied with their presentation by the opposing party.

3. A brief on the merits may not exceed the page limitations specified in Rule 33.1(g). An appendix to a brief may include only relevant material, and counsel are cautioned not to include in an appendix arguments or citations that properly belong in the body of the brief.

4. A reply brief shall conform to those portions of this Rule applicable to the brief for a respondent or an appellee, but, if appropriately divided by topical headings, need not contain a summary of the argument.

5. A reference to the joint appendix or to the record set out in any brief shall indicate the appropriate page number. If the reference is to an exhibit, the page numbers at which the exhibit appears, at which it was offered in evidence, and at which it was ruled on by the judge shall be indicated, e. g., Pl. Exh.14, Record 199, 2134.

6. A brief shall be concise, logically arranged with proper headings, and free of irrelevant, immaterial, or scandalous matter. The Court may disregard or strike a brief that does not comply with this paragraph.

FIGURE 15-1

Supreme Court Rule of Court

15-3 COMMON FEATURES

A memorandum of points and authorities (often referred to by lawyers as "P and A's"), a trial brief, and an appellate brief, contain several common features: a case caption, table of contents, a table of authorities, a statement of facts, a statement of issues or questions presented, an argument, and a conclusion.

Case Caption

filed. To become part of the court record.

caption. A caption identifies the parties to the case, the court in which the case is pending, the docket number and the title of the document.

In all jurisdictions, any document **filed** in a court must contain a case **caption.** A caption identifies the parties to the case, the court in which the case is pending, the docket number, and the title of the document. Review Figure 15-5 and identify the caption.

Table of Contents

table of contents. A list of the sections of a document with the page on which they appear within the document.

A **table of contents** is a list of the various sections found in the document with the corresponding page. The various sections include the following:

- Table of Authorities
- Statement of Facts
- Issues
- Argument: Each point heading, and the page on which it appears, is restated under the argument in the table of contents.
- Conclusion
- Signature

A table of contents is generally required for trial briefs and appellate briefs. It is required in a memorandum of points and authorities only if the memorandum exceeds a certain page length. Local rules of court govern this.

See Figure 15-2 for an example of a table of contents from an appellate brief.

Table of Authorities

table of authorities. A list of primary and secondary authorities cited within a memorandum or brief and the page numbers on which they appear.

A **table of authorities** contains a list of all legal authorities, primary and secondary, that are cited within the document and the page or pages on which the citation appears. There are several acceptable formats for setting up the table of authorities; a common way follows.

Case Law

- Cite all cases, listing them alphabetically, and give *all* pages on which they appear in the memorandum or brief.

Constitutional Provisions and Statutes

- Cite constitutional provisions in the order in which they appear in the Constitution and give all pages on which they appear.
- Cite *United States Code* sections in numerical order and give all pages on which they appear in the document.
- Cite state code sections (either alphabetically or numerically, depending on how the code is cited) and give all pages on which they appear in the documents.
- Cite federal and state regulations.

Miscellaneous Sources

- Cite secondary source material and any other source material used (usually alphabetically); give all pages on which each source appears.

TABLE OF CONTENTS

Summary of Argument   3

Argument   5

I.   Congress Always Intended To Require A
     Federal Defense For Removal   5

     A.   Reading section 1442(a) as a whole
          establishes that Congress required a
          federal defense for removal   5

     B.   The legislative history of section 1442(a)(1)
          demonstrates that Congress always required
          a federal defense for removal   7

          1.   Congress enacted the first federal
               official removal statute solely to provide
               an efficient mechanism to transfer suits
               challenging federal authority to federal
               court before trial   7

          2.   Subsequent reenactments of the federal
               official removal statute maintained
               the federal defense requirement   10

          3.   The addition of section 1442(a)(3) in
               1916 is compelling evidence that
               Congress maintained the federal
               defense requirement   14

ii

FIGURE 15-2 Table of Contents for Appellate Brief

FIGURE 15-2
(continued)

TABLE OF CONTENTS--Continued

iv

FIGURE 15-2
(continued)

Reprinted with permission of the author, Kenneth Rosenblatt, Esq.

See Figure 15-3 for an example of a table of authorities. Note how all primary authority is listed first and how the primary authority is organized and labeled.

TABLE OF AUTHORITIES

Cases:

Arizona v. Manypenny, 451 U.S. 232 (1981) 13, 35, 36
Barr v. Matteo, 360 U.S. 564 (1959) 30
Bigelow v. Forrest, 76 U.S. 339 (1869) 16
Buck v. Colbath, 70 U.S. 334 (1865) 12, 16
City of Aurora v. Erwin, 706 F.2d 295
(10th Cir. 1983) 47-48
Cleveland C. & c. R.R. v. McClung,
119 U.S. 454 (1886) 21-22
Colorado v. Symes, 286 U.S. 510 (1932) . . . 17, 18, 20, 27, 34
Commonwealth of Pennsylvania v. Newcomer,
618 F.2d 246 (3d Cir. 1980) 33-35
Davis v. South Carolina, 107 U.S. 597 (1882) 14, 16, 25
Ellis v. Railway Clerks, 466 U.S. 435 (1984) 36
Erlenbaugh v. United States, 409 U.S. 239 (1972) 20
Fourco Glass Co. v. Transmirra Prod. Corp.,
353 U.S. 222 (1957) 18
Garcia v. United States, 469 U.S. 70 (1984) 6
Gay v. Ruff, 292 U.S. 25 (1934) 12, 15-17, 20
Georgia v. Grady, 10 Fed. Cas. 245 (1876) (No. 5,352) . . 13
Illinois v. Fletcher, 22 F. 776 (N.D. Ill. 1884) 25
In re Debs, 158 U.S. 564 (1895) 45
In re Neagle, 135 U.S. 1 (1890) 13, 14, 49
Jarecki v. Searle & Co., 367 U.S. 303 (1961) 6
Kelly v. Robinson, 479 U.S. __, 107 S.Ct. 353 (1986) 46
Little York Gold-Washing & Water Co. v. Keyes,
96 U.S. 199 (1887) 38
Martin v. Hunter's Lessee, 14 U.S. 304 (1816) 4, 8
Maryland v. Soper (No. 1),
270 U.S. 9 (1926) 2, 18, 20, 23-33, 35, 49

v

FIGURE 15-3 Table of Authorities for Appellate Brief

TABLE OF AUTHORITIES--Continued

vi

FIGURE 15-3
(continued)

TABLE OF AUTHORITIES--Continued

vii

FIGURE 15-3
(continued)

TABLE OF AUTHORITIES--Continued

Miscellaneous authorities:

viii

FIGURE 15-3
(continued)

Like a table of contents, a table of authorities is usually required in trial briefs and appellate briefs. It is generally required in a memorandum of points and authorities only if it exceeds a certain page length. Local rules of court govern this.

Statement of Facts

court record. Documents and transcripts of proceedings in connection with a case.

declaration. A statement under penalty of perjury containing factual statements.

affidavit. A statement under penalty of perjury sworn to before a notary.

A brief statement of the factual dispute before the court is usually presented in any argumentative document. The facts should be supported in the **court record** or in **declarations** or **affidavits** that are attached to the memorandum or brief. Although facts must always be accurate and truthful, the statement of facts is presented in a way most favorable to the party filing the memorandum or brief.

This section of the brief is usually presented after the table of contents and table of authorities. In this way, the reader has the opportunity to become acquainted with what actually happened before the legal issues or the argument is presented. (Although sometimes, the question presented may appear first. In fact, in a brief to the U.S. Supreme Court, the question presented is placed first, even before the table of contents and table of authorities.) Remember, all legal issues revolve around the facts. The facts contained in a brief are written so that your client is placed in the best light. Sometimes this is referred to as "slanting the facts to favor your client." *Caution:* Never change the facts, never add facts that do not exist, and never omit damaging facts. Write the facts for the court so that the client is placed in the best possible position. Vocabulary choices and descriptive terms can often produce different pictures of the same event. For example, consider the Rambeaux case. In describing the facts here, Rambeaux's attorney might state the facts as follows:

Facing multiple suspects and fearing for his safety, Rambeaux used a reasonable amount of force in order to effect a legal arrest.

On the other hand, the attorney for the victims might characterize the events as follows:

Rambeaux maliciously, violently, and unreasonably attacked and beat minority individuals, clearly using excessive force in light of the alleged minor infractions.

Damaging facts are downplayed or offset when possible. Writing an effective factual statement is mastered with practice.

Figure 15-4 contains the beginning sections of the Fact Statements presented to the United States Supreme Court in the *United States v. Virginia* (VMI) case. Notice the differences between the Petitioner's statement and the Respondent's statement. Citations to other documents and transcripts have been omitted. Also, read the statement of facts in the Memorandum of Points and Authorities in Figure 15-5. Note how factual statements are supported by references to other court material. The abbreviation PXTX refers to a Preliminary Examination Transcript. The numbers following indicate the page and line number where the information is found.

Statement of Issue(s) or Question(s) Presented

This section of a memorandum or brief states in simple terms the legal question or questions before the court. An issue statement sets forth the legal question *and* it provides the reader with the most significant facts. The issue is often stated as a question. Remember, it is the question presented to the court for resolution. Sometimes there is only one issue. Other times there are many. Each issue should generally be no more than one sentence. Proper identification and statement of the issues are critical to the success of the parties. Failure to raise all important issues or misstating the issue can result in the court's refusing to consider legal authorities or arguments that might favor your client. Proper identification of the issues obviously must

PETITIONER'S STATEMENT OF FACTS

1. The Virginia Military Institute. The Virginia Military Institute (VMI) is a state military college in Lexington, Virginia. Since its founding in 1839, VMI has maintained a policy of admitting only men to its four-year undergraduate degree program. The fourteen other public colleges in Virginia are all coeducational. Approximately 1300 male students are enrolled at VMI.

VMI's mission statement declares that VMI's goal is to produce "citizen-soldiers," described as "educated and honorable men who are suited for leadership in civilian life and who can provide military leadership when necessary." The VMI curriculum includes liberal arts, science and engineering courses, and VMI confers both Bachelor of Arts and Bachelor of Science degrees.

As the district court found, VMI has a strong reputation for producing leaders, and has an exceptionally loyal and powerful alumni network. That network is "enormously influential," especially in the male-dominated fields of engineering, the military, business, and public service in which VMI graduates tend to pursue careers, "VMI alumni overwhelmingly perceive that their VMI educational experience contributed to their obtaining personal goals." VMI enjoys the largest endowment on a per-student basis of any undergraduate institution in the United States.

VMI employs an "adversative" method of character development and leadership training not currently used by any other college-level institution. That method is based on techniques used in "English public schools" and "earlier military training," although it has long been abandoned at the United States military academies. The method "emphasizes physical rigor, mental stress, absolute equality of treatment, absence of privacy, minute regulation of behavior, and indoctrination of values." "As a consequence of completing the rigorous tasks, succeeding, and actually graduating from VMI, VMI cadets have a sense of having overcome almost impossible physical and psychological odds. They have been put through great physical pressures and hazards, and just to have made it yields a feeling of tremendous accomplishment."

VMI's adversative method is implemented through a pervasive military-style system. The system includes the "rat line," which is a seven-month regimen during which first-year cadets, or "rats," are "treated miserably," like "the lowest animal on earth." "Rats" are subjected to a strict system of punishments and rewards that creates "a sense of accomplishment and a bonding to their fellow sufferers and former tormentors." The "rat line" experience is accompanied by "rat training," "a tough physical training program" "designed to foster self-confidence and physical conditioning in fourth classmen [i.e., freshmen] by creating training situations which are stressful enough to show them that they are capable of doing tasks which surpass their previously self-imposed limits."

The "class system" assigns roles to each class of cadets within a hierarchy in order to "cultivate leadership." "After the rat line strips away cadets' old values and behaviors, the class system teaches and reinforces through peer pressure the values and behaviors that VMI exists to promote." VMI's program also includes the "dyke system," an arrangement by which each "rat" is assigned a senior as a mentor to give some "relief from the extreme stress of the rat line." VMI's honor code—providing that a cadet "does not lie, cheat, steal nor tolerate those who do"—provides "the single penalty of expulsion for its violation."

FIGURE 15-4
Petitioner's Statement of Facts in the *Virginia Military Institute* Case

VMI requires cadets to "live within a military framework; they wear the cadet uniform at the Institute, eat most meals in the mess hall, live in a barracks, and regularly take part in parades and drills." "The most important aspects of the VMI educational experience occur in the barracks." There, cadets live at close quarters with one another, three to five together in stark and unattractive rooms, with poor ventilation, unappealing furniture, windowed doors with no locks and no window coverings. "[A] cadet is totally removed from his social background," and placed in an environment the principal object of which is "to induce stress."

Although VMI has always restricted admission to men, some women "would want to attend [VMI] if they had the opportunity." (Recruitment of women would likely yield a 10% female student body at VMI.) Between 1988 and 1990 VMI received 347 letters from women inquiring about admission, or indicating interest in attending VMI. It is not disputed that some women can succeed within the VMI-type methodology and are capable of doing all of the individual activities required of VMI cadets. The district court expressly found that the VMI methodology "could be used to educate women."

RESPONDENT'S STATEMENT OF FACTS

Petitioner's opening brief presents an incomplete picture of the VMI program and glosses over or contradicts crucial facts found by the courts below. This brief sets forth a more accurate and representative statement of the record and the remedial proceedings below.

A. Mary Baldwin College

Mary Baldwin College (MBC), an historically women's college, was founded in 1842. MBC has responded to the changing role of women in society by expanding its curriculum "to include the new options open to women in business and the professions." MBC has "developed an emphasis on career planning," has "computerized the campus," and has added "new state of the art equipment for its science labs." MBC "is committed to the education of women for a world of expanding opportunity."

MBC enrolls over 700 residential undergraduate students, has a Phi Beta Kappa chapter, is accredited by the Southern Association of Colleges and Schools, and is now ranked first among regional liberal arts colleges in the South. See U.S. News & World Rep. 141 (Sept. 18, 1995. MBC's 55-acre campus in Staunton, Virginia, includes the facilities of the former Staunton Military Academy, residence halls, classroom buildings, computer and science laboratories, a 40,000-square-foot physical education facility, playing fields, tennis courts, and a swimming pool.

The student-faculty ratio in MBC's residential program is 11 to 1. MBC offers 28 undergraduate majors, including degrees in mathematics, the sciences, business, and the arts, and also offers pre-law and pre-med programs and a joint-degree engineering program with the University of Virginia. MBC is "geared in the direction of trying to encourage women to persist in math and physics."

MBC enjoys "a record of success in developing new programs and operating distinctive and unique programs within the larger traditional undergraduate residential community." For example, MBC has successfully established a unique residential baccalaureate program for academically gifted, high-school-age students tailored to "the academic, emotional and developmental needs of young women."

FIGURE 15-4
(continued)
Respondent's
Statement of Facts in
the *Virginia Military
Institute* Case

IN THE SUPERIOR COURT OF THE STATE OF CALIFORNIA

IN AND FOR THE COUNTY OF SANTA CLARA

THE PEOPLE OF THE STATE OF CALIFORNIA,	)	Case No. 11111
Plaintiff,	)	
	)	MEMORANDUM OF POINTS AND
vs.	)	AUTHORITIES IN OPPOSITION
	)	TO MOTION TO DISMISS
RANDOLPH RAMBEAUX,	)	
	)	Date: November 20, 2005
Defendant.	)	Time: 9:00 a.m.
	)	Dept: 2

STATEMENT OF FACTS

On April 4, 2005 a preliminary examination in this case was assigned by Department 20, Santa Clara County Municipal Court, in Judge Phillips' department. PXTX 4:10-13. On May 2, 2005 the preliminary examination was heard and the defendant was held to answer on the charge of grand theft with an excessive taking (Penal Code §1022.6(b)) and two counts of tax fraud. Bail remained as previously set. PXTX 3:1-2 and 149:9-14.

Prior to the preliminary examination, Judge Phillips was advised by counsel that there was an unresolved source of bail issue (Penal Code §1275) that counsel were discussing prior to the preliminary examination. PXTX 5:27-28; 6:1-3. As a result, Judge Phillips viewed the

1

FIGURE 15-5
Memorandum of
Points and Authorities

complaint and the defendant's prior criminal history, not the file. PXTX 6:6-8. Thereafter, Judge Phillips stated that he was "inclined" to increase bail. PXTX 5:27-28; 6:1-3.

On or about October 21, 2005 the People were served with the instant motion. For the first time, defendant raises, *inter alia*, the issue of Judge Phillips' alleged prior representation of the defendant.

STATEMENT OF LAW AND ARGUMENT

I

DEFENDANT'S MOTION PURSUANT TO PENAL CODE §995 IS WITHOUT MERIT

In his motion under Penal Code §995, defendant has not contested the sufficiency of the evidence to support the holding order. His sole basis for objection is that Judge Phillips violated various sections of the Code of Civil Procedure and two sections of the Code of Judicial Ethics in failing to disqualify himself from hearing the matter and that therefore his order was void. Defendant raises two separate contentions regarding the disqualification. First, he claims that Judge Phillips showed actual bias or prejudice resulting from his review of the complaint and RAP sheet in the court file prior to the preliminary examination, and by his comments on bail. Second, he claims, for the first time in this motion, that Judge Phillips should be disqualified because he represented the defendant in a criminal case more than 15 years ago. Both of these claims are without merit. First, the record clearly shows that bail issues were discussed with the court and that therefore a review of appropriate documents was justified. Second, nothing in the record suggests that the Judge knew or remembered that he had represented the defendant many years prior. Furthermore, defendant has failed to comply with the requirements of California Code of Civil Procedure §170.3 in that he failed to file a statement of facts detailing the basis for the §170.1 motion as required by the statute. Failure to do so results in a waiver of claim of disqualification.

2

FIGURE 15-5
(continued)

II

JUDGE PHILLIPS WAS QUALIFIED TO HEAR THE PRELIMINARY EXAMINATION AND SHOWED NO BIAS IN REVIEWING LIMITED DOCUMENTS OR IN COMMENTING ON BAIL.

A. Judge Phillips was justified in reviewing documents in the file because of bail issues.

Defendant first claims that Judge Phillips acted improperly in reviewing the court file before the preliminary hearing and such conduct requires that this motion be granted. This is not supported by the facts of this case nor by the law. The record is clear that the parties had discussed bail issues with the court. Defense counsel, on the record, states that he had discussed bail issues with the court, thus justifying the court's review of the above described documents. "I discussed the case briefly, procedural issues, regarding the 1275 motion. At that time the court indicated to me...."(PXTX 5:4-6). The declaration of Mark Hames, attached hereto, also indicates that bail issues were being discussed by counsel and that the court was advised of that fact. It was a logical and natural assumption that the court might be called upon to rule on this matter. Judge Phillips was thus justified in reviewing appropriate documents in the file. As defendant points out in his motion, the Judge clearly stated that he did not review the entire file, only the complaint and RAP sheet. (PXTX 6:6-14).

The case cited by defendant, *O'Neal v. Superior Court* (1986) 185 Cal. App. 3d 1086, 230 Cal. Rptr. 257, supports the People's position on this matter. *O'Neal* holds that where there are bail issues, the review of a court file prior to a preliminary examination does ***not*** require disqualification of the judge, absent a showing of actual prejudice. In *O'Neal*, a magistrate had reviewed the file at the arraignment in connection with a bail. Later that same judge presided over the preliminary examination. The appellate court found that this was not a reason to set aside the ruling.

Defendant further argues that Judge Phillips' comment regarding defendant's past offense proves bias. Such a conclusion is completely unwarranted.

3

FIGURE 15-5
(continued)

B. Judge Phillips' comments regarding his inclination to increase bail do not constitute bias.

A defendant's past criminal history and the current complaint are clearly relevant when setting bail or determining its source. The fact that Judge Phillips mentioned this fact to defense counsel does not indicate bias. It merely indicates that the defendant's position regarding bail was *not* consistent with that of the court. Also controlling here is California Code of Civil Procedure §170.2 which holds that a judge's statement of an opinion regarding legal or factual issues in the proceeding is not grounds for disqualification:

§ 170.2. Grounds not allowed for disqualification

It shall not be grounds for disqualification that the judge...

(b) Has in any capacity expressed a view on a legal or factual issue

presented in the proceeding, except as provided in paragraph (2) of subdivision

(a) of, or subdivision (b) or (c) of, Section 170.1.

In conclusion, Judge Phillips' denial of defendant's motion under §170.1 was correct. Although not raised in defendant's moving papers herein, at the preliminary examination, defendant also based his motion to disqualify Judge Phillips on Code of Civil Procedure §170.6. This motion was clearly not timely, the matter was assigned to Judge Phillips over one month prior to the actual preliminary examination.

III

THIS COURT SHOULD NOT CONSIDER DEFENDANT'S CLAIM THAT JUDGE PHILLIPS REPRESENTED DEFENDANT ON A PRIOR OCCASION AND THEREFORE SHOULD BE DISQUALIFIED

In his moving papers, defendant raises a claim that Judge Phillips should be disqualified because he represented the defendant more than 15 years ago. The preliminary examination in this matter lasted most of a court day, all of which time the defendant was present in court. At no time did defendant or his attorney raise this issue. Furthermore, we knew for approximately

4

FIGURE 15-5
(continued)

one month that this matter had been assigned to Judge Phillips. Although the People strongly

contend that nothing in the record provides any basis for the disqualification of Judge Phillips, if

there were any factual support, the matter was waived. The case of *In re Stephen O* (1991) 229

Cal. App. 3d 46, 279 Cal. Rptr. 868 is on point. In the case of *In re Stephen O*, a case whose

procedural facts are identical to the case at hand, the Juvenile Court Hearing Officer had

previously prosecuted the juvenile in a matter related to the case he was hearing. Neither party

commented on this fact at the hearing and in fact, the issue of judicial disqualification was raised

for the first time on appeal. The defendant claimed that the facts justifying disqualification were

not discovered until review of the transcript for appeal and therefore it was being raised at

the earliest possible time. The appellate court found that because the lower court record was

devoid of any evidence of this, the right to challenge the judge had been impliedly waived. In

discussing petitioner's argument, which is similar to that of defendant in this case, the appellate

court stated:

> All of these statements, however, are factual assertions
> unsupported by the record. Insofar as the record shows anything, it
> indicates Steven was personally present at both the jurisdictional hearing
> on the original petitions...and at the ...hearings on the supplemental
> petitions....
>
> We, of course, cannot resolve any factual questions raised by
> Steven's appellate counsel. The proper forum for presentation and
> resolution of such questions is the lower court. On this record we can only
> conclude Steven failed to comply with Code of Civil Procedure Section
> 170.3 subdivision (c) (1). Accordingly, Steven's challenge to Referee
> Warmerdam, first raised on appeal, is untimely. *Id.* at 54-55.

In reaching its decision, this court was clear to point out that the lower court decision

was not void.

Defense counsel argues that under Code of Civil Procedure 170.3 (b) (1) and (2) Judge

Phillips' disqualification cannot be waived. This code section only limits a waiver in two

situations: (1) if a judge has a personal bias or prejudice concerning the party or (2) if the judge

served as an attorney in the matter in controversy. Neither of those situations is present.

5

FIGURE 15-5
(continued)

Nothing in the record demonstrates that Judge Phillips had any personal bias or prejudice against the defendant. And clearly, the Judge did not represent the defendant in this case, the matter in controversy.

IV

IN ANY EVENT, JUDGE PHILLIPS' PRIOR REPRESENTATION OF DEFENDANT DOES NOT AFFECT THE COMMITMENT ORDER IN THIS CASE

A. Rulings made by a judge before he or she discovers facts that support a disqualification are valid.

   For the first time, in this motion defendant contends that Judge Phillips should have disqualified himself under Code of Civil Procedure §170.1 (a) (1), (2) and (6) because he represented the defendant more than 15 years ago. Nothing in the record indicates that Judge Phillips had any recollection of this fact at the preliminary examination (or for that matter, at any time since the preliminary examination.) In his memorandum of points and authorities defendant states that "Either he forgot that he had previously represented defendant, or knew of the prior representation and neglected to disclose it." (Defendant's Memorandum Pg 9:5-7). Even if Judge Phillips' prior representation of defendant would justify disqualification, it would not justify granting the §995 motion. California Code of Civil Procedure 170.3(b) (4) provides:

> (4) In the event that grounds for disqualification are first learned of or arise after the judge has made one or more rulings in a proceeding but before the judge has completed judicial action in a proceeding, the judge shall, unless the disqualification be waived, disqualify himself or herself, **but in the absence of good cause the rulings he or she has made up to that time shall not be set aside by the judge who replaces the disqualified judge.** (Emphasis added)

6

FIGURE 15-5
(continued)

WRITING TO THE COURT

This is further supported by the *Sincavage* case, so often cited by defendant (*Sincavage v. Superior Court* (1996) 42 Cal. App. 4th 224, 49 Cal. Rptr. 2d 615.) In the *Sincavage* case, the judge assigned to hear a trial had previously been a district attorney. Prior to trial, the parties discovered that the judge had appeared on a calendar involving the defendant. The judge told the defendant that she could nevertheless be fair and impartial. The judge further stated that had she played an active role in the prosecution she would have to excuse herself. The defendant agreed that she could hear the trial, at which the defendant was convicted. After trial, a motion on priors was scheduled before the same judge. Before the motion, the parties discovered that the judge in question had in fact handled the preliminary examination of the previous case now charged as a prior in the current case. Defendants filed an application for a writ of mandate to prevent the judge from hearing the motion on this prior. The appellate court granted the writ on the basis of the judge's statements prior to trial regarding her potential bias. In granting the writ, however, the court made it very clear that all prior proceedings, including the trial verdict, were valid:

> Because of the timing peculiar to the instant motion, disqualification would
> not invalidate the judgment of conviction of the current offenses.
> Under section 170.3, subdivision (b)(4), only proceedings after the grounds for
> disqualification were discovered would be affected. The grounds here were not
> discovered until July 19, 1995, when counsel reviewed the proceedings on the
> priors in preparation for sentencing and a hearing on the motion to strike.

Since the record in this case does not indicate that anyone knew of Judge Phillips' prior representation of defendant prior to this motion, all of his prior rulings are valid, whether or not he should have been disqualified.

B. In any event, Judge Phillips was not obligated to disqualify himself under CCP §170.1

Code of Civil Procedure § 170.1(1) (2) & (6), cited by defendant as relevant to this case, requires that a judge be disqualified under different circumstances. First, a judge must disqualify himself where he or she has personal knowledge of disputed evidentiary facts concerning the

7

FIGURE 15-5
(continued)

proceeding. [Section 170.1 (a) (1)] The record, and all papers filed by defendant, contain no evidence nor any inference that Judge Phillips had knowledge of any disputed evidentiary facts concerning this proceeding. This section is clearly inapplicable. Second, a judge must be disqualified if he or she served as a lawyer for any of the parties in another proceeding that involved the same issues.[Section 170.1 (a) (2)]. Defendant argues that because Judge Phillips represented defendant years prior in a similar criminal case, this section applies. This is not supported by any authority.

   This case does not involve the same issues as the prior case. The current case occurred more than 15 years after the case in which Judge Phillips represented defendant. Furthermore, the first offense has nothing to do with the present charges. Priors are not charged and this is not a "3 Strikes" case.   While it is true that both criminal cases involve embezzlement, the two cases are in no way related to one another. There are no common issues, such as the same victim. Although no cases give any complete definition of what the "same issues" means, several cases do present some guidance. The first is the case of *In re Arthur S.* (1991) 228 Cal. App. 3d 814, 279 Cal. Rptr. 69. In this case a hearing officer in a juvenile proceeding was the prosecuting attorney in a previous case. A petition was filed against the juvenile alleging a criminal offense, battery. Approximately one year later, a subsequent action alleging a different criminal offense, residential burglary, was filed against the same juvenile as a "supplemental petition" in the same case. The court held "that a second juvenile court petition filed under Welfare and Institutions Code section 602, not alleging a violation of probation and not seeking aggregation of confinement time, is not part of the same proceeding arising from the original petition. Thus, the referee hearing the second petition, who served as deputy district attorney prosecuting the first petition, is not necessarily disqualified under Code of Civil Procedure section 170.1." (*Id.* at 816).

   In another case, *Reeve v. Jahn* (1937) 9 Cal. 2d 244, 70 P.2d 610, a judge had represented certain minor children in a partition action, involving the estate of their father. Several years

8

FIGURE 15-5
(continued)

later, one of the children, now an adult, was the plaintiff in a quiet title action involving the estate of his mother. Defendants in the action insisted that, having advised the minor children as to their rights in the estate of their father, the judge was unavoidably prejudiced in their favor in this action. They made a motion to disqualify the judge based on the same grounds as asserted in this case. The California Supreme Court stated that since the property in the partition action was different from the property in the quiet title action, the issues were not in any way the same and the motion to disqualify the judge was properly denied.

In their Memorandum of Points and Authorities, Defendants in this case rely heavily on the case of *Sincavage v. Superior Court* (1996) 42 Cal. App. 4th 224, 49 Cal. Rptr. 2d 615. Although the appellate court does not directly address the question of what constitutes the same issue, the court is clear to point out that in *Sincavage* the prior case had a direct connection with the case at hand. *Sincavage* involved a 3 strikes issue and penalty enhancement as a result of the prior conviction.

Since Judge Phillips did not represent defendant Rambeaux in any case that has a bearing on this case and since the issues in this case are not the same as any issues in the prior case, disqualification is not warranted under Section 170.1 (a) (2)

Defendants further rely on CCP 170.1 (a) (6) and the Code of Judicial Ethics, Canon 2A (Promoting Public Confidence) and 3D (Disqualification). For this argument, defendants rely heavily on the case of *Sincavage v. Superior Court*. The facts in *Sincavage* are clearly distinguishable and inapplicable to the case before this court. In *Sincavage*, the defendant had filed a motion to disqualify a judge from hearing a motion regarding priors. The judge, who was previously a prosecutor, had actually handled the preliminary examination for the very priors in question. Furthermore, the judge in *Sincavage* stated on the record that she would disqualify herself if she had actively participated in the prosecution. Under these circumstances, the court justifiably felt there might be an appearance of impropriety.

9

FIGURE 15-5
(continued)

In the matter before this court, none of the facts present any impression that Judge Phillips was not fair or impartial.   Neither this code section, nor the Canons of Judicial Ethics cited by defense counsel, support defendant's position.

CONCLUSION

It is indeed unfortunate that the defendant so easily attacks the ethics of a judge with this scantness of evidence. Reviewing a complaint and RAP sheet, after being advised of a pending Penal Code §1275 issue, is not only proper but hardly the basis for a 995. The Judge's comment regarding the amount of bail is clearly sanctioned by C.C.P. §170.2 and disagreement with the court's comments does not equal disqualification. Finally, absent actual prejudice in this case, a judge cannot be disqualified on matters *not* known by the judge, counsel, and the defendant.

Respectfully submitted,
By _____
         MARK B. HAMES
         DEPUTY DISTRICT ATTORNEY

10

FIGURE 15-5
(continued)

Reprinted with permission of the author, Mark Hames, Esq.

be done before you finish your research and prior to writing a memorandum or brief. Review carefully the section in Chapter 3 dealing with issue statements. The following is the issue statement found in a brief to the Supreme Court in the case of *Paula Jones v. William Clinton:*

QUESTION PRESENTED

Whether a private civil action for damages against the President of the United States, based on events occuring before the President took office, should be permitted to go forward during the President's term of office.

The following are the questions presented in the *VMI* case, mentioned previously.

Petitioner's Question Presented

Whether the Equal Protection Clause permits a State, as one alternative in a primarily coeducational system of higher education, to afford its citizens the option of receiving the acknowledged benefits of single-sex education through methodologies designed by professional educators to accomplish optimal and substantively comparable pedagogical results for both women and men.

Respondent's Questions Presented

1. Whether a State that provides a rigorous military-style public education program for men can remedy the unconstitutional denial of the same opportunity to women by offering them a different type of single-sex educational program deemed more suited to the typical woman.

2. Whether coeducation is the required remedy in the context of this case.

After reading these questions, can you figure out which party is the petitioner and which is the respondent? What clues are provided in the questions?

Summary of Argument

In lengthy memoranda and in appellate briefs, the court requires that the parties include a brief summary of the argument before the argument itself.

Argument

The **argument** is the main part of any memorandum of points and authorities or brief. This is where the law and facts are analyzed. In the argument section, each issue should be discussed separately, preferably in the order in which the issues are stated in the "Issue" section of the document. Major points are stated in point headings and then discussed in detail following the point heading. Legal authorities are cited and analyzed. (Hence the term "Points and Authorities.") Just as with the "Discussion" section of a memorandum of law, the argument should be outlined and organized prior to the actual writing.

    Proper phrasing of the point headings is an important part of the drafting of this section of the document. Remember you are making an argument, not just identifying the issue under discussion. Your position should thus be stated in positive and conclusionary terms. You tell the court how and why it should rule on the issues or questions presented. Refer back to Figure 15-2, the table of contents, and review the point headings found under "Argument." Note how the headings try to "persuade" the court to rule in a certain way. Also review the point headings found in the memorandum in Figure 15-5.

    The IRAC method of analysis often forms the basis of the argument just as it is in a discussion. However, in more complex cases and in cases of **first impression,** the argument also includes more analysis of the reasoning behind the law. Most often, a reported case opinion includes a detailed analysis of why the court is ruling

argument. The section of a memorandum or brief containing the legal analysis supporting that party's position on a legal issue.

first impression. A case where the legal issue has not previously been decided.

the way it is. In writing an argument, the researcher shows how and why this reasoning applies to his or her case. Short quotations from the reported case help to support this.

Conclusion

Every memorandum and brief should contain a conclusion. Sometimes this is a brief summary of the main points. Other times, especially in appellate briefs where the argument itself contains summaries of the main points, attorneys conclude the legal arguments with this simple paragraph:

"For the foregoing reasons, the petitioner requests that the judgment of the lower court be affirmed."

Signature

Any document submitted to the court must contain the signature of the attorney submitting it. Because this is a legal document filed in court, an attorney—not a paralegal or law clerk—must sign it. However, a research associate can do much of the research for a memorandum or brief. A research associate might even prepare drafts of the final document for review by the attorney.

⇨ **A Point to Remember** A court is obligated to follow authorities that you cite only when those authorities are mandatory authority in your jurisdiction. If you are in a state court, mandatory authority is found in case law from your state courts and constitutional and statutory law of your state. Only if these do **not** exist should you use other authorities. If you are in federal court, and the issue is a constitutional or federal one, then cite cases from the U.S. Supreme Court and federal appellate courts from your circuit. Only if these do not exist should you cite cases from other jurisdictions. If you do not cite mandatory authority, the court can ignore your arguments. Review Chapter 2.

15-4 MEMORANDUM OF POINTS AND AUTHORITIES

As mentioned above, a memorandum of points and authorities is a document filed with a court in which the author is arguing for or against a legal position on a matter. This type of document is often filed in support of or in opposition to a motion. A motion is a request for an order from the court in either criminal or civil cases. It is made when an attorney makes a request in connection with a pending case, such as a motion to dismiss a case, motion for summary judgment, or a motion to suppress evidence that was illegally obtained. A memorandum of points and authorities contains an argument based on the law and the facts of the case.

Unlike a memorandum of law, the object of a memorandum of points and authorities is not to present an obective and thorough treatment of the law. In this document, attorneys advocate their client's position in a matter before the court. While it is an ethical violation to misstate either the law or the facts, attorneys generally try to present the material in a way that is most favorable to their clients.

Even though the purpose is different, in many ways a memorandum of points and authorities resembles a memorandum of law. It generally contains a statement of facts, a statement of issues, legal analysis, and a conclusion. In lieu of a discussion, however, a memorandum of points and authorities contains an argument. Within this argument, the attorney sets forth the points he or she is making and then gives the legal authorities for these points. The IRAC method of analysis is used within the

argument, just as it is in a discussion. The points are usually set out in point headings that precede each section of the argument.

Memoranda of points and authorities are used in adversary proceedings and, therefore, each side has the opportunity to submit a memorandum to the court. Memoranda are filed as follows.

Memorandum of Points and Authorities in Support of the Motion   This is the first memorandum filed by the **moving party,** the party making the motion. In this motion, the party, who may be the plaintiff or the defendant in the action, sets forth the legal argument for the court to grant the motion. This memorandum contains a caption, statement of facts, statement of issues, argument, conclusion, and attorney signature. It may also include a table of contents and table of authorities if it is lengthy.

moving party. The party making a motion.

Memorandum of Points and Authorities in Opposition to the Motion   This motion is filed by the responding party within strict time limits set by law. In this memorandum, the responding party tries to accomplish two goals: (1) set forth the strongest argument in support of his or her position, and (2) refute arguments set forth by the moving party. This document may or may not include a statement of facts and statement of issues. If the responding party is satisfied with the statements set forth in the opening memorandum, it is not necessary to repeat them.

Reply Memorandum   The moving party generally has the opportunity to file a reply memorandum, again within very strict time limits. This document replies to points raised in the responding memorandum.

In addition to rules regarding time limits for filing, many courts have rules regarding the maximum number of pages allowable in the memorandum of points and authorities. Review Figure 15-5 for an example of a memorandum of points and authorities filed in opposition to a motion to dismiss a criminal case. Note that this memorandum does not contain a section setting forth the issues. This is because the memorandum of points and authorities in support of the motion previously filed contained a correct statement of the issues. Also, because this is a relatively short memorandum, no table of contents or table of authorities was required. Review Appendix D, which contains examples of memoranda prepared by research associates and the memorandum of points and authorities drafted by the attorney and based in part on those memoranda.

15-5 DECLARATIONS

The statement of facts in a memorandum or brief must be supported by evidence in the court record. When parties file a memorandum of points and authorities, they often use declarations or affidavits, rather than live testimony, to present the facts to the court. A declaration is a statement made under penalty of perjury. An affidavit is also a statement made under penalty, but it is sworn to before a notary.

Facts contained in a declaration take on a tone quite different from those in a fact statement in a memorandum or brief. The declaration is made by the person having first-hand knowledge of the facts. It may be your client's words or it might be the attorney's statement. This is the declarant's story. A declaration often reads like a narrative of the *events from the client's point of view.* Even though it may be the client's story, and even though it may be signed by the client, it is still drafted by the attorney or the attorney's associate. A well-written declaration may be a powerful tool when combined with a motion. The following is an example of a declaration written in support of a request for a temporary restraining order in a family law matter:

Example

Declaration of Alma Steinman:

1. I am the plaintiff in the above-entitled action.

2. On July 3, 2005, my husband, the Defendant, Robert Steinman, arrived at my home about 11:45 p.m. drunk and angry. At that time, we had been separated and living apart for almost one year. That night he yelled horrible things at me. The children were in their rooms but they could hear him. He said things like, "You will pay for everything you have done," and "I will make sure you never leave me."

3. When I tried to close the door he pushed me to the floor and began slapping me and punching me. I was screaming and crying. Our oldest child, Marcy, called 911 for help. The police came and took my husband away.

4. Since that day he has called my office and home at least six times every day. He continues to threaten me. Some of his threats are really violent. He told me on August 19 that he would "kill me" if I see another man. I am very afraid of him.

I declare that the foregoing is true and correct under penalty of perjury.

You can see that this simple declaration in the client's own words is a powerful statement, much more so than the statement of facts in the memorandum itself. See Figure 15-6 for an example of a declaration by an attorney prepared in connection with a motion.

IN THE SUPERIOR COURT OF THE STATE OF CALIFORNIA

IN AND FOR THE COUNTY OF SANTA CLARA

THE PEOPLE OF THE STATE OF CALIFORNIA,)   Case No. 196239

           Plaintiff,)   DECLARATION OF
)   MARK B. HAMES
   vs.   )   IN OPPOSITION TO
)   MOTION TO DISMISS
RANDOLPH RAMBEAUX,   )
)   Date: November 20, 2005
           Defendant.)   Time: 9:00 a.m.
)   Dept: 2

I, Mark Hames, do declare as follows:

1. I am a Supervising Deputy District Attorney as to the prosecution and preliminary examination of the above-entitled case;

2. On or about May 1, 2005, I received a call from the then attorney for the defendant, to resolve a Penal Code §1275 source of bail issue. As I was not available, I asked to take up the matter on May 2, 2005, as we would both be in Judge Phillips' department for preliminary examination;

3. On May 2, 2005 at 8:30 a.m. counsel and I appeared in Judge Phillips' department. We both advised the court in chambers that we were trying to resolve a Penal Code §1275 issue. These discussions lasted approximately 30 minutes at which time the court took the bench and the preliminary examination started;

4. During he course of the Penal Code §1275 discussions Judge Phillips stated that he had viewed the complaint and prior history and was "inclined" to raise the bail;

5. Thereafter, defendant's counsel made his CCP §170.6 for the first time, it was denied as being untimely;

6. Throughout the preliminary examination, neither counsel nor the defendant stated or implied that Judge Phillips had previously represented the defendant in 1990.

1

FIGURE 15-6

Declaration in Opposition to Motion

Throughout the preliminary examination, Judge Phillips did not state or imply that he had represented the defendant almost 16 years ago.

I declare, under penalty of perjury, that the above is true and correct, and that this declaration was executed in San Jose, California on November 12, 2005.

_____
MARK B. HAMES
Supervising Deputy District Attorney

FIGURE 15-6
(continued)

Reprinted with permission of the author, Mark Hames, Esq.

15-6 TRIAL AND ARBITRATION BRIEFS

A trial brief is a document filed with the trial court, usually immediately prior to the start of the trial. The purpose of this document is to establish the legal support for the party's claims or defenses at trial. A second purpose is to present legal argument for evidentiary issues that a party anticipates will arise during trial. For example, in a medical malpractice case, the defendant, a doctor, might want to be assured that the plaintiff does not present any evidence relating to the doctor's insurance. In a trial brief filed before the case begins, the doctor's attorneys can present legal authorities supporting such a request. Trial briefs can also provide legal support for jury instructions.

In many jurisdictions, trial briefs are not required, but are filed only when attorneys anticipate that legal questions will arise during trial. If a trial brief is filed, it is for the benefit of the judge. If the case is being tried by a jury, the jurors never see the document. Furthermore, because there are no requirements that a party file a trial brief, the plaintiff is not necessarily the first one to file such a document. It is possible for both parties to file a trial brief simultaneously or for the defendant to file first. In any event, if one party has filed a brief, the other will often respond to the issues that are raised. The court might even ask the attorneys to do this.

Today, many cases go to **arbitration** rather than to trial. Arbitration is an out-of-court proceeding that takes place before a neutral party. This neutral party, an arbitrator, hears evidence from both parties and makes a decision. In an arbitration proceeding, parties may file **arbitration briefs,** which are similar to trial briefs and serve the same purposes.

arbitration. An out-of-court proceeding in which parties submit a dispute to a neutral person for resolution.

arbitration brief. A document submitted in an arbitration proceeding addressing the legal issues in the arbitration.

15-7 APPELLATE BRIEFS

When a trial court decision is appealed, the parties are required to file briefs with the reviewing court. The initial brief, filed by the party who appeals, is called the _brief for the petitioner._ The brief filed by the other party is called the _brief for the respondent._ The petitioner, or appellant, also files a reply brief. In the opening, or petitioner's, brief, the appealing party describes legal errors that it contends occurred at trial. These form the basis for the legal issues in the brief that contains legal argument supporting these contentions. The respondent's brief answers these contentions, arguing that no legal errors occurred, or if they did, they were harmless and do not justify a reversal. In the reply brief, the petitioner answers points raised in the respondent's brief. Like a memorandum of points and authorities, an appellate brief

is a persuasive document. Also, as with memoranda of points and authorities, strict time limits govern the filing dates for each brief.

⇨ **A Point to Remember**   *Be careful not to confuse parties in an appellate brief. Often the appellant is called the* petitioner. *This is not the same as the plaintiff at the trial level. The petitioner, or appellant, may be either the plaintiff or the defendant.*

Appellate briefs generally contain the following sections: Table of Contents, Table of Authorities, Statement of Facts, Statement of the Case, Issues or Questions Presented, Summary of Argument, Argument, and Conclusion. A statement of the case, which is usually not included in a memorandum of points and authorities or a trial brief, is a brief summary of the procedural history of the case. In substance, an appellate brief is very similar to a memorandum of points and authorities. The respondent's brief may or may not contain a statement of facts, statement of the case, or issue statement. If the respondent accepts the statements of the petitioners, there is no need to repeat it. Reply briefs generally do not contain any of the above.

Writing an appellate brief requires one step not usually required for a memorandum of points and authorities or for a trial brief. Because the appellate brief deals with what happened at trial, frequent mention is made of testimony or documents from the lower court. When this is done, reference or citation to the testimony or documents must be made in the brief. When a case is appealed, two types of records are prepared, a **clerk's transcript** and a **reporter's transcript.** The clerk's transcript consists of all the documents filed in the case or introduced at trial as exhibits. They are bound together and each page is numbered. The reporter's transcript contains a verbatim record of oral proceedings.

A reference to the clerk's transcript in a brief looks like this:

On September 15, 1998, plaintiff filed a complaint accusing defendant of having violated the Civil Rights Act and asking for damages. (CT 7-12)

A reference to the reporter's transcript in a brief looks like this:

During trial, the judge denied plaintiff's request to admit a videotape of the incident. (RT 125)

In some motions, parties do refer to transcripts of prior court hearings and reference is made to the transcript in the memorandum. Review Figure 15-5 and see if you can identify all references to the transcript.

Another requirment that is unique to appellate briefs is a color-coded cover. Appellate court rules dictate the color of a cover for the particular brief.

clerk's transcript. Copies of all documents filed in a case and compiled by the clerk of the court at a party's request.

reporter's transcript. A verbatim record of oral proceedings in a case.

15-8 ROLE OF THE RESEARCH ASSOCIATE

Any legal memorandum or brief filed in court must bear the signature of an attorney rather than of a paralegal or law clerk. This does not mean, however, that research associates play no role in the preparation of a legal memorandum or brief; indeed the opposite is often true. Tasks performed by paralegals and law clerks include researching the legal issues, drafting memoranda of law explaining their research findings, reviewing and summarizing transcripts that are connected to the proceeding, and cite checking and proofreading the final document. Occasionally, a research associate prepares a draft of a memorandum of points and authorities or brief for the attorney. Review Appendix D for an example of how two research associates helped in the preparation of a memorandum of points and authorities.

BOX 15-1

CLOSE-UP WITH GERALD UELMEN, ATTORNEY—CONSTITUTIONAL LAW SCHOLAR—PROFESSOR OF LAW

Professor Uelmen, who often uses research associates, provides the following insights and advice about legal research and writing.

The *key* to good research is thoroughness. All research must be updated and current. Researchers must use the most current sources available. The research project must be complete. A complete research project includes the "bad news" as well as the law that supports the client's interests. Counter arguments and weaknesses must be thoroughly researched. If a researcher does not explore the entire issue, a "torpedo" may damage the client's legal position.

Professor Uelmen sees tangents and unclear writing as common problems. He advises researchers to strive for clarity. Clarity is an essential element of good writing. Researchers must have a clear idea of where they are going *during* the research process. This initial focus enables the researcher to produce a writing that is clear and well reasoned. When doing his own research, much of his initial effort is through the LEXIS service. He often supplements his computer assisted legal research with various printed materials.

At the time of this interview, Professor Uelmen was one of several defense attorneys working on the Marijuna Club cases in Federal Court in San Francisco, California. The attorneys divided up the issues, with Professor Uelmen focusing on four issues. Law student volunteers performed the initial research and provided memos to Professor Uelmen, which he then transformed into an argument which, as a portion of the Memorandum of Points and Authorities, was filed with the Federal Court. In Appendix D, you will see some of this research and the Memorandum of Points and Authorities that was filed in this case.

Professor Uelmen is former Dean of the School of Law at Santa Clara University. His publications include *Lessons from the Trial: The People v. O. J. Simpson; Disorderly Conduct: Verbatim Excerpts from Actual Cases; Supreme Folly;* and *Drug Abuse and Law: Cases, Text, Materials.* He has litigated many high-profile cases; his former clients include O. J. Simpson and Christian Brando.

TECHNOLOGY CORNER

For examples of briefs/arguments written for the court, there may be no better source than LEXIS and Westlaw. Both databases offer the user the opportunity to view the briefs submitted to the United States Supreme Court over the past few decades. In addition, in newsworthy litigation the pleadings and briefs are often available through these resources.

Note: The transcripts of the oral arguments may be available.

Court TV provides the pleadings and briefs on some current cases. The archives include a wide variety of documents.

www.courttv.com

The 7th Circuit provides a great deal of very useful information. Check the Web site at: www.ca7.uscourts.gov/ (look under Rules and Guides).

CHAPTER SUMMARY

Research memoranda written for the courts are persuasive or argumentative documents in which an attorney advocates a position favorable to the client. These documents, which include a memorandum of points and authorities, a trial brief, and

an appellate brief, are formal documents that must adhere to technical rules of form and content. Rules govern such things as length, content, citation format, and filing deadlines. Rules regarding form and content are often found in rules of court.

Research documents filed in court have several common features. These include a case caption, a table of contents, a table of authorities, a statement of facts, a statement of issues or questions presented, an argument, a conclusion, and a signature. A table of contents and table of authorities are often not required in short documents.

When legal issues arise in a pending case, those issues are addressed in a memorandum of points and authorities, prepared by the attorneys for the disputing parties. These are often used to support or oppose a motion. Trial briefs are used to analyze legal issues anticipated to arise at trial. These include substantive issues in the case as well as anticipated evidentiary problems. Appellate briefs analyze legal questions that form the basis of an appeal. All documents filed in court must bear the signature of an attorney rather than a paralegal or law clerk. However, research associates often help in the preparation of these documents by (1) researching the law, (2) preparing research memoranda, (3) drafting memoranda of points and authorities or briefs for attorney review, (4) summarizing and reviewing transcripts of hearings or trials that are relevant to the issues, (5) checking cites, and (6) proofreading the final document to be filed with the court.

TERMS TO REMEMBER

advocate
memorandum of points and authorities
trial brief
appellate brief
motion
rules of court
local rules of court
filed
caption
table of contents
table of authorities

court record
declaration
affidavit
argument
first impression
moving party
arbitration
arbitration brief
clerk's transcript
reporter's transcript

QUESTIONS FOR REVIEW

1. Briefly describe the three types of research documents submitted to a court.
2. How do rules of court affect research documents?
3. What is the difference between a table of contents and a table of authorities?
4. What are point headings and how are they used in an argument?
5. What type of documents usually require a table of contents and table of authorities?
6. What is the significance of the court record, declarations, or affidavits to research documents?
7. Why must an attorney and not a paralegal or law clerk sign a memorandum or brief that is filed with the court?

8. Describe the three types of memoranda of points and authorities.

9. Compare and contrast a memorandum of law with a memorandum of points and authorities.

10. Compare and contrast a trial brief with an appellate brief.

CAN YOU FIGURE IT OUT?

Review Figure 15-5.

1. The abbreviation PXTX 4:10-13 appears in the statement of facts. What does this mean?

2. List the point headings in outline format.

3. Was the moving party in this motion the plaintiff or the defendant?

4. What documents or records were used to establish the facts?

RESEARCH ASSIGNMENTS AND ACTIVITIES

1. Prepare a table of authorities for the memorandum in Figure 15-5.

2. Prepare a table of contents for the memorandum in Figure 15-5.

CASE PROJECT

Refer to the hypothetical case in Appendix A that you researched in previous chapters. Assume that the case is going to trial. Write a trial brief for either side addressing the legal issues in the case.

Research Problems

RESEARCH FACT PATTERN 1

Flowers v. Mitchells

Peggy Mitchells is an aspiring fiction writer. She responds to a contest in a national magazine, *Sixteen,* and submits a short story. The short story is based on a teenage experience of Peggy revolving around a conflict with another girl, Tiffany Flowers, over a boy. In the short story, which is written in the first person, Peggy describes Tiffany as a "slut." Unfortunately, Peggy did not change Tiffany's name in the story. Tiffany has sued both Peggy and the magazine for libel. Are they liable?

RESEARCH FACT PATTERN 2

Anystate v. Sutter

Sutter, a hospital, and Anystate, an insurance provider, signed a contract regarding health care services. The contract contained a provision requiring binding arbitration in the event of a dispute. Anystate claims that the contract was void and unenforceable and filed a lawsuit for declaratory relief and for rescission. Sutter filed an answer. Soon after the answer was filed, Anystate petitioned the court to require Sutter to submit to binding arbitration. Sutter claims that Anystate waived the arbitration provision by (1) claiming that the contract was void and unenforceable and by (2) filing a lawsuit in court. Is Sutter correct?

1. Assume the contract is governed by state law.
2. Assume the contract is governed by federal law and the Federal Arbitration Act.

RESEARCH FACT PATTERN 3

Matter of Estate of Starr

Marjorie Starr had one natural child, a daughter, Evelyn Starr, and one foster child, Anthony Dilman. Anthony became her foster child when he was 16 years old. Marjorie's daughter Evelyn left home when she turned 18 and only contacted her mother when she needed money. Anthony, on the other hand, remained at home until he completed college. When Marjorie developed a terminal illness, Anthony moved back home and became her primary caregiver. Marjorie was dependent on Anthony for the last 2 years of her life. During this time, Evelyn rarely called and never visited.

When Anthony was 27, Marjorie died. She left no will, but surprisingly left an estate valued in excess of $2 million. Evelyn claims the entire estate as the sole child. Anthony has made a claim, contending that there was an equitable adoption. Pretrial discovery indicates the following facts: Marjorie and Anthony had a very close relationship from the time he first came to live with Marjorie. While in high school, Marjorie attended mother-son events with him and always referred to him as "my boy." She wore a "mother's ring" with the birthstones of both Evelyn and Anthony. However, Anthony was never formally adopted, nor were any attempts made to adopt. Anthony always kept his own name.

RESEARCH FACT PATTERN 4

The *Rambeaux* Matter

Randy Rambeaux, a San Diego city police officer, is facing both civil liability and criminal charges as a result of injuries he caused during a traffic stop. Although he is accused of using excessive force, Rambeaux claims he acted in self-defense and always used an appropriate amount of force. The incident occurred as follows: Rambeaux, who was not on duty at the time, observed a pickup truck with a defective tail light. He was, however, still in uniform since he had just completed his shift. After observing the truck, Rambeaux pulled up along side the truck (Rambeaux was operating his own motorcycle), and motioned for the truck to pull over. The pickup pulled over to the side of the road and stopped. At this point there is some disagreement as to what happened. The accounts of the incident have been taken from a police report filed by Rambeaux, depositions of various parties and statements from witnesses. However, uncontroverted is the fact that the driver of the truck suffered a severe blow to his head, resulting in a serious brain injury from which he has not recovered. One passenger in the truck has also been injured.

The following information was obtained from police reports and depositions of the parties:

Police Report

On March 21 of last year, San Diego Police Officer Randy Rambeaux stopped a 1989 Ford pickup truck with a camper shell, license, 123 ABC, because of defective brake lights. When he approached the vehicle Rambeaux saw numerous individuals crowded together in the camper shell. Rambeaux states that he ordered these individuals out of the vehicle. None of the individuals obeyed the officer's request. The request was repeated and still no one obeyed. Believing that the individuals might not understand English, Officer Rambeaux opened the driver's door, placed his hand on the arm of the driver (later

identified as Jose Alcosta), and gestured for him to exit the vehicle. Alcosta resisted and more force was used to remove him from the vehicle. Fearing attack from the other passengers, Rambeaux removed his baton for self-protection. When Alcosta was pulled from the vehicle, he stumbled and fell, injuring himself. After Alcosta fell, suspect #2, Roberto Alcosta, jumped out of the vehicle. He slipped on the street, scraping his arms and legs. It was later determined that all passengers in the vehicle were in this country illegally. Both Alcostas were taken to San Diego County Hospital so that their injuries could be treated. The individuals in the camper shell, who were all under 18 years of age, were taken to county child protective services.

Deposition of Roberto Alcosta (taken through an interpreter)

Jose Alcosta is a citizen of Mexico who decided to come to the United States. Jose is 19 years old and has worked in construction in Mexico. Roberto is his 17-year-old brother. They lived a life of poverty in Mexico and hoped to find a better life in California. Friends told them that they could find work in California. Neither speaks English.

On the date of the incident, he recalls the following: The Alcosta family, came across the border in a Ford pickup truck with a camper shell. At some point in time, police stopped their vehicle. The officer appeared to be saying something to them, but it was in English and they did not understand. Alcosta told the officer in Spanish that he did not understand him. The officer then grabbed Jose Alcosta and dragged him out of the vehicle. He then hit him repeatedly with a baton. Roberto Alcosta attempted to come to the aid of his brother and was grabbed and thrown to the ground by the officer. Jose suffered a severe blow to the head, a broken right arm, and internal injuries requiring the removal of his spleen. He has not recovered from the head injury. Roberto suffered numerous contusions and abrasions, but no broken bones.

Deposition of Rock MacMillan, Chief of Police

Chief MacMillan testified that it is highly unusual for off-duty police to make traffic stops and they are not encouraged to do so. Chief MacMillan also testified that the following is San Diego office policy regarding the use of force: Police officers are allowed to use reasonable force to effect an arrest or defend themselves. This includes the use of their baton or gun where appropriate. In the past year, the department has received twenty-six citizen complaints of excessive force. Fourteen of these complaints concerned arrests of illegal aliens. Of the twenty-six complaints made, the department determined that only two had any merit. In both cases the officers involved received reprimands.

The police department investigated the Rambeaux matter. Police talked to one witness who told them that Rambeaux ordered the driver and passengers out of the vehicle. Then, without giving them a chance to exit, he reached into the vehicle and pulled the driver out, throwing him on the ground. He drew his baton and struck the driver, saying, "Why don't you guys go back where you came from?"

Other evidence consists of a video showing Rambeaux pulling Jose Alcosta from the car and hitting him with a baton. The video also shows the officer pushing Roberto Alcosta to the ground. There is no sound on the video.

Deposition of Randy Rambeaux

Officer Rambeaux took the Fifth Amendment when deposed.

In addition to the depositions and police report, other discovery (mostly record production) revealed the following about the officer:

Randy Rambeaux is a ten-year veteran with the police department. He is married and has 3 children, ages 4, 7, and 13. He graduated from UCLA with a degree in criminal justice. He graduated cum laude. He had a minor in psychology. He has received two commendations for his work as a police officer. One of the commendations revolved around an incident where he went into a burning building and saved a young child. The child was Latino. On two prior occasions complaints have been made against Rambeaux for use of excessive force. One incident involved two African-American teenagers. The other involved Anglo teenagers. These two incidents were investigated by the department, which found that there was insufficient evidence against Rambeaux to take any action. Both incidents occurred five years ago.

RESEARCH FACT PATTERN 5

People v. Barker

While on routine traffic patrol, police officer Matthew Dillon spotted Sonny Barker driving a late model white Mercedes automobile. Barker was well-known to the police department and was suspected of being a drug dealer, although he had never been convicted of any drug offenses. Barker appeared to be obeying all traffic laws. Officer Dillon then noted that the vehicle did not have current registration tags and decided to stop the car, hoping that he might just see something related to the drug dealing. After stopping the vehicle, Dillon asked to see Barker's driver's license and the car registration. Barker could not produce either his license or the car's registration. Barker told Dillon that the car belonged to his mother. Dillon checked on Barker's driver's license and the car license. There were no warrants and the car had not been reported as stolen. He then asked Barker if he could search the car. Barker said yes. Dillon looked in the glove box and found the following: Barker's wallet, a little over one ounce of what looked like marijuana, and a piece of paper with the following writing—sbarker@digicom.com ("doobie"). Officer Dillon then reached under the front seat and found a large quantity of marijuana in a clear plastic bag. At this point he arrested Barker.

Later, officer Dillon, who happens to be a computer fanatic and recognized the writing on the paper as being an Internet e-mail address, accessed the e-mail of S. Barker (*doobie* being the password). Dillon used his own computer to do this. Barker's e-mail contained the following message, "Sold latest shipment of mary-jane for a cool million; deposited your share in your mutual fund account at Citibank. Love, Ma."

Based on all of the above information, Sonny was charged with possession for sale.

The following issues have been raised in the criminal case.

1. Was the original stop good?
2. Was the search of the car good?
3. Was the officer's accessing Sonny's e-mail proper?

RESEARCH FACT PATTERN 6

Su v. KILR

KILR, a local radio station, sponsored a "treasure chest" type contest. The station had buried a treasure ($5000) and periodically gave clues as to its location. The first one to find the treasure won the money. Steven Shriver heard a clue and was sure he knew the location of the money. However, several clues had been given over a period of time and Shriver was fairly certain that other people would also be able to figure out the clues. In order to get to the treasure first, Shriver therefore ignored the posted speed limits and was travelling 40 mph in a 25 mph zone (largely a residential neighborhood). When Shriver was about five blocks from the "treasure site," he noticed a police car behind him signaling him to pull over. Instead of pulling over, Shriver increased his speed to 50 mph. The police followed. Shriver kept increasing his speed, as did the police car following him. A high speed chase ensued for about three blocks, at which time Shriver ran a stop sign, colliding with another car and injuring the driver of that car. The injured party, Sally Su, has sued Shriver, KILR Radio Station, and Metro City Police Department for her injuries.

Su is a 35-year-old computer programmer. She is married and has two children. As

a result of the accident, she suffered a cervical strain and was unable to work for three weeks following the accident. She did not have her seat belt on at the time of the accident.

Shriver is a 19-year-old college student. He was uninsured at the time of the accident.

RESEARCH FACT PATTERN 7

Lighthand v. Acme Products, Inc.

Gordon Lighthand worked as a security guard for Acme Products, Inc., a software company. A few months ago, the company noted an especially high rate of theft of software products and concluded that its security guards were not very alert. The president of the company thought this might be due to drug use by the security guards. The company, therefore, required all of its security guards to submit to urine testing for drugs. Lighthand refused and was fired. Lighthand has worked for Acme for three years. Acme has a company policy manual that states that after one year, employees will be fired only for good cause. Lighthand has sued Acme Products, claiming Acme violated his federal and state constitutional right to privacy. Acme made a motion for summary judgment based on the following points:

Constitutional rights only protect against *government* intrusion.

Employers have an absolute right to require drug testing.

How should the court rule on the motion for summary judgment?

RESEARCH FACT PATTERN 8

People v. Baxter

In a busy shopping mall, Baxter grabs a bag of merchandise from Simpson. Simpson gives chase. In the course of the chase, Simpson has a heart attack and dies. With what crimes, if any, should Baxter be charged?

RESEARCH FACT PATTERN 9

Drummond v. Jergins

Drummond, a customer in a bar, gets into a heated discussion with the bartender (Bob) over politics. Bob gets very angry and throws a glass of scotch at Drummond, splashing him in the face with the alcohol. The alcohol causes severe burning of Drummond's eyes. Bob then asks Bouncer Bill to eject Drummond from the bar. Bill grabs Drummond, dislocating Drummond's arm. Drummond sues Joe Jergins, the owner of the bar, for $100,000 for the damage to his eyes and his arm. Is Jergins liable for the injuries claimed by Drummond? Inciden-

tally, Bob, the bartender, had worked for Jergins for only two weeks, during which time there were no complaints. Jergins did a background check of Bob before hiring him and found nothing to suggest he had violent tendencies.

RESEARCH FACT PATTERN 10

Owens v. Adams

Adams saw an advertisement on the Internet for the sale of a "wooded real estate lot." This was the only property advertised on this site. The lot was offered at $50,000, and interested parties were asked to e-mail the owner. Adams, who was familiar with the property in question, e-mailed the owner (Owens) as follows.

"To: Owens@aol.com
Re: Purchase of wooded real estate lot as seen on www.woodedlot.com

I am interested in your lot and hereby offer to purchase the property at $45,000, all cash, with the sale to close in 30 days.
M. Adams"

Owens responded as follows:

"To: madams@yahoo.com
Re: Offer to purchase lot

I will sell you the land at $47,500.
Owens"

Adams replied immediately:

"To: owens@aol.com
Re: Offer to purchase lot

Great! We have a deal
☺"

Two weeks later, after doing considerable legal research on the Internet, Adams backed out of the deal, claiming that the transaction did not meet the requirements of the statute of frauds. Is Adams correct?

Basic Citation Reference Guide

This citation information is taken from *THE BLUEBOOK: A Uniform System of Citation* (Harvard 18th ed. 2005).

Learning to cite correctly and consistently is essential. *THE BLUEBOOK* is a reference manual. It has more citation rules than you will ever need to learn. However, this tool is indispensable. The "rules" and conventions are all here. It takes patience to become familiar with *THE BLUEBOOK*. Take the time to look through this tool before you need to find answers quickly. The index to *THE BLUEBOOK* is excellent: Use it.

Note: Many states have their own legal style or citation manual. Check with your instructor for your state guidelines.

CASE LAW

The United States Supreme Court

Most case citations follow this basic format:

Name	Volume	Reporter	Page	Year
Miranda v. Arizona,	384	U.S.	436	(1966)

Miranda v. Arizona is the name of the case. Case names are underlined or italicized. This makes them easy to see on the page.

The *Miranda* case is located in volume 384 of the *United States Reports.* The *United States Reports* is the official reporter for United States Supreme Court cases. It is "official" because it is published by the United States Government. The proper abbreviation for this reporter is: U.S.

In volume 384, the *Miranda* case is located at page 436. The case was decided in 1966. The year is placed in parentheses.

This information allows anyone looking at the citation to locate the actual decision.

All United States Supreme Court cases are located in print form in three separate reporters, published by three different publishers. The full citation for the *Miranda* case is as follows:

Miranda v. Arizona, 384 U.S. 436, 86 S. Ct. 1602, 16 L. Ed. 2d 694 (1966).

86 S. Ct. 1602 and 16 L. Ed. 2d 694 are referred to as *parallel citations.*

⇨ **A Point to Remember**   When you refer to or "cite" a case, be sure to provide your reader with a complete citation. Use the name, volume, reporter, page number, year, and, if necessary, the parallel citations.

GO TO: *The Bluebook,* Table 1 (pages 200–201)

STATE CASE LAW

State cases are cited much the same as Supreme Court cases.

For example, in the state of California, either of the following citations is correct for a California case.

Long Beach v. Superior Court, 64 Cal. App. 3d 65, 134 Cal. Rptr. 468 (1976).

or,

Long Beach v. Superior Court (1976) 64 Cal. App. 3d 65, 134 Cal. Rptr. 468.

In California and other states, there is an unofficial publisher of state case law. In the citation above, Cal. Rptr. is the abbreviation for the California Reporter, published by West Publishing. 134 Cal. Rptr. 468 is the parallel citation.

Sometimes you will see references to "regional reporters." The regional reporter abbreviations follow.

Atlantic Reporter	A.2d
North Eastern Reporter	N.E.2d
North Western Reporter	N.W.2d
Pacific Reporter	P.2d
Southern Reporter	So. 2d
South Eastern Reporter	S.E.2d
South Western Reporter	S.W.2d

The *2d* following the regional reporter abbreviation indicates that each of these reporters is in the second series.

⇨ **A Point to Remember**   Most legal sources follow the general format of
Title
Volume
Book or Reporter (abbreviated)
Page
Year

When you are looking at an unfamiliar citation, try to identify these elements. This will enable you to understand the various citations you come across in your legal studies.

GO TO: *The Bluebook,* Table 1 (pages 193–242)

UNITED STATES CONSTITUTION

The Fourteenth Amendment to the United States Constitution is written as follows:

U.S. Const. amend. XIV.

If you want to indicate a certain section of the Amendment you add:§ 1
The full citation looks like this:

U.S. Const. amend. XIV, § 1.

GO TO: *The Bluebook,* Rule 11 (page 100)

THE UNITED STATES CODE (STATUTES)

The United States Code is cited in the following manner:

Number of Code Title	Code	Section Cited	Date
28	U.S.C.	§ 1291	(XXXX)

The proper cite is 28 U.S.C. § 1291 (XXXX).

GO TO: *The Bluebook,* Rule 12 (pages 101–113)

STATE CODES (STATUTES)

A statute citation must show

1. the numbers of the statutory topic,
2. the abbreviated name of the publication,
3. the specific statute or section of the statute, and
4. the year of the publication.

Examples

Ariz. Rev. Stat. Ann. § ## (XXXX)	Arizona Revised Statutes Annotated
Cal. Educ. Code § ## (XXXX)	California Education Code
Conn. Gen. Stat. § ## (XXXX)	Connecticut General Statutes
Ind. Code § ## (XXXX)	Indiana Code

GO TO: *The Bluebook,* Table 1 (pages 193–242)

THE BLUEBOOK **Index (Eighteenth Edition)**

When Citing	Check Bluebook Page	Rule/Table
A.L.R. Annotation	145	Rule 16.6.6
American Jurisprudence	135	Rule 15.8
Books	129–137	Rule 15
Brackets	69–70	Rule 5.2
Briefs	96–97	Rule 10.8.3
States and the District of Columbia	193–242	T.1
Capitalization	76–78	Rule 8
Case History	92–93	Rule 10.7
Case Names	81–86	Rule 10.2
Constitution, The	100	Rule 11
Corpus Juris Secundum (C.J.S.)	135	Rule 15.8
Dictionaries	135	Rule 15.8
Dissenting Opinions	91–92	Rule 10.6
Federal Cases	193–196	T.1
Federal Rules	110	Rule 12.8.3
Footnotes	59–61	Rule 3.2
Internet Sources	151–158	Rule 18
Introductory Signals	46–48	Rule 1.2
Law Review Articles	138–139	Rule 16
LEXIS	151–153	Rule 18
Looseleaf Services	162–163	Rule 19
Model Codes	111–112	Rule 12.8.5
Newspapers	141	Rule 16.5
Official Reporters	6–13, 86–88, 193–242	B5, Rule 10.3, T.1
Pages	59–61	Rule 3.2
Parenthetical Explanation of Authorities	91–92, 109	Rule 10.6, 12.7
Pending and Unreported Cases	95–96	Rule 10.8.1
Periodical Abbreviations (Law Reviews)	349–372	T.13
Periodicals	138–147	Rule 16
Pinpoint Citations	59–61	Rule 3.2
Quote Marks	68–71	Rule 5
Restatements	111–112	Rule 12.8.5
Short Citation Forms	64–67	Rule 4
State Cases	193–242	T.1
Statutes	101–113	Rule 12
Treatises	129–137	Rule 15
Uniform Acts	111	Rule 12.8.4
United States Supreme Court Cases	79, 193	Rule 10, T.1
Westlaw	151–153	Rule 18

QUOTATIONS

When you quote, you must alert the reader that you are using quoted language. Usually this means you must use quote marks. A citation must follow a quote. This citation lets the reader know where the borrowed material originated. Quotations of fifty words or more are blocked. A blocked quote is single spaced and indented on the left and right margins. No quote marks are used with a blocked quotation.

GO TO: *THE BLUEBOOK,* Rule 5 (page 68–71)

SIGNALS

Signals serve a variety of purposes. Signals indicate support, suggest comparisons, indicate contradictions, or indicate background material. When there is no signal, the cited authority is the source of the quoted material. A common introductory signal is *See.* When the signal *see* is placed in front of the cited authority, it means that the cited authority, clearly supports the proposition found in the quoted language.

GO TO: *THE BLUEBOOK,* Rule 1.2 (pages 46–48)

Information on the Order of Signals is found in *THE BLUEBOOK* at Rule 1.3 (page 48)

ELLIPSIS

When you omit a word or phrase from a quote, you must alert the reader that you have done so. The ellipsis is the tool we use for this purpose. For example: "The motion to suppress, after much heated debate and loud gavel banging, was denied". could become:"The motion to suppress . . . was denied." Do not use an ellipsis at the beginning of a quote. This tool is properly used in the middle of a quoted language or at the end of the quote. When used at the end of a quote you need to use four rather than three points. Never use more than three points internally in a quote. Never use more than four points at the end of a quote. The number of points does not indicate the amount of material omitted.

GO TO: *THE BLUEBOOK,* Rule 5.3 (pages 70–71)

Research Strategies: An Overview

CREATE THE VOCABULARY LIST

Every fact pattern provides an initial vocabulary or terminology list. Sort the terms into two lists: one factual and the other legal.

As you review what you know, some terms are easily placed into your vocabulary list. At this point, do not worry too much about which list a certain fact actually belongs on; just pull out the key terminology. Some terms or concepts may seem to be both legal and factual. Do not let that confuse you. Your research will help you separate the legal from the factual.

From personal experience you may want to add terms or phrases. The important thing is that you have a list of words and phrases identified before you even consider going to the law library. If case law research becomes important, other facts will be important when you begin to compare and contrast the facts of your client's case and the facts of the reported decisions your research produces. You now have a list of terms to take to an index.

FORMULATE THE ISSUE

Attempt to articulate the legal issue. Remember, a well-written legal issue contains the cause of action (or legal problem) and the key facts. However, rather than attempting to write a formal issue statement at this early stage of the research, just ask a simple question.

Your initial research will clarify the cause of action. Once the elements of the cause of action are known, you will be better able to determine which of the facts are most important. This initial research also helps you to articulate the issue in a more formal format, that is, a format acceptable to send to the court. For now, keep it simple and remain focused on the research project.

USE THE LEGAL DICTIONARY AND THESAURUS

Once the initial vocabulary list is complete, take a few moments to consult a legal dictionary and a legal thesaurus. These resources expand your research list. That is, you will have a larger list of terms to take to the indexes of the legal research resources.

With this list of terms you are ready to begin work in the indexes. The questions become "Which set of books?" and "Which index?"

CREATE A RESEARCH PLAN BEFORE GOING TO THE LAW LIBRARY

Before going to the law library, sit down and consider where to begin the research. Make a list of books or sets of books you plan to review. Break that list into primary sources and secondary sources.

Most states have a state legal encyclopedia. This can be a good starting place when you know very little about the topic you are researching. Pleading and practice guides provide good examples. These secondary resources provide the researcher with a foundation to perform the research in primary sources. Once the vocabulary list and a list of library resources are prepared, you are ready to begin the initial research.

TAKE YOUR RESEARCH TERMS/VOCABULARY TO THE INDEXES

Step One

Determine which resource to attack first. Take a moment to look the set over. Notice how much information is on the spine of every volume. Notice that some of the volumes may say "Index" on them. This is a good sign. It means that in addition to a large comprehensive index at the end of the set, there is also a topical index for each topic.

Step Two

Locate the index for the set. The comprehensive index is usually at the end of the set of books. In most instances, the index is a large multivolume set. Sometimes these indexes are called "Descriptive Word Indexes" or "General Index." They are arranged alphabetically. Begin to methodically look up your vocabulary words and phrases. An early understanding of the cause of action provides an overall understanding of the materials you will locate.

EFFECTIVE USE OF THE INDEX VOLUMES

As you look at the index pages, you may locate terms that are not on your initial list, but look interesting. Add them to your list and pursue them.

Legal researchers must be armed with as many vocabulary terms as possible. With this expanded vocabulary list you are ready to begin the actual research in the sources you have chosen.

WHEN TO BEGIN THE RESEARCH IN PRIMARY SOURCES

Although your first inclination may be to begin all research in primary sources, this may not always be the best choice. Remember: Primary sources contain the law, not a discussion or explanation of the law. Primary sources are often annotated, but this information is usually a brief summary of case law, not an explanation or discussion written to educate or inform the reader.

Primary sources are a good place to begin research when you are familiar with the area of law to be researched and you are familiar with the vocabulary involved in the factual situation. In such cases, you may not need to perform foundation research.

Remember to begin with the terms directly produced by the initial fact pattern. However, you may need to expand the list of terms through a dictionary, thesaurus, and various indexes. As the list expands and becomes more complex, your understanding of the terminology may diminish. Good legal researchers work to expand their vocabulary. Take the time to understand all terminology before beginning the research.

With a good foundation of basic vocabulary and a clear legal issue, you are prepared to begin research in the statutes. You will have already used the index to look for terms; while searching for terms, you must begin to make a list of codes that may be applicable to your fact pattern. Methodically, list the code section names and numbers. When the initial list is complete, begin to locate and read the statutes you identified from the index.

In addition to a general index, usually a multivolume set located at the end of the set of books you are researching, there may be an index located at the end of the specific subject within the set of books. For example, if you know your topic is summary judgment motions, and you know that the general information on these motions is found in the civil procedure section of the state code, you could go to the last volume of the civil procedure sections of the state code to find the index to just the civil procedure statutes. This allows the researcher to limit or pinpoint the research. Think of this as a way to filter out other references that may be irrelevant.

WHEN TO BEGIN RESEARCH IN SECONDARY SOURCES

The set you choose to work in reflects how much prior knowledge you bring to the research situation. Legal encyclopedias, *American Law Reports,* and law review articles often provide a great deal of basic information. When a researcher knows very little about the topic, this is a good place to begin to build a research foundation.

Caution: When performing state-specific research, if possible, use your state's legal encyclopedia and try to find articles and *American Law Reports* annotations that include your state. If your issue is federal, you may want to look at the *American Law Reports Federal* edition and search out law review articles that focus on federal issues.

If your topic is somewhat narrow and you must search for case law, consider using the appropriate digest. The digest provides narrow topics listed in alphabetical order. Following each topic are references to specific cases. These references are often referred to as *annotations*.

The specialty sets and pleading and practice sets work well when the researcher is focused and understands the basic vocabulary associated with the topic to be researched.

Make a list of potential resources to be reviewed. Prioritize the list. Start with the set you feel will provide the most efficient path to your answers. Make sure you have thought about what you already know and what you need to know. Remember: Your goal is to locate relevant primary law.

Another approach to locating background information is to locate and read an *American Law Reports* annotation (article). There may even be a specialty set appropriate to your research situation.

As you can see, there are several places to begin your research. With practice, you will develop preferences for certain resources over other, less user-friendly resources. Do not lose sight of the research plan. Create a plan and follow it until you have good reason to believe that the initial plan is not producing reliable results.

TAKE NOTES WHEN WORKING WITH PRINTED MATERIALS

Finding the law is a good starting point. Try not to go too far into the research without slowing down and checking the validity of your research results. In addition, make sure you have the most current information available.

Use *Shepard's* to update and validate your research. *Shepard's* is available in print and on LEXIS. Shepardize any case or statute you feel you may rely on. Do not forget that you may Shepardize law review articles and *A.L.R.* annotations.

In addition to *Shepard's* you should consider using some of the features available through *LEXIS* and *Westlaw*. In LEXIS you may use the Auto-Cite feature, discussed in Chapter 10. Westlaw offers a similar service called KeyCite; this is also introduced in Chapter 10. These services are designed to be used in addition to *Shepard's*.

TAKE NOTES WHEN WORKING WITH PRINTED MATERIALS

ORGANIZATION AND ATTENTION TO DETAIL	
Get ready to take notes.	You need pencils, pens, underliners, self-adhesive notes, paperclips.
Be prepared to take notes.	Get your materials out and ready; be organized at each step of the research process.
Think about the paper you will use.	Loose leaf paper?
	Bound tablet?
	Large index cards?
	Adhesive notes?

Loose leaf paper is easy to shuffle and organize later. It is also easy to misplace. These pages may look a lot like the other notes in your notebooks.

A bound tablet will keep everything in one place, but does not provide much flexibility when shuffling becomes necessary. At some point it becomes necessary to organize the notes in a logical order. Remember: Your research results may not proceed in the same order you will eventually write up your memorandum or brief.

Large index cards, sometimes color-coded, prove useful because of their versatility. Many researchers color-code their issues. All research on a specific issue is placed, for example, on blue 5×7 cards. On the back of each card, the researcher notes the date the research is performed, the source of the data, and any personal notes. It is easy later to shuffle and organize by color. Sometimes a researcher places each case reviewed on a separate card. The notes on each statute are also noted on separate cards. This makes later organization much easier.

Self-adhesive notes are small, come unstuck, and are easily misplaced. Consider using them only in addition to other resources.

Work toward establishing a personal preference. Consider the nature of your research. If you plan to take a good number of written notes, maybe index cards or loose leaf paper will provide you with the ability to easily organize and rearrange your results. Try several approaches and work toward finding a note-taking process that is comfortable and reliable.

TAKE NOTES AND RECORD RESULTS WHEN WORKING WITH ONLINE OR CD-ROM MATERIALS

Instead of making handwritten notes from the screen during online research, consider printing or downloading the relevant information. Some handwritten notes may be necessary, however: keep in mind that the database in which you are researching may be quite expensive and note taking is time consuming.

When working with CD-ROM products, the time element is not critical. Still, you may want to take minimal notes while you print and download the most useful data. Be sure that you note why you printed the material and how you plan to use it.

ORGANIZATION OF PHOTOCOPIED OR DOWNLOADED MATERIALS

Organization of Materials

In the process of legal research, you will photocopy and download many documents, probably too many. It is critical that you organize these documents *as you acquire them*. Staple pages that belong together; do not paperclip them. On the reverse side of every document copied or printed, note the date you acquired the material, the reason you copied it, the source and the issue(s) it pertains to. Over days or weeks of research, you *will* forget why you copied materials and where they originated. You may also find that some of the documents you copy in the early stages of research may not be as relevant as they seemed at the time you copied them. The date notation may help you place perspective on the data.

Create folders or files. Organize the materials issue by issue or separate the documents into groups of case law and statutes. If you organize from the very beginning, the process of creating the written document is made much easier.

Defendants' Joint Memorandum of Points and Authorities in Opposition to Plaintiff's Motions for Preliminary Injunction: Initial Research Memoranda

This appendix is a complex Memorandum of Points and Authorities dealing with a law that purportedly legalized the use of marijuana for medicinal purposes. In part, this Memorandum is based on work done by research associates. Their research memoranda follow the Memorandum of Points and Authorities. Sections II.C, II.D, and II.E.5 of Defendants' Joint Memorandum of Points and Authorities in Opposition to Plaintiff's Motions for Preliminary Injunction incorporate the work of the research associates. Their work is found beginning on page 458.

IN THE UNITED STATES DISTRICT COURT
FOR THE NORTHERN DISTRICT OF CALIFORNIA

UNITED STATES OF AMERICA,	) Nos. C 98-00085 CRB
	) C 98-00086 CRB
Plaintiff,	) C 98-00087 CRB
	) C 98-00088 CRB
v.	) C 98-00089 CRB
	) C 98-20013 CRB
CANNABIS CULTIVATORS' CLUB;	)
and DENNIS PERON,	)
	) DEFENDANTS' JOINT MEMORANDUM
Defendants.	) OF POINTS AND AUTHORITIES IN
	) OPPOSITION TO PLAINTIFF'S
	) MOTIONS FOR PRELIMINARY
AND RELATED ACTIONS.	) INJUNCTION
	)
	Date: March 24, XXXX
	Time: 2:30 p.m.
	Courtroom: 8

TABLE OF CONTENTS

TABLE OF AUTHORITIES

TO THE HONORABLE CHARLES R. BREYER, UNITED STATES DISTRICT JUDGE,
AND TO ALL PARTIES TO THE ABOVE-CAPTIONED ACTION:

Defendants herein, by and through their respective counsel, specially appearing, submit the following Opposition to Plaintiff United States' Motion For Preliminary Injunction And Permanent Injunction And For Summary Judgment:

I. INTRODUCTION

On January 9th 1998, the Government filed the instant suit against six medical cannabis dispensaries pursuant to 21 USC § 882. On January 30, 1998, over the government's objections, this Honorable Court granted defendants' Motion for Continuance and directed defendants to file Memoranda addressing the effect of federal law on defendants' activities protected by Proposition 215, codified as California Health & Safety Code § 11362.5. Defendants submit their Opposition herein.

A.   History of Medical Marijuana

The medicinal use of cannabis can hardly be characterized as a "recent" phenomenon. The first recorded use of marijuana medicinally was over five thousand years ago. During the reign of the Chinese Emperor, Chen Nung, it was written that cannabis provided relief for malaria, constipation, rheumatic pains, and other conditions.

In the *Anatomy of Melancholy*, published in 1621, the English clergyman Robert Burton suggested the use of cannabis in the treatment of depression. The New English Dispensary of 1764 recommended applying a cannabis compress to the skin to relieve inflammation.

Between 1840 and 1900, more than 100 papers were published in Western medical literature concerning the medicinal benefits of cannabis. In 1839, Dr. W. B. O'Shaughnessy, a professor at the medical college of Calcutta wrote that a tincture made of hemp proved to be an effective analgesic.

Cannabis was first listed in the United States Dispensatory in 1854. It was common during that era for commercial cannabis preparations to be available in drugstores. In 1860, Dr. R. R. M'Meens reported numerous medical uses for cannabis to the Ohio State Medical Society. In 1887, H. A. Hare wrote of the benefits of cannabis in the treatment of terminal patients. In 1891, Dr. J. B. Mattison urged physicians to use hemp as an analgesic and to treat such conditions as chronic rheumatism and migraine. In 1937, the United States passed the Marihuana Tax Act at the urging of Harry Anslinger, a government agent who had essentially been put out of business with the repeal of prohibition. Mr. Anslinger was instrumental in convincing the public of the dangers of marijuana through such means as the film "reefer madness."

In 1938, Mayor Fiorello LaGuardia appointed a committee of scientists to study the medical, sociological, and psychological effects of marijuana use in New York. The study was published in 1944, finding no proof that major crime was associated with marijuana, or that it caused any aggressive or antisocial behavior. Harry Anslinger denounced this report and it was essentially ignored by the government.

In 1970, Congress passed the Controlled Substances Act, at which time President Nixon appointed the Presidential Commission on Marihuana and Drug Abuse, aka the Shafer Commission, to study marijuana and report back to Congress. The purpose was to assist Congress in determining the appropriate scheduling of marijuana. When the Commission found that there was no basis for placing marijuana in Schedule I, Congress and the President virtually ignored its scientific judgment.

On September 6, 1988, after a Court order forced the DEA to hold two years of hearings before its own administrative law judge, the Honorable Francis L. Young ruled that approval by a significant

minority of physicians was enough to meet the standard of "currently accepted medical use in treatment in the United States" established by the Controlled Substances Act for a Schedule II drug. Judge Young wrote that "marihuana, in its natural form, is one of the safest therapeutically active substances known to man. . . . One must reasonably conclude that there is accepted safety for use of marihuana under medical supervision. To conclude otherwise, on the record, would be unreasonable, arbitrary, and capricious." Judge Young's findings were, not surprisingly, ignored by the government.

B.   History of Dispensaries

Proposition 215 was not the first effort in California to allow for the use of medicinal marijuana. In two consecutive years, the California legislature passed medical marijuana bills, only to see them vetoed by Gov. Pete Wilson. Finally, in 1996, the voters of the state placed an initiative on the ballot. It passed on November 5, 1996, receiving 56% of the vote. In response to the voters' demand that "seriously ill Californians have the right to obtain and use marijuana for medical purposes where the medical use is deemed appropriate by a physician," numerous medical cannabis dispensaries, including the defendants herein, sprang up to meet the needs of patients. These dispensaries provided safe and affordable medicine that patients had previously only found available on the black market, and then only at exorbitant prices and of questionable quality.

II.   ARGUMENT

Defendants herein contend that the government's pending motion should be denied. Defendants' argument can be summarized as follows:

A.   Substantive Due Process Bars The Government From Enforcing The Sections Of the Controlled Substances Act It Seeks To Apply To Defendants.

B.   The Controlled Substances Act Does Not Reach The Defendants' Activities Which Are Wholly Intrastate In Nature.

C.   Defendants' Activities Are Exempt From Application Of The Controlled Substances Act.

D.   Defendants' Activities Are Justified By The Defense Of Necessity.

E.   The Government Cannot Meet The Standards For The Injunctive Relief It Seeks.

A.   SUBSTANTIVE DUE PROCESS BARS THE GOVERNMENT FROM ENFORCING THE SECTIONS OF THE CONTROLLED SUBSTANCES ACT IT SEEKS TO APPLY TO DEFENDANTS.

1.   Substantive Due Process Protects Individuals from Government Actions That Violate Protected Personal Liberty Interests.

The United States Supreme Court has established that individuals are protected under the Due Process clauses of the Fourteenth and Fifth Amendments from State or Federal intrusions into their "fundamental liberty interests." Substantive Due Process has come to stand for protection of numerous un-enumerated liberties. As Justice Rehnquist recently described in *Washington v. Glucksberg,*____ U.S.____, 117 S.Ct. 2258 (1997).

The Due Process Clause guarantees more than fair process, and the "liberty" it protects includes more than the absence of physical restraint. . . . The Clause also provides heightened protection against government interference with certain fundamental rights and liberty interests. In a long line of cases, we have held that, in addition to the specific freedoms protected by the Bill of Rights, the "liberty" specially protected by the Due Process Clause includes the rights to marry; to have children; to direct the education and upbringing of one's children; to marital privacy; to use contraception; to bodily integrity; and to abortion. We have also assumed, and strongly suggested, that the Due Process Clause protects the traditional right to refuse unwanted lifesaving medical treatment.

Glucksberg, at 2267, (citations omitted).

In applying Substantive Due Process analysis, the Chief Justice in *Glucksberg* explained that government action must be "narrowly tailored to serve a compelling [government] interest" where a "fundamental liberty interest" is involved. Such interests arise where the interest protected is firmly rooted in history and tradition and is carefully described:

Our established method of substantive due process analysis has two primary features: First, we have regularly observed that the Due Process Clause specially protects those fundamental rights and liberties which are, objectively, "deeply rooted in this Nation's history and tradition," ("so rooted in the traditions and conscience of our people as to be ranked as fundamental"), and "implicit in the concept of ordered liberty," such that "neither liberty nor justice would exist if they were sacrificed". . . . Second, we have required in substantive due process cases a "careful description" of the asserted fundamental liberty interest. Our Nation's history, legal traditions, and practices thus provide the crucial "guideposts for responsible decision-making," that direct and restrain our exposition of the Due Process Clause. As we stated recently . . . , the Fourteenth Amendment "forbids the government to infringe . . . 'fundamental' liberty interests at all, no matter what process is provided, unless the infringement is narrowly tailored to serve a compelling state interest."

Glucksberg, at 2268 (citations omitted).

Justice Souter in his concurrence to *Glucksberg* argues the application of Substantive Due Process based on a "concept of 'ordered liberty' . . . comprising a continuum of rights to be free from 'arbitrary impositions and purposeless restraints.'" *Glucksberg*, at 2281–2 (Souter, J., concurring). Justice Souter described his standard for a substantive due process right as follows:

This approach calls for the court to assess the relative "weights" or dignities of the contending interests. . . . [This] method is subject to two important constraints. . . . First, such a court is bound to confine the values that it recognizes to those truly deserving constitutional stature, either to those expressed in constitutional text, or those exemplified by "the traditions from which [the nation] developed" or revealed by contrast with "the traditions from which it broke."

The second constraint, again, simply reflects the fact that constitutional review, not judicial lawmaking, is a court's business here. . . . It is only when the legislation's justifying principle, critically valued, is so far from being commensurate with the individual interest as to be arbitrarily or pointlessly applied that the statute must give way.

Glucksberg, at 2283 (Souter, J., concurring) (citations omitted).

Under either the Rehnquist or Souter standard, the High Court would resolve Defendants' Substantive Due Process claims similarly.

2.   The Due Process Clause Protects Clearly Established Fundamental Liberty Interests.

Defendants' liberty interests meet the first prong of the Rehnquist analysis of Substantive Due Process: The right of patients to obtain physician-recommended treatment that would alleviate pain and preserve life is strongly reflected in our nation's traditions and the Supreme Court's historic Substantive Due Process analysis. The Court has found Due Process interests in preserving life and caring for oneself. *Id.* Moreover, Substantive Due Process analysis indicates that the Fourteenth and Fifth Amendments protect a fundamental interest *to receive palliative treatment for a painful medical condition. Id.*

"Many of the rights and liberties protected by the Due Process Clause sound in personal autonomy." *Glucksberg,* at 2271. There is no liberty more firmly established than the fundamental interest to be free from physical pain imposed by the government for arbitrary and capricious reasons. The highest Court in the land has continuously and persistently measured and evaluated Substantive Due Process claims in terms of the physical pain imposed upon the individual by government restraints. *Furman v. Georgia,* 408 U.S. 238 (1972). (Substantive Due Process implicated where death penalty imposed under a method inflicting "unnecessary pain"); *Doe v. Bolton,* 410 U.S. 179 (1973), (considerations of an individual's Substantive Due Process right to abortion include the fact that pregnancy requires one "to incur pain" and a "higher mortality rate"); *Ingraham v. Wright,* 430 U.S. 651 (1977) (school children's Substantive Due Process violated by corporal punishment, discussed *infra); Los Angeles v. Lyons,* 461 U.S. 95 (1983) (arrestee's Substantive Due Process violated by police utilizing unnecessarily painful chokeholds); *Cruzan v. Director, MDH,* 497 U.S. 261 (1990), (pain suffered by patient in persistent vegetative state relevant to inquiry of fundamental interest to deprive oneself of nutrition and hydration, discussed *infra); Planned Parenthood v. Casey,* 505 U.S. 833 (1992) ("anxieties," "physical constraints," and "pain" of women carrying child to term basis of Substantive Due Process right for a woman to elect an abortion); *Rochin v. California,* 342 U.S. 165 (1952) (violation of Substantive Due Process to pump arrestee's stomach to preserve evidence); and *Washington v. Glucksberg,* ___U.S.___ (1997) (terminally ill patient rights to palliative treatment implicate to Substantive Due Process, discussed *infra*).

In *Ingraham v. Wright, supra,* the Supreme Court cited the long history and tradition of constitutional rights respecting individual integrity:

> The Due Process Clause of the Fifth Amendment, later incorporated into the Fourteenth, was intended to give Americans at least the protection against governmental power that they had enjoyed as Englishmen against the power of the Crown. The liberty preserved from deprivation without due process included the right "generally to enjoy those privileges long recognized at common law as essential to the orderly pursuit of happiness by free men." Among the historic liberties so protected was a *right to be free from, and to obtain judicial relief for, unjustified intrusions on personal security.*

> While the contours of this historic liberty interest in the context of our federal system of government have not been defined precisely, they always have been thought to encompass freedom from bodily restraint and punishment. It is fundamental that the state cannot hold and physically punish an individual except in accordance with due process of law.

> This constitutionally protected liberty interest is at stake in this case. . . . where school authorities, acting under color of state law, inflict *appreciable physical pain,* we hold that [Due Process] liberty interests are implicated.

Ingraham, at 672–3 (footnotes and citations omitted) (*emphasis added*).

Not only is the prevention of unnecessary pain established under the Due Process Clause, but is also clearly established as a basic *enumerated* fundamental right in regard to punishment under the Eighth Amendment barring cruel and unusual punishment. As was true in *Ingraham,* the High Court has drawn from the history of the Eighth Amendment in defining the parameters of Substantive Due

Process. Where the issue of unnecessary pain is involved, Substantive Due Process is often analyzed as a parallel to the Eighth Amendment. Thus, in *Furman v. Georgia*, 408 U.S. (1972), the Court surmised a confluence between the two approaches. "[C]ruel and unusual punishment and substantive due process become so close as to merge." *Furman*, at 359.

The relevance of infliction of pain by the state as the basis for Substantive Due Process claims is not limited to those areas involving discipline or criminal punishment. Pain analysis was also highly relevant to Substantive Due Process analysis in *Cruzan, supra*. There, the Court considered whether the state of Missouri could require "clear and convincing" evidence that a patient wished to terminate artificial nutrition treatment after an automobile accident left her in a persistent vegetative state.

Most recently, the Supreme Court considered whether an individual had a Substantive Due Process right to have the assistance of a physician in committing suicide. *Washington v. Glucksberg, supra.* In that case, four terminally ill patients and their doctors petitioned the court for the permission to proceed with doctor-assisted suicides. As in the previous instances, the notion that the state would subject an individual to unnecessary pain weighed heavy in the minds of the Justices.

Although the Court's opinion in *Glucksberg* was unanimous in result, it was not so in its reasoning. Justice O'Connor and four other Justices filed separate concurrences, each of which supports the position maintained by Defendants herein that Substantive Due Process protects an individual's right to obtain medical treatment that alleviates unnecessary pain. Her opinion makes clear that suffering patients are presumed to have access to any palliative medication that would alleviate pain even where such medication might hasten death. "[A] patient who is suffering from a terminal illness and who is experiencing great pain has *no legal barriers* to obtaining medication, from qualified physicians." *Glucksberg*, at 2303 (emphasis added).

Similarly, Justice Breyer's concurrence turned on issues of a consideration of the pain suffered by patients. Breyer's opinion suggested that a "right to die with dignity" may in fact be protected under the Constitution. He argued that such a right would include a right to "professional medical assistance" and "the avoidance of unnecessary and severe physical suffering." *Glucksberg*, at 2311 (J. Breyer, concurring). Justice Breyer made clear that the presence of pain was a determinative factor in his mind: "[I]n my view, the avoidance of severe physical pain (connected with death) would have to comprise an essential part of any successful claim". *Id.*

Justice Souter's concurrence similarly stresses an individual's right to make decisions with one's own doctor along with considering the pain and incumbent indignity suffered by an individual. Justice Souter writes, "[The] liberty interest in bodily integrity was phrased . . . by [Justice] Cardozo when he said, '[e]very human being of adult years and sound mind has a right to determine what shall be done with his own body' in relation to his medical needs." *Glucksberg* at 2288 (Souter, J., concurring). He explained further,

> [T]he Court [has] recognized that the good physician is not just a mechanic of the human body whose services have no bearing on a person's moral choices, but one who does more than treat symptoms, one who ministers to the patient. . . . This idea of the physician as serving the whole person is a source of the high value traditionally placed on the medical relationship.

Glucksberg, at 2288–89, (citation omitted).

Finally, Justice Stevens asserts with regard to the protected "sphere of substantive liberty":

> Whatever the outer limits of the concept may be, it definitely includes protection for matters "central to personal dignity and autonomy." It includes, "the individual's right to make certain unusually important decisions that will affect his own, or his family's, destiny. The Court has referred to such decisions as implicating 'basic values,' as being 'fundamental,' and as being dignified by history and tradition.

Glucksberg, at 2307 (Stevens, J., concurring) (citation omitted).

Defendants herein assert that they maintain a fundamental liberty interest in physician recommended treatment to alleviate physical pain in the face of governmental restraint. The Defendant dispensaries are cooperatives composed of members who are patients whose doctors have recommended cannabis for medical purposes. Many of the members are terminally ill cancer or AIDS patients. As a result of their conditions, they experience intense pain and nausea. Others are glaucoma patients, threatened with permanent blindness. Defendants can prove that cannabis is unique in its ability to relieve these symptoms. The government now seeks an injunction that would prevent these Defendants from obtaining this necessary treatment.

In a similar vein, Defendants' interests are bolstered by a second established fundamental interest in the *right to provide care for oneself.* Although this right is usually implicated where an individual is incarcerated and does not have access to necessary medical treatment, the argument is equally applicable to a situation where the government denies medical treatment by enacting laws proscribing such:

> [W]hen the State by the affirmative exercise of its power so restrains an individual's liberty that it renders him unable to care for himself, and at the same time fails to provide for his basic human needs—e.g., food, clothing, shelter, *medical care,* and reasonable safety—it transgresses the substantive limits on state action set by the Eighth Amendment and the Due Process Clause. In the substantive due process analysis, it is the State's affirmative act of restraining the individual's freedom to act on his own behalf—through incarceration, institutionalization, or other *similar restraint of personal liberty*—which is the "deprivation of liberty" triggering the protections of the Due Process Clause.

Deshaney v. Winnebago Cty. Soc.Servs. Dept., 489 U.S. 189, 200 (1989) (citation omitted).

The government's restraint on the distribution of cannabis prevents the defendant patients from obtaining medical care for themselves, as protected by *Deshaney.* This is particularly egregious where the treatment sought is that to alleviate pain as discussed above.

The interest of some of these member/patients in preventing unnecessary pain, in treating themselves, and in preserving eyesight, is surpassed only by a third firmly rooted liberty interest, that of preserving life. It is without question that an individual has a liberty interest in preserving his or her life. As the Supreme Court explained in *Cruzan, supra,* "[i]t cannot be disputed that the Due Process Clause protects an interest in life." *Cruzan,* at 281. Many of the cooperative members would needlessly place their lives in jeopardy were they denied the right to the medical use of cannabis. Many chemotherapy patients and AIDS patients are so plagued with nausea and discomfort that they are unable to eat. Without basic nourishment, their conditions are aggravated and they are essentially at risk of starving to death.

Defendants herein present compelling circumstances. The history and traditions of Substantive Due Process make clear that bodily integrity is an area of fundamental importance. The interests protected, relief from pain, self care, and preservation of life, are so ingrained in our nation's traditions and are so firmly rooted in our concepts of ordered liberty that they are fundamental. The right to live, painfree under the care of one's physician without arbitrary interference from the government, is at stake.

3.   The Substantive Due Process Interest At Issue Is Narrowly Defined

The Defendant patients assert Constitutional protection from the federal government's interference with their right legally to obtain cannabis, with a doctor's recommendation, for treatment of painful and life-threatening medical conditions. Unlike the plaintiff doctors in *Glucksberg* various Defendants in the instant action assert personal interests as the Controlled Substances Act applies specifically to them. Each of the Defendant cooperative's members has a medical condition for which a physician has recommended treatment with cannabis. Without the treatment some will suffer pain, some will risk blindness, and others will die of malnutrition. The only barrier to this treatment is the broad federal

proscription against the distribution of marijuana. The interest asserted by Defendants is sufficiently defined to pass the "narrowly described" standard of the Rehnquist analysis.

    4.   The Government Cannot Establish That The Broad Federal Proscription Against Distribution And Use of Marijuana Is Narrowly Tailored To Meet a Compelling State Interest.

As the Court laid out in *Glucksberg,* where fundamental liberty interests that are narrowly described are demonstrated, any restraint on those interests must be narrowly tailored to serve a compelling state interest. Defendants contend that the federal proscription against the possession and distribution of marijuana is unnecessarily overbroad and arbitrary where it restrains the terminally ill and others in chronic pain from obtaining an essential medication to alleviate their pain and in some cases contribute to the preservation of life.[1]

    Congress has recognized and declared that "[m]any . . . drugs . . . have a useful and legitimate medical purpose and are necessary to maintain the health and general welfare of the American people." 21 USC § 801 (1). Congress has also declared that "[t]he illegal importation, manufacture, distribution, and possession and improper use of controlled substances have a substantial and detrimental effect on the health and general welfare of the American people." 21 USC § 801 (2). Thus the government has a legitimate interest both in assuring that appropriate medicines are made available, and in stemming the abuse of controlled substances.

    In the case of numerous other substances, the government has acted to provide for medical use while limiting abuse. In the case of marijuana, however, the means employed by the government abysmally fail to accomplish the purpose stated in 21 USC § 801 (1) and are therefore an affront to the concept of Substantive Due Process.

    B.   The Controlled Substances Act Is
             Not Applicable to Defendants' Activities

    1.   Congress May Only Regulate Those Purely Intrastate Activities Which Have A Substantial Effect On Interstate Commerce.

In determining whether congress may properly regulate an activity pursuant to its power derived under the Commerce Clause, Courts have recognized that the activity to be regulated must fall into one of three categories.

> "First, Congress may regulate the use of the channels of interstate commerce. Second, Congress is empowered to regulate and protect the instrumentalities of interstate commerce, or persons or things in interstate commerce, even though the threat may come only from intrastate activities. Finally, Congress's commerce authority includes the power to regulate those activities having a substantial relation to interstate commerce, i.e., those activities that substantially affect interstate commerce." *Lopez,*_____U.S. at _____, 115 S.Ct. at 1629–30 (citations omitted); see also *Perez,* 402 U.S. at 150, 91 S.Ct. at 1359 (same).

U.S. v. Pappadopoulos, 64 F.3d 522, 525–526 (9th Cir. 1995).

    In the *Lopez* case, the Supreme Court declared the Gun-Free School Zones Act unconstitutional on the basis that the act purported to reach purely intrastate conduct that had no substantial effect on

---

    1. Although Defendants do not present evidence in support of this claim in the present briefing, they certainly will be prepared to do so at an evidentiary hearing. Such evidence would include not only medical evidence verified by volumes of scientific research, but also thousands of testimonials from patients who have obtained relief from pain and other conditions and who have gained a life-saving appetite from the medical use of cannabis.

interstate commerce. *United States v. Lopez*, 514 U.S. 549 (1995). Relying on this holding, this Circuit found that a particular activity may be regulated by the Controlled Substances Act, (21 USC § 801, et seq.), only if it can be found to fall into one of the three categories identified in *Lopez*. *U.S. v. Tisor*, 96 F.3d 370, 374 (9th Cir. 1996).

It cannot be argued that defendants' activities constitute either 1) channels or 2) instrumentalities of interstate commerce. Defendants will be able to prove that their activities are purely intrastate in nature. Thus, in order for Congress to lawfully regulate defendants' activities through the promulgation, and enforcement of the sections of the Controlled Substances Act now advanced by the Government, (21 USC §§ 841, 846, and 856), the Government must establish that defendants' intrastate activities are substantially related to or affect interstate commerce. *Tisor*, at 375.

This Circuit previously considered and rejected Commerce Clause challenges to prosecutions under the Controlled Substances Act, both before and after *Lopez*. However, a review of these cases, when juxtaposed against defendants' activities, establishes that they are materially distinguishable from the matter now before the Court.

a).   Pre-*Lopez* Cases

Prior to the Supreme Court's recent decision in *Lopez*, this Circuit considered four cases in which defendants, charged with one or more of the sections of the Controlled Substances Act now relied upon by the Government, challenged the applicability of the Act to their allegedly intrastate activities: *U.S. v. Rodriquez-Camacho*, 468 F.2d 1220, (9th Cir. 1972), (possession of 99 pounds of marijuana with intent to distribute, in violation of 21 U.S.C. § 841); *U.S. v. Montes-Zarate*, 522 F.2d 1330 (9th Cir. 1977), (possession of marijuana with intent to distribute, in violation of 21 U.S.C. § 841); *U.S. v. Thornton*, 901 F.2d 738 (9th Cir. 1990), (sale of PCP within 1000 feet of a school, in violation of 21 USC § 845a, (currently § 860), which provided for an enhancement to the penalty for violation of § 841); and *U.S. v. Visman*, 919 F.2d 1390 (9th Cir. 1990), (Cultivation of marijuana, in violation of §§ 841, 846, and 856).

In these cases this Circuit recognized that Congress could regulate wholly intrastate activity only if it had an effect on interstate commerce. *Rodriquez-Camacho*, at 1221; see also *Visman*, at 1392.

In finding such a relationship in each case, the court relied on Congressional findings, as set forth in 21 USC § 801, that the intrastate activities in controlled substances affects interstate commerce. *Rodriquez-Camacho*, at 1221; *Montes-Zarate* at 1331; *Thornton*, at 741; *Visman*, at 1392.

This Circuit recognized, however, that the Congressional findings in 21 USC § 801 were not inherently dispositive, but created, in effect, a rebuttable presumption. "This court will certainly not substitute its judgment for that of Congress in such a matter unless the relation of the subject to interstate commerce and its effect upon it are clearly nonexistent. [Citation Omitted]." *Rodriquez-Camacho*, at 1222; *Visman*, at 1393.

b).   Post-*Lopez* Cases

Following the *Lopez*, decision, this Circuit revisited the question of regulation of intrastate activity under the Controlled Substances Act, considering four new challenges: *U.S. v. Staples*, 85 F.3d 461 (9th Cir. 1996), (use of firearm while distributing cocaine, in violation of 18 U.S.C. § 924(c)(1), the underlying offense being a violation of § 841); *U.S. v. Kim*, 94 F.3d 1247, 1248 (9th Cir. 1996), (possession of methamphetamine with the intent to distribute, in violation of 21 USC § 841); *U.S. v. Tisor*, 96 F.3d 370 (9th Cir. 1996), (conspiracy to distribute and distribution of methamphetamine, in violation of §§ 841 and 846); and *U.S. v. Henson* 123 F.3d 1226 (9th Cir. 1997), (distribution of PCP in violation of §§ 841 and 846).

In these cases considered in the aftermath of Lopez, this Circuit noted that Congress could properly regulate intrastate activity that "*substantially* affected interstate commerce." [Emphasis added]. *Staples*, at 463; see also *Tisor*, at 375; *Henson*, at 1233. Once again, the decisions in these cases rested upon

Congressional findings that intrastate drug trafficking has a substantial effect on interstate commerce. *Kim,* at 1250;

As the *Tisor* Court explained:

> The challenged laws are part of a wider regulatory scheme criminalizing interstate and intrastate commerce in drugs. In adopting the Controlled Substances Act, Congress expressly found that intrastate drug trafficking had a "substantial affect" on interstate commerce. Accordingly, we hold that the Controlled Substances Act does not exceed Congressional authority under the Commerce Clause.

Tisor, at 375.

Each of these cases, both pre-and post-*Lopez,* is materially distinguishable from the matter now before the Court on two distinct grounds: 1) each of the above cases involved intrastate activities that inarguably constituted violations of state law, as opposed to the case at bar where the defendants' activities are sanctioned by California Health & Safety Code § 11362.5; and 2) each of these cases involved intrastate illicit drug trafficking activities in the same "class of activities" as those interstate activities prohibited by the Controlled Substances Act, while the defendants now before the Court, as will be established below, are involved in conduct that is not in the "class of activities" prohibited by the sections of the Controlled Substances Act relied upon by the government.

> 2.   Congress Did Not Intend The Controlled Substances Act To Reach
>   Defendants' Activities.

As noted above, Courts have consistently found that Congress may lawfully regulate those purely intrastate activities which substantially affect interstate commerce. In applying this principle to prosecutions under the Controlled Substances Act, Courts have deferred to Congressional findings that intrastate drug trafficking has just such a substantial effect on interstate drug trafficking. Just as consistently, though, it has been recognized that a Court will not defer to this Congressional finding where "the relation of the subject to interstate commerce and its effect upon it are clearly nonexistent." *Stafford v. Wallace,* 258 U.S. 495, 521, (1922); *U.S. v. Rodriquez-Camacho,* 468 F.2d 1220, 1222 (9th Cir. 1972); *U.S. v. Visman,* 919 F.2d 1390, 1392 (9th Cir. 1990).

A review of the Congressional findings to which the Courts refer in the above-referenced decisions, in the context of defendants' conduct herein, is illustrative of the inapplicability of §§ 841, 846, and 856 of the Controlled Substances Act to these defendants.

The first Congressional finding, 21 USC § 801(1), states:

> (1) Many of the drugs included within this subchapter have a useful and legitimate medical purpose and are necessary to maintain the health and general welfare of the American people.

Thus it is clear that Congress has recognized that a drug may serve a legitimate, beneficial medical purpose.[2] In subsection (2), Congress recognized the converse:

> (2) The illegal importation, manufacture, distribution, and possession and improper use of controlled substances have a substantial and detrimental effect on the health and general welfare of the American people.

Here Congress focused specifically on "illegal" and "improper" use which has a "detrimental" effect on health. The conduct of the defendants (providing cannabis for the relief of seriously ill

---

2.   It is interesting to note that the government, in quoting 21 USC § 801 in its Memorandum, left this particular subsection out of its argument. (See e.g. Government Memorandum in Oakland Case, 3:15).

patients who have obtained a recommendation and/or approval of a physician for the medical use of cannabis, all under color of state law) can only rationally be viewed as falling within the activities envisioned by Congress in subsection (1) as opposed to subsection (2).

In subsection (3) Congress declared:

> (3) A major portion of the traffic in controlled substances flows through interstate and foreign commerce. Incidents of the traffic which are not an integral part of the interstate or foreign flow, such as manufacture, local distribution, and possession, nonetheless have a substantial and direct effect upon interstate commerce because—

> (a) after manufacture, many controlled substances are transported in interstate commerce,

> (b) controlled substances distributed locally usually have been transported in interstate commerce immediately before their distribution, and

> (c) controlled substances possessed commonly flow through interstate commerce immediately prior to such possession.

Here Congress identified three distinct grounds for its conclusion that intrastate trafficking in controlled substances substantially effects interstate commerce.

Congress first noted that controlled substances are often transported across state lines after manufacture. Such a concern is not applicable to defendants' activities. Defendants will be able to prove that they distribute individually small amounts of cannabis to a discrete class of persons for relatively immediate medicinal use in California, all in accordance with the state law that specifically prohibits diversion for nonmedical purposes. (See H&S § 11362.5(b)(2)).

Congress next recognized that controlled substances are often transported over state lines immediately prior to their distribution. Again this concern is not applicable to defendants' activities. Defendants will be able to prove that the medicinal cannabis they distribute is cultivated under controlled conditions in California.

Finally Congress found that controlled substances are often transported over state lines immediately prior to their possession. As established above, this concern is equally inapplicable to defendants' activities as defendants will be able to prove that the medicinal cannabis they distribute is grown, distributed, and consumed wholly within the borders of California.

Congress next found, in subsection (4), that:

> (4) local distribution and possession of controlled substances contribute to swelling the interstate traffic in such substances.

In considering this finding it is easy to see how defendants' activities, which are condoned by state law, have no relation to the illicit interstate trafficking Congress sought to proscribe. Unlike the intrastate trafficking considered by this Circuit in previous cases, defendants' activities in providing a medicine to a discreet class of persons do not have any effect on interstate illicit drug trafficking. Judge Fern Smith of this Honorable Court recognized such when she ruled that "the government's fears in this case are exaggerated and without evidentiary support. It is unreasonable to believe that use of medical marijuana by this discrete population for this limited purpose will create a significant drug problem." *Conant v. McCaffrey,* 172 F.R.D. 681, 694 n5 (N.D.Cal. 1997).

Congress next found that:

> (5) Controlled substances manufactured and distributed intrastate cannot be differentiated from controlled substances manufactured and distributed interstate. Thus, it is not

feasible to distinguish, in terms of controls, between controlled substances manufactured and distributed interstate and controlled substances manufactured and distributed intrastate.

If considering intrastate illicit drug trafficking versus interstate illicit drug trafficking, Congress' findings here are clearly applicable. However, the concerns evidenced by Congress in this subsection are once again allayed when viewed in the context of defendants' conduct. Defendants will be able to prove that the medicinal cannabis they distribute is clearly and unambiguously labeled as such. No reasonable person could confuse the labeled medicinal cannabis distributed by the defendants herein with illicit black market marijuana, or vice versa.

In subsection (6) Congress noted that:

> (6) Federal control of the intrastate incidents of the traffic in controlled substances is essential to the effective control of the interstate incidents of such traffic.

Again, it is clear that Congress is concerned with intrastate trafficking effecting interstate trafficking. As noted above and recognized by Judge Smith, the suppression of defendants' activities, clearly separate from and unrelated to black market drug trafficking, be it intrastate or interstate, is not essential to the control of illegal interstate commerce in drugs. In fact, the converse is true: Barring these defendants from providing a safe affordable source of medicinal cannabis will only serve to drive seriously ill patients into the waiting and willing arms of the black marketeers, thus swelling the interstate illicit drug trade. This certainly was not the intention of Congress in promulgating the Controlled Substances Act.

Finally, Congress recognized the international attempt to curb the illicit traffic in drugs, finding that:

> (7) The United States is a party to the single convention on narcotic drugs, 1961, and other international conventions designed to establish effective control over international and domestic traffic in controlled substances.

Here again, the emphasis is on "drug trafficking," a class of activity in which the defendants herein are not involved.

Thus it is readily apparent that the Congressional findings stated in 21 USC § 801 are not applicable to the defendants' conduct herein. When defendants' activities are observed under the illumination of these findings, it is clear that defendants' activities are not within the "class of activities" that adversely effect interstate commerce. (See *U.S. v. Kim*, 94 F.3d 1247, 1249 (9th Cir. 1996); *U.S. v. Visman*, 919 F.2d 1390, 1392–93 (9th Cir. 1990). The Government cannot show that defendants' purely intrastate activities have any substantial effect on interstate commerce. Under these circumstances, the Controlled Substances Act is unconstitutional as applied to these defendants.

C. Defendants' Activities Are Exempt From Application Of The Controlled Substances Act

1.   Joint Acquisition and Use of Cannabis for Medical Purposes Is Not "Distribution" or "Possession for Distribution" under the Federal Controlled Substances Act.

In *United States v. Swiderski*, 548 F.2d. 445 (2nd Cir. 1977), two individuals purchased cocaine together, then shared it. After they were convicted of the federal crime of distribution, the Second Circuit Court of Appeal held that "where two or more individuals simultaneously and jointly acquire possession of a drug for their own use, intending only to share together, the only crime is personal drug

abuse—simple joint possession, without any intent to distribute the drug further." *Id.* at 450. The court reasoned that Congress, in making the penalties much harsher for distributing drugs than for possessing them, was concerned that distribution has the dangerous, unwanted effect of drawing additional participants into the web of drug abuse. *Id.* Because the concerns are not present in a situation of joint purchasers, it was error not to instruct the jury that it could find possession without any distribution. Id. at 452

At a trial on the merits, Defendants herein would be able to demonstrate that under *Swiderski,* they are not guilty of the federal crimes of distribution, or possession for distribution, because their alleged control of medical cannabis is established through a cooperative enterprise, shared equally among all of the members thereto, for the exclusive medicinal use of each of them, individually. Defendants will be able to demonstrate that there are no third parties involved, nor is anyone else being brought into a "web" of drug use.

Further, Defendants will be able to establish that this is an enterprise that is legal under the laws of the State of California. Cooperatives are a commonly authorized legal entity. The activity allegedly being conducted is lawful and authorized under the Compassionate Use Act of 1996 (H&S § 11362.5).

In the context of illicit drug transactions, the Ninth Circuit limited *Swiderski* to its facts in *United States v. Wright,* 593 F.2d 105 (1979), In *Wright,* a person asked the defendant to purchase heroin, and gave him money for that purpose. The defendant went out on his own, procured the heroin, brought it back and then participated in its consumption. The court held that it was not error to deny a jury instruction based on the doctrine of joint possession, because the defendant "facilitated the transfer of the narcotic; he did not simply simultaneously and jointly acquire possession of a drug for their (his and another's) own use. *Id.*

At a trial of this matter on the merits, Defendants in this case will be able to demonstrate that, unlike the situation in *Wright,* defendants do not give money to others for the purposes of procuring drugs for recreational use. Rather, Defendants in this case act in concert as cooperatives to ensure the safe and affordable access to cannabis for medicinal purposes for each of the members. In *Wright,* the Court was concerned with defendants using the *Swiderski* defense in a "typical" drug deal. Here, any cannabis possessed is exclusively for medicinal purposes. The activity is not illicit, because it is medicinal in nature and authorized by California Law.

In *United States v. Rush,* 738 F.2d 497 (1st Cir. 1984), the Court upheld a *Swiderski* instruction in a case involving "tons" of marijuana. The Court concluded, "[T]he *Swiderski* defendants were entitled to pursue whatever factual defense they could support, however implausible it might seem to a finder of fact in this case they may have had a colorable alternative." *Id.* at 514. As the Court noted in *United States v. Escobar De Bright:*

> [T]he general principle is well established that a criminal defendant is entitled to have a jury instruction on any defense which provides a legal defense to the charge against him and which has some foundation in the evidence, even though the evidence be weak, insufficient, inconsistent and doubtful of credibility.

Id., 742 F.2d 1196, 1198 (9th Cir. 1984),

Here, the evidence is strong, sufficient, consistent, and credible and would almost certainly result in an acquittal of the Defendants by a jury.

2. Defendants Are Not in Violation of the Controlled Substances Act, Because They Are "Ultimate Users".

Section 802(27) of the Controlled Substances Act defines an "ultimate user" as "a person who has lawfully obtained, and who possesses a controlled substance for his own use or for the use of a member of his household. . . ." Under the Act, an ultimate user is permitted to possess a Schedule I controlled

substance, including marijuana, without being in violation of the Act and without being required to register with the Attorney General.

At a trial on the merits, Defendants would be able to demonstrate that they fit squarely into the "ultimate user" exemption of the Controlled Substances Act. Defendants could show that California Health & Safety Code § 11362.5 authorizes their possession of cannabis. Further, under *Swiderski, supra,* any medical cannabis possessed by any of the Defendants as members of their respective cooperatives would be for the exclusive medicinal purposes of each of them under the doctrine of joint possession. See also, *United States v. Bartee,* 479 F.2d 1390 (10th Cir. 1973) (ultimate user "obtain[s] the drug for his own use").

D.   Defendants' Activities Are Justified by the Defense of Necessity.

1.   The Defense Of Medical Necessity Provides Complete Justification For The Defendants' Acts.

The common law defense of necessity is well-established as a defense to federal criminal prosecutions not involving homicides. *United States v. Holmes,* 26 Fed. Cas.No. 15, 383, p. 360 (C.C.E.D. Pa. 1842); *United States v. Ashton,* 24 Fed.Cas.No. 14,470 p. 873 (C.C.D. Mass. 1834). In *United States v. Bailey,* 444 U.S. 394, 414 (1980), the Supreme Court held that criminal defendants may assert the defense of necessity when charged with prison escape, provided they proffer the necessary; evidence to support the claim. The defense of medical necessity is simply a specialized application of the common law defense of necessity available in all federal criminal prosecutions. 1 LaFave & Scott, *Substantive Criminal Law,* § 5.4(c)(7), pp. 631–33 (1986). Although neither the Supreme Court nor this Circuit have ruled directly on the issue in the context of marijuana use, ample authority exists to recognize the viability of the defense of medical necessity in prosecutions for possession, distribution, and cultivation of marijuana.

In *United States v. Randall,* 104 Daily Wash.L.Rptr. 2249, 2252 (D.C. Super. 1976), a defendant successfully asserted medical necessity as a defense to a charge of marijuana possession in the Washington D.C. Superior Court. He grew marijuana plants and used them to treat his own condition of glaucoma after conventional medications were ineffective. The court concluded that the defendant's right to preserve his sight outweighed the government's interest in outlawing the drug.

In *United States v. Burton,* 894 F.2d 188 (6th Cir. 1990), the defendant, who also suffered from glaucoma, asserted a defense of medical necessity when charged with three counts of possession of marijuana with intent to distribute. The jury convicted him of the lesser offense of simple possession, however, and on appeal the Court declined to hold that the medical necessity defense was available to the possession charge, while noting, "Medical necessity has been recognized by some courts and by some authority." *Id.* at 191. The reason the court found the defense unavailable was that, subsequent to the *Randall* case, a government program was established to study the effects of marijuana on glaucoma sufferers, and the defendant failed to utilize this "reasonable legal alternative." Since the *Burton* decision, however, that experimental governmental program has been closed to additional applicants. Thus, the "reasonable legal alternative" is no longer available, and the *Burton* court's grudging acceptance of the medical necessity defense remains good law.

The medical necessity defense has received a warmer reception in the Appellate Courts of many states in this Circuit. In *State v. Hasting,* 801 P.2d 563 (Idaho 1990), the Supreme court of Idaho held that a defendant who claimed her use of marijuana was necessary to control the pain and muscle spasms associated with rheumatoid arthritis presented a legitimate defense of necessity, and it was "for the trier of fact to determine whether or not she has met the elements of that defense." *Id.* at 565. In *State v. Diana,* 604 P.2d 1312 (Wash.App. 1979), the Washington Court of Appeals, citing *United States v. Randall,* held that medical necessity was encompassed in the common law defense of necessity:

> The wisdom of the Randall decision was recognized by the legislature in our State when
> it enacted the Controlled Substances Therapeutic Research Act, Laws of Washington

1979, Reg.Sess. Ch. 136, eff. March 27, 1979. That legislation recognizes marijuana as a medicinal drug and makes it available under controlled circumstances to alleviate the effects of glaucoma and cancer chemotherapy. The patient must be certified to the State Board of Pharmacy by a licensed physician. In addition, under the Act other disease groups may be included if pertinent medical data is presented to the Board. We believe that the defendant here should be given the opportunity to demonstrate the alleged beneficial effect, if any, of marijuana on the symptoms of multiple sclerosis. Accordingly, we remand his case to the trial court, here the trier of fact, for determination of whether medical necessity exists.

604 P.2d at 1316–17.

In *State v. Bachman*, 595 P.2d 287 (Hawaii 1979), the Hawaii Supreme court concluded "it is entirely possible that medical necessity could be asserted as a defense to a marijuana charge in a proper case." However, the Court held the defense was properly rejected in that case because the defense failed to proffer competent medical testimony "of the beneficial effects upon the defendant's condition of marijuana use, as well as the absence or ineffectiveness of conventional medical alternatives." *Id.* at 288.

Most recently, the California Court of Appeal, assuming that a medical necessity defense is valid in California, and that it is composed of the same elements as the general necessity defense, concluded that the defendant's offer of proof was insufficient to meet those elements because she failed to establish she had no adequate alternative but to possess and transport the marijuana as charged. Nonetheless, based on the subsequent enactment of H&S § 11362.5 and its retroactive application, the court remanded the case for a limited retrial to determine whether H&S § 1362.5 provided a partial defense to the charges. *People v. Trippet*, 56 Cal.App.4th 1532, (1997).

Thus, clear authority exists for the availability of a medical necessity defense in a federal criminal prosecution for marijuana distribution or possession with intent to distribute. The medical necessity defense is simply a corollary of the fully accepted common law defense of necessity, and presents a factual question for the jury to determine in a particular case.

The Ninth Circuit has established a four part test regarding the availability of the necessity defense. To invoke the necessity defense Defendants must offer proof that: "(1) they were faced with a choice of evils and chose the lesser evil; (2) they acted to prevent imminent harm; (3) they reasonably anticipated a direct causal relationship between their conduct and the harm to be averted; and (4) they had no legal alternatives to violating the law." *United States v. Aguilar*, 883 F.2d 662, 693 (9th Cir.1989), *cert. denied*, 498 U.S. 1046, (1991).

Defendants are able to prove each element of the necessity defense. Defendants faced a choice of evils. Thousands of people within the Defendants' geographic range suffer from debilitating and often deadly diseases, including cancer, AIDS, and glaucoma.

A common cause of death for AIDS patients is wasting syndrome. Those afflicted lose all appetite and literally waste away from starvation. Similarly, chemotherapy often causes intense nausea and loss of appetite. Patients face the choice of quitting chemotherapy or enduring it and risking starvation and malnutrition. For many people afflicted with these two diseases, cannabis provides relief as a pain reliever and, more importantly, as an appetite stimulant. In short, cannabis saves these people's lives. Similarly, many glaucoma patients find that cannabis is the only medication that effectively relieves the intraocular pressure in their eyes, a condition that threatens permanent blindness.

But cannabis is, for many, difficult or impossible to obtain. The Defendants solve this problem by providing cannabis to their members. By doing so they run the risk of potentially running afoul of federal drug laws. Such is the choice of evils, and Defendants have clearly chosen the lesser one.

The Defendants also meet the second and third prongs of the necessity test: The harm sought to be averted was (and continues to be) imminent and life threatening and the act of supplying cannabis is a necessary component to averting that harm.

The fourth prong of the necessity defense is the one the government will most likely insist the Defendants have not met. The Defendants are prepared to show that there are no legal alternatives to the distribution of medical cannabis via the cannabis cooperative. The Defendants will present evidence from doctors and patients showing that for many people Marinol or other "legal" drugs simply do not work in treating their symptoms. Cannabis, however, does work. Defendants will also show that their members have no legal or safe alternative to acquire marijuana from other sources, including the government. Additionally, Defendants will show that they have attempted (and continue to attempt) to change marijuana laws at the local, state, and federal level. Such legal alternatives have, for purposes of a necessity defense, been exhausted. Moreover, even if such legal alternatives as rescheduling were an option, such "alternatives" are not adequate to render the necessity defense unavailable to patients who will likely die, waste away, or go blind long before any rescheduling actually is accomplished.

Defendants' actions fall squarely within those contemplated by the necessity defense as articulated by the Ninth Circuit. As such, Defendants possess a valid defense to the charges underlying the government's motions for an injunction.

2.   The Defense of Entrapment Is Available to the Extent That a Defense of Medical Necessity Would Be Precluded for Distribution to DEA Agents.

The entrapment defense was first recognized by the United States Supreme Court in *Sorrels v. United States*, 287 U.S. 435 (1932). The Court held that the defense should be available when the government instigates criminal activity by an otherwise innocent defendant. This subjective test, focused on the predisposition of the defendant, was reaffirmed in *United States v. Russell*, 411 U.S. 423 (1972).

When examining a defendant's predisposition, the court looks to persistent and extended efforts by government agents to target the defendant. Illustrative is *Sherman v. United States*, 356 U.S. 369 (1958), where the government agent met the defendant while both were undergoing treatment for drug abuse. The government agent claimed he was suffering from withdrawal and repeatedly implored the defendant to provide a source for illicit drugs. The Court found the government conduct so extreme that it ruled Sherman was entrapped as a matter of law. In determining the defendant was not "predisposed," the Court distinguished the "unwary innocent" from the "unwary criminal," and examined both the personal characteristics of the defendant and the persistent and extended government behavior.

Clearly, the defendants in this case were not predisposed to commit any crime. The cannabis dispensaries were established for the sole purpose of providing marijuana to patients with doctors' recommendations, to alleviate the nausea associated with cancer chemotherapy, AIDS treatment, and the symptoms of other debilitating diseases. The DEA initiated an extensive undercover sting operation lasting over seven months, to infiltrate the clubs under the guise of needing medical marijuana. The DEA created phony physician's orders, with an agent posing as a doctor to verify the orders. Similar to the egregious behavior in *Sherman*, the undercover DEA agents falsely simulated illness to gain the sympathy of the defendants, resulting in the entrapment of "unwary innocents."

The defendants' reasonable belief that the marijuana they were providing to the DEA agents would be used for medicinal purposes confirms their lack of predisposition. The Cannabis Buyers' Cooperatives can be analogized to the drug treatment center in *Sherman*. Government infiltration of a humanitarian venture to alleviate pain should be viewed with great skepticism. Certainly a jury would be justified in questioning the vast investment of governmental investigative resources demonstrated here in order to seduce "unwary innocents" whose primary motivation is providing comfort and relief for those who are seriously ill. In part, the entrapment defense is an effective way of controlling the behavior of overzealous police who themselves create the "crime" they are responsible for suppressing.

In *Matthews v. United States*, 485 U.S. 58 (1988), the defendant denied having committed the crime and simultaneously requested an instruction on entrapment. The lower court denied his request to present the entrapment defense to the jury, requiring that he admit the crime before he could assert

the defense of entrapment. The Supreme Court reversed, holding that he was entitled to an entrapment instruction as long as a reasonable juror could find that entrapment existed. The Court restated the well-established rule applicable to all defenses:

> As a general proposition a defendant is entitled to an instruction as to any recognized defense for which there exists evidence sufficient for a reasonable jury to find in his favor.

Id. at 63.

Once the defendant presents some evidence of entrapment, the prosecution bears the burden of proving beyond a reasonable doubt that the defendant was predisposed to commit the crime of which he is charged before he was approached by the government. *Notaro v. United States,* 363 F.2d 169 (9th Cir. 1966); *United States v. Jacobson,* 112 S.Ct. 1535, 1540–41 (1992). Here, the only "predisposition" on the part of the defendants was a humane willingness to respond to the legitimate medical needs of the sick, in the context of a cooperative venture approved by state law. The government inducements to persuade them to provide marijuana to DEA agents who had no legitimate medical need would be entrapment as a matter of law.

E. The Government Cannot Meet the Standards for The Injunctive Relief it Seeks.

1. Traditional Equitable Principles Apply To An Injunction Sought under Section 882.

Section 882 grants federal courts jurisdiction to enjoin violations of the Controlled Substances Act.

> The district courts of the United States and all courts exercising general jurisdiction in the territories and possessions of the United States shall have jurisdiction in proceedings in accordance with the Federal Rules of Civil Procedure to enjoin violations of this subchapter.

21 USC § 882(a).

Although Congress has the power to limit a court's equitable jurisdiction, it has not done so here. The statute contains no language that suggests any limitation on a court's equitable powers. On the contrary, by explicitly stating that injunction proceedings must follow the Federal Rules of Civil Procedure, Congress intended courts to conduct § 882 actions in the same manner as any other civil proceeding in equity.

The Supreme Court squarely addressed the issue of the application of equitable principles to statutory enforcement actions in *Weinberger v. Romero-Barcelo,* 456 U.S. 305 (1982). In *Romero,* the Court explained, "unless a statute in so many words, or by a necessary and inescapable inference, restricts the court's jurisdiction in equity, the full scope of that jurisdiction is to be recognized and applied." *Id.* at 313. As the Court further explained:

> [A] major departure from the long tradition of equity practice should not be lightly implied . . . we construe the statute at issue in favor of that interpretation which affords a full opportunity for equity courts to treat enforcement proceedings . . . in accordance with their traditional practices, as conditioned by the necessities of the public interest which Congress has sought to protect.

Id. at 320.

Section 882 does not restrict the court's jurisdiction in equity, and consequently the full scope of that jurisdiction applies.

2.   The Government Has Failed To Meet The Equitable Criteria For A Preliminary Injunction.

The Ninth Circuit has established a four pronged analysis to use in determining whether to grant a preliminary injunction. A court should consider:

> (1) [T]he likelihood of the moving party's success on the merits; (2) the possibility of irreparable injury to the moving party if relief is not granted; (3) the extent to which the balance of hardships favors the respective parties; and (4) in certain cases, whether the public interest will be advanced by granting the preliminary relief.

Miller v. California Pacific Medical Center, 19 F.3d 449, 456 (9th Cir. 1994) (en banc).
The moving party must show:

> [E]ither (1) a combination of probable success on the merits and the possibility of irreparable harm, or (2) the existence of serious questions going to the merits, the balance of hardships tipping sharply in its favor, and at least a fair chance of success on the merits. These two formulations represent two points on a sliding scale in which the required degree of irreparable harm increases as the probability of success decreases."

Id. at 456.
The government has failed to make the requisite showing under either test to warrant granting it a preliminary injunction.

      a).   The Government Has Failed To Show Probability Of Success On The Merits

The government has not shown probability of success on the merits. To succeed on the merits the government must prove that Defendants violated §§ 841(a)(1), 856(a)(1), and 846 of the Controlled Substances Act. The government in its moving papers has not done so. Even if the facts were, as the government claims, uncontroverted, the government has not shown violations of the Controlled Substances Act. As explained in detail above, the Controlled Substances Act *cannot* constitutionally reach the Defendants' behavior. Even if it could reach the Defendants' behavior, the Controlled Substances Act *does not* reach their behavior in this circumstance. Finally, even if the federal statutes were applied to the Defendants' acts, the Defendants possess valid defenses that would preclude a finding of probability of success on the merits for the government.

      b).   The Government Has Not Established Irreparable Injury

The government claims that it need not prove irreparable injury. It cites *United States v. Odessa Union Warehouse Co-op,* (833 F.2d 172 (9th Cir. 1987)), for the proposition that in statutory enforcement actions irreparable injury is presumed. Such a presumption is limited, however, to situations in which the statutory violation underlying the injunctive action is conceded. The Ninth Circuit sitting en banc clarified the limits of *Odessa Union.*

> There, the traditional requirement of irreparable injury was inapplicable because the parties *conceded* that the federal statute involved was violated. However, when the violation is *disputed* (as it is here), *Odessa Union* does not relieve the governmental agency of its burden of showing that the statutory conditions are met. See *Id.* Rather, as we recently indicated in *United States v. Nutri-Cology, Inc.,* 982 F.2d 394 (9th Cir. 1992), the strength of the government's showing on the likelihood of prevailing on the merits will affect the degree to which it must prove inseparable injury.

Miller, 19.F.3d at 459 (emphasis added).

In *Nutri-Cology,* because the statutory violation was disputed and the government did not establish likelihood of success on the merits, the court held, "the government is not entitled to a presumption, rebuttable or otherwise, of irreparable injury." *Nutri-Cology,* at 398.

In the instant case Defendants do not concede that any federal statute is being violated. Whether or not such statutes are being violated is the central factual and legal issue in this action. Because the government has not shown probability of success on the merits, it is certainly not entitled to a presumption of irreparable injury.

Other than relying on a presumption of irreparable injury, to which it is not entitled, the government has proffered no evidence to show an injury to the public caused by Defendants' acts. The government has made no such showing because it *cannot* make such a showing. As noted above, in a case arising out of another recent attempt by the federal government to interfere with patients' access to medical marijuana, Judge Smith of this Honorable Court found the government's claims of injury and hardship unsubstantiated.

> Moreover, the government's fears in this case are exaggerated and without evidentiary support. It is unreasonable to believe that use of medical marijuana by this discrete population for this limited purpose will create a significant drug problem.

Conant v. McCaffrey, 172 F.R.D. 681, 694 n5 (N.D. Cal. 1997).

If the government truly possessed a good faith belief that the activities of the Defendants was causing irreparable injury, it would not have waited over two years from the opening of the first cooperative to its bringing this suit in equity. Likewise, the government could have brought criminal charges against members of cooperatives and shut them down long ago, rather than waiting to bring this politically opportune case.

The use of medical cannabis by the members of the cooperatives that are defendants in this action cannot rationally be characterized as an irreparable injury to the United States.

c). Balance of Hardships

The government has made no showing that the balance of hardships tips sharply in its favor. Just as with irreparable injury, the government has relied on an inapplicable presumption that the purported statutory violations it wishes to enjoin are *per se* hardships on the public. It has offered no evidence of any actual hardships suffered by the public as a result of the Defendants' operations. Even if the government were entitled to some presumption of hardship in this case, it has not shown that the balance tips sharply in its favor. As in *Conant,* the "government's fears are exaggerated and without evidentiary support." *Id.*

Moreover, the government still possesses an adequate remedy at law. It will suffer no hardship by being denied the extraordinary remedy of an injunction. As with irreparable injury, if the government were truly burdened by the cooperatives' existence it could move to shut them down in criminal proceedings. That it has not attempted to do so makes the government's claims of hardship ring hollow.

Defendants, in contrast, are prepared to show substantial hardships to be suffered by their members and by the general public if this Court were to enjoin the Defendants. Collectively, the six cooperatives the government seeks to shut down serve the medical needs of several thousand patients. Numerous members are afflicted with AIDS, cancer, glaucoma, and other serious illnesses for which, for many, cannabis is the only effective treatment for intractable pain and conditions that could otherwise lead to death, blindness or other permanent debilitation. For the government to assert that such hardships can be alleviated by petitioning the DEA to reschedule marijuana, *Plaintiff's Motion* at p. 18,

(a process in which Defendants have attempted in the past and continue to pursue), shows a lack of compassion and a distorted view of reality that is truly frightening. The patients who Defendants serve suffer hardships that are immediate and life threatening. These cannot be alleviated by an administrative process that all parties agree could take years to effectuate, even if the government abandoned its arbitrary and capricious practices and dealt with this issue in good faith.

d).   Public Interest Favors Denial Of The Government's Motion

Just as it does with irreparable injury and the balancing of hardships, the government relies on unsubstantiated presumptions it claims weigh in its favor. As with those other factors the government is only entitled to such a presumption when it has clearly shown a statutory violation. This Honorable Court must weigh such presumptions against the effect issuance of an injunction would have on the public interest. Inflicting substantial and life-threatening medical and legal hardships on patients who are reliant upon the Defendants surely offends the public interest. Moreover, issuance of an injunction that frustrates the declared intent of the majority of voters in California, that seriously ill people have access to medical marijuana, would clearly run contrary to the public interest.

3.   No Injunction Should Issue.

As demonstrated above, the government has met none of the equitable criteria for the issuance of an injunction against defendants. Even if the government were able to establish that Defendants' actions were violative of the federal law, the facts and circumstances of this case do not, as the government contends, require that an injunction automatically issue. The Supreme Court made this clear in *Romero*. "The grant of jurisdiction to ensure compliance with a statute hardly suggests an absolute duty to do so under any and all circumstances, and a federal judge sitting as chancellor is not mechanically obligated to grant an injunction for every violation of law." *Romero*, at 313. The public interest and the balance of hardships dictate that no injunction should issue here.

4.   Equitable Defenses Preclude Injunctive Relief.

The government's attempt to invoke equitable relief against defendants is barred by the doctrine of unclean hands.

a).   Unclean Hands

The government cannot prevail in its attempt to prohibit the distribution of medical marijuana since it comes to the Court with unclean hands. The applicability of the doctrine to government action was explained by the Ninth Circuit in *Equal Employment Opportunity Commission v. Recruit U.S.A.*, 939 F.2d 746 (1991).

> They [defendants] rely on the "clean hands" doctrine, which insists that one who seeks equity must come to the court without blemish. See, e.g., *Johnson v. Yellow Cab Transit Co.*, 321 U.S. 383, 387, 64 S.Ct. 622, 624, 88 L.Ed. 814 (1944). This maxim "is a self-imposed ordinance that closes the doors of a court of equity to one tainted with an inequitableness or bad faith relative to the matter in which he seeks relief, however improper may have been the behavior of the defendant. "*Precision Instrument Mfg. Co. v. Automotive Maintenance Mach. Co.*, 324 U.S. 806, 814, 65 S.Ct. 993, 997, 89 L.Ed. 1381 (1945). This rule applies to the government as well as to private litigants. See *United States v. Desert Gold Mining Co.*, 448 F.2d 1230, 1231 (9th Cir. 1971).

Id. at 752.

The government's record regarding marijuana in general and medical marijuana specifically demonstrates a pattern of bad faith that should preclude it from attaining equitable relief. The government has at least a twenty-five year history of bad faith and unclean hands in its dealings with medical marijuana. Such behavior is violative of the legislative intent of the Controlled Substances Act and of the United States' obligations under the Single Convention Treaty. It also flies in the face of virtually every comprehensive study commissioned by the government during the twentieth century. Defendants are prepared to show that 1) numerous and uncontroverted scientific studies exist firmly establishing the medical efficacy of marijuana and 2) the government has obstructed, suppressed or ignored all attempts by citizens to reschedule or otherwise make marijuana legally available for medical purposes. Having in bad faith resisted all attempts by Defendants and others to explicitly legalize medical marijuana under federal law, the government cannot now invoke equity in its attempts to squelch Defendants' good faith efforts to legally provide medical marijuana through the cooperatives. One who comes to equity must do so with clean hands. The government, in this instance, does not.

Perhaps the most glaring example of the government's unclean hands is that of the Investigative New Drug (IND) program. Under the IND program the federal government provides marijuana to eight individuals suffering from a variety of ailments including cancer and glaucoma. The government claims in prosecuting this action that there are no medically accepted uses for marijuana, while, simultaneously, the DEA distributes marijuana for those very same medical purposes that the cooperatives serve. The government's own actions demonstrate the falsity of its arguments. Not only does the very existence of the IND program counter the government argument of no legitimate medical use for marijuana, but the government's administration of the program exhibits a complete lack of good faith. Only eight people currently receive marijuana under the program. No new enrollments are accepted. These eight people do not differ from the several thousand members of the cannabis club in any medical sense. Their illnesses are no more or less severe than those of the club members not part of the IND program. The only distinction is political. The IND patients were all enrolled prior to the War on Drugs of the 1980's. They also predate the AIDS epidemic. The government admits that it stopped approving applications under the program because it feared an upswing in applications by AIDS patients would "send the wrong message." The decision had nothing to do with the efficacy of marijuana as medicine. The history of the IND program demonstrates that the federal government has not dealt with medical marijuana in a rational, scientific good faith manner. For the government to seek injunctive relief here, when it has itself failed to treat its ailing citizens in an equitable fashion, runs afoul of all principles upon which equitable jurisdiction is based.

5.   The Government Is Not Entitled To Summary Judgment And A Permanent Injunction.

    a).   Because Genuine Issues of Fact Exist That Are Material to the Defenses Raised By Defendants, Summary Judgment and Permanent Injunctive Relief Are Inappropriate.

If the Court does grant the government's request for a preliminary injunction it must not simultaneously grant its request for summary judgement and a permanent injunction. Even without considering issues of facts, it is apparent that plaintiffs have violated the procedural rules governing summary judgment, and as such, should be precluded from a final judgment. According to the summary judgment rules applicable to claimants, "[a] party seeking to recover upon a claim, . . . may, at any time after the expiration of 20 days from the commencement of the action . . . , move with or without supporting affidavits for a summary judgment in the party's favor upon all or any part thereof." Fed.R.Civ.P.56(a). Defendants were served with plaintiff's *Motion for Preliminary and Permanent Injunction, and for Summary Judgment* on January 8, 1998, thereby commencing this action. As demonstrated by the motion's title,

plaintiffs included with their request for a preliminary injunction a request for summary judgment. Such a procedure of including at the commencement of the action a motion for summary judgment, is barred by the federal rules. To be in compliance, plaintiff was required to wait until 20 days after the filing of the complaint to move for summary judgment. Since the government failed to do so, the motion should be denied.

Aside from plaintiff's procedural error, the existence of issues of material fact also warrants denial of plaintiff's motion. The threshold inquiry in summary judgment motions is "determining whether there is the need for a trial—whether, in other words, there are any factual issues that can be properly resolved only by a finder of fact because they may reasonably be resolved in favor of either party." *Anderson v. Liberty Lobby, Inc.,* 477 US 242, 250, 106 S.Ct. 2505, 91 L.Ed.2d 202 (1986). A factual dispute is genuine if the nonmovant's evidence is substantial enough to require trial. *Id.* at 249–250. All reasonable inferences to be drawn from the facts "must be viewed in the light most favorable to the party opposing the motion." *Matsushita Elec. Indus. Co. v. Zenith Radio Corp.,* 475 U.S. 574, 587 (1986).

Defendants have sustained their burden of identifying for the Court a multitude of facts that illustrate the presence of genuine issues requiring a hearing. In outlining their defenses above, Defendants have made fact specific offers of proof regarding constitutional, legal, and equitable defenses to the government's charges.

Since no legally adequate notice has been provided to Defendants, summary judgement at this juncture would be premature. Moreover, as previously discussed, genuine issues of fact exist which mandate a hearing. By granting summary judgement on the basis of the current record, Defendants would be effectively deprived of their day in court. Thus, the government's motion for summary judgement and permanent injunctive relief should be denied.

F.   The Court Should Fashion Protective Measures to
      Ensure That Defendants' Procedural Due Process
      Rights are Not Violated.

The Government has brought the within action under 21 USC § 882, a novel use of a statute for which there is a dearth of precedence. In so doing, the government has placed the defendants at a critical disadvantage. If the government had sought to prosecute Defendants criminally, Defendants would have been afforded the Constitutional protections of the Fourth, Fifth, and Sixth Amendments. By seeking to enjoin Defendant's lawyers the government is interfering with the right to counsel to such a degree that in a criminal context would surely be a Sixth Amendment violation. Perhaps most importantly, by first bringing a civil proceeding against Defendants, the government has placed them in an unavoidable Fifth Amendment conundrum. Defendants cannot adequately defend the civil proceedings without effectively waiving Constitutional rights against self-incrimination in any future criminal proceedings. At a minimum, before the government can seek equitable relief against defendants it must guarantee them immunity from any possible criminal prosecutions for the acts which it seeks to enjoin. The government cannot fairly contend that legal remedies are unavailable and at the same time waive the hammer of those very same legal remedies over the heads of Defendants.

III.   CONCLUSION

It is unfortunate that the federal government is undertaking this effort to prohibit access to the only supply of affordable, safe medical cannabis on which numerous seriously ill and suffering patients depend for relief. The federal government is acting in direct defiance to the will of the voters of California who clearly and unambiguously mandated that patients who can attain relief through the use of

medical marijuana should be allowed to do so under a physician's care. The citizens of California have called on the federal government to make medical cannabis available. Instead the federal government has responded by initially threatening California physicians. When Judge Smith of this Honorable Court barred the government from making good on its threats, the government aimed its crosshairs at the sick and dying. Accordingly, defendants request that this Honorable Court deny the government's request for a preliminary injunction, permanent injunction and summary judgment.

Dated: February 27, 1998   Respectfully submitted,

Review section II.D.1 of Defendants' Joint Memorandum to see how this work was incorporated into the final product.

MEMORANDUM OF LAW

I.   The Defense of Medical Necessity Provides Complete Justification for the Defendant's Acts

It is well established that the common law defense of necessity is recognized in federal criminal prosecutions that do not involve homicides. In *US v. Bailey*, 444 U.S. 394, 414 (1980), the United States Supreme Court held that criminal defendants may assert the defense of necessity when charged with prison escape provided they proffer the necessary evidence to support the claim. Moreover, in *US v. Lemon*, 824 F.2d 763, 765 (9th Cir. 1987), the Ninth Circuit recognized the common law defense in the context of a charge of unlawful possession of a handgun. Therefore, it is clear that the courts recognize the common law defense in federal criminal prosecutions. The defense of medical necessity is simply a specialized application of the common law defense of necessity available in all federal criminal prosecutions. 1 LaFave & Scott, *Substantive Criminal Law* § 5.4(c) 7, 631–633 (1986). Although neither the United States Supreme Court nor the Ninth Circuit have ruled directly with the issue in the context of marijuana use, authority exists that does recognize the viability of the defense of medical necessity in prosecutions for possession and cultivation of marijuana.

In *US v. Randall*, 104 Wash.D.C.Rep. 2249, 2252, 104 Daily Wash.L.Rptr. 2249 (D.C. Super. 1976), a Washington D.C. Superior Court allowed the defendant to assert medical necessity as a defense for possession of marijuana. There, the defendant grew marijuana plants and used them to treat his own glaucoma because conventional medications were ineffective. The court concluded that the defendant's right to preserve his sight outweighed the government's interest in outlawing the drug. *Id.* at 2252. In *Hawaii v. Bachman*, 61 Haw. 71, 72 (1976), the Hawaii Supreme Court stated that "it is entirely possible that medical necessity could be asserted as a defense to a marijuana possession charge in a proper case." However, in that case, the court rejected the defense because the defendant failed to show by competent medical testimony the beneficial effects upon the his condition of marijuana use. *Id.* at 73.

Moreover, in *Washington v. Diana*, 24 Wash. App. 908, 916 (1979), the court stated that medical necessity was a viable defense in a prosecution for possession of marijuana. There, the defendant used marijuana as treatment for his multiple sclerosis, but was not allowed to present the medical necessity defense at trial. The appellate court remanded the case holding that the defendant should have been permitted to present the defense of medical necessity. *Id.*, at 915–916. Finally, in *Jenks v. Florida*, 582 So. 2d 676, 677 (CA 1991), the defendant, who suffered from AIDS and used marijuana to combat the side effects of AZT treatment, was convicted of cultivation of marijuana. A Florida Court of Appeals reversed the conviction and entered a judgment of acquittal holding that state legislation which forbids all use of marijuana does not automatically preclude the defense of medical necessity to a charge of possession. *Id.* at 679. Therefore, ample persuasive authority exists which recognizes the viability of the defense in state criminal prosecutions.

However, case law does exist where courts have refused to extend the doctrine of medical necessity to federal prosecutions for possession of marijuana. In *U.S. v. Belknap*, 1993 U.S. App. LEXIS 2183 (4th Cir. 1993), the court refused to allow an instruction on medical necessity. There, the defendant was using marijuana to alleviate pain and overcome previous drug addiction. However, the defendant did not offer evidence to support an instruction on medical necessity because he failed to show that his alternatives were limited and testified that he never tried to treat his suffering through legal

means. Additionally, in *U.S. v. Burton,* 894 F.2d 188, 191 (6th Cir. 1990), the court refused to hold that defense of medical necessity was available to a charge of possession with intent to distribute. The court refused to extend the medical necessity defense because the defendant failed to utilize an existing government program under which he could treat his glaucoma with marijuana under the government's supervision. The defendant was aware of this alternative, thus he failed to meet the elements of medical necessity. However, in *Burton,* the Sixth Circuit expressly recognized that authority did exist for allowing the medical necessity defense in federal prosecutions. *Id.* at 191. Thus, although two federal cases have refused to extend the defense, the facts of those cases are insufficient to assert the defense on a basic level.

Notwithstanding *Burton* and *Belknap,* medical necessity is a common law defense which should be available in federal criminal prosecutions. Clear authority exists establishing that the common law defense of necessity is recognized in federal criminal prosecutions. Medical necessity is merely a particular application of common law necessity. A myriad of persuasive authority exists where courts have extended the defense of medical necessity in state criminal prosecutions. Therefore, the defense should be available in federal criminal prosecutions.

Review sections II.C and II.E.5 of the Defendants' Joint Memorandum to see how this work was incorporated into the final product.

MEMORANDUM OF LAW
ARGUMENT FOR CANNABIS CLUB DEFENSE: "JOINT-PURCHASERS"

I.   THE MOTION FOR A SUMMARY JUDGMENT AND REQUEST FOR INJUNCTION SHOULD NOT BE GRANTED BECAUSE IT UNDULY DEPRIVES THE DEFENDANTS OF THE OPPORTUNITY TO PRESENT A LEGALLY VIABLE DEFENSE TO A JURY OF THEIR PEERS

A.   Introduction

The United States is charging the defendants with the crime of distributing marijuana in violation of 21 U.S.C. section 882(a), referred to as the Controlled Substances Act. Instead of charging the defendants criminally, which would afford them the right to present legally viable defenses to a jury of their peers, the United States is attempting to obtain a preliminary and permanent injunction against the Defendants, ultimately depriving them of the right to present their defenses to the alleged criminal violations.

The United States Constitution guarantees the right to trial by jury in order to prevent oppression by the government. U.S.C.A. Const. Amends 6, 14; *Duncan v. State of La.*, 391 U.S. 145, 194 (1968). As such, a right to a jury trial is inherent in our governmental system which purports to guarantee fairness, and the United States is attempting to deprive the defendants of this right by the institution of this motion for a preliminary and permanent injunction. There is a well-established principle that in proceedings for criminal contempt, a defendant has no right to a jury trial for petty crimes such as ones that result in imprisonment of less than six months. *Bloom v. State of Ill.*, 391 U.S. 194 (1968). It seems apparent that the United States is purposely attempting to avoid a traditional criminal prosecution so that they can pursue criminal contempt proceedings against the Defendants for any violations of the requested injunction, ultimately avoiding a jury trial and depriving the Defendants of their right to present any viable defenses.

The case at hand presents an issue never presented to a court before. The case involves Cannabis Clubs who provide marijuana to their members for medicinal purposes which is legal under California law. (Prop. 15) The United States is requesting an injunction to halt this alleged illegal conduct. However, the Defendants have a viable defense to the allegations that they are engaged in the illicit distribution of marijuana. Under *U.S. v. Swiderski*, 548 F.2d 445 (2nd Cir. 1977), it was held that a statutory "transfer" could not occur between two individuals in joint possession of a controlled substance simultaneously acquired for their own use. It is the Defendant's contention that under *Swiderski*, they and their members should be considered "joint purchasers" thus relieving them of any liability for distributing an illicit substance.

At this juncture, the issue is not whether this defense will ultimately persuade a jury, rather the issue is whether the defendants have a guaranteed right to present such a defense to a jury. The Defendants will argue that they should be accorded such a right and by issuing an injunction at this stage, they will be denied any possibility of defending their alleged conduct.

B.   The Defendants Right To Present A Legally Viable Defense To A Jury Of Their Peers Would Be Unduly Denied With The Issuance Of An Injunction

As stated above, the U.S. Constitution affords individuals the right to a jury trial when dealing with legal issues. It is true that a jury trial is not guaranteed to those seeking relief in equity. *Kalish v. Franklin Advisers, Inc.*, 928 F.2d 590 (1991). However, when a case involves both legal and equitable claims, right to trial by jury must be preserved. *Glezos v. Amalfi Ristorante Italiano, Inc.*, 651 F.Supp. 1271 (1987).

In the case at hand, the United States is seeking equitable relief in the form of a preliminary and permanent injunction against the defendants. If the United States were to charge the defendants criminally based on the same alleged conduct, there would be no question to the defendant's right to a jury trial in a criminal action. So, although equitable relief is being sought by the United States, the issues are legal in nature thus supporting the defendant's right to a jury trial.

In fact, "the general principle is well-established that a criminal defendant is entitled to have a jury instruction on any defense which provides a legal defense to the charge against him and which has some foundation in the evidence, even though the evidence may be weak, insufficient, inconsistent, or of doubtful credibility." *U.S. v. Escobar De Bright*, 742 F.2d 1196, 1198 (9th Cir. 1984). So, no matter how insufficient the United States will claim the Defendant's defenses are, if prosecuted a jury would have to be instructed on any viable defenses. It seems obvious that the prosecution is attempting to avoid this by the institution of these proceedings requesting an injunction, so they can ultimately charge the Defendants with criminal contempt without a jury.

C.   The Defendants Should Be Considered "Joint Purchasers" Thus Making It Impossible For Them To Be Charged With Distribution Of An Illicit Substance

In *U.S. v. Swiderski*, 548 F.2d 445 (2d Cir. 1977), two individuals purchased cocaine and then snorted it. After they were charged with distribution, the court held that "where two or more individuals simultaneously and jointly acquire possession of a drug for their own use, intending only to share it together, the only crime is personal drug abuse-simple joint possession, without any intent to distribute the drug further." *Id.* at 450. The court reasoned that Congress, in making the penalties much harsher for distributing narcotics than for just possessing them, was concerned that such conduct tends to have the dangerous, unwanted effect of drawing additional participants into the web of drug abuse. *Id.* Because these concerns were not present in a situation of joint purchasers, it was error for the jury not to be instructed that they could find mere possession without any distribution. *Id.* at 452.

This case presents a factual scenario whereby the Defendants are involved in a cooperative enterprise with the members of their clubs. "Members" of the Defendant's Cannabis clubs jointly obtain marijuana for medicinal purposes. All members are screened and only those with diagnosed medical problems and a doctor's prescription may obtain the marijuana. This is an enterprise that is legal under California law, thus leaving the Defendants without any intent to violate the law. Basically, they jointly acquire the marijuana and jointly use it to treat their medical conditions. The Defendants act as caregivers, making the marijuana available as a remedy for their member's ailments. Alternatively, the members are using the marijuana to alleviate their ailments as a patient would use the medicine his doctor gave him to alleviate his pain. There are no third parties involved. It is simply a joint enterprise that is absolutely legal under California law.

Congress' concerns over drawing additional participants into the web of drug abuse are not jeopardized. As in *Swiderski*, nobody other than the co-purchasers are involved in the marijuana use. The members are not drawn into drug use through the Defendants, rather they seek the drug to alleviate their ailments. These individuals are not using marijuana for recreational purposes. They are merely attempting to alleviate their painful ailments through the use of physician prescribed medicinal marijuana. Basically, there is no distribution taking place, for the clubs and their members jointly acquire the marijuana for medicinal purposes to be shared among them and nobody else. The arrangement actually furthers the federal goal of eliminating illicit drug trafficking, by providing a safe environment for those who frequently suffer from debilitating ailments to conveniently gain access to necessary medication. If these cooperative enterprises are shut down, patients will be left to seek individual transactions with illicit dealers.

In the context of illicit drug transactions, The Ninth Circuit has limited *Swiderski* to its facts. In *U.S. v. Wright,* 593 F.2d 105 (1979), the defendant was asked to purchase heroin and was given money by another. The defendant went out on his own, procured the heroin, brought it to the individual who requested it where they snorted the heroin together. The court held that it was not an error to deny a jury instruction based on the joint purchaser defense presented in *Swiderski, Id.* at 108. The court reasoned that the defendant "facilitated the transfer of the narcotic; he did not simply simultaneously and jointly acquire possession of a drug for their (his and another's) own use." *Id.*

This case presents a factual scenario unlike *Wright.* As opposed to *Wright,* the members of the club do not give money to the Defendants and have them go procure drugs for their recreational use. Rather, the marijuana is originally acquired for the club and its members from the outset. In *Wright,* the court was concerned with defendants using the *Swiderski* defense in a "typical" drug deal. Here, the drugs are not being used for illicit purposes. In fact, the club and its members are engaged in legal activity under state law and the use of the drugs is not for recreational purposes but instead for purely medicinal purposes.

The present case is one of first impression and the Defendants would have the opportunity to present the joint purchaser defense to a jury. *Wright* would not automatically preclude such a defense because the facts of this case are in such discord with the facts of *Wright.* In *U.S. v. Rush,* 738 F.2d 497 (1st Cir. 1984), a group of defendants were in possession of tons of marijuana and argued the *Swiderski* defense. Despite the large amount of marijuana that was retrieved, which usually leads to an inference that they intended to distribute it, the court stated "[T]he *Swiderski* defendants were entitled to pursue whatever factual defense they could support, however implausible it might seem to a finder of fact; in this case they may have had no colorable alternative." *Id.* at 514. Thus, despite *Wright,* the Defendants would still be afforded the opportunity to present the defense to a jury if they were prosecuted criminally. Based on the novel facts of this case as well as the legality of the operation under state law, it cannot be denied that the *Swiderski* defense has direct applicability to these Defendants.

D. Conclusion

Although many courts have decided to limit or even not recognize the defense presented in *Swiderski,* it is still a viable defense. As stated above, a defendant has the right to present any defenses that can be supported by the evidence, no matter how improbable or insufficient it might seem. The reason we have a jury system is to allow a group of our peers to be the ultimate decision-maker. We must trust a jury to ultimately determine if the joint purchaser defense can be applied to the Defendants in this case.

There is no doubt that if the prosecution decided to prosecute the Defendants criminally in this matter, the defense would have the right to present any defense that is allowed under the law or any reasonable extension thereof. In the present case, the situation involving a marijuana club that is involved in a cooperative enterprise with its members to help them get the medicine that their doctors are prescribing is unlike any factual scenario this court has seen before.

As described above, the current situation can be analogized to *Swiderski,* and the cases that have limited the holding have involved situations where individuals were engaged in the illicit use of drugs in direct contravention to Congress' concerns in passing the Controlled Substances Act. Here, those concerns are not raised because the Defendants are operating under a legal scheme under state law. Additionally, marijuana is not being made available to the general public nor those that want marijuana for commercial or recreational purposes. Only those members involved in the cooperative enterprise with the Defendants who have medical prescriptions for marijuana are the ones using the marijuana. This is not a typical drug deal and it would unduly deny the Defendants their rights if they were not allowed to present this defense to a jury of their peers.

Appellate Brief

**IN THE SUPREME COURT
OF THE UNITED STATES**

OCTOBER TERM, 1988

No. 87-1206

KATHRYN ISABELLA MESA, PETITIONER

v.

PEOPLE OF THE STATE OF CALIFORNIA

SHABBIR A. EBRAHIM, PETITIONER

v.

PEOPLE OF THE STATE OF CALIFORNIA

---

*ON WRIT OF CERTIORARI TO THE UNITED STATES
COURT OF APPEALS FOR THE NINTH CIRCUIT*

BRIEF FOR THE RESPONDENT

QUESTION PRESENTED

Whether 28 U.S.C. §1442(a)(1) allows a federal employee charged with committing a traffic offense while on duty to remove the ensuing prosecution to federal court where the employee does not allege a defense to the charges based upon any right, duty, privilege, or immunity provided under federal law?

<u>TABLE OF CONTENTS</u>

TABLE OF AUTHORITIES

Cases:

TABLE OF AUTHORITIES—Continued

STATEMENT

This Court is presented with two otherwise ordinary traffic cases. Petitioner Shabbir A. Ebrahim was given a traffic ticket for speeding and failing to yield after he struck a police car with the mail truck he was driving. Petitioner Kathryn Isabella Mesa was charged with misdemeanor vehicular manslaughter after she struck and killed a bicyclist with the mail truck she was driving.

Each mail carrier filed a petition for removal based solely upon their having been federal employees on duty when the incidents occurred. Neither petitioner alleged that his/her actions were justified by federal law. There has been no suggestion that these prosecutions were motivated by animus toward federal officials or federal law.

The United States District Court for the Northern District of California simultaneously granted the petitions and denied the State of California's motions for remand. California sought review by the Ninth Circuit Court of Appeals by direct appeal and mandamus.

The Ninth Circuit held that mandamus was available to challenge the District Court's decision, and petitioners do not challenge that ruling. The Ninth Circuit found that removal was prohibited by this Court's decision in *Maryland v. Soper (No. 1)*, 270 U.S. 9, 33–35 (1926), which required that the employee have alleged in his petition a defense to the state charges based upon federal law. *People of the State of California v. Mesa*, 813 F.2d 960 (9th Cir. 1987). This Court granted certiorari.

SUMMARY OF ARGUMENT

Petitioners seek to expand federal jurisdiction radically at the expense of State sovereignty and common sense. Petitioners' theory would allow federal employees to force local prosecutors to travel hundreds of miles from country seats to federal courthouses to contest traffic tickets and other criminal offenses completely unconnected with federal law or authority. The tactical advantage of such a procedure will ensure its use, and create a separate criminal court for federal employees. District courts will be burdened with new cases presenting purely state law issues. Those cases will generate a disproportionate number of appeals because there is uncertainty concerning the proper incorporation of state procedural and substantive law into federal criminal procedure.

Such an expansion of federal jurisdiction would breach this Court's fundamental policy against federal interference with state criminal prosecutions, and is both unnecessary and contrary to the intent of Congress in enacting section 1442(a)(1). Petitioners rely upon their construction of other statutes dissimilar in language and heritage to section 1442(a)(1). because the structure and history of section 1442 (a)(1) demonstrates that Congress has always required a federal defense for removal. This is not a case where this Court must choose between two plausible statutory constructions based upon the desirability of the result, although the difficulties posed by creating a separate criminal court for federal officials would tip the balance in favor of California. Rather, petitioners' construction of section 1442 (a)(1) renders both section 1442 (a)(3) and the Federal Drivers Act (28 U.S.C. 2679(b)) superfluous. It also ignores the distinction made by Congress between "under color of office" and "in performance of duties". A chronological view of the legislative history illuminates that distinction and demonstrates that Congress has always intended to require a federal defense under section 1442(a)(1).

When it enacted the first federal official removal statute, Congress only intended to protect federal law against defiance or misinterpretation by State courts. Congress did not provide for removal of all torts and petty crimes committed while on duty, as those cases did not present a challenge to federal law. Moreover, that first statute was enacted before it was clear that Article III, section 2, permitted federal jurisdiction over state court judgments presenting *federal* questions. *See Martin v. Hunter's Lessee,* 14 U.S. 304 (1816). Congress would not have provided for removal of cases presenting purely state law issues under those circumstances. Indeed, removal of these cases would still violate Article III because these traffic offenses do not present federal questions.

Petitioners concede that Congress retained its original intent when it enacted subsequent removal statutes. The history of those enactments confirms that Congress intended to protect federal law by requiring a federal defense for removal.

The lack of cases allowing removal confirms that conclusion. There are no reported cases decided before 1980 (when the Third Circuit "reinvented" Congressional intent), allowing removal where the federal employee did not rely upon his enforcement or compliance with federal law as a defense. Certainly officials sued for miscellaneous torts or prosecuted for petty crimes in "hostile" states would have produced hundreds of reported decisions over 165 years had there been no federal defense requirement. The absence of a case explicity allowing removal without a federal defense, combined with the absence of such reported decisions, is only consistent with the federal defense requirement.

Finally, the decision of this Court in both civil and criminal cases uniformly mandate the federal defense requirement once the term "federal defense" is understood as including all cases where the official's defense raises issues of federal law. Petitioners ignore the official's claim of federal immunity in many of those decisions, and are unable to explain this Court's denial of removal to on-duty officials in the remainder.

ARGUMENT

1. Congress Always Intended to Require a Federal Defense for Removal

A. READING SECTION 1442(a) AS A WHOLE ESTABLISHES THAT CONGRESS REQUIRED A FEDERAL DEFENSE FOR REMOVAL

Section 1442(a)(1) allows removal for suits and prosecutions for acts "under color of office". That phrase is inherently ambiguous.[1] Petitioners claim it mandates removal of suits and prosecutions for any acts committed by officials in performance of their duties. But reading section 1442(a) as a whole prohibits that construction. Section 1442(a)(3) allows removal to "[a]ny officer of the courts of the United States, for any Act under color of office *or* in the performance of his duties" (emphasis added). Terms connected in the disjunctive are to be given separate meanings. *See Garcia, v. United States,* 469 U.S. 70, 73 (1984), *Reiter v. Sonotone,* 442 U.S. 330, 339 (1979). Thus, "under color of office" must restrict removal to something less than all acts committed while on duty. The only logical reading of section 1442(a)(1) is that "under color of office" refers to acts which the official seeks to justify or immunize by the laws creating and protecting his exercise of federal authority (i.e. his "office").

In addition, petitioners' reading of the phrase "under color of office" in section 1442(a)(1) must be rejected because it would allow court officers to remove cases based upon any act committed while in performance of their duties under section 1442(a)(1), rendering all of section 1442(a)(3)

---

1. Petitioners do not address the "plain meaning" of "under color of office". Rather, they attempt to construe section 1442(a)(1) *in pari materia* with other statutes purportedly united by a common purpose and legacy. AB 9–12, 27. The failure of that attempt is discussed below after examination of the legislative history of section 1442(a)(1).

superfluous. *See Jarecki v. Searle & Co.,* 367 U.S. 303 (1961) (this Court reads statutes as a whole and seeks to give effect to each section).

> B.   THE LEGISLATIVE HISTORY OF SECTION 1442(a)(1) DEMONSTRATES THAT CONGRESS ALWAYS REQUIRED A FEDERAL DEFENSE FOR REMOVAL

The history of the removal statutes set forth below demonstrates that Congress employed removal sparingly, as befits a threat to State sovereignty. From the outset, Congress crafted the removal statutes to protect only certain federal laws from State misinterpretation or defiance. Congress periodically reenacted removal statutes protecting different classes of federal officials only when the laws which those officials enforced were the subject of State hostility. Protecting federal officials who enforced federal law was the only mechanism available to protect the law itself. Congress provided for removal to protect enforcement of federal law, not to allow federal officials to remove all torts or crimes committed while on duty.

> 1.   Congress enacted the first federal official removal statute solely to provide an efficient mechanism to transfer suits challenging federal authority to federal court before trial.

Section 25 of the Judiciary Act of 1789 (1 Stat. 85) provided for removal after trial of state court judgments purporting to invalidate federal law or authority exercised under federal law. There was no provision for removal of cases lacking federal questions. Indeed, when the first federal official removal statute was enacted in 1815, this Court had yet to rule that federal courts could review *any* state court judgments, even those presenting federal questions. *Compare* Act of February 4, 1815, 3 Stat. 198 ("1815 Act") with *Martin v. Hunter's Lessee,* 14 U.S. 304 (1816) (decided after Congress enacted the 1815 Act). Congress would not have attempted to expand federal jurisdiction to include cases presenting no federal questions under such circumstances. Rather, the legislative history of the 1815 Act demonstrates that it was only a modest and temporary extension of the Judiciary Act.

The 1815 Act was proposed to protect federal customs agents in their enforcement of federal law against States sympathetic to smugglers during the 1812 War. The only available legislative history for that Act consists of a letter from its proponent, the Secretary of the Treasury. *See* Annals of Congress, 13th Cong., 3d Sess. at 757–61 (also appearing in the American State Papers, 1802–15, Finance, at 881). The Secretary related that the Vermont courts were frustrating the enforcement of federal law by routinely granting civil judgments against customs officials for seizures authorized under federal law. Under the Judiciary Act, decisions in such civil cases could only be removed to federal courts *after* the judgement was affirmed by the highest court in the State. That delay would allow Vermont to forestall review until after the war ended.

The Secretary wanted to allow removal of civil cases before adjudication by any State court. *Id.,* at 760. The Secretary only intended to adjust the Judiciary Act for the duration of the war to allow immediate transfer to federal court of State challenges to federal law authorizing searches and seizures by customs inspectors. He quoted section 25 of the Judiciary Act as allowing removal of cases "where is drawn in question the validity of an authority, exercised under the United States (as in the case of an official of the customs,) and the decision is against the validity." *Id.,* at 760 (quoting the Judiciary Act). His proposal mirrors the Judiciary Act, except that he suggested that removal occur before trial.

> "A more effectual provision should be made for transferring, from the State courts to the Federal courts, suits brought against persons *exercising* an authority under the United States, so that such suits may be transferred, as soon as conveniently may be, after they are commenced."

Id., at 761 (emphasis added). Congress passed the 1815 Act, which allowed certain officials and those assisting them to remove civil and criminal cases where the charged acts were "agreeable to the provisions of this act, or under colour thereof" until the war ended. 1815 Act, secs. 8, 13. Thus, Con-

gress allowed removal of suits only where the validity of the authority "exercised" by the official was relied upon as a defense. Congress was only worried about preserving federal law. Protecting officials relying upon that law was necessary to ensure its enforcement.[2]

2.	Subsequent reenactments of the federal official removal statute maintained the federal defense requirement

The provisions of the 1815 Act were revived during the next State-Federal conflict, when South Carolina purported to nullify the federal tariff by passing the Nullification Act in 1832. *See* Act of March 2, 1833, 4 Stat. 632, sec. 3 ("1833 Act"). The Senate debate indicates that Congress did not intend to expand federal jurisdiction.[3] The 1833 Act tracked the language of the 1815 Act. Most important, courts understood that a federal defense was required for removal. *See Salem & L.R. Co. v. Boston & L.R. Co.*, 21 Fed. Cas. 229 (1857) (No. 12, 249) (official must allege facts in petition demonstrating excuse or justification under the revenue laws).

The next federal official removal statute was enacted during the Civil War. The Act of March 3, 1863, sec. 5, 12 Stat. 756, ("1863 Act") provided for removal where the official acted "by virtue or under color of any authority derived from or exercised by or under the President of the United States, or any Act of Congress." *Id.* This statute by its plain terms required a federal defense.

This Court confirmed that requirement in three cases. In *The Mayor v. Cooper*, 73 U.S. 247 (1867), the Court upheld the constitutionality of the 1863 Act[4] based upon the power of federal courts to hear *federal* questions. *Id., see also The Justices v. Murray*, 76 U.S. 274 (1869) (noting that the 1863 Act only allowed removal of federal questions). In *McKee v. Rains*, 77 U.S. 22 (1870), a United States Marshal was sued for trespass after entering a dwelling and seizing property pursuant to a writ of execution. This Court rejected his petition for removal under the 1863 Act because "[n]o Act of Congress has been cited from which authority can be derived to the Marshal of any court of the United States to seize the goods of one person for the satisfaction of the debts of another." *Id.*, at 25. Although the Marshal was in performance of his duties when executing a court order, he was denied removal because he could not base his defense upon federal law.[5] Petitioners cannot reconcile *McKee* or the 1863 Act with their theory that Congress always intended to allow removal for acts "in performance of duties."

2.	Although there is no case law construing the 1815 Act, one of the briefs filed in *Osborn v. Bank of the United States*, 22 U.S. 738 (1824), suggests that contemporaries understood that Act to allow removal only when the revenue officer alleged a defense based upon federal law. "A revenue officer may commit a trespass while executing his official duties, and *if he justifies under the statutes of the United States, a question will arise under them*, in which an appellate jurisdiction is given to this court, to correct the errors of the state courts. But could Congress give additional jurisdiction to the federal courts, in all suits brought by or against revenue officers?" *Id.*, at 814 (emphasis added).

The absence of case law is also evidence that Congress maintained a "federal question" requirement. A sudden expansion of jurisdiction to encompass all torts committed by federal employees would have sparked litigation well before the brief was filed in *Osborn* in 1824.

3.	Petitioners rely upon Senator Webster's concern that federal officials would not receive a fair trial from jurors who had sworn allegiance to the Nullification Act. AB 13–14. But the Senator did not suggest that federal officials could not receive a fair trial because of universal hostility to federal officials. Rather, he argued that allowing trial in South Carolina's courts would be futile because jurors were sworn to support the Nullification Act in defiance of the federal *law* upon which the official would rest his defense. Thus, removal was needed to "give a chance to the officer to defend himself *where the authority of the law was recognized* (sic)." 9 Congressional Debates, Part II, 22nd Cong., 2d Sess., at 461 (same remarks of Sen. Daniel Webster) (emphasis added), 419 (statute would frustrate attempts by States to preclude an official from "appealing to the constitution and laws under which he acted") (Sen. Dallas), 260 (Sen. Wilkins).

4.	The Court construed the 1863 Act as amended by the Act of May 11, 1866, 14 Stat 46. The changes to the Act were not significant for the issue presented here.

5.	Although the Marshal was also clearly enforcing federal law by enforcing a court order, the 1863 Act required that the official act under authority "derived from the President of the United States, or from an Act of Congress." Court orders were held not to be covered by the Act. *See Buck v. Colbath*, 70 U.S. 334 (1865). As discussed *infra*, at page 14, this problem prompted Congress in 1916 to add section 1442(a)(3) protecting court officers.

The next removal statutes were part of internal revenue laws.[6] The Act of July 13, 1866 was the first statute to use the phrase "under color of office" in providing for removal. Congress did not discuss this new language, and this Court's view of the federal defense requirement did not change. "That the act of Congress does provide for the removal of criminal offenses against the State laws; *when there arises in them the claim of the Federal right or authority, is too plain to admit of denial.*" *Tennesse v. Davis*, 100 U.S. 257, 261 (1880) (emphasis added). Again, this Court required a federal defense.[7]

3.   The addition of section 1442(a)(3) in 1916 is compelling evidence that Congress maintained the federal defense requirement

Congress added section 1442(a)(3) in 1916. As discussed above, that amendment allows a court officer to remove civil and criminal actions "for or on account of any act done under color of his office *or in the performance of his duties as such officer.*" *Id.* (emphasis added). Petitioners' reading of "under color of office" as referring to all acts in performance of duties not only renders section 1442(a)(3) superfluous as read today, but makes no sense historically.

Petitioners claim that Congress read both phrases as "coterminous." AB 26. But this does not explain why Congress added "in performance of duties" to section (a)(3) if "under color of office" achieved the same result. Nor does it explain why Congress added section (a)(3) at all, instead of simply amending section (a)(1) to include court officers.

This Court's decision in *Gay v. Ruff*, 292 U.S. 25 (1934), indicates that Congress intended both phrases to encompass only those acts justifiable by federal law or authority. Defendant in *Ruff* was a receiver appointed by federal court order to run a railroad. Plaintiff sued the receiver for the death of his son allegedly caused by the negligent operation of a train by railroad employees. The receiver sought removal under section 1442(a)(3) based on his having been a court officer when the incident occurred.

---

6.   The 1833 Act applied only to collection of duties on imports. The Internal Revenue Act of June 30, 1864, ch. 173, section 50, 13 Stat. 241 ("1864 Act"), provided that the 1833 Act was to be "taken and deemed as extended to and embracing all cases arising under the laws for the collection fo [revenue]." That provision was repealed and replaced in 1866 with a different removal statute. *See* Act of July 13, 1866, ch. 184, section 67, 14 Stat. 98, 171 ("1866 Act"), *Gay v. Ruff*, 292 U.S. 25 n.8 (1934). That Act was codified in 1874 as section 643 of the Revised Statutes, and recodified as Section 33 of the Judicial Code of 1911, 36 Stat. 1097.

7.   This Court upheld the constitutionality under Article III of section 643 of the 1874 Revised Statutes (*see supra* note 6) based upon the assumption that a federal defense was required for removal. Petitioners' theory that *Davis* did not require a defense based upon federal authority is refuted by virtually every sentence of that case. *Id.*, at 271, 272 (allowing removal of prosecutions where "there arises a federal question" or in which "there arises a defense under United States law"). Petitioners argue that *Davis* did not require a federal defense because "self-defense" is a "state-law" defense. AB 19–20, n.7. But petitioner concedes that this Court stated in *Maryland v. Soper (No. 2)*, 270 U.S. 36 (1926), that acts of self-defense are "part of the exercise of official authority." *Id.*, at 42. The official in *Davis* relied upon the federal immunity defense, very much a "common law of 'justification' applicable to crimes committed by federal employees in the performance of their duties." AB n.7, *see Arizona v. Manypenny*, 451 U.S. 232, 236–237 (1981), *In re Neagle*, 135 U.S. 1 (1890), Amsterdam, *Criminal Prosecutions Affecting Federally Guaranteed Civil Rights: Federal Removal and Habeas Corpus Jurisdiction to Abort State Court Trial*, 113 U.Pa.L.Rev. 793, 874 n.328 (1965) (*Davis* demonstrates the rule under section 1442(a)(1) that the official must show colorable protection under federal law), Currie, *The Constitution in the Supreme Court, The First Hundred Years, 1789–1889* (1985), 393–94 n.172 (recognizing that *Davis* was a federal immunity case). Although the district court in *Georgia v. Grady*, 10 Fed. Cas. 245 (1876) (No. 5, 352) (AB 20–21) chose to couch the necessary and proper test later set forth in *In re Neagle*, in terms of state law with which the jury might be more familiar, the gravamen of the defense still remains reliance upon federal authority.

The officer in *Davis v. South Carolina*, 107 U.S. 597 (1882), also alleged a federal immunity defense. This Court noted that the official relied upon federal law as justifying his presence at the scene. *Id.*, at 600. The official's petition averred that the shooting occurred only after the fugitive attempted to evade arrest, and that the fugitive's sudden appearance had frightened his horse and caused his firearm to discharge. *Id.*, at 598. Thus, the official alleged that his acts while on duty were necessary and proper because the firearm discharged as a result of his attempt to enforce federal law (i.e. guarding the house when the fugitive emerged). Although this immunity defense might not prevail at trial, it was certainly "colorably" alleged for purposes of removal. *See In re Neagle, Willingham v. Morgan*, 395 U.S. 402 (1969) (discussed in a later section in this brief).

This Court held that the receiver was a court officer for purposes of section 1442(a)(3). *Id.*, at 39. But this Court also noted that the case was *dissimilar* to cases removable under section 1442(a)(3) *because no federal questions were presented. Id.*, at 34. (Petitioners' construction would require removal in the absence of a federal question.) This Court denied removal, holding that Congress only intended "in performance of duties" to protect court officers relying upon the federal authority embodied in the court order. *Id.*, at 35, 38–39. Thus, even that broader phrase requires reliance upon federal authority.

This Court also rejected petitioners' construction of the phrase "under color of office", which appears in sections 1442(a)(1) and (a)(3). Petitioners read "under color of office" as allowing removal for all acts committed while on duty. Under that construction, the receiver in *Ruff* should have been allowed removal because he was accused of negligence in performing his duties. But *Ruff* held that the receiver could not have been acting "under color of office" under section 1442(a)(3) because he had no federal defense. *Id.*, at 39 ("nor is there reason to assume that he will in this case rest his defense on his duty to cause the train to be operated").[8]

Only two years before *Ruff*, this Court had construed *section 1442(a)(1)* as prohibiting removal where the federal official failed to present a federal defense. *See Colorado v. Symes*, 286 U.S. 510 (1932). Petitioners suggest that this Court denied removal because the official did not provide enough information to allow the Court to determine if he acted in "proper discharge of his duty." AB 23–24. But the official's detailed narrative established at the very least that he acted in performance of his duties. *Id.*, at 516–17. This Court denied removal because the official failed to establish a federal immunity defense.[9] Petitioners' construction of "under color office" has been refuted repeatedly by this Court.

4.   Congress did not eliminate the federal defense requirements when it enacted the present statute

Congress amended section 1442(a)(1) to include "[a]ny officer of the United States or any agency thereof" as part of the Revision of the Judicial Code in 1948. The Reviser's Note to that section states only that the Revision extended the right to remove to all federal employees. Petitioners concede that

---

8.   That the two phrases are not "coterminous" is demonstrated by the motive of Congress in adding section 1442(a)(3). Court officers serving arrest warrants for violations of revenue laws could remove to federal court under section 1442(a)(1) by raising a federal immunity defense based upon their duty to enforce those laws. *See Tennessee v. Davis, supra, Davis v. South Carolina, supra*. However, section 1442(a)(1) referred only to revenue laws. Court officers executing court orders where the underlying authority for the order was *not* a revenue law were held to be unprotected by section 1442(a)(1). *See Gay v. Ruff*, 292 U.S. 25, 37–38 (1934). This Court has held that federal law did not protect those court officers when sued in state court for a variety of torts even though those suits were based upon the officer's execution of a court order. *See McKee v. Rains, supra, Bigelow v. Forrest*, 76 U.S. 339, 348 (1869), *Buck v. Colbath*, 70 U.S. 334, 342–44 (1865). The defense of federal immunity per the revenue laws, and thus removal, was unavailable to those officers.
     Congress sought to provide court officers with the same protection afforded to revenue officers *and* to members of Congress. *Ruff*, at 38–39 (quoting House Judiciary Committee report). Since revenue officers were allowed to remove acts committed "under color of office", that phrase was also included within section 1442 (a)(3). But additional protection was needed because of this Court's decisions holding that federal law did not provide a defense to suits challenging the marshal's execution of court orders. Section 1442(a)(4), added in 1875, allows members of Congress to remove any suit on account of "any act in the discharge of his official duty *under an order of such House." Id.* (emphasis added). Congress incorporated this protection of all acts committed pursuant to federal authority into section 1442(a)(3) by adding the phrase "in performance of duties." *Ruff*, at 39.
     Had Congress read "under color of office" as protecting all acts committed while on duty (*see* AB 26), then it would not have added another section to subsection 1442(a). Congress simply would have amended section 1442(a)(1) to include court officers. But Congress needed to add protection that petitioners claim was already present. California's reading of the two phrases is the only reading consistent with *Ruff* and the history and intent of the 1916 Act. Petitioners' reading defies common sense by making "under color of office" broader than "in performance of duties."
9.   "The statements of the petition are so vague, indefinite and uncertain as not to commit petitioner in respect of essential details of the *defense* he claims. They are not sufficient to enable the court to determine whether his *claim of immunity* rests on any substantial basis or is made in good faith." *Id.*, at 521 (emphasis added). As discussed in a later section, this Court in *Maryland v. Soper (No. 1), supra*, required officials seeking to allege an immunity defense to make a complete account of the incident prompting prosecution to ensure that all acts which could form the basis of that prosecution were protected by federal law. In *Symes*, this Court held that the official had failed to give a sufficiently complete account. *Id.*, at 519–20 (citing *Soper (No. 1)*).

the extension of protection to all federal employees did not change the character of that protection. AB 16. This Court has repeatedly held that changes in language made during the 1948 Revision are presumed not to have changed the scope and meaning of the statute unless Congress clearly expressed such an intent in the Reviser's Notes. *See Fourco Glass Co. v. Transmirra Prod. Corp.,* 353 U.S. 222, 226 (1957), *see also Walters v. National Assn. of Radiation Survivors,* 473 U.S. 305, 318 (1985), *Muniz v. Hoffman,* 422 U.S. 454, 467–74 (1975)(collected authority).

    5.   The Federal Drivers Act is further evidence that Congress still requires a federal defense for removal

Congress in 1961 refuted petitioners' vision of federal official removal when it added the Federal Drivers Act (28 U.S.C. 2679 (b)), allowing federal officials to remove *civil* suits arising out of the performance of their duties. The Act provides for removal of civil suits against federal drivers upon certification by the Attorney General that the incident occurred while the official was performing his duties. It does not encompass criminal cases. This section would be superfluous under petitioners' construction of section 1442(a)(1). The Federal Drivers Act was necessary because section 1442(a)(1) does not allow removal in the absence of a federal defense.[10]

    6.   This Court has held that section 1442(a)(1) is not *in pari materia* with civil rights laws

Statutes may be considered in *pari materia* only if they share the same object. *Erlenbaugh v. United States,* 409 U.S. 239, 243–45 (1972). This Court held in *Screws v. United States,* 325 U.S. 91, 111 (1945), that the language "under color of law" in the civil rights statutes cannot be construed *in pari materia* with the phrase "under color of office" in section 1442(a)(1) precisely because the statues were enacted for different purposes. *Id.,* at 111–12. The civil rights laws were enacted to punish state or federal officials who deprived others of their constitutional rights under the assumption of authority. Insistence that the official had acted within his federal authority would have vitiated the statutory purpose of punishing abuse of power. *Id.* Section 1442(a)(1), in contrast, was enacted to protect federal law by protecting officials relying upon that law in state courts. Restricting removal to cases featuring federal defenses makes sense.

    That the dissent would have construed civil rights laws in accordance with section 1442(a)(1) does not help petitioners, since the dissent, *along with the majority,* construed "under color of office" as requiring the official to justify his conduct under federal law. *Id.,* at 111–112, 145–46. Petitioners cannot reconcile *Screws* with their construction of section 1442(a)(1). *See also Gay v. Ruff, supra, Colorado v. Symes, supra, Maryland v. Soper (No. 1), supra, Tennessee v. Davis, The Mayor v. Cooper, The Justices v. Murray, McKee v. Rains, supra.*

    II.   This Court has never Abolished the Federal Defense Requirement

A.   THIS COURT'S DECISION IN *CLEVELAND V. MCCLUNG* IS CONSISTENT WITH THE FEDERAL DEFENSE REQUIREMENT

When a railroad company holding a lien on certain freight informed customs collectors of that lien, federal law required the collectors to notify that railroad before releasing the freight to a consignee or owner. The collectors were not allowed to release the freight until the owner discharged the lien. *Cleveland C. & c. R. R. v. McClung,* 119 U.S. 454, at 454–55. Plaintiff in *McClung* was a railroad holding

---

    10.   Although the Federal Tort Claims Act (28 U.S.C. 1346) provides for removal of tort suits against the United States pursuant to that Act, plaintiffs could still sue employees individually in state courts until 1961. Congress enacted the Federal Drivers Act to protect those employees against suits alleging negligent driving, which did not give rise to a federal defense. *See* Comment, *Katlein, Administrative Claims and the Substitution of the United States as Defendants Under the Federal Drivers Act: The Catch-22 of the Federal Tort Claims Act?,* 29 Emory L. J. 755, 761–63 (1980).

a lien on particular goods. Defendant was the customs collector bearing responsibility for notifying plaintiff and holding those goods once they arrived at the station. Plaintiff alleged that defendant had allowed his deputy on prior occasions to release goods to the consignees after collecting the amounts due on the liens. The deputy would then deliver the money to the railroad. Plaintiff complained that the deputy on one occasion had failed to turn over the money, and sought to hold the defendant responsible for the deputy's omission. *Id.*, at 454–55, 461, 462.

Plaintiffs alleged that defendant had failed to adhere to federal law by allowing his deputy to release the goods without notification. *Id.*, at 456. Defendant's petition stated that he had at all times acted "under color of office". After removal, defendant claimed that it was not his duty under federal law to collect money for the lienholders, and that he was therefore not responsible for his deputy's alleged failure to pay that money to the railroad. *Id.*, at 461. He also claimed that since the money had already been paid and the lien discharged, he had no duty under federal law to notify the railroad or retain the goods. *Id.*, at 458.

This case is confusing because, unlike the instant cases, defendant was accused of violating *federal* law. That allegation necessarily put the interpretation of federal law into issue as a defense. Moreover, while defendant's petition by today's standards was overly cryptic, he alleged a federal defense by stating in effect that he defended the charges based upon his duties (or lack thereof) under federal law. *Id.*, at 456. Thus, the Court proceeded to evaluate the case against the collector in those terms.

> The real question here is, therefore, whether the collection of the carrier's charges was a part of the official duty of the collector. If it was, the collection by the deputy was an official act, and the principal officer is liable accordingly.

Id., at 462. The Court found that the collector's federal defense was valid, and affirmed the lower court's instruction to the jury on that defense. *Id.*, at 463. The Court also stated that the defendant's denial of the allegation did not vitiate his right to removal. That ruling was correct because removal depends upon the allegations in the petition; officials may rely upon any defense at trial. The instant cases present no federal issues because petitioners do not defend their allegedly negligent driving by recourse to federal law.

B.   THE "CAUSAL CONNECTION" TEST EMPLOYED IN *WILLINGHAM* WAS DEVELOPED TO PROVIDE A REMEDY FOR HARASSMENT AND ASSUMES THE FEDERAL DEFENSE REQUIREMENT

Petitioners' interpretation of this Court's recent authority is easily stated. Petitioners observe that *Willingham v. Morgan*, 395 U.S. 402 (1969), granted removal in a civil case where the official had alleged only that he was on duty. They quote the language in *Willingham* stating that the official was entitled to removal because he had established a "causal connection" between the charged act and his official authority. AB 17. And they note that section 1442(a)(1) does not distinguish between civil and criminal cases on its face. Petitioners conclude that this "causal connection" test allows them removal in these criminal cases because they too alleged only that they were on duty.

California *agrees* that the test for removal is identical for civil and criminal cases, but suggests that petitioners misunderstand the "causal connection" test. As discussed herein, this Court has always held that a federal defense is required for all cases. Petitioners' argument collapses because they assume that the "causal connection" test outlined in *Willingham* is the exclusive test for removal. But that test already assumes that the federal official attempts to justify his conduct by relying upon federal law. The "casual connection" test only defines what facts must be alleged to put that federal defense into issue. This distinction is critical and is illustrated by *Maryland v. Soper*, 270 U.S. 9 (1926) ("*Soper (No. 1)*").

The "causal connection" test arose out of the problem posed by petitioners: the official who is harassed by State authorities attempting to frustrate Federal policy. *See* AB 7, 8, 27, 29–30. Petitioners'

suggestion that officials may remove prosecutions without admitting having committed the charged act and alleging that the act was justified under federal law is not new. *Cf.* AB 6, 8, 22–23, 31. But the suggestion arose in a different context.

It was assumed that the official had to allege a defense to the charges based upon federal law. *See Tennessee v. Davis, supra.* However, occasionally an official would be disabled from pleading a federal defense to the prosecution by the usual method, which was to admit having committed the charged act and to justify those acts under federal law. This occurred when the official had no knowledge of the incident prompting the prosecution.

In *Maryland v. Soper (No. 1)*, 270 U.S. 9 (1926), prohibition agents discovered a homicide victim while raiding an illegal still. They reported their discovery to local authorities and were promptly arrested for murder. The agents had a choice. They had no knowledge of the homicide. If they admitted killing the decedent, they falsely incriminated themselves. Moreover, since they had no knowledge of the incident, they were not in a position to assert that the killing was required by their duties. Their other alternative was to deny the killing and claim that they did nothing but their federal duty. But asserting that they did nothing but their duty did not necessarily put a federal defense into issue. One court refused to grant removal to an official who denied having committed the charged act, reasoning that the official, by denying having committed the charged act, had failed to allege a defense relevant to the prosecution. *Compare Illinois v. Fletcher*, 22 F. 776 (N.D. Ill. 1884) with *Oregon v. Wood*, 268 F. 975 (D.Or. 1920), and *State of Alabama v. Peak*, 252 F. 306 (D. Ala. 1918).

Although that ruling may appear unfair, allowing removal based only upon a denial of the charges would have eliminated the federal defense requirement. In most cases, the ruling did not affect officials because they had knowledge of the incident and alleged a federal immunity defense justifying the charged act. *See Tennessee v. Davis, supra, South Carolina v. Davis, supra.* This Court in *Soper (No. 1)* created a means by which officials lacking knowledge of the incident could obtain removal while ensuring that prosecutions based upon acts *unjustifiable* under federal law remained in state courts.

To allow removal by an official lacking knowledge about the incident (the agents), there had to be a means of determining whether the prosecution, either deliberately or mistakenly, had been based solely upon the official's performance of federal duties. Even if the prosecutor's motive was innocently based upon the official's presence at the wrong place at the wrong time (i.e. the agent finding the decedent), such a prosecution would in effect penalize compliance with federal law and violate the Supremacy Clause. The Supremacy Clause would then supply the federal defense justifying removal. Otherwise, States could prosecute federal officials for offenses which they had not committed, knowing that the official would be unaware of the incident and thus be unable to formulate a federal defense sufficient for removal. The problem was how to put this Supremacy Clause defense in issue in the appropriate case.

It was clear that an official claiming no knowledge of the incident should have the burden of producing evidence that his presence and activities as a federal official prompted the prosecution. But too strict a test would require the official to prove his defense in order to proceed to trial in federal court, and would defeat the purpose of removal. And too lax a "causal connection" test would allow any official to obtain removal merely by denying having committed the act and claiming ignorance of the incident prompting prosecution.

The agents in *Soper (No. 1)* denied knowledge of the murder, but argued that they were entitled to removal because they had found the slain man while on duty. This Court fashioned a very strict test allowing the official lacking knowledge about the incident to allege a connection between his federal activities and the prosecution sufficient for removal. The official had to demonstrate the "causal connection" by: 1) detailing all of his actions and showing that each act was in enforcement of federal law; and (2) negating the possibility that he was prosecuted for an act unprotected by federal law.

There must be a "causal connection" between what the officer has done under asserted official authority and the state prosecution. It must appear that the prosecution of him for whatever offense has arisen out of the acts done by him under color of Federal authority *and in*

enforcement of Federal law, and he must by direct averment *exclude the possibility* that it was based on acts or conduct of his, *not justified* by his Federal duty. But the statute does not require that the prosecution must be for the very acts which the officer admits to have been done by him under Federal authority. It is enough that his acts or his presence at the place in performance of his official duty constitute the basis, *though mistaken or false,* of the state prosecution.

* * * *

The defense he is to make is that of his immunity from punishment by the State, *because what he did was justified by his duty under the Federal law,* and because *he did nothing else* on which the prosecution could be based.

Id., at 33, 34 (emphasis added).[11] By showing that each of his acts was indisputably in enforcement of federal law, the official declared that the only basis of the prosecution was either: 1) an act protected by a federal defense;[12] or 2) his mere presence at the scene while enforcing federal law. *Id.* (language quoted above). As noted above, a prosecution based upon his mere presence would provide a Supremacy Clause defense. The phrase "it is enough that his acts or his presence at the place in performance of his official duty constitute the basis, though mistaken or false, of the state prosecution" (*id.*) was intended to govern *only* those cases where the official alleged a lack of knowledge of the events underlying the prosecution.

That "presence" language required more than simply being on duty. Thus, this Court in *Soper (No. 1)* denied the removal petition because "[t]hese averments amount to hardly more than to say that the homicide on account of which they are charged with murder was at a time when they were engaged in performing their official duties." *Id.,* at 33. *Petitioners not only misread Soper (No. 1), but rely upon the same allegation that was rejected in that case.*

The language in *Soper (No. 1)* suggests that in order to obtain removal based solely upon the official's presence at the scene, the official must demonstrate that: 1) he committed no acts other than those required by his duties; 2) there was a discernible reason for his prosecution, even though based upon mistake (or animus toward federal authority); and 3) the reason was connected with his having been present carrying out his duties at the time the charged act was allegedly committed.[13] Petitioners fail to meet this test, and instead rely upon the language used by this Court in *Willingham* to justify removal.

---

11. This Court required officials to waive their Fifth Amendment rights and give a complete account of their role in the incident. *Id.,* at 34, 35. Such a waiver would have been unnecessary if an official could obtain removal by alleging only that he was on duty, as such a statement could not be inculpatory

12. The "causal connection" test also applied where the official acknowledged having committed the charged act but alleged a federal defense. The Court, in the language quoted above, held that in order to put a federal immunity defense into issue, the official had to negate any inference that the prosecution could properly be based upon an act unprotected by federal law. This explains this Court's denial of removal in *Colorado v. Symes, supra. See supra* note 9. This Court later relaxed this part of the "causal connection" test for the official immunity defense in civil cases in *Willingham, supra,* at n.4. *See infra* note 16. Petitioners do not allege any federal defense.

13. Thus, this Court posed the hypothetical of a prosecution commenced "merely on account of the presence of the officer in discharge of his duties in enforcing the law, at or near the place of the killing, under circumstances casting suspicion of guilt on him. He may not even know who did the killing, and yet his being there and his official activities may have led to the indictment." *Id.,* at 33. This Court stated that removal was proper if the prosecution arose out of the officer's acts committed "under authority of Federal law in the discharge of his duty *and only by reason thereof."* *Id.,* at 33 (emphasis added).

It is not enough to show that the prosecution would not have occurred *but for* the official's physical presence at the scene, because such a test would be tautological. Had our petitioners not been at the scene of accidents by virtue of their driving, these prosecutions would not have occurred. The official must demonstrate that his mere presence enforcing or executing federal law was the proximate cause of the prosecution.

The official in *Soper (No. 1)* alleged that his identity and activity as a federal agent (and not just his presence at the scene as the reporter of the crime), was the proximate cause of his prosecution. This Court stated that such a showing might have been sufficient. However, this Court denied removal because the official had failed to provide enough information to negate an inference that he might have committed an act apart from his duties (i.e. by having shot the slain man). *Id.,* at 35–36.

Plaintiff inmate in *Willingham* sued his prison warden and doctor for maltreatment. *Willingham* is confusing because this Court had to reconcile its decision in *Soper (No. 1)* with the relatively new federal defense of official immunity. That doctrine had always shielded legislative and judicial officials for acts performed as part of their judicial functions. But after deciding *Soper (No. 1)*, this Court had expanded that doctrine *for civil suits* to shield all federal officials who could show that the charged acts were committed as part of their official duties. *See Barr v. Matteo*, 360 U.S. 564 (1959).

The official immunity defense is a federal defense because it immunizes federal officials in civil cases; the scope of that immunity is a federal question.[14] However, this federal defense differed fundamentally from other defenses because the official could put it into issue by alleging only that he was performing his duties when he committed the act.[15] This difference posed a problem for lower courts because *Soper (No. 1)* in a criminal case had rejected the idea that an official could obtain removal by alleging only that he was on duty when the charged act was committed. *Soper (No. 1)* required defendant to provide a complete account of the incident and negate any inference that he committed an act unprotected by federal law. That an official was on duty was not enough for removal under *Soper (No. 1)*. And there was no reason to believe that *Soper (No. 1)* did not apply to both civil and criminal cases. Thus, even though Congress intended to allow removal of all federal defenses per section 1442(a)(1), the court below in *Willingham* denied removal because it did not recognize official immunity as such a federal defense in light of *Soper (No. 1)*. *See Morgan v. Willingham*, 383 F.2d 139, 141 (10th Cir. 1967) (distinguishing between the breadth of the immunity defense and the scope of removal jurisdiction) (citing *Soper (No. 1)), reversed* in *Willingham v. Morgan*, 395 U.S. 402 (1969).

This Court in *Willingham* recognized this new defense of official immunity as a federal defense for purposes of section 1442(a)(1). *Id.*, at 406, 407. But, as in *Soper (No. 1)*, this Court had to determine what facts were sufficient to put that federal defense in issue. *See id.*, 407–09. This Court was seeking to define what "causal connection" between the official's acts and the civil suit had to be shown in order to demonstrate that the official had a "colorable" official immunity defense. In *Soper (No. 1)*, this Court had required the officials to meticulously detail all of their actions with regard to the victim to negate the inference that an act unprotected by a federal defense was the basis of the prosecution. But such a strict test imposed a burdensome standard in *Willingham* because the defendant prison officials might have had dozens of contacts with plaintiff. *Id.*, at 408–09.

The solution was simple. The official immunity defense covered acts committed in the performance of duties. Thus, that federal defense could be put into issue by alleging that all contacts between the officials and plaintiffs occurred while the officials were on duty. The Court merely eliminated, *for civil cases only,* the requirement that the official alleging a federal defense negate any inference that he had committed an act unprotected by federal law.[16] But petitioners' confusion arises from the Court's implementation of that decision. This Court elected to employ the "presence" language of the *Soper (No. 1)* decision in allowing removal.[17]

---

14.   This explains the distinction between the instant cases and the hypothetical federal officials posed in petitioners' brief. *See* AB 11–12. The FBI agents, the federal engineer, and the EPA inspector would rely upon official immunity as a defense to a civil suit, and upon federal immunity in a criminal action.

15.   This Court only recently resolved a split among the Circuits by holding that the official must allege that his act was discretionary in addition to having been committed while on duty. *See Westfall v. Erwin*, 484 U.S.__ , 108 S.Ct. 580, 98 L.Ed. 2d 619, n.4 (1988). It was assumed in *Willingham* that the warden and doctor had the discretion to impose medical treatment. This Court ultimately allowed removal without requiring the official to allege that the charged act was discretionary. Whether *Westfall* affects the showing required to put the official immunity defense in issue is not relevant here.

16.   In *Soper (No. 1)*, even those officials who admitted the charged act and asserted federal immunity defenses had to negate any inference that they were prosecuted for acts unprotected by federal law. *See supra* note 12. This Court relaxed that requirement for civil cases, but stated in footnote 4 that it had not decided whether to relax that requirement for criminal cases. That issues is not presented here because petitioners do not present a federal defense.

17.   "Past cases have interpreted the 'color of office' test to require a showing of a 'causal connection' between the charged conduct and asserted official authority. *Maryland v. Soper (No. 1), supra*, at 33. 'It is enough that [petitioners'] acts or [their] presence at the place in performance of [their] official duty constitute the basis, though mistaken or false, of the

In hindsight, that decision was the source of later confusion. Averring that the official was on duty was sufficient to allege the official immunity defense. It was not sufficient to allege other federal defenses (e.g. federal immunity). But this Court in *Willingham* used some of the same language to define the "causal connection" test for the official immunity defense as it had used earlier in *Soper (No. 1)* to define the "causal connection" test for a defense based upon enforcement of federal law. *See supra* note 17. Lower courts considering cases where the official immunity defense was not available (i.e. criminal cases) could fail to understand that *Willingham* only defined the showing required to put the official immunity defense in issue. They could infer that *Willingham* mandated removal in *all* cases where federal employees merely alleged that they "were on duty, at their place of federal employment, at all the relevant times." *Willingham*, at 409.

However, this Court did limit its ruling to civil suits. *Willingham*, at n.4. *See supra* note 16. And there was no reason to believe that this Court had elected to overrule 100 years of precedent and radically expand federal jurisdiction when its purpose was to create a means of removing a new federal defense. Nonetheless, the Third Circuit read *Willingham* as having eliminated the federal defense requirement. *See Commonwealth of Pennsylvania v. Newcomer*, 618 F.2d 246 (3d Cir. 1980) (*Newcomer*).

C.   THE THIRD CIRCUIT'S DECISION ABOLISHING THE FEDERAL DEFENSE REQUIREMENT IGNORED CONGRESSIONAL INTENT AND MISINTERPRETED *WILLINGHAM*

The Third Circuit relied upon two arguments in dismantling the federal defense requirement in *Newcomer*. The Circuit stated that the original removal statutes "were enacted not so much to provide federal forums for federal defenses, as to protect federal officers from interference with the operations of federal government by the state." *Id.*, at 250. But this Court in *Willingham* did not suggest that view of legislative intent, and the Third Circuit presented no legislative history supporting it.[18]

The Circuit's second argument contradicted its first. Instead of relying upon its view of Congressional intent, the Circuit stated that "the liberal construction to be afforded the statute, *see Willingham*, at 406; *Colorado v. Symes*, 286 U.S. at 517, 52 S.Ct. at 637, and the interpretation of 'color of office' supplied by *Willingham compel* our result in this case." *Id.*, at 250 (emphasis added). Specifically, the Circuit relied upon the holdings in *Willingham* and *Soper (No. 1)* that the official need not admit that he committed the charged act in order to obtain removal. The Circuit reasoned that "in such a case, of course, the denial does not involve a federal defense." *Newcomer*, at 250. But *Soper (No. 1)* requires that such a denial must be accompanied by facts establishing a "causal connection" between the prosecution and the official's enforcement of federal law sufficient to implicate the Supremacy Clause. The denial *is* the allegation of a federal defense.

---

state prosecution.' *In this case*, once petitioners had shown that their only contact with respondent occurred inside the penitentiary, while they were performing their duties, we believe that they had demonstrated the required 'causal connection'. The connection consists, simply enough, of the undisputed fact that petitioners were on duty, at their place of federal employment, at all the relevant times." *Id.*, at 490 (brackets in original, emphasis added).

Note, however, that this Court also made clear that the causal connection test was intended only to define the allegations necessary to put *federal defenses* in issue. "Petitioners sufficiently put in issue the questions of official justification and immunity; the validity of their defenses should be determined in the federal courts." *Id.* This Court did not abolish the federal defense requirement.

18.   The Third Circuit relied instead upon *Tennessee v. Davis, supra*, and Amsterdam, *Criminal Prosecutions Affecting Federally Guaranteed Civil Rights: Federal Removal and Habeas Corpus Jurisdiction to Abort State Court Trial*, 113 U.Pa.L.Rev. 793 (1965). As discussed above, the legislative history indicates that Congress was concerned with protecting federal law against State interference. Moreover, Professor Amsterdam cited *Davis* as an example of the rule under section 1442(a)(1) that the official must show colorable protection under federal law. *See supra* note 7. And the Third Circuit conceded that the official in *Davis* had alleged a federal defense. *Newcomer*, at 250.

D.   THIS COURT'S *DICTA* IN *ARIZONA V. MANYPENNY* SUPPORTS THE FEDERAL DEFENSE REQUIREMENT

Petitioners' attempt to deny the importance of federal immunity in *Arizona v. Manypenny*, 451 U.S. 232 (1981), is unconvincing. Although an immunity defense had not been alleged at trial, this Court assumed that the removal petition had made out a claim of federal immunity *and* that such a defense was necessary for removal.

> Federal involvement is necessary in order to insure a federal forum, but it is *limited* to assuring that an impartial setting is provided in which the federal defense of immunity can be considered during prosecution under state law. Thus, while giving full effect to the purpose or removal, this Court retains the highest regard for a State's right to make and enforce its own criminal laws.

Id., at 242–43 (emphasis added).[19]

III. Article III Prohibits Removal of Cases Lacking a Federal Defense

Article III, section 2, extends federal jurisdiction only to those cases "arising under" the laws or Constitution of the United States. *Id.* Article III on its face does not allow removal of these traffic cases because petitioners fail to raise federal defenses. California has argued that a reasonable construction of section 1442(a)(1) avoids the obvious constitutional difficulty posed by the absence of federal issues in these cases. *See Ellis v. Railway Clerks*, 466 U.S. 435, 444 (1984) (this Court will first determine whether a reasonable construction of the statute supporting the constitutionality of the statute exists). Should this Court disagree, California reluctantly requests this Court to declare section 1442(a)(1) unconstitutional insofar as it purports to confer federal jurisdiction in this case.

The dissent below suggests that the cases "arise under" Article III because the officials were employed to perform duties that were authorized by federal law. *See Mesa*, at 968 (Noonan, J., dissenting) (citing *Osborn v. Bank of the United States*, 22 U.S. 738, 823 (1824) ("*Osborn*")). *Osborn* does not support jurisdiction here. The only other basis for jurisdiction beyond *Osborn* is the controversial and dubious theory of "protective jurisdiction".

A.   EVEN THE BROAD READING OF "ARISING UNDER" JURISDICTION PROPOUNDED IN *OSBORN V. BANK OF UNITED STATES* DOES NOT CONFER JURISDICTION IN THIS CASE

Osborn has been described as reflecting a "broad conception" of Article III jurisdiction. *See Verlinden B. V. v. Central Bank of Nigeria*, 461 U.S. 480, 492 (1983). However, this Court has refused to hold that *Osborn* allows Article III jurisdiction over cases presenting only "potential" federal issues. *Verlinden*, at 492–93 (declining to decide whether "a mere speculative possibility that a federal question may arise at some point in the proceeding" is sufficient under Article III). The holding and reasoning of *Osborn* demonstrates that only those "potential" issues which are necessarily implied by plaintiff's complaint "arise" under Article III.

There are two types of cases which must be kept separate. First, there are cases where the character of the action always presents federal issues. These issues are "potential" because they may or may not be asserted, or "raised", by one or both of the parties in the action. Such issues may be so well-settled that it is highly unlikely that they will be "raised" by the parties (e.g. the right of the Bank of the United

---

19.   By "state-law questions", the Court referred to remaining defenses available to defendant under state law in addition to the federal immunity defense (e.g. lack of criminal intent, identity, etc.). *Id.*, at 241–42.

States to sue or contract). However, these issues are present at the outset of the case because it is apparent from the facts presented in the complaint (i.e. the status of the Bank as a federal instrumentality) that the rights of the parties are dependent upon the resolution of those issues. The "original ingredient" test established by *Osborn* confers jurisdiction in such cases.[20]

The second class of cases encompasses suits where the facts of the case stated in the complaint do not automatically raise federal issues. Such cases can "arise under" Article III only if a party "raises" a federal issue that is dispositive of that lawsuit.[21] In the absence of an "original ingredient", *Osborn* does not allow a party to create jurisdiction merely by stating a set of facts from which a federal issue might, or might not, arise upon the development of other facts. *See Little York Gold-Washing & Water Co. v. Keyes*, 96 U.S. 199, 203 (1887) (construing Justice Marshall's language in *Osborn* as preventing removal under the admittedly narrower general federal question removal statute where a federal question only *might* be presented at a later point in the litigation).

Turning to the issue presented here, petitioners' status is not an "original ingredient" in these prosecutions. California is not required to allege that defendants are federal officials. California may prevail without first proving that petitioners did not act in enforcement of federal law, just as a plaintiff in an ordinary contract action need not show that his contract is unaffected by federal law. Furthermore, while the Bank's status created an actual federal issue is *Osborn*, petitioners' status as federal employees does not do so here. Federal employees are not "creatures of federal law" (*Osborn*, at 823), and the fact that they are employed by the United States when they commit the charged act does not create a federal issue. Justice Marshall recognized that the mere status of the Bank as an entity created by the United States could not by itself create federal jurisdiction.

> It is said that a clear distinction exists between the party and the cause; that the party may originate under a law with which the cause has no connection; and that Congress may, with the same propriety, give a naturalized citizen, who is the mere creature of a law, a right to sue in the courts of the United States, as give that right to the bank. *This distinction is not denied.*

Id., at 826–27 (emphasis added). The same must be true for persons employed by an entity created by federal law, or else Article III jurisdiction would extend to all suits by federal employees arising out of off-duty activities. Indeed, Justice Marshall's concession was prompted by the dissent's argument that focusing upon the identity of the party instead of the issues raised by the case would create jurisdiction for any case involving federal officials. *Id.*, at 901–02. Justice Marshall did not rely upon the status of the Bank to create jurisdiction directly, but upon the fact that the Bank's status created federal questions concerning all of its acts, including its right to sue. *Id.*, at 827. Thus, petitioners' employment, without more, cannot serve as the basis for Article III jurisdication.

The petitions also failed to raise a federal issue. Since petitioners did not assert that their charged acts (negligent driving) were justified under the laws authorizing their duties, the issue of whether they acted in their official capacity cannot be in dispute. A case cannot "arise under" a law that is irrelevant to the disposition of the action. To argue that Article III jurisdiction encompasses such acts because they were committed "within the scope of his employment" begs the question. *See e.g. Messa*, at 968 (Noonan, J.,

---

20.　This was the point of contention between the majority and dissent in *Osborn*. Justice Johnson, dissenting, stated that a federal issue did not "arise" for purposes of Article III until a party "raised" the issue *Id.*, at 888–889. Justice Marshall decided that issues necessarily implied by the complaint, though well-settled and not raised by either party, presented federal issues sufficient for jurisdiction. *Id.*, at 824–25. But neither Justice Marshall nor Justice Johnson suggested that issues which were not necessarily implied by plaintiff's complaining, but could conceivably appear later in the action depending upon facts later presented, could serve as the foundation for Article III jurisdiction. *Id.*, at 825. *See Shoshone Mining co. v. Rutter*, 177 U.S. 505, 509–10 (1900) (interpreting *Osborn*).

21.　Although *Osborn* was read in later cases as having provided federal jurisdiction for suits against instrumentalities, that jurisdiction was based upon the requirement that plaintiff allege defendant's corporate and federal status in the complaint. *See Texas & P.R. Co. v. Cody*, 166 U.S. 606, 609–10 (1897).

dissenting). Assume that a mail carrier drives his truck down the sidewalk, running over pedestrians. The mail carrier's actions other than the charged act may have been committed within the scope of his employment. But the issue of whether his hitting pedestrians was within the scope of employment for purposes of a criminal action is an issue to be raised via federal defense (i.e. justification under federal law), and only then decided.

In our cases, simply stating that hitting a bicyclist (or a police car) was an act committed within the "scope of employment" does not put the laws authorizing those duties into issue. Petitioners certainly do not contend that those laws authorized the negligent driving charged herein. (If they do, then the District Court erred by allowing removal based upon such a frivolous defense contrary to 28 U.S.C. 1446(a)(4) and (5)). Rather, petitioner Mesa alleges that the accident occurred "*while* defendant was on duty and acting in the course and scope of her employment." (J.A. 5)(emphasis added). Mr. Ebrahim's petition merely states that he was on duty. (J.A. 10). Stating that the alleged criminal act occurred while they were discharging their duties does not present a federal issue because it says nothing about why the particular charged act was committed; petitioners only tell us that they were doing other proper things when the incident occurred. "Scope of employment" in practice means nothing more than that the official was on duty.

The phrase "scope of employment" appears to have been borrowed from official immunity cases, where the official may assert a federal defense in a *civil* suit by showing that he had the discretion to commit the act by virtue of his federal authority. *See Westfall v. Erwin*, 484 U.S. __, 108 S.Ct. 580, 98 L.Ed. 2d 619 (1988). But facts which raise federal issues in such cases do not necessarily raise them in criminal actions. A simple statement that the official was on duty in a typical case may well raise a federal issue sufficient for removal because it actually alleges a federal defense. *See Willingham v. Morgan*, 395 U.S. 402, 409 (1969). But the same statement in these criminal cases does not raise a federal defense. Thus, federal jurisdiction is lacking.

B. THIS COURT SHOULD DECLINE PETITIONERS' INVITATION TO ADOPT PROTECTIVE JURISDICTION AS A BASIS FOR FEDERAL JURISDICTION OVER TRAFFIC TICKETS

This Court has not found it necessary to embrace protective jurisdiction in the more than 200 years since Article III was written. *See e.g. Verlinden v. Central Bank of Nigeria*, 461 U.S. 480, 491–93 (1983), *Northern Pipeline Construction. Co. v. Marathon Pipeline Co. and United States*, 458 U.S. 50, 72–74 (1982)(rejecting federal jurisdiction based upon Article I). Petitioners invite this Court to abandon a reasonable construction of section 1442(a)(1) to create a special district court for federal employees. To accept this invitation would be unsound because the theory is suspect and the consequences unpredictable.

There appear to be two theories of protective jurisdiction. First, that Congress may provide jurisdiction over any case where it has the power under Article I to enact laws governing the outcome of that case. *See* Wechsler, *Federal Jurisdiction and the Revision of the Judicial Code*, 13 Law and Contemporary Problems, 216, 224–25 (1948). Second, that Congress has the power to create a federal forum to protect federal "interests". *See* Note, *The Theory of Protective Jurisdiction*, 57 N.Y.U.L. Rev. 933 (1982).

Justice Frankfurter discussed the limits of Professor Wechsler's theory.

> But, under the theory of 'protective jurisdiction', the 'arising under' jurisdiction of the federal courts would be vastly extended. For example, every contact or tort arising out of a contract affecting commerce might be a potential cause of action in the federal courts, even though only state law was involved in the decision of the case.

Textile Workers Union v. Lincoln Mills, 353 U.S. 448, 481–82 (1956)(Frankfurter, J., dissenting).[22] More-over, even such an all-inclusive theory does not include our cases because Congress lacks the power under Article I to enact federal criminal laws preempting those state laws which govern prosecution of ordinary traffic offenses.[23] Finally, adherents of this theory indicate that Congress provides jurisdiction by moving to protect its regulation of an area. *See* Mishkin, *The Federal Question in the District Courts,* 53 Colum. L. Rev. 157, at 184–96. Congress has heretofore not invaded State sovereignty over State criminal law, and has no policy concerning federal officials charged with acts unrelated to their federal authority.

The theory that Congress may provide jurisdiction based upon its "interest" in providing a federal forum for federal officials has been rejected by this Court. In *Verlinden B. V. v. State Bank of Nigeria, supra,* this Court noted that a jurisdictional statute could not serve as the federal statute under which the case arises under Article III. *Id.,* at 496. Since this species of protective jurisdiction is based upon a "federal interest", and not an actual federal statute, the only federal law available for the case to "arise under" would be the jurisdictional statute.

In addition, protective jurisdiction stretches the "arising under" language of Article III past the breaking point because cases would not arise under "the law and Constitution", but under "federal interests". "The law and Constitution" is definable; "federal interests" mean whatever Congress or the courts say they mean at a particular time. Moreover, the rationale behind this "forum-based" jurisdiction does not extend to the instant cases because the United States has no legitimate interest in conferring jurisdiction over federal officials acting outside of their official capacity.[24] The United States has no interest in providing federal jurisdiction for those who do not contend that their prosecution seeks to penalize compliance with federal law or obstruct the operations of the United States.

---

22.   *See Northern Pipeline,* at 72–74. The majority in *Lincoln Mills* did not reach our Article III issue because it held that the challenged statute directed federal courts to fashion federal common law in that area. *Id.* Congress did not intend section 1442(a)(1) to create federal law governing suits and/or prosecutions of federal officials.

23.   The Commerce power is unaffected by the choice of forum for prosecution of federal officials for acts unrelated to federal authority. Extending jurisdiction on the basis that a guilty verdict might sideline a federal employee would extend jurisdiction to all cases involving employees arrested while off-duty. This was the result Justice Marshall chose to avoid in *Osborn.* The postal power (Art. 1, sec. 8) is also unaffected by the choice of forum for trial of mail carriers. Indeed, this Court has questioned the constitutionality of federal statutes preventing execution of state felony warrants against carriers actually *delivering* mail. *See United States v. Kirby,* 74 U.S. 482 (1868). The United States fisc cannot be affected by a guilty verdict because the United States cannot be the subject of non-mutual offensive collateral estoppel. *See United States v. Mendoza,* 464 U.S. 154 (1984).

24.   *But see Textile Workers Union v. Lincoln Mills,* 353 U.S. 448, 475 (Frankfurter, J., dissenting). Justice Frankfurter argued that the limits of federal distrust of state courts had to be the Constitution as expressed by Article III (i.e. diversity jurisdiction). As part of that argument, he discussed section 1442(a)(1). He first properly distinguished the removal statute by finding that the statute had been interpreted as requiring a federal defense. *Id.,* at 475 n. 5 ("that put federal law in the forefront as a defense")(interpreting *Tennesses v. Davis, supra*). Thus, petitioners receive no comfort from Justice Frankfurter.

However, Justice Frankfurter also attempted to provide an alternate, and incorrect, rationale accounting for section 1442(a)(1). "In any event, the fact that officers of the Federal Government were parties *may* be considered sufficient to afford access to the federal forum. *See In re Debs,* 158 U.S. 564, 584–86 (1895); Mishkin, 53 Col. L. Rev., at 193: 'Without doubt, a federal forum should be available for all suits involving the Government, its agents and instrumentalities, regardless of the source of the substantive rule.'" *Lincoln Mills,* at 482 n. 5. (emphasis added).

Justice Frankfurter's use of the word "may" indicates some uncertainty about this pronouncement. In addition, he appears to have misinterpreted the quotation from Professor Mishkin's article as referring to federal officials instead of government agencies. *See Mishkin, supra,* at 193. Or Justice Frankfurter may have assumed that federal officials would be acting in their official capacities when suing or being sued. *Id.* He appears not to have considered the possibility that the official might have been on duty but acting outside of his official capacity (i.e. without a federal defense). Thus, Justice Frankfurter's only support for the statement (aside from Mishkin) was *In re Debs, supra,* which held that Congress could apply to the courts for an injunction against activities interfering with its Article I powers over interstate commerce. *Id.*

IV. This Court Should Refuse to Create a Special Federal Court for Federal Employees at the Expense of State Sovereignty

This case turns on the proper construction of a statute. Petitioners' reliance on policy considerations is misplaced because the intent of Congress is clear. However, since petitioners invoke federal interests in support of removal, California urges that allowing removal would burden the federal courts at the expense of State sovereignty.

> The right to formulate and enforce penal sanctions is an important aspect of the sovereignty retained by the States. This Court has emphasized repeatedly "the fundamental policy against federal interference with state criminal prosecutions."

Kelly v. Robinson, 479 U.S. __, 107 S.Ct. 353, 360 (1986) (quoting *Younger v. Harris*. 401 U.S. 37, 46 (1971)). This Court should not abrogate that policy by insulating federal employees from State judicial process where there is no challenge to federal authority.

The instant cases are excellent examples of why this Court should not construe section 1442(a)(1) to allow removal to all on-duty employees. Both are traffic cases; one is a simple traffic ticket. These cases were removed even though petitioners do not allege local or State hostility to mail carriers or federal law. Many federal officials will seek to remove such cases, not because of concerns over harassment, but to gain a tactical advantage.

For example, in California and other large states, the distance between a particular county and the nearest federal court may be measured in hundreds of miles.[25] Very few county prosecutors can afford to spend the time and money necessary to contest minor infractions in federal court. Fewer witnesses will be willing or able to travel long distances. Many offenses may be dismissed or compromised because prosecutions have been removed.

Removal in inappropriate cases injures Federal and State governments. Federal courts will be burdened with hundreds or thousands of new cases each year presenting no issues of federal law, including traffic tickets. *Pro se* litigants with distinctive and uninformed views about our Constitution and legal system can be expected to make a federal case out of a traffic ticket.

The spectacle and expense of a separate criminal court for federal employees are themselves good reasons for restricting removal. But such cases will also generate numerous appeals because there is little guidance available concerning the trial of removed cases in federal courts. It appears that district courts are forced to provide most protections available under State law to criminal defendants even where those protections conflict with federal criminal procedure. *See City of Aurora v. Erwin*, 706 F.2d 295 (10th Cir. 1983) (reversing conviction because defendant was not afforded a jury trial guaranteed under Colorado law.) Conflicts between federal and state criminal procedure will raise issues of first impression and create errors requiring reversal or retrial. Differences between federal procedure and procedure mandated by each of the fifty States' constitutions concerning, *inter alia*, discovery, voir dire, and jury instructions will spawn confusion and appeals.[26]

---

25. In California, the county seat of Del Norte County is Crescent City. Crescent City is in the Northern District of California. The nearest federal court within that district is over 350 miles away in San Francisco. Many other county seats are located over 100 miles away from their respective federal district courts.

26. Any State retaining independent and adequate state grounds based upon its constitution may present conflicts with federal criminal procedure. State Supreme Courts have handed down at least 450 decisions based upon State constitutions which conflict with federal law, and the majority of those decisions involve criminal cases. Collins, Galie, Kincaid, *State High Courts, State Constitutions, and Individual Rights Litigation Since 1980: A Judicial Survey*, 13 Hastings Const. I.Q. 599, 613 (1985–86), Wermiel, *State Supreme Courts Are Feeling Their Oats*, Wall St. Journal, June 15, 1988, at 1, col. 1, (updating the Hastings article), Collins and Galie, State Constitutional Law Insert to The National Law Journal, September 29, 1986, S-8 (listing some of those cases sorted by category). Moreover, the definition of state "substantive law" may encompass state statutes, as well as State constitutional provisions. *See Virginia v. Felts*, 133 F. 85 (C.C. Va. 1904) (suggesting that State rules of evidence, voir dire, and sentencing must prevail over federal law).

Finally, petitioners urge that section 1442(a)(1) and the federal defense requirement will disrupt "federal government functions" and leave officals vulnerable to harassment by States hostile to federal authority. But federal officials alleging harassment have effective remedies. This Court allows federal officials to obtain removal by pleading the facts suggesting harassment. As discussed above, the official need only show that his actions were in enforcement of, or compliance with, federal law and negate the possibility that he was prosecuted for an act unprotected by federal law. *See Soper (No. 1), supra,* at 33–34. Congress can amend section 1442(a)(1) if this standard is considered too burdensome. *See e.g. Maryland v. Soper (No. 2),* 270 U.S. 36, 43–44 (1926). Finally, the Ninth Circuit below specifically stated that it might have allowed removal had petitioners alleged harassment. *Mesa, supra,* at 967.

Moreover, the writ of *habeas copus* is an equally potent weapon against harassment. *See* 28 U.S.C. 2241 (c)(2) and (c)(3). *See In re Neagle,* 135 U.S. 1 (1890). Federal officials may apply for the writ before trial. *United States ex rel. Drury v. Lewis,* 200 U.S. 1 (1906). Instead of having to prevail at an evidentiary hearing and again at trial (*see* 28 U.S.C. 1446(a)), the successful official is released immediately after the hearing on the writ. *Id.* The official need only show that the prosecution was motivated by animus toward the performance of federal duties. *See e.g. People of the State of California v. Morgan,* 743 F.2d 728, 731 (9th Cir. 1984). Thus, this Court's decision reaffirming the federal defense requirement will not affect the remedies available to federal officials claiming harassment.

In sum, requiring a federal defense for removal preserves Congressional intent and over 100 years of this Court's precedent. Affirming the judgment below will protect the legitimate interest of the United States in ensuring enforcement of federal law without invading State sovereignty.

CONCLUSION

For the foregoing reasons, the judgment of the court of appeals should be affirmed.

Respectfully submitted.

LEO HIMMELSBACH
District Attorney for the
County of Santa Clara,
State of California

KENNETH ROSENBLATT
Deputy District Attorney

AUGUST 1988

To read the Court's decision in this case, go to *Mesa v. California,* 489 U.S. 121 (1989).

GLOSSARY

Active Voice   A tool used by writers to shorten sentences; a sentence written in active voice uses the simple subject-verb-object approach

Administrative Procedures   Procedures used by agencies and boards

Advocate   Arguing one side of an issue

Affidavit   A statement under penalty of perjury sworn to before a notary

Affirm   To uphold; in connection with an appeal to uphold the lower court's decision

Affirmative Defenses   Defenses raised by the defendant in the answer; reasons why the plaintiff should not recover even if all of the allegations of the complaint are true

Amend   To change

Annotated   A brief summary of a statute or a case added to explain or clarify

Appeal   Review of a lower court decision

Appellant   One who appeals

Appellate Brief   Written document containing factual and legal contentions prepared by attorneys dealing with an appeal in a case

Appellee   Party in an appeal who did not file the appeal

Arbitration   An out-of-court proceeding in which parties submit a dispute to a neutral person for resolution

Arbitration Brief   A document filed in an arbitration proceeding addressing the legal issues in the arbitration

Argument   The section of a memorandum or brief containing legal analysis supporting that party's position on a legal issue

Bill of Rights   First ten amendments to United States Constitution

Binding Authority   Another term for mandatory authority

Boolean   A special logic used in computerized legal research; utilizes the use of connective words

Brief   A written document that might contain a summary of the facts, issues, rules, and analysis used by a court and a comparison with a client's facts; a case brief is a short summary of a published case

Caption   A caption identifies the parties to the case, the court in which the case is pending, the docket number, and the title of the document

Case Brief   A short summary of a reported case

Case Law   A collection of reported cases

Case Law Reporters   Sets of published volumes of cases decided by various courts

Case Reporters   Books that contain case decisions from the courts

Cause of Action   The basis upon which a lawsuit may be brought to the court

CD-ROM Libraries   Legal materials, either primary or secondary sources, stored on a CD-ROM

Century Digest   Part of the American Digest System; containing case annotations for the years 1688 to 1896

Citators   Research materials used to update or "validate" legal authorities

Cited Authority   The authority you are Shepardizing (updating and validating)

Citing Authority   Authorities you are referred to when you Shepardize

Civil Law   The area of law dealing with private disputes between parties

Clerk's Transcript   A record containing copies of documents filed in connection with a court proceeding prepared by a court clerk

Code   A topical organization of statutes

Code Books   Books that contain codes or statutes and that are topically arranged

Common Law   Body of law developed through the courts

Computer Assisted Legal Research   Legal research done with the use of a computer; includes the use of CD-ROM, online services such as LEXIS, Westlaw, Internet, and intranets

Concurrent Jurisdiction   Jurisdiction or power exercised by two different entities

Connectors   Words such as *and* or *or* used in a search query to show the relationship between key words or terms

Court Record   Documents and transcripts of proceedings in connection with a case

Criminal Law   The area of law dealing with prosecution and defense of crimes

Database   Compilation of electronically stored information

Decennial Digest   Updates to the *Century Digest,* published every ten years

Decision   The formal written resolution of a case; it explains the legal and factual issues, the resolution of the case, and the law used by the court in reaching its resolution

Declaration   A statement under penalty of perjury containing factual statements

De-publish   In rare instances, a court will decide a case and write and release a decision. However, before it is published in the official reporter, the court decides not to publish some or all of the case decision. A de-published case cannot be used as precedent.

Descriptive Word Index   An alphabetical listing of words describing the topics contained in a book or a set of books; refers the researcher to the volume and page where the topic is discussed

Digest   An index to reported cases, arranged by subject; a short summary of cases is provided

Digest Topics   Topics included in an index (digest) to reported case law, arranged by subject

Document   An identifiable item located in a database; can refer to a case or a single code section

Double Jeopardy   Clause in the United States Constitution that generally prevents the government from trying a person more than once for the same offense

Editorial Enhancements   Helpful information included in many unofficial publications; the enhancements assist the researcher to understand the material. Most official publications have little or no editorial enhancements

Electronic Search Query   Words that constitute a search request when using electronically stored data, i.e., information on the Internet or on a CD-ROM

Elements   The components of a cause of action or of a statute

Express Powers   Powers given to the federal government that are expressly stated in the Constitution

Federal Reporter   The set containing all of the federal appellate decisions

Federal Rules Decisions   The set containing federal opinions, decisions, and rulings involving the Federal Rules of Civil Procedure and the Federal Rules of Criminal Procedure

Federal Supplement   The set containing the cases argued and determined in the United States District Courts, the United States Court of International Trade, and the rulings of the Judicial Panel on Multidistrict Litigation

Federalism   A system of government in which the people are regulated by both federal and state governments

File   To become part of the court record

First Impression   A case where the legal issue has not previously been decided

Forms of Pleading and Practice   Form books containing forms for use in connection with litigation

Full-text Search   Legal research method utilized in computer assisted legal research, in which all documents in a database are searched for certain words

General Digest   Updates to the *Decennial Digest*

Good Law   Law that is still in effect or valid and can be cited as authority

Headnote   Editorial enhancement added to the front material of a case; useful summary of most of the legal topics addressed in the case

Holding   The legal principle to be taken from the court's decision

Hornbook   Name given to books published by West that are a type of treatise; commonly used by law students

Implied Powers   Power to make all laws that are necessary and proper for carrying into execution any of the stated or express powers of the government

Index   A list of words and phrases that reflect the topics covered in the book

Intranet   A secure database set up and accessible by a specific group, such as a law firm

Judicial History   The legal (courtroom) history of a case

Jurisdiction   The power or authority to act in a certain situation; the power of a court to hear cases and render judgments

Jury Instructions   Statements of the law read to the jury at the end of trial

Key Numbers   A research aid unique to the West Group materials; these numbers allow a researcher to quickly access specific material in a digest

Law Library   A library dedicated to legal resource material

Law Review   A type of legal periodical published by law schools containing articles on different legal topics

Lawyers' Edition   LEXIS Law Publishing publishes this unofficial (non-government) printing of all United States Supreme Court case law

Legal Analysis   The process of analyzing facts and legal issues in light of existing constitutional, statutory, or case law

Legal Citation   Special abbreviations used to describe resource material

Legal Dictionary   A dictionary defining and explaining legal terms

Legal Encyclopedia   A collection of legal information arranged alphabetically by topic; a secondary source of the law

Legal Error   Application of law to a case in a mistaken way

Legal Issue   A question that must be decided by a court

Legal Thesaurus   A book providing synonyms for legal words

Legislative History   The proceedings that relate to a bill before it becomes law

Legislative Intent   The purpose of the legislature in passing a law

LEXIS   A computer assisted legal research service

Local Rules of Court   Procedural rules adopted by an individual court for practice in that specific court

Looseleaf Service   Legal material published in a binder format, regularly supplemented with replacement pages

Mandatory Authority   Case law that must be followed by a court

Memorandum of Law   An objectively written document in which the researcher informs another of the law governing a specific situation

Memorandum of Points and Authorities   Research document filed with the court containing a legal analysis of disputed issues occurring in a case pending in court; often used to support or oppose motions

Model Codes   A collection of sample laws, created for the states to adopt in whole or in part; helped to create uniformity in law

Motion   A request made to a court; for example, a motion could request temporary support or a change in custody

Motion for Summary Judgment   A request that the trial court decide the case without a trial

Moving Party   The party making a motion

Nutshell Series   Condensed versions of hornbooks

Official Citation   Citation to the official publication of case law for a particular jurisdiction (this is usually a government publication); the official citation includes the name of the case, volume number in which the case is located, the first page of the case, and the year of the decision

Official Reporters   Sets of case law published by the government or the designee of the government

Opinion   A court's decision

Opinion Letter   Formal correspondence from an attorney to a client or other attorney explaining an attorney's interpretation of the law as applied to a factual situation

Parallel Citations   References to unofficial publications given in addition to official citations; simply stated, you may find the exact case in more than one publication

Periodical   Legal material, published at regular intervals, consisting of magazines, journals, and law reviews

Persuasive Authority   Non-binding case law that is nevertheless considered by a court

Petition for Writ of Certiorari   A request for a hearing in the Supreme Court

Petitioner   The person who files a petition with the court

Pleading and Practice Guides   Secondary sources providing sample pleadings and general practice advice; available in most states and for some federal practice areas

Pleadings   The formal written allegations filed with the court by both sides to a lawsuit; claims and defenses are clearly set out so that both parties are placed on notice of the position of the opposing party

Pocket Part Supplement   A removable supplement; includes all changes or additions to the material contained in the hardbound volume

Point Headings   Phrases or sentences found in the discussion or argument sections of memoranda or briefs identifying the topic of the following discussion or argument; these headings are set apart from the text by bolding and/or capitalization and they are usually numbered

Positive Law   Codes that have been enacted into law by Congress

Practice Books   Books for use in federal and state legal practice; these often contain discussions of an area of law and provide forms needed for practice in that legal area

Precedent   The example set by the decision of an earlier court for similar cases or similar legal questions that arise in later cases

Preempt   To assume sole responsibility to regulate

Prefatory Material   Material found in the front of a book or set of books, describing such matters as the purpose of the book and instructions for using the book

***Prima Facie* Case**   On first view or on its face; for example, the plaintiff presented a strong *prima facie* case for establishing the negligence of the defendant

Primary Authority   The resources that provide the actual law; laws are found in constitutions, statutes, some administrative materials, and case law

Primary Sources of Law   A work that contains the law

Private Laws   Laws enacted by Congress that affect only selected individuals

Public Law   Laws enacted by Congress that affect the public in general

Query   Words that constitute a search request when using CD-ROM or online materials

Question Presented   A statement of the legal issue presented to the court for resolution

Rationale   The reasoning or explanation for the court's ultimate resolution of a case

Real Party In Interest   A party who has a true interest in the action

Regional Reporters   A set of published volumes of cases by courts in specific regions of the United States; for example the *Pacific Reporter* or the *North Eastern Reporter*

Remand   To send back

Repeal   To undo; to declare a law no longer in effect

Reported Case   A judicial decision that is published

Reporter's Transcript   A verbatim record of the oral proceedings in court prepared by the court reporter

Respondent   The party who answers the Petitioner's petition

Reverse   To change

Rules of Court   Procedural rules adopted by all courts regulating practice in the court

Secondary Sources of Law   Tools used to understand the law; one such tool is a legal encyclopedia that explains the law

Session Laws   Laws from state legislatures, published in chronological order

Shepardize   To check the validity of a citation in one of the *Shepard's* citations

Shepard's   System used to update, validate, and expand research results

Slip Law   First publication of a law; usually in pamphlet form

Specialized Reporters   Collections of cases grouped by specific topics rather than by level of court or jurisdiction

Stare Decisis   "It stands decided"; another term for *precedent*

Statutory Law   Law enacted through the legislative process

Statutory Requirements   Various requirements or elements of a statute that must be met before the statute will apply to a situation

Strategy   A well-thought-out plan or approach to a project

Style Manual   A manual illustrating the proper citation format for a particular state

Superseded   Replaced

Supplemented   Kept up-to-date

Supremacy Clause   Clause in the U.S. Constitution providing that the U.S. Constitution is the supreme law of the land

Supreme Court Reporter   Printed by West Group, this is an unofficial publication of all U.S. Supreme Court case law

Table of Abbreviations   A common feature of legal publications containing an explanation of all abbreviations found in the book

Table of Authorities   A list of primary and secondary authorities cited with a memorandum or brief and the page numbers on which they appear

Table of Cases   A common feature of legal publications containing the names of all cases cited in the book or document

Table of Contents   An outline of the material covered in the book or document

Table of Statutes   A common feature of legal publications containing a list of all statutes or codes that are referenced in the book or document

Thesis Paragraph   Lays a solid foundation for the reader; this paragraph sets forth the client's problem, states the legal issue, briefly explains the legal rules governing the issues, and states the legal conclusion

Topic and Key Number   System used by West Group to integrate its various primary and secondary resource materials

Topic Sentence   Introduces the issues or subissues and connects back to the thesis paragraph

Topical Index   An index arranged by subject matter topics

Transaction Forms   Books that contain forms for use in connection with business and personal transactions

Treatise   Either one book or a multivolume series of books dealing with one legal topic

Trial   A court proceeding before a judge or jury wherein each side presents evidence of the facts that form the basis for the lawsuit or the defense to the lawsuit

Trial Brief   Document submitted to the court; contains a statement of facts, the issues, and the party's legal argument

Trial Court   Where cases originate and where the factual dispute is resolved at trial

Uniform Laws   Similar laws that are adopted by the legislatures of different states (i.e., Uniform Commercial Code); intended to create uniformity in the law

Uniform System of Citation   A reference manual, it contains the rules for proper citation format; often called *THE BLUEBOOK*

United States Reports   Official publication of all U.S. Supreme Court case law; published by the federal government

Unofficial Publication   Material not published by a government entity or a government designee

Unofficial Reporters   Collections of printed decisions that are not government publications or sanctioned by government

Validate   To verify that an authority is still good law

Westlaw   A computer assisted legal research service provided by West Group

Writ of Habeas Corpus   An order directing the release of one who is in custody

Writ of Mandate   Order from higher court to lower court to take some action

INDEX